Weygandt • Kieso • Kimmel

Accounting Principles

8th Edition

Volume 2

Principles of Accounting 2
BU 102

Queensborough Community College

Bicentennial Logo Design: Richard J. Pacifico

To order books or for customer service, please call 1(800)-CALL-WILEY (225-5945).

Printed in the United States of America.

ISBN 978-0-470-89826-0

10 9 8 7 6 5 4 3 2 1

BRIEF CONTENTS

RAPID REVIEW
Chapter Content

BASIC ACCOUNTING EQUATION (Chapter 2)

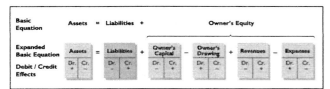

ADJUSTING ENTRIES (Chapter 3)

	Type		Adjusting Entry	
Deferrals	1. Prepaid expenses		Dr. Expenses	Cr. Assets
	2. Unearned revenues		Dr. Liabilities	Cr. Revenues
Accruals	1. Accrued revenues		Dr. Assets	Cr. Revenues
	2. Accrued expenses		Dr. Expenses	Cr. Liabilities

Note: Each adjusting entry will affect one or more income statement accounts and one or more balance sheet accounts.

Interest Computation

Interest = Face value of note × Annual interest rate × Time in terms of one year

CLOSING ENTRIES (Chapter 4)

Purpose: (1) Update the Owner's Capital account in the ledger by transferring net income (loss) and Owner's Drawing to Owner's Capital. (2) Prepare the temporary accounts (revenue, expense, Owner's Drawing) for the next period's postings by reducing their balances to zero.

Process

1. Debit each revenue account for its balance (assuming normal balances), and credit Income Summary for total revenues.
2. Debit Income Summary for total expenses, and credit each expense account for its balance (assuming normal balances).

    STOP AND CHECK: Does the balance in your Income Summary Account equal the net income (loss) reported in the income statement?

3. Debit (credit) Income Summary, and credit (debit) Owner's Capital for the amount of net income (loss).
4. Debit Owner's Capital for the balance in the Owner's Drawing account and credit Owner's Drawing for the same amount.

    STOP AND CHECK: Does the balance in your Owner's Capital account equal the ending balance reported in the balance sheet and the owner's equity statement? Are all of your temporary account balances zero?

ACCOUNTING CYCLE (Chapter 4)

Optional steps: If a worksheet is prepared, steps 4, 5, and 6 are incorporated in the worksheet. If reversing entries are prepared, they occur between steps 9 and 1 as discussed below.

INVENTORY (Chapters 5 and 6)

Ownership

Freight Terms	Ownership of goods on public carrier resides with:
FOB Shipping point	Buyer
FOB Destination	Seller

Perpetual vs. Periodic Journal Entries

Event	Perpetual	Periodic*
Purchase of goods	Inventory Cash (A/P)	Purchases Cash (A/P)
Freight (shipping point)	Inventory Cash	Freight-In Cash
Return of goods	Cash (or A/P) Inventory	Cash (or A/P) Purchase Returns and Allowances
Sale of goods	Cash (or A/R) Sales Cost of Goods Sold Inventory	Cash (or A/R) Sales No entry
End of period	No entry	Closing or adjusting entry required

Cost Flow Methods

- Specific identification
- First-in, first-out (FIFO)
- Weighted average
- Last-in, first-out (LIFO)

INTERNAL CONTROL AND CASH (Chapter 8)

Principles of Internal Control

- Establishment of responsibility
- Segregation of duties
- Documentation procedures
- Physical, mechanical, and electronic controls
- Independent internal verification
- Other controls

Bank Reconciliation

Bank	Books
Balance per bank statement Add: Deposit in transit	Balance per books Add: Unrecorded credit memoranda from bank statement
Deduct: Outstanding checks	Deduct: Unrecorded debit memoranda from bank statement
Adjusted cash balance	Adjusted cash balance

Note: 1. Errors should be offset (added or deducted) on the side that made the error.
2. Adjusting journal entries should only be made on the books.

STOP AND CHECK: Does the adjusted cash balance in the Cash account equal the reconciled balance?

RECEIVABLES (Chapter 9)

Methods to Account for Uncollectible Accounts

Direct write-off method	Record bad debts expense when the company determines a particular account to be uncollectible.
Allowance methods: Percentage-of-sales	At the end of each period estimate the amount of credit sales uncollectible. Debit Bad Debts Expense and credit Allowance for Doubtful Accounts for this amount. As specific accounts become uncollectible, debit Allowance for Doubtful Accounts and credit Accounts Receivable.
Percentage-of-receivables	At the end of each period estimate the amount of uncollectible receivables. Debit Bad Debts Expense and credit Allowance for Doubtful Accounts in an amount that results in a balance in the allowance account equal to the estimate of uncollectibles. As specific accounts become uncollectible, debit Allowance for Doubtful Accounts and credit Accounts Receivable.

*Items with an asterisk are covered in a chapter-end appendix.

RAPID REVIEW
Chapter Content

PLANT ASSETS (Chapter 10)

Presentation

Tangible Assets	Intangible Assets
Property, plant, and equipment	Intangible assets (Patents, copyrights, trademarks, franchises, goodwill)
Natural resources	

Computation of Annual Depreciation Expense

Straight-line	$\dfrac{\text{Cost} - \text{Salvage value}}{\text{Useful life (in years)}}$
Units-of-activity	$\dfrac{\text{Depreciable cost}}{\text{Useful life (in units)}} \times$ Units of activity during year
Declining-balance	Book value at beginning of year $\times$ Declining balance rate* *Declining-balance rate = $1 \div$ Useful life (in years)

Note: If depreciation is calculated for partial periods, the straight-line and declining-balance methods must be adjusted for the relevant proportion of the year. Multiply the annual depreciation expense by the number of months expired in the year divided by 12 months.

SHAREHOLDERS' EQUITY (Chapter 13)

Comparison of Equity Accounts

Proprietorship	Partnership	Corporation
Owner's equity Name, Capital	Partner's equity Name, Capital Name, Capital	Stockholders' equity Common stock Retained earnings

No-Par Value vs. Par Value Stock Journal Entries

No-Par Value	Par Value
Cash Common Stock	Cash Common Stock (par value) Paid-in Capital in Excess of Par Value

DIVIDENDS (Chapter 14)

Comparison of Dividend Effects

	Cash	Common Stock	Retained Earnings
Cash dividend	↓	No effect	↓
Stock dividend	No effect	↑	↓
Stock split	No effect	No effect	No effect

BONDS (Chapter 15)

Premium	Market interest rate < Contractual interest rate
Face Value	Market interest rate = Contractual interest rate
Discount	Market interest rate > Contractual interest rate

INVESTMENTS (Chapter 16)

Comparison of Long-Term Bond Investment and Liability Journal Entries

Event	Investor	Investee

Purchase / issue of bonds	Debt Investments
	     Cash
		Cash
		     Bonds Payable

Interest receipt / payment	Cash
	     Interest Revenue
		Interest Expense
		     Cash

Comparison of Cost and Equity Methods of Accounting for Long-Term Stock Investments

Event	Cost	Equity

Acquisition	Stock Investments
	     Cash
		Stock Investments
		     Cash

Investee reports earnings	No entry	Stock Investments Investment Revenue

Investee pays dividends	Cash
	     Dividend Revenue
		Cash
		     Stock Investments

Trading and Available-for-Sale Securities

Trading	Report at fair value with changes reported in net income.
Available-for-sale	Report at fair value with changes reported in the stockholders' equity section.

STATEMENT OF CASH FLOWS (Chapter 17)

Cash flows from operating activities (**indirect method**)
Net income

Add:	Losses on disposals of assets	$ X
	Amortization and depreciation	X
	Decreases in current assets	X
	Increases in current liabilities	X
Deduct:	Gains on disposals of assets	(X)
	Increases in current assets	(X)
	Decreases in current liabilities	(X)
Net cash provided (used) by operating activities		$ X

Cash flows from operating activities (**direct method**)
Cash receipts
  (Examples: from sales of goods and services to customers, from receipts of interest and dividends on loans and investments) $ X
Cash payments
  (Examples: to suppliers, for operating expenses, for interest, for taxes)   (X)
Cash provided (used) by operating activities $ X

PRESENTATION OF NON-TYPICAL ITEMS (Chapter 18)

Prior period adjustments (Chapter 14)	Statement of retained earnings (adjustment of beginning retained earnings)
Discontinued operations	Income statement (presented separately after "Income from continuing operations")
Extraordinary items	Income statement (presented separately after "Income before extraordinary items")
Changes in accounting principle	In most instances, use the new method in current period and restate previous years results using new method. For changes in depreciation and amortization methods, use the new method in the current period, but do not restate previous periods.

RAPID REVIEW
Chapter Content

MANAGERIAL ACCOUNTING (Chapter 19)

Characteristics of Managerial Accounting

Primary Users	Internal users
Reports	Internal reports issued as needed
Purpose	Special purpose for a particular user
Content	Pertains to subunits, may be detailed, use of relevant data
Verification	No independent audits

Types of Manufacturing Costs

Direct materials	Raw materials directly associated with finished product
Direct labor	Work of employees directly associated with turning raw materials into finished product
Manufacturing overhead	Costs indirectly associated with manufacture of finished product

JOB ORDER AND PROCESS COSTING (Chapters 20 and 21)

Types of Accounting Systems

Job order	Costs are assigned to each unit or each batch of goods
Process cost	Costs are applied to similar products that are mass-produced in a continuous fashion

Job Order and Process Cost Flow

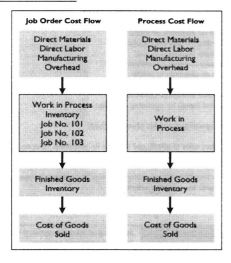

COST-VOLUME-PROFIT (Chapter 22)

Types of Costs

Variable costs	Vary in total directly and proportionately with changes in activity level
Fixed costs	Remain the same in total regardless of change in activity level
Mixed costs	Contain both a fixed and a variable element

CVP Income Statement Format

	Total	Per Unit
Sales	$xx	$xx
Variable costs	xx	xx
Contribution margin	xx	$xx
Fixed costs	xx	
Net income	$xx	

Breakeven Point

$$\text{Breakeven point in units} = \text{Fixed costs} \div \text{Contribution margin per unit}$$

Target Net Income

$$\text{Required sales in units} = (\text{Fixed costs} + \text{Target net income}) \div \text{Contribution margin per unit}$$

BUDGETS (Chapter 23)

Components of the Master Budget

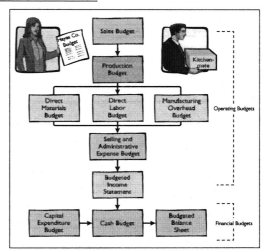

RESPONSIBILITY ACCOUNTING (Chapter 24)

Types of Responsibility Centers

Cost	Profit	Investment
Expenses only	Expenses and Revenues	Expenses and Revenues and ROI

Return on Investment

$$\begin{array}{c} \text{Return on} \\ \text{investment} \\ \text{(ROI)} \end{array} = \dfrac{\text{Investment center}}{\text{controllable margin}} \div \begin{array}{c} \text{Average} \\ \text{investment center} \\ \text{operating assets} \end{array}$$

STANDARD COSTS (Chapter 25)

Standard Cost Variances

$$\begin{array}{c} \text{Total} \\ \text{materials} \\ \text{variance} \end{array} = \begin{array}{c} \text{Materials} \\ \text{price} \\ \text{variance} \end{array} + \begin{array}{c} \text{Materials} \\ \text{quantity} \\ \text{variance} \end{array}$$

$$\begin{array}{c} \text{Total} \\ \text{labor} \\ \text{variance} \end{array} = \begin{array}{c} \text{Labor} \\ \text{price} \\ \text{variance} \end{array} + \begin{array}{c} \text{Labor} \\ \text{quantity} \\ \text{variance} \end{array}$$

$$\begin{array}{c} \text{Total} \\ \text{overhead} \\ \text{variance} \end{array} = \begin{array}{c} \text{Overhead} \\ \text{controllable} \\ \text{variance} \end{array} + \begin{array}{c} \text{Overhead} \\ \text{volume} \\ \text{variance} \end{array}$$

Materials price variance $= \boxed{AQ \times AP} - \boxed{AQ \times SP}$

Materials quantity variance $= \boxed{AQ \times SP} - \boxed{SQ \times SP}$

Labor price variance $= \boxed{AH \times AR} - \boxed{AH \times SR}$

Labor quantity variance $= \boxed{AH \times SR} - \boxed{SH \times SR}$

Overhead controllable variance $= \boxed{\text{Actual overhead}} - \boxed{\text{Overhead budgeted}}$

Overhead volume variance $= \boxed{\text{Fixed overhead rate}} \times \boxed{\begin{array}{c} \text{Normal capacity} - \\ \text{Standard hours allowed} \end{array}}$

INCREMENTAL ANALYSIS AND CAPITAL BUDGETING (Chapter 26)

Annual Rate of Return

$$\begin{array}{c} \text{Annual rate} \\ \text{of return} \end{array} = \begin{array}{c} \text{Expected annual} \\ \text{net income} \end{array} \div \begin{array}{c} \text{Average} \\ \text{investment} \end{array}$$

Cash Payback

$$\begin{array}{c} \text{Cash payback} \\ \text{period} \end{array} = \begin{array}{c} \text{Cost of capital} \\ \text{investment} \end{array} \div \begin{array}{c} \text{Annual} \\ \text{cash inflow} \end{array}$$

Discounted Cash Flow Approaches

Net Present Value	Internal Rate of Return
Compute net present value (a dollar amount). If net present value is zero or positive, accept the proposal. If net present value is negative, reject the proposal.	Compute internal rate of return (a percentage). If internal rate of return is equal to or greater than the minimum required rate of return, accept the proposal. If internal rate of return is less than the minimum rate, reject the proposal.

Incremental Analysis

1. Identify the relevant costs associated with each alternative. Relevant costs are those costs and revenues that differ across alternatives. Choose the alternative that maximizes net income.
2. Opportunity costs are those benefits that are given up when one alternative is chosen instead of another one. Opportunity costs are relevant costs.
3. Sunk costs have already been incurred and will not be changed or avoided by any future decision. Sunk costs are not relevant costs.

RAPID REVIEW
Financial Statements

Order of Preparation

Statement Type	Date
1. Income statement	For the period ended
2. Retained earnings statement	For the period ended
3. Balance sheet	As of the end of the period
4. Statement of cash flows	For the period ended

Income Statement (perpetual inventory system)

Name of Company Income Statement For the Period Ended		
Sales revenues		
Sales	$ X	
Less: Sales returns and allowances	X	
Sales discounts	X	
Net sales		$ X
Cost of goods sold		X
Gross profit		X
Operating expenses		
(Examples: store salaries, advertising, delivery, rent, depreciation, utilities, insurance)		X
Income from operations		X
Other revenues and gains		
(Examples: interest, gains)	X	
Other expenses and losses		
(Examples: interest, losses)	X	X
Income before income taxes		X
Income tax expense		X
Net income		$ X

Income Statement (periodic inventory system)

Name of Company Income Statement For the Period Ended			
Sales revenues			
Sales		$ X	
Less: Sales returns and allowances		X	
Sales discounts		X	
Net sales			$ X
Cost of goods sold			
Beginning inventory		X	
Purchases	$ X		
Less: Purchase returns and allowances	X		
Net purchases	X		
Add: Freight in	X		
Cost of goods purchased		X	
Cost of goods available for sale		X	
Less: Ending inventory		X	
Cost of goods sold			X
Gross profit			X
Operating expenses			
(Examples: store salaries, advertising, delivery, rent, depreciation, utilities, insurance)			X
Income from operations			X
Other revenues and gains			
(Examples: interest, gains)		X	
Other expenses and losses			
(Examples: interest, losses)		X	X
Income before income taxes			X
Income tax expense			X
Net income			$ X

Retained Earnings Statement

Name of Company Retained Earnings Statement For the Period Ended	
Retained earnings, beginning of period	$ X
Add: Net income (or deduct net loss)	X
	X
Deduct: Dividends	X
Retained earnings, end of period	$ X

STOP AND CHECK: Net income (loss) presented on the retained earnings statement must equal the net income (loss) presented on the income statement.

Balance Sheet

Name of Company Balance Sheet As of the End of the Period			
Assets			
Current assets			
(Examples: cash, short-term investments, accounts receivable, merchandise inventory, prepaids)			$ X
Long-term investments			
(Examples: investments in bonds, investments in stocks)			X
Property, plant, and equipment			
Land		$ X	
Buildings and equipment	$ X		
Less: Accumulated depreciation	X	X	X
Intangible assets			X
Total assets			$ X
Liabilities and Stockholders' Equity			
Liabilities			
Current liabilities			
(Examples: notes payable, accounts payable, accruals, unearned revenues, current portion of notes payable)			$ X
Long-term liabilities			
(Examples: notes payable, bonds payable)			X
Total liabilities			X
Stockholders' equity			
Common stock			X
Retained earnings			X
Total liabilities and stockholders' equity			$ X

STOP AND CHECK: Total assets on the balance sheet must equal total liabilities and stockholders' equity; and, ending retained earnings on the balance sheet must equal ending retained earnings on the retained earnings statement.

Statement of Cash Flows

Name of Company Statement of Cash Flows For the Period Ended	
Cash flows from operating activities	
Note: May be prepared using the direct or indirect method	
Cash provided (used) by operating activities	$ X
Cash flows from investing activities	
(Examples: purchase / sale of long-term assets)	
Cash provided (used) by investing activities	X
Cash flows from financing activities	
(Examples: issue / repayment of long-term liabilities, issue of stock, payment of dividends)	
Net cash provided (used) by financing activities	X
Net increase (decrease) in cash	X
Cash, beginning of the period	X
Cash, end of the period	$ X

STOP AND CHECK: Cash, end of the period, on the statement of cash flows must equal cash presented on the balance sheet.

RAPID REVIEW
Using the Information in the Financial Statements

Ratio	Formula	Purpose or Use
Liquidity Ratios		
1. Current ratio	$\dfrac{\text{Current assets}}{\text{Current liabilities}}$	Measures short-term debt-paying ability.
2. Acid-test (quick) ratio	$\dfrac{\text{Cash + Short-term investments + Receivables (net)}}{\text{Current liabilities}}$	Measures immediate short-term liquidity.
3. Receivables turnover	$\dfrac{\text{Net credit sales}}{\text{Average net receivables}}$	Measures liquidity of receivables.
4. Inventory turnover	$\dfrac{\text{Cost of goods sold}}{\text{Average inventory}}$	Measures liquidity of inventory.
Profitability Ratios		
5. Profit margin	$\dfrac{\text{Net income}}{\text{Net sales}}$	Measures net income generated by each dollar of sales.
6. Gross profit margin	$\dfrac{\text{Gross profit}}{\text{Net sales}}$	Measures gross margin generated by each dollar of sales.
7. Asset turnover	$\dfrac{\text{Net sales}}{\text{Average assets}}$	Measures how efficiently assets are used to generate sales.
8. Return on assets	$\dfrac{\text{Net income}}{\text{Average total assets}}$	Measures overall profitability of assets.
9. Return on common stockholders' equity	$\dfrac{\text{Net income − Preferred stock dividends}}{\text{Average common stockholders' equity}}$	Measures profitability of stockholders' investment.
10. Book value per share	$\dfrac{\text{Total stockholders' equity}}{\text{Number of common shares outstanding}}$	Measures the equity in net assets of each share of common stock.
11. Earnings per share (EPS)	$\dfrac{\text{Net income − Preferred stock dividends}}{\text{Weighted average common shares outstanding}}$	Measures net income earned on each share of common stock.
12. Price-earnings (P-E) ratio	$\dfrac{\text{Market price per share of stock}}{\text{Earnings per share}}$	Measures ratio of the market price per share to earnings per share.
13. Payout ratio	$\dfrac{\text{Cash dividends}}{\text{Net income}}$	Measures percentage of earnings distributed in the form of cash dividends.
Solvency Ratios		
14. Debt to total assets ratio	$\dfrac{\text{Total debt}}{\text{Total assets}}$	Measures percentage of total assets provided by creditors.
15. Times interest earned	$\dfrac{\text{Income before income taxes and interest expense}}{\text{Interest expense}}$	Measures ability to meet interest payments as they come due.
16. Free cash flow	Cash provided by operating activities − Capital expenditures − Cash dividends	Measures the amount of cash generated during the current year that is available for the payment of additional dividends or for expansion.

Success in Accounting is just a click away...

With *WileyPLUS*, students and instructors will experience success in the classroom.

When students succeed—when they stay on-task and make the breakthrough that turns confusion into confidence—they are empowered to realize the possibilities for greatness that lie within each of them. Our goal is to create an environment where students reach their full potential and experience the exhilaration of academic success that will last them a lifetime. *WileyPLUS* can help you reach that goal.

Wiley**PLUS** is an online suite of resources—including the complete text—that will help your students:

- come to class better prepared for your lectures
- get immediate feedback and context-sensitive help on assignments and quizzes
- track progress throughout the course

"I just wanted to say how much this program helped me in studying… I was able to actually see my mistakes and correct them. … I really think that other students should have the chance to use *WileyPLUS*."

Ashlee Krisko, *Oakland University*

www.wiley.com/college/wileyplus

85% of students surveyed said it improved their understanding of the material. *

*Based on a spring 2005 survey of 972 student users of *WileyPLUS*

WileyPLUS is built around the activities you perform

Prepare & Present

Create outstanding class presentations using a wealth of resources, such as PowerPoint™ slides, interactive simulations, and more. Plus you can easily upload any materials you have created into your course, and combine them with the resources contained in *WileyPLUS*.

Create Assignments

Automate the assigning and grading of homework or quizzes by using the provided question banks, or by writing your own. Student results will be automatically graded and recorded in your gradebook. *WileyPLUS* also links homework problems to relevant sections of the online text, hints, or solutions— context-sensitive help where students need it most!

TO THE STUDENT

You have the potential to make a difference!

WileyPLUS is a powerful online system packed with features to help you make the most of your potential, and get the best grade you can!

With Wiley**PLUS** you get:

A complete online version of your text and other study resources

Study more effectively and get instant feedback when you practice on your own. Resources like self-assessment quizzes, tutorials, and animations bring the subject matter to life, and help you master the material.

Problem-solving help, instant grading, and feedback on your homework and quizzes

You can keep all of your assigned work in one location, making it easy for you to stay on task. Plus, many homework problems contain direct links to the relevant portion of your text to help you deal with problem-solving obstacles at the moment they come up.

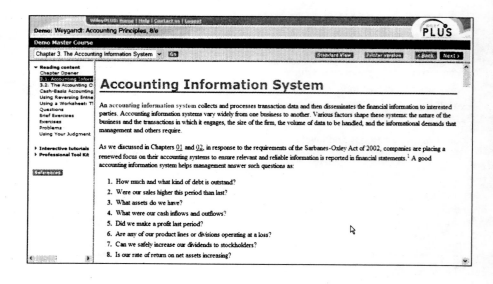

The ability to track your progress and grades throughout the term.

A personal gradebook allows you to monitor your results from past assignments at any time. You'll always know exactly where you stand.

If your instructor uses *WileyPLUS*, you will receive a URL for your class. If not, your instructor can get more information about *WileyPLUS* by visiting www.wiley.com/college/wileyplus

"It has been a great help, and I believe it has helped me to achieve a better grade."

Michael Morris, *Columbia Basin College*

69% of students surveyed said it helped them get a better grade. *

n a spring 2005 survey of 972 student users of *WileyPLUS*

8th Edition

Accounting Principles

Jerry J. Weygandt PhD, CPA

Arthur Andersen Alumni Professor of Accounting
University of Wisconsin
Madison, Wisconsin

Donald E. Kieso PhD, CPA

KPMG Emeritus Professor of Accountancy
Northern Illinois University
DeKalb, Illinois

Paul D. Kimmel PhD, CPA

Associate Professor of Accounting
University of Wisconsin—Milwaukee
Milwaukee, Wisconsin

BICENTENNIAL
1807
WILEY
2007
BICENTENNIAL

John Wiley & Sons, Inc.

Dedicated to
Amaya, Christina, and Max, and their grandmother Enid
Morgan, Cole, and Erin, and their grandmother Donna
Croix, Marais, and Kale, and their mother Merlynn

Publisher   Donald Fowley
Executive Editor   Christopher DeJohn
Associate Editor   Brian Kamins
Executive Marketing Manager   Clay Stone
Senior Production Editor   Valerie A. Vargas
Senior Media Editor   Allie K. Morris
Development Editor   Ann Torbert
Production Management   Ingrao Associates
Creative Director   Harry Nolan
Senior Designer   Madelyn Lesure
Project Editor   Ed Brislin
Text and Cover Designer   Jerry Wilke
Senior Photo Editor   Elle Wagner
Senior Illustration Editor   Sandra Rigby
Editorial Assistant   Karolina Zarychta
Marketing Assistant   Tierra Morgan
Cover Photo   © Peter Turner/The Image Bank/Getty Images

This book was set in Times Ten by GTS/Techbooks and printed and bound by Von Hoffmann Press. The cover was printed by Von Hoffmann Press.

STUDENT OWNERS MANUAL

How to Use the Study Aids in This Book

Chapter 7

Accounting Information Systems

STUDY OBJECTIVES

After studying this chapter, you should be able to:

1. Identify the basic concepts of an accounting information system.
2. Describe the nature and purpose of a subsidiary ledger.
3. Explain how companies use special journals in journalizing.
4. Indicate how companies post a multi-column journal.

✓ The Navigator

Scan **Study Objectives**
Read **Feature Story**
Read **Preview**
Read text and answer **Before You Go On** p. 297   p. 311
Work **Demonstration Problem**
Review **Summary of Study Objectives**
Answer **Self-Study Questions**
Complete **Assignments**

The Navigator is a learning system designed to guide you through the chapter and help you succeed in learning the material. It consists of (1) a checklist at the beginning of the chapter, which outlines text features and study aids you will need, and (2) a series of check boxes that prompt you to use the chapter's learning aids and set priorities as you study.

Feature Story

QUICKBOOKS® HELPS THIS RETAILER SELL GUITARS

Starting a small business requires many decisions. For example, you have to decide where to locate, how much space you need, how much inventory to have, how many employees to hire, and where to advertise. Small business owners are typically so concerned about the product and sales side of their business that they often do not give enough thought to something that is critical to their success—how to keep track of financial results.

Small business owners today can choose either manual or computerized accounting systems. For example, Paul and Laura West are the owners of the first independent dealership of Carvin guitars and professional audio equipment. When they founded their company, in Sacramento, California, they

290

The **Feature Story** helps you picture how the chapter topic relates to the real world of accounting and business. References to the Feature Story throughout the chapter will help you put new ideas in context, organize them, and remember them.

Study Objectives at the beginning of each chapter give you a framework for learning the specific concepts in the chapter. Each study objective reappears in the margin where the concept is discussed. You can review the study objectives in the **Summary** at the end of the chapter text.

decided to purchase a computerized accounting system that would integrate many aspects of their retail operations. They wanted their accounting software to manage their inventory of guitars and amplifiers, ring up sales, record and report financial data, and process credit card and debit card transactions. They evaluated a number of options and chose QuickBooks® by Intuit Inc.

QuickBooks®, like most other popular software packages, has programs designed for the needs of a specific business, which in this case is retailing. This QuickBooks® retailing package automatically collects sales information from its point-of-sale scanning devices. It also keeps track of inventory levels and automatically generates purchase orders for popular items when re-order points are reached. It even supports sales efforts by compiling a customer database from which the Wests send out targeted direct mailings to potential customers. The computerized system enables data files to be emailed to the company's accountant. This keeps costs down and makes it easier and more efficient to generate financial reports as needed. The Wests believe that the investment in the computerized system has saved them time and money and allowed them to spend more time on other aspects of their business.

Source: Intuit Inc., "QuickBooks® and ProAdvisor® Help Make Guitar Store a Hit," *Journal of Accountancy,* May 2006, p. 101.

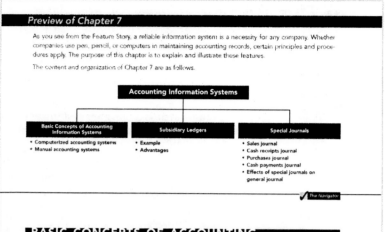

The **Preview** links the Feature Story with the major topics of the chapter and describes the purpose of the chapter.

A **graphic outline** provides a visual preview of the chapter topics. Together, the narrative and visual previews help you organize the information you are learning.

Study Objectives reappear in the margins next to the text discussion of the related topic. End-of-chapter assignments are keyed to study objectives.

Helpful Hints in the margins further clarify concepts being discussed. They are like having an instructor with you as you read.

Ethics Notes point out ethical issues related to the nearby text discussion.

---

202   Chapter 5 Accounting for Merchandising Operations

HELPFUL HINT
The merchandiser credits the Sales account only for sales of goods held for resale. Sales of assets not held for resale, such as equipment or land, are credited directly to the asset account.

ETHICS NOTE
Many companies are trying to improve the quality of their financial reporting. For example, General Electric now provides more detail on its revenues and operating profits.

For internal decision-making purposes, merchandising companies may use more than one sales account. For example, PW Audio Supply may decide to keep separate sales accounts for its sales of TV sets, DVD recorders, and satellite radio receivers. Wal-Mart might use separate accounts for sporting goods, children's clothing, and hardware—or it might have even more narrowly defined accounts. By using separate sales accounts for major product lines, rather than a single combined sales account, company management can more closely monitor sales trends and respond more strategically to changes in sales patterns. For example, if HDTV sales are increasing while DVD-player sales are decreasing, PW Audio Supply might reevaluate both its advertising and pricing policies on these items to ensure they are optimal.

On its income statement presented to outside investors, a merchandising company normally would provide only a single sales figure—the sum of all of its individual sales accounts. This is done for two reasons. First, providing detail on all of its individual sales accounts would add considerable length to its income statement. Second, companies do not want their competitors to know the details of their operating results. However, Microsoft recently expanded its disclosure of revenue from three to five types. The reason: The additional categories will better enable financial statement users to evaluate the growth of the company's consumer and Internet businesses.

Sales Returns and Allowances

We now look at the "flipside" of purchase returns and allowances, which the seller records as sales returns and allowances. PW Audio Supply's entries to record credit for returned goods involve (1) an increase in Sales Returns and Allowances and a decrease in Accounts Receivable at the $300 selling price, and (2) an increase in

---

ETHICS INSIGHT

Curbing Fraudulent Activity with Software

The Sarbanes-Oxley Act (SOX) of 2002 requires that companies demonstrate that they have adequate controls in place to detect significant fraudulent behavior by employees. As of November 2005 about 15% of publicly traded companies reported at least one material weakness in their controls that needed to be remedied.

The SOX requirements have created a huge market for software that can monitor and trace every recorded transaction and adjusting entry. This enables companies to pinpoint who used the accounting system and when they used it. These systems also require "electronic signatures" by employees for all significant transactions. Such signatures verify that employees have followed all required procedures, and that all actions are properly authorized. SOX-related technology spending was estimated to be approximately $2 billion in 2005. One firm that specializes in compliance software had 10 clients prior to SOX and 250 after SOX.

Source: W. M. Bulkeley and C. Forelle, "Anti-Crime Program: How Corporate Scandals Gave Tech Firms a New Business Line," *Wall Street Journal*, December 9, 2005, p. A1.

Why might this software help reduce fraudulent activity by employees?

Insight **examples** give you more glimpses into how actual companies make decisions using accounting information. These high-interest boxes focus on various themes—ethics, international, investor concerns, and management.

A **critical thinking question** asks you to apply your accounting learning to the story in the example. *Guideline answers* appear at the end of the chapter.

Accounting Across the Organization examples show the use of accounting by people in non-accounting functions—such as finance, marketing, or management.

Guideline answers to the critical thinking questions appear at the end of the chapter.

ACCOUNTING ACROSS THE ORGANIZATION

New Xbox Contributes to Profitability

Bryan Lee is head of finance at Microsoft's Home and Entertainment Division. In recent years the division has lost over $4 billion, mostly due to losses on the original Xbox videogame player. With the new Xbox 360 videogame player, Mr. Lee hopes the division will become profitable. He has set strict goals for sales, revenue, and profit. "A manager seeking to spend more on a feature such as a disk drive has to find allies in the group to cut spending elsewhere, or identify new revenue to offset the increase," he explains.

For example, Microsoft originally designed the new Xbox to have 256 megabytes of memory. But the design department said that amount of memory wouldn't support the best special effects. The purchasing department said that adding more memory would cost $30—which is 10% of the estimated selling price of $300. But the marketing department determined that adding the memory would let Microsoft reduce marketing costs and attract more game developers, boosting royalty revenue. It would also extend the life of the console, generating more sales." Microsoft doubled the memory to 512 megabytes.

Source: Robert A. Guth, "New Xbox Aim for Microsoft: Profitability," *Wall Street Journal*, May 24, 2005, p. C1.

In what ways is this Microsoft division using accounting to assist in its effort to become more profitable?

Review It questions marked with the PepsiCo icon direct you to find information in PepsiCo, Inc.'s 2005 annual report, printed in Appendix A. Answers to these questions appear on the last page of the chapter.

Before You Go On...

REVIEW IT

1. What are the two criteria for classifying a debt as a current liability?
2. Identify the liabilities classified as current by PepsiCo. The answer to this question appears on page 511.
3. What entries does a company make for an interest-bearing note payable?
4. How do retailers record sales taxes? Identify three unearned revenues.
5. How may the liquidity of a company be analyzed?
6. What are the accounting guidelines for contingent liabilities?

DO IT

You and several classmates are studying for the next accounting examination. They ask you to answer the following questions: (1) How is the sales tax amount determined when the cash register total includes sales taxes? (2) When should a company record a contingency in the accounts?

Action Plan

■ Remove the sales tax from the total sales.
■ Identify the criteria for recording and disclosing contingent liabilities.

Solution

(1) First, divide the total proceeds by 100% plus the sales tax percentage to find the sales amount. Second, subtract the sales amount from the total proceeds to determine the sales taxes.
(2) A company should record a contingency when it is *probable* that it will incur a liability *and* it can *reasonably* estimate the amount.

Related exercise material: BE11-1, BE11-6, E11-3, E11-5, and E11-6.

Before You Go On sections follow each key topic. **Review It** questions prompt you to stop and review the key points you have just studied. If you cannot answer these questions, you should go back and read the section again.

Brief **Do It** exercises ask you to put to work your newly acquired knowledge. They outline an **Action Plan** necessary to complete the exercise, and they show a **Solution**.

Accounting equation analyses appear next to key journal entries. They will help you understand the impact of an accounting transaction on the components of the accounting equation, on the owner's equity accounts, and on the company's cash flows.

A	=	L	+	OE
+36				
		+36		

Cash Flows
+36

A	=	L	+	OE
+425.60				
−425.60				

Cash Flows
−425.60

Book Error. The cash disbursements journal shows that check no. 443 was a payment on account to Andrea Company, a supplier. The correcting entry is:

Apr. 30	Cash	36.00	
	Accounts Payable—Andrea Company		36.00
	(To correct error in recording check no. 443)		

NSF Check. As indicated earlier, an NSF check becomes an account receivable to the depositor. The entry is:

Apr. 30	Accounts Receivable—J. R. Baron	425.60	
	Cash		425.60
	(To record NSF check)		

Owner's Equity

The content of the owner's equity section varies with the form of business organization. In a proprietorship, there is one capital account. In a partnership, there is a capital account for each partner. Corporations divide owners' equity into two accounts—Capital Stock and Retained Earnings. Corporations record stockholders' investments in the company by debiting an asset account and crediting the Capital Stock account. They record in the Retained Earnings account income retained for use in the business. Corporations combine the Capital Stock and Retained Earnings accounts and report them on the balance sheet as stockholders' equity. (We'll learn more about these corporation accounts in later chapters.) Nordstrom, Inc. recently reported its stockholders' equity section as follows.

Illustration 4-25
Stockholders' equity section

NORDSTROM, INC.
Balance Sheet (partial)
($ in thousands)

Stockholders' equity	
Common stock, 271,331 shares	$ 685,934
Retained earnings	1,406,747
Total stockholders' equity	$2,092,681

Be sure to read **ALL ABOUT YOU: *Your Personal Balance Sheet*** on page 165 for information on how topics in this chapter apply to you.

Financial statements appear regularly. Those from actual companies are identified by a company logo or a photo.

An ***All About You* feature** links some aspect of the chapter topic to your personal life, and often to some financial situation you are likely to face now or in the near future. We offer our own *opinions* about the situation near the end of the chapter.

all about YOU

Should You Be Carrying Plastic?

Smart business people carefully consider their use of credit. They evaluate who they lend to, and how they finance their own operations. They know that getting overextended on credit can destroy their business.

Individuals need to evaluate their personal credit positions using the same thought processes used by business people. Some of you might consider the idea of not having a credit card a ridiculous proposition. But the reality is that the misuse of credit cards brings financial hardship to millions of Americans each year. Credit card companies aggressively market their cards with images of glamour and happiness. But there isn't much glamour in paying an 18% to 21% interest rate, and there is very little happiness to be found in filing for personal bankruptcy.

✪ About the Numbers

Presented below is a chart that shows the major causes of personal financial problems. Note the excessive use of credit, which is cited as the number-one cause. This often translates into addiction to credit cards.

Causes of Personal Financial Problems

- Excessive use of credit/Over-obligation 39%
- Reduced income/Unemployment 24%
- Poor money management 15%
- Divorce/Separation 8%
- Other 14%

Source: Debt Solutions of America, www.becomedebtfree.com (accessed May 2008).

✪ Some Facts

* About 70% of undergraduates at 4-year colleges carry at least one credit card in their own name. Approximately 22% of college students got their first credit cards in high school.

* The average monthly debt on a college student's charge account, according to one study, is close to $2,000.

* In a recent year, Americans charged more than $1 trillion in purchases with their credit cards. That was more than they spent in cash.

* During one quarter in 2006, the percentage of delinquent credit card payments rose to 5% from 4.3%. Card write-offs increased from 5.6% to 6.4%. Until this year, both numbers were declining.

* Significant increases in consumer bankruptcy filings occurred in every region of the country. There were 2,043,535 new filings in 2005, up 31.6% from 1,552,967 in 2004 — that is, one in every 53 households filed a bankruptcy petition.

✪ What Do You Think?

Should you cut up your credit card(s)?

YES: Americans are carrying huge personal debt burdens. Credit cards encourage unnecessary, spontaneous expenditures. The interest rates on credit cards are extremely high, which causes debt problems to escalate exponentially.

NO: Credit cards are a necessity for transactions in today's economy. In fact, many transactions are difficult or impossible to carry out without a credit card. People should learn to use credit cards responsibly.

Sources: Debtsmart, www.debtsmart.com/pages/debt_stats.html; Robin Marantz Henig, "Teen Credit Cards Actually Teach Responsibility," USAToday.com, July 30, 2007.

Demonstration Problem

Cassandra Wilson Company uses a six-column cash receipts journal with the following columns:

Cash (Dr.)	Other Accounts (Cr.)
Sales Discounts (Dr.)	Cost of Goods Sold (Dr.) and
Accounts Receivable (Cr.)	Merchandise Inventory (Cr.)
Sales (Cr.)	

Cash receipts transactions for the month of July 2008 are as follows.

July 3 Cash sales total $5,800 (cost, $3,480).
5 Received a check for $6,370 from Jeltz Company in payment of an invoice dated June 26 for $6,500, terms 2/10, n/30.
9 Cassandra Wilson, the proprietor, made an additional investment of $5,000 in cash in the business.
10 Cash sales total $12,519 (cost, $7,511).
12 Received a check for $7,275 from R. Eliot & Co. in payment of a $7,500 invoice dated July 3, terms 3/10, n/30.
15 Received a customer advance of $700 cash for future sales.
20 Cash sales total $15,472 (cost, $9,283).
22 Received a check for $5,880 from Beck Company in payment of $6,000 invoice dated July 13, terms 2/10, n/30.
29 Cash sales total $17,660 (cost, $10,596).
31 Received cash of $200 on interest earned for July.

Instructions

(a) Journalize the transactions in the cash receipts journal.
(b) Contrast the posting of the Accounts Receivable and Other Accounts columns.

action plan

- Record all cash receipts in the cash receipts journal.
- The "account credited" indicates items posted individually to the subsidiary ledger or general ledger.
- Record cash sales in the cash receipts journal—not in the sales journal.
- The total debits must equal the total credits.

A **Demonstration Problem** is a review of key concepts and a warm-up before you begin homework. These sample problems provide you with an **Action Plan** in the margin that lists the strategies needed to approach and solve the problem.

The **Solution to the Demonstration Problem** demonstrates both the form and content of complete answers.

Solution to Demonstration Problem

(a)

CASSANDRA WILSON COMPANY
Cash Receipts Journal

Date	Account Credited	Ref.	Cash Dr.	Sales Discounts Dr.	Accounts Receivable Cr.	Sales Cr.	Other Accoun. Cr.
2008							
7/3			5,800			5,800	
5	Jeltz Company		6,370	130	6,500		
9	C. Wilson, Capital		5,000				5,000

The **Summary of Study Objectives** reviews the main points related to the study objectives. It provides you with an opportunity to review what you have learned and to see how the key topics within the chapter fit together.

SUMMARY OF STUDY OBJECTIVES

1 Describe the steps in determining inventory quantities. The steps are (1) take a physical inventory of goods on hand and (2) determine the ownership of goods in transit or on consignment.

2 Explain the accounting for inventories and apply the inventory cost flow methods. The primary basis of accounting for inventories is cost. Cost of goods available for sale includes (a) cost of beginning inventory and (b) cost of goods purchased. The inventory cost flow methods are: specific identification and three assumed cost flow methods—FIFO, LIFO, and average-cost.

3 Explain the financial effects of the inventory cost flow assumptions. Companies may allocate the cost of goods available for sale to cost of goods sold and ending inventory by specific identification or by a method based on an assumed cost flow. When prices are rising, the first-in, first-out (FIFO) method results in lower cost of goods sold and higher net income than the other methods. The reverse is true when prices are falling. In the balance sheet, FIFO results in an ending inventory that is closest to current value; inventory under LIFO is the farthest from current value. LIFO results in the lowest income taxes.

4 Explain the lower-of-cost-or-market basis of accounting for inventories. Companies may use the lower-of-cost-or-market (LCM) basis when the current replacement cost (market) is less than cost. Under LCM, companies recognize the loss in the period in which the price decline occurs.

5 Indicate the effects of inventory errors on the financial statements. In the income statement of the current year: (a) An error in beginning inventory will have a reverse effect on net income. (b) An error in ending inventory will have a similar effect on net income. If ending inventory errors are not corrected in the following period, their effect on net income for that period is reversed, and total net income for the two years will be correct.

In the balance sheet: Ending inventory errors will have the same effect on total assets and total stockholders' equity and no effect on liabilities.

6 Compute and interpret the inventory turnover ratio. The inventory turnover ratio is cost of goods sold divided by average inventory. To convert it to average days in inventory, divide 365 days by the inventory turnover ratio.

✓ The Navigator

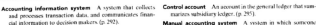

GLOSSARY

Accounting information system A system that collects and processes transaction data, and communicates financial information to decision makers. (p. 292).

Accounts payable (creditors') subsidiary ledger A subsidiary ledger that collects transaction data of individual creditors. (p. 295).

Accounts receivable (customers') subsidiary ledger A subsidiary ledger that collects transaction data of individual customers. (p. 295).

Cash payments (disbursements) journal A special journal that records all cash paid. (p. 307).

Cash receipts journal A special journal that records all cash received. (p. 301).

Control account An account in the general ledger that summarizes subsidiary ledgers. (p. 295).

Manual accounting system A system in which someone performs each of the steps in the accounting cycle by hand. (p. 295).

Purchases journal A special journal that records all purchases of merchandise on account. (p. 305).

Sales journal A special journal that records all sales of merchandise on account. (p. 299).

Special journal A journal that records similar types of transactions, such as all credit sales. (p. 298).

Subsidiary ledger A group of accounts with a common characteristic. (p. 295).

The **Glossary** defines all the **key terms** and **concepts** introduced in the chapter. Page references help you find any terms you need to study further.

The **WileyPLUS icon** here and throughout the end-of-chapter material identifies resources for further reading, study, and practice that can be accessed via WileyPLUS.

SELF-STUDY QUESTIONS

Answers are at the end of the chapter.

1. The basic principles of an accounting information system include all of the following *except:*
   a. cost effectiveness.
   b. flexibility.
   c. useful output.
   d. periodicity.

2. Which of the following is *not* an advantage of computerized accounting systems?
   a. Data is entered only once in computerized accounting systems.
   b. Computerized accounting systems provide up-to-date information.
   c. Computerized accounting systems eliminate entering of transaction information.
   d. Computerized accounting systems eliminate many errors resulting from human intervention.

3. Which of the following is *incorrect* concerning subsidiary ledgers?
   a. The purchases ledger is a common subsidiary ledger for creditor accounts.
   b. The accounts receivable ledger is a subsidiary ledger.
   c. A subsidiary ledger is a group of accounts with a common characteristic.
   d. An advantage of the subsidiary ledger is that it permits a division of labor in posting.

4. A sales journal will be used for:

	Credit Sales	Cash Sales	Sales Discounts
a.	no	yes	yes
b.	yes	no	yes
c.	yes	no	no
d.	yes	yes	no

Self-Study Questions provide a practice test, keyed to study objectives, with which you can check your knowledge of important chapter topics. *Answers* appear on the last page of the chapter.

QUESTIONS

1. (a) "The steps in the accounting cycle for a merchandising company are different from the accounting cycle for a service company." Do you agree or disagree? (b) Is the measurement of net income for a merchandising company conceptually the same as for a service company? Explain.

2. Why is the normal operating cycle for a merchandising company likely to be longer than for a service company?

3. (a) How do the components of revenues and expenses differ between merchandising and service companies? (b) Explain the income measurement process in a merchandising company.

4. How does income measurement differ between a merchandising and a service company?

5. When is cost of goods sold determined in a perpetual inventory system?

Give the journal entry on July 24 to record payment of the balance due within the discount period using a perpetual inventory system.

9. Joan Roland believes revenues from credit sales may be earned before they are collected in cash. Do you agree? Explain.

10. (a) What is the primary source document for recording (1) cash sales, (2) credit sales. (b) Using XXs for amounts, give the journal entry for each of the transactions in part (a).

11. A credit sale is made on July 10 for $900, terms 2/10, n/30. On July 12, $100 of goods are returned for credit. Give the journal entry on July 19 to record the receipt of the balance due within the discount period.

12. Explain why the Merchandise Inventory account will usually require adjustment at year-end.

Questions focus your study on understanding concepts and relationships from the chapter. Use them to help prepare for class discussion and tests.

BRIEF EXERCISES

BE4-1 The steps in using a worksheet are presented in random order below. List the steps in the proper order by placing numbers 1–5 in the blank spaces.
(a) _____ Prepare a trial balance on the worksheet.
(b) _____ Enter adjusted balances.
(c) _____ Extend adjusted balances to appropriate statement columns.
(d) _____ Total the statement columns, compute net income (loss), and complete the worksheet.
(e) _____ Enter adjustment data.

List the steps in preparing a worksheet.
(SO 1)

BE4-2 The ledger of Ley Company includes the following unadjusted balances: Prepaid Insurance $3,000, Service Revenue $58,000, and Salaries Expense $25,000. Adjusting entries are required for (a) expired insurance $1,200; (b) services provided $1,100, but unbilled and uncollected; and (c) accrued salaries payable $800. Enter the unadjusted balances and adjustments into a worksheet and complete the worksheet for all accounts. *Note:* You will need to add the following accounts: Accounts Receivable, Salaries Payable, and Insurance Expense.

Prepare partial worksheet.
(SO 1)

BE4-3 The following selected accounts appear in the adjusted trial balance columns of the worksheet for Batan Company: Accumulated Depreciation; Depreciation Expense; N. Batan, Capital; N. Batan, Drawing; Service Revenue; Supplies; and Accounts Payable. Indicate the financial statement column (income statement Dr., balance sheet Cr., etc.) to which each balance should be extended.

Identify worksheet columns for selected accounts.
(SO 1)

Brief Exercises focus on one study objective at a time. They help build confidence in your basic skills and knowledge.

EXERCISES

Analyze statements about accounting and the recording process.
(SO 1)

E2-1 Josh Cephus has prepared the following list of statement[s]
1. An account is an accounting record of either a specific ass[et]
2. An account shows only increases, not decreases, in the item it relates to.
3. Some items, such as Cash and Accounts Receivable, are combined into one account.
4. An account has a left, or credit side, and a right, or debit side.
5. A simple form of an account consisting of just the account title, the left side, and the right side, is called a T-account.

Instructions
Identify each statement as true or false. If false, indicate how to correct the statement.

Identify debits, credits, and normal balances.
(SO 2)

E2-2 Selected transactions for D. Reyes, an interior decorator, in her first month of business, are as follows.

Jan. 2 Invested $10,000 cash in business.
   3 Purchased used car for $4,000 cash for use in business.
   9 Purchased supplies on account for $500.
   11 Billed customers $1,800 for services performed.
   16 Paid $200 cash for advertising.
   20 Received $700 from customers billed on January 11.
   23 Paid creditor $300 cash on balance owed.
   28 Withdrew $1,000 cash for personal use by owner.

Instructions
For each transaction indicate the following.
(a) The basic type of account debited and credited (asset, liability, owner's equity).
(b) The specific account debited and credited (cash, rent expense, service revenue, etc.).
(c) Whether the specific account is increased or decreased.
(d) The normal balance of the specific account.

Exercises are slightly more difficult than Brief Exercises, and may combine two or more study objectives. They help you continue to build confidence in your ability to combine and use the material learned in the chapter.

EXERCISES: SET B

Visit the book's website at **www.wiley.com/college/weygandt**, and choose the Student Companion site, to access Exercise Set B.

A set of **B Exercises**, closely related to the Exercises in the book, appears at the book's *companion website*, for additional practice.

Each **Problem** helps you pull together and apply several concepts from the chapter.

An icon identifies **Exercises** and **Problems** that can be solved using Excel templates at the student website.

Selected problems, identified by this icon, can be solved using the **General Ledger Software (GLS)** package.

Problems marked with the **Peachtree** icon can be worked using *Peachtree Complete Accounting® to Accompany Accounting Principles.*

Check figures in the margin provide key numbers to let you know you're on the right track as you work the problems.

PROBLEMS: SET A

Journalize purchase and sales transactions under a perpetual inventory system.
(SO 2, 3)

P5-1A Sansomite Co. distributes suitcases to retail stores and extends credit terms of 1/10, n/30 to all of its customers. At the end of June, Sansomite's inventory consisted of 40 suitcases purchased at $30 each. During the month of July the following merchandising transactions occurred.

July 1 Purchased 60 suitcases on account for $30 each from Trunk Manufacturers, FOB destination, terms 2/10, n/30. The appropriate party also made a cash payment of $100 for freight on this date.
    3 Sold 40 suitcases on account to Satchel World for $50 each.
    9 Paid Trunk Manufacturers in full.
   12 Received payment in full from Satchel World.
   17 Sold 30 suitcases on account to The Going Concern for $50 each.
   18 Purchased 60 suitcases on account for $1,700 from Kingman Manufacturers, FOB shipping point, terms 1/10, n/30. The appropriate party also made a cash payment of $100 for freight on this date.
   20 Received $300 credit (including freight) for 10 suitcases returned to Kingman Manufacturers.
   21 Received payment in full from The Going Concern.
   22 Sold 45 suitcases on account to Fly-By-Night for $50 each.
   30 Paid Kingman Manufacturers in full.
   31 Granted Fly-By-Night $200 credit for 4 suitcases returned costing $120.

Sansomite's chart of accounts includes the following: No. 101 Cash, No. 112 Accounts Receivable, No. 120 Merchandise Inventory, No. 201 Accounts Payable, No. 401 Sales, No. 412 Sales Returns and Allowances, No. 414 Sales Discounts, No. 505 Cost of Goods Sold.

Instructions
Journalize the transactions for the month of July for Sansomite using a perpetual inventory system.

Journalize, post, and prepare a partial income statement.
(SO 2, 3, 5, 6)

P5-2A Olaf Distributing Company completed the following merchandising transactions in the month of April. At the beginning of April, the ledger of Olaf showed Cash of $9,000 and M. Olaf, Capital of $9,000.

Apr. 2 Purchased merchandise on account from Dakota Supply Co. $6,900, terms 1/10, n/30.
    4 Sold merchandise on account $5,500, FOB destination, terms 1/10, n/30. The cost of the merchandise sold was $4,100.
    5 Paid $240 freight on April 4 sale.
    6 Received credit from Dakota Supply Co. for merchandise returned $500.
   11 Paid Dakota Supply Co. in full, less discount.
   13 Received collections in full, less discounts, from customers billed on April 4.
   14 Purchased merchandise for cash $3,800.
   16 Received refund from supplier for returned goods on cash purchase of April 14, $500.
   18 Purchased merchandise from Skywalker Distributors $4,500, FOB shipping point, terms 2/10, n/30.
   20 Paid freight on April 18 purchase $100.
   23 Sold merchandise for cash $6,400. The merchandise sold had a cost of $5,120.
   26 Purchased merchandise for cash $2,300.
   27 Paid Skywalker Distributors in full, less discount.
   29 Made refunds to cash customers for defective merchandise $90. The returned merchandise had a scrap value of $30.
   30 Sold merchandise on account $3,700, terms n/30. The cost of the merchandise sold was $2,800.

Olaf Company's chart of accounts includes the following: No. 101 Cash, No. 112 Accounts Receivable, No. 120 Merchandise Inventory, No. 201 Accounts Payable, No. 301 M. Olaf, Capital, No. 401 Sales, No. 412 Sales Returns and Allowances, No. 414 Sales Discounts, No. 505 Cost of Goods Sold, and No. 644 Freight-out.

Instructions
(a) Journalize the transactions using a perpetual inventory system.
(b) Enter the beginning cash and capital balances, and post the transactions. (Use J1 for the journal reference.)
(c) Prepare the income statement through gross profit for the month of April 2008.

PROBLEMS: SET B

Journalize purchase and sales transactions under a perpetual inventory system.
(SO 2, 3)

P5-1B Sorvino Book Warehouse distributes hardcover books to retail stores and extends credit terms of 2/10, n/30 to all of its customers. At the end of May, Sorvino's inventory consisted of 240 books purchased at $1,200. During the month of June the following merchandising transactions occurred.

June 1 Purchased 180 books on account for $5 each from Atkinson Publishers, FOB destination, terms 2/10, n/30. The appropriate party also made a cash payment of $50 for the freight on this date.
    3 Sold 120 books on account to Readers-R-Us for $10 each.
    6 Received $50 credit for 10 books returned to Atkinson Publishers.
    9 Paid Atkinson Publishers in full, less discount.
   15 Received payment in full from Readers-R-Us.
   17 Sold 150 books on account to Bargain Books for $10 each.
   20 Purchased 120 books on account for $5 each from Bookem Publishers, FOB destination, terms 2/15, n/30. The appropriate party also made a cash payment of $50 for the freight on this date.
   24 Received payment in full from Bargain Books.
   26 Paid Bookem Publishers in full, less discount.
   28 Sold 110 books on account to Read-n-Weep Bookstore for $10 each.
   30 Granted Read-n-Weep Bookstore $150 credit for 15 books returned costing $75.

Sorvino Book Warehouse's chart of accounts includes the following: No. 101 Cash, No. 112 Accounts Receivable, No. 120 Merchandise Inventory, No. 201 Accounts Payable, No. 401 Sales, No. 412 Sales Returns and Allowances, No. 414 Sales Discounts, No. 505 Cost of Goods Sold.

Instructions
Journalize the transactions for the month of June for Sorvino Book Warehouse using a perpetual inventory system.

In the book, two similar sets of **Problems—A** and **B**—are keyed to the same study objectives.

An additional parallel set of **C Problems** appears at the book's companion site.

PROBLEMS: SET C

Visit the book's website at **www.wiley.com/college/weygandt**, and choose the Student Companion site, to access Problem Set C.

COMPREHENSIVE PROBLEM: CHAPTERS 2 TO 4

Julie Molony opened Julie's Maids Cleaning Service on July 1, 2008. During July, the company completed the following transactions.

July 1 Invested $14,000 cash in the business.
    1 Purchased a used truck for $10,000, paying $3,000 cash and the balance on account.
    3 Purchased cleaning supplies for $800 on account.
    5 Paid $1,800 on a one-year insurance policy, effective July 1.
   12 Billed customers $3,800 for cleaning services.
   18 Paid $1,000 of amount owed on truck, and $400 of amount owed on cleaning supplies.
   20 Paid $1,600 for employee salaries.
   21 Collected $1,400 from customers billed on July 12.
   25 Billed customers $1,500 for cleaning services.

Comprehensive Problems in six chapters combine concepts covered across multiple chapters.

CONTINUING COOKIE CHRONICLE

CCC1 Natalie Koebel spent much of her childhood learning the art of cookie-making from her grandmother. They passed many happy hours mastering every type of cookie imaginable and later creating new recipes that were both healthy and delicious. Now at the start of her second year in college, Natalie is investigating various possibilities for starting her own business as part of the requirements of the entrepreneurship program in which she is enrolled.

A long-time friend insists that Natalie has to somehow include cookies in her business plan. After a series of brainstorming sessions, Natalie settles on the idea of operating a cookie-making school. She will start on a part-time basis and offer her services in people's homes. Now that she has started thinking about it, the possibilities seem endless. During the fall, she will concentrate on holiday cookies. She will offer individual lessons and group sessions (which will probably be more entertainment than education for the participants). Natalie also decides to include children in her target market.

The first difficult decision is coming up with the perfect name for her business. In the end, she settles on "Cookie Creations" and then moves on to more important issues.

Instructions

(a) What form of business organization—proprietorship, partnership, or corporation—do you recommend that Natalie use for her business? Discuss the benefits and weaknesses of each form and give the reasons for your choice.

(b) Will Natalie need accounting information? If yes, what information will she need and why? How often will she need this information?

(c) Identify specific asset, liability, and equity accounts that Cookie Creations will likely use to record its business transactions.

(d) Should Natalie open a separate bank account for the business? Why or why not?

The **Continuing Cookie Chronicle** exercise follows the continuing saga of accounting for a small business begun by an entrepreneurial student.

BROADENING YOUR PERSPECTIVE

FINANCIAL REPORTING AND ANALYSIS

Financial Reporting Problem
PepsiCo, Inc.

BYP1-1 The actual financial statements of PepsiCo, as presented in the company's 2005 Annual Report, are contained in Appendix A (at the back of the textbook).

Instructions
Refer to PepsiCo's financial statements and answer the following questions.

(a) What were PepsiCo's total assets at December 31, 2005? At December 25, 2004?

(b) How much cash (and cash equivalents) did PepsiCo have on December 31, 2005?

(c) What amount of accounts payable did PepsiCo report on December 31, 2005? On December 25, 2004?

(d) What were PepsiCo's net sales in 2003? In 2004? In 2005?

(e) What is the amount of the change in PepsiCo's net income

The **Broadening Your Perspective** section helps you pull together concepts from the chapter and apply them to real-world business situations.

The **Financial Reporting Problem** focuses on reading and understanding the financial statements of PepsiCo, Inc., which are printed in Appendix A.

A **Comparative Analysis Problem** compares and contrasts the financial reporting of PepsiCo with its competitor The Coca-Cola Company.

Comparative Analysis Problem
PepsiCo, Inc. vs. The Coca-Cola Company

BYP5-2 PepsiCo's financial statements are presented in Appendix A. Coca-Cola's financial statements are presented in Appendix B.

Instructions
(a) Based on the information contained in these financial statements, determine each of the following for each company.
(1) Gross profit for 2005.
(2) Gross profit rate for 2005.
(3) Operating income for 2005.
(4) Percent change in operating income from 2004 to 2005.
(b) What conclusions concerning the relative profitability of the two companies can you draw from these data?

Exploring the Web

BYP5-3 No financial decision maker should ever rely solely on the financial information reported in the annual report to make decisions. It is important to keep abreast of financial news. This activity demonstrates how to search for financial news on the Web.

Address: biz.yahoo.com/i, or go to **www.wiley.com/college/weygandt**

Steps:
1. Type in either PepsiCo or Coca-Cola.
2. Choose **News.**
3. Select an article that sounds interesting to you.

Instructions
(a) What was the source of the article? (For example, Reuters, Businesswire, PR Newswire.)
(b) Pretend that you are a personal financial planner and that one of your clients owns stock in the company. Write a brief memo to your client, summarizing the article and explaining the implications of the article for their investment.

Exploring the Web exercises guide you to websites where you can find and analyze information related to the chapter topic.

CRITICAL THINKING

Decision Making Across the Organization

BYP5-4 Three years ago, Carrie Dungy and her brother-in-law Luke Barber opened FedCo Department Store. For the first two years, business was good, but the following condensed income results for 2007 were disappointing.

FEDCO DEPARTMENT STORE
Income Statement
For the Year Ended December 31, 2007

Net sales		$700,000
Cost of goods sold		553,000
Gross profit		147,000
Operating expenses		
Selling expenses	$100,000	
Administrative expenses	20,000	120,000
Net income		$ 27,000

Decision Making Across the Organization helps you build decision-making skills by analyzing accounting information in a less structured situation. These cases require teams of students to evaluate a manager's decision or lead to a decision among alternative courses of action.

Communication Activity

BYP8-5 As a new auditor for the CPA firm of Croix, Marais, and Kale, you have been assigned to review the internal controls over mail cash receipts of Manhattan Company. Your review reveals the following: Checks are promptly endorsed "For Deposit Only," but no list of the checks is prepared by the person opening the mail. The mail is opened either by the cashier or by the employee who maintains the accounts receivable records. Mail receipts are deposited in the bank weekly by the cashier.

Instructions
Write a letter to Jerry Mays, owner of the Manhattan Company, explaining the weaknesses in internal control and your recommendations for improving the system.

Communication Activities help you build business communication skills by asking you to engage in real-world business situations using writing, speaking, or presentation skills.

Ethics Cases ask you to reflect on typical ethical dilemmas, analyze the stakeholders and the issues involved, and decide on an appropriate course of action.

Ethics Case

BYP3-6 Bluestem Company is a pesticide manufacturer. Its sales declined greatly this year due to the passage of legislation outlawing the sale of several of Bluestem's chemical pesticides. In the coming year, Bluestem will have environmentally safe and competitive chemicals to replace these discontinued products. Sales in the next year are expected to greatly exceed any prior year's. The decline in sales and profits appears to be a one-year aberration. But even so, the company president fears a large dip in the current year's profits. He believes that such a dip could cause a significant drop in the market price of Bluestem's stock and make the company a takeover target.

To avoid this possibility, the company president calls in Cathi Bell, controller, to discuss this period's year-end adjusting entries. He urges her to accrue every possible revenue and to defer as many expenses as possible. He says to Cathi, "We need the revenues this year, and next year can easily absorb expenses deferred from this year. We can't let our stock price be hammered down!" Cathi didn't get around to recording the adjusting entries until January 17, but she dated the entries December 31 as if they were recorded then. Cathi also made every effort to comply with the president's request.

Instructions
(a) Who are the stakeholders in this situation?
(b) What are the ethical considerations of (1) the president's request and (2) Cathi's dating the adjusting entries December 31?
(c) Can Cathi accrue revenues and defer expenses and still be ethical?

The **"All About You" Activity** offers another opportunity to explore the All About You topic in a homework assignment.

"All About You" Activity

BYP3-7 In the **All About You** feature in this chapter (p. 113), you learned how important it is that companies report or disclose information about all liabilities, including potential liabilities related to environmental clean-up. There are many situations in which you will be asked to provide personal financial information about your assets, liabilities, revenue, and expenses. Sometimes you will face difficult decisions regarding what to disclose and how to disclose it.

Instructions
Suppose that you are putting together a loan application to purchase a home. Based on your income and assets, you qualify for the mortgage loan, but just barely. How would you address each of the following situations in reporting your financial position for the loan application? Provide responses for each of the following questions.
(a) You signed a guarantee for a bank loan that a friend took out for $20,000. If your friend doesn't pay, you will have to pay. Your friend has made all of the payments so far, and it appears he will be able to pay in the future.
(b) You were involved in an auto accident in which you were at fault. There is the possibility that you may have to pay as much as $50,000 as part of a settlement. The issue will not be resolved before the bank processes your mortgage request.
(c) The company at which you work isn't doing very well, and it has recently laid off employees. You are still employed, but it is quite possible that you will lose your job in the next few months.

Answers to Insight and Accounting Across the Organization Questions

p. 386 Be Sure to Read the Fine Print
Q: Why are credit card companies willing to offer relaxed repayment options?
A: *Credit card companies generate their income primarily from interest charges on cardholders' balances. The larger the outstanding balances, the greater the interest income.*

p. 392 When Investors Ignore Warning Signs
Q: When would it be appropriate for a company to lower its allowance for doubtful accounts as a percentage of its receivables?
A: *It could do so if the company's collection experience had improved, or was expected to improve, and therefore the company expected lower defaults as a percentage of receivables.*

p. 395 How Does a Credit Card Work?
Q: Assume that Nordstrom prepares a bank reconciliation at the end of each month. If some credit card sales have not been processed by the bank, how should Nordstrom treat these transactions on its bank reconciliation?
A: *Nordstrom would treat the credit card receipts as deposits in transit. It has already recorded the receipts as cash. Its bank will increase Nordstrom's cash account when it receives the receipts.*

p. 400 Who Gets Credit?
Q: How would reported net income likely differ during the first year of this promotion if Mitsubishi used the direct write-off method versus the allowance method?
A: *Under the direct write-off method, Mitsubishi would not record bad debt expense until a customer defaulted on a loan. Under the allowance method, it would estimate how many of its loans would default rather than waiting until they default. The direct write-off method would have resulted in higher net income during the first year of the promotion.*

Authors' Comments on *All About You*: Should You Be Carrying Plastic? (p. 403)

We aren't going to tell you to cut up your credit card. Well, we aren't going to tell *all* of you to do so. Credit cards, when used properly, can serve a very useful purpose. They provide great convenience, are widely accepted, and can be a source of security in an emergency. But too many Americans use credit cards inappropriately. When businesses purchase short-term items such as inventory and supplies, they use short-term credit, which they expect to pay back very quickly. The same should be true of your credit card. When you make purchases of everyday items, you should completely pay off those items within a month or two. If you don't, you are living beyond your means, and you will soon dig yourself a deep financial pit.

Longer-term items should not be purchased with credit cards, since the interest rate is too high. If you currently have a large balance on your credit card(s), we encourage you to cut up your card(s) until you have paid off your balance(s).

Answers to Insight and Accounting Across the Organization questions offer guideline answers for questions in the boxed real-world examples.

Authors' Comments on *All About You* provide the author's opinions and further discussion about financial literacy topic in the chapter.

The **Answer to PepsiCo Review It Question**, based on the PepsiCo financial statements, appears here.

Answers to Self-Study Questions provide feedback on your understanding of the chapter's basic concepts.

Answer to PepsiCo Review It Question 4, p. 13
PepsiCo's accounting equation is:

Assets	=	Liabilities	+	Owners' (Stockholders') Equity
$31,727,000,000	=	$17,476,000,000	+	$14,251,000,000

(Owners' equity includes preferred stock.)

Answers to Self-Study Questions
1. b   2. d   3. c   4. b   5. d   6. b   7. a   8. b   9. c   10. a

✓ *Remember to go back to the Navigator box on the chapter-opening page and check off your completed work.*

After you complete your homework assignments, it's a good idea to go back to **The Navigator** checklist at the start of the chapter to see if you have used all the chapter's study aids.

SPECIAL STUDENT SUPPLEMENTS

That Help You Get the Best Grade You Can

The Accounting Principles Website

The book's website at **www.wiley.com/college/weygandt** provides a wealth of materials that will help you develop a conceptual understanding and increase your ability to solve problems. For example, you will find PowerPoint™ presentations and web quizzing. Be sure to check the site often.

Working Papers

Working papers are partially completed accounting forms (templates) for all end-of-chapter brief exercises, exercises, problems, and cases. They are a convenient resource for organizing and completing homework assignments, and they demonstrate how to correctly set up solution formats. The Working Papers are available in various groupings, so take care to order the set that matches the book you are using (check the number of chapters in your book). Also available on CD-ROM is an electronic version of the print working papers, which are Excel-formatted templates that will help you learn to properly format and present end-of-chapter textbook solutions.

Study Guide

The Study Guide is a comprehensive review of accounting. It guides you through chapter content, tied to study objectives. Each chapter of the Study Guide includes a chapter review (20 to 30 key points); a demonstration problem; and for extra practice, true/false, multiple-choice, and matching questions, and additional exercises, with solutions. The Study Guide is an excellent tool for use on a regular basis during the course and also when preparing for exams. The Study Guide is available in two volumes, Volume I for Chapters 1–12 and Volume II for Chapters 13–26.

Problem-Solving Survival Guide

This tutorial is designed to improve your success rates in solving homework assignments and exam questions. Each chapter includes an overview of key topics; a purpose statement and link to study objectives for each homework assignment; numerous review tips to alert you to common pitfalls and misconceptions; and reminders to concepts and principles. Multiple-choice exercises and cases similar to common homework assignments or exam questions enhance your problem-solving proficiency. Solutions not only explain answers but also discuss an approach to similar types of accounting problems. The Problem-Solving Survival Guide comes in two volumes, Volume I (Chapters 1–12) and Volume II (Chapters 13–26).

General Ledger Software for Windows

GLS The General Ledger Software program allows you to use a computerized accounting system to solve the end-of-chapter text problems that are identified by the icon shown here.

Peachtree Complete® Accounting

A workbook and accompanying CD teach you how to use Peachtree Complete® Accounting Software. Selected problems in the book, denoted by the Peachtree icon, can be solved using this supplementary software package.

Solving Accounting Principles Problems Using Excel

A manual guides you step-by-step from an introduction to computers and Excel, to completion of preprogrammed spreadsheets, to design of your own spreadsheets. Accompanying spreadsheet templates allow you to complete selected end-of-chapter exercises and problems, identified by the icon shown here.

Practice Sets

Practice sets expose you to real-world simulations of maintaining a complete set of accounting records for a business. They integrate the business events, accounting concepts, procedures, and records covered within the textbook, and they reinforce the concepts and procedures learned. Four different practice sets are available: Campus Cycle Shop; Heritage Home Furniture; University Bookstore; and Custom Party Associates.

For more information on any of these student supplements, check with your professor or bookstore, or go to the companion website at **www.wiley.com/college/weygandt**.

Jerry J. Weygandt, PhD, CPA, is Arthur Andersen Alumni Professor of Accounting at the University of Wisconsin—Madison. He holds a Ph.D. in accounting from the University of Illinois. Articles by Professor Weygandt have appeared in the *Accounting Review, Journal of Accounting Research, Accounting Horizons, Journal of Accountancy,* and other academic and professional journals. These articles have examined such financial reporting issues as accounting for price-level adjustments, pensions, convertible securities, stock option contracts, and interim reports. Professor Weygandt is author of other accounting and financial reporting books and is a member of the American Accounting Association, the American Institute of Certified Public Accountants, and the Wisconsin Society of Certified Public Accountants. He has seved on numerous committees of the American Accounting Association and as a member of the editorial board of the *Accounting Review*; he also has served as President and Secretary-Treasurer of the American Accounting Association. In addition, he has been actively involved with the American Institute of Certified Public Accountants and has been a member of the Accounting Standards Executive Committee (AcSEC) of that organization. He has served on the FASB task force that examined the reporting issues related to accounting for income taxes and served as a trustee of the Financial Accounting Foundation. Professor Weygandt has received the Chancellor's Award for Excellence in Teaching and the Beta Gamma Sigma Dean's Teaching Award. He is on the board of directors of M & I Bank of Southern Wisconsin. He is the recipient of the Wisconsin Institute of CPA's Outstanding Educator's Award and the Lifetime Achievement Award. In 2001 he received the American Accounting Association's Outstanding Accounting Educator Award.

Donald E. Kieso, PhD, CPA, received his bachelor's degree from Aurora University and his doctorate in accounting from the University of Illinois. He has served as chairman of the Department of Accountancy and is currently the KPMG Emeritus Professor of Accountancy at Northern Illinois University. He has public accounting experience with Price Waterhouse & Co. (San Francisco and Chicago) and Arthur Andersen & Co. (Chicago) and research experience with the Research Division of the American Institute of Certified Public Accountants (New York). He has done postdoctorate work as a Visiting Scholar at the University of California at Berkeley and is a recipient of NIU's Teaching Excellence Award and four Golden Apple Teaching Awards. Professor Kieso is the author of other accounting and business books and is a member of the American Accounting Association, the American Institute of Certified Public Accountants, and the Illinois CPA Society. He has served as a member of the Board of Directors of the Illinois CPA Society, the AACSB's Accounting Accreditation Committees, the State of Illinois Comptroller's Commission, as Secretary-Treasurer of the Federation of Schools of Accountancy, and as Secretary-Treasurer of the American Accounting Association. Professor Kieso is currently serving on the Board of Trustees and Executive Committee of Aurora University, as a member of the Board of Directors of Kishwaukee Community Hospital, and as Treasurer and Director of Valley West Community Hospital. From 1989 to 1993 he served as a charter member of the national Accounting Education Change Commission. He is the recipient of the Outstanding Accounting Educator Award from the Illinois CPA Society, the FSA's Joseph A. Silvoso Award of Merit, the NIU Foundation's Humanitarian Award for Service to Higher Education, a Distinguished Service Award from the Illinois CPA Society, and in 2003 an honorary doctorate from Aurora University.

Paul D. Kimmel, PhD, CPA, received his bachelor's degree from the University of Minnesota and his doctorate in accounting from the University of Wisconsin. He is an Associate Professor at the University of Wisconsin—Milwaukee, and has public accounting experience with Deloitte & Touche (Minneapolis). He was the recipient of the UWM School of Business Advisory Council Teaching Award, the Reggie Taite Excellence in Teaching Award, and a three-time winner of the Outstanding Teaching Assistant Award at the University of Wisconsin. He is also a recipient of the Elijah Watts Sells Award for Honorary Distinction for his results on the CPA exam. He is a member of the American Accounting Association and the Institute of Management Accountants and has published articles in *Accounting Review, Accounting Horizons, Advances in Management Accounting, Managerial Finance, Issues in Accounting Education, Journal of Accounting Education*, as well as other journals. His research interests include accounting for financial instruments and innovation in accounting education. He has published papers and given numerous talks on incorporating critical thinking into accounting education, and helped prepare a catalog of critical thinking resources for the Federated Schools of Accountancy.

This questionnaire aims to find out something about your preferences for the way you work with information. You will have a preferred learning style, and one part of that learning style is your preference for the intake and output of ideas and information.

Choose the answer which best explains your preference. You can select more than one response if a single answer does not match your perception. Leave blank any question that does not apply.

1. You are about to give directions to a person who is standing with you. She is staying in a hotel in town and wants to visit your house later. She has a rental car. You would:
   a. draw or provide a map on paper.
   b. tell her the directions.
   c. write down the directions (without a map).
   d. pick her up from the hotel in a car.

2. You are not sure whether a word should be spelled "dependent" or "dependant." You would:
   c. look it up in the dictionary.
   a. see the word in your mind and choose by the way it looks
   b. sound it out in your mind.
   d. write both versions down on paper and choose one.

3. You have just received a copy of your itinerary for a world trip. This is of interest to some friends. You would:
   b. phone, text, or email them and tell them about it.
   c. send them a copy of the printed itinerary.
   a. show them on a map of the world.
   d. describe what you plan to do at each place on the itinerary.

4. You are going to cook something as a special treat for your family. You would:
   d. cook something familiar without the need for instructions.
   a. thumb through the cookbook looking for ideas from the pictures.
   c. refer to a specific cookbook where there is a good recipe.

5. A group of tourists has been assigned to you to find out about wildlife reserves or parks. You would:
   d. drive them to a wildlife reserve or park.
   a. show them slides and photographs.
   c. give them pamphlets or a book on wildlife reserves or parks.
   b. give them a talk on wildlife reserves or parks.

6. You are about to purchase a new CD player. Other than price, what would most influence your decision?
   b. The salesperson telling you what you want to know.
   c. Reading the details about it.
   d. Playing with the controls and listening to it.
   a. It looks really smart and fashionable.

7. Recall a time in your life when you learned how to do something like playing a new board game. Try to avoid choosing a very physical skill, e.g. riding a bike. You learned best by:
   a. visual clues – pictures, diagrams and charts.
   c. written instructions.
   b. listening to somebody explaining it.
   d. doing it or trying it.

8. You have a knee problem. You would prefer that the doctor:
   b. told you what was wrong.
   a. showed you a diagram of what was wrong.
   d. used a model of a knee to show you what was wrong.

9. You are about to learn to use a new program on a computer. You would:
   d. sit down at the keyboard and experiment with the program.
   c. read the manual that came with the program.
   b. telephone or text a friend and ask questions about the program.

10. You are staying in a hotel and have a rental car. You would like to visit friends whose address/location you do not know. You would like them to:
    a. draw you a map on paper or provide a map from the Internet.
    b. tell you the directions.
    c. write down the directions (without a map).
    d. pick you up from the hotel in a car.

11. Apart from the price, what would most influence your decision to buy a particular textbook?
    d. You have used a copy before.
    b. A friend talking about it.
    c. Quickly reading parts of it.
    a. The way it looks is appealing.

12. A new movie has arrived in town. What would most influence your decision to go (or not go)?
    b. You heard a review about it on the radio.
    c. You read a review about it.
    a. You saw a preview of it.

13. You prefer a teacher who likes to use:
    c. a textbook, handouts, and reading.
    a. flow diagrams, charts, and graphs.
    d. field trips, models, laboratories, and practical sessions.
    b. class or email discussion, online chat groups, and guest speakers.

Count your choices:

a.	b.	c.	d.
☐	☐	☐	☐
V	A	R	K

Now match the letter or letters you have recorded most to the same letter or letters in the Learning Styles Chart. You may have more than one learning style preference—many people do. Next to each letter in the chart are suggestions that will refer you to different learning aids throughout this text.

LEARNING STYLES CHART

	Intake: To take in the information	To make a study package

Visual

Intake:
- Pay close attention to charts, drawings, and handouts your instructors use.
- Underline.
- Use different colors.
- Use symbols, flow charts, graphs, different arrangements on the page, white spaces.

To make a study package:
Convert your lecture notes into "page pictures." To do this:
- Use the "Intake" strategies.
- Reconstruct images in different ways.
- Redraw pages from memory.
- Replace words with symbols and initials.
- Look at your pages.

Aural

Intake:
- Attend lectures and tutorials.
- Discuss topics with students and instructors.
- Explain new ideas to other people.
- Use a tape recorder.
- Leave spaces in your lecture notes for later recall.
- Describe overheads, pictures, and visuals to somebody who was not in class.

To make a study package:
You may take poor notes because you prefer to listen. Therefore:
- Expand your notes by talking with others and with information from your textbook.
- Tape-record summarized notes and listen.
- Read summarized notes out loud.
- Explain your notes to another "aural" person.

Reading/ Writing

Intake:
- Use lists and headings.
- Use dictionaries, glossaries, and definitions.
- Read handouts, textbooks, and supplementary library readings.
- Use lecture notes.

To make a study package:
- Write out words again and again.
- Reread notes silently.
- Rewrite ideas and principles into other words.
- Turn charts, diagrams, and other illustrations into statements.

Kinesthetic

Intake:
- Use all your senses.
- Go to labs, take field trips.
- Listen to real-life examples.
- Pay attention to applications.
- Use hands-on approaches.
- Use trial-and-error methods.

To make a study package:
You may take poor notes because topics do not seem concrete or relevant. Therefore:
- Put examples in your summaries.
- Use case studies and applications to help with principles and abstract concepts.
- Talk about your notes with another "kinesthetic" person.
- Use pictures and photographs that illustrate an idea.

Source: Adapted from VARK pack. © Copyright 2001–2006 Neil D. Fleming. This material may be used for faculty or student development if attribution is given. It may not be published in either paper or electronic form without consent of the authors. There is a VARK website at **www.vark-learn.com.**

The Navigator/Feature Story/Preview
Infographics/Illustrations
Accounting Equation Analyses
Highlighted words
Graph in *All About You*
Demonstration Problem/Action Plan
Questions/Exercises/Problems
Financial Reporting Problem
Comparative Analysis Problem
Exploring the Web

* Recall your "page pictures."
* Draw diagrams where appropriate.
* Practice turning your visuals back into words.

Visual

Preview
Insight Boxes
Review It/Do It/Action Plan
"What Do You Think?" in *All About You*
Summary of Study Objectives
Glossary
Demonstration Problem/Action Plan
Self-Study Questions
Questions/Exercises/Problems
Financial Reporting Problem
Comparative Analysis Problem
Exploring the Web
Group Decision Case
Communication Activity
Ethics Case

* Talk with the instructor.
* Spend time in quiet places recalling the ideas.
* Practice writing answers to old exam questions.
* Say your answers out loud.

Aural

The Navigator/Feature Story/Study
    Objectives/Preview
Review It/Do It/Action Plan
Summary of Study Objectives
Glossary/Self-Study Questions
Questions/Exercises/Problems
Writing Problems
Financial Reporting Problem
Comparative Analysis Problem
"All About You" Activity
Exploring the Web
Group Decision Case
Communication Activity

* Write exam answers.
* Practice with multiple-choice questions.
* Write paragraphs, beginnings and endings.
* Write your lists in outline form.
* Arrange your words into hierarchies and points.

Reading/ Writing

The Navigator/Feature Story/Preview
Infographics/Illustrations
Review It/Do It/Action Plan
Summary of Study Objectives
Demonstration Problem/Action Plan
Self-Study Questions
Questions/Exercises/Problems
Financial Reporting Problem
Comparative Analysis Problem
Exploring the Web
Group Decision Case
Communication Activity
"All About You" Activity

* Write practice answers.
* Role-play the exam situation.

Kinesthetic

For all learning styles: Be sure to use the book's website to enhance your understanding of the concepts and procedures of the text.

ACKNOWLEDGMENTS

From the first edition and onward, we have benefited greatly from feedback provided by numerous instructors and students of accounting principles courses throughout the country. We offer our thanks to those many people for their criticism, constructive suggestions, and innovative ideas. We are indebted to the following reviewers and focus group participants for their contributions to the most recent editions of the book.

Seventh Edition

Matt Anderson, *Michigan State University;* Yvonne Baker, *Cincinnati State Tech Community College;* Peter Battelle, *University of Vermont;* Michael Blackett, *National American University;* David Boyd, *Arkansas State University;* Leon Button, *Scottsdale Community College;* Trudy Chiaravelli, *Lansing Community College;* Kenneth Couvillion, *San Joaquin Delta College.*

Thomas Davies, *University of South Dakota;* Peggy DeJong, *Kirkwood Community College;* Kevin Dooley, *Kapi'olani Community College;* Edmond Douville, *Indiana University Northwest;* Pamela Druger, *Augustana College;* John Eagan, *Erie Community College;* Richard Ellison, *Middlesex Community College;* Richard Ghio, *San Joaquin Delta College.*

Jeannie Harrington, *Middle Tennessee State University;* William Harvey, *Henry Ford Community College;* Zach Holmes, *Oakland Community College;* Paul Holt, *Texas A&M–Kingsville;* Verne Ingram, *Red Rocks Community College;* Mark Johnston, *Washtenaw Community College;* Shirly Kleiner, *Johnson County Community College;* Jo Koehn, *Central Missouri State University.*

Robert Laycock, *Montgomery College;* Maureen McBeth, *College of DuPage;* Jerry Martens, *Community College of Aurora;* Shea Mears, *Des Moines Area Community College;* Pam Meyer, *University of Louisiana–Lafayette;* Robin Nelson, *Community College of Southern Nevada;* George Palz, *Erie Community College;* Bill Rencher, *Seminole Community College;* Renee Rigoni, *Monroe Community College;* Jill Russell, *Camden County College.*

Alice Sineath, *Forsyth Tech Community College;* Jeff Slater, *North Shore Community College;* Ken Sinclair, *Lehigh University;* James Smith, *Ivy Tech State College;* Carol Springer, *Georgia State University;* Lynda Thompson, *Massasoit Community College;* Sue Van Boven, *Paradise Valley Community College;* and Christian Widmer, *Tidewater Community College.*

Eighth Edition

Sylvia Allen, *Los Angeles Valley College*; Alan Applebaum, *Broward Community College*; Juanita Ardavany, *Los Angeles Valley College*; Jim Benedum, *Milwaukee Area Technical College;* Bernard Bieg, *Bucks County College*; Barry Bomboy, *J. Sargeant Reynolds Community College;* Greg Brookins, *Santa Monica College;* Kent D. Bowen, *Butler County Community College*; Kurt H. Buerger, *Angelo State University.*

Steve Carlson, *University of North Dakota;* Fatma Cebenoyan, *Hunter College;* Shifei Chung, *Rowan University;* Siu Chung, *Los Angeles Valley College;* Lisa Cole, *Johnson County Community College;* Alan B. Czyzewski, *Indiana State University*; John Delaney, *Augustana College*; Pamela Druger, *Augustana College*; Russell Dunn, *Broward Community College;* Mary Falkey, *Prince George Community College;* Raymond Gardner, *Ocean County College.*

Amy Haas, *Kingsborough Community College, CUNY;* Bonnie Harrison, *College of Southern Maryland*; Michelle Heard, *Metropolitan Community College;* Ruth Henderson, *Union Community College;* Ed Hess, *Butler County Community College*; Kathy Hill, *Leeward Community College*; Patty Holmes, *Des Moines Area Community College;* Audrey Hunter, *Broward Community College.*

Joanne Johnson, *Caldwell Community College*; Naomi Karolinski, *Monroe Community College*; Anil Khatri, *Bowie State University*; Ken Koerber, *Bucks County Community College*; Adriana Kulakowski, *Mynderse Academy*; Natasha Librizzi, *Madison Area Technical College*; William P. Lovell, *Cayuga Community College/ Fulton Campus.*

Melanie Mackey, *Ocean County College;* Francis T. McCloskey, *Community College of Philadelphia* Chris McNamara, *Finger Lakes Community College*; Edwin Mah, *University of Maryland, University College*; Thomas Marsh, *Northern Virginia Community College—Annandale;* Cathy Montesarchio, *Broward Community College*; Robin Nelson, *Community College of Southern Nevada;* Joseph M. Nicassio, *Westmoreland County Community College;* Michael O'Neill, *Seattle Central Community College.*

Mike Palma, *Gwinnett Tech*; Michael Papke, *Kellogg Community College*; Ruth Parks, *Kellogg Community College*; Al Partington, *Los Angeles Pierce College*; Jennifer Patty, *Des Moines Area Community College*; Jan Pitera, *Broome Community College*; Laura M. Prosser, *Black Hills State University;* Jenny Resnick, Santa Monica College; Renee Rigoni, *Monroe Community College*; Kathie Rogers, *SUNY Suffolk;* Al Ruggiero, *SUNY Suffolk.*

Roger Sands, *Milwaukee Area Technical College;* Marcia Sandvold, *Des Moines Area Community College;* Kent Schneider, *East Tennessee State University*; Karen Searle; Paul J. Shinal, *Cayuga Community College;* Leon Singleton, *Santa Monica College;* Michael S. Skaff, *College of the Sequoias;* Lois Slutsky, *Broward Community College*; Dan Small, *J. Sargeant Reynolds Community College;* Lee Smart, *Southwest Tennessee Community College;* Jeff

Spoelman, *Grand Rapids Community College;* Norman Sunderman, *Angelo State University.*

Donald Terpstra, *Jefferson Community College*; Wanda Wong, *Chabot College*; Pat Walczak, *Lansing Community College;* Carol N. Welsh, *Rowan University*; Idalene Williams, *Metropolitan Community College;* Gloria Worthy, *Southwest Tennessee Community College;* and Cathy Xanthaky, *Middlesex Community College*

Special Thanks

Our thanks also go to the authors of the Eighth Edition supplements:

Mel Coe, *DeVry Institute of Technology, Atlanta* – Peachtree Workbook

Joan Cook, *Milwaukee Area Technical College* – Heritage Home Furniture Practice Set

Larry Falcetto, *Emporia State University* – Test Bank, Instructor's Manual, Campus Cycle Practice Set

Coby Harmon, University of California, Santa Barbara – PowerPoint Presentations

Marilyn Hunt, *University of Central Florida* – Problem-Solving Survival Guide

Douglas W. Kieso, *Aurora University* – Study Guide

Rex A. Schildhouse, Miramar College, *San Diego Community College District Campus* – Peachtree Workbook, Excel Workbook and Templates

Dick Wasson, *Southwestern College* – Excel Working Papers, Working Papers

We also thank those who have ensured the accuracy of our supplements:

Cynthia Ash, *Davenport University*
Irene Bembenista, *Davenport University*
Jack Borke, *University of Wisconsin – Platteville*
Terry Elliott, *Morehead State University*
James Emig, *Villanova University*
Larry Falcetto, *Emporia State University*
A. Anthony Falgiani, *Western Illinois University*
Lori Grady, *Bucks County Community College*
Jennifer Laudermilch, *PricewaterhouseCoopers*
Kevin McNelis, *New Mexico State University*
Barbara Muller, *Arizona State University*
Anne Oppegard, *Augustana College*
Renee Rigoni, *Monroe Community College*
Paul Robertson, *Henderson State University*
Rex A. Schildhouse, Miramar College, *San Diego Community College District*
Alice Sineath, *Forsyth Tech Community College*
Teresa Speck, *St. Mary's University*
Sheila Viel, *University of Wisconsin–Milwaukee*
Dick Wasson, *Southwestern College*
Bernie Weinrich, *Lindenwood University*

In addition, special recognition goes to Karen Huffman of Palomar College for her assessment of the text's

pedagogy and her suggestions on how to increase its helpfulness to students; to Gary R., Morrison of Wayne State University for his review of the instructional design; and to Nancy Galli of Palomar College for her work on learning styles. Thanks also to "perpetual reviewers" Robert Benjamin of Taylor University; Charles Malone, Tammy Wend, and Carol Wysocki, all of Columbia Basin College; and William Gregg of Montgomery College for their continuing interest in the book and their regular contributions of ideas to improve it. Finally, special thanks to Wayne Higley of Buena Vista University for his technical proofing.

Our thanks to the publishing "pros" who contribute to our efforts to publish high-quality products that benefit both teachers and students: project editor Ed Brislin, associate editor Brian Kamins, editorial assistant Karolina Zarychta, senior media editor Allie Morris, senior production editor Valerie Vargas, director of production and manufacturing Pam Kennedy, vice president of higher education production and manufacturing Ann Berlin, designer Maddy Lesure, illustration editor Sandra Rigby, photo editor Elle Wagner, project manager Suzanne Ingrao of Ingrao Associates, permissions editor Karyn Morrison, product manager Jane Shifflet at TechBooks, and project manager Kim Nichols at Elm Street Publishing Services. They provided innumerable services that helped this project take shape.

We wish to acknowledge the outstanding work of our development editor, Ann Torbert, whose expertise, encouragement, and patience have helped us immeasurably.

We also appreciate the exemplary support and professional commitment given us by Executive Editor Chris DeJohn. A special thanks to Susan Elbe, who has been our publisher for many years and who has provided exceptional support, and guidance. We wish her well in her new assignment, and we look forward to working with her in her new role.

Finally, our thanks for the support provided by Joe Heider, Vice President of Product and e-Business Development, Bonnie Lieberman, Senior Vice President of the College Division, and Will Pesce, President and Chief Executive Officer.

We thank PepsiCo, Inc. and The Coca-Cola Company for permitting us the use of their 2005 annual reports for our specimen financial statements and accompanying notes.

We will appreciate suggestions and comments from users—instructors and students alike. You can send your thoughts to us via email at:
AccountingAuthors@yahoo.com.

Jerry J. Weygandt
Madison, Wisconsin

Donald E. Kieso
DeKalb, Illinois

Paul D. Kimmel
Milwaukee, Wisconsin

BRIEF CONTENTS

APPENDIXES

DETAILED CONTENTS

5 Accounting for Merchandising Operations 192

6 Inventories 242

7 Accounting Information Systems 290

8 Internal Control and Cash 336

26 Incremental Analysis and Capital Budgeting   1132

The new *"All About You"* features, one in each chapter, promote financial literacy. They are intended to get students thinking and talking about how accounting impacts their personal lives. Students are more likely to understand the accounting concept being made within the textbook when accounting material is linked to a familiar topic. Each *All About You* box presents a high-interest issue related to the chapter topic, offers facts about it, poses a situation for students to think about, and offers brief opposing answers as a starting place for further discussion. As a feedback mechanism, the authors' comments and opinions about the situation appear at the end of the chapter.

An *"All About You"* Activity, located in the *Broadening Your Perspective* section near the end of the assignment material, offers further opportunity to explore aspects of a high-interest topic in a homework assignment.

CHAPTER 1 Accounting in Action
Ethics: Managing Personal Financial Reporting
Compares filing for financial aid, especially the FAFSA form, to corporate financial reporting. Presents facts about student debt loads. Asks whether students should present a negative financial picture to increase the chance of receiving financial aid. *AAY Activity* further examines ethics of financial aid and corporate reporting.

CHAPTER 2 The Recording Process
Your Personal Annual Report
Likens a student's résumé to a company's annual report. Presents facts about prominent people with inaccurate résumés. Asks students to consider whether firing Radio Shack's CEO for résumé falsehoods was warranted. *AAY Activity* explores short-term career goals and résumé presentation.

CHAPTER 3 Adjusting the Accounts
Is Your Old Computer a Liability?
Discusses the responsibility for disposing of old electronic equipment and presents facts about the extent of that problem nationally. Asks if companies should consider environmental clean-up costs as liabilities. *AAY Activity* asks students to evaluate different liability-disclosure scenarios.

CHAPTER 4 Completing the Accounting Cycle
Your Personal Balance Sheet
Walks students through identification of personal assets and personal liabilities. Presents facts about Americans' wealth and attitudes toward saving versus spending. Asks if college is a good time to prepare a personal balance sheet. *AAY Activity* gives students practice preparing a personal balance sheet.

CHAPTER 5 Accounting for Merchandising Operations
When Is a Sale Not a Sale?
Discusses channel stuffing as a way to manipulate revenue recognition. Presents facts about companies that improperly recognized revenue and the percentage that restated earnings to correct errors. Asks students to think through what they would do if a boss asked them to engage in channel stuffing. *AAY Activity* presents ethical situations related to revenue recognition.

CHAPTER 6 Inventories
Employee Theft—An Inside Job
Discusses the problem of inventory theft, and how companies keep it in check. Presents facts about inventory theft. Asks for students' opinions on the use of video cameras to reduce theft. *AAY Activity* involves an Internet search for stories on inventory fraud.

CHAPTER 7 Accounting Information Systems
Keeping Track of the Documents in Your Life
Discusses personal record-keeping and documents students may need to keep. Presents facts about what records to keep, and where, as well as back-up contingencies. Asks students to think about their own record-keeping. *AAY Activity* explores a general ledger software program.

CHAPTER 8 Internal Control and Cash
Protecting Yourself from Identity Theft
Likens corporate internal controls to individuals' efforts to protect themselves from identity thieves. Presents facts about how thieves obtain stolen data and how they use it. Asks students about the safety of storing personal financial data on computers. *AAY Activity* asks students to take an online quiz on identity theft.

CHAPTER 9 Accounting for Receivables
Should You Be Carrying Plastic?
Discusses the need for individuals to evaluate their credit positions as thoughtfully as companies do. Presents facts about college-student debt, Americans' use of credit cards, and recent bankruptcy filings. Asks whether students should cut up their credit cards. *AAY Activity* asks students to evaluate credit card terms.

CHAPTER 10 Plant Assets, Natural Resources, and Intangible Assets
Buying a Wreck of Your Own
Presents information about costs and financing of new versus used cars. Asks whether students could improve their economic well-being by buying a used car. The *AAY Activity* tests knowledge of famous trade names.

CHAPTER 11 Current Liabilities and Payroll Accounting
Your Boss Wants to Know If You Jogged Today
Discusses ways to contain cost of health-care benefits. Presents facts on costs and spending on health care. Asks students to consider whose responsibility it is to maintain healthy lifestyles to control health-care costs. *AAY Activity* looks at an employee's other major cost—taxes—and has students calculate various types of taxes.

CHAPTER 12 Accounting for Partnerships
How Well Do You Know Your Partner?
Focuses on the importance of the right business partner. Presents facts about partnerships and other forms of business organization. Asks students to evaluate the risks of a possible partnership siutation. *AAY Activity* asks students to research organizational forms of local businesses.

CHAPTER 13   Corporations: Organization and Capital Stock Transactions
Home-Equity Loans
Compares equity-reducing transactions of companies to use of home-equity loans by individuals. Presents facts about home-equity loans, including tax benefits and variable interest rates. Asks students to assess use of a home-equity loan for a dream vacation. *AAY Activity* asks students to navigate through an annual report like a shareholder would.

CHAPTER 14   Corporations: Dividends, Retained Earnings, and Income Reporting
Corporations Have Governance Structures—Do You?
Discusses the idea of codes of ethics in business and at college. Presents facts about use and abuse of codes of ethics in the workplace, and responses of stockholders. Asks students for opinions on whether schools' codes of ethics serve a useful purpose. *AAY Activity* has students evaluate a code of ethics, and make recommendations to improve it.

CHAPTER 15   Long-Term Liabilities
The Risks of Adjustable Rates
Describes benefits and drawbacks of adjustable-rate mortgages (ARMs). Presents facts about use of ARMs and fixed-rate mortgages. Asks students to evaluate a home-buying scenario and whether to use adjustable-rate financing. *AAY Activity* has students research articles about warning signs of personal-debt trouble.

CHAPTER 16   Investments
A Good Day to Start Saving
Lists excuses not to save, and encourages students to begin saving now. Presents facts about U.S. savings rates and the difference made by starting early. Asks students to assess whether to pay off credit cards before contributing to a 401(k). *AAY Activity* sends students to the SEC's websites to define investment terms and for a quiz on investment "smarts."

CHAPTER 17   The Statement of Cash Flows
Where Does the Money Go?
Discusses the need to know how one spends one's cash. Presents facts about college students' spending patterns. Asks students to analyze a personal cash flow statement and decide whether, and where, cuts should be made. *AAY Activity* has students read an article at The Motley Fool site and discuss how much money to set aside for short-term needs.

CHAPTER 18   Financial Statement Analysis
Should I Play the Market Yet?
Discusses when to begin investing in the stock market. Presents facts about stock ownership in the U.S. Asks students to decide whether a young working person should invest in her employer's stock. *AAY Activity* asks students to complete a questionnaire about appropriate types of mutual funds.

CHAPTER 19   Managerial Accounting
Outsourcing and Jobs
Discusses trends in outsourcing. Presents facts about outsourcing by U.S. companies and top foreign employers in the U.S. Asks students to assess the outsourcing of tax-prep services overseas. *AAY Activity* has students identify personal situations to which managerial accounting techniques apply.

CHAPTER 20   Job Order Cost Accounting
Minding Your Own Business
Focuses on how small business owners calculate product costs. Presents facts about sole proprietorships and franchises. Poses a start-up business idea and asks students to evaluate the cost of labor input. *AAY Activity* sends students to SBA website to take quiz on readiness to start a small business.

CHAPTER 21   Process Cost Accounting
Wal-Mart Is on the Phone
Describes cost accounting for a small company with a possible Wal-Mart deal. Presents facts about Wal-Mart's desirability as an outlet and potential risks for its suppliers. Ask students to evaluate whether a small company should accept a distribution offer. *AAY Activity* asks students to identify activities and cost drivers in a service company.

CHAPTER 22   Cost-Volume-Profit
A Hybrid Dilemma
Explores the cost tradeoffs of hybrid vehicles. Presents facts about sales, costs, and fuel efficiency of hybrid vehicles. Asks students to evaluate the pros and cons of buying a hybrid vehicle. *AAY Activity* asks students to do a break-even analysis on the decision to buy a hybrid.

CHAPTER 23   Budgetary Planning
Avoiding Personal Financial Disaster
Explores personal budgets for college students. Presents facts about the average family budget. Asks students to look at a budgeting calculator and consider whether student loans should be considered a source of income. *AAY Activity* has students compute and analyze a personal budget, using assumed data.

CHAPTER 24   Budgetary Control and Responsibility Accounting
Budgeting for Housing Costs
Applies performance evaluation to personal budgeting, via control of routine expenses, especially housing costs. Presents facts about expenses for childrearing, medical, and housing costs. Asks students to consider the pros and cons of buying a house immediately out of college. *AAY Activity* explores the strategy of "envelope budgeting."

CHAPTER 25   Performance Evaluation Through Standard Costs
Balancing Costs and Quality in Health Care
Applies the concept of standard costs to balancing costs and quality in health care. Presents facts about medical costs and incentives for physicians to reduce costs and maintain quality care. Asks students to consider whether doctors should have to meet standard-cost targets. *AAY Activity* explores using standardized tests to measure college students' learning.

CHAPTER 26   Incremental Analysis and Capital Budgeting
What Is a Degree Worth?
Explores the decision to stay in college as an example of incremental analysis and capital budgeting. Presents facts about the cost of college, and benefits of a college education. Asks students to consider the value of a college education. *AAY Activity* applies incremental analysis to the problem of chronic homelessness.

THE WILEY BICENTENNIAL—KNOWLEDGE FOR GENERATIONS

*E*ach generation has its unique needs and aspirations. When Charles Wiley first opened his small printing shop in lower Manhattan in 1807, it was a generation of boundless potential searching for an identity. And we were there, helping to define a new American literary tradition. Over half a century later, in the midst of the Second Industrial Revolution, it was a generation focused on building the future. Once again, we were there, supplying the critical scientific, technical, and engineering knowledge that helped frame the world. Throughout the 20th Century, and into the new millennium, nations began to reach out beyond their own borders and a new international community was born. Wiley was there, expanding its operations around the world to enable a global exchange of ideas, opinions, and know-how.

For 200 years, Wiley has been an integral part of each generation's journey, enabling the flow of information and understanding necessary to meet their needs and fulfill their aspirations. Today, bold new technologies are changing the way we live and learn. Wiley will be there, providing you the must-have knowledge you need to imagine new worlds, new possibilities, and new opportunities.

Generations come and go, but you can always count on Wiley to provide you the knowledge you need, when and where you need it!

William J. Pesce

PRESIDENT AND CHIEF EXECUTIVE OFFICER

Peter Booth Wiley

CHAIRMAN OF THE BOARD

8th Edition

Accounting Principles

Jerry J. Weygandt PhD, CPA
Arthur Andersen Alumni Professor of Accounting
University of Wisconsin
Madison, Wisconsin

Donald E. Kieso PhD, CPA
KPMG Emeritus Professor of Accountancy
Northern Illinois University
DeKalb, Illinois

Paul D. Kimmel PhD, CPA
Associate Professor of Accounting
University of Wisconsin—Milwaukee
Milwaukee, Wisconsin

BICENTENNIAL
1807
WILEY
2007
BICENTENNIAL

John Wiley & Sons, Inc.

Chapter 6

Inventories

Feature Story

WHERE IS THAT SPARE BULLDOZER BLADE?

Let's talk inventory—big, bulldozer-size inventory. Caterpillar Inc. (*www.cat.com*) is the world's largest manufacturer of construction and mining equipment, diesel and natural gas engines, and industrial gas turbines. It sells its products in over 200 countries, making it one of the most successful U.S. exporters. More than 70% of its productive assets are located domestically, and nearly 50% of its sales are foreign.

During the 1980s Caterpillar's profitability suffered, but today it is very successful. A big part of this turnaround can be attributed to effective management of its inventory. Imagine what a bulldozer costs. Now imagine what it costs Caterpillar to have too many bulldozers sitting around in inventory—a situation the company definitely wants to avoid. Conversely, Caterpillar must make sure it has enough inventory to meet demand.

During a recent 7-year period, Caterpillar's sales increased by 100%, while its inventory increased by only 50%. To achieve this dramatic reduction in the amount of resources tied up in inventory, while continuing to meet customers' needs, Caterpillar used a two-pronged approach. First, it completed a factory modernization program, which dramatically increased its production efficiency. The program reduced by 60% the amount of inventory the company processed at any one time. It also reduced by an incredible 75% the time it takes to manufacture a part.

Second, Caterpillar dramatically improved its parts distribution system. It ships more than 100,000 items daily from its 23 distribution centers strategically located around the world (10 *million* square feet of warehouse space—remember, we're talking bulldozers). The company can virtually guarantee that it can get any part to anywhere in the world within 24 hours. Although this network services 550,000 part numbers, Caterpillar is able to ship 99.7% of its orders within hours. In fact, Caterpillar's distribution system is so advanced that it created a subsidiary, Caterpillar Logistics Services, Inc., that warehouses and distributes other companies' products. This subsidiary distributes products as diverse as running shoes, computer software, and auto parts all around the world.

In short, how Caterpillar manages and accounts for its inventory goes a long way in explaining how profitable it is.

✔ The Navigator

Inside Chapter 6...

In the previous chapter, we discussed the accounting for merchandise inventory using a perpetual inventory system. In this chapter, we explain the methods used to calculate the cost of inventory on hand at the balance sheet date and the cost of goods sold.

The content and organization of this chapter are as follows.

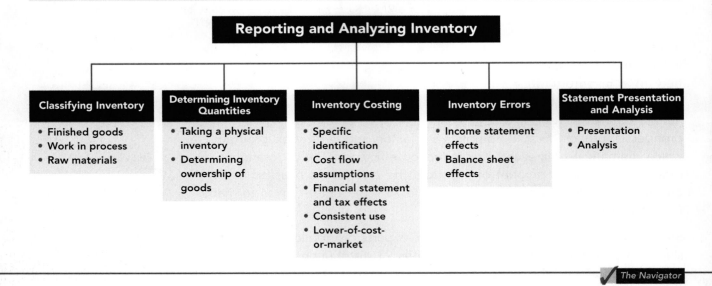

CLASSIFYING INVENTORY

How a company classifies its inventory depends on whether the firm is a merchandiser or a manufacturer. In a **merchandising** company, such as those described in Chapter 5, inventory consists of many different items. For example, in a grocery store, canned goods, dairy products, meats, and produce are just a few of the inventory items on hand. These items have two common characteristics: (1) They are owned by the company, and (2) they are in a form ready for sale to customers in the ordinary course of business. Thus, merchandisers need only one inventory classification, **merchandise inventory**, to describe the many different items that make up the total inventory.

In a **manufacturing** company, some inventory may not yet be ready for sale. As a result, manufacturers usually classify inventory into three categories: finished goods, work in process, and raw materials. **Finished goods inventory** is manufactured items that are completed and ready for sale. **Work in process** is that portion of manufactured inventory that has been placed into the production process but is not yet complete. **Raw materials** are the basic goods that will be used in production but have not yet been placed into production.

For example, Caterpillar classifies earth-moving tractors completed and ready for sale as **finished goods**. It classifies the tractors on the assembly line in various stages of production as **work in process**. The steel, glass, tires, and other components that are on hand waiting to be used in the production of tractors are identified as **raw materials**.

By observing the levels and changes in the levels of these three inventory types, financial statement users can gain insight into management's production plans. For example, low levels of raw materials and high levels of finished goods suggest that management believes it has enough inventory on hand, and production will be slowing down—perhaps in anticipation of a recession. On the other hand, high levels of raw materials and low levels of finished goods probably indicate that management is planning to step up production.

HELPFUL HINT

Regardless of the classification, companies report all inventories under Current Assets on the balance sheet.

Many companies have significantly lowered inventory levels and costs using **just-in-time (JIT) inventory** methods. Under a just-in-time method, companies manufacture or purchase goods just in time for use. Dell is famous for having developed a system for making computers in response to individual customer requests. Even though it makes each computer to meet each customer's particular specifications, Dell is able to assemble the computer and put it on a truck in less than 48 hours. By integrating its information systems with those of its suppliers, Dell reduced its inventories to nearly zero. This is a huge advantage in an industry where products become obsolete nearly overnight.

The accounting concepts discussed in this chapter apply to the inventory classifications of both merchandising and manufacturing companies. Our focus here is on merchandise inventory.

ACCOUNTING ACROSS THE ORGANIZATION

How Wal-Mart Tracks Inventory

Wal-Mart improved its inventory control in 2004 with the introduction of electronic product codes (EPCs). Much like bar codes, which tell a retailer the number of boxes of a specific product it has, EPCs go a step farther, helping to distinguish one box of a specific product from another. EPCs use radio frequency identification (RFID) technology, the same technology behind keyless remotes used to unlock car doors.

Companies currently use EPCs to track shipments from supplier to distribution center to store. Other potential uses include help with monitoring product expiration dates and acting quickly on product recalls. Wal-Mart also anticipates faster returns and warranty processing using EPCs. This technology will further assist Wal-Mart managers in their efforts to ensure that their stores have just the right type of inventory, in just the right amount, in just the right place.

 Why is inventory control important to managers such as those at Wal-Mart?

DETERMINING INVENTORY QUANTITIES

No matter whether they are using a periodic or perpetual inventory system, all companies need to determine inventory quantities at the end of the accounting period. When using a perpetual system, companies take a physical inventory for two purposes: The first purpose is to check the accuracy of their perpetual inventory records. The second is to determine the amount of inventory lost due to wasted raw materials, shoplifting, or employee theft.

STUDY OBJECTIVE 1
Describe the steps in determining inventory quantities.

Companies using a periodic inventory system must take a physical inventory for two *different* purposes: to determine the inventory on hand at the balance sheet date, and to determine the cost of goods sold for the period.

Determining inventory quantities involves two steps: (1) taking a physical inventory of goods on hand and (2) determining the ownership of goods.

Taking a Physical Inventory

Taking a physical inventory involves actually counting, weighing, or measuring each kind of inventory on hand. In many companies, taking an inventory is a formidable task. Retailers such as Target, True Value Hardware, or Home Depot have thousands of different inventory items. An inventory count is generally more accurate when goods are not being sold or received during the counting. Consequently, companies often "take inventory" when the business is closed or when business is slow. Many retailers close early on a chosen day in January—after the holiday sales and returns, when inventories are at their lowest level—to count inventory. Recall from Chapter 5 that Wal-Mart had a year-end of January 31. Companies take the physical inventory at the end of the accounting period.[1]

E T H I C S   I N S I G H T

"Fill 'Em Up—With Water, Not Oil"

Over the years inventory has played a role in many fraud cases. A classic case involved salad oil. Management of a salad-oil company filled storage tanks mostly with water. Since oil rises to the top, the auditors thought the tanks were full of oil. In addition, management said they had more tanks than they really did—they repainted numbers on the tanks to confuse auditors.

More recently, managers at women's apparel maker Leslie Fay were convicted of falsifying inventory records to boost net income—and consequently to boost management bonuses.

? What effect does an overstatement of inventory have on a company's financial statements?

Determining Ownership of Goods

One challenge in computing inventory quantities is determining what inventory a company owns. To determine ownership of goods, two questions must be answered: Do all of the goods included in the count belong to the company? Does the company own any goods that were not included in the count?

GOODS IN TRANSIT

A complication in determining ownership is **goods in transit** (on board a truck, train, ship, or plane) at the end of the period. The company may have purchased goods that have not yet been received, or it may have sold goods that have not yet been delivered. To arrive at an accurate count, the company must determine ownership of these goods.

Goods in transit should be included in the inventory of the company that has legal title to the goods. Legal title is determined by the terms of the sale, as shown in Illustration 6-1 and described below.

1. When the terms are **FOB (free on board) shipping point**, ownership of the goods passes to the buyer when the public carrier accepts the goods from the seller.
2. When the terms are **FOB destination**, ownership of the goods remains with the seller until the goods reach the buyer.

If goods in transit at the statement date are ignored, inventory quantities may be seriously miscounted. Assume, for example, that Hargrove Company has 20,000 units of inventory on hand on December 31. It also has the following goods in transit: (1) sales of 1,500 units shipped December 31 FOB destination, and (2) purchases of 2,500 units shipped FOB shipping point by the seller on December 31. Hargrove has legal title to both the 1,500 units sold and the 2,500 units purchased. If the

---

[1]To estimate the cost of inventory when a physical inventory cannot be taken (e.g., the inventory is destroyed) or when it is inconvenient (e.g., during interim periods), companies can use estimation methods. We discuss these methods—gross profit method and retail inventory method—in Appendix 6B.

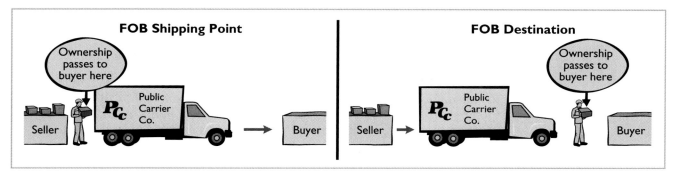

Illustration 6-1
Terms of sale

company ignores the units in transit, it would understate inventory quantities by 4,000 units (1,500 + 2,500).

As we will see later in the chapter, inaccurate inventory counts affect not only the inventory amount shown on the balance sheet but also the cost of goods sold calculation on the income statement.

CONSIGNED GOODS

In some lines of business, it is common to hold the goods of other parties and try to sell the goods for them for a fee, but without taking ownership of the goods. These are called **consigned goods**.

For example, you might have a used car that you would like to sell. If you take the item to a dealer, the dealer might be willing to put the car on its lot and charge you a commission if it is sold. Under this agreement the dealer **would not take ownership** of the car, which would still belong to you. Therefore, if an inventory count were taken, the car would not be included in the dealer's inventory.

Many car, boat, and antique dealers sell goods on consignment to keep their inventory costs down and to avoid the risk of purchasing an item that they won't be able to sell. Today even some manufacturers are making consignment agreements with their suppliers in order to keep their inventory levels low.

> **ETHICS NOTE**
>
> **Employees of** Craig Consumer Electronics allegedly overstated the company's inventory figures by improperly classifying defective goods as either new or refurbished. They also were accused of stating that the company owned goods from suppliers when in fact the company did not own the shipments, or the shipments did not even exist.

Before You Go On...

REVIEW IT

1. What steps are involved in determining inventory quantities? *goods in transit @ the end of a period*
2. How is ownership determined for goods in transit at the balance sheet date?
3. Who has title to consigned goods? *the owner*

DO IT

Hasbeen Company completed its inventory count. It arrived at a total inventory value of $200,000. As a new member of Hasbeen's accounting department, you have been given the information listed below. Discuss how this information affects the reported cost of inventory.

1. Hasbeen included in the inventory goods held on consignment for Falls Co., costing $15,000.
2. The company did not include in the count purchased goods of $10,000 which were in transit (terms: FOB shipping point).
3. The company did not include in the count sold inventory with a cost of $12,000 which was in transit (terms: FOB shipping point).

Action Plan

■ Apply the rules of ownership to goods held on consignment.

■ Apply the rules of ownership to goods in transit FOB shipping point.

Solution The goods of $15,000 held on consignment should be deducted from the inventory count. The goods of $10,000 purchased FOB shipping point should be added to the inventory count. Sold goods of $12,000 which were in transit FOB shipping point should not be included in the ending inventory. Thus, inventory should be carried at $195,000.

Related exercise material: *BE6-1, E6-1, and E6-2.*

 The Navigator

INVENTORY COSTING

STUDY OBJECTIVE 2

Explain the accounting for inventories and apply the inventory cost flow methods.

After a company has determined the quantity of units of inventory, it applies unit costs to the quantities to compute the total cost of the inventory and the cost of goods sold. This process can be complicated if a company has purchased inventory items at different times and at different prices.

For example, assume that Crivitz TV Company purchases three identical 46-inch TVs on different dates at costs of $700, $750, and $800. During the year Crivitz sold two sets at $1,200 each. These facts are summarized in Illustration 6-2.

Illustration 6-2
Data for inventory costing example

Purchases			
February 3	1 TV	at	$700
March 5	1 TV	at	$750
May 22	1 TV	at	$800
Sales			
June 1	2 TVs	for	$2,400 ($1,200 × 2)

Cost of goods sold will differ depending on which two TVs the company sold. For example, it might be $1,450 ($700 + $750), or $1,500 ($700 + $800), or $1,550 ($750 + $800). In this section we discuss alternative costing methods available to Crivitz.

Specific Identification

If Crivitz sold the TVs it purchased on February 3 and May 22, then its cost of goods sold is $1,500 ($700 + $800), and its ending inventory is $750. If Crivitz can positively identify which particular units it sold and which are still in ending inventory, it can use the **specific identification method** of inventory costing (see Illustration 6-3, page 249). Using this method, companies can accurately determine ending inventory and cost of goods sold.

Specific identification requires that companies keep records of the original cost of each individual inventory item. Historically, specific identification was possible only when a company sold a limited variety of high-unit-cost items that could be identified clearly from the time of purchase through the time of sale. Examples of such products are cars, pianos, or expensive antiques.

Today, bar coding, electronic product codes, and radio frequency identification make it theoretically possible to do specific identification with nearly any type of product. The reality is, however, that this practice is still relatively

ETHICS NOTE

A major disadvantage of the specific identification method is that management may be able to manipulate net income. For example, it can boost net income by selling units purchased at a low cost, or reduce net income by selling units purchased at a high cost.

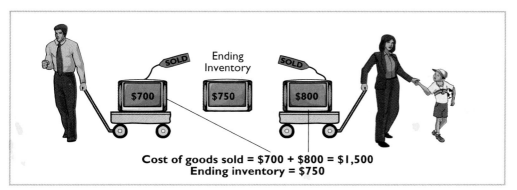

Illustration 6-3
Specific identification
method

rare. Instead, rather than keep track of the cost of each particular item sold, most companies make assumptions, called **cost flow assumptions**, about which units were sold.

Cost Flow Assumptions

Because specific identification is often impractical, other cost flow methods are permitted. These differ from specific identification in that they **assume** flows of costs that may be unrelated to the physical flow of goods. There are three assumed cost flow methods:

1. First-in, first-out (FIFO)
2. Last-in, first-out (LIFO)
3. Average-cost

There is no accounting requirement that the cost flow assumption be consistent with the physical movement of the goods. Company management selects the appropriate cost flow method.

To illustrate these three inventory cost flow methods, we will assume that Houston Electronics uses a periodic inventory system and has the information shown in Illustration 6-4 for its Astro condenser.[2] (An appendix to this chapter presents the use of these methods under a perpetual system.)

Illustration 6-4
Cost of goods available
for sale

HOUSTON ELECTRONICS
Astro Condensers

Date	Explanation	Units	Unit Cost	Total Cost
Jan. 1	Beginning inventory	100	$10	$ 1,000
Apr. 15	Purchase	200	11	2,200
Aug. 24	Purchase	300	12	3,600
Nov. 27	Purchase	400	13	5,200
	Total	1,000		$12,000

The company had a total of 1,000 units available that it could have sold during the period. The total cost of these units was $12,000. A physical inventory at the end

---

[2]We have chosen to use the periodic approach for a number of reasons. First, many companies that use a perpetual inventory system use it to keep track of units on hand, but then determine cost of goods sold at the end of the period using one of the three cost flow approaches applied under essentially a periodic approach. In addition, because of the complexity, few companies use average cost on a perpetual basis. Also, most companies that use perpetual LIFO employ dollar-value LIFO, which is presented in more advanced texts. Furthermore, FIFO gives the same results under either perpetual or periodic. And finally, it is easier to demonstrate the cost flow assumptions under the periodic system, which makes it more pedagogically appropriate.

of the year determined that during the year Houston sold 550 units and had 450 units in inventory at December 31. The question then is how to determine what prices to use to value the goods sold and the ending inventory. The sum of the cost allocated to the units sold plus the cost of the units in inventory must be $12,000, the total cost of all goods available for sale.

FIRST-IN, FIRST-OUT (FIFO)

The **FIFO (first-in, first-out) method** assumes that the **earliest goods** purchased are the first to be sold. FIFO often parallels the actual physical flow of merchandise; it generally is good business practice to sell the oldest units first. Under the FIFO method, therefore, the **costs** of the earliest goods purchased are the first to be recognized in determining cost of goods sold. (This does not necessarily mean that the oldest units *are* sold first, but that the costs of the oldest units are *recognized* first. In a bin of picture hangers at the hardware store, for example, no one really knows, nor would it matter, which hangers are sold first.) Illustration 6-5 shows the allocation of the cost of goods available for sale at Houston Electronics under FIFO.

Illustration 6-5
Allocation of costs—FIFO method

HELPFUL HINT
Note the sequencing of the allocation: (1) Compute ending inventory, and (2) determine cost of goods sold.

HELPFUL HINT
Another way of thinking about the calculation of FIFO ending inventory is the *LISH assumption*—last in still here.

COST OF GOODS AVAILABLE FOR SALE

Date	Explanation	Units	Unit Cost	Total Cost
Jan. 1	Beginning inventory	100	$10	$ 1,000
Apr. 15	Purchase	200	11	2,200
Aug. 24	Purchase	300	12	3,600
Nov. 27	Purchase	400	13	5,200
	Total	1,000		**$12,000**

STEP 1: ENDING INVENTORY

Date	Units	Unit Cost	Total Cost
Nov. 27	400	$13	$5,200
Aug. 24	50	12	600
Total	450		**$5,800**

STEP 2: COST OF GOODS SOLD

Cost of goods available for sale	$12,000
Less: Ending inventory	5,800
Cost of goods sold	**$ 6,200**

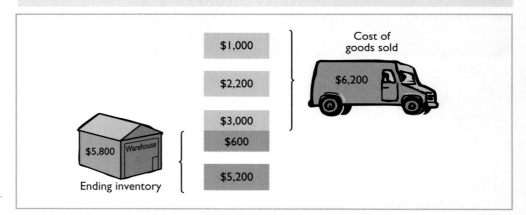

Under FIFO, since it is assumed that the first goods purchased were the first goods sold, ending inventory is based on the prices of the most recent units purchased. That is, **under FIFO, companies obtain the cost of the ending inventory by taking the unit cost of the most recent purchase and working backward until all units of inventory have been costed**. In this example, Houston Electronics prices the 450 units of ending inventory using the *most recent* prices. The last purchase was 400 units at $13 on November 27. The remaining 50 units are priced using the unit cost of the second most recent purchase, $12, on August 24. Next, Houston

Electronics calculates cost of goods sold by subtracting the cost of the units **not sold** (ending inventory) from the cost of all goods available for sale.

Illustration 6-6 demonstrates that companies also can calculate cost of goods sold by pricing the 550 units sold using the prices of the first 550 units acquired. Note that of the 300 units purchased on August 24, only 250 units are assumed sold. This agrees with our calculation of the cost of ending inventory, where 50 of these units were assumed unsold and thus included in ending inventory.

Date	Units	Unit Cost	Total Cost
Jan. 1	100	$10	$1,000
Apr. 15	200	11	2,200
Aug. 24	250	12	3,000
Total	550		$6,200

Illustration 6-6
Proof of cost of goods sold

LAST-IN, FIRST-OUT (LIFO)

The **LIFO (last-in, first-out) method** assumes that the **latest goods** purchased are the first to be sold. LIFO seldom coincides with the actual physical flow of inventory. (Exceptions include goods stored in piles, such as coal or hay, where goods are removed from the top of the pile as they are sold.) Under the LIFO method, the **costs** of the latest goods purchased are the first to be recognized in determining cost of goods sold. Illustration 6-7 shows the allocation of the cost of goods available for sale at Houston Electronics under LIFO.

Illustration 6-7
Allocation of costs—LIFO method

COST OF GOODS AVAILABLE FOR SALE

Date	Explanation	Units	Unit Cost	Total Cost
Jan. 1	Beginning inventory	100	$10	$ 1,000
Apr. 15	Purchase	200	11	2,200
Aug. 24	Purchase	300	12	3,600
Nov. 27	Purchase	400	13	5,200
	Total	1,000		$12,000

STEP 1: ENDING INVENTORY   STEP 2: COST OF GOODS SOLD

Date	Units	Unit Cost	Total Cost		
Jan. 1	100	$10	$1,000	Cost of goods available for sale	$12,000
Apr. 15	200	11	2,200	Less: Ending inventory	5,000
Aug. 24	150	12	1,800	Cost of goods sold	$ 7,000
Total	450		$5,000		

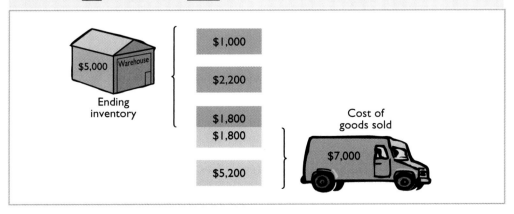

HELPFUL HINT
Another way of thinking about the calculation of LIFO **ending inventory** is the *FISH assumption*—first in still here.

Under LIFO, since it is assumed that the first goods sold were those that were most recently purchased, ending inventory is based on the prices of the oldest units purchased. That is, **under LIFO, companies obtain the cost of the ending inventory by taking the unit cost of the earliest goods available for sale and working forward until all units of inventory have been costed**. In this example, Houston Electronics prices the 450 units of ending inventory using the *earliest* prices. The first purchase was 100 units at $10 in the January 1 beginning inventory. Then 200 units were purchased at $11. The remaining 150 units needed are priced at $12 per unit (August 24 purchase). Next, Houston Electronics calculates cost of goods sold by subtracting the cost of the units **not sold** (ending inventory) from the cost of all goods available for sale.

Illustration 6-8 demonstrates that companies also can calculate cost of goods sold by pricing the 550 units sold using the prices of the last 550 units acquired. Note that of the 300 units purchased on August 24, only 150 units are assumed sold. This agrees with our calculation of the cost of ending inventory, where 150 of these units were assumed unsold and thus included in ending inventory.

Illustration 6-8
Proof of cost of goods sold

Date	Units	Unit Cost	Total Cost
Nov. 27	400	$13	$5,200
Aug. 24	150	12	1,800
Total	550		**$7,000**

Under a periodic inventory system, which we are using here, **all goods purchased during the period are assumed to be available for the first sale, regardless of the date of purchase**.

AVERAGE-COST

The **average-cost method** allocates the cost of goods available for sale on the basis of the **weighted average unit cost** incurred. The average-cost method assumes that goods are similar in nature. Illustration 6-9 presents the formula and a sample computation of the weighted-average unit cost.

Illustration 6-9
Formula for weighted average unit cost

Cost of Goods Available for Sale	÷	Total Units Available for Sale	=	Weighted Average Unit Cost
$12,000	÷	1,000	=	**$12.00**

The company then applies the weighted average unit cost to the units on hand to determine the cost of the ending inventory. Illustration 6-10 shows the allocation of the cost of goods available for sale at Houston Electronics using average cost.

We can verify the cost of goods sold under this method by multiplying the units sold times the weighted average unit cost ($550 \times \$12 = \$6,600$). Note that this method does not use the average of the unit costs. That average is $11.50 ($10 + $11 + $12 + $13 = $46; $46 ÷ 4). The average cost method instead uses the average **weighted by** the quantities purchased at each unit cost.

COST OF GOODS AVAILABLE FOR SALE

Date	Explanation	Units	Unit Cost	Total Cost
Jan. 1	Beginning inventory	100	$10	$ 1,000
Apr. 15	Purchase	200	11	2,200
Aug. 24	Purchase	300	12	3,600
Nov. 27	Purchase	400	13	5,200
	Total	1,000		$12,000

Illustration 6-10
Allocation of costs—average-cost method

STEP 1: ENDING INVENTORY

$12,000 ÷ 1,000 = $12.00

Units	Unit Cost	Total Cost
450	$12.00	$5,400

STEP 2: COST OF GOODS SOLD

Cost of goods available for sale	$12,000
Less: Ending inventory	5,400
Cost of goods sold	$ 6,600

$$\frac{\$12,000}{1,000 \text{ units}} = \$12 \text{ per unit}$$

Cost per unit

450 units × $12 = $5,400   Warehouse

Ending inventory

$12,000 − $5,400 = $6,600

Cost of goods sold

Financial Statement and Tax Effects of Cost Flow Methods

Each of the three assumed cost flow methods is acceptable for use. For example, Reebok International Ltd. and Wendy's International currently use the FIFO method of inventory costing. Campbell Soup Company, Krogers, and Walgreen Drugs use LIFO for part or all of their inventory. Bristol-Myers Squibb, Starbucks, and Motorola use the average-cost method. In fact, a company may also use more than one cost flow method at the same time. Black & Decker Manufacturing Company, for example, uses LIFO for domestic inventories and FIFO for foreign inventories. Illustration 6-11 (in the margin) shows the use of the three cost flow methods in the 600 largest U.S. companies.

The reasons companies adopt different inventory cost flow methods are varied, but they usually involve one of three factors: (1) income statement effects, (2) balance sheet effects, or (3) tax effects.

INCOME STATEMENT EFFECTS
To understand why companies might choose a particular cost flow method, let's examine the effects of the different cost flow assumptions on the financial statements of Houston Electronics. The condensed income statements in Illustration 6-12 (page 254) assume that Houston sold its 550 units for $11,500, had operating expenses of $2,000, and is subject to an income tax rate of 30%.

33% LIFO   44% FIFO   19% Average Cost   4% Other

Illustration 6-11
Use of cost flow methods in major U.S. companies

Illustration 6-12
Comparative effects of cost
flow methods

HOUSTON ELECTRONICS
Condensed Income Statements

	FIFO	LIFO	Average Cost
Sales	$11,500	$11,500	$11,500
Beginning inventory	1,000	1,000	1,000
Purchases	11,000	11,000	11,000
Cost of goods available for sale	12,000	12,000	12,000
Ending inventory	5,800	5,000	5,400
Cost of goods sold	6,200	7,000	6,600
Gross profit	5,300	4,500	4,900
Operating expenses	2,000	2,000	2,000
Income before income taxes[3]	3,300	2,500	2,900
Income tax expense (30%)	990	750	870
Net income	$ 2,310	$ 1,750	$ 2,030

Note the cost of goods available for sale ($12,000) is the same under each of the three inventory cost flow methods. However, the ending inventories and the costs of goods sold are different. This difference is due to the unit costs that the company allocated to cost of goods sold and to ending inventory. Each dollar of difference in ending inventory results in a corresponding dollar difference in income before income taxes. For Houston, an $800 difference exists between FIFO and LIFO cost of goods sold.

In periods of changing prices, the cost flow assumption can have a significant impact on income and on evaluations based on income. In most instances, prices are rising (inflation). In a period of inflation, FIFO produces a higher net income because the lower unit costs of the first units purchased are matched against revenues. In a period of rising prices (as is the case in the Houston example), FIFO reports the highest net income ($2,310) and LIFO the lowest ($1,750); average cost falls in the middle ($2,030). If prices are falling, the results from the use of FIFO and LIFO are reversed: FIFO will report the lowest net income and LIFO the highest.

To management, higher net income is an advantage: It causes external users to view the company more favorably. In addition, management bonuses, if based on net income, will be higher. Therefore, when prices are rising (which is usually the case), companies tend to prefer FIFO because it results in higher net income.

Some argue that the use of LIFO in a period of inflation enables the company to avoid reporting **paper** (or **phantom**) **profit** as economic gain. To illustrate, assume that Kralik Company buys 200 units of a product at $20 per unit on January 10 and 200 more on December 31 at $24 each. During the year, Kralik sells 200 units at $30 each. Illustration 6-13 shows the results under FIFO and LIFO.

Illustration 6-13
Income statement effects
compared

	FIFO		LIFO	
Sales (200 × $30)	$6,000		$6,000	
Cost of goods sold	4,000	(200 × $20)	4,800	(200 × $24)
Gross profit	$2,000		$1,200	

[3]We are assuming that Houston Electronics is a corporation, and corporations are required to pay income taxes.

Under LIFO, Kralik Company has recovered the current replacement cost ($4,800) of the units sold. Thus, the gross profit in economic terms is real. However, under FIFO, the company has recovered only the January 10 cost ($4,000). To replace the units sold, it must reinvest $800 (200 × $4) of the gross profit. Thus, $800 of the gross profit is said to be phantom or illusory. As a result, reported net income is also overstated in real terms.

BALANCE SHEET EFFECTS

A major advantage of the FIFO method is that in a period of inflation, the costs allocated to ending inventory will approximate their current cost. For example, for Houston Electronics, 400 of the 450 units in the ending inventory are costed under FIFO at the higher November 27 unit cost of $13.

Conversely, a major shortcoming of the LIFO method is that in a period of inflation, the costs allocated to ending inventory may be significantly understated in terms of current cost. The understatement becomes greater over prolonged periods of inflation if the inventory includes goods purchased in one or more prior accounting periods. For example, Caterpillar has used LIFO for 50 years. Its balance sheet shows ending inventory of $4,675 million. But the inventory's actual current cost if FIFO had been used is $6,799 million.

TAX EFFECTS

We have seen that both inventory on the balance sheet and net income on the income statement are higher when companies use FIFO in a period of inflation. Yet, many companies have selected LIFO. Why? The reason is that LIFO results in the lowest income taxes (because of lower net income) during times of rising prices. For example, at Houston Electronics, income taxes are $750 under LIFO, compared to $990 under FIFO. The tax savings of $240 makes more cash available for use in the business.

> **HELPFUL HINT**
>
> A tax rule, often referred to as the *LIFO conformity rule*, requires that if companies use LIFO for tax purposes they must also use it for financial reporting purposes. This means that if a company chooses the LIFO method to reduce its tax bills, it will also have to report lower net income in its financial statements.

Using Inventory Cost Flow Methods Consistently

Whatever cost flow method a company chooses, it should use that method consistently from one accounting period to another. This approach is often referred to as the **consistency principle**, which means that a company uses the same accounting principles and methods from year to year. Consistent application enhances the comparability of financial statements over successive time periods. In contrast, using the FIFO method one year and the LIFO method the next year would make it difficult to compare the net incomes of the two years.

Although consistent application is preferred, it does not mean that a company may *never* change its inventory costing method. When a company adopts a different method, it should disclose in the financial statements the change and its effects on net income. Illustration 6-14 shows a typical disclosure, using information from financial statements of Quaker Oats (now a unit of PepsiCo).

QUAKER OATS
Notes to the Financial Statements

Note 1: Effective July 1, the Company adopted the LIFO cost flow assumption for valuing the majority of U.S. Grocery Products inventories. The Company believes that the use of the LIFO method better matches current costs with current revenues. The effect of this change on the current year was to decrease net income by $16.0 million.

Illustration 6-14
Disclosure of change in cost flow method

Lower-of-Cost-or-Market

STUDY OBJECTIVE 4

Explain the lower-of-cost-or-market basis of accounting for inventories.

The value of inventory for companies selling high-technology or fashion goods can drop very quickly due to changes in technology or fashions. These circumstances sometimes call for inventory valuation methods other than those presented so far. For example, purchasing managers at Ford decided to make a large purchase of palladium, a precious metal used in vehicle emission devices. They made this purchase because they feared a future shortage. The shortage did not materialize, and by the end of the year the price of palladium had plummeted. Ford's inventory was then worth $1 billion less than its original cost. Do you think Ford's inventory should have been stated at cost, in accordance with the cost principle, or at its lower replacement cost?

As you probably reasoned, this situation requires a departure from the cost basis of accounting. When the value of inventory is lower than its cost, companies can "write down" the inventory to its market value. This is done by valuing the inventory at the **lower-of-cost-or-market (LCM)** in the period in which the price decline occurs. LCM is an example of the accounting concept of **conservatism**, which means that the best choice among accounting alternatives is the method that is least likely to overstate assets and net income.

Companies apply LCM to the items in inventory after they have used one of the cost flow methods (specific identification, FIFO, LIFO, or average cost) to determine cost. Under the LCM basis, market is defined as **current replacement cost**, not selling price. For a merchandising company, market is the cost of purchasing the same goods at the present time from the usual suppliers in the usual quantities. Current replacement cost is used because a decline in the replacement cost of an item usually leads to a decline in the selling price of the item.

To illustrate the application of LCM, assume that Ken Tuckie TV has the following lines of merchandise with costs and market values as indicated. LCM produces the results shown in Illustration 6-15. Note that the amounts shown in the final column are the lower of cost or market amounts for each item.

Illustration 6-15
Computation of lower-of-cost-or-market

	Cost	Market	Lower-of-Cost-or-Market
Flatscreen TVs	$ 60,000	$ 55,000	$ 55,000
Satellite radios	45,000	52,000	45,000
DVD recorders	48,000	45,000	45,000
DVDs	15,000	14,000	14,000
Total inventory	$168,000	$166,000	**$159,000**

Before You Go On...

REVIEW IT

1. What factors should management consider in selecting an inventory cost flow method? *income statement effects, balance sheet effect & tax effects*
2. What inventory cost flow method does PepsiCo use for its inventories? (*Hint:* You will need to examine the notes for PepsiCo's financial statements.) The answers to these questions appear on page 289.
3. Which inventory cost flow method produces the highest net income in a period of rising prices? Which results in the lowest income taxes? *FIFO ... LIFO*
4. When should inventory be reported at a value other than cost? *A decline in market*

DO IT
The accounting records of Shumway Ag Implement show the following data.

Beginning inventory	4,000 units at $ 3
Purchases	6,000 units at $ 4
Sales	7,000 units at $12

Determine the cost of goods sold during the period under a periodic inventory system using (a) the FIFO method, (b) the LIFO method, and (c) the average-cost method.

Action Plan
- Understand the periodic inventory system.
- Allocate costs between goods sold and goods on hand (ending inventory) for each cost flow method.
- Compute cost of goods sold for each cost flow method.

Solution

Cost of goods available for sale = (4,000 × $3) + (6,000 × $4) = $36,000
Ending inventory = 10,000 − 7,000 = 3,000 units
(a) FIFO: $36,000 − (3,000 × $4) = $24,000
(b) LIFO: $36,000 − (3,000 × $3) = 27,000
(c) Average-cost: [(4,000 @ $3) + (6,000 @ $4)] ÷ 10,000
        = ($12,000 + $24,000) ÷ 10,000
        = $3.60 per unit; 7,000 @ $3.60 = $25,200

Related exercise material: *BE6-3, BE6-4, BE6-5, E6-3, E6-4, E6-5, E6-6, E6-7, and E6-8.*

✓ The Navigator

INVENTORY ERRORS

Unfortunately, errors occasionally occur in accounting for inventory. In some cases, errors are caused by failure to count or price the inventory correctly. In other cases, errors occur because companies do not properly recognize the transfer of legal title to goods that are in transit. When errors occur, they affect both the income statement and the balance sheet.

Income Statement Effects

As you know, both the beginning and ending inventories appear in the income statement. The ending inventory of one period automatically becomes the beginning inventory of the next period. Thus, inventory errors affect the computation of cost of goods sold and net income in two periods.

The effects on cost of goods sold can be computed by entering incorrect data in the formula in Illustration 6-16 and then substituting the correct data.

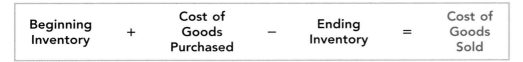

Illustration 6-16
Formula for cost of goods sold

If the error understates *beginning* inventory, cost of goods sold will be understated. If the error understates *ending* inventory, cost of goods sold will be overstated. Illustration 6-17 (page 258) shows the effects of inventory errors on the current year's income statement.

Illustration 6-17
Effects of inventory errors on current year's income statement

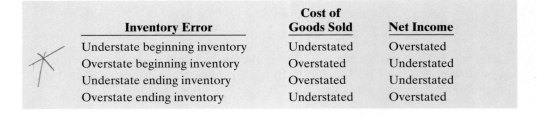

Inventory Error	Cost of Goods Sold	Net Income
Understate beginning inventory	Understated	Overstated
Overstate beginning inventory	Overstated	Understated
Understate ending inventory	Overstated	Understated
Overstate ending inventory	Understated	Overstated

ETHICS NOTE

Inventory fraud increases during recessions. Such fraud includes pricing inventory at amounts in excess of its actual value, or claiming to have inventory when no inventory exists. Inventory fraud usually overstates ending inventory, thereby understating cost of goods sold and creating higher income.

So far, the effects of inventory errors are fairly straightforward. Now, though, comes the (at first) surprising part: An error in the ending inventory of the current period will have a **reverse effect on net income of the next accounting period**. Illustration 6-18 shows this effect. As you study the illustration, you will see that the reverse effect comes from the fact that understating ending inventory in 2008 results in understating beginning inventory in 2009 and overstating net income in 2009.

Over the two years, though, total net income is correct because the errors **offset each other**. Notice that total income using incorrect data is $35,000 ($22,000 + $13,000), which is the same as the total income of $35,000 ($25,000 + $10,000) using correct data. Also note in this example that an error in the beginning inventory does not result in a corresponding error in the ending inventory for that period. The correctness of the ending inventory depends entirely on the accuracy of taking and costing the inventory at the balance sheet date under the periodic inventory system.

Illustration 6-18
Effects of inventory errors on two years' income statements

SAMPLE COMPANY
Condensed Income Statements

	2008 Incorrect		2008 Correct		2009 Incorrect		2009 Correct	
Sales		$80,000		$80,000		$90,000		$90,000
Beginning inventory	$20,000		$20,000		$12,000		$15,000	
Cost of goods purchased	40,000		40,000		68,000		68,000	
Cost of goods available for sale	60,000		60,000		80,000		83,000	
Ending inventory	12,000		15,000		23,000		23,000	
Cost of goods sold		48,000		45,000		57,000		60,000
Gross profit		32,000		35,000		33,000		30,000
Operating expenses		10,000		10,000		20,000		20,000
Net income		$22,000		$25,000		$13,000		$10,000

$(3,000)
Net income
understated

$3,000
Net income
overstated

The errors cancel. Thus the combined total income for the 2-year period is correct.

Balance Sheet Effects

Companies can determine the effect of ending inventory errors on the balance sheet by using the basic accounting equation: Assets = Liabilities + Stockholders' equity. Errors in the ending inventory have the effects shown in Illustration 6-19.

Ending Inventory Error	Assets	Liabilities	Stockholders' Equity
Overstated	Overstated	No effect	Overstated
Understated	Understated	No effect	Understated

Illustration 6-19
Effects of ending inventory errors on balance sheet

STATEMENT PRESENTATION AND ANALYSIS

Presentation

As indicated in Chapter 5, inventory is classified as a current asset after receivables in the balance sheet. In a multiple-step income statement, cost of goods sold is subtracted from sales. There also should be disclosure of (1) the major inventory classifications, (2) the basis of accounting (cost, or lower of cost or market), and (3) the costing method (FIFO, LIFO, or average).

Wal-Mart, for example, in its January 31, 2006, balance sheet reported inventories of $32,191 million under current assets. The accompanying notes to the financial statements, as shown in Illustration 6-20, disclosed the following information.

WAL★MART
WAL-MART STORES, INC.
Notes to the Financial Statements

Illustration 6-20
Inventory disclosures by Wal-Mart

Note 1. Summary of Significant Accounting Policies

Inventories

The company values inventories at the lower-of-cost-or-market as determined primarily by the retail method of accounting, using the last-in, first-out ("LIFO") method for substantially all merchandise inventories in the United States, except SAM'S CLUB merchandise and merchandise in our distribution warehouses, which is based on cost LIFO method. Inventories of foreign operations are primarily valued by the retail method of accounting, using the first-in, first-out ("FIFO") method. At January 31, 2006 and 2005, our inventories valued at LIFO approximate those inventories as if they were valued at FIFO.

As indicated in this note, Wal-Mart values its inventories at the lower-of-cost-or-market using LIFO and FIFO.

Analysis

The amount of inventory carried by a company has significant economic consequences. And inventory management is a double-edged sword that requires constant attention. On the one hand, management wants to have a great variety and quantity on hand so that customers have a wide selection and items are always in stock. But such a policy may incur high carrying costs (e.g., investment, storage, insurance, obsolescence, and damage). On the other hand, low inventory levels lead to stockouts and lost sales. Common ratios used to manage and evaluate inventory levels are inventory turnover and a related measure, days in inventory.

Inventory turnover measures the number of times on average the inventory is sold during the period. Its purpose is to measure the liquidity of the inventory. The inventory turnover is computed by dividing cost of goods sold by the average inventory during the period. Unless seasonal factors are significant, average inventory can be computed from the beginning and ending inventory balances. For example, Wal-Mart reported in its 2006 annual report a beginning inventory of $29,762 million, an ending inventory of $32,191 million,

STUDY OBJECTIVE 6
Compute and interpret the inventory turnover ratio.

and cost of goods sold for the year ended January 31, 2006, of $240,391 million. The inventory turnover formula and computation for Wal-Mart are shown below.

Illustration 6-21
Inventory turnover formula and computation for Wal-Mart

Cost of Goods Sold	÷	Average Inventory	=	Inventory Turnover
$240,391	÷	$\dfrac{\$29,762 + \$32,191}{2}$	=	7.8 times

A variant of the inventory turnover ratio is **days in inventory**. This measures the average number of days inventory is held. It is calculated as 365 divided by the inventory turnover ratio. For example, Wal-Mart's inventory turnover of 7.8 times divided into 365 is approximately 47 days. This is the approximate time that it takes a company to sell the inventory once it arrives at the store.

There are typical levels of inventory in every industry. Companies that are able to keep their inventory at lower levels and higher turnovers and still satisfy customer needs are the most successful.

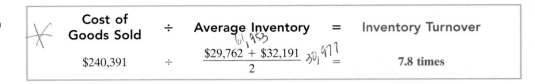

ACCOUNTING ACROSS THE ORGANIZATION

Samsung Uses a Different Strategy

Demand for cell phones typically falls during the first quarter of each year. It is a widely held principle that a company should cut back its production and inventory levels when it anticipates that demand will decrease. Thus many industry observers were surprised when Samsung Electronics Co. chose to increase production during the first quarter of the year, for the third year in a row.

Why did Samsung do this? Its executives felt that this approach would enable it to stand out against competitors by putting "a slew of new cell phones on shelves next to graying models from its rivals." It is clear that even with just-in-time inventory techniques and highly efficient inventory systems, management still must make many critical strategic decisions regarding inventory.

Source: Evan Ramstad, "Samsung to Report Whether Counterintuitive Move Paid Off," *Wall Street Journal*, April 24, 2005, p. B3.

? If Samsung isn't successful in selling the units, what steps will it have to take, and how will this show up in its financial statements?

Before You Go On...

REVIEW IT
1. How do inventory errors affect financial statements?
2. What is the purpose of the inventory turnover ratio?
3. What is the relationship between the inventory turnover ratio and average days in inventory?

The Navigator

 Be sure to read **ALL ABOUT YOU:** *Employee Theft—An Inside Job* on page 261 for information on how topics in this chapter apply to you.

Employee Theft—An Inside Job

Inventory theft is a huge problem for many businesses. Few employees would be as bold as the character in a Johnny Cash song, who while working on an assembly line in Detroit, steals an entire car, one piece at a time, over the course of many years (*www.lyricsdomain.com/10/johnny_cash/one_piece_at_a_time.html*). Nonetheless, at most companies, employees are the primary culprits. While you might think that a free pizza or steak at the end of your shift isn't hurting anybody, the statistics below show that such pilferage really adds up.

Many companies use sophisticated technologies to monitor their customers and employees in order to keep their inventory from walking off. Examples include closed-circuit video cameras and radio frequency identification (RFID). Other companies use techniques that don't rely on technology, such as taking frequent (in some cases daily) inventory counts, having employees keep all personal belongings and bags in a separate changing room, and making surprise checks of employees' bags as they leave. An increasing number of companies are setting up 800 numbers that employees or customers can call to report suspicious behavior, sometimes for a reward.

✹ Some Facts

The National Food Service Security Council estimates that employee theft costs U.S. restaurants $15 billion to $25 billion annually.

The average supermarket has inventory shrinkage losses of 2.28% of sales, or $224,808 per year. Average net profit is only 1.1% of sales, so inventory shrinkage is twice the level of profits.

Fear of getting caught and being fired ranks among one of the top reasons employees give, in surveys of reasons why they do not steal from their employer.

Tips from customers are the No. 1 way that many stores catch thieving employees.

The average employee caught stealing costs his or her company $1,341, while the average loss from a shoplifting incident is only $207.

✹ About the Numbers

Where Did the Inventory Go?

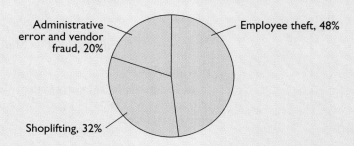

Administrative error and vendor fraud, 20%

Employee theft, 48%

Shoplifting, 32%

Source: Data from 2003 National Retail Security Survey, University of Florida.

✹ What Do You Think?

Suppose you own a number of wine shops selling mid-level as well as expensive bottled wine. You have been experiencing significant losses from theft at your stores. You suspect that it is a combination of both employee and customer theft. Assuming that it would be cost-effective, would you install video cameras to reduce both employee theft and customer theft?

YES: Most employees and customers are honest. However, some will steal if given the opportunity. Management has a responsibility to employ reasonable, cost-effective approaches to safeguard company assets.

NO: The use of video technology to monitor employees and customers sends a message of distrust. You run the risk of alienating your employees (who may well figure out a way around the cameras anyway). Cameras might also reduce the welcoming atmosphere for your customers, who might find the cameras offensive.

Sources: Bob Ingram, "Shrink Has Shrunk," *Supermarket Business*, September 15, 2000, p. 65; Lisa Bertagnoli, "Wrapping up Shrink," *Restaurants & Institutions*, May 1, 2005, pp. 89–90; Naomi R. Kooker, "Taking Aim at Crime," *Nation's Restaurant News*, May 22, 2000, pp. 114–118.

The authors' comments on this situation appear on page 289.

Demonstration Problem 1

Gerald D. Englehart Company has the following inventory, purchases, and sales data for the month of March.

Inventory: March 1	200 units @ $4.00	$ 800	
Purchases:			
	March 10	500 units @ $4.50	2,250
	March 20	400 units @ $4.75	1,900
	March 30	300 units @ $5.00	1,500
Sales:			
	March 15	500 units	
	March 25	400 units	

The physical inventory count on March 31 shows 500 units on hand.

Instructions

Under a **periodic inventory system**, determine the cost of inventory on hand at March 31 and the cost of goods sold for March under (a) (FIFO), (b) (LIFO), and (c) average-cost.

action plan

✔ Compute the cost of inventory under the periodic FIFO method by allocating to the units on hand the **latest costs**.

✔ Compute the cost of inventory under the periodic LIFO method by allocating to the units on hand the **earliest costs**.

✔ Compute the cost of inventory under the periodic average-cost method by allocating to the units on hand a **weighted-average cost**.

Solution to Demonstration Problem 1

The cost of goods available for sale is $6,450, as follows.

Inventory:		200 units @ $4.00	$ 800
Purchases:			
	March 10	500 units @ $4.50	2,250
	March 20	400 units @ $4.75	1,900
	March 30	300 units @ $5.00	1,500
Total cost of goods available for sale			$6,450

Under a **periodic inventory system**, the cost of goods sold under each cost flow method is as follows.

FIFO Method

Ending inventory:

Date	Units	Unit Cost	Total Cost	
March 30	300	$5.00	$1,500	
March 20	200	4.75	950	$2,450

Cost of goods sold: $6,450 − $2,450 = $4,000

LIFO Method

Ending inventory:

Date	Units	Unit Cost	Total Cost	
March 1	200	$4.00	$ 800	
March 10	300	4.50	1,350	$2,150

Cost of goods sold: $6,450 − $2,150 = $4,300

Average-Cost Method

Average unit cost: $6,450 ÷ 1,400 = $4.607
Ending inventory: 500 × $4.607 = $2,303.50

Cost of goods sold: $6,450 − $2,303.50 = $4,146.50

SUMMARY OF STUDY OBJECTIVES

1 Describe the steps in determining inventory quantities. The steps are (1) take a physical inventory of goods on hand and (2) determine the ownership of goods in transit or on consignment.

2 Explain the accounting for inventories and apply the inventory cost flow methods. The primary basis of accounting for inventories is cost. Cost of goods available for sale includes (a) cost of beginning inventory and (b) cost of goods purchased. The inventory cost flow methods are: specific identification and three assumed cost flow methods—FIFO, LIFO, and average-cost.

3 Explain the financial effects of the inventory cost flow assumptions. Companies may allocate the cost of goods available for sale to cost of goods sold and ending inventory by specific identification or by a method based on an assumed cost flow. When prices are rising, the first-in, first-out (FIFO) method results in lower cost of goods sold and higher net income than the other methods. The reverse is true when prices are falling. In the balance sheet, FIFO results in an ending inventory that is closest to current value; inventory under LIFO is the farthest from current value. LIFO results in the lowest income taxes.

4 Explain the lower-of-cost-or-market basis of accounting for inventories. Companies may use the lower-of-cost-or-market (LCM) basis when the current replacement cost (market) is less than cost. Under LCM, companies recognize the loss in the period in which the price decline occurs.

5 Indicate the effects of inventory errors on the financial statements. *In the income statement of the current year:* (a) An error in beginning inventory will have a reverse effect on net income. (b) An error in ending inventory will have a similar effect on net income. If ending inventory errors are not corrected in the following period, their effect on net income for that period is reversed, and total net income for the two years will be correct.

In the balance sheet: Ending inventory errors will have the same effect on total assets and total stockholders' equity and no effect on liabilities.

6 Compute and interpret the inventory turnover ratio. The inventory turnover ratio is cost of goods sold divided by average inventory. To convert it to average days in inventory, divide 365 days by the inventory turnover ratio.

✓ *The Navigator*

GLOSSARY

Average-cost method Inventory costing method that uses the weighted average unit cost to allocate to ending inventory and cost of goods sold the cost of goods available for sale. (p. 252).

Conservatism Concept that dictates that when in doubt, choose the method that will be least likely to overstate assets and net income. (p. 256).

Consigned goods Goods held for sale by one party (the consignee) although ownership of the goods is retained by another party (the consignor). (p. 247).

Consistency principle Dictates that a company use the same accounting principles and methods from year to year. (p. 255).

Current replacement cost The current cost to replace an inventory item. (p. 256).

Days in inventory Measure of the average number of days inventory is held; calculated as 365 divided by inventory turnover ratio. (p. 260).

Finished goods inventory Manufactured items that are completed and ready for sale. (p. 244).

First-in, first-out (FIFO) method Inventory costing method that assumes that the costs of the earliest goods purchased are the first to be recognized as cost of goods sold. (p. 250).

FOB (free on board) destination Freight terms indicating that ownership of the goods passes to the buyer when the public carrier accepts the goods from the seller. (p. 246).

FOB (free on board) shipping point Freight terms indicating that ownership of the goods remains with the seller until the goods reach the buyer. (p. 246).

Inventory turnover ratio A ratio that measures the number of times on average the inventory sold during the period; computed by dividing cost of goods sold by the average inventory during the period. (p. 259).

Just-in-time (JIT) inventory method Inventory system in which companies manufacture or purchase goods just in time for use. (p. 245).

Last-in, first-out (LIFO) method Inventory costing method that assumes the costs of the latest units purchased are the first to be allocated to cost of goods sold. (p. 251).

Lower-of-cost-or-market (LCM) basis A basis whereby inventory is stated at the lower of either its cost or its market value as determined by current replacement cost. (p. 256).

Raw materials Basic goods that will be used in production but have not yet been placed into production. (p. 244).

Specific identification method An actual physical flow costing method in which items still in inventory are specifically costed to arrive at the total cost of the ending inventory. (p. 248).

Weighted average unit cost Average cost that is weighted by the number of units purchased at each unit cost. (p. 252).

Work in process That portion of manufactured inventory that has been placed into the production process but is not yet complete. (p. 244).

APPENDIX 6A Inventory Cost Flow Methods in Perpetual Inventory Systems

What inventory cost flow methods do companies employ if they use a perpetual inventory system? Simple—they can use any of the inventory cost flow methods described in the chapter. To illustrate the application of the three assumed cost flow methods (FIFO, LIFO, and average-cost), we will use the data shown in Illustration 6A-1 and in this chapter for Houston Electronic's Astro Condenser.

Illustration 6A-1
Inventoriable units and costs

HOUSTON ELECTRONICS
Astro Condensers

Date	Explanation	Units	Unit Cost	Total Cost	Balance in Units
1/1	Beginning inventory	100	$10	$ 1,000	100
4/15	Purchases	200	11	2,200	300
8/24	Purchases	300	12	3,600	600
9/10	Sale	550			50
11/27	Purchases	400	13	5,200	450
				$12,000	

First-In, First-Out (FIFO)

Under FIFO, the company charges to cost of goods sold the cost of the earliest goods on hand **prior to each sale**. Therefore, the cost of goods sold on September 10 consists of the units on hand January 1 and the units purchased April 15 and August 24. Illustration 6A-2 shows the inventory under a FIFO method perpetual system.

Illustration 6A-2
Perpetual system—FIFO

Date	Purchases	Cost of Goods Sold	Balance (in units and cost)
January 1			(100 @ $10) $ 1,000
April 15	(200 @ $11) $2,200		(100 @ $10) (200 @ $11) } $ 3,200
August 24	(300 @ $12) $3,600		(100 @ $10) (200 @ $11) (300 @ $12) } $ 6,800
September 10		(100 @ $10) (200 @ $11) (250 @ $12)	(50 @ $12) $ 600
		$6,200	
November 27	(400 @ $13) $5,200		(50 @ $12) (400 @ $13) } **$5,800**

Cost of goods sold

Ending inventory

The ending inventory in this situation is $5,800, and the cost of goods sold is $6,200 [(100 @ $10) + (200 @ $11) + (250 @ $12)].

Compare Illustrations 6-5 (page 250) and 6A-2. You can see that the results under FIFO in a perpetual system are the **same as in a periodic system**. In both cases, the ending inventory is $5,800 and cost of goods sold is $6,200. Regardless of the system, the first costs in are the costs assigned to cost of goods sold.

Last-In, First-Out (LIFO)

Under the LIFO method using a perpetual system, the company charges to cost of goods sold the cost of the most recent purchase prior to sale. Therefore, the cost of the goods sold on September 10 consists of all the units from the August 24 and April 15 purchases plus 50 of the units in beginning inventory. Illustration 6A-3 shows the computation of the ending inventory under the LIFO method.

Date	Purchases	Cost of Goods Sold	Balance (in units and cost)	
January 1			(100 @ $10)	$1,000
April 15	(200 @ $11) $2,200		(100 @ $10) (200 @ $11)	$3,200
August 24	(300 @ $12) $3,600		(100 @ $10) (200 @ $11) (300 @ $12)	$6,800
September 10		(300 @ $12) (200 @ $11) (50 @ $10)	(50 @ $10)	$ 500
		$6,300		Cost of goods sold
November 27	(400 @ $13) $5,200		(50 @ $10) (400 @ $13)	**$5,700**

Illustration 6A-3
Perpetual system—LIFO

Ending inventory

The use of LIFO in a perpetual system will usually produce cost allocations that differ from those using LIFO in a periodic system. In a perpetual system, the company allocates the latest units purchased *prior to each sale* to cost of goods sold. In contrast, in a periodic system, the latest units purchased *during the period* are allocated to cost of goods sold. Thus, when a purchase is made after the last sale, the LIFO periodic system will apply this purchase to the previous sale. Compare Illustrations 6-8 (page 252) and 6A-3. Illustration 6-8 shows that the 400 units at $13 purchased on November 27 applied to the sale of 550 units on September 10. Under the LIFO perpetual system in Illustration 6A-3, the 400 units at $13 purchased on November 27 are all applied to the ending inventory.

The ending inventory in this LIFO perpetual illustration is $5,700, and cost of goods sold is $6,300, as compared to the LIFO periodic illustration (on page 251) where the ending inventory is $5,000 and cost of goods sold is $7,000.

Average-Cost

The average-cost method in a perpetual inventory system is called the **moving-average method**. Under this method the company computes a new average **after each purchase**, by dividing the cost of goods available for sale by the units on hand. They then apply the average cost to: (1) the units sold, to determine the cost of goods sold, and (2) the remaining units on hand, to determine the ending inventory amount. Illustration 6A-4 shows the application of the average-cost method by Houston Electronics.

Date	Purchases	Cost of Goods Sold	Balance (in units and cost)	
January 1			(100 @ $10)	$1,000
April 15	(200 @ $11) $2,200		(300 @ $10.667)	$3,200
August 24	(300 @ $12) $3,600		(600 @ $11.333)	$6,800
September 10		(550 @ $11.333)	(50 @ $11.333)	$ 567
		$6,233		Cost of goods sold
November 27	(400 @ $13) $5,200		(450 @ $12.816)	**$5,767**

Illustration 6A-4
Perpetual system—average-cost method

Ending inventory

As indicated above, Houston Electronics computes **a new average each time it makes a purchase**. On April 15, after it buys 200 units for $2,200, a total of 300 units costing $3,200 ($1,000 + $2,200) are on hand. The average unit cost is $10.667 ($3,200 ÷ 300). On August 24, after Houston Electronics buys 300 units for $3,600, a total of 600 units costing $6,800 ($1,000 + $2,200 + $3,600) are on hand, at an average cost per unit of $11.333 ($6,800 ÷ 600). Houston Electronics uses this unit cost of $11.333 in costing sales until it makes another purchase, when the company computes a new unit cost. Accordingly, the unit cost of the 550 units sold on September 10 is $11.333, and the total cost of goods sold is $6,233. On November 27, following the purchase of 400 units for $5,200, there are 450 units on hand costing $5,767 ($567 + $5,200) with a new average cost of $12.816 ($5,767 ÷ 450).

Compare this moving-average cost under the perpetual inventory system to Illustration 6-10 (on page 253) showing the weighted-average method under a periodic inventory system.

Demonstration Problem 2

Demonstration Problem 1 on page 262 showed cost of goods sold computations under a periodic inventory system. Now let's assume that Gerald D. Englehart Company uses a perpetual inventory system. The company has the same inventory, purchases, and sales data for the month of March as shown earlier:

Inventory:	March 1	200 units @ $4.00	$ 800
Purchases:	March 10	500 units @ $4.50	2,250
	March 20	400 units @ $4.75	1,900
	March 30	300 units @ $5.00	1,500
Sales:	March 15	500 units	
	March 25	400 units	

The physical inventory count on March 31 shows 500 units on hand.

Instructions

Under a **perpetual inventory system**, determine the cost of inventory on hand at March 31 and the cost of goods sold for March under (a) FIFO, (b) LIFO, and (c) average-cost.

Solution to Demonstration Problem 2

The cost of goods available for sale is $6,450, as follows.

Inventory:		200 units @ $4.00	$ 800
Purchases:	March 10	500 units @ $4.50	2,250
	March 20	400 units @ $4.75	1,900
	March 30	300 units @ $5.00	1,500
	Total cost of goods available for sale		$6,450

Under a **perpetual inventory system**, the cost of goods sold under each cost flow method is as follows.

FIFO Method

Date	Purchases	Cost of Goods Sold	Balance
March 1			(200 @ $4.00) $ 800
March 10	(500 @ $4.50) $2,250		(200 @ $4.00)⎫ $3,050 (500 @ $4.50)⎭
March 15		(200 @ $4.00) (300 @ $4.50) ——— $2,150	(200 @ $4.50) $ 900

action plan

✔ Compute the cost of goods sold under the perpetual FIFO method by allocating to the goods sold the **earliest** cost of goods purchased.

✔ Compute the cost of goods sold under the perpetual LIFO method by allocating to the goods sold the **latest** cost of goods purchased.

✔ Compute the cost of goods sold under the perpetual average-cost method by allocating to the goods sold a **moving-average** cost.

Date	Purchases	Cost of Goods Sold	Balance
March 20	(400 @ $4.75) $1,900		(200 @ $4.50) ⎱ $2,800 (400 @ $4.75) ⎰
March 25		(200 @ $4.50) (200 @ $4.75) ‾‾‾‾‾‾‾ $1,850	(200 @ $4.75) $ 950
March 30	(300 @ $5.00) $1,500		(200 @ $4.75) ⎱ $2,450 (300 @ $5.00) ⎰

Ending inventory, $2,450   Cost of goods sold: $2,150 + $1,850 = $4,000

LIFO Method

Date	Purchases	Cost of Goods Sold	Balance
March 1			(200 @ $4.00) $ 800
March 10	(500 @ $4.50) $2,250		(200 @ $4.00) ⎱ $3,050 (500 @ $4.50) ⎰
March 15		(500 @ $4.50) $2,250	(200 @ $4.00) $ 800
March 20	(400 @ $4.75) $1,900		(200 @ $4.00) ⎱ $2,700 (400 @ $4.75) ⎰
March 25		(400 @ $4.75) $1,900	(200 @ $4.00) $ 800
March 30	(300 @ $5.00) $1,500		(200 @ $4.00) ⎱ $2,300 (300 @ $5.00) ⎰

Ending inventory, $2,300   Cost of goods sold: $2,250 + $1,900 = $4,150

Moving-Average Cost Method

Date	Purchases	Cost of Goods Sold	Balance
March 1			(200 @ $ 4.00) $ 800
March 10	(500 @ $4.50) $2,250		(700 @ $4.357) $3,050
March 15		(500 @ $4.357) $2,179	(200 @ $4.357) $ 871
March 20	(400 @ $4.75) $1,900		(600 @ $4.618) $2,771
March 25		(400 @ $4.618) $1,847	(200 @ $4.618) $ 924
March 30	(300 @ $5.00) $1,500		(500 @ $4.848) $2,424

Ending inventory, $2,424   Cost of goods sold: $2,179 + $1,847 = $4,026

✔ The Navigator

7 Apply the inventory cost flow methods to perpetual inventory records. Under FIFO and a perpetual inventory system, companies charge to cost of goods sold the cost of the earliest goods on hand prior to each sale. Under LIFO and a perpetual system, companies charge to cost of goods sold the cost of the most recent purchase prior to sale. Under the moving-average (average cost) method and a perpetual system, companies compute a new average cost after each purchase.

APPENDIX 6B Estimating Inventories

In the chapter we assumed that a company would be able to physically count its inventory. What if it cannot? What if the inventory were destroyed by fire or flood, for example? In that case, the company would use an estimate.

STUDY OBJECTIVE 8
Describe the two methods of estimating inventories.

Two circumstances explain why companies sometimes estimate inventories. First, a casualty such as fire, flood, or earthquake may make it impossible to take a physical inventory. Second, managers may want monthly or quarterly financial statements, but a physical inventory is taken only annually. The need for estimating inventories occurs primarily with a periodic inventory system because of the absence of perpetual inventory records.

There are two widely used methods of estimating inventories: (1) the gross profit method, and (2) the retail inventory method.

Gross Profit Method

The gross profit method estimates the cost of ending inventory by applying a gross profit rate to net sales. This method is relatively simple, but effective. It will detect large errors. Accountants, auditors, and managers frequently use the gross profit method to test the reasonableness of the ending inventory amount.

To use this method, a company needs to know its net sales, cost of goods available for sale, and gross profit rate. With the gross profit rate, the company can estimate its gross profit for the period. Illustration 6B-1 shows the formulas for using the gross profit method.

Illustration 6B-1
Gross profit method formulas

To illustrate, assume that Kishwaukee Company wishes to prepare an income statement for the month of January. Its records show net sales of $200,000, beginning inventory $40,000, and cost of goods purchased $120,000. In the preceding year, the company realized a 30% gross profit rate. It expects to earn the same rate this year. Given these facts and assumptions, Kishwaukee can compute the estimated cost of the ending inventory at January 31 under the gross profit method as follows.

Illustration 6B-2
Example of gross profit method

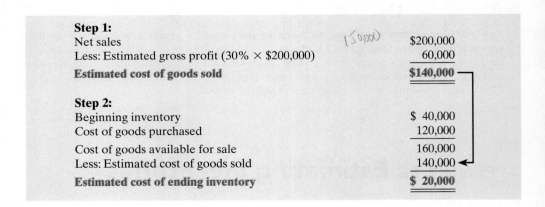

The gross profit method is based on the assumption that the gross profit rate will remain constant. But it may not remain constant, due to a change in merchandising policies or in market conditions. In such cases, the company should adjust the rate to reflect current operating conditions. In some cases, companies can obtain a more accurate estimate by applying this method on a department or product-line basis.

Note that companies should not use the gross profit method to prepare financial statements at the end of the year. These statements should be based on a physical inventory count.

Retail Inventory Method

A retail store such as Home Depot, Ace Hardware, or Wal-Mart has thousands of different types of merchandise at low unit costs. In such cases it is difficult and time-consuming to apply unit costs to inventory quantities. An alternative is to use the **retail inventory method** to estimate the cost of inventory. Most retail companies can establish a relationship between cost and sales price. The company then applies the cost-to-retail percentage to the ending inventory at retail prices to determine inventory at cost.

Under the retail inventory method, a company's records must show both the cost and retail value of the goods available for sale. Illustration 6B-3 presents the formulas for using the retail inventory method.

Step 1:	Goods Available for Sale at Retail	−	Net Sales	=	Ending Inventory at Retail	
Step 2:	Goods Available for Sale at Cost _210,000_	÷	Goods Available for Sale at Retail _300,000_	=	Cost-to-Retail Ratio	
Step 3:	Ending Inventory at Retail _80,000_	×	Cost-to-Retail Ratio	=	Estimated Cost of Ending Inventory	

Illustration 6B-3
Retail inventory method formulas

We can demonstrate the logic of the retail method by using unit-cost data. Assume that Ortiz Inc. has marked 10 units purchased at $7 to sell for $10 per unit. Thus, the cost-to-retail ratio is 70% ($70 ÷ $100). If four units remain unsold, their retail value is $40 (4 × $10), and their cost is $28 ($40 × 70%). This amount agrees with the total cost of goods on hand on a per unit basis (4 × $7).

Illustration 6B-4 shows application of the retail method for Valley West Co. Note that it is not necessary to take a physical inventory to determine the estimated cost of goods on hand at any given time.

	At Cost	At Retail
Beginning inventory	$14,000	$ 21,500
Goods purchased	61,000	78,500
Goods available for sale	$75,000	100,000
Net sales		70,000
Step (1) Ending inventory at retail =		$ 30,000
Step (2) Cost-to-retail ratio $75,000 ÷ $100,000 = 75%		
Step (3) Estimated cost of ending inventory = $30,000 × 75% = $22,500		

Illustration 6B-4
Application of retail inventory method

HELPFUL HINT

In determining inventory at retail, companies use selling prices of the units.

The retail inventory method also facilitates taking a physical inventory at the end of the year. Valley West can value the goods on hand at the prices marked on the merchandise, and then apply the cost-to-retail ratio to the goods on hand at retail to determine the ending inventory at cost.

The major disadvantage of the retail method is that it is an averaging technique. Thus, it may produce an incorrect inventory valuation if the mix of the ending inventory is not representative of the mix in the goods available for sale. Assume, for example, that the cost-to-retail ratio of 75% for Valley West Co. consists of equal proportions of inventory items that have cost-to-retail ratios of 70%, 75%, and 80%. If the ending inventory contains only items with a 70% ratio, an incorrect inventory cost will result. Companies can minimize this problem by applying the retail method on a department or product-line basis.

SUMMARY OF STUDY OBJECTIVE FOR APPENDIX 6B

8 Describe the two methods of estimating inventories. The two methods of estimating inventories are the gross profit method and the retail inventory method. Under the gross profit method, companies apply a gross profit rate to net sales to determine estimated cost of goods sold. They then subtract estimated cost of goods sold from cost of goods available for sale to determine the estimated cost of the ending inventory.

Under the retail inventory method, companies compute a cost-to-retail ratio by dividing the cost of goods available for sale by the retail value of the goods available for sale. They then apply this ratio to the ending inventory at retail to determine the estimated cost of the ending inventory.

GLOSSARY FOR APPENDIX 6B

Gross profit method   A method for estimating the cost of the ending inventory by applying a gross profit rate to net sales and subtracting the result from cost of goods available for sale. (p. 268).

Retail inventory method   A method for estimating the cost of the ending inventory by applying a cost-to-retail ratio to the ending inventory at retail. (p. 269).

*Note: All **asterisked** Questions, Exercises, and Problems relate to material in the appendixes to the chapter.

SELF-STUDY QUESTIONS

Answers are at the end of the chapter.

(SO 1) **1.** Which of the following should *not* be included in the physical inventory of a company?
 a. Goods held on consignment from another company.
 b. Goods shipped on consignment to another company.
 c. Goods in transit from another company shipped FOB shipping point.
 d. None of the above.

(SO 2) **2.** Cost of goods available for sale consist of two elements: beginning inventory and
 a. ending inventory.
 b. cost of goods purchased.
 c. cost of goods sold.
 d. all of the above.

(SO 2) **3.** Tinker Bell Company has the following:

	Units	Unit Cost
Inventory, Jan. 1	8,000	$11
Purchase, June 19	13,000	12
Purchase, Nov. 8	5,000	13

If Tinker Bell has 9,000 units on hand at December 31, the cost of the ending inventory under FIFO is:
 a. $99,000.
 b. $108,000.
 c. $113,000.
 d. $117,000.

(SO   **4.** Using the data in (3) above, the cost of the ending inventory under LIFO is:
 a. $113,000.
 b. $108,000.
 c. $99,000.
 d. $100,000.

(SO   **5.** In periods of rising prices, LIFO will produce:
 a. higher net income than FIFO.
 b. the same net income as FIFO.
 c. lower net income than FIFO.
 d. higher net income than average costing.

(SO   **6.** Factors that affect the selection of an inventory costing method do *not* include:
 a. tax effects.
 b. balance sheet effects.
 c. income statement effects.
 d. perpetual vs. periodic inventory system.

⊃ 4)   **7.** Rickety Company purchased 1,000 widgets and has 200 widgets in its ending inventory at a cost of $91 each and a current replacement cost of $80 each. The ending inventory under lower of cost or market is:
   a. $91,000.
   b. $80,000.
   c. $18,200.
   d. $16,000.

⊃ 5)   **8.** Atlantis Company's ending inventory is understated $4,000. The effects of this error on the current year's cost of goods sold and net income, respectively, are:
   a. understated, overstated.
   b. overstated, understated.
   c. overstated, overstated.
   d. understated, understated.

⊃ 6)   **9.** Which of these would cause the inventory turnover ratio to increase the most?
   a. Increasing the amount of inventory on hand.
   b. Keeping the amount of inventory on hand constant but increasing sales.
   c. Keeping the amount of inventory on hand constant but decreasing sales.

   d. Decreasing the amount of inventory on hand and increasing sales.

*10. Songbird Company has sales of $150,000 and cost of goods available for sale of $135,000. If the gross profit rate is 30%, the estimated cost of the ending inventory under the gross profit method is: (SO 8)
   a. $15,000.
   b. $30,000.
   c. $45,000.
   d. $75,000.

*11. In a perpetual inventory system,   (SO 7)
   a. LIFO cost of goods sold will be the same as in a periodic inventory system.
   b. average costs are based entirely on unit cost averages.
   c. a new average is computed under the average cost method after each sale.
   d. FIFO cost of goods sold will be the same as in a periodic inventory system.

Go to the book's website,
www.wiley.com/college/weygandt,
for Additional Self-Study questions.

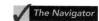 The Navigator

QUESTIONS

1. "The key to successful business operations is effective inventory management." Do you agree? Explain.

2. An item must possess two characteristics to be classified as inventory by a merchandiser. What are these two characteristics?

3. Your friend Tom Witt has been hired to help take the physical inventory in Hawkeye Hardware Store. Explain to Tom Witt what this job will entail.

4. (a) Reeves Company ships merchandise to Cox Company on December 30. The merchandise reaches the buyer on January 6. Indicate the terms of sale that will result in the goods being included in (1) Reeves's December 31 inventory, and (2) Cox's December 31 inventory.
   (b) Under what circumstances should Reeves Company include consigned goods in its inventory?

5. Jim's Hat Shop received a shipment of hats for which it paid the wholesaler $2,970. The price of the hats was $3,000 but Jim's was given a $30 cash discount and required to pay freight charges of $50. In addition, Jim's paid $130 to cover the travel expenses of an employee who negotiated the purchase of the hats. What amount will Jim's record for inventory? Why?

6. Identify the distinguishing features of an income statement for a merchandiser.

7. David Shannon believes that the allocation of inventoriable costs should be based on the actual physical flow of the goods. Explain to David why this may be both impractical and inappropriate.

8. What is a major advantage and a major disadvantage of the specific identification method of inventory costing?

9. "The selection of an inventory cost flow method is a decision made by accountants." Do you agree? Explain.

Once a method has been selected, what accounting requirement applies?

10. Which assumed inventory cost flow method:
   (a) usually parallels the actual physical flow of merchandise?
   (b) assumes that goods available for sale during an accounting period are identical?
   (c) assumes that the latest units purchased are the first to be sold?

11. In a period of rising prices, the inventory reported in Plato Company's balance sheet is close to the current cost of the inventory. Cecil Company's inventory is considerably below its current cost. Identify the inventory cost flow method being used by each company. Which company has probably been reporting the higher gross profit?

12. Casey Company has been using the FIFO cost flow method during a prolonged period of rising prices. During the same time period, Casey has been paying out all of its net income as dividends. What adverse effects may result from this policy?

13. Peter Lunde is studying for the next accounting mid-term examination. What should Peter know about (a) departing from the cost basis of accounting for inventories and (b) the meaning of "market" in the lower-of-cost-or-market method?

14. Garitson Music Center has 5 CD players on hand at the balance sheet date. Each cost $400. The current replacement cost is $380 per unit. Under the lower-of-cost-or-market basis of accounting for inventories, what value should be reported for the CD players on the balance sheet? Why?

15. Ruthie Stores has 20 toasters on hand at the balance sheet data. Each cost $27. The current replacement cost is

$30 per unit. Under the lower-of-cost-or-market basis of accounting for inventories, what value should Ruthie report for the toasters on the balance sheet? Why?

16. Mintz Company discovers in 2008 that its ending inventory at December 31, 2007, was $7,000 understated. What effect will this error have on (a) 2007 net income, (b) 2008 net income, and (c) the combined net income for the 2 years?

17. Willingham Company's balance sheet shows Inventories $162,800. What additional disclosures should be made?

18. Under what circumstances might inventory turnover be too high? That is, what possible negative consequences might occur?

*19. "When perpetual inventory records are kept, the results under the FIFO and LIFO methods are the same as they would be in a periodic inventory system." Do you agree? Explain.

*20. How does the average-cost method of inventory costing differ between a perpetual inventory system and a periodic inventory system?

*21. When is it necessary to estimate inventories?

*22. Both the gross profit method and the retail inventory method are based on averages. For each method, indicate the average used, how it is determined, and how it is applied.

*23. Maureen Company has net sales of $400,000 and cost of goods available for sale of $300,000. If the gross profit rate is 35%, what is the estimated cost of the ending inventory? Show computations.

*24. Milo Shoe Shop had goods available for sale in 2008 with a retail price of $120,000. The cost of these goods was $84,000. If sales during the period were $80,000, what is the ending inventory at cost using the retail inventory method?

BRIEF EXERCISES

Identify items to be included in taking a physical inventory.

(SO 1)

BE6-1   Smart Company identifies the following items for possible inclusion in the taking of a physical inventory. Indicate whether each item should be included or excluded from the inventory taking.

(a) Goods shipped on consignment by Smart to another company. Yes
(b) Goods in transit from a supplier shipped FOB destination. No
(c) Goods sold but being held for customer pickup. No
(d) Goods held on consignment from another company. No

Identify the components of goods available for sale.

(SO 2)

BE6-2   The ledger of Gomez Company includes the following items: (a) Freight-in, (b) Purchase Returns and Allowances, (c) Purchases, (d) Sales Discounts, (e) Purchase Discounts. Identify which items are included in goods available for sale.

Compute ending inventory using FIFO and LIFO.

(SO 2)

BE6-3   In its first month of operations, Quirk Company made three purchases of merchandise in the following sequence: (1) 300 units at $6, (2) 400 units at $7, and (3) 200 units at $8. Assuming there are 360 units on hand, compute the cost of the ending inventory under the (a) FIFO method and (b) LIFO method. Quirk uses a periodic inventory system.

Compute the ending inventory using average-cost.

(SO 2)

BE6-4   Data for Quirk Company are presented in BE6-3. Compute the cost of the ending inventory under the average-cost method, assuming there are 360 units on hand.

Explain the financial statement effect of inventory cost flow assumptions.

(SO 3)

BE6-5   The management of Hoyt Corp. is considering the effects of various inventory-costing methods on its financial statements and its income tax expense. Assuming that the price the company pays for inventory is increasing, which method will:

(a) provide the highest net income? FIFO
(b) provide the highest ending inventory? FIFO
(c) result in the lowest income tax expense? LIFO
(d) result in the most stable earnings over a number of years? Average Cost

Explain the financial statement effect of inventory cost flow assumptions.

(SO 3)

BE6-6   In its first month of operation, Gulletson Company purchased 100 units of inventory for $6, then 200 units for $7, and finally 150 units for $8. At the end of the month, 180 units remained. Compute the amount of phantom profit that would result if the company used FIFO rather than LIFO. Explain why this amount is referred to as phantom profit. The company uses the periodic method.

Determine the LCM valuation using inventory categories.

(SO 4)

BE6-7   Alou Appliance Center accumulates the following cost and market data at December 31.

Inventory Categories	Cost Data	Market Data
Cameras	$12,000	$12,100
Camcorders	9,500	9,700
VCRs	14,000	12,800

Compute the lower-of-cost-or-market valuation for the company's total inventory.

BE6-8   Cody Company reports net income of $90,000 in 2008. However, ending inventory was understated $10,000. What is the correct net income for 2008? What effect, if any, will this error have on total assets as reported in the balance sheet at December 31, 2008?

Determine correct income statement amounts.
(SO 5)

BE6-9   At December 31, 2008, the following information was available for J. Graff Company: ending inventory $40,000, beginning inventory $60,000, cost of goods sold $270,000, and sales revenue $380,000. Calculate inventory turnover and days in inventory for J. Graff Company.

Compute inventory turnover and days in inventory.
(SO 6)

*BE6-10   Jensen's Department Store uses a perpetual inventory system. Data for product E2-D2 include the following purchases.

Apply cost flow methods to perpetual inventory records.
(SO 7)

Date	Number of Units	Unit Price
May 7	50	$10
July 28	30	13

On June 1 Jensen's sold 30 units, and on August 27, 40 more units. Prepare the perpetual inventory schedule for the above transactions using (1) FIFO, (2) LIFO, and (3) average-cost.

*BE6-11   At May 31, Creole Company has net sales of $330,000 and cost of goods available for sale of $230,000. Compute the estimated cost of the ending inventory, assuming the gross profit rate is 35%.

Apply the gross profit method.
(SO 8)

*BE6-12   On June 30, Fabre Fabrics has the following data pertaining to the retail inventory method: Goods available for sale: at cost $35,000, at retail $50,000; net sales $40,000, and ending inventory at retail $8,000. Compute the estimated cost of the ending inventory using the retail inventory method.

Apply the retail inventory method.
(SO 8)

EXERCISES

E6-1   Premier Bank and Trust is considering giving Lima Company a loan. Before doing so, they decide that further discussions with Lima's accountant may be desirable. One area of particular concern is the inventory account, which has a year-end balance of $297,000. Discussions with the accountant reveal the following.

Determine the correct inventory amount.
(SO 1)

1. Lima sold goods costing $38,000 to Comerica Company, FOB shipping point, on December 28. The goods are not expected to arrive at Comerica until January 12. The goods were not included in the physical inventory because they were not in the warehouse.
2. The physical count of the inventory did not include goods costing $95,000 that were shipped to Lima FOB destination on December 27 and were still in transit at year-end.
3. Lima received goods costing $22,000 on January 2. The goods were shipped FOB shipping point on December 26 by Galant Co. The goods were not included in the physical count.
4. Lima sold goods costing $35,000 to Emerick Co., FOB destination, on December 30. The goods were received at Emerick on January 8. They were not included in Lima's physical inventory.
5. Lima received goods costing $44,000 on January 2 that were shipped FOB destination on December 29. The shipment was a rush order that was supposed to arrive December 31. This purchase was included in the ending inventory of $297,000.

Instructions
Determine the correct inventory amount on December 31.

E6-2   Kale Thompson, an auditor with Sneed CPAs, is performing a review of Strawser Company's inventory account. Strawser did not have a good year and top management is under pressure to boost reported income. According to its records, the inventory balance at year-end was $740,000. However, the following information was not considered when determining that amount.

Determine the correct inventory amount.
(SO 1)

1. Included in the company's count were goods with a cost of $250,000 that the company is holding on consignment. The goods belong to Superior Corporation.
2. The physical count did not include goods purchased by Strawser with a cost of $40,000 that were shipped FOB destination on December 28 and did not arrive at Strawser's warehouse until January 3.

3. Included in the inventory account was $17,000 of office supplies that were stored in the warehouse and were to be used by the company's supervisors and managers during the coming year.
4. The company received an order on December 29 that was boxed and was sitting on the loading dock awaiting pick-up on December 31. The shipper picked up the goods on January 1 and delivered them on January 6. The shipping terms were FOB shipping point. The goods had a selling price of $40,000 and a cost of $30,000. The goods were not included in the count because they were sitting on the dock.
5. On December 29 Strawser shipped goods with a selling price of $80,000 and a cost of $60,000 to District Sales Corporation FOB shipping point. The goods arrived on January 3. District Sales had only ordered goods with a selling price of $10,000 and a cost of $8,000. However, a sales manager at Strawser had authorized the shipment and said that if District wanted to ship the goods back next week, it could.
6. Included in the count was $40,000 of goods that were parts for a machine that the company no longer made. Given the high-tech nature of Strawser's products, it was unlikely that these obsolete parts had any other use. However, management would prefer to keep them on the books at cost, "since that is what we paid for them, after all."

Instructions

Prepare a schedule to determine the correct inventory amount. Provide explanations for each item above, saying why you did or did not make an adjustment for each item.

Calculate cost of goods sold using specific identification and FIFO.

(SO 2, 3)

E6-3 On December 1, Bargain Electronics Ltd. has three DVD players left in stock. All are identical, all are priced to sell at $150. One of the three DVD players left in stock, with serial #1012, was purchased on June 1 at a cost of $100. Another, with serial #1045, was purchased on November 1 for $90. The last player, serial #1056, was purchased on November 30 for $80.

Instructions

(a) Calculate the cost of goods sold using the FIFO periodic inventory method assuming that two of the three players were sold by the end of December, Bargain Electronic's year-end.
(b) If Bargain Electronics used the specific identification method instead of the FIFO method, how might it alter its earnings by "selectively choosing" which particular players to sell to the two customers? What would Bargain's cost of goods sold be if the company wished to minimize earnings? Maximize earnings?
(c) Which inventory method do you recommend that Bargain use? Explain why.

Compute inventory and cost of goods sold using FIFO and LIFO.

(SO 2)

E6-4 Boarders sells a snowboard, Xpert, that is popular with snowboard enthusiasts. Below is information relating to Boarders's purchases of Xpert snowboards during September. During the same month, 121 Xpert snowboards were sold. Boarders uses a periodic inventory system.

Date	Explanation	Units	Unit Cost	Total Cost
Sept. 1	Inventory	26	$ 97	$ 2,522
Sept. 12	Purchases	45	102	4,590
Sept. 19	Purchases	20	104	2,080
Sept. 26	Purchases	50	105	5,250
	Totals	141		$14,442

Instructions

(a) Compute the ending inventory at September 30 and cost of goods sold using the FIFO and LIFO methods. Prove the amount allocated to cost of goods sold under each method.
(b) For both FIFO and LIFO, calculate the sum of ending inventory and cost of goods sold. What do you notice about the answers you found for each method?

Compute inventory and cost of goods sold using FIFO and LIFO.

(SO 2)

E6-5 Catlet Co. uses a periodic inventory system. Its records show the following for the month of May, in which 65 units were sold.

		Units	Unit Cost	Total Cost
May 1	Inventory	30	$ 8	$240
15	Purchases	25	11	275
24	Purchases	35	12	420
	Totals	90		$935

Instructions

Compute the ending inventory at May 31 and cost of goods sold using the FIFO and LIFO methods. Prove the amount allocated to cost of goods sold under each method.

E6-6   Yount Company reports the following for the month of June.

		Units	Unit Cost	Total Cost
June 1	Inventory	200	$5	$1,000
12	Purchase	300	6	1,800
23	Purchase	500	7	3,500
30	Inventory	120		

Compute inventory and cost of goods sold using FIFO and LIFO.

(SO 2, 3)

Instructions

(a) Compute the cost of the ending inventory and the cost of goods sold under (1) FIFO and (2) LIFO.
(b) Which costing method gives the higher ending inventory? Why?
(c) Which method results in the higher cost of goods sold? Why?

E6-7   Jones Company had 100 units in beginning inventory at a total cost of $10,000. The company purchased 200 units at a total cost of $26,000. At the end of the year, Jones had 80 units in ending inventory.

Compute inventory under FIFO, LIFO, and average-cost.

(SO 2, 3)

Instructions

(a) Compute the cost of the ending inventory and the cost of goods sold under (1) FIFO, (2) LIFO, and (3) average-cost.
(b) Which cost flow method would result in the highest net income?
(c) Which cost flow method would result in inventories approximating current cost in the balance sheet?
(d) Which cost flow method would result in Jones paying the least taxes in the first year?

E6-8   Inventory data for Yount Company are presented in E6-6.

Compute inventory and cost of goods sold using average-cost.

(SO 2, 3)

Instructions

(a) Compute the cost of the ending inventory and the cost of goods sold using the average-cost method.
(b) Will the results in (a) be higher or lower than the results under (1) FIFO and (2) LIFO?
(c) Why is the average unit cost not $6?

E6-9   Americus Camera Shop uses the lower-of-cost-or-market basis for its inventory. The following data are available at December 31.

Determine ending inventory under LCM.

(SO 4)

Item	Units	Unit Cost	Market
Cameras:			
Minolta	5	$170	$156
Canon	6	150	152
Light meters:			
Vivitar	12	125	115
Kodak	14	120	135

Instructions

Determine the amount of the ending inventory by applying the lower-of-cost-or-market basis.

E6-10   Conan Company applied FIFO to its inventory and got the following results for its ending inventory.

Compute lower-of-cost-or-market.

(SO 4)

VCRs	100 units at a cost per unit of $65
DVD players	150 units at a cost per unit of $75
iPods	125 units at a cost per unit of $80

The cost of purchasing units at year-end was VCRs $71, DVD players $69, and iPods $78.

Instructions

Determine the amount of ending inventory at lower-of-cost-or-market.

Determine effects of inventory errors.

(SO 5)

E6-11 Lebo Hardware reported cost of goods sold as follows.

	2008	2009
Beginning inventory	$ 20,000	$ 30,000
Cost of goods purchased	150,000	175,000
Cost of goods available for sale	170,000	205,000
Ending inventory	30,000	35,000
Cost of goods sold	$140,000	$170,000

Lebo made two errors: (1) 2008 ending inventory was overstated $3,000, and (2) 2009 ending inventory was understated $6,000.

Instructions

Compute the correct cost of goods sold for each year.

Prepare correct income statements.

(SO 5)

E6-12 Staley Watch Company reported the following income statement data for a 2-year period.

	2008	2009
Sales	$210,000	$250,000
Cost of goods sold		
Beginning inventory	32,000	44,000
Cost of goods purchased	173,000	202,000
Cost of goods available for sale	205,000	246,000
Ending inventory	44,000	52,000
Cost of goods sold	161,000	194,000
Gross profit	$ 49,000	$ 56,000

Staley uses a periodic inventory system. The inventories at January 1, 2008, and December 31, 2009, are correct. However, the ending inventory at December 31, 2008, was overstated $5,000.

Instructions

(a) Prepare correct income statement data for the 2 years.

(b) What is the cumulative effect of the inventory error on total gross profit for the 2 years?

(c) ━━━━ Explain in a letter to the president of Staley Company what has happened—i.e., the nature of the error and its effect on the financial statements.

Compute inventory turnover, days in inventory, and gross profit rate.

(SO 6)

E6-13 This information is available for Santo's Photo Corporation for 2007, 2008, and 2009.

	2007	2008	2009
Beginning inventory	$ 100,000	$ 300,000	$ 400,000
Ending inventory	300,000	400,000	480,000
Cost of goods sold	900,000	1,120,000	1,300,000
Sales	1,200,000	1,600,000	1,900,000

Instructions

Calculate inventory turnover, days in inventory, and gross profit rate (from Chapter 5) for Santo's Photo Corporation for 2007, 2008, 2009. Comment on any trends.

Compute inventory turnover and days in inventory.

(SO 6)

E6-14 The cost of goods sold computations for O'Brien Company and Weinberg Company are shown below.

	O'Brien Company	Weinberg Company
Beginning inventory	$ 45,000	$ 71,000
Cost of goods purchased	200,000	290,000
Cost of goods available for sale	245,000	361,000
Ending inventory	55,000	69,000
Cost of goods sold	$190,000	$292,000

Instructions

(a) Compute inventory turnover and days in inventory for each company.

(b) Which company moves its inventory more quickly?

*E6-15   Klugman Appliance uses a perpetual inventory system. For its flat-screen television sets, the January 1 inventory was 3 sets at $600 each. On January 10, Klugman purchased 6 units at $660 each. The company sold 2 units on January 8 and 4 units on January 15.

Apply cost flow methods to perpetual records.

(SO 7)

Instructions

Compute the ending inventory under (1) FIFO, (2) LIFO, and (3) average-cost.

*E6-16   Yount Company reports the following for the month of June.

Calculate inventory and cost of goods sold using three cost flow methods in a perpetual inventory system.

(SO 7)

Date	Explanation	Units	Unit Cost	Total Cost
June 1	Inventory	200	$5	$1,000
12	Purchase	300	6	1,800
23	Purchase	500	7	3,500
30	Inventory	120		

Instructions

(a) Calculate the cost of the ending inventory and the cost of goods sold for each cost flow assumption, using a perpetual inventory system. Assume a sale of 400 units occurred on June 15 for a selling price of $8 and a sale of 480 units on June 27 for $9.

(b) How do the results differ from E6-6 and E6-8?

(c) Why is the average unit cost not $6 [($5 + $6 + $7) ÷ 3 = $6]?

*E6-17   Information about Boarders is presented in E6-4. Additional data regarding Boarders' sales of Xpert snowboards are provided below. Assume that Boarders uses a perpetual inventory system.

Apply cost flow methods to perpetual records.

(SO 7)

Date		Units	Unit Price	Total Cost
Sept. 5	Sale	12	$199	$ 2,388
Sept. 16	Sale	50	199	9,950
Sept. 29	Sale	59	209	12,331
	Totals	121		$24,669

Instructions

(a) Compute ending inventory at September 30 using FIFO, LIFO, and average cost.

(b) Compare ending inventory using a perpetual inventory system to ending inventory using a periodic inventory system (from E6-4).

(c) Which inventory cost flow method (FIFO, LIFO) gives the same ending inventory value under both periodic and perpetual? Which method gives different ending inventory values?

*E6-18   Doc Gibbs Company reported the following information for November and December 2008.

Use the gross profit method to estimate inventory.

(SO 8)

	November	December
Cost of goods purchased	$500,000	$ 610,000
Inventory, beginning-of-month	100,000	120,000
Inventory, end-of-month	120,000	????
Sales	800,000	1,000,000

Doc Gibbs's ending inventory at December 31 was destroyed in a fire.

Instructions

(a) Compute the gross profit rate for November.

(b) Using the gross profit rate for November, determine the estimated cost of inventory lost in the fire.

*E6-19   The inventory of Faber Company was destroyed by fire on March 1. From an examination of the accounting records, the following data for the first 2 months of the year are obtained: Sales $51,000, Sales Returns and Allowances $1,000, Purchases $31,200, Freight-in $1,200, and Purchase Returns and Allowances $1,400.

Determine merchandise lost using the gross profit method of estimating inventory.

(SO 8)

Instructions

Determine the merchandise lost by fire, assuming:

(a) A beginning inventory of $20,000 and a gross profit rate of 40% on net sales.

(b) A beginning inventory of $30,000 and a gross profit rate of 30% on net sales.

Determine ending inventory at cost using retail method.

(SO 8)

*E6-20 Quayle Shoe Store uses the retail inventory method for its two departments, Women's Shoes and Men's Shoes. The following information for each department is obtained.

Item	Women's Department	Men's Department
Beginning inventory at cost	$ 32,000	$ 45,000
Cost of goods purchased at cost	148,000	136,300
Net sales	178,000	185,000
Beginning inventory at retail	46,000	60,000
Cost of goods purchased at retail	179,000	185,000

Instructions

Compute the estimated cost of the ending inventory for each department under the retail inventory method.

EXERCISES: SET B

Visit the book's website at **www.wiley.com/college/weygandt**, and choose the Student Companion site, to access Exercise Set B.

PROBLEMS: SET A

Determine items and amounts to be recorded in inventory.

(SO 1)

P6-1A Heath Limited is trying to determine the value of its ending inventory at February 28, 2008, the company's year end. The accountant counted everything that was in the warehouse as of February 28, which resulted in an ending inventory valuation of $48,000. However, she didn't know how to treat the following transactions so she didn't record them.

(a) On February 26, Heath shipped to a customer goods costing $800. The goods were shipped FOB shipping point, and the receiving report indicates that the customer received the goods on March 2.

(b) On February 26, Seller Inc. shipped goods to Heath FOB destination. The invoice price was $350. The receiving report indicates that the goods were received by Heath on March 2.

(c) Heath had $500 of inventory at a customer's warehouse "on approval." The customer was going to let Heath know whether it wanted the merchandise by the end of the week, March 4.

(d) Heath also had $400 of inventory on consignment at a Jasper craft shop.

(e) On February 26, Heath ordered goods costing $750. The goods were shipped FOB shipping point on February 27. Heath received the goods on March 1.

(f) On February 28, Heath packaged goods and had them ready for shipping to a customer FOB destination. The invoice price was $350; the cost of the items was $250. The receiving report indicates that the goods were received by the customer on March 2.

(g) Heath had damaged goods set aside in the warehouse because they are no longer saleable. These goods originally cost $400 and, originally, Heath expected to sell these items for $600.

Instructions

For each of the above transactions, specify whether the item in question should be included in ending inventory, and if so, at what amount. For each item that is not included in ending inventory, indicate who owns it and what account, if any, it should have been recorded in.

Determine cost of goods sold and ending inventory using FIFO, LIFO, and average-cost with analysis.

(SO 2, 3)

P6-2A Glanville Distribution markets CDs of the performing artist Harrilyn Clooney. At the beginning of March, Glanville had in beginning inventory 1,500 Clooney CDs with a unit cost of $7. During March Glanville made the following purchases of Clooney CDs.

March 5	3,000 @ $8	March 21	4,000 @ $10
March 13	5,500 @ $9	March 26	2,000 @ $11

During March 12,500 units were sold. Glanville uses a periodic inventory system.

Instructions

(a) Determine the cost of goods available for sale.

(b) Determine (1) the ending inventory and (2) the cost of goods sold under each of the assumed cost flow methods (FIFO, LIFO, and average-cost). Prove the accuracy of the cost of goods sold under the FIFO and LIFO methods.

(c) Which cost flow method results in (1) the highest inventory amount for the balance sheet and (2) the highest cost of goods sold for the income statement?

(b)(2) Cost of goods sold:
FIFO $109,000
LIFO $119,500
Average $114,062

P6-3A   Eddings Company had a beginning inventory of 400 units of Product XNA at a cost of $8.00 per unit. During the year, purchases were:

Determine cost of goods sold and ending inventory using FIFO, LIFO, and average-cost with analysis.

(SO 2, 3)

| Feb. 20 | 600 units at $9 | Aug. 12 | 300 units at $11 |
| May 5 | 500 units at $10 | Dec. 8 | 200 units at $12 |

Eddings Company uses a periodic inventory system. Sales totaled 1,500 units.

Instructions

(a) Determine the cost of goods available for sale.

(b) Determine (1) the ending inventory, and (2) the cost of goods sold under each of the assumed cost flow methods (FIFO, LIFO, and average). Prove the accuracy of the cost of goods sold under the FIFO and LIFO methods.

(c) Which cost flow method results in (1) the lowest inventory amount for the balance sheet, and (2) the lowest cost of goods sold for the income statement?

(b) Cost of goods sold:
FIFO $13,600
LIFO $15,200
Average $14,475

P6-4A   The management of Morales Co. is reevaluating the appropriateness of using its present inventory cost flow method, which is average-cost. They request your help in determining the results of operations for 2008 if either the FIFO method or the LIFO method had been used. For 2008, the accounting records show the following data.

Compute ending inventory, prepare income statements, and answer questions using FIFO and LIFO.

(SO 2, 3)

Inventories		Purchases and Sales	
Beginning (15,000 units)	$32,000	Total net sales (215,000 units)	$865,000
Ending (30,000 units)		Total cost of goods purchased	
		(230,000 units)	595,000

Purchases were made quarterly as follows.

Quarter	Units	Unit Cost	Total Cost
1	60,000	$2.40	$144,000
2	50,000	2.50	125,000
3	50,000	2.60	130,000
4	70,000	2.80	196,000
	230,000		$595,000

Operating expenses were $147,000, and the company's income tax rate is 34%.

Instructions

(a) Prepare comparative condensed income statements for 2008 under FIFO and LIFO. (Show computations of ending inventory.)

(b) ➡ Answer the following questions for management.

(1) Which cost flow method (FIFO or LIFO) produces the more meaningful inventory amount for the balance sheet? Why?

(2) Which cost flow method (FIFO or LIFO) produces the more meaningful net income? Why?

(3) Which cost flow method (FIFO or LIFO) is more likely to approximate actual physical flow of the goods? Why?

(4) How much additional cash will be available for management under LIFO than under FIFO? Why?

(5) Will gross profit under the average-cost method be higher or lower than (a) FIFO and (b) LIFO? (*Note*: It is not necessary to quantify your answer.)

(a) Net income
FIFO $115,500
LIFO $104,940
(b)(4) $5,440

Calculate ending inventory, cost of goods sold, gross profit, and gross profit rate under periodic method; compare results.

(SO 2, 3)

P6-5A You are provided with the following information for Pavey Inc. for the month ended October 31, 2008. Pavey uses a periodic method for inventory.

Date	Description	Units	Unit Cost or Selling Price
October 1	Beginning inventory	60	$25
October 9	Purchase	120	26
October 11	Sale	100	35
October 17	Purchase	70	27
October 22	Sale	60	40
October 25	Purchase	80	28
October 29	Sale	110	40

Instructions

(a)(iii) Gross profit:
LIFO $3,050
FIFO $3,230
Average $3,141

(a) Calculate (i) ending inventory, (ii) cost of goods sold, (iii) gross profit, and (iv) gross profit rate under each of the following methods.
  (1) LIFO.
  (2) FIFO.
  (3) Average-cost.
(b) Compare results for the three cost flow assumptions.

Compare specific identification, FIFO and LIFO under periodic method; use cost flow assumption to influence earnings.

(SO 2, 3)

P6-6A You have the following information for Bernelli Diamonds. Bernelli Diamonds uses the periodic method of accounting for its inventory transactions. Bernelli only carries one brand and size of diamonds—all are identical. Each batch of diamonds purchased is carefully coded and marked with its purchase cost.

March 1 Beginning inventory 150 diamonds at a cost of $300 per diamond.
March 3 Purchased 200 diamonds at a cost of $350 each.
March 5 Sold 180 diamonds for $600 each.
March 10 Purchased 350 diamonds at a cost of $375 each.
March 25 Sold 400 diamonds for $650 each.

Instructions

(a) Gross profit:
(1) Maximum $166,750

(2) Minimum $157,750

(a) Assume that Bernelli Diamonds uses the specific identification cost flow method.
  (1) Demonstrate how Bernelli Diamonds could maximize its gross profit for the month by specifically selecting which diamonds to sell on March 5 and March 25.
  (2) Demonstrate how Bernelli Diamonds could minimize its gross profit for the month by selecting which diamonds to sell on March 5 and March 25.
(b) Assume that Bernelli Diamonds uses the FIFO cost flow assumption. Calculate cost of goods sold. How much gross profit would Bernelli Diamonds report under this cost flow assumption?
(c) Assume that Bernelli Diamonds uses the LIFO cost flow assumption. Calculate cost of goods sold. How much gross profit would the company report under this cost flow assumption?
(d) Which cost flow method should Bernelli Diamonds select? Explain.

Compute ending inventory, prepare income statements, and answer questions using FIFO and LIFO.

(SO 2, 3)

P6-7A The management of Utley Inc. asks your help in determining the comparative effects of the FIFO and LIFO inventory cost flow methods. For 2008 the accounting records show these data.

Inventory, January 1 (10,000 units)	$ 35,000
Cost of 120,000 units purchased	504,500
Selling price of 100,000 units sold	665,000
Operating expenses	130,000

Units purchased consisted of 35,000 units at $4.00 on May 10; 60,000 units at $4.20 on August 15; and 25,000 units at $4.50 on November 20. Income taxes are 28%.

Instructions

Gross profit:
FIFO $259,000
LIFO $240,500

(a) Prepare comparative condensed income statements for 2008 under FIFO and LIFO. (Show computations of ending inventory.)
(b) ▬▬▬ Answer the following questions for management in the form of a business letter.
  (1) Which inventory cost flow method produces the most meaningful inventory amount for the balance sheet? Why?

(2) Which inventory cost flow method produces the most meaningful net income? Why?

(3) Which inventory cost flow method is most likely to approximate the actual physical flow of the goods? Why?

(4) How much more cash will be available for management under LIFO than under FIFO? Why?

(5) How much of the gross profit under FIFO is illusionary in comparison with the gross profit under LIFO?

*P6-8A   Vasquez Ltd. is a retailer operating in Edmonton, Alberta. Vasquez uses the perpetual inventory method. All sales returns from customers result in the goods being returned to inventory; the inventory is not damaged. Assume that there are no credit transactions; all amounts are settled in cash. You are provided with the following information for Vasquez Ltd. for the month of January 2008.

Calculate cost of goods sold and ending inventory for FIFO, average-cost, and LIFO under the perpetual system; compare gross profit under each assumption.

(SO 7)

Date	Description	Quantity	Unit Cost or Selling Price
December 31	Ending inventory	150	$17
January 2	Purchase	100	21
January 6	Sale	150	40
January 9	Sale return	10	40
January 9	Purchase	75	24
January 10	Purchase return	15	24
January 10	Sale	50	45
January 23	Purchase	100	28
January 30	Sale	110	50

Instructions

(a) For each of the following cost flow assumptions, calculate (i) cost of goods sold, (ii) ending inventory, and (iii) gross profit.

(1) LIFO.   **(2)** FIFO.   **(3)** Moving-average-cost.

(b) Compare results for the three cost flow assumptions.

Gross profit:
LIFO $6,330
FIFO $7,500
Average $7,090

*P6-9A   Sandoval Appliance Mart began operations on May 1. It uses a perpetual inventory system. During May the company had the following purchases and sales for its Model 25 Sureshot camera.

Determine ending inventory under a perpetual inventory system.

(SO 7)

Date	Purchases Units	Purchases Unit Cost	Sales Units
May 1	7	$150	
4			4
8	8	$170	
12			5
15	6	$185	
20			3
25			4

Instructions

(a) Determine the ending inventory under a perpetual inventory system using (1) FIFO, (2) average-cost, and (3) LIFO.

(b) Which costing method produces (1) the highest ending inventory valuation and (2) the lowest ending inventory valuation?

(a) FIFO $925
Average $874
LIFO $790

*P6-10A   Saffordville Company lost 70% of its inventory in a fire on March 25, 2008. The accounting records showed the following gross profit data for February and March.

Estimate inventory loss using gross profit method.

(SO 8)

	February	March (to 3/25)
Net sales	$300,000	$250,000
Net purchases	197,800	191,000
Freight-in	2,900	4,000
Beginning inventory	4,500	13,200
Ending inventory	13,200	?

Saffordville Company is fully insured for fire losses but must prepare a report for the insurance company.

Instructions

(a) Compute the gross profit rate for the month of February.

(b) Using the gross profit rate for February, determine both the estimated total inventory and inventory lost in the fire in March.

Compute ending inventory using retail method.

(SO 8)

*P6-11A Neer Department Store uses the retail inventory method to estimate its monthly ending inventories. The following information is available for two of its departments at August 31, 2008.

	Sporting Goods		Jewelry and Cosmetics	
	Cost	Retail	Cost	Retail
Net sales		$1,000,000		$1,160,000
Purchases	$675,000	1,066,000	$741,000	1,158,000
Purchase returns	(26,000)	(40,000)	(12,000)	(20,000)
Purchase discounts	(12,360)	—	(2,440)	—
Freight-in	9,000	—	14,000	—
Beginning inventory	47,360	74,000	39,440	62,000

At December 31, Neer Department Store takes a physical inventory at retail. The actual retail values of the inventories in each department are Sporting Goods $95,000, and Jewelry and Cosmetics $44,000.

Instructions

(a) Determine the estimated cost of the ending inventory for each department on **August 31**, 2008, using the retail inventory method.

(b) Compute the ending inventory at cost for each department at **December 31**, assuming the cost-to-retail ratios are 60% for Sporting Goods and 64% for Jewelry and Cosmetics.

PROBLEMS: SET B

Determine items and amounts to be recorded in inventory.

(SO 1)

Peachtree

P6-1B Slaymakker Country Limited is trying to determine the value of its ending inventory as of February 28, 2008, the company's year-end. The following transactions occurred, and the accountant asked your help in determining whether they should be recorded or not.

(a) On February 26, Slaymakker shipped goods costing $800 to a customer and charged the customer $1,000. The goods were shipped with terms FOB destination and the receiving report indicates that the customer received the goods on March 2.

(b) On February 26, Seller Inc. shipped goods to Slaymakker under terms FOB shipping point. The invoice price was $350 plus $25 for freight. The receiving report indicates that the goods were received by Slaymakker on March 2.

(c) Slaymakker had $500 of inventory isolated in the warehouse. The inventory is designated for a customer who has requested that the goods be shipped on March 10.

(d) Also included in Slaymakker's warehouse is $400 of inventory that Craft Producers shipped to Slaymakker on consignment.

(e) On February 26, Slaymakker issued a purchase order to acquire goods costing $750. The goods were shipped with terms FOB destination on February 27. Slaymakker received the goods on March 2.

(f) On February 26, Slaymakker shipped goods to a customer under terms FOB shipping point. The invoice price was $350 plus $25 for freight; the cost of the items was $300. The receiving report indicates that the goods were received by the customer on March 2.

Instructions

For each of the above transactions, specify whether the item in question should be included in ending inventory, and if so, at what amount.

Determine cost of goods sold and ending inventory using FIFO, LIFO, and average-cost with analysis.

(SO 2, 3)

P6-2B Carrington Distribution markets CDs of the performing artist Christina Spears. At the beginning of October, Carrington had in beginning inventory 1,000 Spears CDs with a unit cost of $5. During October Carrington made the following purchases of Spears CDs.

| Oct. 3 | 3,500 @ $6 | Oct. 19 | 2,000 @ $8 |
| Oct. 9 | 4,000 @ $7 | Oct. 25 | 2,000 @ $9 |

During October 9,500 units were sold. Carrington uses a periodic inventory system.

Instructions
(a) Determine the cost of goods available for sale.
(b) Determine (1) the ending inventory and (2) the cost of goods sold under each of the assumed cost flow methods (FIFO, LIFO, and average-cost). Prove the accuracy of the cost of goods sold under the FIFO and LIFO methods.
(c) Which cost flow method results in (1) the highest inventory amount for the balance sheet and (2) the highest cost of goods sold for the income statement?

(b)(2) Cost of goods sold:
  FIFO $62,000
  LIFO $71,000
  Average $66,880

P6-3B Shellankamp Company had a beginning inventory on January 1 of 100 units of Product WD-44 at a cost of $21 per unit. During the year, the following purchases were made.

| Mar. 15 | 300 units at $24 | Sept. 4 | 300 units at $28 |
| July 20 | 200 units at $25 | Dec. 2 | 100 units at $30 |

800 units were sold. Shellankamp Company uses a periodic inventory system.

Determine cost of goods sold and ending inventory, using FIFO, LIFO, and average-cost with analysis.

(SO 2, 3)

Instructions
(a) Determine the cost of goods available for sale.
(b) Determine (1) the ending inventory, and (2) the cost of goods sold under each of the assumed cost flow methods (FIFO, LIFO, and average-cost). Prove the accuracy of the cost of goods sold under the FIFO and LIFO methods.
(c) Which cost flow method results in (1) the highest inventory amount for the balance sheet, and (2) the highest cost of goods sold for the income statement?

(b)(2) Cost of goods sold:
  FIFO $19,900
  LIFO $21,200
  Average $20,560

P6-4B The management of Groneman Inc. is reevaluating the appropriateness of using its present inventory cost flow method, which is average-cost. The company requests your help in determining the results of operations for 2008 if either the FIFO or the LIFO method had been used. For 2008 the accounting records show these data:

Compute ending inventory, prepare income statements, and answer questions using FIFO and LIFO.

(SO 2, 3)

Inventories		Purchases and Sales	
Beginning (10,000 units)	$22,800	Total net sales (220,000 units)	$865,000
Ending (20,000 units)		Total cost of goods purchased	
		(230,000 units)	578,500

Purchases were made quarterly as follows.

Quarter	Units	Unit Cost	Total Cost
1	60,000	$2.30	$138,000
2	50,000	2.50	125,000
3	50,000	2.60	130,000
4	70,000	2.65	185,500
	230,000		$578,500

Operating expenses were $147,000, and the company's income tax rate is 32%.

Instructions
(a) Prepare comparative condensed income statements for 2008 under FIFO and LIFO. (Show computations of ending inventory.)
(b) ▬▬▬▬▶ Answer the following questions for management.
  (1) Which cost flow method (FIFO or LIFO) produces the more meaningful inventory amount for the balance sheet? Why?
  (2) Which cost flow method (FIFO or LIFO) produces the more meaningful net income? Why?
  (3) Which cost flow method (FIFO or LIFO) is more likely to approximate the actual physical flow of goods? Why?
  (4) How much more cash will be available for management under LIFO than under FIFO? Why?
  (5) Will gross profit under the average-cost method be higher or lower than FIFO? Than LIFO? (*Note*: It is not necessary to quantify your answer.)

(a) Gross profit:
  FIFO $316,700
  LIFO $309,500

Calculate ending inventory, cost of goods sold, gross profit, and gross profit rate under periodic method; compare results.

(SO 2, 3)

P6-5B You are provided with the following information for Charlote Inc. for the month ended June 30, 2008. Charlote uses the periodic method for inventory.

Date	Description	Quantity	Unit Cost or Selling Price
June 1	Beginning inventory	25	$60
June 4	Purchase	85	64
June 10	Sale	70	90
June 11	Sale return	10	90
June 18	Purchase	35	68
June 18	Purchase return	5	68
June 25	Sale	40	95
June 28	Purchase	20	72

Instructions

(a)(iii) Gross profit:
LIFO $2,520
FIFO $2,900
Average $2,687.50

(a) Calculate (i) ending inventory, (ii) cost of goods sold, (iii) gross profit, and (iv) gross profit rate under each of the following methods.

   (1) LIFO.   **(2)** FIFO.   **(3)** Average-cost.

(b) Compare results for the three cost flow assumptions.

Compare specific identification, FIFO, and LIFO under periodic method; use cost flow assumption to justify price increase.

(SO 2, 3)

P6-6B You are provided with the following information for Rondelli Inc. Rondelli Inc. uses the periodic method of accounting for its inventory transactions.

March 1   Beginning inventory 1,500 litres at a cost of 40¢ per litre.
March 3   Purchased 2,000 litres at a cost of 45¢ per litre.
March 5   Sold 1,800 litres for 60¢ per litre.
March 10   Purchased 3,500 litres at a cost of 49¢ per litre.
March 20   Purchased 2,000 litres at a cost of 55¢ per litre.
March 30   Sold 4,500 litres for 70¢ per litre.

Instructions

(a) Prepare partial income statements through gross profit, and calculate the value of ending inventory that would be reported on the balance sheet, under each of the following cost flow assumptions.

(a)(1) Gross profit:
Specific identification
$1,256

   (1) Specific identification method assuming:

     (i) the March 5 sale consisted of 900 litres from the March 1 beginning inventory and 900 litres from the March 3 purchase; and

     (ii) the March 30 sale consisted of the following number of units sold from beginning inventory and each purchase: 400 litres from March 1; 500 litres from March 3; 2,600 litres from March 10; 1,000 litres from March 20.

(2) FIFO $1,358
(3) LIFO $1,055

   (2) FIFO.
   (3) LIFO.

(b) How can companies use a cost flow method to justify price increases? Which cost flow method would best support an argument to increase prices?

Compute ending inventory, prepare income statements, and answer questions using FIFO and LIFO.

(SO 2, 3)

P6-7B The management of Dains Co. asks your help in determining the comparative effects of the FIFO and LIFO inventory cost flow methods. For 2008, the accounting records show the following data.

Inventory, January 1 (10,000 units)	$ 37,000
Cost of 110,000 units purchased	479,000
Selling price of 90,000 units sold	630,000
Operating expenses	120,000

Units purchased consisted of 40,000 units at $4.20 on May 10; 50,000 units at $4.40 on August 15; and 20,000 units at $4.55 on November 20. Income taxes are 30%.

Instructions

(a) Net income
FIFO $90,300
LIFO $80,500

(a) Prepare comparative condensed income statements for 2008 under FIFO and LIFO. (Show computations of ending inventory.)

(b) ━━━▶ Answer the following questions for management.

   (1) Which inventory cost flow method produces the most meaningful inventory amount for the balance sheet? Why?

(2) Which inventory cost flow method produces the most meaningful net income? Why?

(3) Which inventory cost flow method is most likely to approximate actual physical flow of the goods? Why?

(4) How much additional cash will be available for management under LIFO than under FIFO? Why?

(5) How much of the gross profit under FIFO is illusory in comparison with the gross profit under LIFO?

*P6-8B   Fechter Inc. is a retailer operating in Dartmouth, Nova Scotia. Fechter uses the perpetual inventory method. All sales returns from customers result in the goods being returned to inventory; the inventory is not damaged. Assume that there are no credit transactions; all amounts are settled in cash. You are provided with the following information for Fechter Inc. for the month of January 2008.

Calculate cost of goods sold and ending inventory under LIFO, FIFO, and average-cost under the perpetual system; compare gross profit under each assumption.

(SO 7)

Date	Description	Quantity	Unit Cost or Selling Price
January 1	Beginning inventory	50	$12
January 5	Purchase	100	14
January 8	Sale	80	25
January 10	Sale return	10	25
January 15	Purchase	30	18
January 16	Purchase return	5	18
January 20	Sale	75	25
January 25	Purchase	10	20

Instructions

(a) For each of the following cost flow assumptions, calculate (i) cost of goods sold, (ii) ending inventory, and (iii) gross profit.

(1) LIFO.   **(2)** FIFO.   **(3)** Moving-average-cost.

(b) Compare results for the three cost flow assumptions.

Gross profit:
LIFO $1,535
FIFO $1,695
Average $1,608

*P6-9B   Falco Co. began operations on July 1. It uses a perpetual inventory system. During July the company had the following purchases and sales.

Determine ending inventory under a perpetual inventory system.

(SO 7)

Date	Units	Unit Cost	Sales Units
	Purchases		
July 1	4	$ 90	
July 6			3
July 11	5	$ 99	
July 14			2
July 21	6	$106	
July 27			5

Instructions

(a) Determine the ending inventory under a perpetual inventory system using (1) FIFO, (2) average-cost, and (3) LIFO.

(b) Which costing method produces the highest ending inventory valuation?

(a) Ending inventory
FIFO $530
Avg. $513
LIFO $493

*P6-10B   Hannigan Company lost all of its inventory in a fire on December 26, 2008. The accounting records showed the following gross profit data for November and December.

Compute gross profit rate and inventory loss using gross profit method.

(SO 8)

	November	December (to 12/26)
Net sales	$500,000	$400,000
Beginning inventory	34,100	31,100
Purchases	334,975	246,000
Purchase returns and allowances	11,800	5,000
Purchase discounts	7,577	6,000
Freight-in	6,402	3,700
Ending inventory	31,100	?

Hannigan is fully insured for fire losses but must prepare a report for the insurance company.

Instructions

(a) Compute the gross profit rate for November.

(b) Using the gross profit rate for November, determine the estimated cost of the inventory lost in the fire.

Compute ending inventory using retail method.

(SO 8)

*P6-11B Frontenac Books uses the retail inventory method to estimate its monthly ending inventories. The following information is available for two of its departments at October 31, 2008.

	Hardcovers		**Paperbacks**	
	Cost	**Retail**	**Cost**	**Retail**
Beginning inventory	$ 256,000	$ 400,000	$ 65,000	$ 90,000
Purchases	1,180,000	1,825,000	266,000	380,000
Freight-in	4,000		2,000	
Purchase discounts	16,000		4,000	
Net sales		1,827,000		385,000

At December 31, Frontenac Books takes a physical inventory at retail. The actual retail values of the inventories in each department are Hardcovers $395,000 and Paperbacks $88,000.

Instructions

(a) Determine the estimated cost of the ending inventory for each department at **October 31, 2008**, using the retail inventory method.

(b) Compute the ending inventory at cost for each department at **December 31**, assuming the cost-to-retail ratios for the year are 65% for hardcovers and 70% for paperbacks.

PROBLEMS: SET C

Visit the book's website at **www.wiley.com/college/weygandt**, and choose the Student Companion site, to access Problem Set C.

CONTINUING COOKIE CHRONICLE

(*Note:* This is a continuation of the Cookie Chronicle from Chapters 1 through 5.)

CCC6 Natalie is busy establishing both divisions of her business (cookie classes and mixer sales) and completing her business degree. Her goals for the next 11 months are to sell one mixer per month and to give two to three classes per week.

The cost of the fine European mixers is expected to increase. Natalie has just negotiated new terms with Kzinski that include shipping costs in the negotiated purchase price (mixers will be shipped FOB destination). Natalie must choose a cost flow assumption for her mixer inventory.

Go to the book's website,
www.wiley.com/college/weygandt,
to see the completion of this problem.

BROADENING YOUR PERSPECTIVE

FINANCIAL REPORTING AND ANALYSIS

Financial Reporting Problem

PepsiCo, Inc.

BYP6-1 The notes that accompany a company's financial statements provide informative details that would clutter the amounts and descriptions presented in the statements. Refer to the financial statements of PepsiCo and the Notes to Consolidated Financial Statements in Appendix A.

Instructions

Answer the following questions. Complete the requirements in millions of dollars, as shown in PepsiCo's annual report.

(a) What did PepsiCo report for the amount of inventories in its consolidated balance sheet at December 31, 2005? At December 25, 2004?

(b) Compute the dollar amount of change and the percentage change in inventories between 2004 and 2005. Compute inventory as a percentage of current assets at December 31, 2005.

(c) How does PepsiCo value its inventories? Which inventory cost flow method does PepsiCo use? (See Notes to the Financial Statements.)

(d) What is the cost of sales (cost of goods sold) reported by PepsiCo for 2005, 2004, and 2003? Compute the percentage of cost of sales to net sales in 2005.

Comparative Analysis Problem

PepsiCo, Inc. vs. The Coca-Cola Company

BYP6-2 PepsiCo's financial statements are presented in Appendix A. Coca-Cola's financial statements are presented in Appendix B.

Instructions

(a) Based on the information contained in these financial statements, compute the following 2005 ratios for each company.
  (1) Inventory turnover ratio
  (2) Days in inventory

(b) What conclusions concerning the management of the inventory can you draw from these data?

Exploring the Web

BYP6-3 A company's annual report usually will identify the inventory method used. Knowing that, you can analyze the effects of the inventory method on the income statement and balance sheet.

Address: www.cisco.com, or go to **www.wiley.com/college/weygandt**

Instructions

Answer the following questions based on the current year's Annual Report on Cisco's Web site.

(a) At Cisco's fiscal year-end, what was the inventory on the balance sheet?
(b) How has this changed from the previous fiscal year-end?
(c) How much of the inventory was finished goods?
(d) What inventory method does Cisco use?

CRITICAL THINKING

Decision Making Across the Organization

BYP6-4 On April 10, 2008, fire damaged the office and warehouse of Inwood Company. Most of the accounting records were destroyed, but the following account balances were determined as of March 31, 2008: Merchandise Inventory, January 1, 2008, $80,000; Sales (January 1–March 31, 2008), $180,000; Purchases (January 1–March 31, 2008) $94,000.

The company's fiscal year ends on December 31. It uses a periodic inventory system.

From an analysis of the April bank statement, you discover cancelled checks of $4,200 for cash purchases during the period April 1–10. Deposits during the same period totaled $18,500. Of that amount, 60% were collections on accounts receivable, and the balance was cash sales.

Correspondence with the company's principal suppliers revealed $12,400 of purchases on account from April 1 to April 10. Of that amount, $1,600 was for merchandise in transit on April 10 that was shipped FOB destination.

Correspondence with the company's principal customers produced acknowledgments of credit sales totaling $37,000 from April 1 to April 10. It was estimated that $5,600 of credit sales will never be acknowledged or recovered from customers.

Inwood Company reached an agreement with the insurance company that its fire-loss claim should be based on the average of the gross profit rates for the preceding 2 years. The financial statements for 2006 and 2007 showed the following data.

	2007	2006
Net sales	$600,000	$480,000
Cost of goods purchased	404,000	356,000
Beginning inventory	60,000	40,000
Ending inventory	80,000	60,000

Inventory with a cost of $17,000 was salvaged from the fire.

Instructions
With the class divided into groups, answer the following.

(a) Determine the balances in (1) Sales and (2) Purchases at April 10.
*(**b**) Determine the average profit rate for the years 2006 and 2007. (*Hint*: Find the gross profit rate for each year and divide the sum by 2.)
*(**c**) Determine the inventory loss as a result of the fire, using the gross profit method.

Communication Activity

BYP6-5   You are the controller of Small Toys Inc. Janice LeMay, the president, recently mentioned to you that she found an error in the 2007 financial statements which she believes has corrected itself. She determined, in discussions with the Purchasing Department, that 2007 ending inventory was overstated by $1 million. Janice says that the 2008 ending inventory is correct. Thus she assumes that 2008 income is correct. Janice says to you, "What happened has happened—there's no point in worrying about it anymore."

Instructions
You conclude that Janice is incorrect. Write a brief, tactful memo to Janice, clarifying the situation.

Ethics Case

BYP6-6   B. J. Ortiz Wholesale Corp. uses the LIFO method of inventory costing. In the current year, profit at B. J. Ortiz is running unusually high. The corporate tax rate is also high this year, but it is scheduled to decline significantly next year. In an effort to lower the current year's net income and to take advantage of the changing income tax rate, the president of B. J. Ortiz Wholesale instructs the plant accountant to recommend to the purchasing department a large purchase of inventory for delivery 3 days before the end of the year. The price of the inventory to be purchased has doubled during the year, and the purchase will represent a major portion of the ending inventory value.

Instructions
(a) What is the effect of this transaction on this year's and next year's income statement and income tax expense? Why?
(b) If B. J. Ortiz Wholesale had been using the FIFO method of inventory costing, would the president give the same directive?
(c) Should the plant accountant order the inventory purchase to lower income? What are the ethical implications of this order?

 # "All About You" Activity

BYP6-7   Some of the largest business frauds ever perpetrated have involved the misstatement of inventory. Two classics were at Leslie Fay Cos, and McKesson Corporation.

Instructions
There is considerable information regarding inventory frauds available on the Internet. Search for information about one of the two cases mentioned above, or inventory fraud at any other company, and prepare a short explanation of the nature of the inventory fraud.

Chapter 12

Accounting for Partnerships

Feature Story

FROM TRIALS TO THE TOP TEN

In 1990 Cliff Chenfield and Craig Balsam gave up the razors, ties, and six-figure salaries they had become accustomed to as New York lawyers. Instead, they set up a partnership, Razor & Tie Music (*www.razorandtie.com*), in Cliff's living room. Ten years later, it became the only record company in the country that had achieved success in selling music both on television and in stores. Razor & Tie's entertaining and effective TV commercials have yielded unprecedented sales for multi-artist music compilations. At the same time, its hot retail label has been behind some of the most recent original, progressive releases.

Razor & Tie may be best known for its wildly popular *Kidz Bop* CD series, the top-selling children's audio product in the United States. Advertised on Nickelodeon, the Cartoon Network, and elsewhere, *Kidz Bop* titles have sold over 7 million copies. Seven of the 11 releases in the series have "gone Gold."

Razor & Tie got its start with its first TV release, *Those Fabulous '70s* (100,000 copies sold), followed by *Disco Fever* (over 300,000 sold). These albums generated so much publicity that partners Cliff and Craig were guests on dozens of TV interview shows.

After restoring the respectability of the oft-maligned music of the 1970s, the partners forged into the musical '80s with the same zeal that elicited success with their first releases. In 1993, Razor & Tie released *Totally '80s*, a collection of Top-10 singles from the 1980s that has sold over 450,000 units. Featuring the tag line, "The greatest hits from the decade when communism died and music videos were born," *Totally '80s* was the best-selling direct-response album in the country in 1993.

In 1995, Razor & Tie broke into the contemporary music world with *Living in the '90s*, the most successful record in the history of the company. Featuring a number of songs that were still hits on the radio at the time the package initially aired, *Living in the '90s* was a blockbuster. It received Gold certification in less than nine months and rewrote the rules on direct-response albums. For the first time, contemporary music was available through an album offered only through direct-response spots. Razor & Tie pursued that same strategy with its 2002 introduction of the *Kidz Bop* titles.

How has Razor & Tie carved out its sizable piece of the market? Through the complementary talents of the two partners. Their imagination and savvy, along with exciting new releases planned for the coming years, ensure Razor & Tie continued growth.

✓ The Navigator

Inside Chapter 12...

- **Limited Liability Companies Gain in Popularity** (p. 516)

- **How to Part Ways Nicely** (p. 518)

- **Start-Up Seeks to Share R&D Costs, and Profits** (p. 523)

- ***All About You:* How Well Do You Know Your Partner?** (p. 530)

It is not surprising that when Cliff Chenfield and Craig Balsam began Razor & Tie, they decided to use the partnership form of organization. Both saw the need for hands-on control of their product and its promotion. In this chapter, we will discuss reasons why businesses select the partnership form of organization. We also will explain the major issues in accounting for partnerships.

The content and organization of Chapter 12 are as follows.

Accounting for Partnerships

Partnership Form of Organization	Basic Partnership Accounting	Liquidation of a Partnership
• Characteristics • Organizations with partnership characteristics • Advantages/disadvantages • Partnership agreement	• Forming a partnership • Dividing net income/loss • Financial statements	• No capital deficiency • Capital deficiency

✓ The Navigator

PARTNERSHIP FORM OF ORGANIZATION

A **partnership** is an association of two or more persons to carry on as co-owners of a business for profit. Partnerships are sometimes used in small retail, service, or manufacturing companies. Also accountants, lawyers, and doctors find it desirable to form partnerships with other professionals in the field.

Characteristics of Partnerships

STUDY OBJECTIVE 1

Identify the characteristics of the partnership form of business organization.

Partnerships are fairly easy to form. People form partnerships simply by a verbal agreement, or more formally, by written agreement. We explain the principal characteristics of partnerships in the following sections.

ASSOCIATION OF INDIVIDUALS

A partnership is a legal entity. A partnership can own property (land, buildings, equipment), and can sue or be sued. **A partnership also is an accounting entity.** Thus, the personal assets, liabilities, and transactions of the partners are excluded from the accounting records of the partnership, just as they are in a proprietorship.

The net income of a partnership is not taxed as a separate entity. But, a partnership must file an information tax return showing partnership net income and each partner's share of that net income. Each partner's share is taxable at **personal tax rates**, regardless of the amount of net income each withdraws from the business during the year.

Association of Individuals

MUTUAL AGENCY

Mutual agency means that <u>each</u> partner acts on behalf of the partnership when engaging in partnership business. The act of any partner is binding on all other partners. This is true even when partners act beyond the scope of their authority, so long as the act appears to be appropriate for the partnership. For example, a part-

Mutual Agency

ner of a grocery store who purchases a delivery truck creates a binding contract in the name of the partnership, even if the partnership agreement denies this authority. On the other hand, if a partner in a law firm purchased a snowmobile for the partnership, such an act would not be binding on the partnership. The purchase is clearly outside the scope of partnership business.

LIMITED LIFE

Corporations have unlimited life. Partnerships do not. A partnership may be ended voluntarily at any time through the acceptance of a new partner or the withdrawal of a partner. It may be ended involuntarily by the death or incapacity of a partner. **Partnership dissolution** occurs whenever a partner withdraws or a new partner is admitted. Dissolution does not necessarily mean that the business ends. If the continuing partners agree, operations can continue without interruption by forming a new partnership.

Limited Life

UNLIMITED LIABILITY

Each partner is **personally and individually liable** for all partnership liabilities. Creditors' claims attach first to partnership assets. If these are insufficient, the claims then attach to the personal resources of any partner, irrespective of that partner's equity in the partnership. Because each partner is responsible for all the debts of the partnership, each partner is said to have **unlimited liability**.

CO-OWNERSHIP OF PROPERTY

Partners jointly own partnership assets. If the partnership is dissolved, each partner has a claim on total assets equal to the balance in his or her respective capital account. This claim does not attach to **specific assets** that an individual partner contributed to the firm. Similarly, if a partner invests a building in the partnership valued at $100,000 and the building is later sold at a gain of $20,000, the partners all share in the gain.

Unlimited Liability

Partnership net income (or net loss) is also co-owned. **If the partnership contract does not specify to the contrary, all net income or net loss is shared equally by the partners.** As you will see later, though, partners may agree to unequal sharing of net income or net loss.

Co-ownership of Property

Organizations with Partnership Characteristics

If you are starting a business with a friend and each of you has little capital and your business is not risky, you probably want to use a partnership. As indicated above, the partnership is easy to establish and its cost is minimal. These types of partnerships are often called **regular partnerships**. However if your business is risky—say, roof repair or providing some type of professional service—you will want to limit your liability and not use a regular partnership. As a result, special forms of business organizations with partnership characteristics are now often used to provide protection from unlimited liability for people who wish to work together in some activity.

The special partnership forms are: limited partnerships, limited liability partnerships, and limited liability companies. These special forms use the same accounting procedures as those described for a regular partnership. In addition, for taxation purposes, all the profits and losses pass through these organizations (similar to the regular partnership) to the owners, who report their share of partnership net income or losses on their personal tax returns.

LIMITED PARTNERSHIPS

In a **limited partnership**, one or more partners have **unlimited liability** and one or more partners have **limited liability** for the debts of the firm. Those with unlimited liability are **general partners**. Those with limited liability are **limited partners**. Limited partners are responsible for the debts of the partnership up to the limit of their investment in the firm.

The words "Limited Partnership," or "Ltd.," or "LP" identify this type of organization. For the privilege of limited liability, the limited partner usually accepts less compensation than a general partner and exercises less influence in the affairs of the firm. If the limited partners get involved in management, they risk their liability protection.

LIMITED LIABILITY PARTNERSHIP

Most states allow professionals such as lawyers, doctors, and accountants to form a **limited liability partnership** or "LLP." The LLP is designed to protect innocent partners from malpractice or negligence claims resulting from the acts of another partner. LLPs generally carry large insurance policies as protection against malpractice suits. These professional partnerships vary in size from a medical partnership of three to five doctors, to 150 to 200 partners in a large law firm, to more than 2,000 partners in an international accounting firm.

LIMITED LIABILITY COMPANIES

A hybrid form of business organization with certain features like a corporation and others like a limited partnership is the **limited liability company**, or "LLC." An LLC usually has a limited life. The owners, called **members**, have limited liability like owners of a corporation. Whereas limited partners do not actively participate in the management of a limited partnership (LP), the members of a limited liability company (LLC) can assume an active management role. For income tax purposes, the IRS usually classifies an LLC as a partnership.

ACCOUNTING ACROSS THE ORGANIZATION

Limited Liability Companies Gain in Popularity

The proprietorship form of business organization is still the most popular, followed by the corporate form. But whenever a group of individuals wants to form a partnership, the limited liability company is usually the popular choice.

One other form of business organization is a *subchapter S corporation*. A subchapter S corporation has many of the characteristics of a partnership—especially, taxation as a partnership—but it is losing its popularity. The reason: It involves more paperwork and expense than a limited liability company, which in most cases offers similar advantages.

 Why do you think that the use of the limited liability company is gaining in popularity?

Illustration 12-1 summarizes different forms of organizations that have partnership characteristics.

Advantages and Disadvantages of Partnerships

Why do people choose partnerships? One major advantage of a partnership is to combine the skills and resources of two or more individuals. In addition, partnerships are easily formed and are relatively free from government regulations and restrictions. A partnership does not have to contend with the "red tape" that a

	Major Advantages	Major Disadvantages
Regular Partnership General Partners	Simple and inexpensive to create and operate.	Owners (partners) personally liable for business debts.
Limited Partnership General Limited Partners Partners	Limited partners have limited personal liability for business debts as long as they do not participate in management. General partners can raise cash without involving outside investors in management of business.	General partners personally liable for business debts. More expensive to create than regular partnership. Suitable mainly for companies that invest in real estate.
Limited Liability Partnership	Mostly of interest to partners in old-line professions such as law, medicine, and accounting. Owners (partners) are not personally liable for the malpractice of other partners.	Unlike a limited liability company, owners (partners) remain personally liable for many types of obligations owed to business creditors, lenders, and landlords. Often limited to a short list of professions.
Limited Liability Company	Owners have limited personal liability for business debts even if they participate in management.	More expensive to create than regular partnership.

Source: *www.nolo.com* (accessed June 2006).

Illustration 12-1
Different forms of organizations with partnership characteristics

corporation must face. Also, partners generally can make decisions quickly on substantive business matters without having to consult a board of directors.

On the other hand, partnerships also have some major disadvantages. **Unlimited liability** is particularly troublesome. Many individuals fear they may lose not only their initial investment but also their personal assets, if those assets are needed to pay partnership creditors.

Illustration 12-2 summarizes the advantages and disadvantages of the regular partnership form of business organization. As indicated in the previous section, different types of partnership forms have evolved to reduce some of the disadvantages.

Advantages	Disadvantages
Combining skills and resources of two or more individuals	Mutual agency
Ease of formation	Limited life
Freedom from governmental regulations and restrictions	Unlimited liability
Ease of decision making	

Illustration 12-2
Advantages and disadvantages of a partnership

The Partnership Agreement

Ideally, the agreement of two or more individuals to form a partnership should be expressed in a written contract, called the **partnership agreement** or **articles of co-partnership**. The partnership agreement contains such basic information as the name and principal location of the firm, the purpose of the business, and date of inception. In addition, it should specify relationships among the partners, such as:

1. Names and capital contributions of partners.
2. Rights and duties of partners.
3. Basis for sharing net income or net loss.
4. Provision for withdrawals of assets.
5. Procedures for submitting disputes to arbitration.
6. Procedures for the withdrawal or addition of a partner.
7. Rights and duties of surviving partners in the event of a partner's death.

We cannot overemphasize the importance of a written contract. The agreement should attempt to anticipate all possible situations, contingencies, and disagreements. The help of a lawyer is highly desirable in preparing the agreement.

ACCOUNTING ACROSS THE ORGANIZATIO

How to Part Ways Nicely

What should you do when you and your business partner do not agree on things, to the point where you are no longer on speaking terms? Given how heated business situations can get, this is not an unusual occurrence. Unfortunately, in many instances the partners do everything they can to undermine the other partner, eventually destroying the business. In some instances people even steal from the partnership because they either feel that they "deserve it" or they assume that the other partners are stealing from them.

It would be much better to follow the example of Jennifer Appel and her partner. They found that after opening a successful bakery and writing a cookbook, they couldn't agree on how the business should be run. The other partner bought out Ms. Appel's share of the business, and Ms. Appel went on to start her own style of bakery, which she ultimately franchised.

Source: Paulette Thomas, "As Partnership Sours, Parting Is Sweet," *Wall Street Journal,* July 6, 2004, p. A20.

? How can partnership conflicts be minimized and more easily resolved?

Before You Go On...

REVIEW IT
1. What are the distinguishing characteristics of a partnership?
2. What are the principal advantages and disadvantages of a partnership? Why is PepsiCo not a partnership? The answer to this question appears on page 552.
3. What is the difference between a regular partnership and a limited liability company?
4. What are the major items in a partnership agreement?

✓ *The Navigator*

■BASIC PARTNERSHIP ACCOUNTING■

We now turn to the basic accounting for partnerships. The major accounting issues relate to forming the partnership, dividing income or loss, and preparing financial statements.

Forming a Partnership

STUDY OBJECTIVE 2

Explain the accounting entries for the formation of a partnership.

Each partner's initial investment in a partnership is entered in the partnership records. The partnership should record these investments at the **fair market value of the assets at the date of their transfer to the partnership**. All partners must agree to the values assigned.

To illustrate, assume that A. Rolfe and T. Shea combine their proprietorships to start a partnership named U.S. Software. The firm will specialize in developing financial modeling software packages. Rolfe and Shea have the following assets prior to the formation of the partnership.

	Book Value		Market Value	
	A. Rolfe	**T. Shea**	**A. Rolfe**	**T. Shea**
Cash	$ 8,000	$ 9,000	$ 8,000	$ 9,000
Office equipment	5,000		4,000	
Accumulated depreciation	(2,000)			
Accounts receivable		4,000		4,000
Allowance for doubtful accounts		(700)		(1,000)
	$11,000	$12,300	$12,000	$12,000

Illustration 12-3
Book and market values of assets invested

The partnership records the investments as follows.

Investment of A. Rolfe

Cash	8,000	
Office Equipment	4,000	
A. Rolfe, Capital		12,000
(To record investment of Rolfe)		

*Items under **owners' equity** (**OE**) in the accounting equation analyses (in margins) are not labeled in this partnership chapter. Nearly all affect partners' **capital** accounts.*

A	=	L	+	OE
+8,000				
+4,000				
				+12,000

Cash Flows
+8,000

Investment of T. Shea

Cash	9,000	
Accounts Receivable	4,000	
Allowance for Doubtful Accounts		1,000
T. Shea, Capital		12,000
(To record investment of Shea)		

A	=	L	+	OE
+9,000				
+4,000				
−1,000				
				+12,000

Cash Flows
+9,000

Note that the partnership records neither the original cost of the office equipment ($5,000) nor its book value ($5,000 − $2,000). It records the equipment at its fair market value, $4,000. The partnership does not carry forward any accumulated depreciation from the books of previous entities (in this case, the two proprietorships).

In contrast, the gross claims on customers ($4,000) are carried forward to the partnership. The partnership adjusts the allowance for doubtful accounts to $1,000, to arrive at a cash (net) realizable value of $3,000. A partnership may start with an allowance for doubtful accounts because it will continue to collect existing accounts receivable, some of which are expected to be uncollectible. In addition, this procedure maintains the control and subsidiary relationship between Accounts Receivable and the accounts receivable subsidiary ledger.

After formation of the partnership, the accounting for transactions is similar to any other type of business organization. For example, the partners record all transactions with outside parties, such as the purchase or sale of merchandise inventory and the payment or receipt of cash, the same as would a sole proprietor.

The steps in the accounting cycle described in Chapter 4 for a proprietorship also apply to a partnership. For example, the partnership prepares a trial balance and journalizes and posts adjusting entries. A worksheet may be used. There are minor differences in journalizing and posting closing entries and in preparing financial statements, as we explain in the following sections. The differences occur because there is more than one owner.

Dividing Net Income or Net Loss

Partners equally share partnership net income or net loss unless the partnership contract indicates otherwise. The same basis of division usually applies to both net income and net loss. It is customary to refer to this basis as the **income ratio**, the **income and loss ratio**, or the **profit and loss (P&L) ratio**. Because of its wide acceptance, we will use the term income ratio to identify the basis for dividing net income and net loss. The partnership recognizes a partner's share of net income or net loss in the accounts through closing entries.

CLOSING ENTRIES

As in the case of a proprietorship, a partnership must make four entries in preparing closing entries. The entries are:

1. Debit each revenue account for its balance, and credit Income Summary for total revenues.
2. Debit Income Summary for total expenses, and credit each expense account for its balance.
3. Debit Income Summary for its balance, and credit each partner's capital account for his or her share of net income. Or, credit Income Summary, and debit each partner's capital account for his or her share of net loss.
4. Debit each partner's capital account for the balance in that partner's drawing account, and credit each partner's drawing account for the same amount.

The first two entries are the same as in a proprietorship. The last two entries are different because (1) there are two or more owners' capital and drawing accounts, and (2) it is necessary to divide net income (or net loss) among the partners.

To illustrate the last two closing entries, assume that AB Company has net income of $32,000 for 2008. The partners, L. Arbor and D. Barnett, share net income and net loss equally. Drawings for the year were Arbor $8,000 and Barnett $6,000. The last two closing entries are:

A = L + OE
−32,000
+16,000
+16,000

Cash Flows
no effect

Dec. 31	Income Summary	32,000	
	L. Arbor, Capital ($32,000 × 50%)		16,000
	D. Barnett, Capital ($32,000 × 50%)		16,000
	(To transfer net income to partners' capital accounts)		

A = L + OE
−8,000
−6,000
+8,000
+6,000

Cash Flows
no effect

Dec. 31	L. Arbor, Capital	8,000	
	D. Barnett, Capital	6,000	
	L. Arbor, Drawing		8,000
	D. Barnett, Drawing		6,000
	(To close drawing accounts to capital accounts)		

Assume that the beginning capital balance is $47,000 for Arbor and $36,000 for Barnett. After posting the closing entries, the capital and drawing accounts will appear as shown in Illustration 12-4.

Illustration 12-4
Partners' capital and drawing accounts after closing

L. Arbor, Capital			
12/31 **Clos.**	**8,000**	1/1 Bal.	47,000
		12/31 **Clos.**	**16,000**
		12/31 Bal.	55,000

L. Arbor, Drawing			
12/31 Bal.	8,000	12/31 **Clos.**	**8,000**

D. Barnett, Capital			
12/31 **Clos.**	**6,000**	1/1 Bal.	36,000
		12/31 **Clos.**	**16,000**
		12/31 Bal.	46,000

D. Barnett, Drawing			
12/31 Bal.	6,000	12/31 **Clos.**	**6,000**

As in a proprietorship, the partners' capital accounts are permanent accounts; their drawing accounts are temporary accounts. Normally, the capital accounts will have credit balances, and the drawing accounts will have debit balances. Drawing accounts are debited when partners withdraw cash or other assets from the partnership for personal use.

INCOME RATIOS

As noted earlier, the partnership agreement should specify the basis for sharing net income or net loss. The following are typical income ratios.

1. A fixed ratio, expressed as a proportion (6:4), a percentage (70% and 30%), or a fraction (2/3 and 1/3).
2. A ratio based either on capital balances at the beginning of the year or on average capital balances during the year.
3. Salaries to partners and the remainder on a fixed ratio.
4. Interest on partners' capital balances and the remainder on a fixed ratio.
5. Salaries to partners, interest on partners' capital, and the remainder on a fixed ratio.

The objective is to settle on a basis that will equitably reflect the partners' capital investment and service to the partnership.

A **fixed ratio** is easy to apply, and it may be an equitable basis in some circumstances. Assume, for example, that Hughes and Lane are partners. Each contributes the same amount of capital, but Hughes expects to work full-time in the partnership and Lane expects to work only half-time. Accordingly, the partners agree to a fixed ratio of 2/3 to Hughes and 1/3 to Lane.

A **ratio based on capital balances** may be appropriate when the funds invested in the partnership are considered the critical factor. Capital ratios may also be equitable when the partners hire a manager to run the business and do not plan to take an active role in daily operations.

The three remaining ratios (items 3, 4, and 5) give specific recognition to differences among partners. These ratios provide salary allowances for time worked and interest allowances for capital invested. Then, the partnership allocates any remaining net income or net loss on a fixed ratio.

Salaries to partners and interest on partners' capital are not expenses of the partnership. Therefore, these items do not enter into the matching of expenses with revenues and the determination of net income or net loss. For a partnership, as for other entities, salaries expense pertains to the cost of services performed by employees. Likewise, interest expense relates to the cost of borrowing from creditors. But partners, as owners, are not considered either **employees** or **creditors**. When the partnership agreement permits the partners to make monthly withdrawals of cash based on their "salary," the partnership debits these withdrawals to the partner's drawing account.

SALARIES, INTEREST, AND REMAINDER ON A FIXED RATIO

Under income ratio (5) in the list above, the partnership must apply salaries and interest **before** it allocates the remainder on the specified fixed ratio. **This is true even if the provisions exceed net income. It is also true even if the partnership has suffered a net loss for the year.** The partnership's income statement should show, below net income, detailed information concerning the division of net income or net loss.

To illustrate, assume that King and Lee are co-partners in the Kingslee Company. The partnership agreement provides for: (1) salary allowances of $8,400 to King and $6,000 to Lee, (2) interest allowances of 10% on capital balances at the beginning of the year, and (3) the remainder equally. Capital balances on January 1 were King $28,000, and Lee $24,000. In 2008, partnership net income is $22,000. The division of net income is as follows.

Illustration 12-5
Income statement with division of net income

KINGSLEE COMPANY			
Income Statement (partial)			
For the Year Ended December 31, 2008			

Sales		$200,000	
Net income		$ 22,000	

Division of Net Income

	Sara King	Ray Lee	Total
Salary allowance	$ 8,400	$6,000	$14,400
Interest allowance on partners' capital			
Sara King ($28,000 × 10%)	2,800		
Ray Lee ($24,000 × 10%)		2,400	
Total interest allowance			5,200
Total salaries and interest	11,200	8,400	19,600
Remaining income, $2,400			
($22,000 − $19,600)			
Sara King ($2,400 × 50%)	1,200		
Ray Lee ($2,400 × 50%)		1,200	
Total remainder			2,400
Total division of net income	$12,400	$9,600	$22,000

Kingslee records the division of net income as follows.

A	=	L	+	OE
				−22,000
				+12,400
				+9,600

Cash Flows
no effect

Dec. 31	Income Summary	22,000	
	Sara King, Capital		12,400
	Ray Lee, Capital		9,600
	(To close net income to partners' capital)		

Now let's look at a situation in which the salary and interest allowances *exceed* net income. Assume that Kingslee Company's net income is only $18,000. In this case, the salary and interest allowances will create a deficiency of $1,600 ($19,600 − $18,000). The computations of the allowances are the same as those in the preceding example. Beginning with total salaries and interest, we complete the division of net income as shown in Illustration 12-6.

	Sara King	Ray Lee	Total
Total salaries and interest	$11,200	$8,400	$19,600
Remaining deficiency ($1,600)			
($18,000 − $19,600)			
Sara King ($1,600 × 50%)	(800)		
Ray Lee ($1,600 × 50%)		(800)	
Total remainder			(1,600)
Total division	**$10,400**	**$7,600**	**$18,000**

Illustration 12-6
Division of net income—income deficiency

ACCOUNTING ACROSS THE ORGANIZATION

Start-Up Seeks to Share R&D Costs, and Profits

A biotech company named Curis has a promising new product to combat baldness. In order to bring the product to market, the company decided to form partnerships with some much larger companies in order minimize its legal exposure and maximize its research firepower. Says CEO Daniel Passeri, "Any quality-of-life drug is going to be looked at very carefully" by the U.S. Food and Drug Administration (FDA). "The FDA is likely to require big safety studies—broader than we can subsidize ourselves." The company had struggled to minimize its losses during the years when its research and development costs were huge and its sales were minimal. Although the company would have liked to retain all of the profits from its new product for itself, forming partnerships with other companies seemed like its only viable option.

Source: Arlene Weintraub, "Bristling with Promise," *BusinessWeek,* May 15, 2005, p. 57.

? What advantages does Curis achieve by forming agreements with other companies?

Partnership Financial Statements

The financial statements of a partnership are similar to those of a proprietorship. The differences are due to the number of owners involved. The income statement for a partnership is identical to the income statement for a proprietorship except for the division of net income, as shown earlier.

STUDY OBJECTIVE 4
Describe the form and content of partnership financial statements.

The <u>owners' equity statement for a partnership</u> is called the **partners' capital statement.** It explains the changes in each partner's capital account and in total partnership capital during the year. Illustration 12-7 (page 524) shows the partners' capital statement for Kingslee Company. It is based on the division of $22,000 of net income in Illustration 12-5. The statement includes assumed data for the additional investment and drawings. The partnership prepares the partners' capital statement from the income statement and the partners' capital and drawing accounts.

Illustration 12-7
Partners' capital statement

KINGSLEE COMPANY
Partners' Capital Statement
For the Year Ended December 31, 2008

	Sara King	Ray Lee	Total
Capital, January 1	$28,000	$24,000	$52,000
Add: Additional investment	2,000		2,000
Net income	12,400	9,600	22,000
	42,400	33,600	76,000
Less: Drawings	7,000	5,000	12,000
Capital, December 31	**$35,400**	**$28,600**	**$64,000**

The balance sheet for a partnership is the same as for a proprietorship except for the owner's equity section. For a partnership, the balance sheet shows the capital balances of each partner. The owners' equity section for Kingslee Company would show the following.

Illustration 12-8
Owners' equity section of a partnership balance sheet

KINGSLEE COMPANY
Balance Sheet (partial)
December 31, 2008

Total liabilities (assumed amount)		$115,000
Owners' equity		
Sara King, Capital	$35,400	
Ray Lee, Capital	28,600	
Total owners' equity		64,000
Total liabilities and owners' equity		$179,000

Before You Go On...

REVIEW IT

1. How should a partnership value a partner's initial investment of assets?
2. What are the closing entries for a partnership?
3. What types of income ratios might a partnership use?
4. How do partnership financial statements differ from proprietorship financial statements?

DO IT

LeeMay Company reports net income of $57,000. The partnership agreement provides for salaries of $15,000 to L. Lee and $12,000 to R. May. They will share the remainder on a 60:40 basis (60% to Lee). L. Lee asks your help to divide the net income between the partners and to prepare the closing entry.

Action Plan

- Compute net income exclusive of any salaries to partners and interest on partners' capital.
- Deduct salaries to partners from net income.

- Apply the partners' income ratios to the remaining net income.
- Prepare the closing entry distributing net income or net loss among the partners' capital accounts.

Solution   The division of net income is as follows.

	L. Lee	R. May	Total
Salary allowance	$15,000	$12,000	$27,000
Remaining income $30,000 ($57,000 − $27,000)			
L. Lee (60% × $30,000)	18,000		
R. May (40% × $30,000)		12,000	
Total remaining income			30,000
Total division of net income	$33,000	$24,000	$57,000

The closing entry for net income therefore is:

Income Summary	57,000	
L. Lee, Capital		33,000
R. May, Capital		24,000
(To close net income to partners' capital accounts)		

Related exercise material: *BE12-3, BE12-4, BE12-5, E12-4, and E12-5.*

✓ The Navigator

LIQUIDATION OF A PARTNERSHIP

Liquidation of a business involves selling the assets of the firm, paying liabilities, and distributing any remaining assets. Liquidation may result from the sale of the business by mutual agreement of the partners, from the death of a partner, or from bankruptcy. **Partnership liquidation** ends both the legal and economic life of the entity.

> **STUDY OBJECTIVE 5**
> Explain the effects of the entries to record the liquidation of a partnership.

From an accounting standpoint, the partnership should complete the accounting cycle for the final operating period prior to liquidation. This includes preparing adjusting entries and financial statements. It also involves preparing closing entries and a post-closing trial balance. Thus, only balance sheet accounts should be open as the liquidation process begins.

In liquidation, the sale of noncash assets for cash is called **realization**. Any difference between book value and the cash proceeds is called the **gain or loss on realization**. To liquidate a partnership, it is necessary to:

1. Sell noncash assets for cash and recognize a gain or loss on realization.
2. Allocate gain/loss on realization to the partners based on their income ratios.
3. Pay partnership liabilities in cash.
4. Distribute remaining cash to partners on the basis of their **capital balances**.

Each of the steps must be performed in sequence. The partnership must pay creditors **before** partners receive any cash distributions. Also, an accounting entry must record each step.

When a partnership is liquidated, all partners may have credit balances in their capital accounts. This situation is called **no capital deficiency**. Or, one or more partners may have a debit balance in the capital account. This situation is termed a **capital deficiency**. To illustrate each of these conditions, assume that Ace Company is liquidated when its ledger shows the following assets, liabilities, and owners' equity accounts.

Illustration 12-9
Account balances prior to liquidation

Assets		Liabilities and Owners' Equity	
Cash	$ 5,000	Notes payable	$15,000
Accounts receivable	15,000	Accounts payable	16,000
Inventory	18,000	R. Arnet, Capital	15,000
Equipment	35,000	P. Carey, Capital	17,800
Accum. depr.—equipment	(8,000)	W. Eaton, Capital	1,200
	$65,000		$65,000

No Capital Deficiency

The partners of Ace Company agree to liquidate the partnership on the following terms: (1) The partnership will sell its noncash assets to Jackson Enterprises for $75,000 cash. (2) The partnership will pay its partnership liabilities. The income ratios of the partners are 3 : 2 : 1, respectively. The steps in the liquidation process are as follows.

1. Ace sells the noncash assets (accounts receivable, inventory, and equipment) for $75,000. The book value of these assets is $60,000 ($15,000 + $18,000 + $35,000 − $8,000). Thus Ace realizes a gain of $15,000 on the sale. The entry is:

(1)

Cash	75,000	
Accumulated Depreciation–Equipment	8,000	
Accounts Receivable		15,000
Inventory		18,000
Equipment		35,000
Gain on Realization		15,000
(To record realization of noncash assets)		

A	=	L	+	OE
+75,000				
+8,000				
−15,000				
−18,000				
−35,000				
				+15,000

Cash Flows
+75,000

2. Ace allocates the $15,000 gain on realization to the partners on their income ratios, which are 3:2:1. The entry is:

(2)

Gain on Realization	15,000	
R. Arnet, Capital ($15,000 × 3/6)		7,500
P. Carey, Capital ($15,000 × 2/6)		5,000
W. Eaton, Capital ($15,000 × 1/6)		2,500
(To allocate gain to partners' capital accounts)		

A	=	L	+	OE
		−15,000		
				+7,500
				+5,000
				+2,500

Cash Flows
no effect

3. Partnership liabilities consist of Notes Payable $15,000 and Accounts Payable $16,000. Ace pays creditors in full by a cash payment of $31,000. The entry is:

(3)

Notes Payable	15,000	
Accounts Payable	16,000	
Cash		31,000
(To record payment of partnership liabilities)		

A	=	L	+	OE
		−15,000		
		−16,000		
−31,000				

Cash Flows
−31,000

4. Ace distributes the remaining cash to the partners on the basis of **their capital balances**. After posting the entries in the first three steps, all partnership accounts, including Gain on Realization, will have zero balances except for four accounts: Cash $49,000; R. Arnet, Capital $22,500; P. Carey, Capital $22,800; and W. Eaton, Capital $3,700, as shown on the next page.

Cash				R. Arnet, Capital		P. Carey, Capital		W. Eaton, Capital	
Bal.	5,000	(3)	31,000	Bal.	15,000	Bal.	17,800	Bal.	1,200
(1)	75,000			(2)	7,500	(2)	5,000	(2)	2,500
Bal.	49,000			Bal.	22,500	Bal.	22,800	Bal.	3,700

Ace records the distribution of cash as follows.

(4)

R. Arnet, Capital	22,500	
P. Carey, Capital	22,800	
W. Eaton, Capital	3,700	
Cash		49,000
(To record distribution of cash to partners)		

After posting this entry, all partnership accounts will have zero balances.

A word of caution: **Partnerships should not distribute remaining cash to partners on the basis of their income-sharing ratios.** On this basis, Arnet would receive three-sixths, or $24,500, which would produce an erroneous debit balance of $2,000. The income ratio is the proper basis for allocating net income or loss. **It is not a proper basis for making the final distribution of cash to the partners.**

SCHEDULE OF CASH PAYMENTS

The **schedule of cash payments** shows the distribution of cash to the partners in a partnership liquidation. A cash payments schedule is sometimes prepared to determine the distribution of cash to the partners in the liquidation of a partnership. The schedule of cash payments is organized around the basic accounting equation. Illustration 12-11 shows the schedule for Ace Company. The numbers in parentheses refer to the four required steps in the liquidation of a partnership. They also identify the accounting entries that Ace must make. The cash payments schedule is especially useful when the liquidation process extends over a period of time.

Illustration 12-10
Ledger balances before distribution of cash

A	=	L	+	OE
				−22,500
				−22,800
				−3,700
−49,000				

Cash Flows
−49,000

ALTERNATIVE TERMINOLOGY

The schedule of cash payments is sometimes called a *safe cash payments schedule*.

Illustration 12-11
Schedule of cash payments, no capital deficiency

ACE Company.xls

File   Edit   View   Insert   Format   Tools   Data   Window   Help

ACE COMPANY
Schedule of Cash Payments

Item		Cash	+	Noncash Assets	=	Liabilities	+	R. Arnet Capital	+	P. Carey Capital	+	W. Eaton Capital
Balances before liquidation		5,000	+	60,000	=	31,000	+	15,000	+	17,800	+	1,200
Sales of noncash assets and allocation of gain	(1)&(2)	75,000	+	(60,000)	=			7,500	+	5,000	+	2,500
New balances		80,000	+	−0−	=	31,000	+	22,500	+	22,800	+	3,700
Pay liabilities	(3)	(31,000)			=	(31,000)						
New balances		49,000	+	−0−	=	−0−	+	22,500	+	22,800	+	3,700
Cash distribution to partners	(4)	(49,000)			=			(22,500)	+	(22,800)	+	(3,700)
Final balances		−0−		−0−	=	−0−		−0−		−0−		−0−

Capital Deficiency

A capital deficiency may result from recurring net losses, excessive drawings, or losses from realization suffered during liquidation. To illustrate, assume that Ace Company is on the brink of bankruptcy. The partners decide to liquidate by having a "going-out-of-business" sale. They sell merchandise at substantial discounts, and sell the equipment at auction. Cash proceeds from these sales and collections from customers total only $42,000. Thus, the loss from liquidation is $18,000 ($60,000 − $42,000). The steps in the liquidation process are as follows.

1. The entry for the realization of noncash assets is:

Cash Flows
+42,000

(1)

Cash	42,000	
Accumulated Depreciation—Equipment	8,000	
Loss on Realization	18,000	
Accounts Receivable		15,000
Inventory		18,000
Equipment		35,000
(To record realization of noncash assets)		

2. Ace allocates the loss on realization to the partners on the basis of their income ratios. The entry is:

(2)

R. Arnet, Capital ($18,000 × 3/6)	9,000	
P. Carey, Capital ($18,000 × 2/6)	6,000	
W. Eaton, Capital ($18,000 × 1/6)	3,000	
Loss on Realization		18,000
(To allocate loss on realization to partners)		

Cash Flows
no effect

3. Ace pays the partnership liabilities. This entry is the same as the previous one.

(3)

Notes Payable	15,000	
Accounts Payable	16,000	
Cash		31,000
(To record payment of partnership liabilities)		

Cash Flows
−31,000

4. After posting the three entries, two accounts will have debit balances—Cash $16,000, and W. Eaton, Capital $1,800. Two accounts will have credit balances—R. Arnet, Capital $6,000, and P. Carey, Capital $11,800. All four accounts are shown below.

Illustration 12-12
Ledger balances before distribution of cash

Cash				R. Arnet, Capital				P. Carey, Capital				W. Eaton, Capital			
Bal.	5,000	(3)	31,000	(2)	9,000	Bal.	15,000	(2)	6,000	Bal.	17,800	(2)	3,000	Bal.	1,200
(1)	42,000					Bal.	6,000			Bal.	11,800	Bal.	1,800		
Bal.	16,000														

Eaton has a capital deficiency of $1,800, and so owes the partnership $1,800. Arnet and Carey have a legally enforceable claim for that amount against Eaton's personal assets. Note that the distribution of cash is still made on the basis of capital balances. But the amount will vary depending on how Eaton settles the deficiency. Two alternatives are presented in the following sections.

PAYMENT OF DEFICIENCY

If the partner with the capital deficiency pays the amount owed the partnership, the deficiency is eliminated. To illustrate, assume that Eaton pays $1,800 to the partnership. The entry is:

Cash Flows
+1,800

(a)

Cash	1,800	
W. Eaton, Capital		1,800
(To record payment of capital deficiency by Eaton)		

After posting this entry, account balances are as follows.

Illustration 12-13
Ledger balances after
paying capital deficiency

Cash				R. Arnet, Capital				P. Carey, Capital				W. Eaton, Capital			
Bal.	5,000	(3)	31,000	(2)	9,000	Bal.	15,000	(2)	6,000	Bal.	17,800	(2)	3,000	Bal.	1,200
(1)	42,000													(a)	1,800
(a)	1,800					Bal.	6,000			Bal.	11,800				
Bal.	17,800													Bal.	–0–

The cash balance of $17,800 is now equal to the credit balances in the capital accounts (Arnet $6,000 + Carey $11,800). Ace now distributes cash on the basis of these balances. The entry is:

R. Arnet, Capital	6,000	
P. Carey, Capital	11,800	
Cash		17,800
(To record distribution of cash to the partners)		

A	=	L	+	OE
				−6,000
				−11,800
−17,800				

Cash Flows
−17,800

After posting this entry, all accounts will have zero balances.

NONPAYMENT OF DEFICIENCY

If a partner with a capital deficiency is unable to pay the amount owed to the partnership, the partners with credit balances must absorb the loss. The partnership allocates the loss on the basis of the income ratios that exist between the partners with credit balances.

The income ratios of Arnet and Carey are 3 : 2, or 3/5 and 2/5, respectively. Thus, Ace would make the following entry to remove Eaton's capital deficiency.

(a)

R. Arnet, Capital ($1,800 × 3/5)	1,080	
P. Carey, Capital ($1,800 × 2/5)	720	
W. Eaton, Capital		1,800
(To record write-off of capital deficiency)		

A	=	L	+	OE
				−1,080
				−720
				+1,800

Cash Flows
no effect

After posting this entry, the cash and capital accounts will have the following balances.

Cash				R. Arnet, Capital				P. Carey, Capital				W. Eaton, Capital			
Bal.	5,000	(3)	31,000	(2)	9,000	Bal.	15,000	(2)	6,000	Bal.	17,800	(2)	3,000	Bal.	1,200
(1)	42,000			(a)	1,080			(a)	720					(a)	1,800
Bal.	16,000					Bal.	4,920			Bal.	11,080			Bal.	–0–

Illustration 12-14
Ledger balances after nonpayment of capital deficiency

The cash balance ($16,000) now equals the sum of the credit balances in the capital accounts (Arnet $4,920 + Carey $11,080). Ace records the distribution of cash as:

R. Arnet, Capital	4,920	
P. Carey, Capital	11,080	
Cash		16,000
(To record distribution of cash to the partners)		

A	=	L	+	OE
				−4,920
				−11,080
−16,000				

Cash Flows
−16,000

After posting this entry, all accounts will have zero balances.

 Be sure to read **ALL ABOUT YOU:** *How Well Do You Know Your Partner?* on page 530 for information on how topics in this chapter apply to you.

How Well Do You Know Your Partner?

As noted in this chapter, the partnership form of organization is popular for a variety of reasons. A partnership is easy to form, and it has significant tax advantages over the corporate form. But the partnership form is not without its faults. Chief among these is that, in a standard partnership, each partner can be held fully responsible for all of the partnership's obligations—not just his or her share. Because of this, choosing a partner is a big decision, and choosing the wrong partner can have devastating consequences.

✹ About the Numbers

The following graph shows that the most rapid growth in business organizations occurring in limited liability companies (LLCs). The LLC form is the choice of mos new businesses.

Change from Prior Year in Business Organizations

Source of graph: *www.BizStats.com* (accessed June 2006).

✹ Some Facts

* There are about 1.7 million business partnerships in the United States, with an average of 9 partners per partnership.

* Over 72% of all small businesses are sole proprietors. Only 6% are partnerships (including limited liability companies that choose to file tax returns as partnerships).

* A partnership is simple to set up because no legal documents are needed. Partnerships are often formed by an oral agreement between the parties. Potential problems can be averted down the road by drawing up a written legal partnership agreement.

✹ What Do You Think?

Suppose that your best friend has approached you about forming a partne ship to design and build websites. You have a degree in computer programming, and your friend has a degree in marketing. You are very inte ested in starting the business. You know you have the technical abilities, bu you dread having to be a salesperson. Your friend, on the other hand, has a ways been outgoing and assertive—the perfect salesperson. Your friend als however, has an extremely bad credit history, including having filed for pe sonal bankruptcy. Should you form the partnership?

YES: This is a great opportunity. What could be better than working with your best friend?

NO: If the partnership has financial trouble, and your friend cannot pay, then, as a partner you will be responsible for all of the firm's debts, not jus your half.

Sources: BizStats.com; Darrell Zahorsky, "Creating a Winning Business Partnership," *www.sbinformation.about.com* (accessed June 2006); *www.askinc@inc.com* (accessed June 20 *Inc.* Magazine, December 2005, p. 64.

Before You Go On...

REVIEW IT

1. What are the steps in liquidating a partnership?
2. What basis do partnerships use in making final distribution of cash to partners?

 The Navigator

Demonstration Problem

On January 1, 2008, the capital balances in Hollingsworth Company are Lois Holly $26,000, and Jim Worth $24,000. In 2008 the partnership reports net income of $30,000. The income ratio provides for salary allowances of $12,000 for Holly and $10,000 to Worth and the remainder equally. Neither partner had any drawings in 2008.

Instructions

(a) Prepare a schedule showing the distribution of net income in 2008.
(b) Journalize the division of 2008 net income to the partners.

Solution to Demonstration Problem

(a)

Net income   30,000

Division of Net Income

	Lois Holly	Jim Worth	Total
Salary allowance	$12,000	$10,000	$22,000
Remaining income $8,000 ($30,000 − $22,000)			
Lois Holly ($8,000 × 50%)	4,000		
Jim Worth ($8,000 × 50%)		4,000	
Total remainder			8,000
Total division of net income	$16,000	$14,000	$30,000

(b) 12/31/08

		Debit	Credit
Income Summary		30,000	
Lois Holly, Capital			16,000
Jim Worth, Capital			14,000
(To close net income to partners' capital)			

 The Navigator

action plan

✔ Compute the net income of the partnership.
✔ Allocate the partners' salaries.
✔ Divide the remaining net income among the partners, applying the income/loss ratio.
✔ Journalize the division of net income in a closing entry.

SUMMARY OF STUDY OBJECTIVES

1 **Identify the characteristics of the partnership form of business organization.** The principal characteristics of a partnership are: (a) association of individuals, (b) mutual agency, (c) limited life, (d) unlimited liability, and (e) co-ownership of property.

2 **Explain the accounting entries for the formation of a partnership.** When formed, a partnership records each

partner's initial investment at the fair market value of the assets at the date of their transfer to the partnership.

3 **Identify the bases for dividing net income or net loss.** Partnerships divide net income or net loss on the basis of the income ratio, which may be (a) a fixed ratio, (b) a ratio based on beginning or average capital balances, (c) salaries to partners and the remainder on a fixed ratio, (d) interest

on partners' capital and the remainder on a fixed ratio, and (e) salaries to partners, interest on partners' capital, and the remainder on a fixed ratio.

4 **Describe the form and content of partnership financial statements.** The financial statements of a partnership are similar to those of a proprietorship. The principal differences are: (a) The partnership shows the division of net income on the income statement. (b) The owners' equity statement is called a partners' capital statement. (c) The partnership reports each partner's capital on the balance sheet.

5 **Explain the effects of the entries to record the liquidation of a partnership.** When a partnership is liquidated, it is necessary to record the (a) sale of noncash assets, (b) allocation of the gain or loss on realization, (c) payment of partnership liabilities, and (d) distribution of cash to the partners on the basis of their capital balances.

GLOSSARY

Capital deficiency   A debit balance in a partner's capital account after allocation of gain or loss. (p. 525).

General partner   A partner who has unlimited liability for the debts of the firm. (p. 516).

Income ratio   The basis for dividing net income and net loss in a partnership. (p. 520).

Limited liability company   A form of business organization, usually classified as a partnership for tax purposes and usually with limited life, in which partners, who are called *members*, have limited liability. (p. 516).

Limited liability partnership   A partnership of professionals in which partners are given limited liability and the public is protected from malpractice by insurance carried by the partnership. (p. 516).

Limited partner   A partner whose liability for the debts of the firm is limited to that partner's investment in the firm. (p. 516).

Limited partnership   A partnership in which one or more general partners have unlimited liability and one or more partners have limited liability for the obligations of the firm. (p. 515).

No capital deficiency   All partners have credit balances after allocation of gain or loss. (p. 525).

Partners' capital statement   The owners' equity statement for a partnership which shows the changes in each partner's capital account and in total partnership capital during the year. (p. 523).

Partnership   An association of two or more persons to carry on as co-owners of a business for profit. (p. 514).

Partnership agreement   A written contract expressing the voluntary agreement of two or more individuals in a partnership. (p. 518).

Partnership dissolution   A change in partners due to withdrawal or admission, which does not necessarily terminate the business. (p. 515).

Partnership liquidation   An event that ends both the legal and economic life of a partnership. (p. 525).

Schedule of cash payments   A schedule showing the distribution of cash to the partners in a partnership liquidation. (p. 527).

APPENDIX Admission and Withdrawal of Partners

The chapter explained how the basic accounting for a partnership works. We now look at how to account for a common occurrence in partnerships—the addition or withdrawal of a partner.

Admission of a Partner

STUDY OBJECTIVE 6

Explain the effects of the entries when a new partner is admitted.

The admission of a new partner results in the **legal dissolution** of the existing partnership and the beginning of a new one. From an economic standpoint, however, the admission of a new partner (or partners) may be of minor significance in the continuity of the business. For example, in large public accounting or law firms, partners are admitted annually without any change in operating policies. **To recognize the economic effects, it is necessary only to open a capital account for each new partner.** In the entries illustrated in this appendix, we assume that the accounting records of the predecessor firm will continue to be used by the new partnership.

A new partner may be admitted either by (1) purchasing the interest of one or more existing partners or (2) investing assets in the partnership, as shown in Illustration 12A-1. The former affects only the capital accounts of the partners who are parties to the transaction. The latter increases both net assets and total capital of the partnership.

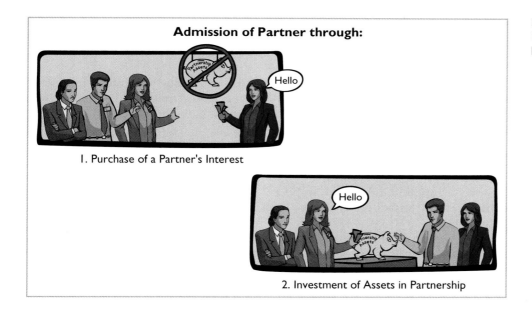

Admission of Partner through:

1. Purchase of a Partner's Interest

2. Investment of Assets in Partnership

Illustration 12A-1
Procedures in adding partners

PURCHASE OF A PARTNER'S INTEREST

The **admission** of a partner **by purchase of an interest** is a personal transaction between one or more existing partners and the new partner. Each party acts as an individual separate from the partnership entity. The individuals involved negotiate the price paid. It may be equal to or different from the capital equity acquired. The purchase price passes directly from the new partner to the partners who are giving up part or all of their ownership claims.

Any money or other consideration exchanged is the personal property of the participants and **not** the property of the partnership. Upon purchase of an interest, the new partner acquires each selling partner's capital interest and income ratio.

Accounting for the purchase of an interest is straightforward. The partnership records record only the changes in partners' capital. **Partners' capital accounts are debited for any ownership claims sold.** At the same time, the new partner's capital account is credited for the capital equity purchased. Total assets, total liabilities, and total capital remain unchanged, as do all individual asset and liability accounts.

To illustrate, assume that L. Carson agrees to pay $10,000 each to C. Ames and D. Barker for 33⅓% (one-third) of their interest in the Ames–Barker partnership. At the time of the admission of Carson, each partner has a $30,000 capital balance. Both partners, therefore, give up $10,000 of their capital equity. The entry to record the admission of Carson is:

C. Ames, Capital	10,000	
D. Barker, Capital	10,000	
L. Carson, Capital		20,000
(To record admission of Carson by purchase)		

HELPFUL HINT

In a purchase of an interest, the partnership is **not** a participant in the transaction. In this transaction, the new partner contributes *no* cash to the partnership.

Illustration 12A-2
Ledger balances after purchase of a partner's interest

The effect of this transaction on net assets and partners' capital is shown below.

Net Assets	C. Ames, Capital	D. Barker, Capital	L. Carson, Capital
60,000	10,000 | 30,000	10,000 | 30,000	20,000
	Bal. 20,000	Bal. 20,000	

Note that net assets remain unchanged at $60,000, and each partner has a $20,000 capital balance. Ames and Barker continue as partners in the firm, but the capital interest of each has changed. The cash paid by Carson goes directly to the individual partners and not to the partnership.

Regardless of the amount paid by Carson for the one-third interest, the entry is exactly the same. If Carson pays $12,000 each to Ames and Barker for one-third of the partnership, the partnership still makes the entry shown on the bottom of page 533.

INVESTMENT OF ASSETS IN A PARTNERSHIP

The admission of a partner by an investment of assets is a transaction between the new partner and the partnership. Often referred to simply as **admission by investment**, the transaction **increases both the net assets and total capital of the partnership**.

Assume, for example, that instead of purchasing an interest, Carson invests $30,000 in cash in the Ames–Barker partnership for a 33⅓% capital interest. In such a case, the entry is:

Cash	30,000	
L. Carson, Capital		30,000
(To record admission of Carson by investment)		

Illustration 12A-3
Ledger balances after investment of assets

The effects of this transaction on the partnership accounts would be:

Net Assets	C. Ames, Capital	D. Barker, Capital	L. Carson, Capital
60,000	30,000	30,000	30,000
30,000			
Bal. 90,000			

Note that both net assets and total capital have increased by $30,000.

Remember that Carson's one-third capital interest might not result in a one-third income ratio. The new partnership agreement should specify Carson's income ratio, and it may or may not be equal to the one-third capital interest.

The comparison of the net assets and capital balances in Illustration 12A-4 shows the different effects of the purchase of an interest and admission by investment.

Illustration 12A-4
Comparison of purchase of an interest and admission by investment

Purchase of an Interest		Admission by Investment	
Net Assets	$60,000	Net Assets	$90,000
Capital		Capital	
C. Ames	$20,000	C. Ames	$30,000
D. Barker	20,000	D. Barker	30,000
L. Carson	20,000	L. Carson	30,000
Total capital	$60,000	Total capital	$90,000

When a new partner purchases an interest, the total net assets and total capital of the partnership *do not change.* When a partner is admitted by investment, both the total net assets and the total capital *change.*

In the case of admission by investment, further complications occur when the new partner's investment differs from the capital equity acquired. When those amounts are not the same, the difference is considered a **bonus** either to (1) the existing (old) partners or (2) the new partner.

Bonus to Old Partners   For both personal and business reasons, the existing partners may be unwilling to admit a new partner without receiving a bonus. In an established firm, existing partners may insist on a bonus as compensation for the work they have put into the company over the years. Two accounting factors underlie the business reason: First, total partners' capital equals the **book value** of the recorded net assets of the partnership. When the new partner is admitted, the fair market values of assets such as land and buildings may be higher than their book values. The bonus will help make up the difference between fair market value and book value. Second, when the partnership has been profitable, goodwill may exist. But, the partnership balance sheet does not report goodwill. In such cases, the new partner is usually willing to pay the bonus to become a partner.

A bonus to old partners results when the new partner's investment in the firm is greater than the capital credit on the date of admittance. The bonus results in **an increase in the capital balances of the old partners. The partnership allocates the bonus to them on the basis of their income ratios before the admission of the new partner.**

To illustrate, assume that the Bart–Cohen partnership, owned by Sam Bart and Tom Cohen, has total capital of $120,000. Lea Eden acquires a 25% ownership (capital) interest in the partnership by making a cash investment of $80,000. The procedure for determining Eden's capital credit and the bonus to the old partners is as follows.

1. **Determine the total capital of the new partnership:** Add the new partner's investment to the total capital of the old partnership. In this case the total capital of the new firm is $200,000, computed as follows.

Total capital of existing partnership	$120,000
Investment by new partner, Eden	80,000
Total capital of new partnership	$200,000

2. **Determine the new partner's capital credit:** Multiply the total capital of the new partnership by the new partner's ownership interest. Eden's capital credit is $50,000 ($200,000 × 25%).

3. **Determine the amount of bonus:** Subtract the new partner's capital credit from the new partner's investment. The bonus in this case is $30,000 ($80,000 − $50,000).

4. **Allocate the bonus to the old partners on the basis of their income ratios:** Assuming the ratios are Bart 60%, and Cohen 40%, the allocation is: Bart $18,000 ($30,000 × 60%) and Cohen $12,000 ($30,000 × 40%).

The entry to record the admission of Eden is:

Cash	80,000	
Sam Bart, Capital		18,000
Tom Cohen, Capital		12,000
Lea Eden, Capital		50,000
(To record admission of Eden and bonus to old		
partners)		

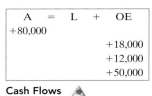

A	=	L	+	OE
+80,000				
				+18,000
				+12,000
				+50,000

Cash Flows
+80,000

Bonus to New Partner A bonus to a new partner results when the new partner's investment in the firm is less than his or her capital credit. This may occur when the new partner possesses resources or special attributes that the partnership wants. For example, the new partner may be able to supply cash that the firm urgently needs for expansion or to meet maturing debts. Or the new partner may be a recognized expert or authority in a relevant field. Thus, an engineering firm may be willing to give a renowned engineer a bonus to join the firm. The partners of a restaurant may offer a bonus to a sports celebrity in order to add the athlete's name to the partnership. A bonus to a new partner may also result when recorded book values on the partnership books are higher than their market values.

A bonus to a new partner results in a **decrease in the capital balances of the old partners. The amount of the decrease for each partner is based on the income ratios before the admission of the new partner.** To illustrate, assume that Lea Eden invests $20,000 in cash for a 25% ownership interest in the Bart–Cohen partnership. The computations for Eden's capital credit and the bonus are as follows, using the four procedures described in the preceding section.

Illustration 12A-5
Computation of capital credit and bonus to new partner

1.	Total capital of Bart–Cohen partnership	$120,000
	Investment by new partner, Eden	20,000
	Total capital of new partnership	$140,000
2.	**Eden's capital credit** (25% × $140,000)	$ 35,000
3.	**Bonus to Eden** ($35,000 − $20,000)	$ 15,000
4.	Allocation of bonus to old partners:	
	Bart ($15,000 × 60%) $9,000	
	Cohen ($15,000 × 40%) 6,000	$ 15,000

The partnership records the admission of Eden as follows:

```
A  =  L  +  OE
+20,000
              −9,000
              −6,000
             +35,000
```

Cash Flows
+20,000

Cash	20,000	
Sam Bart, Capital	9,000	
Tom Cohen, Capital	6,000	
Lea Eden, Capital		35,000
(To record Eden's admission and bonus)		

Withdrawal of a Partner

STUDY OBJECTIVE 7

Describe the effects of the entries when a partner withdraws from the firm.

Now let's look at the opposite situation—the withdrawal of a partner. A partner may withdraw from a partnership **voluntarily**, by selling his or her equity in the firm. Or, he or she may withdraw **involuntarily**, by reaching mandatory retirement age or by dying. The withdrawal of a partner, like the admission of a partner, legally dissolves the partnership. The legal effects may be recognized by dissolving the firm. However, it is customary to record only the economic effects of the partner's withdrawal, while the firm continues to operate and reorganizes itself legally.

As indicated earlier, the partnership agreement should specify the terms of withdrawal. As Illustration 12A-6 shows, the withdrawal of a partner may be accomplished by (1) payment from partners' personal assets or (2) payment from partnership assets. The former affects only the partners' capital accounts. The latter decreases total net assets and total capital of the partnership.

Withdrawal of Partner through:

1. Payment from Partners' Personal Assets

2. Payment from Partnership Assets

Illustration 12A-6
Procedures in partnership
withdrawal

PAYMENT FROM PARTNERS' PERSONAL ASSETS

<u>Withdrawal by payment from partners' personal assets</u> is a personal transaction between the partners. **It is the direct opposite of admitting a new partner who purchases a partner's interest.** The remaining partners pay the retiring partner directly from their personal assets. **Partnership assets are not involved in any way, and total capital does not change.** The effect on the partnership is limited to changes in the partners' capital balances.

To illustrate, assume that partners Morz, Nead, and Odom have capital balances of $25,000, $15,000, and $10,000, respectively. Morz and Nead agree to buy out Odom's interest. Each of them agrees to pay Odom $8,000 in exchange for one-half of Odom's total interest of $10,000. The entry to record the withdrawal is:

J. Odom, Capital	10,000	
A. Morz, Capital		5,000
M. Nead, Capital		5,000
(To record purchase of Odom's interest)		

A	=	L	+	OE
				−10,000
				+5,000
				+5,000

Cash Flows
no effect

The effect of this entry on the partnership accounts is shown below.

Net Assets		A. Morz, Capital		M. Nead, Capital		J. Odom, Capital	
50,000			25,000		15,000	10,000	10,000
			5,000		5,000		Bal. −0−
			Bal. 30,000		Bal. 20,000		

Illustration 12A-7
Ledger balances after
payment from partners'
personal assets

Note that net assets and total capital remain the same at $50,000.

What about the $16,000 paid to Odom? You've probably noted that it is not recorded. The entry debited Odom's capital only for $10,000, not for the $16,000 that she received. Similarly, both Morz and Nead credit their capital accounts for only $5,000, not for the $8,000 they each paid.

After Odom's withdrawal, Morz and Nead will share net income or net loss equally unless they specifically indicate another income ratio in the partnership agreement.

PAYMENT FROM PARTNERSHIP ASSETS

Withdrawal by payment from partnership assets is a transaction that involves the partnership. **Both partnership net assets and total capital decrease as a result.** Using partnership assets to pay for a withdrawing partner's interest is the **reverse** of admitting a partner through the investment of assets in the partnership.

Many partnership agreements provide that the amount paid should be based on the fair market value of the assets at the time of the partner's withdrawal. When this basis is required, some maintain that any differences between recorded asset balances and their fair market values should be (1) recorded by an adjusting entry, and (2) allocated to all partners on the basis of their income ratios. This position has serious flaws. Recording the revaluations violates the cost principle, which requires that assets be stated at original cost. It also is a departure from the going-concern assumption, which assumes the entity will continue indefinitely. The terms of the partnership contract should not dictate the accounting for this event.

In accounting for a withdrawal by payment from partnership assets, the partnership should not record asset revaluations. Instead, it should consider any difference between the amount paid and the withdrawing partner's capital balance as **a bonus** to the retiring partner or to the remaining partners.

Bonus to Retiring Partner A partnership may pay a bonus to a retiring partner when:

1. The fair market value of partnership assets is more than their book value,
2. There is unrecorded goodwill resulting from the partnership's superior earnings record, or
3. The remaining partners are eager to remove the partner from the firm.

The partnership deducts the bonus from the remaining partners' capital balances on the basis of their income ratios at the time of the withdrawal.

To illustrate, assume that the following capital balances exist in the RST partnership: Roman $50,000, Sand $30,000, and Terk $20,000. The partners share income in the ratio of 3 : 2 : 1, respectively. Terk retires from the partnership and receives a cash payment of $25,000 from the firm. The procedure for determining the bonus to the retiring partner and the allocation of the bonus to the remaining partners is as follows.

1. **Determine the amount of the bonus:** Subtract the retiring partner's capital balance from the cash paid by the partnership. The bonus in this case is $5,000 ($25,000 − $20,000).
2. **Allocate the bonus to the remaining partners on the basis of their income ratios:** The ratios of Roman and Sand are 3 : 2. Thus, the allocation of the $5,000 bonus is: Roman $3,000 ($5,000 × 3/5) and Sand $2,000 ($5,000 × 2/5).

The partnership records the withdrawal of Terk as follows.

B. Terk, Capital	20,000	
F. Roman, Capital	3,000	
D. Sand, Capital	2,000	
Cash		25,000
(To record withdrawal of and bonus to Terk)		

HELPFUL HINT

Compare this entry to the one on page 539.

A	=	L	+	OE
				−20,000
				−3,000
				−2,000
−25,000				

Cash Flows
−25,000

The remaining partners, Roman and Sand, will recover the bonus given to Terk as the partnership sells or uses the undervalued assets.

Bonus to Remaining Partners The retiring partner may give a bonus to the remaining partners when:

1. Recorded assets are overvalued,
2. The partnership has a poor earnings record, or
3. The partner is eager to leave the partnership.

In such cases, the cash paid to the retiring partner will be less than the retiring partner's capital balance. **The partnership allocates (credits) the bonus to the capital accounts of the remaining partners on the basis of their income ratios.**

To illustrate, assume (instead of the example above) that the partnership pays Terk only $16,000 for her $20,000 equity when she withdraws from the partnership. In that case:

1. The bonus to remaining partners is $4,000 ($20,000 − $16,000).
2. The allocation of the $4,000 bonus is: Roman $2,400 ($4,000 × 3/5) and Sand $1,600 ($4,000 × 2/5).

Under these circumstances, the entry to record the withdrawal is:

B. Terk, Capital	20,000	
F. Roman, Capital		2,400
D. Sand, Capital		1,600
Cash		16,000
(To record withdrawal of Terk and bonus to remaining partners)		

Note that if Sand had withdrawn from the partnership, Roman and Terk would divide any bonus on the basis of their income ratio, which is 3 : 1 or 75% and 25%.

HELPFUL HINT

Compare this entry to the one on page 538.

A	=	L	+	OE
				−20,000
				+2,400
				+1,600
−16,000				

Cash Flows
−16,000

DEATH OF A PARTNER

The death of a partner dissolves the partnership. But partnership agreements usually contain a provision for the surviving partners to continue operations. When a partner dies, it usually is necessary to determine the partner's equity at the date of death. This is done by (1) determining the net income or loss for the year to date, (2) closing the books, and (3) preparing financial statements. The partnership agreement may also require an independent audit of the financial statements and a revaluation of assets by an appraisal firm.

The surviving partners may agree to purchase the deceased partner's equity from their personal assets. Or they may use partnership assets to settle with the deceased partner's estate. In both instances, the entries to record the withdrawal of the partner are similar to those presented earlier.

To facilitate payment from partnership assets, some partnerships obtain life insurance policies on each partner, with the partnership named as the beneficiary. The partnership then uses the proceeds from the insurance policy on the deceased partner to settle with the estate.

SUMMARY OF STUDY OBJECTIVES FOR APPENDIX

6 **Explain the effects of the entries when a new partner is admitted.** The entry to record the admittance of a new partner by purchase of a partner's interest affects only partners' capital accounts. The entries to record the admittance by investment of assets in the partnership (a) increase both net assets and total capital and (b) may result in recognition of a bonus to either the old partners or the new partner.

7 **Describe the effects of the entries when a partner withdraws from the firm.** The entry to record a withdrawal from the firm when the partners pay from their personal assets affects only partners' capital accounts. The entry to record a withdrawal when payment is made from partnership assets (a) decreases net assets and total capital and (b) may result in recognizing a bonus either to the retiring partner or the remaining partners.

GLOSSARY FOR APPENDIX

Admission by investment Admission of a partner by investing assets in the partnership, causing both partnership net assets and total capital to increase. (p. 534).

Admission by purchase of an interest Admission of a partner in a personal transaction between one or more existing partners and the new partner; does not change total partnership assets or total capital. (p. 533).

Withdrawal by payment from partners' personal assets Withdrawal of a partner in a personal transaction between partners; does not change total partnership assets or total capital. (p. 537).

Withdrawal by payment from partnership assets Withdrawal of a partner in a transaction involving the partnership, causing both partnership net assets and total capital to decrease. (p. 538).

*Note: All **asterisked** Questions, Exercises, and Problems relate to material in the appendix to the chapter.

SELF-STUDY QUESTIONS

Answers are at the end of the chapter.

(SO 1) **1.** Which of the following is *not* a characteristic of a partnership?
  a. Taxable entity
  b. Co-ownership of property
  c. Mutual agency
  d. Limited life

(SO 1) **2.** The advantages of a partnership do *not* include:
  a. ease of formation.
  b. unlimited liability.
  c. freedom from government regulation.
  d. ease of decision making.

(SO 2) **3.** Upon formation of a partnership, each partner's initial investment of assets should be recorded at their:
  a. book values.
  b. cost.
  c. market values.
  d. appraised values.

(SO 3) **4.** The NBC Company reports net income of $60,000. If partners N, B, and C have an income ratio of 50%, 30%, and 20%, respectively, C's share of the net income is:
  a. $30,000.
  b. $12,000.
  c. $18,000.
  d. No correct answer is given.

(SO 3) **5.** Using the data in (4) above, what is B's share of net income if the percentages are applicable after each partner receives a $10,000 salary allowance?
  a. $12,000
  b. $20,000
  c. $19,000
  d. $21,000

(SO 4) **6.** Which of the following statements about partnership financial statements is true?
  a. Details of the distribution of net income are shown in the owners' equity statement.
  b. The distribution of net income is shown on the balance sheet.
  c. Only the total of all partner capital balances is shown in the balance sheet.
  d. The owners' equity statement is called the partners' capital statement.

(SO 4) **7.** In the liquidation of a partnership it is necessary to (1) distribute cash to the partners, (2) sell noncash assets, (3) allocate any gain or loss on realization to the partners, and (4) pay liabilities. These steps should be performed in the following order:
  a. (2), (3), (4), (1).
  b. (2), (3), (1), (4).
  c. (3), (2), (1), (4).
  d. (3), (2), (4), (1).

*8. Louisa Santiago purchases 50% of Leo Lemon's capital (SO interest in the K & L partnership for $22,000. If the capital balance of Kate Kildare and Leo Lemon are $40,000 and $30,000, respectively, Santiago's capital balance following the purchase is:
  a. $22,000.
  b. $35,000.
  c. $20,000.
  d. $15,000.

*9. Capital balances in the MEM partnership are Mary Capital (SO $60,000, Ellen Capital $50,000, and Mills Capital $40,000, and income ratios are 5 : 3 : 2, respectively. The MEMO partnership is formed by admitting Oleg to the firm with a cash investment of $60,000 for a 25% capital interest. The bonus to be credited to Mills Capital in admitting Oleg is:
  a. $10,000.
  b. $7,500.
  c. $3,750.
  d. $1,500.

*10. Capital balances in the MURF partnership are Molly (SO Capital $50,000, Ursula Capital $40,000, Ray Capital $30,000, and Fred Capital $20,000, and income ratios are 4 : 3 : 2 : 1, respectively. Fred withdraws from the firm following payment of $29,000 in cash from the partnership. Ursula's capital balance after recording the withdrawal of Fred is:
  a. $36,000.
  b. $37,000.
  c. $38,000.
  d. $40,000.

Go to the book's website,
www.wiley.com/college/weygandt,
for Additional Self-Study questions.

The Navigator

QUESTIONS

1. The characteristics of a partnership include the following: (a) association of individuals, (b) limited life, and (c) co-ownership of property. Explain each of these terms.

2. Jerry Kerwin is confused about the partnership characteristics of (a) mutual agency and (b) unlimited liability. Explain these two characteristics for Jerry.

3. Brent Houghton and Dick Kreibach are considering a business venture. They ask you to explain the advantages and disadvantages of the partnership form of organization.

4. Why might a company choose to use a limited partnership?

5. Sampson and Stevens form a partnership. Sampson contributes land with a book value of $50,000 and a fair market value of $65,000. Sampson also contributes equipment with a book value of $52,000 and a fair market value of $57,000. The partnership assumes a $20,000 mortgage on the land. What should be the balance in Sampson's capital account upon formation of the partnership?

6. W. Mantle, N. Cash, and W. DiMaggio have a partnership called Outlaws. A dispute has arisen among the partners. Mantle has invested twice as much in assets as the other two partners, and he believes net income and net losses should be shared in accordance with the capital ratios. The partnership agreement does not specify the division of profits and losses. How will net income and net loss be divided?

7. Blue and Grey are discussing how income and losses should be divided in a partnership they plan to form. What factors should be considered in determining the division of net income or net loss?

8. M. Carson and R. Leno have partnership capital balances of $40,000 and $80,000, respectively. The partnership agreement indicates that net income or net loss should be shared equally. If net income for the partnership is $36,000, how should the net income be divided?

9. S. McMurray and F. Kohl share net income and net loss equally. (a) Which account(s) is (are) debited and credited to record the division of net income between the partners? (b) If S. McMurray withdraws $30,000 in cash for personal use in lieu of salary, which account is debited and which is credited?

10. Partners T. Evans and R. Meloy are provided salary allowances of $30,000 and $25,000, respectively. They divide the remainder of the partnership income in a ratio of 60 : 40. If partnership net income is $45,000, how much is allocated to Evans and Meloy?

11. Are the financial statements of a partnership similar to those of a proprietorship? Discuss.

12. How does the liquidation of a partnership differ from the dissolution of a partnership?

13. Bobby Donal and Bill Spader are discussing the liquidation of a partnership. Bobby maintains that all cash should be distributed to partners on the basis of their income ratios. Is he correct? Explain.

14. In continuing their discussion from Question 13, Bill says that even in the case of a capital deficiency, all cash should still be distributed on the basis of capital balances. Is Bill correct? Explain.

15. Lowery, Keegan, and Feeney have income ratios of 5 : 3 : 2 and capital balances of $34,000, $31,000, and $28,000, respectively. Noncash assets are sold at a gain. After creditors are paid, $109,000 of cash is available for distribution to the partners. How much cash should be paid to Keegan?

16. Before the final distribution of cash, account balances are: Cash $23,000; S. Penn, Capital $19,000 (Cr.); L. Pattison, Capital $12,000 (Cr.); and M. Jeter, Capital $8,000 (Dr.). Jeter is unable to pay any of the capital deficiency. If the income-sharing ratios are 5 : 3 : 2, respectively, how much cash should be paid to L. Pattison?

*17. Linda Ratzlaff decides to purchase from an existing partner for $50,000 a one-third interest in a partnership. What effect does this transaction have on partnership net assets?

*18. Steve Renn decides to invest $25,000 in a partnership for a one-sixth capital interest. How much do the partnership's net assets increase? Does Renn also acquire a one-sixth income ratio through this investment?

*19. Kate Robidou purchases for $72,000 Grant's interest in the Sharon-Grant partnership. Assuming that Grant has a $66,000 capital balance in the partnership, what journal entry is made by the partnership to record this transaction?

*20. Tracy Harper has a $39,000 capital balance in a partnership. She sells her interest to Kim Remington for $45,000 cash. What entry is made by the partnership for this transaction?

*21. Debbie Perry retires from the partnership of Garland, Newlin, and Perry. She receives $85,000 of partnership assets in settlement of her capital balance of $77,000. Assuming that the income-sharing ratios are 5 : 3 : 2, respectively, how much of Perry's bonus is debited to Newlin's capital account?

*22. Your roommate argues that partnership assets should be revalued in situations like those in question 21. Why is this generally not done?

*23. How is a deceased partner's equity determined?

BRIEF EXERCISES

BE12-1 Jennifer DeVine and Stanley Farrin decide to organize the ALL-Star partnership. DeVine invests $15,000 cash, and Farrin contributes $10,000 cash and equipment having a book value of $3,500. Prepare the entry to record Farrin's investment in the partnership, assuming the equipment has a fair market value of $5,000.

Journalize entries in forming a partnership.

(SO 2)

Prepare portion of opening balance sheet for partnership.
(SO 2)

BE12-2 Beck and Cey decide to merge their proprietorships into a partnership called Fresh Start Company. The balance sheet of Cey Co. shows:

Accounts receivable	$16,000	
Less: Allowance for doubtful accounts	1,200	$14,800
Equipment	20,000	
Less: Accumulated depreciation	7,000	13,000

The partners agree that the net realizable value of the receivables is $13,500 and that the fair market value of the equipment is $11,000. Indicate how the four accounts should appear in the opening balance sheet of the partnership.

Journalize the division of net income using fixed income ratios.
(SO 3)

BE12-3 Held Bond Co. reports net income of $70,000. The income ratios are Held 60% and Bond 40%. Indicate the division of net income to each partner, and prepare the entry to distribute the net income.

Compute division of net income with a salary allowance and fixed ratios.
(SO 3)

BE12-4 ESU Co. reports net income of $55,000. Partner salary allowances are Espino $15,000, Sears $5,000, and Utech $5,000. Indicate the division of net income to each partner, assuming the income ratio is 50 : 30 : 20, respectively.

Show division of net income when allowances exceed net income.
(SO 3)

BE12-5 Joe & Sam Co. reports net income of $28,000. Interest allowances are Joe $7,000 and Sam $5,000; salary allowances are Joe $15,000 and Sam $10,000; the remainder is shared equally. Show the distribution of income on the income statement.

Journalize final cash distribution in liquidation.
(SO 5)

BE12-6 After liquidating noncash assets and paying creditors, account balances in the Heartley Co. are Cash $19,000, A Capital (Cr.) $8,000, L Capital (Cr.) $7,000, and F Capital (Cr.) $4,000. The partners share income equally. Journalize the final distribution of cash to the partners.

Journalize admission by purchase of an interest.
(SO 6)

*BE12-7 In Alpha Co. capital balances are: Ace $30,000, Bly $25,000, and Cox $20,000. The partners share income equally. Day is admitted to the firm by purchasing one-half of Cox's interest for $13,000. Journalize the admission of Day to the partnership.

Journalize admission by investment.
(SO 6)

*BE12-8 In Decker Co., capital balances are Menke $40,000 and Hibbett $50,000. The partners share income equally. Kosko is admitted to the firm with a 45% interest by an investment of cash of $52,000. Journalize the admission of Kosko. *0-142,000*

Journalize withdrawal paid by personal assets.
(SO 7)

*BE12-9 Capital balances in Midway Co. are Messer $40,000, Isch $30,000, and Denny $18,000. Messer and Isch each agree to pay Denny $12,000 from their personal assets. Messer and Isch each receive 50% of Denny's equity. The partners share income equally. Journalize the withdrawal of Denny.

Journalize withdrawal paid by partnership assets.
(SO 7)

*BE12-10 Data pertaining to Midway Co. are presented in BE12-9. Instead of payment from personal assets, assume that Denny receives $24,000 from partnership assets in withdrawing from the firm. Journalize the withdrawal of Denny.

EXERCISES

Identify characteristics of partnership.
(SO 1)

E12-1 Shani Davis has prepared the following list of statements about partnerships.

1. A partnership is an association of three or more persons to carry on as co-owners of a business for profit. *True False*
2. The legal requirements for forming a partnership can be quite burdensome. *False*
3. A partnership is not an entity for financial reporting purposes. *False*
4. The net income of a partnership is taxed as a separate entity. *False*
5. The act of any partner is binding on all other partners, even when partners perform business acts beyond the scope of their authority. *True*
6. Each partner is personally and individually liable for all partnership liabilities. *True*
7. When a partnership is dissolved, the assets legally revert to the original contributor. *False*
8. In a limited partnership, one or more partners have unlimited liability and one or more partners have limited liability for the debts of the firm. *True*
9. Mutual agency is a major advantage of the partnership form of business. *False disadvantage*

Instructions
Identify each statement on page 542 as true or false. If false, indicate how to correct the statement.

E12-2   K. Meissner, S. Cohen, and E. Hughes are forming a partnership. Meissner is transferring $50,000 of personal cash to the partnership. Cohen owns land worth $15,000 and a small building worth $80,000, which she transfers to the partnership. Hughes transfers to the partnership cash of $9,000, accounts receivable of $32,000 and equipment worth $19,000. The partnership expects to collect $29,000 of the accounts receivable.

Journalize entry for formation of a partnership.
(SO 2)

Instructions   202,000
(a) Prepare the journal entries to record each of the partners' investments.
(b) What amount would be reported as total owners' equity immediately after the investments?

E12-3   Jack Herington has owned and operated a proprietorship for several years. On January 1, he decides to terminate this business and become a partner in the firm of Herington and Kaspar. Herington's investment in the partnership consists of $12,000 in cash, and the following assets of the proprietorship: accounts receivable $14,000 less allowance for doubtful accounts of $2,000, and equipment $20,000 less accumulated depreciation of $4,000. It is agreed that the allowance for doubtful accounts should be $3,000 for the partnership. The fair market value of the equipment is $13,500.   36,500

Journalize entry for formation of a partnership.
(SO 2)

Instructions
Journalize Herington's admission to the firm of Kaspar and Herington.

E12-4   F. Calvert and G. Powers have capital balances on January 1 of $50,000 and $40,000, respectively. The partnership income-sharing agreement provides for (1) annual salaries of $20,000 for Calvert and $12,000 for Powers, (2) interest at 10% on beginning capital balances, and (3) remaining income or loss to be shared 60% by Calvert and 40% by Powers.

Prepare schedule showing distribution of net income and closing entry.
(SO 3)

Instructions
(a) Prepare a schedule showing the distribution of net income, assuming net income is (1) $50,000 and (2) $36,000.
(b) Journalize the allocation of net income in each of the situations above.

E12-5   O. Guillen (beginning capital, $60,000) and K. Williams (beginning capital $90,000) are partners. During 2008, the partnership earned net income of $70,000, and Guillen made drawings of $18,000 while Williams made drawings of $24,000.

Prepare journal entries to record allocation of net income.
(SO 3)

Instructions
(a) Assume the partnership income-sharing agreement calls for income to be divided 45% to Guillen and 55% to Williams. Prepare the journal entry to record the allocation of net income.
(b) Assume the partnership income-sharing agreement calls for income to be divided with a salary of $30,000 to Guillen and $25,000 to Williams, with the remainder divided 45% to Guillen and 55% to Williams. Prepare the journal entry to record the allocation of net income.
(c) Assume the partnership income-sharing agreement calls for income to be divided with a salary of $40,000 to Guillen and $35,000 to Williams, interest of 10% on beginning capital, and the remainder divided 50%–50%. Prepare the journal entry to record the allocation of net income.
(d) Compute the partners' ending capital balances under the assumption in part (c).

E12-6   For Starrite Co., beginning capital balances on January 1, 2008, are Gary Stark $20,000 and Jim Nyland $18,000. During the year, drawings were Stark $8,000 and Nyland $5,000. Net income was $30,000, and the partners share income equally.

Prepare partners' capital statement and partial balance sheet.
(SO 4)

Instructions
(a) Prepare the partners' capital statement for the year.
(b) Prepare the owners' equity section of the balance sheet at December 31, 2008.

E12-7   Moe, Larry, and Curly are forming The Stooges Partnership. Moe is transferring $30,000 of personal cash and equipment worth $25,000 to the partnership. Larry owns land worth $18,000 and a small building worth $75,000, which he transfers to the partnership. There is a long-term mortgage of $20,000 on the land and building, which the partnership assumes. Curly transfers cash of $7,000, accounts receivable of $36,000, supplies worth $3,000, and equipment worth $22,000 to the partnership. The partnership expects to collect $32,000 of the accounts receivable.

Prepare a classified balance sheet of a partnership.
(SO 4)

Instructions

Prepare a classified balance sheet for the partnership after the partners' investments on December 31, 2008.

Prepare cash distribution schedule.

(SO 5)

E12-8   The Best Company at December 31 has cash $20,000, noncash assets $100,000, liabilities $55,000, and the following capital balances: Rodriguez $45,000 and Escobedo $20,000. The firm is liquidated, and $110,000 in cash is received for the noncash assets. Rodriguez and Escobedo income ratios are 60% and 40%, respectively.

Instructions

Prepare a cash distribution schedule.

Journalize transactions in a liquidation.

(SO 5)

E12-9   Data for The Best partnership are presented in E12-8.

Instructions

Prepare the entries to record:

(a) The sale of noncash assets.
(b) The allocation of the gain or loss on liquidation to the partners.
(c) Payment of creditors.
(d) Distribution of cash to the partners.

Journalize transactions with a capital deficiency.

(SO 5)

E12-10   Prior to the distribution of cash to the partners, the accounts in the NJF Company are: Cash $28,000, Newell Capital (Cr.) $17,000, Jennings Capital (Cr.) $15,000, and Farley Capital (Dr.) $4,000. The income ratios are 5 : 3 : 2, respectively.

Instructions

(a) Prepare the entry to record (1) Farley's payment of $4,000 in cash to the partnership and (2) the distribution of cash to the partners with credit balances.
(b) Prepare the entry to record (1) the absorption of Farley's capital deficiency by the other partners and (2) the distribution of cash to the partners with credit balances.

Journalize admission of a new partner by purchase of an interest.

(SO 6)

E12-11   J. Lynn, M. Oller, and F. Tate share income on a 5 : 3 : 2 basis. They have capital balances of $30,000, $26,000, and $18,000, respectively, when Doc Duran is admitted to the partnership.

Instructions

Prepare the journal entry to record the admission of Doc Duran under each of the following assumptions.

(a) Purchase of 50% of Lynn's equity for $19,000.
(b) Purchase of 50% of Oller's equity for $12,000.
(c) Purchase of 33⅓% of Tate's equity for $9,000.

Journalize admission of a new partner by investment.

(SO 6)

E12-12   G. Olde and R. Young share income on a 6 : 4 basis. They have capital balances of $100,000 and $70,000, respectively, when K. Twener is admitted to the partnership.

Instructions

Prepare the journal entry to record the admission of K. Twener under each of the following assumptions.

(a) Investment of $90,000 cash for a 30% ownership interest with bonuses to the existing partners.
(b) Investment of $50,000 cash for a 30% ownership interest with a bonus to the new partner.

Journalize withdrawal of a partner with payment from partners' personal assets.

(SO 7)

E12-13   B. Cates, V. Elder, and S. Nguyen have capital balances of $50,000, $40,000, and $32,000, respectively. Their income ratios are 5 : 3 : 2. Nguyen withdraws from the partnership under each of the following independent conditions.

1. Cates and Elder agree to purchase Nguyen's equity by paying $17,000 each from their personal assets. Each purchaser receives 50% of Nguyen's equity.
2. Elder agrees to purchase all of Nguyen's equity by paying $22,000 cash from her personal assets.
3. Cates agrees to purchase all of Nguyen's equity by paying $26,000 cash from her personal assets.

Instructions

Journalize the withdrawal of Nguyen under each of the assumptions above.

*E12-14   H. Barrajas, T. Dingler, and R. Fisk have capital balances of $95,000, $75,000, and $60,000, respectively. They share income or loss on a 5 : 3 : 2 basis. Fisk withdraws from the partnership under each of the following conditions.

Journalize withdrawal of a partner with payment from partnership assets.

(SO 7)

1. Fisk is paid $68,000 in cash from partnership assets, and a bonus is granted to the retiring partner.
2. Fisk is paid $56,000 in cash from partnership assets, and bonuses are granted to the remaining partners.

Instructions
Journalize the withdrawal of Fisk under each of the assumptions above.

*E12-15   Carson, Letterman, and O'Brien are partners who share profits and losses 50%, 30%, and 20%, respectively. Their capital balances are $100,000, $60,000, and $40,000, respectively.

Journalize entry for admission and withdrawal of partners.

(SO 6, 7)

Instructions
(a) Assume Stewart joins the partnership by investing $80,000 for a 25% interest with bonuses to the existing partners. Prepare the journal entry to record his investment.
(b) Assume instead that Carson leaves the partnership. Carson is paid $120,000 with a bonus to the retiring partner. Prepare the journal entry to record Carson's withdrawal.

EXERCISES: SET B

Visit the book's website at **www.wiley.com/college/weygandt**, and choose the Student Companion site, to access Exercise Set B.

PROBLEMS: SET A

P12-1A   The post-closing trial balances of two proprietorships on January 1, 2008, are presented below.

Prepare entries for formation of a partnership and a balance sheet.

(SO 2, 4)

	Patrick Company		Samuelson Company	
	Dr.	**Cr.**	**Dr.**	**Cr.**
Cash	$ 14,000		$12,000	
Accounts receivable	17,500		26,000	
Allowance for doubtful accounts		$ 3,000		$ 4,400
Merchandise inventory	26,500		18,400	
Equipment	45,000		29,000	
Accumulated depreciation—equipment		24,000		11,000
Notes payable		18,000		15,000
Accounts payable		22,000		31,000
Patrick, Capital		36,000		
Samuelson, Capital				24,000
	$103,000	$103,000	$85,400	$85,400

Patrick and Samuelson decide to form a partnership, Pasa Company, with the following agreed upon valuations for noncash assets.

	Patrick Company	Samuelson Company
Accounts receivable	$17,500	$26,000
Allowance for doubtful accounts	4,500	4,000
Merchandise inventory	28,000	20,000
Equipment	23,000	16,000

All cash will be transferred to the partnership, and the partnership will assume all the liabilities of the two proprietorships. Further, it is agreed that Patrick will invest an additional $5,000 in cash, and Samuelson will invest an additional $19,000 in cash.

(a) Patrick, Capital $38,000
Samuelson, Capital
$24,000

(c) Total assets $172,000

Journalize divisions of net income and prepare a partners' capital statement.

(SO 3, 4)

(a) (1) Caplin $18,000
(2) Caplin $19,000
(3) Caplin $15,700

(c) Caplin $40,700

Prepare entries with a capital deficiency in liquidation of a partnership.

(SO 5)

Instructions

(a) Prepare separate journal entries to record the transfer of each proprietorship's assets and liabilities to the partnership.

(b) Journalize the additional cash investment by each partner.

(c) Prepare a balance sheet for the partnership on January 1, 2008.

P12-2A   At the end of its first year of operations on December 31, 2008, CNU Company's accounts show the following.

Partner	Drawings	Capital
Reese Caplin	$23,000	$48,000
Phyllis Newell	14,000	30,000
Betty Uhrich	10,000	25,000

The capital balance represents each partner's initial capital investment. Therefore, net income or net loss for 2008 has not been closed to the partners' capital accounts.

Instructions

(a) Journalize the entry to record the division of net income for the year 2008 under each of the following independent assumptions.

  (1) Net income is $30,000. Income is shared 6 : 3 : 1.

  (2) Net income is $37,000. Caplin and Newell are given salary allowances of $15,000 and $10,000, respectively. The remainder is shared equally.

  (3) Net income is $19,000. Each partner is allowed interest of 10% on beginning capital balances. Caplin is given a $12,000 salary allowance. The remainder is shared equally.

(b) Prepare a schedule showing the division of net income under assumption (3) above.

(c) Prepare a partners' capital statement for the year under assumption (3) above.

P12-3A   The partners in New Yorker Company decide to liquidate the firm when the balance sheet shows the following.

NEW YORKER COMPANY
Balance Sheet
May 31, 2008

Assets		Liabilities and Owners' Equity	
Cash	$ 27,500	Notes payable	$ 13,500
Accounts receivable	25,000	Accounts payable	27,000
Allowance for doubtful accounts	(1,000)	Wages payable	4,000
Merchandise inventory	34,500	M. Mantle, Capital	33,000
Equipment	21,000	W. Mays, Capital	21,000
Accumulated depreciation—equipment	(5,500)	D. Snider, Capital	3,000
Total	$101,500	Total	$101,500

The partners share income and loss 5 : 3 : 2. During the process of liquidation, the following transactions were completed in the following sequence.

1. A total of $55,000 was received from converting noncash assets into cash.

2. Liabilities were paid in full.

3. D. Snider paid his capital deficiency.

4. Cash was paid to the partners with credit balances.

Instructions

(a) Loss on realization
$19,000
Cash paid: to Mantle
$23,500; to Mays
$15,300

Journalize admission of a partner under different assumptions.

(SO 6)

(a) Prepare the entries to record the transactions.

(b) Post to the cash and capital accounts.

(c) Assume that Snider is unable to pay the capital deficiency.

  (1) Prepare the entry to allocate Snider's debit balance to Mantle and Mays.

  (2) Prepare the entry to record the final distribution of cash.

*P12-4A   At April 30, partners' capital balances in SKG Company are: S. Seger $52,000, J. Kensington $54,000, and T. Gomez $18,000. The income sharing ratios are 5:4:1, respectively. On May 1, the SKGA Company is formed by admitting D. Atchley to the firm as a partner.

Instructions

(a) Journalize the admission of Atchley under each of the following independent assumptions.

   (1) Atchley purchases 50% of Gomez's ownership interest by paying Gomez $16,000 in cash.

   (2) Atchley purchases 33⅓% of Kensington's ownership interest by paying Kensington $15,000 in cash.

   (3) Atchley invests $66,000 for a 30% ownership interest, and bonuses are given to the old partners.

   (4) Atchley invests $46,000 for a 30% ownership interest, which includes a bonus to the new partner.

(b) Kensington's capital balance is $32,000 after admitting Atchley to the partnership by investment. If Kensington's ownership interest is 20% of total partnership capital, what were (1) Atchley's cash investment and (2) the bonus to the new partner?

(a) (1) Atchley $9,000
(2) Atchley $18,000
(3) Atchley $57,000
(4) Atchley $51,000

*P12-5A   On December 31, the capital balances and income ratios in FAD Company are as follows.

Journalize withdrawal of a partner under different assumptions.

(SO 7)

Partner	Capital Balance	Income Ratio
J. Fagan	$60,000	50%
P. Ames	40,000	30%
K. Durham	26,000	20%

Instructions

(a) Journalize the withdrawal of Durham under each of the following assumptions.

   (1) Each of the continuing partners agrees to pay $18,000 in cash from personal funds to purchase Durham's ownership equity. Each receives 50% of Durham's equity.

   (2) Ames agrees to purchase Durham's ownership interest for $25,000 cash.

   (3) Durham is paid $34,000 from partnership assets, which includes a bonus to the retiring partner.

   (4) Durham is paid $22,000 from partnership assets, and bonuses to the remaining partners are recognized.

(b) If Ames's capital balance after Durham's withdrawal is $42,400 what were (1) the total bonus to the remaining partners and (2) the cash paid by the partnership to Durham?

(a) (1) Ames, Capital $13,000
(2) Ames, Capital $26,000
(3) Bonus $8,000
(4) Bonus $4,000

PROBLEMS: SET B

P12-1B   The post-closing trial balances of two proprietorships on January 1, 2008, are presented below.

Prepare entries for formation of a partnership and a balance sheet.

(SO 2, 4)

	Free Company		Will Company	
	Dr.	Cr.	Dr.	Cr.
Cash	$ 9,500		$ 6,000	
Accounts receivable	15,000		23,000	
Allowance for doubtful accounts		$ 2,500		$ 4,000
Merchandise inventory	28,000		17,000	
Equipment	50,000		30,000	
Accumulated depreciation—equipment		24,000		13,000
Notes payable		25,000		
Accounts payable		20,000		37,000
Free, Capital		31,000		
Will, Capital				22,000
	$102,500	$102,500	$76,000	$76,000

Free and Will decide to form a partnership, Free-Will Company, with the following agreed upon valuations for noncash assets.

	Free Company	Will Company
Accounts receivable	$15,000	$23,000
Allowance for doubtful accounts	3,500	5,000
Merchandise inventory	32,000	21,000
Equipment	28,000	18,000

All cash will be transferred to the partnership, and the partnership will assume all the liabilities of the two proprietorships. Further, it is agreed that Free will invest an additional $3,000 in cash, and Will will invest an additional $13,000 in cash.

Instructions

(a) Prepare separate journal entries to record the transfer of each proprietorship's assets and liabilities to the partnership.

(b) Journalize the additional cash investment by each partner.

(c) Prepare a balance sheet for the partnership on January 1, 2008.

(a) Free, Capital $36,000
Will, Capital $26,000

(c) Total assets $160,000

Journalize divisions of net income and prepare a partners' capital statement.

(SO 3, 4)

P12-2B At the end of its first year of operations on December 31, 2008, the RAF Company's accounts show the following.

Partner	Drawings	Capital
J. Reno	$12,000	$33,000
L. Augustine	9,000	20,000
J. Fritz	4,000	10,000

The capital balance represents each partner's initial capital investment. Therefore, net income or net loss for 2008 has not been closed to the partners' capital accounts.

Instructions

(a) Journalize the entry to record the division of net income for 2008 under each of the following independent assumptions.

(1) Net income is $40,000. Income is shared 5:3:2.

(2) Net income is $30,000. Reno and Augustine are given salary allowances of $11,000 and $10,000, respectively. The remainder is shared equally.

(3) Net income is $27,000. Each partner is allowed interest of 10% on beginning capital balances. Reno is given an $18,000 salary allowance. The remainder is shared equally.

(b) Prepare a schedule showing the division of net income under assumption (3) above.

(c) Prepare a partners' capital statement for the year under assumption (3) above.

(a) (1) Reno $20,000
(2) Reno $14,000
(3) Reno $22,200

(c) Reno $43,200

Prepare entries and schedule of cash payments in liquidation of a partnership

(SO 5)

P12-3B The partners in Shawnee Company decide to liquidate the firm when the balance sheet shows the following.

SHAWNEE COMPANY
Balance Sheet
April 30, 2008

Assets		Liabilities and Owners' Equity	
Cash	$28,000	Notes payable	$16,000
Accounts receivable	19,000	Accounts payable	24,000
Allowance for doubtful accounts	(1,000)	Wages payable	2,000
Merchandise inventory	28,000	Neeley, Capital	23,000
Equipment	17,000	Hannah, Capital	11,200
Accumulated depreciation—equipment	(10,000)	Doonan, Capital	4,800
Total	$81,000	Total	$81,000

The partners share income and loss 5:3:2. During the process of liquidation, the transactions below were completed in the following sequence.

1. A total of $43,000 was received from converting noncash assets into cash.
2. Liabilities were paid in full.
3. Cash was paid to the partners with credit balances.

Instructions

(a) Prepare a cash distribution schedule.

(b) Prepare the entries to record the transactions.

(c) Post to the cash and capital accounts.

(a) Loss on realization $10,000
Cash paid: to Neeley
$18,000; to Doonan $2,800

Journalize admission of a partner under different assumptions.

(SO 6)

*P12-4B At April 30, partners' capital balances in ANR Company are: Alexander $49,000. Norrison $26,000, and Rothlisberger $24,000. The income-sharing ratios are 5:3:2, respectively. On May 1, the ANRW Company is formed by admitting Wamser to the firm as a partner.

Instructions

(a) Journalize the admission of Wamser under each of the following independent assumptions.

    (1) Wamser purchases 50% of Rothlisberger's ownership interest by paying Rothlisberger $9,000 in cash.

    (2) Wamser purchases 50% of Norrison's ownership interest by paying Norrison $15,000 in cash.

    (3) Wamser invests $46,000 cash in the partnership for a 40% ownership interest that includes a bonus to the new partner.

    (4) Wamser invests $30,000 in the partnership for a 20% ownership interest, and bonuses are given to the old partners.

(b) Rothlisberger's capital balance is $27,000 after admitting Wamser to the partnership by investment. If Rothlisberger's ownership interest is 15% of total partnership capital, what were (1) Wamser's cash investment and (2) the total bonus to the old partners?

(a) (1) Wamser Capital
$12,000
(2) Wamser $13,000
(3) Wamser $58,000
(4) Wamser $25,800

*P12-5B   On December 31, the capital balances and income ratios in the Poker Company are as follows.

Journalize withdrawal of a partner under different assumptions.

(SO 7)

Partner	Capital Balance	Income Ratio
A. King	$70,000	60%
L. Queen	30,000	30
B. Jack	20,000	10

Instructions

(a) Journalize the withdrawal of Jack under each of the following independent assumptions.

    (1) Each of the remaining partners agrees to pay $13,000 in cash from personal funds to purchase Jack's ownership equity. Each receives 50% of Jack's equity.

    (2) Queen agrees to purchase Jack's ownership interest for $18,000 in cash.

    (3) From partnership assets, Jack is paid $26,000, which includes a bonus to the retiring partner.

    (4) Jack is paid $11,000 from partnership assets. Bonuses to the remaining partners are recognized.

(b) If Queen's capital balance after Jack's withdrawal is $32,000, what were (1) the total bonus to the remaining partners and (2) the cash paid by the partnership to Jack?

(a) (1) Queen, Capital $10,000
(2) Queen, Capital $20,000
(3) Bonus $6,000
(4) Bonus $9,000

PROBLEMS: SET C

Visit the book's website at **www.wiley.com/college/weygandt**, and choose the Student Companion site, to access Problem Set C.

CONTINUING COOKIE CHRONICLE

(*Note:* This is a continuation of the Cookie Chronicle from Chapters 1 through 11.)

CCC12   Natalie's high school friend, Katy Peterson, has been operating a bakery for approximately 18 months. Because Natalie has been so successful operating Cookie Creations, Katy would like to have Natalie become her partner. Katy believes that together they will create a thriving cookie-making business. Natalie is quite happy with her current business set-up. Up until now, she had not considered joining forces with anyone. However, Natalie thinks that it may be a good idea to establish a partnership with Katy, and decides to look into it.

Go to the book's website,
www.wiley.com/college/weygandt,
to see the completion of this problem.

BROADENING YOUR PERSPECTIVE

FINANCIAL REPORTING AND ANALYSIS

Exploring the Web

BYP12-1 This exercise is an introduction to the Big Four accounting firms, all of which are partnerships.

Addresses

Deloitte & Touche	**www.deloitte.com/**
Ernst & Young	**www.ey.com/**
KPMG	**www.us.kpmg.com/**
PricewaterhouseCoopers	**www.pw.com/**

or go to **www.wiley.com/college/weygandt**

Steps
1. Select a firm that is of interest to you.
2. Go to the firm's homepage.

Instructions
(a) Name two services provided by the firm.
(b) What is the firm's total annual revenue?
(c) How many clients does it service?
(d) How many people are employed by the firm?
(e) How many partners are there in the firm?

CRITICAL THINKING

Decision Making Across the Organization

BYP12-2 Richard Powers and Jane Keckley, two professionals in the finance area, have worked for Eberhart Leasing for a number of years. Eberhart Leasing is a company that leases high-tech medical equipment to hospitals. Richard and Jane have decided that, with their financial expertise, they might start their own company to provide consulting services to individuals interested in leasing equipment. One form of organization they are considering is a partnership.

If they start a partnership, each individual plans to contribute $50,000 in cash. In addition, Richard has a used IBM computer that originally cost $3,700, which he intends to invest in the partnership. The computer has a present market value of $1,500.

Although both Richard and Jane are financial wizards, they do not know a great deal about how a partnership operates. As a result, they have come to you for advice.

Instructions
With the class divided into groups, answer the following.

(a) What are the major disadvantages of starting a partnership?
(b) What type of document is needed for a partnership, and what should this document contain?
(c) Both Richard and Jane plan to work full-time in the new partnership. They believe that net income or net loss should be shared equally. However, they are wondering how they can provide compensation to Richard Powers for his additional investment of the computer. What would you tell them?
(d) Richard is not sure how the computer equipment should be reported on his tax return. What would you tell him?
(e) As indicated above, Richard and Jane have worked together for a number of years. Richard's skills complement Jane's and vice versa. If one of them dies, it will be very difficult for the other to maintain the business, not to mention the difficulty of paying the deceased partner's estate for his or her partnership interest. What would you advise them to do?

Communication Activity

BYP12-3   You are an expert in the field of forming partnerships. Daniel Ortman and Sue Stafford want to establish a partnership to start "Pasta Shop," and they are going to meet with you to discuss their plans. Prior to the meeting you will send them a memo discussing the issues they need to consider before their visit.

Instructions
Write a memo in good form to be sent to Ortman and Stafford.

Ethics Case

BYP12-4   Elizabeth and Laurie operate a beauty salon as partners who share profits and losses equally. The success of their business has exceeded their expectations; the salon is operating quite profitably. Laurie is anxious to maximize profits and schedules appointments from 8 a.m. to 6 p.m. daily, even sacrificing some lunch hours to accommodate regular customers. Elizabeth schedules her appointments from 9 a.m. to 5 p.m. and takes long lunch hours. Elizabeth regularly makes significantly larger withdrawals of cash than Laurie does, but, she says, "Laurie, you needn't worry, I never make a withdrawal without you knowing about it, so it is properly recorded in my drawing account and charged against my capital at the end of the year." Elizabeth's withdrawals to date are double Laurie's.

Instructions
(a) Who are the stakeholders in this situation?
(b) Identify the problems with Elizabeth's actions and discuss the ethical considerations of her actions.
(c) How might the partnership agreement be revised to accommodate the differences in Elizabeth's and Laurie's work and withdrawal habits?

"All About You" Activity

BYP12-5   As the **All About You** feature in this chapter (p. 530) indicates, the partnership form of organization has advantages and disadvantages. The chapter noted that different types of partnerships have been developed to minimize some of these disadvantages. Alternatively, an individual or company can choose the proprietorship or corporate form of organization.

Instructions
Go to two local businesses that are different, such as a restaurant, a retailer, a construction company, a professional office (dentist, doctor, etc.), and find the answers to the following questions.

(a) What form of organization do you use in your business?
(b) What do you believe are the two major advantages of this form of organization for your business?
(c) What do you believe are the two major disadvantages of this form of organization for your business?
(d) Do you believe that eventually you may choose another form of organization?
(e) Did you have someone help you form this organization (attorney, accountant, relative, etc.)?

Answers to Insight and Accounting Across the Organization Questions

p. 516 Limited Liability Companies Gain in Popularity
Q: Why do you think that the use of the limited liability company is gaining in popularity?
A: *The LLC is gaining in popularity because owners in such companies have limited liability for business debts even if they participate in management. As a result, the LLC form has a distinct advantage over regular partnerships. In addition, the other limited type partnerships discussed in Illustration 12-1 are restrictive as to their use. As a result, it is not surprising that limited liability companies are now often used as the form of organization when individuals want to set up a partnership.*

p. 518 How to Part Ways Nicely

Q: How can partnership conflicts be minimized and more easily resolved?

A: *First, it is important to develop a business plan that all parties agree to. Second, it is vital to have a well-thought-out partnership agreement. Third, it can be useful to set up a board of mutually agreed upon and respected advisors to consult when making critical decisions.*

p. 523 Start-Up Seeks to Share R&D Costs, and Profits

Q: What advantages does Curis achieve by forming agreements with other companies?

A: *Research and development for new pharmaceutical products can be extremely costly. In addition, product lawsuits from negative side-effects can completely wipe out a company. By forming agreements with much larger companies, Curis expands its research capabilities and legal defense resources.*

Authors' Comments on *All About You:* How Well Do You Know Your Partner? (p. 530)

The answer to this question depends in part on the cause of your friend's financial hardship. Was it bad luck, or irresponsibility? A high percentage of personal bankruptcies in the United States are the result of an inability to pay medical bills. If this was the case with your friend, then your concerns would be lessened. On the other hand, if the personal bankruptcy was the result of irresponsible spending, then perhaps your friend would not be a good person to own a business with.

If you do decide to form the business, you might need to consider a different organizational form to ensure that you do not get stuck with an undue portion of the legal liability. If limiting your legal liability is a concern, then you should investigate the option of forming a limited liability company. Under this form, you can avoid the legal liabilities of a partnership, but you can still get the benefits of partnership taxation, along with a very flexible organizational structure. This option is not available in all states, and is not allowable for certain types of businesses.

Answer to PepsiCo Review It Question 2, p. 518

Mutual agency, limited life, unlimited liability, and co-ownership of property are major characteristics of a partnership. As a company like PepsiCo becomes very large, it becomes difficult to remain as a partnership because of these factors. Unlimited liability is particularly troublesome because owners may lose not only their initial investment but also their personal assets, if those assets are needed to pay partnership creditors. Also, it is much easier to change owners of a corporation than it is to change owners in a partnership.

Answers to Self-Study Questions

1. a **2.** b **3.** c **4.** b **5.** c **6.** d **7.** a ***8.** d ***9.** d ***10.** b

Chapter 13

Corporations: Organization and Capital Stock Transactions

STUDY OBJECTIVES

After studying this chapter, you should be able to:

1 Identify the major characteristics of a corporation.
2 Differentiate between paid-in capital and retained earnings.
3 Record the issuance of common stock.
4 Explain the accounting for treasury stock.
5 Differentiate preferred stock from common stock.
6 Prepare a stockholders' equity section.
7 Compute book value per share.

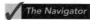 The Navigator

✔ The Navigator

Scan **Study Objectives**	▪
Read **Feature Story**	▪
Read **Preview**	▪
Read text and answer **Before You Go On** p. 562 ▪ p. 565 ▪ p. 568 ▪ p. 572 ▪ p. 576 ▪	
Work **Demonstration Problem**	▪
Review **Summary of Study Objectives**	▪
Answer **Self-Study Questions**	▪
Complete **Assignments**	▪

Feature Story

"HAVE YOU DRIVEN A FORD LATELY?"

A company that has produced such renowned successes as the Model T and the Mustang, and such a dismal failure as the Edsel, would have some interesting tales to tell. Henry Ford was a defiant visionary from the day he formed Ford Motor Company (*www.ford.com*) in 1903. His goal from day one was to design a car he could mass-produce and sell at a price that was affordable to the masses. In short order he accomplished this goal. By 1920,

60% of all vehicles on U.S. roads were Fords.

Henry Ford was intolerant of anything that stood between him and success. In the early years Ford had issued shares to the public in order to finance the company's exponential growth. In 1916 he decided not to pay a dividend in order to increase the funds available to expand the company.

The shareholders sued. Henry Ford's reaction was swift and direct: If the shareholders didn't see things his way, he would get rid of them. In 1919 the Ford family purchased 100 percent of the outstanding shares of Ford, eliminating any outside "interference." It was over 35 years before the company again issued shares to the public.

Ford Motor Company has continued to evolve and grow over the years into one of the largest international corporations. Today there are nearly a billion shares of publicly traded Ford stock outstanding. But some aspects of the company have changed very little: The chairman and chief executive of the company is a member of the Ford family. Also, the Ford family still retains a significant stake in Ford Motor Company. In a move Henry Ford might have supported, top management recently decided to centralize decision making—that is, to have more key decisions made by top management, rather than by division managers. And, reminiscent of Henry Ford's most famous car, the company is attempting to make a "global car"—a mass-produced car that can be sold around the world with only minor changes.

✓ *The Navigator*

Inside Chapter 13...

Corporations like Ford Motor Company have substantial resources. In fact, the corporation is the dominant form of business organization in the United States in terms of number of employees and dollar volume of sales and earnings. All of the 500 largest companies in the United States are corporations. In this chapter we will explain the essential features of a corporation and the accounting for a corporation's capital stock transactions. In Chapter 14 we will look at other issues related to accounting for corporations.

The content and organization of Chapter 13 are as follows.

Corporations: Organization and Capital Stock Transactions				
The Corporate Form of Organization	**Accounting for Common Stock Issues**	**Accounting for Treasury Stock**	**Preferred Stock**	**Statement Presentation and Analysis**
• Characteristics • Formation • Stockholder rights • Stock issue considerations • Corporate capital	• Issuing par value stock • Issuing no-par stock • Issuing stock for services or noncash assets	• Purchase of treasury stock • Disposal of treasury stock	• Dividend preferences • Liquidation preference	• Presentation • Analysis—Book value per share

The Navigator

THE CORPORATE FORM OF ORGANIZATION

In 1819, Chief Justice John Marshall defined a corporation as "an artificial being, invisible, intangible, and existing only in contemplation of law." This definition is the foundation for the prevailing legal interpretation that a **corporation** is an **entity separate and distinct from its owners**.

A corporation is created by law, and its continued existence depends upon the statutes of the state in which it is incorporated. As a legal entity, a corporation has most of the rights and privileges of a person. The major exceptions relate to privileges that only a living person can exercise, such as the right to vote or to hold public office. A corporation is subject to the same duties and responsibilities as a person. For example, it must abide by the laws, and it must pay taxes.

Two common ways to classify corporations are by purpose and by ownership. A corporation may be organized for the purpose of making a **profit**, or it may be **not-for-profit**. For-profit corporations include such well-known companies as McDonald's, Ford Motor Company, PepsiCo, and Google. Not-for-profit corporations are organized for charitable, medical, or educational purposes. Examples are the Salvation Army, the American Cancer Society, and the Bill & Melinda Gates Foundation.

Classification by **ownership** distinguishes between publicly held and privately held corporations. A **publicly held corporation** may have thousands of stockholders. Its stock is regularly traded on a national securities exchange such as the New York Stock Exchange. Most of the largest U.S. corporations are publicly held. Examples of publicly held corporations are Intel, IBM, Caterpillar Inc., and General Electric.

In contrast, a **privately held corporation** usually has only a few stockholders, and does not offer its stock for sale to the general public. Privately held companies are generally much smaller than publicly held companies, although some notable exceptions exist. Cargill Inc., a private corporation that trades in grain and other commodities, is one of the largest companies in the United States.

Characteristics of a Corporation

A number of characteristics distinguish corporations from proprietorships and partnerships. We explain the most important of these characteristics below.

STUDY OBJECTIVE 1

Identify the major characteristics of a corporation.

SEPARATE LEGAL EXISTENCE

As an entity separate and distinct from its owners, the corporation acts under its own name rather than in the name of its stockholders. Ford Motor Company may buy, own, and sell property. It may borrow money, and may enter into legally binding contracts in its own name. It may also sue or be sued, and it pays its own taxes.

Remember that in a partnership the acts of the owners (partners) bind the partnership. In contrast, the acts of its owners (stockholders) do not bind the corporation unless such owners are **agents** of the corporation. For example, if you owned shares of Ford Motor Company stock, you would not have the right to purchase automobile parts for the company unless you were appointed as an agent of the company, such as a purchasing manager.

Legal existence separate from owners

LIMITED LIABILITY OF STOCKHOLDERS

Since a corporation is a separate legal entity, creditors have recourse only to corporate assets to satisfy their claims. The liability of stockholders is normally limited to their investment in the corporation. Creditors have no legal claim on the personal assets of the owners unless fraud has occurred. Even in the event of bankruptcy, stockholders' losses are generally limited to their capital investment in the corporation.

Limited liability of stockholders

TRANSFERABLE OWNERSHIP RIGHTS

Shares of capital stock give ownership in a corporation. These shares are transferable units. Stockholders may dispose of part or all of their interest in a corporation simply by selling their stock. Remember that the transfer of an ownership interest in a partnership requires the consent of each owner. In contrast, the transfer of stock is entirely at the discretion of the stockholder. It does not require the approval of either the corporation or other stockholders.

The transfer of ownership rights between stockholders normally has no effect on the daily operating activities of the corporation. Nor does it affect the corporation's assets, liabilities, and total ownership equity. The transfer of these ownership rights is a transaction between individual owners. After it first issues the capital stock, the company does not participate in such transfers.

Transferable ownership rights

ABILITY TO ACQUIRE CAPITAL

It is relatively easy for a corporation to obtain capital through the issuance of stock. Investors buy stock in a corporation to earn money over time as the share price grows, and because a stockholder has limited liability and shares of stock are readily transferable. Also, individuals can become stockholders by investing relatively small amounts of money. In sum, the ability of a successful corporation to obtain capital is virtually unlimited.

Ability to acquire capital

CONTINUOUS LIFE

The life of a corporation is stated in its charter. The life may be perpetual, or it may be limited to a specific number of years. If it is limited, the company can extend the life through renewal of the charter. Since a corporation is a separate legal entity, its

Continuous life

continuance as a going concern is not affected by the withdrawal, death, or incapacity of a stockholder, employee, or officer. As a result, a successful enterprise can have a continuous and perpetual life.

CORPORATION MANAGEMENT

As in Ford Motor Company, stockholders legally own the corporation. But they manage the corporation indirectly through a board of directors they elect. The board, in turn, formulates the operating policies for the company. The board also selects officers, such as a president and one or more vice presidents, to execute policy and to perform daily management functions.

Illustration 13-1 presents a typical organization chart showing the delegation of responsibility. The chief executive officer (CEO) has overall responsibility for managing the business. As the organization chart shows, the CEO delegates responsibility to other officers.

Illustration 13-1
Corporation organization chart

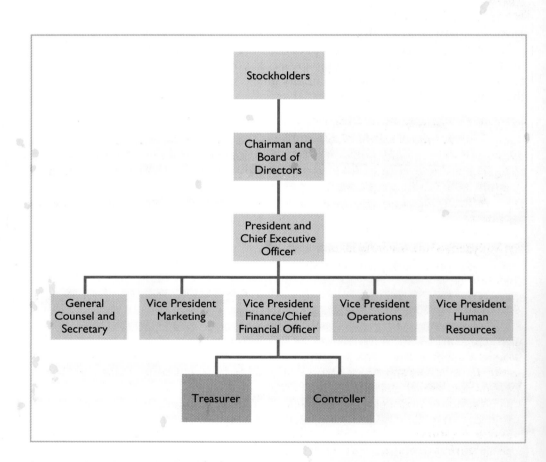

The chief accounting officer is the **controller**. The controller's responsibilities include (1) maintaining the accounting records, (2) maintaining an adequate system of internal control, and (3) preparing financial statements, tax returns, and internal reports. The **treasurer** has custody of the corporation's funds and is responsible for maintaining the company's cash position.

The organizational structure of a corporation enables a company to hire professional managers to run the business. On the other hand, the separation of ownership and management prevents owners from having an active role in managing the company, which some owners like to have.

ETHICS NOTE

Managers who are not owners are often compensated based on the performance of the firm. They thus may be tempted to exaggerate firm performance by inflating income figures.

ETHICS INSIGHT

Directors Take on More Accountability

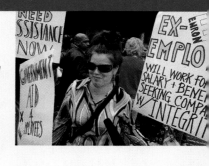

In the wake of Enron's collapse, the members of Enron's board of directors were questioned and scrutinized to determine what they knew, and when they knew it. A *Wall Street Journal* story reported that Enron's board contends it was "kept in the dark" by management and by Arthur Andersen—Enron's longtime auditors—and didn't learn about the company's troublesome accounting until October 2001. But, the *Wall Street Journal* reported that according to outside attorneys, "directors on at least two occasions waived Enron's ethical code of conduct to approve partnerships between Enron and its chief financial officer. Those partnerships kept significant debt off of Enron's books and masked actual company finances."

Since Enron's demise, passage of the Sarbanes-Oxley Act and proposals by the SEC and the stock exchanges have created a new corporate-governance climate: Stronger boards, with more independent directors, are now in favor.

Source: Carol Hymowitz, "Serving on a Board Now Means Less Talk, More Accountability," *Wall Street Journal*, January 29, 2002.

? Was Enron's board of directors fulfilling its role in a corporate organization when it waived Enron's ethical code on two occasions?

GOVERNMENT REGULATIONS

A corporation is subject to numerous state and federal regulations. State laws usually prescribe the requirements for issuing stock, the distributions of earnings permitted to stockholders, and the effects of retiring stock. Federal securities laws govern the sale of capital stock to the general public. Also, most publicly held corporations are required to make extensive disclosure of their financial affairs to the Securities and Exchange Commission (SEC) through quarterly and annual reports. In addition, when a corporation lists its stock on organized securities exchanges, it must comply with the reporting requirements of these exchanges. Government regulations are designed to protect the owners of the corporation.

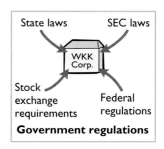

ADDITIONAL TAXES

Neither proprietorships nor partnerships pay income taxes separate from the owner's share of earnings. Sole proprietors and partners report earnings on their personal income tax returns and pay taxes on this amount. Corporations, on the other hand, must pay federal and state income taxes **as a separate legal entity**. These taxes are substantial.

In addition, stockholders must pay taxes on cash dividends (pro rata distributions of net income). Thus, many argue that the government taxes corporate income **twice (double taxation)**—once at the corporate level, and again at the individual level.

In summary, we can identify the following advantages and disadvantages of a corporation compared to a proprietorship and a partnership.

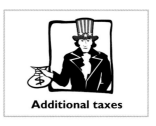

Additional taxes

Advantages	Disadvantages
Separate legal existence	Corporation management—separation of
Limited liability of stockholders	ownership and management
Transferable ownership rights	Government regulations
Ability to acquire capital	Additional taxes
Continuous life	
Corporation management—professional	
managers	

Illustration 13-2
Advantages and disadvantages of a corporation

Forming a Corporation

The initial step in forming a corporation is to file an application with the Secretary of State in the state in which incorporation is desired. The application contains such information as: (1) the name and purpose of the proposed corporation; (2) amounts, kinds, and number of shares of capital stock to be authorized; (3) the names of the incorporators; and (4) the shares of stock to which each has subscribed.

After the state approves the application, it grants a **charter**. The charter may be an approved copy of the application form, or it may be a separate document containing the same basic data. The issuance of the charter creates the corporation. Upon receipt of the charter, the corporation develops its by-laws. The **by-laws** establish the internal rules and procedures for conducting the affairs of the corporation. They also indicate the powers of the stockholders, directors, and officers of the enterprise.[1]

ALTERNATIVE TERMINOLOGY

The charter is often referred to as the *articles of incorporation.*

Regardless of the number of states in which a corporation has operating divisions, it is incorporated in only one state. It is to the company's advantage to incorporate in a state whose laws are favorable to the corporate form of business organization. General Motors, for example, is incorporated in Delaware, whereas Qualcomm is a New Jersey corporation. Many corporations choose to incorporate in states with rules favorable to existing management. For example, Gulf Oil at one time changed its state of incorporation to Delaware to thwart possible unfriendly takeovers. There, state law allows boards of directors to approve certain defensive tactics against takeovers without a vote by shareholders.

Corporations engaged in interstate commerce must also obtain a license from each state in which they do business. The license subjects the corporation's operating activities to the corporation laws of the state.

Costs incurred in the formation of a corporation are called **organization costs**. These costs include legal and state fees, and promotional expenditures involved in the organization of the business. **Corporations expense organization costs as incurred.** To determine the amount and timing of future benefits is so difficult that it is standard procedure to take a conservative approach of expensing these costs immediately.

Ownership Rights of Stockholders

When chartered, the corporation may begin selling ownership rights in the form of shares of stock. When a corporation has only one class of stock, it is **common stock**. Each share of common stock gives the stockholder the ownership rights pictured in Illustration 13-3. A corporation's articles of incorporation or its by-laws state the ownership rights of a share of stock.

Proof of stock ownership is evidenced by a form known as a **stock certificate**. As Illustration 13-4 shows, the face of the certificate shows the name of the corporation, the stockholder's name, the class and special features of the stock, the number of shares owned, and the signatures of authorized corporate officials. Prenumbered certificates facilitate accountability. They may be issued for any quantity of shares.

---

[1]Following approval by two-thirds of the stockholders, the by-laws become binding upon all stockholders, directors, and officers. Legally, a corporation is regulated first by the laws of the state, second by its charter, and third by its by-laws. Corporations must take care to ensure that the provisions of the by-laws are not in conflict with either state laws or the charter.

Stockholders have the right to:

1. Vote in election of board of directors at annual meeting and vote on actions that require stockholder approval.

2. Share the corporate earnings through receipt of dividends.

3. Keep the same percentage ownership when new shares of stock are issued (**preemptive right**[2]).

4. Share in assets upon liquidation in proportion to their holdings. This is called a **residual claim:** owners are paid with assets that remain after all creditors' claims have been paid.

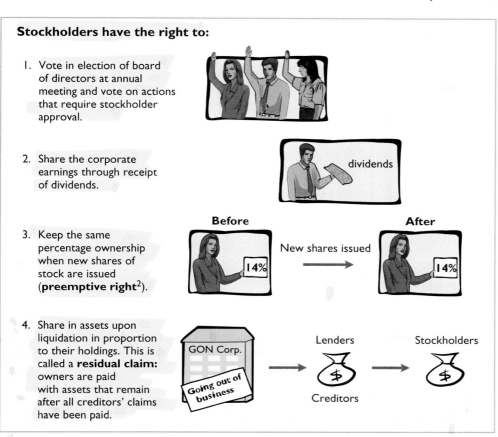

Illustration 13-3
Ownership rights of stockholders

Illustration 13-4
A stock certificate

---

[2]A number of companies have eliminated the preemptive right, because they believe it makes an unnecessary and cumbersome demand on management. For example, by stockholder approval, IBM has dropped its preemptive right for stockholders.

Before You Go On...

REVIEW IT

1. What are the advantages and disadvantages of a corporation compared to a proprietorship and a partnership?
2. Identify the principal steps in forming a corporation.
3. What rights are inherent in owning a share of stock in a corporation?

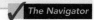 The Navigator

Stock Issue Considerations

In considering the issuance of stock, a corporation must resolve a number of basic questions: How many shares should it authorize for sale? How should it issue the stock? At what price should it issue the shares? What value should the corporation assign to the stock? These questions are addressed in the following sections.

AUTHORIZED STOCK

The charter indicates the amount of stock that a corporation is **authorized** to sell. The total amount of authorized stock at the time of incorporation normally anticipates both initial and subsequent capital needs. As a result, the number of shares authorized generally exceeds the number initially sold. If it sells all authorized stock, a corporation must obtain consent of the state to amend its charter before it can issue additional shares.

The authorization of capital stock does not result in a formal accounting entry. This event has no immediate effect on either corporate assets or stockholders' equity. However, the number of authorized shares is often reported in the stockholders' equity section. It is then simple to determine the number of unissued shares that the corporation can issue without amending the charter: subtract the total shares issued from the total authorized. For example, if Advanced Micro was authorized to sell 100,000 shares of common stock and issued 80,000 shares, 20,000 shares would remain unissued.

ISSUANCE OF STOCK

A corporation can issue common stock **directly** to investors. Or it can issue the stock **indirectly** through an investment banking firm that specializes in bringing securities to market. Direct issue is typical in closely held companies. Indirect issue is customary for a publicly held corporation.

In an indirect issue, the investment banking firm may agree to **underwrite** the entire stock issue. In this arrangement, the investment banker buys the stock from the corporation at a stipulated price and resells the shares to investors. The corporation thus avoids any risk of being unable to sell the shares. Also, it obtains immediate use of the cash received from the underwriter. The investment banking firm, in turn, assumes the risk of reselling the shares, in return for an underwriting fee.[3] For example, Google (the world's number 1 Internet search engine) used underwriters when it issued a highly successful initial public offering, raising $1.67 billion. The underwriters charged a 3% underwriting fee (approximately $50 million) on Google's stock offering.

How does a corporation set the price for a new issue of stock? Among the factors to be considered are: (1) the company's anticipated future earnings, (2) its

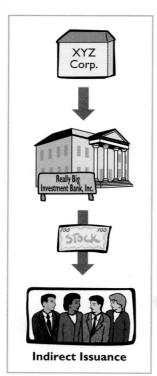

Indirect Issuance

---

[3]Alternatively, the investment banking firm may agree only to enter into a **best-efforts** contract with the corporation. In such cases, the banker agrees to sell as many shares as possible at a specified price. The corporation bears the risk of unsold stock. Under a best-efforts arrangement, the banking firm is paid a fee or commission for its services.

expected dividend rate per share, (3) its current financial position, (4) the current state of the economy, and (5) the current state of the securities market. The calculation can be complex and is properly the subject of a finance course.

MARKET VALUE OF STOCK

The stock of publicly held companies is traded on organized exchanges. The interaction between buyers and sellers determines the prices per share. In general, the prices set by the marketplace tend to follow the trend of a company's earnings and dividends. But, factors beyond a company's control, such as an oil embargo, changes in interest rates, and the outcome of a presidential election, may cause day-to-day fluctuations in market prices.

INVESTOR INSIGHT

How to Read Stock Quotes

The volume of trading on national and international exchanges is heavy. Shares in excess of a billion are often traded daily on the New York Stock Exchange (NYSE) alone. For each listed stock, the *Wall Street Journal* and other financial media report the total volume of stock traded for a given day, the high and low price for the day, the closing market price, and the net change for the day. A recent stock quote for PepsiCo, listed on the NYSE under the ticker symbol PEP, is shown below.

Stock	Volume	High	Low	Close	Net Change
PepsiCo	4,305,600	60.30	59.32	60.02	+0.41

These numbers indicate that PepsiCo's trading volume was 4,305,600 shares. The high, low, and closing prices for that date were $60.30, $59.32, and $60.02, respectively. The net change for the day was an increase of $0.41 per share.

? For stocks traded on organized stock exchanges, how are the dollar prices per share established? What factors might influence the price of shares in the marketplace?

The trading of capital stock on securities exchanges involves the transfer of **already issued shares** from an existing stockholder to another investor. These transactions have **no impact** on a corporation's stockholders' equity.

PAR AND NO-PAR VALUE STOCKS

Par value stock is capital stock to which the charter has assigned a value per share. Years ago, par value determined the **legal capital** per share that a company must retain in the business for the protection of corporate creditors; that amount was not available for withdrawal by stockholders. Thus, in the past, most states required the corporation to sell its shares at par or above.

However, par value was often immaterial relative to the value of the company's stock—even at the time of issue. Thus, its usefulness as a protective device to creditors was questionable. For example, Reebok's par value is $0.01 per share, yet a new issue in 2006 would have sold at a **market value** in the $33 per share range. Thus, par has no relationship with market value; in the vast majority of cases, it is an immaterial amount. As a consequence, today many states do not require a par value. Instead, they use other means to determine legal capital to protect creditors.

No-par value stock is capital stock to which the charter has not assigned a value. No-par value stock is quite common today. For example, Nike, Procter & Gamble, and North American Van Lines all have no-par stock. In many states the board of directors assigns a **stated value** to no-par shares.

Corporate Capital

Owners' equity is identified by various names: **stockholders' equity**, **shareholders' equity**, or **corporate capital**. The stockholders' equity section of a corporation's balance sheet consists of two parts: (1) paid-in (contributed) capital and (2) retained earnings (earned capital).

The distinction between **paid-in capital** and **retained earnings** is important from both a legal and a financial point of view. Legally, corporations can make distributions of earnings (declare dividends) out of retained earnings in all states. However, in many states they cannot declare dividends out of paid-in capital. Management, stockholders, and others often look to retained earnings for the continued existence and growth of the corporation.

PAID-IN CAPITAL

Paid-in capital is the total amount of cash and other assets paid in to the corporation by stockholders in exchange for capital stock. As noted earlier, when a corporation has only one class of stock, it is **common stock**.

RETAINED EARNINGS

Retained earnings is net income that a corporation retains for future use. Net income is recorded in Retained Earnings by a closing entry that debits Income Summary and credits Retained Earnings. For example, assuming that net income for Delta Robotics in its first year of operations is $130,000, the closing entry is:

A	=	L	+	SE
				−130,000 Inc
				+130,000 RE

Cash Flows
no effect

Income Summary	130,000	
Retained Earnings		130,000
(To close Income Summary and transfer net income		
to retained earnings)		

If Delta Robotics has a balance of $800,000 in common stock at the end of its first year, its stockholders' equity section is as follows.

Illustration 13-5
Stockholders' equity section

DELTA ROBOTICS
Balance Sheet (partial)

Stockholders' equity		
Paid-in capital		
Common stock	$800,000	
Retained earnings	130,000	
Total stockholders' equity		$930,000

The following illustration compares the owners' equity (stockholders' equity) accounts reported on a balance sheet for a proprietorship, a partnership, and a corporation.

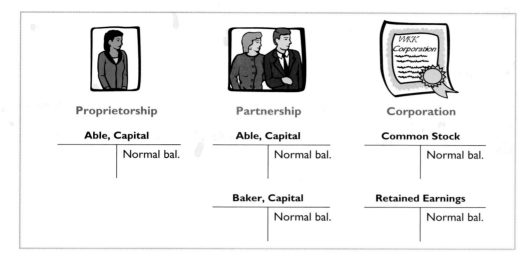

Illustration 13-6
Comparison of owners' equity accounts

Before You Go On...

REVIEW IT
1. Of what significance to a corporation is the amount of authorized stock?
2. What alternative approaches may a corporation use in issuing stock?
3. Distinguish between par value and market value.

DO IT
At the end of its first year of operation, Doral Corporation has $750,000 of common stock and net income of $122,000. Prepare (a) the closing entry for net income and (b) the stockholders' equity section at year-end.

Action Plan
■ Record net income in Retained Earnings by a closing entry in which Income Summary is debited and Retained Earnings is credited.
■ In the stockholders' equity section, show (1) paid-in capital and (2) retained earnings.

Solution
(a) Income Summary | 122,000 |
    Retained Earnings | | 122,000
      (To close Income Summary and transfer net income to retained earnings)

(b) Stockholders' equity
  Paid-in capital
    Common stock $750,000
  Retained earnings   122,000
    Total stockholders' equity $872,000

Related exercise material: *BE13-2.*

The Navigator

ACCOUNTING FOR COMMON STOCK ISSUES

Let's now look at how to account for issues of common stock. The primary objectives in accounting for the issuance of common stock are: (1) to identify the specific sources of paid-in capital, and (2) to maintain the

STUDY OBJECTIVE 3
Record the issuance of common stock.

distinction between paid-in capital and retained earnings. **The issuance of common stock affects only paid-in capital accounts.**

Issuing Par Value Common Stock for Cash

As discussed earlier, par value does not indicate a stock's market value. Therefore, the cash proceeds from issuing par value stock may be equal to, greater than, or less than par value. When the company records issuance of common stock for cash, it credits to Common Stock the par value of the shares. It records in a separate paid-in capital account the portion of the proceeds that is above or below par value.

To illustrate, assume that Hydro-Slide, Inc. issues 1,000 shares of $1 par value common stock at par for cash. The entry to record this transaction is:

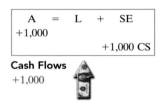

Cash	1,000	
Common Stock		1,000
(To record issuance of 1,000 shares of $1 par common stock at par)		

If Hydro-Slide issues an additional 1,000 shares of the $1 par value common stock for cash at $5 per share, the entry is:

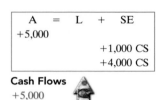

Cash	5,000	
Common Stock		1,000
Paid-in Capital in Excess of Par Value		4,000
(To record issuance of 1,000 shares of $1 par common stock)		

The total paid-in capital from these two transactions is $6,000, and the legal capital is $2,000. Assuming Hydro-Slide, Inc. has retained earnings of $27,000, Illustration 13-7 shows the company's stockholders' equity section.

Illustration 13-7
Stockholders' equity—paid-in capital in excess of par value

HYDRO-SLIDE, INC.	
Balance Sheet (partial)	
Stockholders' equity	
Paid-in capital	
Common stock	$ 2,000
Paid-in capital in excess of par value	**4,000**
Total paid-in capital	6,000
Retained earnings	27,000
Total stockholders' equity	$33,000

ALTERNATIVE TERMINOLOGY

Paid-in Capital in Excess of Par is also called *Premium on Stock.*

When a corporation issues stock for less than par value, it debits the account Paid-in Capital in Excess of Par Value, if a credit balance exists in this account. If a credit balance does not exist, then the corporation debits to Retained Earnings the amount less than par. This situation occurs only rarely: Most states do not permit the sale of common stock below par value, because stockholders may be held personally liable for the difference between the price paid upon original sale and par value.

Issuing No-Par Common Stock for Cash

When no-par common stock has a stated value, the entries are similar to those illustrated for par value stock. The corporation credits the stated value to Common Stock. Also, when the selling price of no-par stock exceeds stated value, the corporation credits the excess to Paid-in Capital in Excess of Stated Value.

For example, assume that instead of $1 par value stock, Hydro-Slide, Inc. has $5 stated value no-par stock and the company issues 5,000 shares at $8 per share for cash. The entry is:

Cash	40,000	
Common Stock		25,000
Paid-in Capital in Excess of Stated Value		15,000
(To record issue of 5,000 shares of $5 stated value no-		
par stock)		

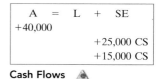

A = L + SE
+40,000
            +25,000 CS
            +15,000 CS

Cash Flows
+40,000

Hydro-Slide, Inc. reports Paid-in Capital in Excess of Stated Value as part of paid-in capital in the stockholders' equity section.

What happens when no-par stock does not have a stated value? In that case, the corporation credits the entire proceeds to Common Stock. Thus, if Hydro-Slide does not assign a stated value to its no-par stock, it would record the issuance of the 5,000 shares at $8 per share for cash as follows.

Cash	40,000	
Common Stock		40,000
(To record issue of 5,000 shares of no-par stock)		

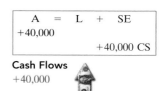

A = L + SE
+40,000
            +40,000 CS

Cash Flows
+40,000

Issuing Common Stock for Services or Noncash Assets

Corporations also may issue stock for services (compensation to attorneys or consultants) or for noncash assets (land, buildings, and equipment). In such cases, what cost should be recognized in the exchange transaction? To comply with the **cost principle**, in a noncash transaction **cost is the cash equivalent price**. Thus, **cost is either the fair market value of the consideration given up, or the fair market value of the consideration received**, whichever is more clearly determinable.

To illustrate, assume that attorneys have helped Jordan Company incorporate. They have billed the company $5,000 for their services. They agree to accept 4,000 shares of $1 par value common stock in payment of their bill. At the time of the exchange, there is no established market price for the stock. In this case, the market value of the consideration received, $5,000, is more clearly evident. Accordingly, Jordan Company makes the following entry:

Organization Expense	5,000	
Common Stock		4,000
Paid-in Capital in Excess of Par Value		1,000
(To record issuance of 4,000 shares of $1 par value		
stock to attorneys)		

A = L + SE
            −5,000 Exp
            +4,000 CS
            +1,000 CS

Cash Flows
no effect

As explained on page 560, organization costs are expensed as incurred.

In contrast, assume that Athletic Research Inc. is an existing publicly held corporation. Its $5 par value stock is actively traded at $8 per share. The company issues 10,000 shares of stock to acquire land recently advertised for sale at $90,000. The most clearly evident value in this noncash transaction is the market price of the consideration given, $80,000. The company records the transaction as follows.

Land	80,000	
Common Stock		50,000
Paid-in Capital in Excess of Par Value		30,000
(To record issuance of 10,000 shares of $5 par value		
stock for land)		

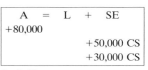

A = L + SE
+80,000
            +50,000 CS
            +30,000 CS

Cash Flows
no effect

As illustrated in these examples, **the par value of the stock is never a factor in determining the cost of the assets received**. This is also true of the stated value of no-par stock.

Before You Go On...

REVIEW IT

1. Explain the accounting for par and no-par common stock issued for cash.
2. Explain the accounting for the issuance of stock for services or noncash assets.
3. What is the par or stated value per share of PepsiCo's common stock? How many shares has PepsiCo issued at December 31, 2005? The answers to these questions appear on page 593.

DO IT

Cayman Corporation begins operations on March 1 by issuing 100,000 shares of $10 par value common stock for cash at $12 per share. On March 15 it issues 5,000 shares of common stock to attorneys in settlement of their bill of $50,000 for organization costs. Journalize the issuance of the shares, assuming the stock is not publicly traded.

Action Plan

■ In issuing shares for cash, credit Common Stock for par value per share.
■ Credit any additional proceeds in excess of par value to a separate paid-in capital account.
■ When stock is issued for services, use the cash equivalent price.
■ For the cash equivalent price use either the fair market value of what is given up or the fair market value of what is received, whichever is more clearly determinable.

Solution

Mar. 1	Cash	1,200,000	
	Common Stock		1,000,000
	Paid-in Capital in Excess of Par Value		200,000
	(To record issuance of 100,000 shares at $12 per share)		
Mar. 15	Organization Expense	50,000	
	Common Stock		50,000
	(To record issuance of 5,000 shares for attorneys' fees)		

Related exercise material: *BE13-3, BE13-4, BE13-5, E13-3, E13-4, and E13-6.*

✓ The Navigator

ACCOUNTING FOR TREASURY STOCK

STUDY OBJECTIVE 4

Explain the accounting for treasury stock.

Treasury stock is a corporation's own stock that it has issued and subsequently reacquired from shareholders, but not retired. A corporation may acquire treasury stock for various reasons:

1. To reissue the shares to officers and employees under bonus and stock compensation plans.
2. To signal to the stock market that management believes the stock is underpriced, in the hope of enhancing its market value.

3. To have additional shares available for use in the acquisition of other companies.

4. To reduce the number of shares outstanding and thereby increase earnings per share.

5. To rid the company of disgruntled investors, perhaps to avoid a takeover, as illustrated in the Ford Motor Company Feature Story.

HELPFUL HINT

Treasury shares do not have dividend rights or voting rights.

Many corporations have treasury stock. One survey of 600 U.S. companies found that approximately two-thirds have treasury stock.[4] Buybacks are becoming more popular. For example, ExxonMobil Corp., Microsoft Corp., and Time Warner Inc. purchased a combined $14.37 billion of their shares in the first quarter of 2005.

Purchase of Treasury Stock

Companies generally account for treasury stock by **the cost method**. This method uses the cost of the shares purchased to value the treasury stock. Under the cost method, the company debits **Treasury Stock** for the **price paid to reacquire the shares**.

When the company disposes of the shares, it credits to Treasury Stock **the same amount** it paid to reacquire the shares. To illustrate, assume that on January 1, 2008, the stockholders' equity section of Mead, Inc. has 100,000 shares of $5 par value common stock outstanding (all issued at par value) and Retained Earnings of $200,000. The stockholders' equity section before purchase of treasury stock is as follows.

MEAD, INC. Balance Sheet (partial)		
Stockholders' equity		
Paid-in capital		
Common stock, $5 par value, 100,000 shares		
issued and outstanding	$500,000	
Retained earnings	200,000	
Total stockholders' equity	$700,000	

Illustration 13-8
Stockholders' equity with no treasury stock

On February 1, 2008, Mead acquires 4,000 shares of its stock at $8 per share. The entry is:

Feb. 1	Treasury Stock	32,000	
	Cash		32,000
	(To record purchase of 4,000 shares of treasury stock at $8 per share)		

A	=	L	+	SE
				−32,000 TS
−32,000				

Cash Flows
−32,000

Note that Mead debits Treasury Stock for the cost of the shares purchased. Is the original paid-in capital account, Common Stock, affected? No, because the number of issued shares does not change. In the stockholders' equity section of the balance sheet, Mead deducts treasury stock from total paid-in capital and retained earnings. Treasury Stock is a **contra stockholders' equity account**. Thus, the acquisition of treasury stock reduces stockholders' equity.

[4]*Accounting Trends & Techniques 2005* (New York: American Institute of Certified Public Accountants).

The stockholders' equity section of Mead, Inc. after purchase of treasury stock is as follows.

Illustration 13-9
Stockholders' equity with treasury stock

MEAD, INC. Balance Sheet (partial)	
Stockholders' equity	
Paid-in capital	
Common stock, $5 par value, 100,000 shares issued and 96,000 shares outstanding	$500,000
Retained earnings	200,000
Total paid-in capital and retained earnings	700,000
Less: Treasury stock (4,000 shares)	**32,000**
Total stockholders' equity	$668,000

ETHICS NOTE

The purchase of treasury stock reduces the cushion for creditors and preferred stockholders. A restriction for the cost of treasury stock purchased is often required. The restriction is usually applied to retained earnings.

In the balance sheet, Mead discloses both the number of shares issued (100,000) and the number in the treasury (4,000). The difference between these two amounts is the number of shares of stock outstanding (96,000). The term **outstanding stock** means the number of shares of issued stock that are being held by stockholders.

Some maintain that companies should report treasury stock as an asset because it can be sold for cash. Under this reasoning, companies should also show unissued stock as an asset, clearly an erroneous conclusion. Rather than being an asset, treasury stock reduces stockholder claims on corporate assets. This effect is correctly shown by reporting treasury stock as a deduction from total paid-in capital and retained earnings.

ACCOUNTING ACROSS THE ORGANIZATIO

Why Did Reebok Buy Its Own Stock?

In a bold (and some would say risky) move, Reebok at one time bought back nearly a *third* of its shares. This repurchase of shares dramatically reduced Reebok's available cash. In fact, the company borrowed significant funds to accomplish the repurchase. In a press release, management stated that it was repurchasing the shares because it believed its stock was severely underpriced. The repurchase of so many shares was meant to signal management's belief in good future earnings.

Skeptics, however, suggested that Reebok's management was repurchasing shares to make it less likely that another company would acquire Reebok (in which case Reebok's top managers would likely lose their jobs). By depleting its cash, Reebok became a less likely acquisition target. Acquiring companies like to purchase companies with large cash balances so they can pay off debt used in the acquisition.

? What signal might a large stock repurchase send to investors regarding management's belief about the company's growth opportunities?

Disposal of Treasury Stock

Treasury stock is usually sold or retired. The accounting for its sale differs when treasury stock is sold above cost than when it is sold below cost.

SALE OF TREASURY STOCK ABOVE COST

If the selling price of the treasury shares is equal to their cost, the company records the sale of the shares by a debit to Cash and a credit to Treasury Stock. When the selling price of the shares is greater than their cost, the company credits the difference to Paid-in Capital from Treasury Stock.

To illustrate, assume that on July 1, Mead sells for $10 per share the 1,000 shares of its treasury stock, previously acquired at $8 per share. The entry is as follows.

July 1	Cash	10,000	
	Treasury Stock		8,000
	Paid-in Capital from Treasury Stock		2,000
	(To record sale of 1,000 shares of treasury stock above cost)		

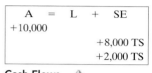

A	=	L	+	SE
+10,000				
				+8,000 TS
				+2,000 TS

Cash Flows
+10,000

Mead does not record a $2,000 gain on sale of treasury stock for two reasons: (1) Gains on sales occur when **assets** are sold, and treasury stock is not an asset. (2) A corporation does not realize a gain or suffer a loss from stock transactions with its own stockholders. Thus, companies should not include in net income any paid-in capital arising from the sale of treasury stock. Instead, they report Paid-in Capital from Treasury Stock separately on the balance sheet, as a part of paid-in capital.

SALE OF TREASURY STOCK BELOW COST

When a company sells treasury stock below its cost, it usually debits to Paid-in Capital from Treasury Stock the excess of cost over selling price. Thus, if Mead, Inc. sells an additional 800 shares of treasury stock on October 1 at $7 per share, it makes the following entry.

Oct. 1	Cash	5,600	
	Paid-in Capital from Treasury Stock	800	
	Treasury Stock		6,400
	(To record sale of 800 shares of treasury stock below cost)		

A	=	L	+	SE
+5,600				
				−800 TS
				+6,400 TS

Cash Flows
+5,600

Observe the following from the two sales entries: (1) Mead credits Treasury Stock at cost in each entry. (2) Mead uses Paid-in Capital from Treasury Stock for the difference between cost and the resale price of the shares. (3) The original paid-in capital account, Common Stock, is not affected. **The sale of treasury stock increases both total assets and total stockholders' equity.**

After posting the foregoing entries, the treasury stock accounts will show the following balances on October 1.

Illustration 13-10
Treasury stock accounts

Treasury Stock				Paid-in Capital from Treasury Stock			
Feb. 1	32,000	July 1	8,000	Oct. 1	800	July 1	2,000
		Oct. 1	6,400				
						Oct. 1 Bal.	1,200
Oct. 1 Bal.	17,600						

When a company fully depletes the credit balance in Paid-in Capital from Treasury Stock, it debits to Retained Earnings any additional excess of cost over selling price. To illustrate, assume that Mead, Inc. sells its remaining 2,200 shares at $7 per share on December 1. The excess of cost over selling price is $2,200 [2,200 × ($8 − $7)]. In this case, Mead debits $1,200 of the excess to Paid-in

Capital from Treasury Stock. It debits the remainder to Retained Earnings. The entry is:

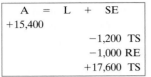

Dec. 1	Cash		15,400	
	Paid-in Capital from Treasury Stock		1,200	
	Retained Earnings		1,000	
	Treasury Stock			17,600
	(To record sale of 2,200 shares of treasury stock at $7 per share)			

A = L + SE
+15,400
            −1,200 TS
            −1,000 RE
            +17,600 TS

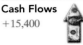

Cash Flows
+15,400

Before You Go On...

REVIEW IT

1. What is treasury stock, and why do companies acquire it?
2. How do companies record treasury stock?
3. Where do companies report treasury stock in the financial statements? Does a company record gains and losses on treasury stock transactions? Explain.
4. How many shares of treasury stock did PepsiCo have at December 31, 2005 and at December 25, 2004? The answer to this question appears on page 593.

DO IT

Santa Anita Inc. purchases 3,000 shares of its $50 par value common stock for $180,000 cash on July 1. It will hold the shares in the treasury until resold. On November 1, the corporation sells 1,000 shares of treasury stock for cash at $70 per share. Journalize the treasury stock transactions.

Action Plan
■ Record the purchase of treasury stock at cost.
■ When treasury stock is sold above its cost, credit the excess of the selling price over cost to Paid-in Capital from Treasury Stock.
■ When treasury stock is sold below its cost, debit the excess of cost over selling price to Paid-in Capital from Treasury Stock.

Solution

July 1	Treasury Stock		180,000	
	Cash			180,000
	(To record the purchase of 3,000 shares at $60 per share)			
Nov. 1	Cash		70,000	
	Treasury Stock			60,000
	Paid-in Capital from Treasury Stock			10,000
	(To record the sale of 1,000 shares at $70 per share)			

Related exercise material: *BE13-6, E13-6, and E13-7.*

 The Navigator

PREFERRED STOCK

STUDY OBJECTIVE 5
Differentiate preferred stock from common stock.

To appeal to more investors, a corporation may issue an additional class of stock, called preferred stock. **Preferred stock** has provisions that give it some preference or priority over common stock. Typically, preferred stockholders have a priority as to (1) distributions of earnings (dividends) and (2) assets in the event of liquidation. However, they generally do not have voting rights.

Like common stock, corporations may issue preferred stock for cash or for noncash assets. The entries for these transactions are similar to the entries for common stock. When a corporation has more than one class of stock, each paid-in capital account title should identify the stock to which it relates. A company might have the following accounts: Preferred Stock, Common Stock, Paid-in Capital in Excess of Par Value—Preferred Stock, and Paid-in Capital in Excess of Par Value—Common Stock. For example, if Stine Corporation issues 10,000 shares of $10 par value preferred stock for $12 cash per share, the entry to record the issuance is:

Cash	120,000	
Preferred Stock		100,000
Paid-in Capital in Excess of Par Value–Preferred Stock		20,000
(To record the issuance of 10,000 shares of $10 par		
value preferred stock)		

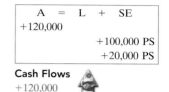

A = L + SE
+120,000
        +100,000 PS
        +20,000 PS

Cash Flows
+120,000

Preferred stock may have either a par value or no-par value. In the stockholders' equity section of the balance sheet, companies list preferred stock first because of its dividend and liquidation preferences over common stock.

We discuss various features associated with the issuance of preferred stock on the following pages.

Dividend Preferences

As noted earlier, **preferred stockholders have the right to receive dividends before common stockholders**. For example, if the dividend rate on preferred stock is $5 per share, common shareholders will not receive any dividends in the current year until preferred stockholders have received $5 per share. The first claim to dividends does not, however, guarantee the payment of dividends. Dividends depend on many factors, such as adequate retained earnings and availability of cash. If a company does not pay dividends to preferred stockholders, it cannot of course pay dividends to common stockholders.

The per share dividend amount is stated as a percentage of the preferred stock's par value or as a specified amount. For example, at one time Crane Company specified a 3¾% dividend on its $100 par value preferred ($100 × 3¾% = $3.75 per share). PepsiCo has a $5.46 series of no-par preferred stock.

I hope there is some money left when it's my turn.

Preferred   Common
stockholders stockholders

Dividend Preference

CUMULATIVE DIVIDEND

Preferred stock often contains a **cumulative dividend** feature. This means that preferred stockholders must be paid both current-year dividends and any unpaid prior-year dividends before common stockholders receive dividends. When preferred stock is cumulative, preferred dividends not declared in a given period are called **dividends in arrears**.

To illustrate, assume that Scientific Leasing has 5,000 shares of 7%, $100 par value, cumulative preferred stock outstanding. The annual dividend is $35,000 (5,000 × $7 per share), but dividends are two years in arrears. In this case, preferred stockholders are entitled to receive the following dividends in the current year.

Dividends in arrears ($35,000 × 2)	$ 70,000
Current-year dividends	35,000
Total preferred dividends	**$105,000**

Illustration 13-11
Computation of total dividends to preferred stock

Payment of a Cumulative Dividend

Dividend in arrears

Current dividend

Preferred stockholders

The company cannot pay dividends to common stockholders until it pays the entire preferred dividend. In other words, companies cannot pay dividends to common stockholders while any preferred stock is in arrears.

Are dividends in arrears considered a liability? **No—no payment obligation exists until the board of directors declares a dividend**. However, companies should disclose in the notes to the financial statements the amount of dividends in arrears. Doing so enables investors to assess the potential impact of this commitment on the corporation's financial position.

Companies that are unable to meet their dividend obligations are not looked upon favorably by the investment community. As a financial officer noted in discussing one company's failure to pay its cumulative preferred dividend for a period of time, "Not meeting your obligations on something like that is a major black mark on your record." The accounting entries for preferred stock dividends are explained in Chapter 14.

Liquidation Preference

Most preferred stocks also have a preference on corporate assets if the corporation fails. This feature provides security for the preferred stockholder. The preference to assets may be for the par value of the shares or for a specified liquidating value. For example, EarthLink's preferred stock entitles its holders to receive $20.83 per share, plus accrued and unpaid dividends, in the event of involuntary liquidation. The liquidation preference establishes the respective claims of creditors and preferred stockholders.

STATEMENT PRESENTATION AND ANALYSIS

STUDY OBJECTIVE 6
Prepare a stockholders' equity section.

Companies report paid-in capital and retained earnings in the stockholders' equity section of the balance sheet. They identify the specific sources of paid-in capital. Within paid-in capital, companies use the following classifications.

ALTERNATIVE TERMINOLOGY

Paid-in capital is sometimes called *contributed capital*.

1. **Capital stock.** This category consists of preferred and common stock. Preferred stock appears before common stock because of its preferential rights. Companies report par value, shares authorized, shares issued, and shares outstanding for each class of stock.
2. **Additional paid-in capital.** This category includes the excess of amounts paid in over par or stated value and paid-in capital from treasury stock.

Presentation

The stockholders' equity section of Connally Inc. in Illustration 13-12 (next page) includes most of the accounts discussed in this chapter. The disclosures pertaining to Connally's common stock indicate that: the company issued 400,000 shares; 100,000 shares are unissued (500,000 authorized less 400,000 issued); and 390,000 shares are outstanding (400,000 issued less 10,000 shares in treasury).

Published annual reports often combine and report as a single amount the individual sources of additional paid-in capital, as shown in Illustration 13-13 (next page). In addition, authorized shares are sometimes not reported.

In practice, companies sometimes use the term "Capital surplus" in place of "Additional paid-in capital," and "Earned surplus" in place of "Retained earnings." The use of the term "surplus" suggests that the company has available an excess amount of funds. Such is not necessarily the case. Therefore, **the term**

Illustration 13-12
Stockholders' equity section

CONNALLY INC.
Balance Sheet (partial)

Stockholders' equity
  Paid-in capital
    Capital stock

9% preferred stock, $100 par value cumulative, 10,000 shares authorized, 6,000 shares issued and outstanding		$ 600,000
Common stock, no par, $5 stated value, 500,000 shares authorized, 400,000 shares issued, and 390,000 outstanding		2,000,000
Total capital stock		2,600,000
Additional paid-in capital		
In excess of par value—preferred stock	$ 30,000	
In excess of stated value—common stock	860,000	
From treasury stock	140,000	
Total additional paid-in capital		1,030,000
Total paid-in capital		3,630,000
Retained earnings		1,058,000
Total paid-in capital and retained earnings		4,688,000
Less: Treasury stock—common (10,000 shares) (at cost)		(80,000)
Total stockholders' equity		$4,608,000

Illustration 13-13
Published stockholders'
equity section

KELLOGG COMPANY
Balance Sheet (partial)
($ in millions)

Stockholders' equity	
Common stock, $0.25 par value, 1,000,000,000 shares authorized	
Issued: 418,451,198 shares	$ 104.6
Capital in excess of par value	58.9
Retained earnings	3,266.1
Treasury stock, at cost	
13,121,446 shares	(569.8)
Accumulated other comprehensive income	(576.1)
Total stockholders' equity	$2,283.7

"surplus" should not be employed in accounting. Unfortunately, a number of financial statements still do use it.

Analysis—Book Value Per Share

You have learned about a number of per share amounts in this chapter. Another per share amount of some importance is **book value per share**. It represents **the equity a common stockholder has in the net assets of the corporation** from owning one share of stock. Remember that the net assets of a corporation must be equal to total stockholders' equity. Therefore, the formula for computing book value per share when a company has only one class of stock outstanding is:

STUDY OBJECTIVE 7
Compute book value per share.

Illustration 13-14
Book value per share
formula

Total Stockholders' Equity	÷	Number of Common Shares Outstanding	=	Book Value per Share

Thus, if Marlo Corporation has total stockholders' equity of $1,500,000 (common stock $1,000,000 and retained earnings $500,000) and 50,000 shares of common stock outstanding, book value per share is $30 ($1,500,000 ÷ 50,000).[5]

BOOK VALUE VERSUS MARKET VALUE

Be sure you understand that **book value per share generally does not equal market value per share**. Book value generally is based on recorded costs. Market value reflects the subjective judgments of thousands of stockholders and prospective investors about a company's potential for future earnings and dividends.

Market value per share may exceed book value per share, but that fact does not necessarily mean that the stock is overpriced. The correlation between book value and the annual range of a company's market value per share is often remote, as indicated by the following recent data.

Illustration 13-15
Book and market values
compared

Company	Book Value (year-end)	Market Range (for year 2005)
The Limited, Inc.	$13.38	$31.03–$22.89
H. J. Heinz Company	$ 7.48	$40.61–$34.53
Cisco Systems	$ 3.66	$21.24–$17.01
Wal-Mart Stores	$12.79	$50.87–$42.31

Book value per share is useful in determining the trend of a stockholder's per share equity in a corporation. It is also significant in many contracts and in court cases where the rights of individual parties are based on cost information.

Before You Go On...

REVIEW IT

1. Identify the classifications within the paid-in capital section and the totals stated in the stockholders' equity section of a balance sheet.
2. What is the method for computing book value per share when only common stock is outstanding?

 The Navigator

 Be sure to read **ALL ABOUT YOU:** *Home-Equity Loans* on the next page for information on how topics in this chapter apply to you.

---

[5]When a company has both preferred and common stock, the computation of book value is a bit more complex. Since preferred stockholders have a prior claim on net assets over common stockholders, their equity must be deducted from total stockholders' equity.

Home-Equity Loans

In this chapter you learned that companies sometimes reduce their stockholders' equity by buying treasury stock or paying dividends. They do this for a variety of reasons—some good, and some not so good. Individuals who own homes sometimes engage in equity reducing transactions by using home-equity loans. Home-equity loans use the equity existing in the home as collateral for borrowing additional monies.

Many banks encourage people to take out home-equity loans. As a result of the dramatic increase in home values in the United States in recent years, many people have significant equity in their homes. Thus, many people have chosen to use home-equity loans to finance vacations, new cars, improvements to the home, educational pursuits, and so on, or to consolidate debt. However, by taking out a home-equity loan, a homeowner is reducing the equity in that home.

✸ Some Facts

PNC Financial Services Group Inc. offered gifts—in some cases, two airline tickets—to borrowers who took out a new home-equity loan.

Many banks are extending the length of home-equity loans. Regions Financial Corp. introduced a fixed-rate home-equity loan with a term of up to 15 years. It had previously been five years.

While home-equity loans tend to have fixed rates, home-equity lines of credit, which allow the homeowner to borrow up to a certain amount whenever they want to, have variable rates. Rates on home-equity lines of credit averaged 8.33% in April 2006, versus about 14% for credit card debt.

Home-equity loan interest is tax deductible (like home mortgage interest). Interest on car loans, most student loans, and credit cards is not.

✸ About the Numbers

Home-equity loans can be very tempting. Suppose that you wanted to borrow $5,000 to take a vacation. You could spread your payments over 15 years and you would have to pay only about $50 per month. But look what your total payments would be over the life of the 15-year loan. Some vacation!

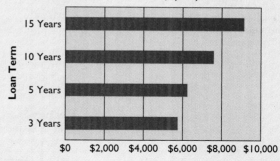

Source: Data from Marc Eisenson and Nancy Castleman, "When Mining Your Home for Money, Beware of Fool's Gold," Good Advice Press, *www.goodadvicepress.com/omhomeequity.htm* (accessed June 20, 2006).

✸ What Do You Think?

Your home has increased in value by $50,000 during the last five years. You have very little savings outside of the equity in your home. You desperately need a vacation, and you are considering taking out a $5,000 home-equity loan to finance a two-week dream vacation in Europe. Is this is a bad idea?

YES: This represents a significant portion of your savings. Home-equity loans should be used to finance investments of a lasting nature, not items of a fleeting nature like vacations.

NO: You need a vacation. If you use a little of the equity in your home now, you can make it up when your house increases in value in the future.

Source: Ruth Simon, "Lenders Push Home-Equity Deals," *Wall Street Journal*, April 27, 2006, page D1; Marc Eisenson and Nancy Castleman, "When Mining Your Home for Money, Beware of Fool's Gold," Good Advice Press, *www.goodadvicepress.com/omhomeequity.htm* (accessed June 20, 2006).

Demonstration Problem

The Rolman Corporation is authorized to issue 1,000,000 shares of $5 par value common stock. In its first year, the company has the following stock transactions.

Jan. 10   Issued 400,000 shares of stock at $8 per share.
July 1   Issued 100,000 shares of stock for land. The land had an asking price of $900,000. The stock is currently selling on a national exchange at $8.25 per share.
Sept. 1   Purchased 10,000 shares of common stock for the treasury at $9 per share.
Dec. 1   Sold 4,000 shares of the treasury stock at $10 per share.

Instructions

(a) Journalize the transactions.
(b) Prepare the stockholders' equity section assuming the company had retained earnings of $200,000 at December 31.

action plan

✔ When common stock has a par value, credit Common Stock for par value.

✔ Use fair market value in a noncash transaction.

✔ Debit and credit the Treasury Stock account at cost.

✔ Record differences between the cost and selling price of treasury stock in stockholders' equity accounts, not as gains or losses.

Solution to Demonstration Problem

(a)

Jan. 10	Cash	3,200,000	
	Common Stock		2,000,000
	Paid-in Capital in Excess of Par Value		1,200,000
	(To record issuance of 400,000 shares of $5 par value stock)		
July 1	Land	825,000	
	Common Stock		500,000
	Paid-in Capital in Excess of Par Value		325,000
	(To record issuance of 100,000 shares of $5 par value stock for land)		
Sept. 1	Treasury Stock	90,000	
	Cash		90,000
	(To record purchase of 10,000 shares of treasury stock at cost)		
Dec. 1	Cash	40,000	
	Treasury Stock		36,000
	Paid-in Capital from Treasury Stock		4,000
	(To record sale of 4,000 shares of treasury stock above cost)		

(b)

ROLMAN CORPORATION
Balance Sheet (partial)

Stockholders' equity
  Paid-in capital
    Capital stock

Common stock, $5 par value, 1,000,000 shares authorized, 500,000 shares issued, 494,000 shares outstanding		$2,500,000
Additional paid-in capital		
In excess of par value	$1,525,000	
From treasury stock	4,000	
Total additional paid-in capital		1,529,000
Total paid-in capital		4,029,000
Retained earnings		200,000
Total paid-in capital and retained earnings		4,229,000
Less: Treasury stock (6,000 shares)		(54,000)
Total stockholders' equity		$4,175,000

SUMMARY OF STUDY OBJECTIVES

1 Identify the major characteristics of a corporation. The major characteristics of a corporation are separate legal existence, limited liability of stockholders, transferable ownership rights, ability to acquire capital, continuous life, corporation management, government regulations, and additional taxes.

2 Differentiate between paid-in capital and retained earnings. Paid-in capital is the total amount paid in on capital stock. It is often called contributed capital. Retained earnings is net income retained in a corporation. It is often called earned capital.

3 Record the issuance of common stock. When companies record the issuance of common stock for cash, they credit the par value of the shares to Common Stock. They record in a separate paid-in capital account the portion of the proceeds that is above or below par value. When no-par common stock has a stated value, the entries are similar to those for par value stock. When no-par stock does not have a stated value, companies credit the entire proceeds to Common Stock.

4 Explain the accounting for treasury stock. The cost method is generally used in accounting for treasury stock. Under this approach, companies debit Treasury Stock at the price paid to reacquire the shares. They credit the same amount to Treasury Stock when they sell the shares. The difference between the sales price and cost is recorded in stockholders' equity accounts, not in income statement accounts.

5 Differentiate preferred stock from common stock. Preferred stock has contractual provisions that give it priority over common stock in certain areas. Typically, preferred stockholders have a preference (1) to dividends and (2) to assets in liquidation. They usually do not have voting rights.

6 Prepare a stockholders' equity section. In the stockholders' equity section, companies report paid-in capital and retained earnings and identify specific sources of paid-in capital. Within paid-in capital, two classifications are shown: capital stock and additional paid-in capital. If a corporation has treasury stock, it deducts the cost of treasury stock from total paid-in capital and retained earnings to obtain total stockholders' equity.

7 Compute book value per share. Book value per share represents the equity a common stockholder has in the net assets of a corporation from owning one share of stock. When there is only common stock outstanding, the formula for computing book value is: Total stockholders' equity ÷ Number of common shares outstanding = Book value per share.

✓ *The Navigator*

GLOSSARY

Authorized stock   The amount of stock that a corporation is authorized to sell as indicated in its charter. (p. 562).

Book value per share   The equity a common stockholder has in the net assets of the corporation from owning one share of stock. (p. 575).

By-laws   The internal rules and procedures for conducting the affairs of a corporation. (p. 560).

Charter   A document that creates a corporation. (p. 560).

Corporation   A business organized as a legal entity separate and distinct from its owners under state corporation law. (p. 556).

Cumulative dividend   A feature of preferred stock entitling the stockholder to receive current and unpaid prior-year dividends before common stockholders receive dividends. (p. 573).

No-par value stock   Capital stock that has not been assigned a value in the corporate charter. (p. 564).

Organization costs   Costs incurred in the formation of a corporation. (p. 560).

Outstanding stock   Capital stock that has been issued and is being held by stockholders. (p. 570).

Paid-in capital   Total amount of cash and other assets paid in to the corporation by stockholders in exchange for capital stock. (p. 564).

Par value stock   Capital stock that has been assigned a value per share in the corporate charter. (p. 563).

Preferred stock   Capital stock that has some preferences over common stock. (p. 572).

Privately held corporation   A corporation that has only a few stockholders and whose stock is not available for sale to the general public. (p. 556).

Publicly held corporation   A corporation that may have thousands of stockholders and whose stock is regularly traded on a national securities exchange. (p. 556).

Retained earnings   Net income that is retained in the corporation. (p. 564).

Stated value   The amount per share assigned by the board of directors to no-par stock. (p. 564).

Treasury stock   A corporation's own stock that has been issued and subsequently reacquired from shareholders by the corporation but not retired. (p. 568).

Answers are at the end of the chapter.

(SO 1) **1.** Which of the following is *not* a major advantage of a corporation?
  a. Separate legal existence.
  b. Continuous life.
  c. Government regulations.
  d. Transferable ownership rights.

(SO 1) **2.** A major disadvantage of a corporation is:
  a. limited liability of stockholders.
  b. additional taxes.
  c. transferable ownership rights.
  d. none of the above.

(SO 2) **3.** Which of the following statements is *false*?
  a. Ownership of common stock gives the owner a voting right.
  b. The stockholders' equity section begins with paid-in capital.
  c. The authorization of capital stock does not result in a formal accounting entry.
  d. Legal capital per share applies to par value stock but not to no-par value stock.

(SO 2) **4.** The account Retained Earnings is:
  a. a subdivision of paid-in capital.
  b. net income retained in the corporation.
  c. reported as an expense in the income statement.
  d. closed to capital stock.

(SO 3) **5.** ABC Corporation issues 1,000 shares of $10 par value common stock at $12 per share. In recording the transaction, credits are made to:
  a. Common Stock $10,000 and Paid-in Capital in Excess of Stated Value $2,000.
  b. Common Stock $12,000.
  c. Common Stock $10,000 and Paid-in Capital in Excess of Par Value $2,000.
  d. Common Stock $10,000 and Retained Earnings $2,000.

(SO 4) **6.** XYZ, Inc. sells 100 shares of $5 par value treasury stock at $13 per share. If the cost of acquiring the shares was $10 per share, the entry for the sale should include credits to:

a. Treasury Stock $1,000 and Paid-in Capital from Treasury Stock $300.
b. Treasury Stock $500 and Paid-in Capital from Treasury Stock $800.
c. Treasury Stock $1,000 and Retained Earnings $300.
d. Treasury Stock $500 and Paid-in Capital in Excess of Par Value $800.

7. In the stockholders' equity section, the cost of treasury (SO) stock is deducted from:
  a. total paid-in capital and retained earnings.
  b. retained earnings.
  c. total stockholders' equity.
  d. common stock in paid-in capital.

8. Preferred stock may have priority over common stock (SO) *except* in:
  a. dividends.
  b. assets in the event of liquidation.
  c. cumulative dividend features.
  d. voting.

9. Which of the following is *not* reported under additional (SO) paid-in capital?
  a. Paid-in capital in excess of par value.
  b. Common stock.
  c. Paid-in capital in excess of stated value.
  d. Paid-in capital from treasury stock.

10. The ledger of JFK, Inc. shows common stock, common (SO) treasury stock, and no preferred stock. For this company, the formula for computing book value per share is:
  a. Total paid-in capital and retained earnings divided by the number of shares of common stock issued.
  b. Common stock divided by the number of shares of common stock issued.
  c. Total stockholders' equity divided by the number of shares of common stock outstanding.
  d. Total stockholders' equity divided by the number of shares of common stock issued.

Go to the book's website,
www.wiley.com/college/weygandt,
for Additional Self-Study questions.

QUESTIONS

1. Eric Fink, a student, asks your help in understanding the following characteristics of a corporation: (a) separate legal existence, (b) limited liability of stockholders, and (c) transferable ownership rights. Explain these characteristics to Eric.

2. (a) Your friend Vicky Biel cannot understand how the characteristic of corporation management is both an advantage and a disadvantage. Clarify this problem for Vicky.
  (b) Identify and explain two other disadvantages of a corporation.

3. (a) The following terms pertain to the forming of a corporation: (1) charter, (2) by-laws, and (3) organization costs. Explain the terms.
  (b) Linda Merando believes a corporation must be incorporated in the state in which its headquarters office is located. Is Linda correct? Explain.

4. What are the basic ownership rights of common stockholders in the absence of restrictive provisions?

5. (a) What are the two principal components of stockholders' equity?
  (b) What is paid-in capital? Give three examples.

6. How do the financial statements for a corporation differ from the statements for a proprietorship?

7. The corporate charter of Hawes Corporation allows the issuance of a maximum of 100,000 shares of common stock. During its first two years of operations, Hawes sold 70,000 shares to shareholders and reacquired 7,000 of these shares. After these transactions, how many shares are authorized, issued, and outstanding?

8. Which is the better investment—common stock with a par value of $5 per share, or common stock with a par value of $20 per share? Why?

9. What factors help determine the market value of stock?

10. What effect does the issuance of stock at a price above par value have on the issuer's net income? Explain.

11. Why is common stock usually not issued at a price that is less than par value?

12. Land appraised at $80,000 is purchased by issuing 1,000 shares of $20 par value common stock. The market price of the shares at the time of the exchange, based on active trading in the securities market, is $95 per share. Should the land be recorded at $20,000, $80,000, or $95,000? Explain.

13. For what reasons might a company like IBM repurchase some of its stock (treasury stock)?

14. Kwun, Inc. purchases 1,000 shares of its own previously issued $5 par common stock for $12,000. Assuming the shares are held in the treasury, what effect does this transaction have on (a) net income, (b) total assets, (c) total paid-in capital, and (d) total stockholders' equity?

15. The treasury stock purchased in question 14 is resold by Kwun, Inc. for $18,000. What effect does this transaction have on (a) net income, (b) total assets, (c) total paid-in capital, and (d) total stockholders' equity?

16. (a) What are the principal differences between common stock and preferred stock?
(b) Preferred stock may be cumulative. Discuss this feature.
(c) How are dividends in arrears presented in the financial statements?

17. What is the formula for computing book value per share when a corporation has only common stock?

18. Ruiz Inc.'s common stock has a par value of $1, a book value of $29, and a current market value of $15. Explain why these amounts are all different.

19. Indicate how each of the following accounts should be classified in the stockholders' equity section.
(a) Common stock
(b) Paid-in capital in excess of par value
(c) Retained earnings
(d) Treasury stock
(e) Paid-in capital from treasury stock
(f) Paid-in capital in excess of stated value
(g) Preferred stock

BRIEF EXERCISES

BE13-1 Ken Fritz is studying for his accounting midterm examination. Identify for Ken the advantages and disadvantages of the corporate form of business organization.

List the advantages and disadvantages of a corporation. (SO 1)

BE13-2 At December 31, Kunkel Corporation reports net income of $450,000. Prepare the entry to close net income.

Prepare closing entries for a corporation. (SO 2)

BE13-3 On May 10, Mazili Corporation issues 2,000 shares of $10 par value common stock for cash at $18 per share. Journalize the issuance of the stock.

Prepare entries for issuance of par value common stock. (SO 3)

BE13-4 On June 1, Mendoza Inc. issues 3,000 shares of no-par common stock at a cash price of $6 per share. Journalize the issuance of the shares assuming the stock has a stated value of $1 per share.

Prepare entries for issuance of no-par value common stock. (SO 3)

BE13-5 Kane Inc.'s $10 par value common stock is actively traded at a market value of $15 per share. Kane issues 5,000 shares to purchase land advertised for sale at $85,000. Journalize the issuance of the stock in acquiring the land.

Prepare entries for issuance of stock in a noncash transaction. (SO 3)

BE13-6 On July 1, Goetz Corporation purchases 500 shares of its $5 par value common stock for the treasury at a cash price of $8 per share. On September 1, it sells 300 shares of the treasury stock for cash at $11 per share. Journalize the two treasury stock transactions.

Prepare entries for treasury stock transactions. (SO 4)

BE13-7 Acker Inc. issues 5,000 shares of $100 par value preferred stock for cash at $130 per share. Journalize the issuance of the preferred stock.

Prepare entries for issuance of preferred stock. (SO 5)

BE13-8 Ermler Corporation has the following accounts at December 31: Common Stock, $10 par, 5,000 shares issued, $50,000; Paid-in Capital in Excess of Par Value $20,000; Retained Earnings $45,000; and Treasury Stock—Common, 500 shares, $11,000. Prepare the stockholders' equity section of the balance sheet.

Prepare stockholders' equity section. (SO 6)

BE13-9 The balance sheet for Gambino Inc. shows the following: total paid-in capital and retained earnings $870,000, total stockholders' equity $820,000, common stock issued 44,000 shares, and common stock outstanding 40,000 shares. Compute the book value per share.

Compute book value per share. (SO 7)

EXERCISES

Identify characteristics of a corporation.

(SO 1)

E13-1   Jeff Lynne has prepared the following list of statements about corporations.

1. A corporation is an entity separate and distinct from its owners.
2. As a legal entity, a corporation has most of the rights and privileges of a person.
3. Most of the largest U.S. corporations are privately held corporations.
4. Corporations may buy, own, and sell property; borrow money; enter into legally binding contracts; and sue and be sued.
5. The net income of a corporation is not taxed as a separate entity.
6. Creditors have a legal claim on the personal assets of the owners of a corporation if the corporation does not pay its debts.
7. The transfer of stock from one owner to another requires the approval of either the corporation or other stockholders.
8. The board of directors of a corporation legally owns the corporation.
9. The chief accounting officer of a corporation is the controller.
10. Corporations are subject to less state and federal regulations than partnerships or proprietorships.

Instructions
Identify each statement as true or false. If false, indicate how to correct the statement.

Identify characteristics of a corporation.

(SO 1, 2)

E13-2   Jeff Lynne (see E13-1) has studied the information you gave him in that exercise and has come to you with more statements about corporation.

1. Corporation management is both an advantage and a disadvantage of a corporation compared to a proprietorship or a partnership.
2. Limited liability of stockholders, government regulations, and additional taxes are the major disadvantages of a corporation.
3. When a corporation is formed, organization costs are recorded as an asset.
4. Each share of common stock gives the stockholder the ownership rights to vote at stockholder meetings, share in corporate earnings, keep the same percentage ownership when new shares of stock are issued, and share in assets upon liquidation.
5. The number of issued shares is always greater than or equal to the number of authorized shares. *True*
6. A journal entry is required for the authorization of capital stock.
7. Publicly held corporations usually issue stock directly to investors. *False*
8. The trading of capital stock on a securities exchange involves the transfer of already issued shares from an existing stockholder to another investor.
9. The market value of common stock is usually the same as its par value. *False*
10. Retained earnings is the total amount of cash and other assets paid in to the corporation by stockholders in exchange for capital stock. *False*

Instructions
Identify each statement as true or false. If false, indicate how to correct the statement.

Journalize issuance of common stock.

(SO 3)

E13-3   During its first year of operations, Harlan Corporation had the following transactions pertaining to its common stock.

Jan. 10   Issued 70,000 shares for cash at $5 per share.   *350,000*
July 1   Issued 40,000 shares for cash at $7 per share.

Instructions   *280000*
(a) Journalize the transactions, assuming that the common stock has a par value of $5 per share.
(b) Journalize the transactions, assuming that the common stock is no-par with a stated value of $1 per share.

Journalize issuance of common stock.

(SO 3)

E13-4   Grossman Corporation issued 1,000 shares of stock.

Instructions
Prepare the entry for the issuance under the following assumptions.
(a) The stock had a par value of $5 per share and was issued for a total of $52,000.
(b) The stock had a stated value of $5 per share and was issued for a total of $52,000.

A) Total paid in of cap. in excess of par value $ 80,000
Par value $ 80,000 in capital
B) Total paid in stated in class of stated
in class of stated value $ 520,000

(c) The stock had no par or stated value and was issued for a total of $52,000.

(d) The stock had a par value of $5 per share and was issued to attorneys for services during incorporation valued at $52,000.

(e) The stock had a par value of $5 per share and was issued for land worth $52,000.

E13-5   Leone Co. had the following transactions during the current period.

Mar. 2   Issued 5,000 shares of $5 par value common stock to attorneys in payment of a bill for $30,000 for services provided in helping the company to incorporate.

June 12   Issued 60,000 shares of $5 par value common stock for cash of $375,000.

July 11   Issued 1,000 shares of $100 par value preferred stock for cash at $110 per share.

Nov. 28   Purchased 2,000 shares of treasury stock for $80,000.

Journalize issuance of common and preferred stock and purchase of treasury stock.

(SO 3, 4, 5)

Mar. 2 Organ. expense 30000

Instructions
Journalize the transactions.

E13-6   As an auditor for the CPA firm of Bunge and Dodd, you encounter the following situations in auditing different clients.

Journalize noncash common stock transactions.

(SO 3)

1) LAND 115,000   2) LAND 240,000

1. Desi Corporation is a closely held corporation whose stock is not publicly traded. On December 5, the corporation acquired land by issuing 5,000 shares of its $20 par value common stock. The owners' asking price for the land was $120,000, and the fair market value of the land was $115,000.

2. Lucille Corporation is a publicly held corporation whose common stock is traded on the securities markets. On June 1, it acquired land by issuing 20,000 shares of its $10 par value stock. At the time of the exchange, the land was advertised for sale at $250,000. The stock was selling at $12 per share.

Instructions
Prepare the journal entries for each of the situations above.

E13-7   On January 1, 2008, the stockholders' equity section of Nunez Corporation shows: Common stock ($5 par value) $1,500,000; paid-in capital in excess of par value $1,000,000; and retained earnings $1,200,000. During the year, the following treasury stock transactions occurred.

Journalize treasury stock transactions.

(SO 4)

Mar. 1   Purchased 50,000 shares for cash at $15 per share.

July 1   Sold 10,000 treasury shares for cash at $17 per share.

Sept. 1   Sold 8,000 treasury shares for cash at $14 per share.

A) PAID IN CAPITAL FROM TREASURY stock $12,000
b) RETAINED EARNINGS $4,000 (Debit)

Instructions
(a) Journalize the treasury stock transactions.

(b) Restate the entry for September 1, assuming the treasury shares were sold at $12 per share.

E13-8   Mad City Corporation purchased from its stockholders 5,000 shares of its own previously issued stock for $250,000. It later resold 2,000 shares for $54 per share, then 2,000 more shares for $49 per share, and finally 1,000 shares for $40 per share.

Journalize treasury stock transactions.

(SO 4)

Instructions
Prepare journal entries for the purchase of the treasury stock and the three sales of treasury stock.

E13-9   Polzin Corporation is authorized to issue both preferred and common stock. The par value of the preferred is $50. During the first year of operations, the company had the following events and transactions pertaining to its preferred stock.

Journalize preferred stock transactions and indicate statement presentation.

(SO 5, 6)

Feb. 1   Issued 20,000 shares for cash at $53 per share.

July 1   Issued 12,000 shares for cash at $57 per share.

B) Preferred Stock $1,600,000; PAID IN CAP. of par
value preferred $144,000

Instructions
(a) Journalize the transactions.

(b) Post to the stockholders' equity accounts.

(c) Indicate the financial statement presentation of the related accounts.

E13-10   AI Corporation issued 100,000 shares of $20 par value, cumulative, 8% preferred stock on January 1, 2007, for $2,100,000. In December 2009, AI declared its first dividend of $500,000.

Differentiate between preferred and common stock.

(SO 5)

Instructions

(a) Prepare AI's journal entry to record the issuance of the preferred stock.

(b) If the preferred stock is *not* cumulative, how much of the $500,000 would be paid to **common** stockholders?

(c) If the preferred stock is cumulative, how much of the $500,000 would be paid to **common** stockholders?

Prepare correct entries for capital stock transactions.

(SO 3, 4, 5)

E13-11   Roemer Corporation recently hired a new accountant with extensive experience in accounting for partnerships. Because of the pressure of the new job, the accountant was unable to review his textbooks on the topic of corporation accounting. During the first month, the accountant made the following entries for the corporation's capital stock.

May 2		Cash	130,000	
		Capital Stock		130,000
		(Issued 10,000 shares of $10 par value common stock at $13 per share)		
	10	Cash	600,000	
		Capital Stock		600,000
		(Issued 10,000 shares of $50 par value preferred stock at $60 per share)		
	15	Capital Stock	15,000	
		Cash		15,000
		(Purchased 1,000 shares of common stock for the treasury at $15 per share)		
	31	Cash	8,000	
		Capital Stock		5,000
		Gain on Sale of Stock		3,000
		(Sold 500 shares of treasury stock at $16 per share)		

Instructions

On the basis of the explanation for each entry, prepare the entry that should have been made for the capital stock transactions.

Prepare a stockholders' equity section.

(SO 6)

E13-12   The following stockholders' equity accounts, arranged alphabetically, are in the ledger of Freeze Corporation at December 31, 2008.

Common Stock ($5 stated value)	$1,700,000
Paid-in Capital in Excess of Par Value—Preferred Stock	280,000
Paid-in Capital in Excess of Stated Value—Common Stock	900,000
Preferred Stock (8%, $100 par, noncumulative)	500,000
Retained Earnings	1,134,000
Treasury Stock—Common (10,000 shares)	120,000

Instructions

Prepare the stockholders' equity section of the balance sheet at December 31, 2008.

Answer questions about stockholders' equity section.

(SO 3, 4, 5, 6)

E13-13   The stockholders' equity section of Jarvis Corporation at December 31 is as follows.

JARVIS CORPORATION
Balance Sheet (partial)

Paid-in capital	
Preferred stock, cumulative, 10,000 shares authorized, 6,000 shares issued	
and outstanding	$ 300,000
Common stock, no par, 750,000 shares authorized, 600,000 shares issued	1,200,000
Total paid-in capital	1,500,000
Retained earnings	1,858,000
Total paid-in capital and retained earnings	3,358,000
Less: Treasury stock (10,000 common shares)	(64,000)
Total stockholders' equity	$3,294,000

Instructions

From a review of the stockholders' equity section, as chief accountant, write a memo to the president of the company answering the following questions.

(a) How many shares of common stock are outstanding?
(b) Assuming there is a stated value, what is the stated value of the common stock?
(c) What is the par value of the preferred stock?
(d) If the annual dividend on preferred stock is $30,000, what is the dividend rate on preferred stock?
(e) If dividends of $60,000 were in arrears on preferred stock, what would be the balance in Retained Earnings?

E13-14   In a recent year, the stockholders' equity section of Aluminum Company of America (Alcoa) showed the following (in alphabetical order): additional paid-in capital $6,101, common stock $925, preferred stock $55, retained earnings $7,428, and treasury stock 2,828. All dollar data are in millions.

Prepare a stockholders' equity section.

(SO 6)

The preferred stock has 557,740 shares authorized, with a par value of $100 and an annual $3.75 per share cumulative dividend preference. At December 31, 557,649 shares of preferred are issued and 546,024 shares are outstanding. There are 1.8 billion shares of $1 par value common stock authorized, of which 924.6 million are issued and 844.8 million are outstanding at December 31.

Instructions

Prepare the stockholders' equity section, including disclosure of all relevant data.

E13-15   The ledger of Mathis Corporation contains the following accounts: Common Stock, Preferred Stock, Treasury Stock—Common, Paid-in Capital in Excess of Par Value—Preferred Stock, Paid-in Capital in Excess of Stated Value—Common Stock, Paid-in Capital from Treasury Stock, and Retained Earnings.

Classify stockholders' equity accounts.

(SO 6)

Instructions

Classify each account using the following table headings.

	Paid-in Capital			
Account	Capital Stock	Additional	Retained Earnings	Other

E13-16   At December 31, Penny Corporation has total stockholders' equity of $5,500,000. There are no shares of preferred stock outstanding. At year-end, 250,000 shares of common stock are outstanding and 20,000 shares are in treasury.

Compute book value per share.

(SO 7)

Instructions

Compute the book value per share of common stock.

EXERCISES: SET B

Visit the book's website at **www.wiley.com/college/weygandt**, and choose the Student Companion site, to access Exercise Set B.

PROBLEMS: SET A

P13-1A   Franco Corporation was organized on January 1, 2008. It is authorized to issue 10,000 shares of 8%, $100 par value preferred stock, and 500,000 shares of no-par common stock with a stated value of $2 per share. The following stock transactions were completed during the first year.

Journalize stock transactions, post, and prepare paid-in capital section.

(SO 3, 5, 6)

Peachtree

Jan. 10   Issued 80,000 shares of common stock for cash at $4 per share.
Mar. 1   Issued 5,000 shares of preferred stock for cash at $105 per share.
Apr. 1   Issued 24,000 shares of common stock for land. The asking price of the land was $90,000. The fair market value of the land was $85,000.

May   1   Issued 80,000 shares of common stock for cash at $4.50 per share.
Aug. 1   Issued 10,000 shares of common stock to attorneys in payment of their bill of $30,000 for services provided in helping the company organize.
Sept. 1   Issued 10,000 shares of common stock for cash at $5 per share.
Nov. 1   Issued 1,000 shares of preferred stock for cash at $109 per share.

Instructions
(a) Journalize the transactions.

(c) Total paid-in capital $1,479,000

(b) Post to the stockholders' equity accounts. (Use J5 as the posting reference.)
(c) Prepare the paid-in capital section of stockholders' equity at December 31, 2008.

Journalize and post treasury stock transactions, and prepare stockholders' equity section.

(SO 4, 6)

P13-2A   Jacobsen Corporation had the following stockholders' equity accounts on January 1, 2008: Common Stock ($5 par) $500,000, Paid-in Capital in Excess of Par Value $200,000, and Retained Earnings $100,000. In 2008, the company had the following treasury stock transactions.

Mar. 1   Purchased 5,000 shares at $9 per share.
June 1   Sold 1,000 shares at $12 per share.
Sept. 1   Sold 2,000 shares at $10 per share.
Dec. 1   Sold 1,000 shares at $6 per share.

Jacobsen Corporation uses the cost method of accounting for treasury stock. In 2008, the company reported net income of $30,000.

Instructions
(a) Journalize the treasury stock transactions, and prepare the closing entry at December 31, 2008, for net income.

(b) Treasury Stock $9,000

(c) Total stockholders' equity $823,000

(b) Open accounts for (1) Paid-in Capital from Treasury Stock, (2) Treasury Stock, and (3) Retained Earnings. Post to these accounts using J10 as the posting reference.
(c) Prepare the stockholders' equity section for Jacobsen Corporation at December 31, 2008.

Journalize and post transactions, prepare stockholders' equity section.

(SO 2, 3, 4, 5, 6)

GLS

P13-3A   The stockholders' equity accounts of Neer Corporation on January 1, 2008, were as follows.

Preferred Stock (8%, $50 par, cumulative, 10,000 shares authorized)	$ 400,000
Common Stock ($1 stated value, 2,000,000 shares authorized)	1,000,000
Paid-in Capital in Excess of Par Value—Preferred Stock	100,000
Paid-in Capital in Excess of Stated Value—Common Stock	1,450,000
Retained Earnings	1,816,000
Treasury Stock—Common (10,000 shares)	50,000

During 2008, the corporation had the following transactions and events pertaining to its stockholders' equity.

Feb. 1   Issued 25,000 shares of common stock for $120,000.
Apr. 14   Sold 6,000 shares of treasury stock—common for $33,000.
Sept. 3   Issued 5,000 shares of common stock for a patent valued at $35,000.
Nov. 10   Purchased 1,000 shares of common stock for the treasury at a cost of $6,000.
Dec. 31   Determined that net income for the year was $452,000.

No dividends were declared during the year.

Instructions
(a) Journalize the transactions and the closing entry for net income.
(b) Enter the beginning balances in the accounts, and post the journal entries to the stockholders' equity accounts. (Use J5 for the posting reference.)

(c) Total stockholders' equity $5,350,000

(c) Prepare a stockholders' equity section at December 31, 2008, including the disclosure of the preferred dividends in arrears.

Journalize and post stock transactions, and prepare stockholders' equity section.

(SO 2, 3, 5, 6)

P13-4A   Vargas Corporation is authorized to issue 20,000 shares of $50 par value, 10% preferred stock and 125,000 shares of $3 par value common stock. On January 1, 2008, the ledger contained the following stockholders' equity balances.

Preferred Stock (10,000 shares)	$500,000
Paid-in Capital in Excess of Par Value—Preferred	75,000
Common Stock (70,000 shares)	210,000
Paid-in Capital in Excess of Par Value—Common	700,000
Retained Earnings	300,000

During 2008, the following transactions occurred.

Feb.	1	Issued 2,000 shares of preferred stock for land having a fair market value of $125,000.
Mar.	1	Issued 1,000 shares of preferred stock for cash at $65 per share.
July	1	Issued 16,000 shares of common stock for cash at $7 per share.
Sept.	1	Issued 400 shares of preferred stock for a patent. The asking price of the patent was $30,000. Market values were preferred stock $70 and patent indeterminable.
Dec.	1	Issued 8,000 shares of common stock for cash at $7.50 per share.
Dec.	31	Net income for the year was $260,000. No dividends were declared.

Instructions

(a) Journalize the transactions and the closing entry for net income.

(b) Enter the beginning balances in the accounts, and post the journal entries to the stockholders' equity accounts. (Use J2 for the posting reference.)

(c) Total stockholders' equity $2,435,000

(c) Prepare a stockholders' equity section at December 31, 2008.

P13-5A   The following stockholders' equity accounts arranged alphabetically are in the ledger of Tyner Corporation at December 31, 2008.

Prepare stockholders' equity section.

(SO 6)

Common Stock ($5 stated value)	$2,000,000
Paid-in Capital from Treasury Stock	10,000
Paid-in Capital in Excess of Stated Value—Common Stock	1,600,000
Paid-in Capital in Excess of Par Value—Preferred Stock	679,000
Preferred Stock (8%, $50 par, noncumulative)	800,000
Retained Earnings	1,748,000
Treasury Stock—Common (10,000 shares)	130,000

Instructions

Prepare a stockholders' equity section at December 31, 2008.

Total stockholders' equity $6,707,000

P13-6A   Palmaro Corporation has been authorized to issue 20,000 shares of $100 par value, 10%, noncumulative preferred stock and 1,000,000 shares of no-par common stock. The corporation assigned a $2.50 stated value to the common stock. At December 31, 2008, the ledger contained the following balances pertaining to stockholders' equity.

Prepare entries for stock transactions and prepare stockholders' equity section.

(SO 3, 4, 5, 6)

Preferred Stock	$120,000
Paid-in Capital in Excess of Par Value—Preferred	20,000
Common Stock	1,000,000
Paid-in Capital in Excess of Stated Value—Common	1,800,000
Treasury Stock—Common (1,000 shares)	13,000
Paid-in Capital from Treasury Stock	500
Retained Earnings	82,000

The preferred stock was issued for land having a fair market value of $140,000. All common stock issued was for cash. In November, 1,500 shares of common stock were purchased for the treasury at a per share cost of $13. In December, 500 shares of treasury stock were sold for $14 per share. No dividends were declared in 2008.

Instructions

(a) Prepare the journal entries for the:
  (1) Issuance of preferred stock for land.
  (2) Issuance of common stock for cash.
  (3) Purchase of common treasury stock for cash.
  (4) Sale of treasury stock for cash.

(b) Total stockholders' equity $3,009,500

(b) Prepare the stockholders' equity section at December 31, 2008.

PROBLEMS: SET B

P13-1B   Scribner Corporation was organized on January 1, 2008. It is authorized to issue 20,000 shares of 6%, $50 par value preferred stock, and 500,000 shares of no-par common stock with a stated value of $1 per share. The following stock transactions were completed during the first year.

Journalize stock transactions, post, and prepare paid-in capital section.

(SO 3, 5, 6)

Jan.	10	Issued 100,000 shares of common stock for cash at $3 per share.
Mar.	1	Issued 10,000 shares of preferred stock for cash at $55 per share.

Apr.   1   Issued 25,000 shares of common stock for land. The asking price of the land was $90,000. The company's estimate of fair market value of the land was $75,000.
May   1   Issued 75,000 shares of common stock for cash at $4 per share.
Aug.   1   Issued 10,000 shares of common stock to attorneys in payment of their bill for $50,000 for services provided in helping the company organize.
Sept.   1   Issued 5,000 shares of common stock for cash at $6 per share.
Nov.   1   Issued 2,000 shares of preferred stock for cash at $60 per share.

Instructions
(a) Journalize the transactions.

(c) Total paid-in capital $1,425,000

(b) Post to the stockholders' equity accounts. (Use J1 as the posting reference.)
(c) Prepare the paid-in capital section of stockholders' equity at December 31, 2008.

Journalize and post treasury stock transactions, and prepare stockholders' equity section.

(SO 4, 6)

P13-2B   Inwood Corporation had the following stockholders' equity accounts on January 1, 2008: Common Stock ($1 par) $400,000, Paid-in Capital in Excess of Par Value $500,000, and Retained Earnings $100,000. In 2008, the company had the following treasury stock transactions.

Mar.   1   Purchased 5,000 shares at $8 per share.
June   1   Sold 1,000 shares at $10 per share.
Sept.   1   Sold 2,000 shares at $9 per share.
Dec.   1   Sold 1,000 shares at $5 per share.

Inwood Corporation uses the cost method of accounting for treasury stock. In 2008, the company reported net income of $50,000.

Instructions
(a) Journalize the treasury stock transactions, and prepare the closing entry at December 31, 2008, for net income.

(b) Treasury Stock $8,000

(c) Total stockholders' equity $1,043,000

(b) Open accounts for (1) Paid-in Capital from Treasury Stock, (2) Treasury Stock, and (3) Retained Earnings. Post to these accounts using J12 as the posting reference.
(c) Prepare the stockholders' equity section for Inwood Corporation at December 31, 2008.

Journalize and post transactions, prepare stockholders' equity section.

(SO 2, 3, 4, 5, 6)

P13-3B   The stockholders' equity accounts of Litke Corporation on January 1, 2008, were as follows.

Preferred Stock (10%, $100 par, noncumulative, 5,000 shares authorized)	$ 300,000
Common Stock ($5 stated value, 300,000 shares authorized)	1,000,000
Paid-in Capital in Excess of Par Value—Preferred Stock	20,000
Paid-in Capital in Excess of Stated Value—Common Stock	425,000
Retained Earnings	488,000
Treasury Stock—Common (5,000 shares)	35,000

During 2008, the corporation had the following transactions and events pertaining to its stockholders' equity.

Feb.   1   Issued 3,000 shares of common stock for $24,000.
Mar. 20   Purchased 1,500 additional shares of common treasury stock at $7 per share.
June 14   Sold 4,000 shares of treasury stock—common for $36,000.
Sept.   3   Issued 2,000 shares of common stock for a patent valued at $17,000.
Dec. 31   Determined that net income for the year was $320,000.

Instructions
(a) Journalize the transactions and the closing entry for net income.

(c) Total stockholders' equity $2,584,500

(b) Enter the beginning balances in the accounts and post the journal entries to the stockholders' equity accounts. (Use J1 as the posting reference.)
(c) Prepare a stockholders' equity section at December 31, 2008.

Journalize and post stock transactions, and prepare stockholders' equity section.

(SO 2, 3, 5, 6)

P13-4B   Mendez Corporation is authorized to issue 10,000 shares of $50 par value, 10% preferred stock and 200,000 shares of $2 par value common stock. On January 1, 2008, the ledger contained the following stockholders' equity balances.

Preferred Stock (4,000 shares)	$200,000
Paid-in Capital in Excess of Par Value—Preferred	60,000
Common Stock (70,000 shares)	140,000
Paid-in Capital in Excess of Par Value—Common	700,000
Retained Earnings	300,000

During 2008, the following transactions occurred.

Feb.	1	Issued 1,000 shares of preferred stock for land having a fair market value of $65,000.
Mar.	1	Issued 2,000 shares of preferred stock for cash at $60 per share.
July	1	Issued 20,000 shares of common stock for cash at $5.80 per share.
Sept.	1	Issued 800 shares of preferred stock for a patent. The asking price of the patent was $60,000. Market values were preferred stock $65 and patent, indeterminable.
Dec.	1	Issued 10,000 shares of common stock for cash at $6 per share.
Dec. 31		Net income for the year was $210,000. No dividends were declared.

Instructions

(a) Journalize the transactions and the closing entry for net income.

(b) Enter the beginning balances in the accounts, and post the journal entries to the stockholders' equity accounts. (Use J2 as the posting reference.)

(c) Prepare a stockholders' equity section at December 31, 2008.

(c) Total stockholders' equity $2,023,000

P13-5B   The following stockholders' equity accounts arranged alphabetically are in the ledger of Parnell Corporation at December 31, 2008.

Prepare stockholders' equity section.

(SO 6)

Common Stock ($10 stated value)	$1,200,000
Paid-in Capital from Treasury Stock	6,000
Paid-in Capital in Excess of Stated Value—Common Stock	690,000
Paid-in Capital in Excess of Par Value—Preferred Stock	288,400
Preferred Stock (8%, $100 par, noncumulative)	400,000
Retained Earnings	876,000
Treasury Stock—Common (8,000 shares)	88,000

Instructions

Prepare a stockholders' equity section at December 31, 2008.

Total stockholders' equity $3,372,400

P13-6B   Colyer Corporation has been authorized to issue 40,000 shares of $100 par value, 8%, noncumulative preferred stock and 2,000,000 shares of no-par common stock. The corporation assigned a $5 stated value to the common stock. At December 31, 2008, the ledger contained the following balances pertaining to stockholders' equity.

Prepare entries for stock transactions and prepare stockholders' equity section.

(SO 3, 4, 5, 6)

Preferred Stock	$ 240,000
Paid-in Capital in Excess of Par Value—Preferred	56,000
Common Stock	2,000,000
Paid-in Capital in Excess of Stated Value—Common	5,200,000
Treasury Stock—Common (1,000 shares)	24,000
Paid-in Capital from Treasury Stock	2,000
Retained Earnings	560,000

The preferred stock was issued for land having a fair market value of $296,000. All common stock issued was for cash. In November, 1,500 shares of common stock were purchased for the treasury at a per share cost of $24. In December, 500 shares of treasury stock were sold for $28 per share. No dividends were declared in 2008.

Instructions

(a) Prepare the journal entries for the:
   (1) Issuance of preferred stock for land.
   (2) Issuance of common stock for cash.
   (3) Purchase of common treasury stock for cash.
   (4) Sale of treasury stock for cash.

(b) Prepare the stockholders' equity section at December 31, 2008.

(b) Total stockholders' equity $8,034,000

PROBLEMS: SET C

Visit the book's website at **www.wiley.com/college/weygandt**, and choose the Student Companion site, to access Problem Set C.

CONTINUING COOKIE CHRONICLE

(Note: This is a continuation of the Cookie Chronicle from Chapters 1 through 12.)

CCC13 Natalie's friend, Curtis Lesperance, decides to meet with Natalie after hearing that her discussions about a possible business partnership with her friend Katy Peterson have failed. Because Natalie has been so successful with Cookie Creations and Curtis has been just as successful with his coffee shop, they both conclude that they could benefit from each other's business expertise. Curtis and Natalie next evaluate the different types of business organization, and because of the advantage of limited personal liability, decide to form a corporation. Natalie and Curtis are very excited about this new business venture. They come to you with information about their businesses and with a number of questions.

Go to the book's website,
www.wiley.com/college/weygandt,
to see the completion of this problem.

BROADENING YOUR PERSPECTIVE

FINANCIAL REPORTING AND ANALYSIS

Financial Reporting Problem:
PepsiCo, Inc.

BYP13-1 The stockholders' equity section for PepsiCo is shown in Appendix A. You will also find data relative to this problem on other pages of the appendix.

Instructions
(a) What is the par or stated value per share of PepsiCo's common stock?
(b) What percentage of PepsiCo's authorized common stock was issued at December 31, 2005?
(c) How many shares of common stock were outstanding at December 31, 2005, and at December 25, 2004?
(d) What was book value per share at December 31, 2005, and at December 25, 2004?
(e) What was the high and low market price per share in the fourth quarter of fiscal 2005, as reported under Selected Financial Data?

Comparative Analysis Problem:
PepsiCo, Inc. vs. The Coca-Cola Company

BYP13-2 PepsiCo's financial statements are presented in Appendix A. Coca-Cola's financial statements are presented in Appendix B.

Instructions
(a) Based on the information contained in these financial statements, compute the 2005 book value per share for each company. (*Hint:* Use the value reported for "common shareholders' equity" as the numerator for PepsiCo.)
(b) Compare the market value per share for each company to the book value per share at year-end 2005. Assume that the market value of Coca-Cola's stock was $40.31 at year-end 2005.
(c) Why are book value and market value per share different?

Exploring the Web

BYP13-3 SEC filings of publicly traded companies are available to view online.

Address: http://biz.yahoo.com/i, or go to **www.wiley.com/college/weygandt**

Steps
1. Pick a company and type in the company's name.
2. Choose **Quote**.

Instructions
Answer the following questions.

(a) What company did you select?
(b) What is its stock symbol?
(c) What was the stock's trading range today?
(d) What was the stock's trading range for the year?

CRITICAL THINKING

Decision Making Across the Organization

BYP13-4   The stockholders' meeting for Strauder Corporation has been in progress for some time. The chief financial officer for Strauder is presently reviewing the company's financial statements and is explaining the items that comprise the stockholders' equity section of the balance sheet for the current year. The stockholders' equity section of Strauder Corporation at December 31, 2008, is as follows.

STRAUDER CORPORATION
Balance Sheet (partial)
December 31, 2008

Paid-in capital		
Capital stock		
Preferred stock, authorized 1,000,000 shares cumulative, $100 par value, $8 per share, 6,000 shares issued and outstanding		$ 600,000
Common stock, authorized 5,000,000 shares, $1 par value, 3,000,000 shares issued, and 2,700,000 outstanding		3,000,000
Total capital stock		3,600,000
Additional paid-in capital		
In excess of par value—preferred stock	$ 50,000	
In excess of par value—common stock	25,000,000	
Total additional paid-in capital		25,050,000
Total paid-in capital		28,650,000
Retained earnings		900,000
Total paid-in capital and retained earnings		29,550,000
Less: Common treasury stock (300,000 shares)		9,300,000
Total stockholders' equity		$20,250,000

At the meeting, stockholders have raised a number of questions regarding the stockholders' equity section.

Instructions
With the class divided into groups, answer the following questions as if you were the chief financial officer for Strauder Corporation.

(a) "What does the cumulative provision related to the preferred stock mean?"
(b) "I thought the common stock was presently selling at $29.75, but the company has the stock stated at $1 per share. How can that be?"
(c) "Why is the company buying back its common stock? Furthermore, the treasury stock has a debit balance because it is subtracted from stockholders' equity. Why is treasury stock not reported as an asset if it has a debit balance?"
(d) "Why is it necessary to show additional paid-in capital? Why not just show common stock at the total amount paid in?"

Communication Activity

BYP13-5 Sid Hosey, your uncle, is an inventor who has decided to incorporate. Uncle Sid knows that you are an accounting major at U.N.O. In a recent letter to you, he ends with the question, "I'm filling out a state incorporation application. Can you tell me the difference in the following terms: (1) authorized stock, (2) issued stock, (3) outstanding stock, (4) preferred stock?"

Instructions
In a brief note, differentiate for Uncle Sid among the four different stock terms. Write the letter to be friendly, yet professional.

Ethics Case

BYP13-6 The R&D division of Marco Chemical Corp. has just developed a chemical for sterilizing the vicious Brazilian "killer bees" which are invading Mexico and the southern states of the United States. The president of Marco is anxious to get the chemical on the market to boost Marco's profits. He believes his job is in jeopardy because of decreasing sales and profits. Marco has an opportunity to sell this chemical in Central American countries, where the laws are much more relaxed than in the United States.

The director of Marco's R&D division strongly recommends further testing in the laboratory for side-effects of this chemical on other insects, birds, animals, plants, and even humans. He cautions the president, "We could be sued from all sides if the chemical has tragic side-effects that we didn't even test for in the labs." The president answers, "We can't wait an additional year for your lab tests. We can avoid losses from such lawsuits by establishing a separate wholly owned corporation to shield Marco Corp. from such lawsuits. We can't lose any more than our investment in the new corporation, and we'll invest just the patent covering this chemical. We'll reap the benefits if the chemical works and is safe, and avoid the losses from lawsuits if it's a disaster." The following week Marco creates a new wholly owned corporation called Brecht Inc., sells the chemical patent to it for $10, and watches the spraying begin.

Instructions
(a) Who are the stakeholders in this situation?
(b) Are the president's motives and actions ethical?
(c) Can Marco shield itself against losses of Brecht Inc.?

 # "All About You" Activity

BYP13-7 A high percentage of Americans own stock in corporations. As a shareholder in a corporation, you will receive an annual report. One of the goals of this course is for you to learn how to navigate your way around an annual report.

Instructions
Use the annual report provided in Appendix A to answer the following questions.

(a) What CPA firm performed the audit of PepsiCo's financial statements?
(b) What was the amount of PepsiCo's earnings per share in 2005?
(c) What are the company's net sales to foreign countries?
(d) What were net sales in 2001?
(e) How many shares of treasury stock did the company have at the end of 2005?
(f) How much cash did PepsiCo spend on capital expenditures in 2005?
(g) Over what life does the company depreciate its buildings?
(h) What was the total amount of dividends paid in 2005?

 # Answers to Insight and Accounting Across the Organization Questions

p. 559 Directors Take on More Accountability

Q: Was Enron's board of directors fulfilling its role in a corporate organization when it waived Enron's ethical code on two occasions?

A: *The board of directors is elected by the owners (stockholders) of the corporation to manage the corporation. One of its roles is to formulate the ethical and operating policies for the* *company and to assume an oversight responsibility on behalf of the stockholders and other third parties. It was the responsibility of the board of directors to enforce the corporation's ethical code, not to waive it.*

p. 563 How to Read Stock Quotes

Q: For stocks traded on organized stock exchanges, how are the dollar prices per share established?

A: *The dollar prices per share are established by the interaction between buyers and sellers of the shares.*

Q: What factors might influence the price of shares in the marketplace?

A: *The price of shares is influenced by a company's earnings and dividends as well as by factors beyond a company's control, such as changes in interest rates, labor strikes, scarcity of supplies or resources, and politics. The number of willing buyers and sellers (demand and supply) also plays a part in the price of shares.*

p. 570 Why Did Reebok Buy Its Own Stock?

Q: What signal might a large stock repurchase send to investors regarding management's belief about the company's growth opportunities?

A: *When a company has many growth opportunities it will normally conserve its cash in order to be better able to fund expansion. A large use of cash to buy back stock (and essentially shrink the company) would suggest that management was not optimistic about its growth opportunities.*

Authors' Comments on *All About You:* Home Equity Loans (p. 577)

The reasons why people reduce the equity in their homes with home-equity loans are as varied as the reasons why companies reduce their stockholders' equity by buying treasury stock or paying dividends. There are good and bad reasons to buy treasury stock and pay dividends, and there are good and bad reasons to use a home-equity loan.

Suppose you are considering putting an addition on your house which would increase its value. That may be a good use of a home-equity loan, since it increases the value of your investment. Or suppose that you need to buy a new car. Financing the purchase with a home-equity loan can make good financial sense, since the interest on a home-equity loan is tax-deductible, while the interest on a car loan is not. But you should be sure you repay the home-equity loan over the same time period that you would have repaid the car loan. As the graphs in the box show, if you spread the loan over a long period you could end up owing more money than the car is worth when it comes time to sell it.

Borrowing against the equity in your home to go on a vacation is not a financially prudent thing to do. If you want to go on a vacation, you should set up a separate travel fund as part of your personal budget, and go on the vacation only when you can actually afford it.

The bottom line is this: Reducing equity, either corporate or personal, increases reliance on debt and therefore increases risk. It is a decision that should be carefully considered.

Answers to PepsiCo Review It Question 3, p. 568, and Question 4, p. 572

3. The par value of PepsiCo's common stock is $0.0166 per share. On December 31, 2005, PepsiCo had issued 1,782 million shares.

4. Treasury shares held by PepsiCo on December 31, 2005, were 126 million, and on December 25, 2004, were 103 million.

Answers to Self-Study Questions

1. c   **2.** b   **3.** d   **4.** b   **5.** c   **6.** a   **7.** a   **8.** d   **9.** b   **10.** c

Chapter 14

Corporations: Dividends, Retained Earnings, and Income Reporting

STUDY OBJECTIVES

After studying this chapter, you should be able to:

1 Prepare the entries for cash dividends and stock dividends.
2 Identify the items reported in a retained earnings statement.
3 Prepare and analyze a comprehensive stockholders' equity section.
4 Describe the form and content of corporation income statements.
5 Compute earnings per share.

 The Navigator

✓ The Navigator

Scan **Study Objectives**	■
Read **Feature Story**	■
Read **Preview**	■
Read text and answer **Before You Go On** p. 603 ■ p. 608 ■ p. 611 ■	
Work **Demonstration Problem**	■
Review **Summary of Study Objectives**	■
Answer **Self-Study Questions**	■
Complete **Assignments**	■

Feature Story

WHAT'S COOKING?

What major U.S. corporation got its start 35 years ago with a waffle iron? Hint: It doesn't sell food. Another hint: Swoosh. Another hint: "Just do it." That's right, Nike (*www.nike.com*). In 1971 Nike cofounder Bill Bowerman put a piece of rubber into a kitchen waffle iron, and the trademark waffle sole was born.

Nike was cofounded by Bowerman and Phil Knight, a member of Bowerman's University of Oregon track team. Each began in the shoe business independently

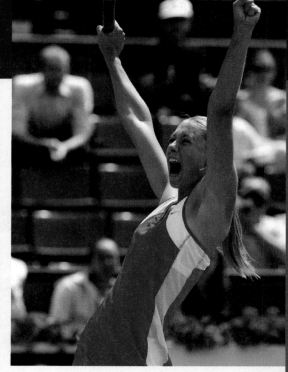

during the early 1960s. Bowerman got his start by making hand-crafted running shoes for his university track team. Knight, after completing graduate school, started a small business importing low-cost, high-quality shoes from Japan. In 1964 the two joined forces. Each contributed $500, and formed Blue Ribbon Sports, a partnership.

At first they marketed Japanese shoes. It wasn't until 1971 that the company began manufacturing its own line of shoes. With the new shoes came a new corporate name—Nike—the Greek goddess of victory. It is hard to imagine that the company that now enlists promoters such as Tiger Woods, Maria Sharapova, Dwayne Wade, and Lance Armstrong at one time had part-time employees selling shoes out of car trunks.

By 1980 Nike was sufficiently established that it was able to issue its first stock to the public. In that same year it also created a stock ownership program that allowed its employees to share in the company's success. Since then Nike has enjoyed phenomenal growth. Sales in 2005 were $13.74 billion. Its dividend per share to shareholders increased from 15 cents per share in 1992 to 95 cents per share in 2005.

Nike is not alone in its quest for the top of the sport shoe world. Reebok (*www.reebok.com*) pushes Nike every step of the way. It's a race to see who will dominate the sports shoe industry. Currently Nike is outpacing Reebok. But is the race over? Probably not. The shoe market is fickle, with new styles becoming popular almost daily. Whether one of these two giants, or some other shoe brand, does eventually take control of the planet remains to be seen. Meanwhile the shareholders sit anxiously in the stands as this Olympic-size drama unfolds.

✓ *The Navigator*

Inside Chapter 14...

As indicated in the Feature Story, a profitable corporation like Nike often distributes substantial portions of corporate income to owners (stockholders), in the form of dividends. In addition, it often reinvests a portion of its earnings in the business. This chapter discusses dividends, retained earnings, corporation income statements, and earnings per share.

The content and organization of Chapter 14 are as follows.

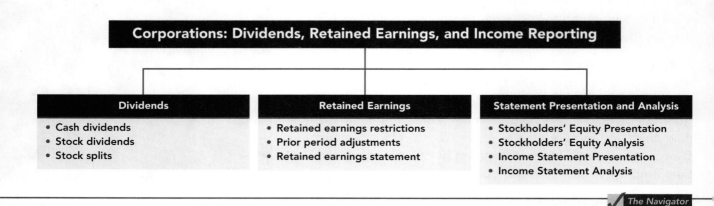

Corporations: Dividends, Retained Earnings, and Income Reporting

Dividends	Retained Earnings	Statement Presentation and Analysis
• Cash dividends • Stock dividends • Stock splits	• Retained earnings restrictions • Prior period adjustments • Retained earnings statement	• Stockholders' Equity Presentation • Stockholders' Equity Analysis • Income Statement Presentation • Income Statement Analysis

✓ The Navigator

DIVIDENDS

STUDY OBJECTIVE 1

Prepare the entries for cash dividends and stock dividends.

A dividend is a corporation's distribution of cash or stock to its stockholders on a pro rata (proportional) basis. Investors are very interested in a company's dividend policies and practices. Dividends can take four forms: cash, property, scrip (a promissory note to pay cash), or stock. Cash dividends predominate in practice. Also, companies declare stock dividends with some frequency. These two forms of dividends will be the focus of discussion in this chapter.

Dividends may be expressed in two ways: (1) as a percentage of the par or stated value of the stock, or (2) as a dollar amount per share. The financial press generally reports **dividends as a dollar amount per share**. For example, Boeing Company's dividend rate is $1.05 a share, Hershey Foods Corp.'s is $0.93, and Nike's is $0.95.

Cash Dividends

A **cash dividend** is a pro rata distribution of cash to stockholders. For a corporation to pay a cash dividend, it must have:

1. **Retained earnings.** The legality of a cash dividend depends on the laws of the state in which the company is incorporated. Payment of cash dividends from retained earnings is legal in all states. In general, cash dividend distributions from only the balance in common stock (legal capital) are illegal.

    A dividend declared out of paid-in capital is termed a **liquidating dividend**. Such a dividend reduces or "liquidates" the amount originally paid in by stockholders. Statutes vary considerably with respect to cash dividends based on paid-in capital in excess of par or stated value. Many states permit such dividends.

2. **Adequate cash.** The legality of a dividend and the ability to pay a dividend are two different things. For example, Nike, with retained earnings of over $3

billion, could legally declare a dividend of at least $3 billion. But Nike's cash balance is only $198 million.

Before declaring a cash dividend, a company's board of directors must carefully consider both current and future demands on the company's cash resources. In some cases, current liabilities may make a cash dividend inappropriate. In other cases, a major plant expansion program may warrant only a relatively small dividend.

3. **A declaration of dividends.** A company does not pay dividends unless its board of directors decides to do so, at which point the board "declares" the dividend. The board of directors has full authority to determine the amount of income to distribute in the form of a dividend and the amount to retain in the business. Dividends do not accrue like interest on a note payable, and they are not a liability until declared.

The amount and timing of a dividend are important issues. The payment of a large cash dividend could lead to liquidity problems for the company. On the other hand, a small dividend or a missed dividend may cause unhappiness among stockholders. Many stockholders expect to receive a reasonable cash payment from the company on a periodic basis. Many companies declare and pay cash dividends quarterly.

ENTRIES FOR CASH DIVIDENDS

Three dates are important in connection with dividends: (1) the declaration date, (2) the record date, and (3) the payment date. Normally, there are two to four weeks between each date. Companies make accounting entries on two of the dates—the declaration date and the payment date.

On the declaration date, the board of directors formally declares (authorizes) the cash dividend and announces it to stockholders. Declaration of a cash dividend **commits the corporation to a legal obligation**. The obligation is binding and cannot be rescinded. The company makes an entry to recognize the decrease in retained earnings and the increase in the liability Dividends Payable.

To illustrate, assume that on December 1, 2008, the directors of Media General declare a 50¢ per share cash dividend on 100,000 shares of $10 par value common stock. The dividend is $50,000 (100,000 × 50¢) The entry to record the declaration is:

Declaration Date

Dec. 1	Retained Earnings	50,000	
	Dividends Payable		50,000
	(To record declaration of cash dividend)		

A = L + SE
−50,000 Div
+50,000

Cash Flows
no effect

Dividends Payable is a current liability: it will normally be paid within the next several months.

Instead of debiting Retained Earnings, the company may debit the account Dividends. This account provides additional information in the ledger. Also, a company may have separate dividend accounts for each class of stock. When using a dividend account, the company transfers the balance of that account to Retained Earnings at the end of the year by a closing entry. Whichever account is used for the dividend declaration, the effect is the same: Retained earnings decreases, and a current liability increases. *For homework problems, you should use the Retained Earnings account for recording dividend declarations.*

At the record date, the company determines ownership of the outstanding shares for dividend purposes. The records maintained by the corporation supply this information. In the interval between the declaration date and the record date, the corporation updates its stock ownership records. For Media General, the record date is December 22. No entry is required on this date because the corporation's liability recognized on the declaration date is unchanged.

Record Date

Dec. 22 | No entry necessary

On the **payment date**, the company mails dividend checks to the stockholders and records the payment of the dividend. Assuming that the payment date is January 20 for Media General, the entry on that date is:

Payment Date

Jan. 20	Dividends Payable	50,000	
	Cash		50,000
	(To record payment of cash dividend)		

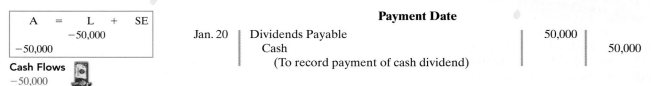

Note that payment of the dividend reduces both current assets and current liabilities. It has no effect on stockholders' equity. The **cumulative effect** of the **declaration and payment** of a cash dividend is to **decrease both stockholders' equity and total assets**. Illustration 14-1 summarizes the three important dates associated with dividends for Media General.

Illustration 14-1
Key dividend dates

ALLOCATING CASH DIVIDENDS BETWEEN PREFERRED AND COMMON STOCK

As explained in Chapter 13, preferred stock has priority over common stock in regard to dividends. Holders of cumulative preferred stock must be paid any unpaid prior-year dividends before common stockholders receive dividends.

To illustrate, assume that at December 31, 2008, IBR Inc. has 1,000 shares of 8%, $100 par value cumulative preferred stock. It also has 50,000 shares of $10 par value common stock outstanding. The dividend per share for preferred stock is $8 ($100 par value × 8%). The required annual dividend for preferred stock is therefore $8,000 (1,000 × $8). At December 31, 2008, the directors declare a $6,000 cash dividend. In this case, the entire dividend amount goes to preferred stockholders because of their dividend preference. The entry to record the declaration of the dividend is:

Dec. 31	Retained Earnings	6,000	
	Dividends Payable		6,000
	(To record $6 per share cash dividend		
	to preferred stockholders)		

A	=	L	+	SE	
					−6,000 Div
		+6,000			

Cash Flows
no effect

Because of the cumulative feature, dividends of $2 per share are in arrears on preferred stock for 2008. The company must pay these dividends to preferred stockholders before it can pay any future dividends to common stockholders. IBR should disclose dividends in arrears in the financial statements.

At December 31, 2009, IBR declares a $50,000 cash dividend. The allocation of the dividend to the two classes of stock is as follows.

Total dividend		$50,000
Allocated to preferred stock		
Dividends in arrears, 2008 (1,000 × $2)	**$2,000**	
2009 dividend (1,000 × $8)	**8,000**	10,000
Remainder allocated to common stock		$40,000

Illustration 14-2
Allocating dividends to preferred and common stock

The entry to record the declaration of the dividend is:

Dec. 31	Retained Earnings	50,000	
	Dividends Payable		50,000
	(To record declaration of cash dividends		
	of $10,000 to preferred stock and $40,000		
	to common stock)		

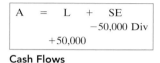

A	=	L	+	SE	
					−50,000 Div
		+50,000			

Cash Flows
no effect

What if IBR's preferred stock were not cumulative? In that case preferred stockholders would have received only $8,000 in dividends in 2009. Common stockholders would have received $42,000.

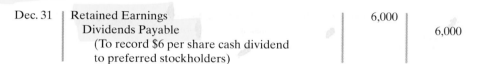

ACCOUNTING ACROSS THE ORGANIZATION

Why Are Companies Increasing Their Dividends?

The decision whether to pay a cash dividend, and how much to pay, is a very important management decision. During 2004 cash dividend payments were a record $181 billion—not including a one-time $32.6 billion dividend by Microsoft. The $181 billion does include a 44% dividend increase by Wal-Mart and a doubling of the dividend payment by Intel.

One explanation for the increase is that Congress lowered, from 39% to 15%, the tax rate paid by investors on dividends received, making dividends more attractive to investors. Another driving force for the dividend increases was that companies were sitting on record amounts of cash. Because they did not see a lot of good expansion opportunities, companies decided to return the cash to shareholders.

Bigger dividends are still possible in the future. Large companies paid out 34% of their earnings as dividends in 2004—well below the historical average payout of 54% of earnings.

Source: Alan Levinsohn, "Divine Dividends," *Strategic Finance,* May 2005, pp. 59–60.

 What factors must management consider in deciding how large a dividend to pay?

Stock Dividends

A **stock dividend** is a pro rata distribution to stockholders of the corporation's own stock. Whereas a company pays cash in a cash dividend, a company issues shares of stock in a stock dividend. **A stock dividend results in a decrease in retained earnings and an increase in paid-in capital.** Unlike a cash dividend, a stock dividend does not decrease total stockholders' equity or total assets.

To illustrate, assume that you have a 2% ownership interest in Cetus Inc.; you own 20 of its 1,000 shares of common stock. If Cetus declares a 10% stock dividend, it would issue 100 shares (1,000 × 10%) of stock. You would receive two shares (2% × 100). Would your ownership interest change? No, it would remain at 2% (22 ÷ 1,100). **You now own more shares of stock, but your ownership interest has not changed.** Illustration 14-3 shows the effect of a stock dividend for stockholders.

Illustration 14-3
Effect of stock dividend for stockholders

Before stock dividend   **After stock dividend**

"I owned 40 shares before and I own 120 shares now, but I still own only ¼ of the company!"

Number of shares owned increases, but percentage of company owned remains the same.

The company has disbursed no cash, and has assumed no liabilities. What are the purposes and benefits of a stock dividend? Corporations issue stock dividends generally for one or more of the following reasons.

1. To satisfy stockholders' dividend expectations without spending cash.
2. To increase the marketability of the corporation's stock. When the number of shares outstanding increases, the market price per share decreases. Decreasing the market price of the stock makes it easier for smaller investors to purchase the shares.
3. To emphasize that a portion of stockholders' equity has been permanently reinvested in the business (and is unavailable for cash dividends).

When the dividend is declared, the board of directors determines the size of the stock dividend and the value assigned to each dividend. Generally, if the company issues a **small stock dividend** (less than 20–25% of the corporation's issued stock), the value assigned to the dividend is the fair market value per share. This treatment is based on the assumption that a small stock dividend will have little effect on the market price of the outstanding shares. Many stockholders consider small stock dividends to be distributions of earnings equal to the fair market value of the shares distributed. If a company issues a **large stock dividend** (greater than 20–25%), the value assigned to the dividend is the par or stated value. Small stock dividends predominate in practice. Thus, we will illustrate only entries for small stock dividends.

ENTRIES FOR STOCK DIVIDENDS

To illustrate the accounting for small stock dividends, assume that Medland Corporation has a balance of $300,000 in retained earnings. It declares a 10% stock dividend on its 50,000 shares of $10 par value common stock. The current fair market value of its stock is $15 per share. The number of shares to be issued is 5,000 (10% × 50,000). Therefore the total amount to be debited to Retained Earnings is $75,000 (5,000 × $15). The entry to record the declaration of the stock dividend is as follows.

Retained Earnings	75,000	
Common Stock Dividends Distributable		50,000
Paid-in Capital in Excess of Par Value		25,000
(To record declaration of 10% stock dividend)		

```
A  =  L  +   SE
          -75,000 Div
          +50,000 CS
          +25,000 CS
```
Cash Flows
no effect

Medland debits Retained Earnings for the fair market value of the stock issued ($15 × 5,000). It credits to Common Stock Dividends Distributable the par value of the dividend shares ($10 × 5,000), and credits to Paid-in Capital in Excess of Par Value the excess over par ($5 × 5,000).

Common Stock Dividends Distributable is a **stockholders' equity account**. It is not a liability because assets will not be used to pay the dividend. If the company prepares a balance sheet before it issues the dividend shares, it reports the distributable account under Paid-in capital as shown in Illustration 14-4.

Paid-in capital		
Common stock	$500,000	
Common stock dividends distributable	**50,000**	$550,000

Illustration 14-4
Statement presentation of common stock dividends distributable

When Medland issues the dividend shares, it debits Common Stock Dividends Distributable, and credits Common Stock, as follows.

Common Stock Dividends Distributable	50,000	
Common Stock		50,000
(To record issuance of 5,000 shares in a stock dividend)		

```
A  =  L  +   SE
          -50,000 CS
          +50,000 CS
```
Cash Flows
no effect

EFFECTS OF STOCK DIVIDENDS

How do stock dividends affect stockholders' equity? They **change the composition of stockholders' equity**, because they transfer to paid-in capital a portion of retained earnings. However, **total stockholders' equity remains the same**. Stock dividends also have no effect on the par or stated value per share. But the number of shares outstanding increases, and the book value per share decreases. Illustration 14-5 shows these effects for Medland Corporation.

	Before Dividend	After Dividend
Stockholders' equity		
Paid-in capital		
Common stock, $10 par	$500,000	$550,000
Paid-in capital in excess of par value	—	25,000
Total paid-in capital	500,000	575,000
Retained earnings	300,000	225,000
Total stockholders' equity	**$800,000**	**$800,000**
Outstanding shares	**50,000**	**55,000**
Book value per share	**$16.00**	**$14.55**

Illustration 14-5
Stock dividend effects

In this example, total paid-in capital increases by $75,000, and retained earnings decreases by the same amount. Note also that total stockholders' equity remains unchanged at $800,000.

Stock Splits

A **stock split**, like a stock dividend, involves issuance of additional shares to stockholders according to their percentage ownership. **A stock split results in a reduction in the par or stated value per share.** The purpose of a stock split is to increase the marketability of the stock by lowering its market value per share.

The effect of a split on market value is generally *inversely proportional* to the size of the split. For example, after a recent 2-for-1 stock split, the market value of Nike's stock fell from $111 to approximately $55. The lower market value stimulated market activity, and within one year the stock was trading above $100 again.

In a stock split, the number of shares increases in the same proportion that par or stated value per share decreases. For example, in a 2-for-1 split, one share of $10 par value stock is exchanged for two shares of $5 par value stock. **A stock split does not have any effect on total paid-in capital, retained earnings, or total stockholders' equity.** But the number of shares outstanding increases, and book value per share decreases. Illustration 14-6 shows these effects for Medland Corporation, assuming that it splits its 50,000 shares of common stock on a 2-for-1 basis.

> **HELPFUL HINT**
>
> A stock split changes the par value per share but does not affect any balances in stockholders' equity.

Illustration 14-6
Stock split effects

	Before Stock Split	After Stock Split
Stockholders' equity		
Paid-in capital		
Common stock	$500,000	$500,000
Paid-in capital in excess of par value	–0–	–0–
Total paid-in capital	500,000	500,000
Retained earnings	300,000	300,000
Total stockholders' equity	**$800,000**	**$800,000**
Outstanding shares	**50,000**	**100,000**
Book value per share	**$16.00**	**$8.00**

A stock split does not affect the balances in any stockholders' equity accounts. Therefore **it is not necessary to journalize a stock split**.

Illustration 14-7 summarizes the significant differences between stock splits and stock dividends.

Illustration 14-7
Differences between the effects of stock splits and stock dividends

Item	Stock Split	Stock Dividend
Total paid-in capital	No change	Increase
Total retained earnings	No change	Decrease
Total par value (common stock)	No change	Increase
Par value per share	Decrease	No change

INVESTOR INSIGHT

Would You Pay $92,100 for One Share of Stock?

A handful of U.S. companies have no intention of keeping their stock trading in a range accessible to mere mortals. These companies never split their stock, no matter how high their stock price gets. The king is investment company Berkshire Hathaway's Class A stock, which sells for a pricey $92,100—per share! The company's Class B stock is a relative bargain at roughly $3,071 per share.

? How does the effect on share price following a stock split compare to the effect on share price of treasury shares acquired?

Before You Go On...

REVIEW IT

1. What entries do companies make for cash dividends on (a) the declaration date, (b) the record date, and (c) the payment date?
2. Distinguish between a small and large stock dividend, and indicate the basis for valuing each kind of dividend.
3. Contrast the effects of a small stock dividend and a 2-for-1 stock split on (a) stockholders' equity, (b) outstanding shares, and (c) book value per share.
4. What were the amounts of the dividends PepsiCo declared per share of common stock during the years 2001 to 2005? Is the trend in dividends consistent with the company's net income trend during that period? The answers to these questions appear on page 628.

DO IT

Sing CD Company has had five years of record earnings. Due to this success, the market price of its 500,000 shares of $2 par value common stock has tripled from $15 per share to $45. During this period, paid-in capital remained the same at $2,000,000. Retained earnings increased from $1,500,000 to $10,000,000. CEO Joan Elbert is considering either (1) a 10% stock dividend or (2) a 2-for-1 stock split. She asks you to show the before-and-after effects of each option on (a) retained earnings and (b) book value per share.

Action Plan

- Calculate the stock dividend's effect on retained earnings by multiplying the number of new shares times the market price of the stock (or par value for a large stock dividend).
- Recall that a stock dividend increases the number of shares without affecting total equity, thus decreasing the book value per share.
- Recall that a stock split only increases the number of shares outstanding and decreases the par value per share.

Solution

(a) (1) The stock dividend amount is $2,250,000 [(500,000 × 10%) × $45]. The new balance in retained earnings is $7,750,000 ($10,000,000 − $2,250,000).

   (2) The retained earnings balance after the stock split would be the same as it was before the split: $10,000,000.

(b) The book value effects are as follows:

	Original Balances	After Dividend	After Split
Paid-in capital	$ 2,000,000	$ 4,250,000	$ 2,000,000
Retained earnings	10,000,000	7,750,000	10,000,000
Total stockholders' equity	$12,000,000	$12,000,000	$12,000,000
Shares outstanding	500,000	550,000	1,000,000
Book value per share	$24	$21.82	$12

Related exercise material: *BE14-2, BE14-3, E14-3, and E14-4.*

✔ *The Navigator*

RETAINED EARNINGS

STUDY OBJECTIVE 2

Identify the items reported in a retained earnings statement.

As you learned in Chapter 13, retained earnings is net income that a company retains for use in the business. The balance in retained earnings is part of the stockholders' claim on the total assets of the corporation. It does not, though, represent a claim on any specific asset. Nor can the amount of retained earnings be associated with the balance of any asset account. For example, a $100,000 balance in retained earnings does not mean that there should be $100,000 in cash. The reason is that the company may have used the cash resulting from the excess of revenues over expenses to purchase buildings, equipment, and other assets.

To demonstrate that retained earnings and cash may be quite different, Illustration 14-8 shows recent amounts of retained earnings and cash in selected companies.

Illustration 14-8
Retained earnings and cash balances

	(in millions)	
Company	**Retained Earnings**	**Cash**
Disney Co.	$17,775	$1,723
Intel Corp.	29,810	7,324
Kellogg Co.	3,266.1	219.1
Amazon.com	(2,027)	1,013

HELPFUL HINT

Remember that Retained Earnings is a stockholders' equity account, whose normal balance is a credit.

Remember from Chapter 13 that when a company has net income, it closes net income to retained earnings. The closing entry is a debit to Income Summary and a credit to Retained Earnings.

When a company has a **net loss** (expenses exceed revenues), it also closes this amount to retained earnings. The closing entry in this case is a debit to Retained Earnings and a credit to Income Summary. This is done even if it results in a debit balance in Retained Earnings. **Companies do not debit net losses to paid-in capital accounts.** To do so would destroy the distinction between paid-in and earned capital. A debit balance in Retained Earnings is identified as a deficit. It is reported as a deduction in the stockholders' equity section, as shown below.

Illustration 14-9
Stockholders' equity with deficit

Balance Sheet (partial)	
Stockholders' equity	
Paid-in capital	
Common stock	$800,000
Retained earnings (deficit)	**(50,000)**
Total stockholders' equity	$750,000

Retained Earnings Restrictions

The balance in retained earnings is generally available for dividend declarations. Some companies state this fact. For example, Lockheed Martin Corporation states the following in the notes to its financial statements.

LOCKHEED MARTIN CORPORATION
Notes to the Financial Statements

Illustration 14-10
Disclosure of unrestricted retained earnings

At December 31, retained earnings were unrestricted and available for dividend payments.

In some cases, there may be **retained earnings restrictions**. These make a portion of the retained earnings balance currently unavailable for dividends. Restrictions result from one or more of the following causes.

1. **Legal restrictions.** Many states require a corporation to restrict retained earnings for the cost of treasury stock purchased. The restriction keeps intact the corporation's legal capital that is being temporarily held as treasury stock. When the company sells the treasury stock, the restriction is lifted.

2. **Contractual restrictions.** Long-term debt contracts may restrict retained earnings as a condition for the loan. The restriction limits the use of corporate assets for payment of dividends. Thus, it increases the likelihood that the corporation will be able to meet required loan payments.

3. **Voluntary restrictions.** The board of directors may voluntarily create retained earnings restrictions for specific purposes. For example, the board may authorize a restriction for future plant expansion. By reducing the amount of retained earnings available for dividends, the company makes more cash available for the planned expansion.

Companies generally disclose **retained earnings restrictions** in the notes to the financial statements. For example, Tektronix Inc., a manufacturer of electronic measurement devices, had total retained earnings of $774 million, but the unrestricted portion was only $223.8 million.

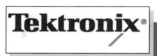

TEKTRONIX INC.
Notes to the Financial Statements

Illustration 14-11
Disclosure of restriction

Certain of the Company's debt agreements require compliance with debt covenants. Management believes that the Company is in compliance with such requirements. The Company had unrestricted retained earnings of $223.8 million after meeting those requirements.

Prior Period Adjustments

Suppose that a corporation has closed its books and issued financial statements. The corporation then discovers that it made a material error in reporting net income of a prior year. How should the company record this situation in the accounts and report it in the financial statements?

The correction of an error in previously issued financial statements is known as a **prior period adjustment**. The company makes the correction directly to Retained

Earnings, because the effect of the error is now in this account. The net income for the prior period has been recorded in retained earnings through the journalizing and posting of closing entries.

To illustrate, assume that General Microwave discovers in 2008 that it understated depreciation expense in 2007 by $300,000 due to computational errors. These errors overstated both net income for 2007 and the current balance in retained earnings. The entry for the prior period adjustment, ignoring all tax effects, is as follows.

Cash Flows
no effect

Retained Earnings	300,000	
Accumulated Depreciation		300,000
(To adjust for understatement of depreciation in a		
prior period)		

A debit to an income statement account in 2008 is incorrect because the error pertains to a prior year.

Companies report prior period adjustments in the retained earnings statement.[1] They add (or deduct, as the case may be) these adjustments from the beginning retained earnings balance. This results in an adjusted beginning balance. For example, assuming a beginning balance of $800,000 in retained earnings, General Microwave reports the prior period adjustment as follows.

Illustration 14-12
Statement presentation of prior period adjustments

GENERAL MICROWAVE	
Retained Earnings Statement (partial)	
Balance, January 1, as reported	$ 800,000
Correction for overstatement of net income	
in prior period (depreciation error)	(300,000)
Balance, January 1, as adjusted	$ 500,000

Again, reporting the correction in the current year's income statement would be incorrect because it applies to a prior year's income statement.

Retained Earnings Statement

The **retained earnings statement** shows the changes in retained earnings during the year. The company prepares the statement from the Retained Earnings account. Illustration 14-13 shows (in account form) transactions that affect retained earnings.

Illustration 14-13
Debits and credits to retained earnings

Retained Earnings	
1. Net loss	1. Net income
2. Prior period adjustments for overstatement of net income	2. Prior period adjustments for understatement of net income
3. Cash dividends and stock dividends	
4. Some disposals of treasury stock	

As indicated, net income increases retained earnings, and a net loss decreases retained earnings. Prior period adjustments may either increase or decrease retained earnings. Both cash dividends and stock dividends decrease retained earnings. The

---

[1] A complete retained earnings statement is shown in Illustration 14-14 on the next page.

circumstances under which treasury stock transactions decrease retained earnings are explained in Chapter 13, page 571.

A complete retained earnings statement for Graber Inc., based on assumed data, is as follows.

Illustration 14-14
Retained earnings statement

GRABER INC.
Retained Earnings Statement
For the Year Ended December 31, 2008

Balance, January 1, as reported		$1,050,000
Correction for understatement of net income in prior period (inventory error)		50,000
Balance, January 1, as adjusted		1,100,000
Add: Net income		360,000
		1,460,000
Less: Cash dividends	$100,000	
Stock dividends	200,000	300,000
Balance, December 31		$1,160,000

STATEMENT PRESENTATION AND ANALYSIS

Stockholders' Equity Presentation

Illustration 14-15 presents the stockholders' equity section of Graber Inc.'s balance sheet. Note the following: (1) "Common stock dividends distributable" is shown under "Capital stock," in "Paid-in capital." (2) A note (Note R) discloses a retained earnings restriction.

STUDY OBJECTIVE 3

Prepare and analyze a comprehensive stockholders' equity section.

Illustration 14-15
Comprehensive stockholders' equity section

GRABER INC.
Balance Sheet (partial)

Stockholders' equity		
Paid-in capital		
Capital stock		
9% Preferred stock, $100 par value, cumulative, callable at $120, 10,000 shares authorized, 6,000 shares issued and outstanding		$ 600,000
Common stock, no par, $5 stated value, 500,000 shares authorized, 400,000 shares issued and 390,000 outstanding	$2,000,000	
Common stock dividends distributable	50,000	2,050,000
Total capital stock		2,650,000
Additional paid-in capital		
In excess of par value—preferred stock	30,000	
In excess of stated value—common stock	1,050,000	
Total additional paid-in capital		1,080,000
Total paid-in capital		3,730,000
Retained earnings (see Note R)		1,160,000
Total paid-in capital and retained earnings		4,890,000
Less: Treasury stock—common (10,000 shares)		80,000
Total stockholders' equity		$4,810,000

Note R: Retained earnings is restricted for the cost of treasury stock, $80,000.

Instead of presenting a detailed stockholders' equity section in the balance sheet and a retained earnings statement, many companies prepare a **stockholders' equity statement**. This statement shows the changes (1) in each stockholders' equity account and (2) in total that occurred during the year. An example of a stockholders' equity statement appears in PepsiCo's financial statements in Appendix A (page A8).

Stockholders' Equity Analysis

Investors and analysts can measure profitability from the viewpoint of the common stockholder by the **return on common stockholders' equity**. This ratio shows how many dollars of net income the company earned for each dollar invested by the stockholders. It is computed by dividing **net income available to common stockholders** (which is net income minus preferred stock dividends) by average common stockholders' equity.

To illustrate, Kellogg Company's beginning-of-the-year and end-of-the-year common stockholders' equity were $1,443.2 and $2,257.2 million respectively. Its net income was $890.6 million, and no preferred stock was outstanding. The return on common stockholders' equity ratio is computed as follows.

Illustration 14-16
Return on common stockholders' equity ratio and computation

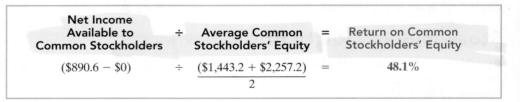

Net Income Available to Common Stockholders	÷	Average Common Stockholders' Equity	=	Return on Common Stockholders' Equity
($890.6 − $0)	÷	$\dfrac{(\$1{,}443.2 + \$2{,}257.2)}{2}$	=	48.1%

As shown above, if a company has preferred stock, we would deduct the amount of **preferred dividends** from the company's net income to compute income available to common stockholders. Also, the par value of preferred stock is deducted from total average stockholders' equity to arrive at the amount of common stockholders' equity.

Before You Go On...

REVIEW IT

1. How do companies generally report retained earnings restrictions?
2. What is a prior period adjustment, and how is it reported?
3. What are the principal sources of debits and credits to Retained Earnings?
4. How do companies report stock dividends distributable in the stockholders' equity section?
5. Explain the return on common stockholders' equity ratio.

DO IT

Vega Corporation has retained earnings of $5,130,000 on January 1, 2008. During the year, Vega earns $2,000,000 of net income. It declares and pays a $250,000 cash dividend. In 2008, Vega records an adjustment of $180,000 due to the understatement of 2007 depreciation expense from a mathematical error. Prepare a retained earnings statement for 2008.

Action Plan

- Recall that a retained earnings statement begins with retained earnings, as reported at the end of the previous year.
- Add or subtract any prior period adjustments to arrive at the adjusted beginning figure.
- Add net income and subtract dividends declared to arrive at the ending balance in retained earnings.

Solution

VEGA CORPORATION
Retained Earnings Statement
For the Year Ended December 31, 2008

Balance, January 1, as reported	$5,130,000
Correction for overstatement of net income in prior period (depreciation error)	(180,000)
Balance, January 1, as adjusted	4,950,000
Add: Net income	2,000,000
	6,950,000
Less: Cash dividends	250,000
Balance, December 31	$6,700,000

Related exercise material: *BE14-4, BE14-5, BE14-6, BE14-7, E14-8, E14-9, E14-10, and E14-11.*

✓ *The Navigator*

Income Statement Presentation

Income statements for **corporations are the same as the statements for proprietorships or partnerships except for one thing: the reporting of income taxes**. For income tax purposes, corporations are a separate legal entity. As a result, corporations report **income tax expense** in a separate section of the corporation income statement, before net income. The condensed income statement for Leads Inc. in Illustration 14-17 shows a typical presentation. Note that the corporation reports income before income taxes as one line item and income tax expense as another.

LEADS INC.
Income Statement
For the Year Ended December 31, 2008

Sales	$800,000
Cost of goods sold	600,000
Gross profit	200,000
Operating expenses	50,000
Income from operations	150,000
Other revenues and gains	10,000
Other expenses and losses	(4,000)
Income before income taxes	**156,000**
Income tax expense	**46,800**
Net income	$109,200

Illustration 14-17
Income statement with income taxes

Companies record income tax expense and the related liability for income taxes payable as part of the adjusting process. Using the data for Leads Inc., in Illustration 14-17, the adjusting entry for income tax expense at December 31, 2008, is:

A = L + SE
          −46,800 Exp
   +46,800

Cash Flows
no effect

Income Tax Expense	46,800	
Income Taxes Payable		46,800
(To record income taxes for 2008)		

The income statement of PepsiCo in Appendix A presents another illustration of income taxes.

Income Statement Analysis

STUDY OBJECTIVE 5
Compute earnings per share.

The financial press frequently reports earnings data. Stockholders and potential investors widely use these data in evaluating the profitability of a company. A convenient measure of earnings is **earnings per share (EPS)**, which indicates the net income earned by each share of outstanding **common stock**.

EPS AND PREFERRED DIVIDENDS

The existence of preferred dividends slightly complicates the calculation of EPS. When a corporation has both preferred and common stock, we must subtract the current year's preferred dividend from net income, to arrive at **income available to common stockholders**. Illustration 14-18 shows the formula for computing EPS.

Illustration 14-18
Formula for earnings per share

Net Income minus Preferred Dividends	÷	Weighted-Average of Common Shares Outstanding	=	Earnings per Share

ETHICS NOTE

In order to meet market expectations for EPS, some managers engage in elaborate treasury stock transactions. These transactions can be very costly for the remaining shareholders.

To illustrate, assume that Rally Inc. reports net income of $211,000 on its 102,500 weighted-average common shares.[2] During the year it also declares a $6,000 dividend on its preferred stock. Therefore, the amount Rally has available for common stock dividends is $205,000 ($211,000 − $6,000). Earnings per share is $2 ($205,000 ÷ 102,500). If the preferred stock is cumulative, Rally deducts the dividend for the current year, whether or not it is declared. Remember that companies report **earnings per share only for common stock**.

Investors often attempt to link earnings per share to the market price per share of a company's stock.[3] Because of the importance of earnings per share, most companies must report it on the face of the income statement. Generally companies

---

[2]The calculation of the weighted average of common shares outstanding is discussed in advanced accounting courses.

[3]The ratio of the market price per share to the earnings per share is called the *price/earnings (P/E) ratio*. The financial media report this ratio for common stocks listed on major stock exchanges.

simply report this amount below net income on the statement. For Rally Inc. the presentation is as follows.

RALLY INC.	
Income Statement (partial)	
Net income	$211,000
Earnings per share	$2.00

Illustration 14-19
Basic earnings per share disclosure

INVESTOR INSIGHT

Yahoo! and Costco Feel the Impact of Earnings per Share

When a company publicly announces its latest earnings per share figure, a change in the company's stock price will often follow. The change in stock price will be most pronounced if the company's net income figure differs from what investors were expecting. When Yahoo! announced earnings per share that exceeded investor expectations, its stock price jumped 14% in a single day. When retail giant Costco Wholesale Corporation announced earnings per share only 1 cent below analysts' expectations, its stock price fell 22% in a single day. To avoid "earnings surprises" and the resultant wide swings in share prices, companies continually try to keep investors informed.

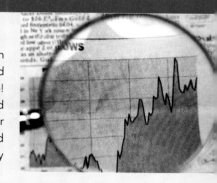

? Why do you think the prices of these companies changed as indicated?

Before You Go On...

REVIEW IT

1. What is the unique feature of a corporation income statement?
2. Explain the components of the formula for computing earnings per share when there is only common stock and outstanding shares are unchanged during the year.
3. What effects may preferred stock have on the formula for computing earnings per share?

 The Navigator

 Be sure to read **ALL ABOUT YOU:** *Corporations Have Governance Structures—Do You?* on page 612 for information on how topics in this chapter apply to you.

Corporations Have Governance Structures—Do You

As discussed previously in this text, the scandals and bankruptcies at Enron, WorldCom, and other companies brought many changes to the way America does business. One of the primary lessons has been that companies need to take corporate governance and management oversight more seriously. As part of this effort, many companies have developed a code of ethics. The purpose of a code of ethics is to clearly specify standards of conduct to deter wrongdoing and promote honest and ethical conduct. It also is intended to be an expression by top management of its "tone at the top" —that is, to indicate that top management takes ethics seriously. Many other organizations, including university student groups, also have formulated ethics codes.

✷ About the Numbers

Stockholders often lose money as a result of unethical behavior by manageme When they do, they often file lawsuits against the company in an effort to reco these losses. The graph below shows just how expensive these class-action la suits can be for companies.

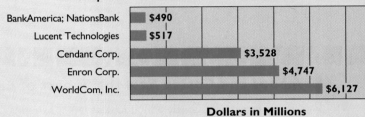

Top Class-Action Securities Settlements

	Dollars in Millions
BankAmerica; NationsBank	$490
Lucent Technologies	$517
Cendant Corp.	$3,528
Enron Corp.	$4,747
WorldCom, Inc.	$6,127

Source: Elaine Buckberg, Todd Foster, and Ronald I. Miller, "Recent Trends in Shareholder Class Action Litigation: Are WorldCom and Enron the New Standard?" NERA Economic Consulting, *www.nera.com* (accessed June 26, 2006).

✷ Some Facts

* Under Sarbanes-Oxley, a company must disclose in its annual report whether it has a code of ethics. It must also disclose any changes to or waivers of the code of ethics.

* Enron had a code of ethics. In a number of instances, Enron's board of directors knowingly waived requirements of the code so that the CFO could set up and run special purpose entities. Ultimately these waivers contributed to Enron's downfall.

* In some instances U.S. federal prosecutors have pressured companies to not pay the legal-defense bills of employees accused of wrong-doing, thus making it harder for the employees to defend themselves.

* In a recent survey of 1,436 workers, 34% said that they have seen unethical activities at their workplace, but only 47% said they are likely to report these activities. Many cited fear of retaliation by their bosses as the reason for not reporting.

✷ What Do You Think

Many universities have become concerned about student cheating. In p ticular, the prevalence of digital documents on the Internet has made it very easy to plagiarize. Many schools now have student ethics codes. Do you think that these ethics codes serve a useful purpose?

YES: Anything that will reduce unethical behavior is a good thing. A ethics code establishes what is and is not acceptable behavior, which he universities maintain ethical standards for academic work and weed out those students who try to get ahead by non-ethical means.

NO: The existence of an ethics code won't affect student behavior. If students have a propensity to cheat, a document that tells them what is and is not good behavior is not going to be a deterrent. Students alread know what cheating is, and that it is wrong.

Sources: "Whistleblowing Workers: Becoming an Endangered Species?" *HR Focus,* June 200 p. 9; Lauren Etter, "The Enron Trial Finally Begins," *Wall Street Journal,* February 4, 2006, p.

The authors' comments on this situation appear on page 627.

Demonstration Problem

On January 1, 2008, Hayslett Corporation had the following stockholders' equity accounts.

Common Stock ($10 par value, 260,000 shares issued and outstanding)	$2,600,000
Paid-in Capital in Excess of Par Value	1,500,000
Retained Earnings	3,200,000

During the year, the following transactions occurred.

April	1	Declared a $1.50 cash dividend per share to stockholders of record on April 15, payable May 1.
May	1	Paid the dividend declared in April.
June	1	Announced a 2-for-1 stock split. Prior to the split, the market price per share was $24.
Aug.	1	Declared a 10% stock dividend to stockholders of record on August 15, distributable August 31. On August 1, the market price of the stock was $10 per share.
	31	Issued the shares for the stock dividend.
Dec.	1	Declared a $1.50 per share dividend to stockholders of record on December 15, payable January 5, 2009.
	31	Determined that net income for the year was $600,000.

Instructions

(a) Journalize the transactions and the closing entry for net income.
(b) Prepare a stockholders' equity section at December 31.

Solution to Demonstration Problem

(a)

Apr. 1	Retained Earnings (260,000 × $1.50)	390,000	
	Dividends Payable		390,000
May 1	Dividends Payable	390,000	
	Cash		390,000
June 1	Memo—two-for-one stock split increases number of shares to 520,000 (260,000 × 2) and reduces par value to $5 per share.		
Aug. 1	Retained Earnings (52,000* × $10)	520,000	
	Common Stock Dividends Distributable (52,000 × $5)		260,000
	Paid-in Capital in Excess of Par Value (52,000 × $5)		260,000
	*520,000 × .10		
31	Common Stock Dividends Distributable	260,000	
	Common Stock		260,000
Dec. 1	Retained Earnings (572,000** × $1.50)	858,000	
	Dividends Payable		858,000
	**(260,000 × 2) + 52,000		
31	Income Summary	600,000	
	Retained Earnings		600,000

action plan

✔ Award dividends to outstanding shares only.

✔ Adjust the par value and number of shares for stock splits, but make no journal entry.

✔ Use market value of stock to determine the value of a small stock dividend.

✔ Close Income Summary to Retained Earnings.

(b)

HAYSLETT CORPORATION

Stockholders' equity	
Paid-in capital	
Capital stock	
Common stock, $5 par value, 572,000	
shares issued and outstanding	$2,860,000
Additional paid-in capital in excess of par value	1,760,000
Total paid-in capital	4,620,000
Retained earnings	2,032,000
Total stockholders' equity	$6,652,000

SUMMARY OF STUDY OBJECTIVES

1 Prepare the entries for cash dividends and stock dividends. Companies make entries for both cash and stock dividends at the declaration date and at the payment date. At the *declaration date* the entries are: cash dividend—debit Retained Earnings, and credit Dividends Payable; small stock dividend—debit Retained Earnings, credit Paid-in Capital in Excess of Par (or Stated) Value, and credit Common Stock Dividends Distributable. At the *payment date*, the entries for cash and stock dividends are: cash dividend—debit Dividends Payable and credit Cash; small stock dividend—debit Common Stock Dividends Distributable and credit Common Stock.

2 Identify the items reported in a retained earnings statement. Companies report each of the individual debits and credits to retained earnings in the retained earnings statement. Additions consist of net income and prior period adjustments to correct understatements of prior years' net income. Deductions consist of net loss, adjustments to correct overstatements of prior years' net income, cash and stock dividends, and some disposals of treasury stock.

3 Prepare and analyze a comprehensive stockholders' equity section. A comprehensive stockholders' equity

section includes all stockholders' equity accounts. It consists of two sections: paid-in capital and retained earnings. It should also include notes to the financial statements that explain any restrictions on retained earnings and any dividends in arrears. One measure of profitability is the return on common stockholders' equity. It is calculated by dividing net income minus preferred stock dividends by average common stockholders' equity.

4 Describe the form and content of corporation income statements. The form and content of corporation income statements are similar to the statements of proprietorships and partnerships with one exception: Corporations must report income taxes or income tax expense in a separate section before net income in the income statement.

5 Compute earnings per share. Companies compute earnings per share by dividing net income by the weighted-average number of common shares outstanding during the period. When preferred stock dividends exist, they must be deducted from net income in order to calculate EPS.

GLOSSARY

Cash dividend A pro rata distribution of cash to stockholders. (p. 596).

Declaration date The date the board of directors formally declares a dividend and announces it to stockholders. (p. 597).

Deficit A debit balance in retained earnings. (p. 604).

Dividend A corporation's distribution of cash or stock to its stockholders on a pro rata (proportional) basis. (p. 596).

Earnings per share The net income earned by each share of outstanding common stock. (p 610)

Liquidating dividend A dividend declared out of paid-in capital. (p. 596).

Payment date The date dividend checks are mailed to stockholders. (p. 598).

Prior period adjustment The correction of an error in previously issued financial statements. (p. 605).

Record date The date when ownership of outstanding shares is determined for dividend purposes. (p. 597).

Retained earnings Net income that is retained in the business. (p. 604).

Retained earnings restrictions   Circumstances that make a portion of retained earnings currently unavailable for dividends. (p. 605).

Retained earnings statement   A financial statement that shows the changes in retained earnings during the year. (p. 606).

Return on common stockholders' equity   A measure of profitability that shows how many dollars of net income were earned for each dollar invested by the owners; computed as net income minus preferred dividends divided by average common stockholders' equity. (p. 608).

Stock dividend   A pro rata distribution to stockholders of the corporation's own stock. (p. 600).

Stockholders' equity statement   A statement that shows the changes in each stockholders' equity account and in total stockholders' equity during the year. (p. 608).

Stock split   The issuance of additional shares of stock to stockholders according to their percentage ownership; is accompanied by a reduction in the par or stated value per share. (p. 602).

SELF-STUDY QUESTIONS

Answers are at the end of the chapter.

1) **1.** Entries for cash dividends are required on the:
   a. declaration date and the payment date.
   b. record date and the payment date.
   c. declaration date, record date, and payment date.
   d. declaration date and the record date.

1) **2.** Which of the following statements about small stock dividends is true?
   a. A debit to Retained Earnings for the par value of the shares issued should be made.
   b. A small stock dividend decreases total stockholders' equity.
   c. Market value per share should be assigned to the dividend shares.
   d. A small stock dividend ordinarily will have no effect on book value per share of stock.

1) **3.** Which of the following statements about a 3-for-1 stock split is true?
   a. It will triple the market value of the stock.
   b. It will triple the amount of total stockholders' equity.
   c. It will have no effect on total stockholders' equity.
   d. It requires the company to distribute cash.

2) **4.** Which of the following can cause a restriction in retained earnings?
   a. State laws regarding treasury stock.
   b. Long-term debt contract terms.
   c. Authorizations by the board of directors in light of planned expansion of corporate facilities.
   d. All of the above.

2) **5.** All *but one* of the following is reported in a retained earnings statement. The exception is:
   a. cash and stock dividends.
   b. net income and net loss.
   c. some disposals of treasury stock below cost.
   d. sales of treasury stock above cost.

2) **6.** A prior period adjustment is:
   a. reported in the income statement as a nontypical item.
   b. a correction of an error that is made directly to retained earnings.

   c. reported directly in the stockholders' equity section.
   d. reported in the retained earnings statement as an adjustment of the ending balance of retained earnings.

7. In the stockholders' equity section, Common Stock (SO 3) Dividends Distributable is reported as a(n):
   a. deduction from total paid-in capital and retained earnings.
   b. addition to additional paid-in capital.
   c. deduction from retained earnings.
   d. addition to capital stock.

8. Corporation income statements may be the same as the (SO 4) income statements for unincorporated companies *except* for:
   a. gross profit.
   b. income tax expense.
   c. operating income.
   d. net sales.

9. The return on common stockholders' equity is defined as: (SO 3)
   a. Net income divided by total assets.
   b. Cash dividends divided by average common stockholders' equity.
   c. Income available to common stockholders divided by average common stockholders' equity.
   d. None of these is correct.

10. The income statement for Nadeen, Inc. shows income be- (SO 5) fore income taxes $700,000, income tax expense $210,000, and net income $490,000. If Nadeen has 100,000 shares of common stock outstanding throughout the year, earnings per share is:
   a. $7.00.
   b. $4.90.
   c. $2.10.
   d. No correct answer is given.

Go to the book's website,
www.wiley.com/college/weygandt,
for Additional Self-Study questions.

QUESTIONS

1. (a) What is a dividend? (b) "Dividends must be paid in cash." Do you agree? Explain.

2. Sue DeVine maintains that adequate cash is the only requirement for the declaration of a cash dividend. Is Sue correct? Explain.

3. (a) Three dates are important in connection with cash dividends. Identify these dates, and explain their significance to the corporation and its stockholders.
   (b) Identify the accounting entries that are made for a cash dividend and the date of each entry.

4. Conger Inc. declares a $45,000 cash dividend on December 31, 2008. The required annual dividend on preferred stock is $10,000. Determine the allocation of the dividend to preferred and common stockholders assuming the preferred stock is cumulative and dividends are 1 year in arrears.

5. Contrast the effects of a cash dividend and a stock dividend on a corporation's balance sheet.

6. Todd Huebner asks, "Since stock dividends don't change anything, why declare them?" What is your answer to Todd?

7. Meenen Corporation has 30,000 shares of $10 par value common stock outstanding when it announces a 2-for-1 stock split. Before the split, the stock had a market price of $120 per share. After the split, how many shares of stock will be outstanding? What will be the approximate market price per share?

8. The board of directors is considering either a stock split or a stock dividend. They understand that total stockholders' equity will remain the same under either action. However, they are not sure of the different effects of the two types of actions on other aspects of stockholders' equity. Explain the differences to the directors.

9. What is a prior period adjustment, and how is it reported in the financial statements?

10. KSU Corporation has a retained earnings balance of $210,000 on January 1. During the year, a prior period adjustment of $50,000 is recorded because of the understatement of depreciation in the prior period. Show the retained earnings statement presentation of these data.

11. What is the purpose of a retained earnings restriction? Identify the possible causes of retained earnings restrictions.

12. How are retained earnings restrictions generally reported in the financial statements?

13. Identify the events that result in debits and credits to retained earnings.

14. Juan Ortega believes that both the beginning and ending balances in retained earnings are shown in the stockholders' equity section. Is Juan correct? Discuss.

15. Gene Remington, who owns many investments in common stock, says, "I don't care what a company's net income is. The stock price tells me everything I need to know!" How do you respond to Gene?

16. What is the unique feature of a corporation income statement? Illustrate this feature, using assumed data.

17. Why must preferred stock dividends be subtracted from net income in computing earnings per share?

BRIEF EXERCISES

Prepare entries for a cash dividend.
(SO 1)

BE14-1 Eidman Corporation has 80,000 shares of common stock outstanding. It declares a $1 per share cash dividend on November 1 to stockholders of record on December 1. The dividend is paid on December 31. Prepare the entries on the appropriate dates to record the declaration and payment of the cash dividend.

Prepare entries for a stock dividend.
(SO 1)

BE14-2 Tidwell Corporation has 50,000 shares of $10 par value common stock outstanding. It declares a 10% stock dividend on December 1 when the market value per share is $16. The dividend shares are issued on December 31. Prepare the entries for the declaration and payment of the stock dividend.

Show before and after effects of a stock dividend.
(SO 1)

BE14-3 The stockholders' equity section of O'Vear Corporation consists of common stock ($10 par) $2,000,000 and retained earnings $500,000. A 10% stock dividend (20,000 shares) is declared when the market value per share is $14. Show the before and after effects of the dividend on the following.

(a) The components of stockholders' equity.
(b) Shares outstanding.
(c) Book value per share.

Prepare a retained earnings statement.
(SO 2)

BE14-4 For the year ending December 31, 2008, Kerns Inc. reports net income $140,000 and dividends $85,000. Prepare the retained earnings statement for the year assuming the balance in retained earnings on January 1, 2008, was $220,000.

Prepare a retained earnings statement.
(SO 2)

BE14-5 The balance in retained earnings on January 1, 2008, for Persinger Inc, was $800,000. During the year, the corporation paid cash dividends of $90,000 and distributed a stock dividend of $8,000. In addition, the company determined that it had understated its depreciation expense in prior years by $50,000. Net income for 2008 was $120,000. Prepare the retained earnings statement for 2008.

BE14-6 SUPERVALU, one of the largest grocery retailers in the United States, is headquartered in Minneapolis. The following financial information (in millions) was taken from the company's 2005 annual report. Net sales $19,543; net income $386; beginning stockholders' equity $2,210; ending stockholders' equity $2,510. Compute the return on common stockholders' equity ratio.

Calculate the return on common stockholders' equity.
(SO 3)

BE14-7 Fuentes Corporation reported net income of $152,000, declared dividends on common stock of $50,000, and had an ending balance in retained earnings of $360,000. Stockholders' equity was $700,000 at the beginning of the year and $820,000 at the end of the year. Compute the return on common stockholders' equity.

Compute return on common stockholders' equity.
(SO 3)

BE14-8 The following information is available for Dixen Corporation for the year ended December 31, 2008: Cost of goods sold $205,000; Sales $450,000; Other revenues and gains $50,000; Operating expenses $75,000. Assuming a corporate tax rate of 30%, prepare an income statement for the company.

Prepare a corporate income statement.
(SO 4)

BE14-9 Quayle Corporation reports net income of $380,000 and a weighted average of 200,000 shares of common stock outstanding for the year. Compute the earnings per share of common stock.

Compute earnings per share.
(SO 5)

BE14-10 Income and common stock data for Quayle Corporation are presented in BE14-9. Assume also that Quayle has cumulative preferred stock dividends for the current year of $20,000 that were declared and paid. Compute the earnings per share of common stock.

Compute earnings per share with cumulative preferred stock.
(SO 5)

EXERCISES

E14-1 On January 1, Molini Corporation had 95,000 shares of no-par common stock issued and outstanding. The stock has a stated value of $5 per share. During the year, the following occurred.

Journalize cash dividends; indicate statement presentation.
(SO 1)

Apr. 1 Issued 25,000 additional shares of common stock for $17 per share.
June 15 Declared a cash dividend of $1 per share to stockholders of record on June 30.
July 10 Paid the $1 cash dividend.
Dec. 1 Issued 2,000 additional shares of common stock for $19 per share.
     15 Declared a cash dividend on outstanding shares of $1.20 per share to stockholders of record on December 31.

Instructions
(a) Prepare the entries, if any, on each of the three dividend dates. *total DIVIDEND declared 266,400*
(b) How are dividends and dividends payable reported in the financial statements prepared at December 31?

E14-2 Perez Corporation was organized on January 1, 2007. During its first year, the corporation issued 2,000 shares of $50 par value preferred stock and 100,000 shares of $10 par value common stock. At December 31, the company declared the following cash dividends: 2007, $6,000, 2008, $12,000, and 2009, $28,000.

Allocate cash dividends to preferred and common stock.
(SO 1)

Instructions
(a) Show the allocation of dividends to each class of stock, assuming the preferred stock dividend is 7% and not cumulative. *2009 Preferred Dividend $7,000*
(b) Show the allocation of dividends to each class of stock, assuming the preferred stock dividend is 8% and cumulative. *2009 Preferred Dividend $8,000*
(c) Journalize the declaration of the cash dividend at December 31, 2009, under part (b).

E14-3 On January 1, 2008, Deweese Corporation had $1,000,000 of common stock outstanding that was issued at par. It also had retained earnings of $750,000. The company issued 40,000 shares of common stock at par on July 1 and earned net income of $400,000 for the year.

Journalize stock dividends.
(SO 1)

Instructions

Journalize the declaration of a 15% stock dividend on December 10, 2008, for the following independent assumptions.

[handwritten: Debit Retained earnings (a) 378,000

(b) 120,000]

1. Par value is $10, and market value is $18.
2. Par value is $5, and market value is $20.

Compare effects of a stock dividend and a stock split.

(SO 1)

E14-4 On October 31, the stockholders' equity section of Huth Company consists of common stock $300,000 and retained earnings $900,000. Huth is considering the following two courses of action: (1) declaring a 5% stock dividend on the 30,000, $10 par value shares outstanding, or (2) effecting a 2-for-1 stock split that will reduce par value to $5 per share. The current market price is $14 per share.

Instructions

Prepare a tabular summary of the effects of the alternative actions on the components of stockholders' equity, outstanding shares, and book value per share. Use the following column headings: Before Action, After Stock Dividend, and After Stock Split. *[handwritten: Book value after Stock Dividend $38.10, after stock split $20.00]*

Compute book value per share; indicate account balances after a stock dividend.

(SO 1, 3)

E14-5 On October 1, Kosko Corporation's stockholders' equity is as follows.

Common stock, $5 par value	$400,000
Paid-in capital in excess of par value	25,000
Retained earnings	155,000
Total stockholders' equity	$580,000

[handwritten: 400,000 ÷ 5 = 80,000]

On October 1, Kosko declares and distributes a 10% stock dividend when the market value of the stock is $15 per share.

Instructions

(a) Compute the book value per share (1) before the stock dividend and (2) after the stock dividend. (Round to two decimals.) *[handwritten: Book value (1) $7.25, (2) 6.59]*

(b) Indicate the balances in the three stockholders' equity accounts after the stock dividend shares have been distributed. *[handwritten: Common stock $440,000, Retained earnings $35,000]*

Indicate the effects on stockholders' equity components.

(SO 1, 2, 3)

E14-6 During 2008, Jester Corporation had the following transactions and events.

1. Declared a cash dividend.
2. Issued par value common stock for cash at par value.
3. Completed a 2-for-1 stock split in which $10 par value stock was changed to $5 par value stock.
4. Declared a small stock dividend when the market value was higher than par value.
5. Made a prior period adjustment for overstatement of net income.
6. Issued the shares of common stock required by the stock dividend declaration in item no. 4 above.
7. Paid the cash dividend in item no. 1 above.
8. Issued par value common stock for cash above par value.

Instructions

Indicate the effect(s) of each of the foregoing items on the subdivisions of stockholders' equity. Present your answer in tabular form with the following columns. Use (I) for increase, (D) for decrease, and (NE) for no effect. Item no. 1 is given as an example.

| | **Paid-in Capital** | | |
| | Capital | | Retained |
Item	Stock	Additional	Earnings
1	NE	NE	D

Prepare correcting entries for dividends and a stock split.

(SO 1)

E14-7 Before preparing financial statements for the current year, the chief accountant for Reynolds Company discovered the following errors in the accounts.

1. The declaration and payment of $50,000 cash dividend was recorded as a debit to Interest Expense $50,000 and a credit to Cash $50,000.
2. A 10% stock dividend (1,000 shares) was declared on the $10 par value stock when the market value per share was $18. The only entry made was: Retained Earnings (Dr.) $10,000 and Dividend Payable (Cr.) $10,000. The shares have not been issued.

3. A 4-for-1 stock split involving the issue of 400,000 shares of $5 par value common stock for 100,000 shares of $20 par value common stock was recorded as a debit to Retained Earnings $2,000,000 and a credit to Common Stock $2,000,000.

Instructions

Prepare the correcting entries at December 31.

E14-8 On January 1, 2008, Felter Corporation had retained earnings of $550,000. During the year, Felter had the following selected transactions.

Prepare a retained earnings statement.

(SO 2)

1. Declared cash dividends $120,000.
2. Corrected overstatement of 2007 net income because of depreciation error $40,000.
3. Earned net income $350,000.
4. Declared stock dividends $60,000.

Instructions

Prepare a retained earnings statement for the year.

E14-9 Sasha Company reported retained earnings at December 31, 2007, of $310,000. Sasha had 200,000 shares of common stock outstanding throughout 2008.

Prepare a retained earnings statement.

(SO 2)

The following transactions occurred during 2008.

1. An error was discovered: in 2006, depreciation expense was recorded at $70,000, but the correct amount was $50,000.
2. A cash dividend of $0.50 per share was declared and paid.
3. A 5% stock dividend was declared and distributed when the market price per share was $15 per share.
4. Net income was $285,000.

Instructions

Prepare a retained earnings statement for 2008.

E14-10 Kelly Groucutt Company reported the following balances at December 31, 2007: common stock $400,000; paid-in capital in excess of par value $100,000; retained earnings $250,000. During 2008, the following transactions affected stockholder's equity.

Prepare stockholders' equity section.

(SO 3)

1. Issued preferred stock with a par value of $125,000 for $200,000.
2. Purchased treasury stock (common) for $40,000.
3. Earned net income of $140,000.
4. Declared and paid cash dividends of $56,000.

Instructions

Prepare the stockholders' equity section of Kelly Groucutt Company's December 31, 2008, balance sheet.

E14-11 The following accounts appear in the ledger of Ortiz Inc. after the books are closed at December 31.

Prepare a stockholders' equity section.

(SO 3)

total stock equity 2,750000

Common Stock, no par, $1 stated value, 400,000 shares authorized; 300,000 shares issued	$ 300,000
Common Stock Dividends Distributable	30,000
Paid-in Capital in Excess of Stated Value—Common Stock	1,200,000
Preferred Stock, $5 par value, 8%, 40,000 shares authorized; 30,000 shares issued	150,000
Retained Earnings	800,000
Treasury Stock (10,000 common shares)	74,000
Paid-in Capital in Excess of Par Value—Preferred Stock	344,000

Instructions

Prepare the stockholders' equity section at December 31, assuming retained earnings is restricted for plant expansion in the amount of $100,000.

E14-12 The following information is available for Patel Corporation for the year ended December 31, 2008: Sales $800,000; Other revenues and gains $92,000; Operating expenses $110,000; Cost of goods sold $465,000; Other expenses and losses $32,000; Preferred stock dividends $30,000. The company's tax rate was 20%, and it had 50,000 shares outstanding during the entire year.

Prepare an income statement and compute earnings per share.

(SO 4, 5)

Instructions
(a) Prepare a corporate income statement.
(b) Calculate earnings per share.

Prepare an income statement and compute return on equity.
(SO 3, 4)

E14-13 In 2008, Mike Singletary Corporation had net sales of $600,000 and cost of goods sold of $360,000. Operating expenses were $153,000, and interest expense was $7,500. The corporation's tax rate is 30%. The corporation declared preferred dividends of $15,000 in 2008, and its average common stockholders' equity during the year was $200,000.

Instructions
(a) Prepare an income statement for Mike Singletary Corporation.
(b) Compute Mike Singletary Corporation's return on common stockholders' equity for 2008.

Compute EPS.
(SO 4, 5)

E14-14 McCoy Corporation has outstanding at December 31, 2008, 50,000 shares of $20 par value, cumulative, 8% preferred stock and 200,000 shares of $5 par value common stock. All shares were outstanding the entire year. During 2008, McCoy earned total revenues of $2,000,000 and incurred total expenses (except income taxes) of $1,200,000. McCoy's income tax rate is 30%.

Instructions
Compute McCoy's 2008 earnings per share.

Calculate ratios to evaluate earnings performance.
(SO 3, 5)

E14-15 The following financial information is available for Cheney Corporation.

	2008	**2007**
Average common stockholders' equity	$1,200,000	$900,000
Dividends paid to common stockholders	50,000	30,000
Dividends paid to preferred stockholders	20,000	20,000
Net income	290,000	200,000
Market price of common stock	20	15

The weighted average number of shares of common stock outstanding was 80,000 for 2007 and 100,000 for 2008.

2008 EPS $2.70

Instructions
Calculate earnings per share and return on common stockholders' equity for 2008 and 2007.

Calculate ratios to evaluate earnings performance.
(SO 3, 5)

E14-16 This financial information is available for Hoyle Corporation.

	2008	**2007**
Average common stockholders' equity	$1,800,000	$1,900,000
Dividends paid to common stockholders	90,000	70,000
Dividends paid to preferred stockholders	20,000	20,000
Net income	290,000	248,000
Market price of common stock	20	25

The weighted-average number of shares of common stock outstanding was 180,000 for 2007 and 150,000 for 2008.

2008 EPS $1.80

Instructions
Calculate earnings per share and return on common stockholders' equity for 2008 and 2007.

Compute earnings per share under different assumptions.
(SO 5)

E14-17 At December 31, 2008, Cali Corporation has 2,000 shares of $100 par value, 8%, preferred stock outstanding and 100,000 shares of $10 par value common stock issued. Cali's net income for the year is $241,000.

Instructions
Compute the earnings per share of common stock under the following independent situations. (Round to two decimals.)

(a) The dividend to preferred stockholders was declared. There has been no change in the number of shares of common stock outstanding during the year.

(b) The dividend to preferred stockholders was not declared. The preferred stock is cumulative. Cali held 10,000 shares of common treasury stock throughout the year.

EXERCISES: SET B

Visit the book's website at **www.wiley.com/college/weygandt**, and choose the Student Companion site, to access Exercise Set B.

PROBLEMS: SET A

P14-1A   On January 1, 2008, Carolinas Corporation had the following stockholders' equity accounts.

Common Stock ($20 par value, 60,000 shares issued and outstanding)	$1,200,000
Paid-in Capital in Excess of Par Value	200,000
Retained Earnings	600,000

Prepare dividend entries and stockholders' equity section.

(SO 1, 3)

During the year, the following transactions occurred.

Feb. 1   Declared a $1 cash dividend per share to stockholders of record on February 15, payable March 1.
Mar. 1   Paid the dividend declared in February.
Apr. 1   Announced a 2-for-1 stock split. Prior to the split, the market price per share was $36.
July 1   Declared a 10% stock dividend to stockholders of record on July 15, distributable July 31. On July 1, the market price of the stock was $13 per share.
     31   Issued the shares for the stock dividend.
Dec. 1   Declared a $0.50 per share dividend to stockholders of record on December 15, payable January 5, 2009.
     31   Determined that net income for the year was $350,000.

Instructions
(a) Journalize the transactions and the closing entry for net income.
(b) Enter the beginning balances, and post the entries to the stockholders' equity accounts. (*Note*: Open additional stockholders' equity accounts as needed.)
(c) Prepare a stockholders' equity section at December 31.

(c) Total stockholders' equity $2,224,000

P14-2A   The stockholders' equity accounts of Hashmi Company at January 1, 2008, are as follows.

Preferred Stock, 6%, $50 par	$600,000
Common Stock, $5 par	800,000
Paid-in Capital in Excess of Par Value—Preferred Stock	200,000
Paid-in Capital in Excess of Par Value—Common Stock	300,000
Retained Earnings	800,000

Journalize and post transactions; prepare retained earnings statement and stockholders' equity section.

(SO 1, 2, 3)

There were no dividends in arrears on preferred stock. During 2008, the company had the following transactions and events.

July 1   Declared a $0.50 cash dividend on common stock.
Aug. 1   Discovered $25,000 understatement of 2007 depreciation. Ignore income taxes.
Sept. 1   Paid the cash dividend declared on July 1.
Dec. 1   Declared a 10% stock dividend on common stock when the market value of the stock was $18 per share.
     15   Declared a 6% cash dividend on preferred stock payable January 15, 2009.
     31   Determined that net income for the year was $355,000.
     31   Recognized a $200,000 restriction of retained earnings for plant expansion.

Instructions
(a) Journalize the transactions, events, and closing entries.
(b) Enter the beginning balances in the accounts, and post to the stockholders' equity accounts. (*Note*: Open additional stockholders' equity accounts as needed.)
(c) Prepare a retained earnings statement for the year.
(d) Prepare a stockholders' equity section at December 31, 2008.

(c) Ending balance $726,000

(d) Total stockholders' equity $2,914,000

Prepare retained earnings statement and stockholders' equity section, and compute earnings per share.

(SO 1, 2, 3, 5)

P14-3A The post-closing trial balance of Dold Corporation at December 31, 2008, contains the following stockholders' equity accounts.

Preferred Stock (15,000 shares issued)	$ 750,000
Common Stock (250,000 shares issued)	2,500,000
Paid-in Capital in Excess of Par Value—Preferred	250,000
Paid-in Capital in Excess of Par Value—Common	400,000
Common Stock Dividends Distributable	250,000
Retained Earnings	1,042,000

A review of the accounting records reveals the following.

1. No errors have been made in recording 2008 transactions or in preparing the closing entry for net income.
2. Preferred stock is $50 par, 6%, and cumulative; 15,000 shares have been outstanding since January 1, 2007.
3. Authorized stock is 20,000 shares of preferred, 500,000 shares of common with a $10 par value.
4. The January 1 balance in Retained Earnings was $1,170,000.
5. On July 1, 20,000 shares of common stock were sold for cash at $16 per share.
6. On September 1, the company discovered an understatement error of $90,000 in computing depreciation in 2007. The net of tax effect of $63,000 was properly debited directly to Retained Earnings.
7. A cash dividend of $250,000 was declared and properly allocated to preferred and common stock on October 1. No dividends were paid to preferred stockholders in 2007.
8. On December 31, a 10% common stock dividend was declared out of retained earnings on common stock when the market price per share was $16.
9. Net income for the year was $585,000.
10. On December 31, 2008, the directors authorized disclosure of a $200,000 restriction of retained earnings for plant expansion. (Use Note X.)

Instructions
(a) Reproduce the Retained Earnings account for the year.
(b) Prepare a retained earnings statement for the year.

(c) Total stockholders' equity, $5,192,000

(c) Prepare a stockholders' equity section at December 31.
(d) Compute the earnings per share of common stock using 240,000 as the weighted average shares outstanding for the year.
(e) Compute the allocation of the cash dividend to preferred and common stock.

Prepare the stockholders' equity section, reflecting dividends and stock split.

(SO 1, 2, 3)

P14-4A On January 1, 2008, Pattini Corporation had the following stockholders' equity accounts.

Common Stock (no par value, 90,000 shares issued and outstanding)	$1,400,000
Retained Earnings	500,000

During the year, the following transactions occurred.

Feb.	1	Declared a $1 cash dividend per share to stockholders of record on February 15, payable March 1.
Mar.	1	Paid the dividend declared in February.
Apr.	1	Announced a 4-for-1 stock split. Prior to the split, the market price per share was $36.
July	1	Declared a 5% stock dividend to stockholders of record on July 15, distributable July 31. On July 1, the market price of the stock was $13 per share.
	31	Issued the shares for the stock dividend.
Dec.	1	Declared a $0.50 per share dividend to stockholders of record on December 15, payable January 5, 2009.
	31	Determined that net income for the year was $350,000.

Instructions

(d) Total stockholders' equity $1,971,000

Prepare the stockholders' equity section of the balance sheet at: (a) March 31, (b) June 30, (c) September 30, and (d) December 31, 2008.

Prepare the stockholders' equity section, reflecting various events.

(SO 1, 3)

P14-5A On January 1, 2008, Yadier Inc. had the following stockholders' equity account balances.

Common Stock, no-par value (500,000 shares issued)	$1,500,000
Common Stock Dividends Distributable	200,000
Retained Earnings	600,000

During 2008, the following transactions and events occurred.

1. Issued 50,000 shares of common stock as a result of a 10% stock dividend declared on December 15, 2007.
2. Issued 30,000 shares of common stock for cash at $6 per share.
3. Corrected an error that had understated the net income for 2006 by $70,000.
4. Declared and paid a cash dividend of $80,000.
5. Earned net income of $300,000.

Instructions
Prepare the stockholders' equity section of the balance sheet at December 31, 2008.

Total stockholders' equity
$2,770,000

PROBLEMS: SET B

P14-1B   On January 1, 2008, Verlin Corporation had the following stockholders' equity accounts.

Prepare dividend entries and stockholders' equity section.

(SO 1, 3)

Common Stock ($10 par value, 100,000 shares issued and outstanding)	$1,000,000
Paid-in Capital in Excess of Par Value	200,000
Retained Earnings	540,000

During the year, the following transactions occurred.

Jan. 15   Declared a $1 cash dividend per share to stockholders of record on January 31, payable February 15.
Feb. 15   Paid the dividend declared in January.
Apr. 15   Declared a 10% stock dividend to stockholders of record on April 30, distributable May 15. On April 15, the market price of the stock was $15 per share.
May 15   Issued the shares for the stock dividend.
July 1   Announced a 2-for-1 stock split. The market price per share prior to the announcement was $17. (The new par value is $5.)
Dec. 1   Declared a $0.50 per share cash dividend to stockholders of record on December 15, payable January 10, 2009.
    31   Determined that net income for the year was $250,000.

Instructions
(a) Journalize the transactions and the closing entry for net income.
(b) Enter the beginning balances, and post the entries to the stockholders' equity accounts. (*Note*: Open additional stockholders' equity accounts as needed.)
(c) Prepare a stockholders' equity section at December 31.

(c) Total stockholders' equity
$1,780,000

P14-2B   The stockholders' equity accounts of Holmes Inc., at January 1, 2008, are as follows.

Journalize and post transactions; prepare retained earnings statement and stockholders' equity section.

(SO 1, 2, 3)

Preferred Stock, $100 par, 7%	$500,000
Common Stock, $10 par	800,000
Paid-in Capital in Excess of Par Value—Preferred Stock	100,000
Paid-in Capital in Excess of Par Value—Common Stock	200,000
Retained Earnings	500,000

There were no dividends in arrears on preferred stock. During 2008, the company had the following transactions and events.

July 1   Declared a $0.50 cash dividend on common stock.
Aug. 1   Discovered a $72,000 overstatement of 2007 depreciation. Ignore income taxes.
Sept. 1   Paid the cash dividend declared on July 1.
Dec. 1   Declared a 10% stock dividend on common stock when the market value of the stock was $16 per share.
    15   Declared a 7% cash dividend on preferred stock payable January 31, 2009.
    31   Determined that net income for the year was $350,000.

Instructions
(a) Journalize the transactions and the closing entry for net income.
(b) Enter the beginning balances in the accounts and post to the stockholders' equity accounts. (*Note*: Open additional stockholders' equity accounts as needed.)

(c) Ending balance $719,000

(d) Total stockholders' equity $2,447,000

Prepare retained earnings statement and stockholders' equity section, and compute earnings per share.

(SO 1, 2, 3, 5)

(c) Prepare a retained earnings statement for the year.
(d) Prepare a stockholders' equity section at December 31, 2008.

P14-3B The ledger of Taguci Corporation at December 31, 2008, after the books have been closed, contains the following stockholders' equity accounts.

Preferred Stock (10,000 shares issued)	$1,000,000
Common Stock (400,000 shares issued)	2,000,000
Paid-in Capital in Excess of Par Value—Preferred	200,000
Paid-in Capital in Excess of Stated Value—Common	1,180,000
Common Stock Dividends Distributable	200,000
Retained Earnings	2,330,000

A review of the accounting records reveals the following.

1. No errors have been made in recording 2008 transactions or in preparing the closing entry for net income.
2. Preferred stock is 6%, $100 par value, noncumulative, and callable at $125. Since January 1, 2007, 10,000 shares have been outstanding; 20,000 shares are authorized.
3. Common stock is no-par with a stated value of $5 per share; 600,000 shares are authorized.
4. The January 1 balance in Retained Earnings was $2,450,000.
5. On October 1, 100,000 shares of common stock were sold for cash at $8 per share.
6. A cash dividend of $600,000 was declared and properly allocated to preferred and common stock on November 1. No dividends were paid to preferred stockholders in 2007.
7. On December 31, a 10% common stock dividend was declared out of retained earnings on common stock when the market price per share was $9.
8. Net income for the year was $840,000.
9. On December 31, 2008, the directors authorized disclosure of a $100,000 restriction of retained earnings for plant expansion. (Use Note A.)

Instructions
(a) Reproduce the Retained Earnings account (T-account) for the year.
(b) Prepare a retained earnings statement for the year.

(c) Total stockholders' equity: $6,910,000

(c) Prepare a stockholders' equity section at December 31.
(d) Compute the earnings per share of common stock using 325,000 as the weighted average shares outstanding for the year.
(e) Compute the allocation of the cash dividend to preferred and common stock.

Prepare the stockholders' equity section, reflecting dividends and stock split.

(SO 1, 2, 3)

P14-4B On January 1, 2008, Erwin Corporation had the following stockholders' equity accounts.

Common Stock (no-par value, 150,000 shares issued and outstanding)	$2,800,000
Retained Earnings	1,000,000

During the year, the following transactions occurred.

Feb.	1	Declared a $1 cash dividend per share to stockholders of record on February 15, payable March 1.
Mar.	1	Paid the dividend declared in February.
Apr.	1	Announced a 4-for-1 stock split. Prior to the split, the market price per share was $36.
July	1	Declared a 5% stock dividend to stockholders of record on July 15, distributable July 31. On July 1, the market price of the stock was $13 per share.
	31	Issued the shares for the stock dividend.
Dec.	1	Declared a $0.50 per share dividend to stockholders of record on December 15, payable January 5, 2009.
	31	Determined that net income for the year was $700,000.

Instructions

(d) Total, stockholders' equity $4,035,000

Prepare the stockholders' equity section of the balance sheet at: (a) March 31, (b) June 30, (c) September 30, and (d) December 31, 2008.

Prepare the stockholders' equity section, reflecting various events.

(SO 1, 3)

P14-5B On January 1, 2008, Morales Inc. had the following shareholders' equity balances.

Common Stock, no-par value (1,000,000 shares issued)	$3,000,000
Common Stock Dividends Distributable	400,000
Retained Earnings	1,200,000

During 2008, the following transactions and events occurred.

1. Issued 100,000 shares of common stock as a result of a 10% stock dividend declared on December 15, 2007.
2. Issued 40,000 shares of common stock for cash at $5 per share.
3. Corrected an error that had understated the net income for 2006 by $140,000.
4. Declared and paid a cash dividend of $500,000.
5. Earned net income of $600,000.

Instructions
Prepare the stockholders' equity section of the balance sheet at December 31, 2008.

Total stockholders' equity
$5,040,000

PROBLEMS: SET C

Visit the book's website at **www.wiley.com/college/weygandt**, and choose the Student Companion site, to access Problem Set C.

CONTINUING COOKIE CHRONICLE

(Note: This is a continuation of the Cookie Chronicle from Chapters 1 through 13.)

CCC14 After establishing their company's fiscal year end to be October 31, Natalie and Curtis began operating Cookie & Coffee Creations Inc. on November 1, 2008. On that date, they issued both preferred and common stock. After the first year of operations, Natalie and Curtis want to prepare financial information for the year.

Go to the book's website,
www.wiley.com/college/weygandt,
to see the completion of this problem.

BROADENING YOUR PERSPECTIVE

FINANCIAL REPORTING AND ANALYSIS

Financial Reporting Problem:
PepsiCo, Inc.

BYP14-1 The financial statements of PepsiCo are presented in Appendix A.

Instructions
Refer to PepsiCo's financial statements and answer the following questions.
  What amount did PepsiCo declare in dividends on common stock in the year ended December 31, 2005? How does this amount compare with dividends declared on common stock in the year ended December 25, 2004?

Comparative Analysis Problem:
PepsiCo, Inc. vs. The Coca-Cola Company

BYP14-2 PepsiCo's financial statements are presented in Appendix A. Coca-Cola's financial statements are presented in Appendix B.

Instructions
(a) Compute earnings per share and return on common stockholders' equity for both companies for the year ending December 31, 2005. Assume PepsiCo's weighted average shares were 1,669 million and Coca-Cola's weighted average shares were 2,392 million. Can these measures be used to compare the profitability of the two companies? Why or why not?
(b) What was the total amount of dividends paid by each company in 2005?

Exploring the Web

BYP14-3   Use the stockholders' equity section of an annual report and identify the major components.

Address: www.reportgallery.com, or go to **www.wiley.com/college/weygandt**

Steps
1. From Report Gallery Homepage, choose **Search by Alphabet**, and choose a letter.
2. Select a particular company.
3. Choose Annual Report.
4. Follow instructions below.

Instructions
Answer the following questions.

(a) What is the company's name?
(b) What classes of capital stock has the company issued?
(c) For each class of stock:
   (1) How many shares are authorized, issued, and/or outstanding?
   (2) What is the par value?
(d) What are the company's retained earnings?
(e) Has the company acquired treasury stock? How many shares?

CRITICAL THINKING

Decision Making Across the Organization

BYP14-4   The stockholders' equity accounts of Fernandez, Inc., at January 1, 2008, are as follows.

Preferred Stock, no par, 4,000 shares issued	$400,000
Common Stock, no par, 140,000 shares issued	700,000
Retained Earnings	500,000

During 2008, the company had the following transactions and events.

July 1   Declared a $0.50 cash dividend on common stock.
Aug. 1   Discovered a $72,000 overstatement of 2007 depreciation expense. (Ignore income taxes.)
Sept. 1   Paid the cash dividend declared on July 1.
Dec. 1   Declared a 10% stock dividend on common stock when the market value of the stock was $12 per share.
    15   Declared a $9 per share cash dividend on preferred stock, payable January 31, 2009.
    31   Determined that net income for the year was $320,000.

Instructions
With the class divided into groups, answer the following questions.

(a) Prepare a retained earnings statement for the year. There are no preferred dividends in arrears.
(b) Discuss why the overstatement of 2007 depreciation expense is not treated as an adjustment of the current year's income.
(c) Discuss the reasons why a company might decide to issue a stock dividend rather than a cash dividend.

Communication Activity

BYP14-5   In the past year, Cormier Corporation declared a 10% stock dividend, and Fegan, Inc. announced a 2-for-1 stock split. Your parents own 100 shares of each company's $50 par value common stock. During a recent phone call, your parents ask you, as an accounting student, to explain the differences between the two events.

Instructions
Write a letter to your parents that explains the effects of the two events to them as stockholders and the effects of each event on the financial statements of each corporation.

Ethics Case

BYP14-6   Garcia Corporation has paid 60 consecutive quarterly cash dividends (15 years). The last 6 months, however, have been a cash drain on the company, as profit margins have been greatly narrowed by increasing competition. With a cash balance sufficient to meet only day-to-day operating needs, the president, Tom Henson, has decided that a stock dividend instead of a cash dividend should be declared. He tells Garcia's financial vice president, Andrea Lane, to issue a press release stating that the company is extending its consecutive dividend record with the issuance of a 5% stock dividend. "Write the press release convincing the stockholders that the stock dividend is just as good as a cash dividend," he orders. "Just watch our stock rise when we announce the stock dividend; it must be a good thing if that happens."

Instructions
(a) Who are the stakeholders in this situation?
(b) Is there anything unethical about Henson's intentions or actions?
(c) What is the effect of a stock dividend on a corporation's stockholders' equity accounts? Which would you rather receive as a stockholder—a cash dividend or a stock dividend? Why?

"All About You" Activity

BYP14-7   In the **All About You** feature in this chapter (p. 612), you learned that in response to the Sarbanes-Oxley Act, many companies have implemented formal ethics codes. Many other organizations also have ethics codes.

Instructions
Obtain the ethics code from an organization that you belong to (e.g., student organization, business school, employer, or a volunteer organization). Evaluate the ethics code based on how clearly it identifies proper and improper behavior. Discuss its strengths, and how it might be improved.

Answers to Insight and Accounting Across the Organization Questions

p. 599 Why Are Companies Increasing Their Dividends?
Q: What factors must management consider in deciding how large a dividend to pay?
A: *Management must consider the size of its retained earnings balance, the amount of available cash, its expected near-term cash needs, its growth opportunities, and what level of dividend it will be able to sustain based upon its expected future earnings.*

p. 603 Would You Pay $92,100 for One Share of Stock?
Q: How does the effect on share price following a stock split compare to the effect on share price of treasury shares acquired?
A: *A stock split and the acquisition of treasury shares have the opposite effects on share price: A stock split decreases the share price, whereas the acquisition of treasury shares increases the share price.*

p. 611 Yahoo! and Costco Feel the Impact of Earnings per Share
Q: Why do you think the prices of these companies changed as indicated?
A: *Stock prices are a function of expected future cash flows. The price of a company's stock is based on investors' expectations of a certain level of future cash flows. If the company exceeds these expectations, its stock price will rise. If it does not meet these expectations, the stock price will fall.*

Authors' Comments on *All About You:* Corporations Have Governance Structures—Do You? p. 612

Before we address the usefulness of a student code of ethics, let's first ask whether a corporate code of ethics will ensure that employees no longer commit fraud. The answer is, "Clearly not." Does that mean a code of ethics is a waste of time? No. A code of ethics is a useful statement by the leaders of an organization about what kind of behavior is expected of the members of that organization. It provides a concrete reference point by which wrongdoing can be identified and evaluated.

Now, suppose that you were taking an exam and that you observed a number of people cheating. It would be very frustrating if you thought that your instructor, the school administrators, and other students didn't care that people were cheating. Ultimately this would encourage even more people to cheat. But if the school has defined unethical behavior, stated that it won't be tolerated, and created the necessary mechanisms for detecting and punishing unethical behavior, then it has begun the first steps in creating a more ethical environment. For an example of an ethics code for university students, see the ethics section of the Student Resources at **www.bus.wisc.edu/accounting**.

Answers to PepsiCo Review It Question 4, p. 603

Dividends per share of common stock declared by PepsiCo were $0.575 in 2001; $0.595 in 2002; $0.630 in 2003; $0.850 in 2004; and $1.01 in 2005. During this same period net income increased in a similar fashion, except from 2004 and 2005 when net income declined.

Answers to Self-Study Questions

1. a   **2.** c   **3.** c   **4.** d   **5.** d   **6.** b   **7.** d   **8.** b   **9.** c   **10.** b

Chapter 15

Long-Term Liabilities

STUDY OBJECTIVES

After studying this chapter, you should be able to:

1 Explain why bonds are issued.

2 Prepare the entries for the issuance of bonds and interest expense.

3 Describe the entries when bonds are redeemed or converted.

4 Describe the accounting for long-term notes payable.

5 Contrast the accounting for operating and capital leases.

6 Identify the methods for the presentation and analysis of long-term liabilities.

✓ *The Navigator*

✓ The Navigator

Scan **Study Objectives**	■
Read **Feature Story**	■
Read **Preview**	■
Read text and answer **Before You Go On** p. 637 ■ p. 640 ■ p. 642 ■ p. 647 ■	
Work **Demonstration Problem**	■
Review **Summary of Study Objectives**	■
Answer **Self-Study Questions**	■
Complete **Assignments**	■

Feature Story

THANK GOODNESS FOR BANKRUPTCY

One piece of baggage America's first settlers carried with them from England was the belief that not repaying one's debts was a moral failure. As in England, the colonists' penalty for such wickedness was often prison.

The theory behind jailing debtors was that the threat of incarceration might persuade them to reveal hidden assets. Or their families might take pity and pay their ransom. But if the debtor was truly penniless, he could be sentenced to what amounted to life in prison. Unlike murderers, rapists, and thieves, the debtors were also responsible for paying their own upkeep, thus putting them even further into debt. . . .

The colonies gradually developed more forgiving laws on debt, recognizing that owing money could be the result of bad luck rather than evidence of fraud or indolence. "Crops fail, prices fall, ships sink, warehouses burn, owners die, partners steal, pirates pillage, wars ravage, and people simply make mistakes," wrote Bruce Mann in his 2002 book *Republic of Debtors*. "Failure was the down side of entrepreneurial risk. This made failure the potential common fate of all merchants." . . .

Colonial lawmakers began taking a more charitable view toward debtors, but they were likelier to excuse a rich defaulter than a poor one. . . . Indeed, when some large speculative financial schemes collapsed after the Revolutionary War, many wealthy men were suddenly bankrupt. One of them, Robert Morris, who had signed the Declaration of Independence and provided critical financing for the war, lost his fortune speculating on land. Sentenced to debtors' prison in Philadelphia, Morris rented the best room in the jail and outfitted it with a settee, writing desks, a bed, a trunk of clothes and other comforts of home.

However lavishly they could outfit their prison cells, though, rich and poor faced the same dim future. There was no way an insolvent could get a fresh start—the "holy grail of debt relief," as Mr. Mann put it. In prison or out, debtors were expected to repay every penny they owed their creditors, even if it took them the rest of their lives. . . .

Congress passed a bankruptcy law in 1800 but then repealed it three years later. Not until 1831 did New York abolish prison for most debtors; Pennsylvania kept its debtors' prisons open until 1842. . . .

Source: Excerpted from Cynthia Crossen, "Early Debtors Faced Jail at Own Expense Until All Was Repaid," *Wall Street Journal*, January 30, 2006, p. B1. By permission.

✓ The Navigator

Inside Chapter 15...

As you can see from the Feature Story, having liabilities can be dangerous in difficult economic times. In this chapter we will explain the accounting for the major types of long-term liabilities reported on the balance sheet. **Long-term liabilities** are obligations that are expected to be paid after one year. These liabilities may be bonds, long-term notes, or lease obligations.

The content and organization of Chapter 15 are as follows.

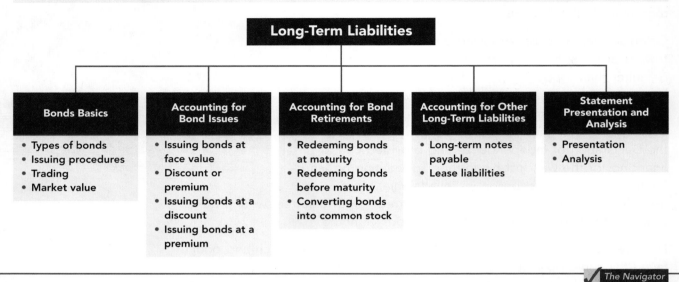

✓ *The Navigator*

BOND BASICS

Bonds are a form of interest-bearing notes payable. To obtain **large amounts of long-term capital**, corporate management usually must decide whether to issue common stock (equity financing) or bonds. Bonds offer three advantages over common stock, as shown in Illustration 15-1.

Illustration 15-1
Advantages of bond financing over common stock

Bond Financing	Advantages
	1. **Stockholder control is not affected.** Bondholders do not have voting rights, so current owners (stockholders) retain full control of the company.
	2. **Tax savings result.** Bond interest is deductible for tax purposes; dividends on stock are not.
	3. **Earnings per share may be higher.** Although bond interest expense reduces net income, earnings per share on common stock often is higher under bond financing because no additional shares of common stock are issued.

As the illustration shows, one reason to issue bonds is that they do not affect stockholder control. Because bondholders do not have voting rights, owners can raise capital with bonds and still maintain corporate control. In addition, bonds are attractive to corporations because the cost of bond interest is tax-deductible. As a result of this tax treatment, which stock dividends do not offer, bonds may result in lower cost of capital than equity financing.

To illustrate the third advantage, on earnings per share, assume that Microsystems, Inc. is considering two plans for financing the construction of a new $5 million plant. Plan A involves issuance of 200,000 shares of common stock at the current market price of $25 per share. Plan B involves issuance of $5 million, 8% bonds at face value. Income before interest and taxes on the new plant will be $1.5 million. Income taxes are expected to be 30%. Microsystems currently has 100,000 shares of common stock outstanding. Illustration 15-2 shows the alternative effects on earnings per share.

	Plan A Issue Stock	Plan B Issue Bonds
Income before interest and taxes	$1,500,000	$1,500,000
Interest (8% × $5,000,000)	—	400,000
Income before income taxes	1,500,000	1,100,000
Income tax expense (30%)	450,000	330,000
Net income	$1,050,000	$ 770,000
Outstanding shares	300,000	100,000
Earnings per share	$3.50	$7.70

Illustration 15-2
Effects on earnings per share—stocks vs. bonds

Note that net income is $280,000 less ($1,050,000 − $770,000) with long-term debt financing (bonds). However, earnings per share is higher because there are 200,000 fewer shares of common stock outstanding.

One disadvantage in using bonds is that the company must **pay interest** on a periodic basis. In addition, the company must also **repay the principal** at the due date. A company with fluctuating earnings and a relatively weak cash position may have great difficulty making interest payments when earnings are low.

A corporation may also obtain long-term financing from notes payable and leasing. However, notes payable and leasing are seldom sufficient to furnish the amount of funds needed for plant expansion and major projects like new buildings.

Bonds are sold in relatively small denominations (usually $1,000 multiples). As a result of their size, and the variety of their features, bonds attract many investors.

Types of Bonds

Bonds may have many different features. In the following sections, we describe the types of bonds commonly issued.

SECURED AND UNSECURED BONDS

Secured bonds have specific assets of the issuer pledged as collateral for the bonds. A bond secured by real estate, for example, is called a mortgage bond. A bond secured by specific assets set aside to retire the bonds is called a sinking fund bond.

HELPFUL HINT

Besides corporations, governmental agencies and universities also issue bonds to raise capital.

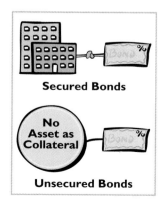

Secured Bonds

No Asset as Collateral

Unsecured Bonds

Unsecured bonds, also called debenture bonds, are issued against the general credit of the borrower. Companies with good credit ratings use these bonds extensively. For example, in a recent annual report, DuPont reported over $2 billion of debenture bonds outstanding.

TERM AND SERIAL BONDS

Bonds that mature—are due for payment—at a single specified future date are term bonds. In contrast, bonds that mature in installments are serial bonds.

REGISTERED AND BEARER BONDS

Bonds issued in the name of the owner are registered bonds. Interest payments on registered bonds are made by check to bondholders of record. Bonds not registered are bearer (or coupon) bonds. Holders of bearer bonds must send in coupons to receive interest payments. Most bonds issued today are registered bonds.

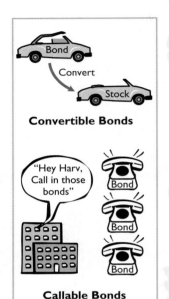

Convertible Bonds

Callable Bonds

CONVERTIBLE AND CALLABLE BONDS

Bonds that can be converted into common stock at the bondholder's option are convertible bonds. The conversion feature generally is attractive to bond buyers. Bonds that the issuing company can retire at a stated dollar amount prior to maturity are callable bonds. A call feature is included in nearly all corporate bond issues.

Issuing Procedures

State laws grant corporations the power to issue bonds. Both the board of directors and stockholders usually must approve bond issues. **In authorizing the bond issue, the board of directors must stipulate the number of bonds to be authorized, total face value, and contractual interest rate.** The total bond authorization often exceeds the number of bonds the company originally issues. This gives the corporation the flexibility to issue more bonds, if needed, to meet future cash requirements.

The face value is the amount of principal the issuing company must pay at the maturity date. The contractual interest rate, often referred to as the stated rate, is the rate used to determine the amount of cash interest the borrower pays and the investor receives. Usually the contractual rate is stated as an annual rate. Interest is generally paid semiannually.

The terms of the bond issue are set forth in a legal document called a bond indenture. The indenture shows the terms and summarizes the rights of the bondholders and their trustees, and the obligations of the issuing company. The trustee (usually a financial institution) keeps records of each bondholder, maintains custody of unissued bonds, and holds conditional title to pledged property.

ETHICS NOTE

Some companies try to minimize the amount of debt reported on their balance sheet by not reporting certain types of commitments as liabilities. This subject is of intense interest in the financial community.

In addition, the issuing company arranges for the printing of bond certificates. The indenture and the certificate are separate documents. As shown in Illustration 15-3, a bond certificate provides the following information: name of the issuer, face value, contractual interest rate, and maturity date. An investment company that specializes in selling securities generally sells the bonds for the issuing company.

Bond Trading

Bondholders have the opportunity to convert their holdings into cash at any time by selling the bonds at the current market price on national securities exchanges. **Bond prices are quoted as a percentage of the face value of the bond, which is usually $1,000.** A $1,000 bond with a quoted price of 97 means that the selling price of

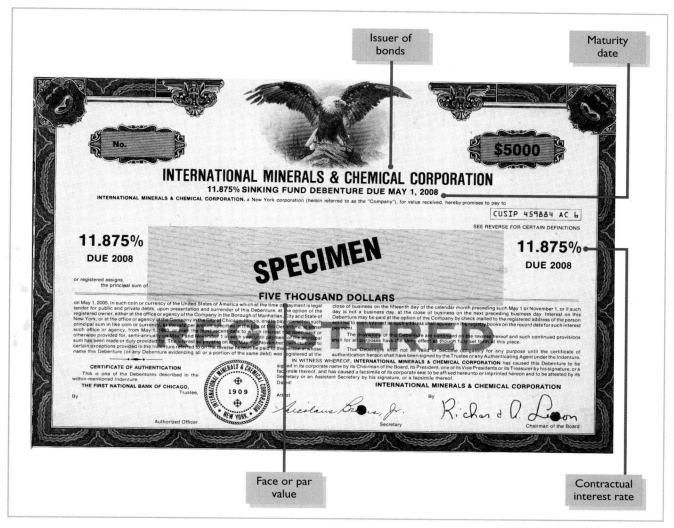

Illustration 15-3
Bond certificate

the bond is 97% of face value, or $970. Newspapers and the financial press publish bond prices and trading activity daily as illustrated by the following.

Bonds	Maturity	Close	Yield	Est. Volume (000)
Boeing Co. 5.125	Feb. 15, 2011	96.595	5.747	33,965

Illustration 15-4
Market information for bonds

This bond listing indicates that Boeing Co. has outstanding 5.125%, $1,000 bonds that mature in 2011. They currently yield a 5.747% return. On this day, $33,965,000 of these bonds were traded. At the close of trading, the price was 96.595% of face value, or $965.95.

A corporation makes journal entries **only when it issues or buys back bonds**, or when bondholders convert bonds into common stock. For example, DuPont **does not journalize** transactions between its bondholders and other investors. If Tom Smith sells his DuPont bonds to Faith Jones, DuPont does not journalize the transaction. (DuPont or its trustee does, however, keep records of the names of bondholders in the case of registered bonds.)

HELPFUL HINT
(1) What is the price of a $1,000 bond trading at 95¼?
(2) What is the price of a $1,000 bond trading at 101⅞?
Answers: (1) $952.50.
(2) $1,018.75.

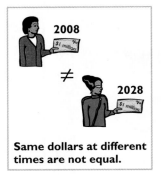

Same dollars at different times are not equal.

Determining the Market Value of Bonds

If you were an investor wanting to purchase a bond, how would you determine how much to pay? To be more specific, assume that Coronet, Inc. issues a **zero-interest bond** (pays no interest) with a face value of $1,000,000 due in 20 years. For this bond, the only cash you receive is a million dollars at the end of 20 years. Would you pay a million dollars for this bond? We hope not! A million dollars received 20 years from now is not the same as a million dollars received today.

The reason you should not pay a million dollars for Coronet's bond relates to what is called the **time value of money**. If you had a million dollars today, you would invest it. From that investment, you would earn interest such that at the end of 20 years, you would have much more than a million dollars. If someone is going to pay you a million dollars 20 years from now, you would want to find its equivalent today. In other words, you would want to determine how much you must invest today at current interest rates to have a million dollars in 20 years. The amount that must be invested today at a given rate of interest over a specified time is called **present value**.

The present value of a bond is the value at which it should sell in the marketplace. Market value therefore is a function of the three factors that determine present value: (1) the dollar amounts to be received, (2) the length of time until the amounts are received, and (3) the market rate of interest. The **market interest rate** is the rate investors demand for loaning funds. Appendix 15A discusses the process of finding the present value for bonds. Appendix C near the end of the book also provides additional material for time value of money computations.

ACCOUNTING ACROSS THE ORGANIZATIO

When to Go Long-Term

A decision that all companies must make is to what extent to rely on short-term versus long-term financing. The critical nature of this decision was highlighted in the fall of 2001, after the World Trade Center disaster. Prior to September 11, short-term interest rates had been extremely low relative to long-term rates. In order to minimize interest costs, many companies were relying very heavily on short-term financing to purchase things they normally would have used long-term debt for. The problem with short-term financing is that it requires companies to continually find new financing as each loan comes due. This makes them vulnerable to sudden changes in the economy.

After September 11, lenders and short-term investors became very reluctant to loan money. This put the squeeze on many companies: as short-term loans came due, they were unable to refinance. Some were able to get other financing, but at extremely high rates (for example, 12% as compared to 3%). Others were unable to get loans and instead had to sell assets to generate cash for their immediate needs.

Source: Henny Sender, "Firms Feel Consequences of Short-Term Borrowing," *Wall Street Journal Online* (October 12, 2001).

 Based on this story, what is a good general rule to use in choosing between short-term and long-term financing?

Before You Go On...

REVIEW IT

1. What are the advantages of bond versus stock financing?
2. What are secured versus unsecured bonds, term versus serial bonds, registered versus bearer bonds, and callable versus convertible bonds?
3. Explain the terms face value, contractual interest rate, and bond indenture.
4. Explain why you would prefer to receive $1 million today rather than five years from now.

The Navigator

ACCOUNTING FOR BOND ISSUES

Bonds may be issued at face value, below face value (at a discount), or above face value (at a premium).

STUDY OBJECTIVE 2

Prepare the entries for the issuance of bonds and interest expense.

Issuing Bonds at Face Value

To illustrate the accounting for bonds, assume that on January 1, 2008, Candlestick Corporation issues $100,000, five-year, 10% bonds at 100 (100% of face value). The entry to record the sale is:

Jan. 1	Cash	100,000	
	Bonds Payable		100,000
	(To record sale of bonds at face value)		

A	=	L	+	SE
+100,000				
				+100,000

Cash Flows
+100,000

Candlestick reports bonds payable in the long-term liabilities section of the balance sheet because the maturity date is more than one year away.

Over the term (life) of the bonds, companies make entries to record bond interest. Interest on bonds payable is computed in the same manner as interest on notes payable, as explained in Chapter 11 (page 473). Assume that interest is payable semiannually on January 1 and July 1 on the bonds described above. In that case, Candlestick must pay interest of $5,000 ($100,000 × 10% × 6/12) on July 1, 2008. The entry for the payment, assuming no previous accrual of interest, is:

July 1	Bond Interest Expense	5,000	
	Cash		5,000
	(To record payment of bond interest)		

A	=	L	+	SE
				−5,000 Exp
−5,000				

Cash Flows
−5,000

At December 31, Candlestick recognizes the $5,000 of interest expense incurred since July 1 with the following adjusting entry:

Dec. 31	Bond Interest Expense	5,000	
	Bond Interest Payable		5,000
	(To accrue bond interest)		

A	=	L	+	SE
				−5,000 Exp
		+5,000		

Cash Flows
no effect

Companies classify bond interest payable as a current liability, because it is scheduled for payment within the next year. When Candlestick pays the interest on January 1, 2009, it debits (decreases) Bond Interest Payable and credits (decreases) Cash for $5,000.

Discount or Premium on Bonds

In the Candlestick illustrations above, we assumed that the contractual (stated) interest rate paid on the bonds and the market (effective) interest rate were the same.

Recall that the **contractual interest rate** is the rate applied to the face (par) value to arrive at the interest paid in a year. The **market interest rate** is the rate investors demand for loaning funds to the corporation. When the contractual interest rate and the market interest rate are the same, bonds sell **at face value**.

However, market interest rates change daily. The type of bond issued, the state of the economy, current industry conditions, and the company's performance all affect market interest rates. Contractual and market interest rates often differ. As a result, bonds often sell below or above face value.

To illustrate, suppose that a company issues 10% bonds at a time when other bonds of similar risk are paying 12%. Investors will not be interested in buying the 10% bonds, so their value will fall below their face value. In this case, we say the 10% bonds are **selling at a discount**. As a result of the decline in the bonds' selling price, the actual interest rate incurred by the company increases to the level of the current market interest rate.

Conversely, if the market rate of interest is **lower than** the contractual interest rate, investors will have to pay more than face value for the bonds. That is, if the market rate of interest is 8% but the contractual interest rate on the bonds is 10%, the issuer will require more funds from the investor. In these cases, **bonds sell at a premium**. Illustration 15-5 shows these relationships graphically.

Illustration 15-5
Interest rates and bond prices

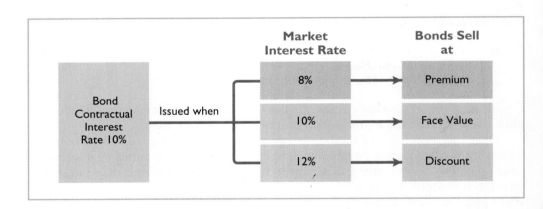

Issuing bonds at an amount different from face value is quite common. By the time a company prints the bond certificates and markets the bonds, it will be a coincidence if the market rate and the contractual rate are the same. Thus, the sale of bonds at a discount does not mean that the issuer's financial strength is suspect. Nor does the sale of bonds at a premium indicate exceptional financial strength.

Issuing Bonds at a Discount

To illustrate issuance of bonds at a discount, assume that on January 1, 2008, Candlestick, Inc. sells $100,000, five-year, 10% bonds for $92,639 (92.639% of face value). Interest is payable on July 1 and January 1. The entry to record the issuance is:

Jan. 1	Cash		92,639	
	Discount on Bonds Payable		7,361	
	Bonds Payable			100,000
	(To record sale of bonds at a discount)			

HELPFUL HINT

Discount on Bonds Payable

Increase Debit ↓ Normal Balance	Decrease Credit

A	=	L	+	SE
+92,639				
		−7,361		
		+100,000		

Cash Flows
+92,639

Although Discount on Bonds Payable has a debit balance, **it is not an asset**. Rather, it is a **contra account**. This account is **deducted from bonds payable** on the balance sheet, as shown in Illustration 15-6.

CANDLESTICK, INC.
Balance Sheet (partial)

Illustration 15-6
Statement presentation of
discount on bonds payable

Long-term liabilities
  Bonds payable $100,000
  Less: Discount on bonds payable   7,361 $92,639

The $92,639 represents the **carrying (or book) value** of the bonds. On the date of issue this amount equals the market price of the bonds.

    The issuance of bonds below face value—at a discount—causes the total cost of borrowing to differ from the bond interest paid. That is, the issuing corporation must pay not only the contractual interest rate over the term of the bonds, but also the face value (rather than the issuance price) at maturity. Therefore, the difference between the issuance price and face value of the bonds—the discount—is an **additional cost of borrowing**. The company records this additional cost as **bond interest expense** over the life of the bonds. Appendixes 15B and 15C show the procedures for recording this additional cost.

    The total cost of borrowing $92,639 for Candlestick, Inc. is $57,361, computed as follows.

> **HELPFUL HINT**
> Carrying value (book value) of bonds issued at a discount is determined by subtracting the balance of the discount account from the balance of the Bonds Payable account.

Bonds Issued at a Discount

Semiannual interest payments	
($100,000 × 10% × ½ = $5,000; $5,000 × 10)	$50,000
Add: Bond discount ($100,000 − $92,639)	7,361
Total cost of borrowing	**$57,361**

Illustration 15-7
Total cost of borrowing—
bonds issued at a discount

Alternatively, we can compute the total cost of borrowing as follows.

Bonds Issued at a Discount

Principal at maturity	$100,000
Semiannual interest payments ($5,000 × 10)	50,000
Cash to be paid to bondholders	150,000
Cash received from bondholders	92,639
Total cost of borrowing	**$ 57,361**

Illustration 15-8
Alternative computation of
total cost of borrowing—
bonds issued at a discount

Issuing Bonds at a Premium

To illustrate the issuance of bonds at a premium, we now assume the Candlestick, Inc. bonds described above sell for $108,111 (108.111% of face value) rather than for $92,639. The entry to record the sale is:

Jan. 1	Cash	108,111	
	Bonds Payable		100,000
	Premium on Bonds Payable		8,111
	(To record sale of bonds at a premium)		

A	=	L	+	SE
+108,111				
		+100,000		
		+8,111		

Cash Flows
+108,111

Candlestick adds the premium on bonds payable **to the bonds payable amount** on the balance sheet, as shown in Illustration 15-9 on the next page.

Illustration 15-9
Statement presentation of
bond premium

CANDLESTICK, INC.		
Balance Sheet (partial)		
Long-term liabilities		
Bonds payable	$100,000	
Add: Premium on bonds payable	**8,111**	$108,111

The sale of bonds above face value causes the total cost of borrowing to be **less than the bond interest paid**. The bond premium is considered to be **a reduction in the cost of borrowing**. The company credits the bond premium to Bond Interest Expense over the life of the bonds. Appendixes 15B and 15C show the procedures for recording this reduction in the cost of borrowing. The total cost of borrowing $108,111 for Candlestick, Inc. is computed as follows.

Illustration 15-10
Total cost of borrowing—
bonds issued at a premium

Bonds Issued at a Premium	
Semiannual interest payments	
($100,000 × 10% × ½ = $5,000; $5,000 × 10)	$50,000
Less: Bond premium ($108,111 − $100,000)	8,111
Total cost of borrowing	**$41,889**

Alternatively, we can compute the cost of borrowing as follows.

Illustration 15-11
Alternative computation of
total cost of borrowing—
bonds issued at a premium

Bonds Issued at a Premium	
Principal at maturity	$100,000
Semiannual interest payments ($5,000 × 10)	50,000
Cash to be paid to bondholders	150,000
Cash received from bondholders	108,111
Total cost of borrowing	**$ 41,889**

Before You Go On...

REVIEW IT
1. What entry would a company make to record the issuance of bonds payable of $1 million at 100? At 96? At 102?
2. Why do bonds sell at a discount? At a premium? At face value?

Related exercise material: *BE15-2, BE15-3, BE15-4, E15-3, E15-4, and E15-7.*

✓ *The Navigator*

ACCOUNTING FOR BOND RETIREMENTS

STUDY OBJECTIVE 3
Describe the entries when bonds are redeemed or converted.

An issuing corporation retires bonds either when it redeems the bonds or when bondholders convert them into common stock. We explain the entries for these transactions in the following sections.

Redeeming Bonds at Maturity

Regardless of the issue price of bonds, the book value of the bonds at maturity will equal their face value. Assuming that the company pays and records separately the interest for the last interest period, Candlestick records the redemption of its bonds at maturity as follows:

Bonds Payable	100,000	
Cash		100,000
(To record redemption of bonds at maturity)		

A	=	L	+	SE
		−100,000		
−100,000				

Cash Flows
−100,000

Redeeming Bonds before Maturity

Bonds also may be redeemed before maturity. A company may decide to retire bonds before maturity to reduce interest cost and to remove debt from its balance sheet. A company should retire debt early only if it has sufficient cash resources.

When a company retires bonds before maturity, it is necessary to: (1) eliminate the carrying value of the bonds at the redemption date; (2) record the cash paid; and (3) recognize the gain or loss on redemption. The carrying value of the bonds is the face value of the bonds less unamortized bond discount or plus unamortized bond premium at the redemption date.

To illustrate, assume that Candlestick, Inc. has sold its bonds at a premium. At the end of the eighth period, Candlestick retires these bonds at 103 after paying the semiannual interest. Assume also that the carrying value of the bonds at the redemption date is $101,623. Candlestick makes the following entry to record the redemption at the end of the eighth interest period (January 1, 2012):

Jan. 1	Bonds Payable	100,000	
	Premium on Bonds Payable	1,623	
	Loss on Bond Redemption	1,377	
	Cash		103,000
	(To record redemption of bonds at 103)		

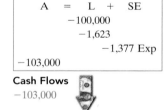

A	=	L	+	SE
		−100,000		
		−1,623		
				−1,377 Exp
−103,000				

Cash Flows
−103,000

Note that the loss of $1,377 is the difference between the cash paid of $103,000 and the carrying value of the bonds of $101,623.

Converting Bonds into Common Stock

Convertible bonds have features that are attractive both to bondholders and to the issuer. The conversion often gives bondholders an opportunity to benefit if the market price of the common stock increases substantially. Until conversion, though, the bondholder receives interest on the bond. For the issuer of convertible bonds, the bonds sell at a higher price and pay a lower rate of interest than comparable debt securities without the conversion option. Many corporations, such as USAir, USX Corp., and DaimlerChrysler Corporation, have convertible bonds outstanding.

When the issuing company records a conversion, the company ignores the current market prices of the bonds and stock. Instead, the company transfers the **carrying value** of the bonds to paid-in capital accounts. **No gain or loss is recognized.**

To illustrate, assume that on July 1 Saunders Associates converts $100,000 bonds sold at face value into 2,000 shares of $10 par value common stock. Both the bonds and the common stock have a market value of $130,000. Saunders makes the following entry to record the conversion:

A	=	L	+	SE
		−100,000		
				+20,000 CS
				+80,000 CS

Cash Flows
no effect

July 1	Bonds Payable	100,000	
	Common Stock		20,000
	Paid-in Capital in Excess of Par Value		80,000
	(To record bond conversion)		

Note that the company does not consider the current market price of the bonds and stock ($130,000) in making the entry. This method of recording the bond conversion is often referred to as the **carrying (or book) value method**.

Before You Go On...

REVIEW IT

1. Explain the accounting for redemption of bonds at maturity, before maturity by payment in cash, and by conversion into common stock.
2. Did PepsiCo redeem any of its debt during the fiscal year ended December 31, 2005? (*Hint:* Examine PepsiCo's statement of cash flows. The answer to this question appears on page 680.)

DO IT

R & B Inc. issued $500,000, 10-year bonds at a premium. Prior to maturity, when the carrying value of the bonds is $508,000, the company retires the bonds at 102. Prepare the entry to record the redemption of the bonds.

Action Plan

■ Determine and eliminate the carrying value of the bonds.
■ Record the cash paid.
■ Compute and record the gain (loss) (the difference between the first two items).

Solution There is a loss on redemption: The cash paid, $510,000 ($500,000 × 102%), is greater than the carrying value of $508,000. The entry is:

Bonds Payable	500,000	
Premium on Bonds Payable	8,000	
Loss on Bond Redemption	2,000	
Cash		510,000
(To record redemption of bonds at 102)		

Related exercise material: *BE15-5, E15-5, E15-6, E15-8, and E15-9.*

ACCOUNTING FOR OTHER LONG-TERM LIABILITIES

Other common types of long-term obligations are notes payable and lease liabilities. The accounting for these liabilities is explained in the following sections.

Long-Term Notes Payable

STUDY OBJECTIVE 4
Describe the accounting for long-term notes payable.

The use of notes payable in long-term debt financing is quite common. **Long-term notes payable** are similar to short-term interest-bearing notes payable except that the term of the notes exceeds one year.

A long-term note may be secured by a **mortgage** that pledges title to specific assets as security for a loan. Individuals widely use mortgage notes payable to purchase homes, and many small and some large companies use them to acquire plant assets. At one time, approximately 18% of McDonald's long-term debt related to mortgage notes on land, buildings, and improvements.

Mortgage loan terms may stipulate either a **fixed** or an **adjustable** interest rate. The interest rate on a fixed-rate mortgage remains the same over the life of the mortgage. The interest rate on an adjustable-rate mortgage is adjusted periodically to reflect changes in the market rate of interest. Typically, the terms require the borrower to make installment payments over the term of the loan. Each payment consists of (1) interest on the unpaid balance of the loan and (2) a reduction of loan principal. The interest decreases each period, while the portion applied to the loan principal increases.

Companies initially record mortgage notes payable at face value. They subsequently make entries for each installment payment. To illustrate, assume that Porter Technology Inc. issues a $500,000, 12%, 20-year mortgage note on December 31, 2008, to obtain needed financing for a new research laboratory. The terms provide for semiannual installment payments of $33,231 (not including real estate taxes and insurance). The installment payment schedule for the first two years is as follows.

Semiannual Interest Period	(A) Cash Payment	(B) Interest Expense (D) × 6%	(C) Reduction of Principal (A) − (B)	(D) Principal Balance (D) − (C)
12/31/08				$500,000
06/30/09	$33,231	$30,000	$3,231	496,769
12/31/09	33,231	29,806	3,425	493,344
06/30/10	33,231	29,601	3,630	489,714
12/31/10	33,231	29,383	3,848	485,866

Illustration 15-12
Mortgage installment payment schedule

Porter records the mortgage loan and first installment payment as follows.

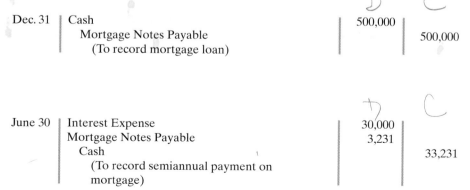

Dec. 31	Cash	500,000	
	Mortgage Notes Payable		500,000
	(To record mortgage loan)		

June 30	Interest Expense	30,000	
	Mortgage Notes Payable	3,231	
	Cash		33,231
	(To record semiannual payment on mortgage)		

In the balance sheet, the company reports the reduction in principal for the next year as a current liability, and it classifies the remaining unpaid principal balance as a long-term liability. At December 31, 2009, the total liability is $493,344. Of that amount, $7,478 ($3,630 + $3,848) is current, and $485,866 ($493,344 − $7,478) is long-term.

ACCOUNTING ACROSS THE ORGANIZATIO

Search for Your Best Rate

Companies spend a great deal of time shopping for the best loan terms. You should do the same. Suppose that you have a used car that you are planning to trade in on the purchase of a new car. Experts suggest that you view this deal as three separate transactions: (1) the purchase of a new car, (2) the trade in or sale of an old car, and (3) shopping for an interest rate.

Studies suggest that too many people neglect transaction number 3. One survey found that 63% of people planned on shopping for the best car-loan interest rate online the next time they bought a car. But a separate study found that only 15% of people who bought a car actually shopped around for the best online rate. Too many people simply take the interest rate offered at the car dealership. Many lenders will pre-approve you for a loan up to a specific dollar amount, and many will then give you a blank check (negotiable for up to that amount) that you can take to the car dealer.

Source: Ron Lieber, "How to Haggle the Best Car Loan," *Wall Street Journal*, March 25, 2006, p. B1.

? What should you do if the dealer "trash-talks" your lender, or refuses to sell you the car for the agreed-upon price unless you get your car loan through the dealer?

Lease Liabilities

As indicated in Chapter 10, a lease is a contractual arrangement between a lessor (owner of the property) and a lessee (renter of the property). It grants the right to use specific property for a period of time in return for cash payments. Leasing is big business. U.S. companies leased an estimated $125 billion of capital equipment in a recent year. This represents approximately one-third of equipment financed that year. The two most common types of leases are operating leases and capital leases.

OPERATING LEASES

The renting of an apartment and the rental of a car at an airport are examples of **operating leases. In an operating lease the intent is temporary use of the property by the lessee, while the lessor continues to own the property.**

In an operating lease, the lessee records the lease (or rental) payments as an expense. The lessor records the payments as revenue. For example, assume that a sales representative for Western Inc. leases a car from Hertz Car Rental at the Los Angeles airport and that Hertz charges a total of $275. Western, the lessee, records the rental as follows:

A	=	L	+	SE
				−275 Exp
−275				

Cash Flows
−275

Car Rental Expense	275	
Cash		275
(To record payment of lease rental charge)		

The lessee may incur other costs during the lease period. For example, in the case above, Western will generally incur costs for gas. Western would report these costs as an expense.

CAPITAL LEASES

In most lease contracts, the lessee makes a periodic payment and records that payment in the income statement as rent expense. In some cases, however, the lease contract transfers to the lessee substantially all the benefits and risks of ownership. Such a lease is in effect a purchase of the property. This type of lease is a **capital lease**. Its name comes from the fact that the company capitalizes the present value of the cash payments for the lease and records that amount as an asset. Illustration 15-13 indicates the major difference between operating and capital leases.

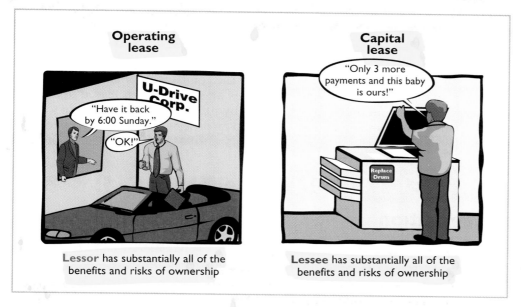

Illustration 15-13
Types of leases

HELPFUL HINT
A capital lease situation is one that, although legally a rental case, is *in substance* an installment purchase by the lessee. Accounting standards require that substance over form be used in such a situation.

If **any one** of the following conditions exists, the lessee must record a lease **as an asset**—that is, as a capital lease:

1. **The lease transfers ownership of the property to the lessee.** *Rationale:* If during the lease term the lessee receives ownership of the asset, the lessee should report the leased asset as an asset on its books.

2. **The lease contains a bargain purchase option.** *Rationale:* If during the term of the lease the lessee can purchase the asset at a price substantially below its fair market value, the lessee will exercise this option. Thus, the lessee should report the lease as a leased asset on its books.

3. **The lease term is equal to 75% or more of the economic life of the leased property.** *Rationale:* If the lease term is for much of the asset's useful life, the lessee should report the asset as a leased asset on its books.

4. **The present value of the lease payments equals or exceeds 90% of the fair market value of the leased property.** *Rationale:* If the present value of the lease payments is equal to or almost equal to the fair market value of the asset, the lessee has essentially purchased the asset. As a result, the lessee should report the leased asset as an asset on its books.

To illustrate, assume that Gonzalez Company decides to lease new equipment. The lease period is four years; the economic life of the leased equipment is estimated to be five years. The present value of the lease payments is $190,000, which is equal to the fair market value of the equipment. There is no transfer of ownership during the lease term, nor is there any bargain purchase option.

In this example, Gonzalez has essentially purchased the equipment. Conditions 3 and 4 have been met. First, the lease term is 75% or more of the economic life of

A	=	L	+	SE
+190,000				
		+190,000		

Cash Flows
no effect

the asset. Second, the present value of cash payments is equal to the equipment's fair market value. Gonzalez records the transaction as follows.

Leased Asset—Equipment	190,000	
Lease Liability		190,000
(To record leased asset and lease liability)		

The lessee reports a leased asset on the balance sheet under plant assets. It reports the lease liability on the balance sheet as a liability. **The portion of the lease liability expected to be paid in the next year is a current liability. The remainder is classified as a long-term liability.**

Most lessees do not like to report leases on their balance sheets. Why? Because the lease liability increases the company's total liabilities. This, in turn, may make it more difficult for the company to obtain needed funds from lenders. As a result, companies attempt to keep leased assets and lease liabilities off the balance sheet by structuring leases so as not to meet any of the four conditions mentioned on page 645. The practice of keeping liabilities off the balance sheet is referred to as **off-balance-sheet financing**.

ETHICS NOTE

Accounting standard setters are attempting to rewrite rules on lease accounting because of concerns that abuse of the current standards is reducing the usefulness of financial statements.

STATEMENT PRESENTATION AND ANALYSIS

Presentation

STUDY OBJECTIVE 6

Identify the methods for the presentation and analysis of long-term liabilities.

Companies report long-term liabilities in a separate section of the balance sheet immediately following current liabilities, as shown in Illustration 15-14. Alternatively, companies may present summary data in the balance sheet, with detailed data (interest rates, maturity dates, conversion privileges, and assets pledged as collateral) shown in a supporting schedule. Companies report the current maturities of long-term debt under current liabilities if they are to be paid from current assets.

Illustration 15-14
Balance sheet presentation of long-term liabilities

LAX CORPORATION		
Balance Sheet (partial)		
Long-term liabilities		
Bonds payable 10% due in 2015	$1,000,000	
Less: Discount on bonds payable	80,000	$ 920,000
Mortgage notes payable, 11%, due		
in 2021 and secured by plant assets		500,000
Lease liability		440,000
Total long-term liabilities		$1,860,000

Analysis

Long-term creditors and stockholders are interested in a company's long-run solvency. Of particular interest is the company's ability to pay interest as it comes due and to repay the face value of the debt at maturity. Debt to total assets and times interest earned are two ratios that provide information about debt-paying ability and long-run solvency.

The **debt to total assets ratio** measures the percentage of the total assets provided by creditors. As shown in the formula in Illustration 15-15, it is computed by dividing total debt (both current and long-term liabilities) by total assets. The higher the percentage of debt to total assets, the greater the risk that the company may be unable to meet its maturing obligations.

The **times interest earned ratio** indicates the company's ability to meet interest payments as they come due. It is computed by dividing income before income taxes and interest expense by interest expense.

To illustrate these ratios, we will use data from Kellogg Company's 2005 annual report. The company had total liabilities of $8,290.8 million, total assets of $10,574.5 million, interest expense of $300.3 million, income taxes of $444.7 million, and net income of $980.4 million. Kellogg's debt to total assets ratio and times interest earned ratio are shown below.

Total Debt	÷	Total Assets	=	Debt to Total Assets
$8,290.8	÷	$10,574.5	=	78.4%

Income before Income Taxes and Interest Expense	÷	Interest Expense	=	Times Interest Earned
$980.4 + $444.7 + $300.3	÷	$300.3	=	5.75 times

Illustration 15-15
Debt to total assets and times interest earned ratios, with computations

Kellogg has a relatively high debt to total assets percentage of 78.4%. Its interest coverage of 5.75 times is considered safe.

INVESTOR INSIGHT

They Thought It Was Easy Money

Lending markets change over time. Sometimes it is easy to borrow money, while at other times the credit market dries up. During the spring of 2006 many observers noted that money was flowing very freely. This was a concern to some analysts, who noted that many lenders had cut back on the number and restrictiveness of loan covenants that they required of borrowers. *Covenants* are performance hurdles that companies agree to in order to obtain a loan. For example, many loan covenants specify required values for debt to total assets or times interest earned measures that must be maintained while the debt is outstanding. In the words of one observer, "Credit quality is still strong, but this trend of shrinking covenants is laying the groundwork for the next round of credit problems."

Source: Serena Ng, "Easy Money? Banks Get Lenient on Loans," *Wall Street Journal*, April 7, 2006, p. C1.

What do you think happens when a company violates its debt covenants?

Before You Go On...

REVIEW IT
1. Explain the accounting for long-term mortgage notes payable.
2. What is the difference in accounting for an operating lease versus a capital lease? Explain the four conditions used to determine whether the lease contract transfers substantially all the benefits and risks of ownership.
3. What ratios may be computed to analyze a company's long-run solvency?

 The Navigator

 Be sure to read **ALL ABOUT YOU: *The Risks of Adjustable Rates*** on page 648 for information on how topics in this chapter apply to you.

The Risks of Adjustable Rates

As home prices rose rapidly between 2000 and 2005, many people found that they could not afford to buy a home using traditional fixed interest rate loans. Lenders encouraged some people to use less-conventional loans such as ARMs—adjustable-rate mortgages.

The lender periodically adjusts the interest rate on an ARM to reflect changes in market interest rates. The advantage of ARMs to home buyers is that the initial rate on an ARM is below the rate charged on a fixed-rate loan. This can enable the buyer to purchase a home that he or she otherwise could not afford. If market interest rates rise, however, the rate on the ARM can rise well above the initial rate. This will result in much higher mortgage payments. Rising rates can be a problem for homeowners who have not planned for them.

⊛ Some Facts

* 35% of people with ARMs do not know how much the rate could increase at one time, and 41% are not sure of the maximum rate they could face.

* 28% of people with ARMs do not know which index of interest rates is used to determine their adjustments.

* ARMs represented about one-third of all loans granted during 2004 and 2005, which was substantially higher than most previous years.

* Borrowers with less income or education were more likely not to know their mortgage terms. Borrowers with less income faced the largest change in their ARM payment, as a percentage of income, when interest rates changed.

⊛ About the Numbers

Although a high percentage of loans granted during 2004 and 2005 were adjustable-rate loans, these loans still represent a relatively small percentage of loans outstanding. Many people who are initially granted an adjustable-rate loan subsequently refinance their loan to get a fixed-rate loan that will offer no unpleasant surprises in later years.

Mortgage Types

Other 4%
Adjustable 13%
Fixed 83%

Source: Brian Bucks and Karen Pence, "Do Homeowners Know Their House Values and Mortgage Terms," Federal Reserve Board of Governors, January 2006, *www.federalreserve.gov/pubs/feds/2006/200603/200603pap.pdf.*

⊛ What Do You Think?

Suppose that you are planning to buy your first home for $200,000. The payment on a 30-year, 7% fixed-rate loan of $180,000 (after a down payment of $20,000) would be $1,198 per month, which is more than you qualify for with the lender. The lender has suggested that you could instead use an ARM. The interest rate would be 5.5%, resulting in payments of $1,022 per month for the first three years. After that, the interest rate would be adjusted annually and could increase by as much as 2% each year, with an upper-end rate of 10.5%. Should you buy the home using adjustable-rate financing?

YES: House prices are just going to keep going up, up, up. If you don't into the market now, you may never be able to.

NO: This nontraditional loan has too much uncertainty tied to it. If interest rates go up, your payment could get so high that you wouldn't be able to make the payment, in which case you would lose the house.

Sources: James R. Hagerty, "The Home-Mortgage Muddle; Some Borrowers Are Confused by Terms of Adjustable-Rate Loans," *Wall Street Journal*, March 11, 2006, p. B4.

Demonstration Problem

Snyder Software Inc. has successfully developed a new spreadsheet program. To produce and market the program, the company needed $2 million of additional financing. On January 1, 2009, Snyder borrowed money as follows.

1. Snyder issued $500,000, 11%, 10-year convertible bonds. The bonds sold at face value and pay semiannual interest on January 1 and July 1. Each $1,000 bond is convertible into 30 shares of Snyder's $20 par value common stock.
2. Snyder issued $1 million, 10%, 10-year bonds at face value. Interest is payable semi-annually on January 1 and July 1.
3. Snyder also issued a $500,000, 12%, 15-year mortgage note payable. The terms provide for semiannual installment payments of $36,324 on June 30 and December 31.

Instructions

1. For the convertible bonds, prepare journal entries for:

   (a) The issuance of the bonds on January 1, 2009.
   (b) Interest expense on July 1 and December 31, 2009.
   (c) The payment of interest on January 1, 2010.
   (d) The conversion of all bonds into common stock on January 1, 2010, when the market value of the common stock was $67 per share.

2. For the 10-year, 10% bonds:

   (a) Journalize the issuance of the bonds on January 1, 2009.
   (b) Prepare the journal entries for interest expense in 2009. Assume no accrual of interest on July 1.
   (c) Prepare the entry for the redemption of the bonds at 101 on January 1, 2012, after paying the interest due on this date.

3. For the mortgage note payable:

   (a) Prepare the entry for the issuance of the note on January 1, 2009.
   (b) Prepare a payment schedule for the first four installment payments.
   (c) Indicate the current and noncurrent amounts for the mortgage note payable at December 31, 2009.

Solution to Demonstration Problem

1. (a) 2009

Jan. 1	Cash	500,000	
	Bonds Payable		500,000
	(To record issue of 11%, 10-year		
	convertible bonds at face value)		

(b) 2009

July 1	Bond Interest Expense *500,000*	27,500	
	Cash ($500,000 × 0.055)		27,500
	(To record payment of semiannual		
	interest)		
Dec. 31	Bond Interest Expense	27,500	
	Bond Interest Payable		27,500
	(To record accrual of semiannual		
	bond interest)		

action plan

✔ Compute interest semiannually (six months).

✔ Record the accrual and payment of interest on appropriate dates.

✔ Record the conversion of the bonds into common stock by removing the book (carrying) value of the bonds from the liability account.

(c) 2010

Jan. 1	Bond Interest Payable	27,500	
	Cash		27,500
	(To record payment of accrued interest)		

(d) Jan. 1

	Bonds Payable	500,000	
	Common Stock		300,000*
	Paid-in Capital in Excess of Par Value		200,000
	(To record conversion of bonds into common stock)		
	*($500,000 ÷ $1,000 = 500 bonds;		
	500 × 30 = 15,000 shares;		
	15,000 × $20 = $300,000)		

action plan

✔ Record the issuance of the bonds.

✔ Compute interest expense for each period.

✔ Compute the loss on bond redemption as the excess of the cash paid over the carrying value of the redeemed bonds.

2. (a) 2009

Jan. 1	Cash	1,000,000	
	Bonds Payable		1,000,000
	(To record issuance of bonds)		

(b) 2009

July 1	Bond Interest Expense	50,000	
	Cash		50,000
	(To record payment of semiannual interest)		
Dec. 31	Bond Interest Expense	50,000	
	Bond Interest Payable		50,000
	(To record accrual of semiannual interest)		

(c) 2012

Jan. 1	Bonds Payable	1,000,000	
	Loss on Bond Redemption	10,000*	
	Cash		1,010,000
	(To record redemption of bonds at 101)		
	*($1,010,000 − $1,000,000)		

action plan

✔ Compute periodic interest expense on a mortgage note, recognizing that as the principal amount decreases, so does the interest expense.

✔ Record mortgage payments, recognizing that each payment consists of (1) interest on the unpaid loan balance and (2) a reduction of the loan principal.

3. (a) 2009

Jan. 1	Cash	500,000	
	Mortgage Notes Payable		500,000
	(To record issuance of mortgage note payable)		

(b)

Semiannual Interest Period	Cash Payment	Interest Expense	Reduction of Principal	Principal Balance
Issue date				$500,000
1	$36,324	$30,000	$6,324	493,676
2	36,324	29,621	6,703	486,973
3	36,324	29,218	7,106	479,867
4	36,324	28,792	7,532	472,335

(c) Current liability $14,638 ($7,106 + $7,532)
Long-term liability $472,335

✔ The Navigator

SUMMARY OF STUDY OBJECTIVES

1 Explain why bonds are issued. Companies may sell bonds to investors to raise long-term capital. Bonds offer the following advantages over common stock: (a) stockholder control is not affected, (b) tax savings result, (c) earnings per share of common stock may be higher.

2 Prepare the entries for the issuance of bonds and interest expense. When companies issue bonds, they debit Cash for the cash proceeds, and credit Bonds Payable for the face value of the bonds. The account Premium on Bonds Payable shows a bond premium; Discount on Bonds Payable shows a bond discount.

3 Describe the entries when bonds are redeemed or converted. When bondholders redeem bonds at maturity, the issuing company credits Cash and debits Bonds Payable for the face value of the bonds. When bonds are redeemed before maturity, the issuing company (a) eliminates the carrying value of the bonds at the redemption date, (b) records the cash paid, and (c) recognizes the gain or loss on redemption. When bonds are converted to common stock, the issuing company transfers the carrying (or

book) value of the bonds to appropriate paid-in capital accounts; no gain or loss is recognized.

4 Describe the accounting for long-term notes payable. Each payment consists of (1) interest on the unpaid balance of the loan and (2) a reduction of loan principal. The interest decreases each period, while the portion applied to the loan principal increases.

5 Contrast the accounting for operating and capital leases. For an operating lease, the lessee (renter) records lease (rental) payments as an expense. For a capital lease, the lessee records the asset and related obligation at the present value of the future lease payments.

6 Identify the methods for the presentation and analysis of long-term liabilities. Companies should report the nature and amount of each long-term debt in the balance sheet or in the notes accompanying the financial statements. Stockholders and long-term creditors are interested in a company's long-run solvency. Debt to total assets and times interest earned are two ratios that provide information about debt-paying ability and long-run solvency.

GLOSSARY

Bearer (coupon) bonds Bonds not registered. (p. 634).

Bond certificate A legal document that indicates the name of the issuer, the face value of the bonds, and such other data as the contractual interest rate and maturity date of the bonds. (p. 634).

Bond indenture A legal document that sets forth the terms of the bond issue. (p. 634).

Bonds A form of interest-bearing notes payable issued by corporations, universities, and governmental entities. (p. 632).

Callable bonds Bonds that are subject to retirement at a stated dollar amount prior to maturity at the option of the issuer. (p. 634).

Capital lease A contractual arrangement that transfers substantially all the benefits and risks of ownership to the lessee so that the lease is in effect a purchase of the property. (p.645).

Contractual interest rate Rate used to determine the amount of cash interest the borrower pays and the investor receives. (p. 634).

Convertible bonds Bonds that permit bondholders to convert them into common stock at their option. (p. 634).

Debenture bonds Bonds issued against the general credit of the borrower. Also called unsecured bonds. (p. 634).

Debt to total assets ratio A solvency measure that indicates the percentage of total assets provided by creditors; computed as total debt divided by total assets. (p. 646).

Discount (on a bond) The difference between the face value of a bond and its selling price, when the bond is sold for less than its face value. (p. 638).

Face value Amount of principal the issuer must pay at the maturity date of the bond. (p. 634).

Long-term liabilities Obligations expected to be paid after one year. (p. 632).

Market interest rate The rate investors demand for loaning funds to the corporation. (p. 636).

Mortgage bond A bond secured by real estate. (p. 633).

Mortgage note payable A long-term note secured by a mortgage that pledges title to specific assets as security for a loan. (p. 643).

Operating lease A contractual arrangement giving the lessee temporary use of the property, with continued ownership of the property by the lessor. (p. 644).

Premium (on a bond) The difference between the selling price and the face value of a bond, when the bond is sold for more than its face value. (p. 638).

Registered bonds Bonds issued in the name of the owner. (p. 634).

Secured bonds Bonds that have specific assets of the issuer pledged as collateral. (p. 633).

Serial bonds Bonds that mature in installments. (p. 634).

Sinking fund bonds Bonds secured by specific assets set aside to retire them. (p. 633).

Term bonds Bonds that mature at a single specified future date. (p. 634).

Times interest earned ratio A solvency measure that indicates a company's ability to meet interest payments; computed by dividing income before income taxes and interest expense by interest expense. (p. 647).

Unsecured bonds Bonds issued against the general credit of the borrower. Also called debenture bonds. (p. 634).

APPENDIX 15A **Present Value Concepts Related to Bond Pricing**

Congratulations! You have a winning lottery ticket and the state has provided you with three possible options for payment. They are:

1. Receive $10,000,000 in three years.
2. Receive $7,000,000 immediately.
3. Receive $3,500,000 at the end of each year for three years.

Which of these options would you select? The answer is not easy to determine at a glance. To make a dollar-maximizing choice, you must perform present value computations. A present value computation is based on the concept of time value of money. Time value of money concepts are useful for the lottery situation and for pricing other amounts to be received in the future. This appendix discusses how to use present value concepts to price bonds. It also will tell you how to determine what option you should take as a lottery winner.

Present Value of Face Value

STUDY OBJECTIVE 7

Compute the market price of a bond.

To illustrate present value concepts, assume that you are willing to invest a sum of money that will yield $1,000 at the end of one year. In other words, what amount would you need to invest today to have $1,000 one year from now? If you want to earn 10%, the investment (or present value) is $909.09 ($1,000 ÷ 1.10). Illustration 15A-1 shows the computation.

Illustration 15A-1
Present value computation—$1,000 discounted at 10% for one year

Present value	**×**	**(1 + Interest rate)**	**=**	**Future amount**
Present value	×	(1 + 10%)	=	$1,000
Present value			=	$1,000 ÷ 1.10
Present value			=	**$909.09**

The future amount ($1,000), the interest rate (10%), and the number of periods (1) are known. We can depict the variables in this situation as shown in the time diagram in Illustration 15A-2.

Illustration 15A-2
Finding present value if discounted for one period

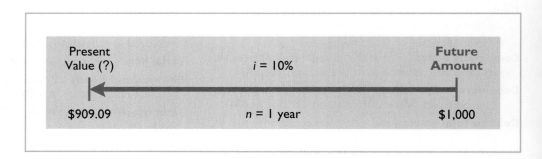

If you are to receive the single future amount of $1,000 **in two years**, discounted at 10%, its present value is $826.45 [($1,000 ÷ 1.10) ÷ 1.10], depicted as follows.

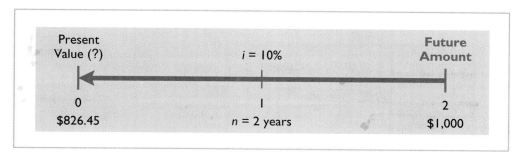

Illustration 15A-3
Finding present value if
discounted for two periods

We also can determine the present value of 1 through tables that show the present value of 1 for *n* periods. In Table 15A-1 below, *n* is the number of discounting periods involved. The percentages are the periodic interest rates, and the 5-digit decimal numbers in the respective columns are the factors for the present value of 1.

When using Table 15A-1, we multiply the future amount by the present value factor specified at the intersection of the number of periods and the interest rate. For example, the present value factor for 1 period at an interest rate of 10% is .90909, which equals the $909.09 ($1,000 × .90909) computed in Illustration 15A-1.

TABLE 15A-1
Present Value of 1

✳ Face Value —

(*n*) Periods	4%	5%	6%	8%	9%	10%	11%	12%	15%
1	.96154	.95238	.94340	.92593	.91743	.90909	.90090	.89286	.86957
2	.92456	.90703	.89000	.85734	.84168	.82645	.81162	.79719	.75614
3	.88900	.86384	.83962	.79383	.77218	.75132	.73119	.71178	.65752
4	.85480	.82270	.79209	.73503	.70843	.68301	.65873	.63552	.57175
5	.82193	.78353	.74726	.68058	.64993	.62092	.59345	.56743	.49718
6	.79031	.74622	.70496	.63017	.59627	.56447	.53464	.50663	.43233
7	.75992	.71068	.66506	.58349	.54703	.51316	.48166	.45235	.37594
8	.73069	.67684	.62741	.54027	.50187	.46651	.43393	.40388	.32690
9	.70259	.64461	.59190	.50025	.46043	.42410	.39092	.36061	.28426
10	.67556	.61391	.55839	.46319	.42241	.38554	.35218	.32197	.24719

For two periods at an interest rate of 10%, the present value factor is .82645, which equals the $826.45 ($1,000 × .82645) computed previously.

Let's now go back to our lottery example. Given the present value concepts just learned, we can determine whether receiving $10,000,000 in three years is better than receiving $7,000,000 today, assuming the appropriate discount rate is 9%. The computation is as follows.

$10,000,000 × PV of 1 due in 3 years at 9% =	
$10,000,000 × .77218 (Table 15A-1)	$7,721,800
Amount to be received from state immediately	7,000,000
Difference	$ 721,800

Illustration 15A-4
Present value of $10,000,000
to be received in three years

What this computation shows you is that you would be $721,800 better off receiving the $10,000,000 at the end of three years rather than taking $7,000,000 immediately.

Present Value of Interest Payments (Annuities)

In addition to receiving the face value of a bond at maturity, an investor also receives periodic interest payments over the life of the bonds. These periodic payments are called **annuities**.

In order to compute the present value of an annuity, we need to know: (1) the interest rate, (2) the number of interest periods, and (3) the amount of the periodic receipts or payments. To illustrate the computation of the present value of an annuity, assume that you will receive $1,000 cash annually for three years and the interest rate is 10%. The time diagram in Illustration 15A-5 depicts this situation.

Illustration 15A-5
Time diagram for a three-year annuity

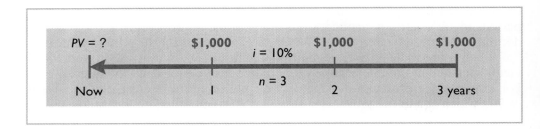

The present value in this situation may be computed as follows.

Illustration 15A-6
Present value of a series of future amounts computation

Future Amount	×	Present Value of 1 Factor at 10%	=	Present Value
$1,000 (1 year away)		.90909		$ 909.09
1,000 (2 years away)		.82645		826.45
1,000 (3 years away)		.75132		751.32
		2.48686		**$2,486.86**

We also can use annuity tables to value annuities. As illustrated in Table 15A-2 below, these tables show the present value of 1 to be received periodically for a given number of periods.

TABLE 15A-2									
Present Value of an Annuity of 1									

(*n*) Periods	4%	5%	6%	8%	9%	10%	11%	12%	15%
1	.96154	.95238	.94340	.92593	.91743	.90909	.90090	.89286	.86957
2	1.88609	1.85941	1.83339	1.78326	1.75911	1.73554	1.71252	1.69005	1.62571
3	2.77509	2.72325	2.67301	2.57710	2.53130	2.48685	2.44371	2.40183	2.28323
4	3.62990	3.54595	3.46511	3.31213	3.23972	3.16986	3.10245	3.03735	2.85498
5	4.45182	4.32948	4.21236	3.99271	3.88965	3.79079	3.69590	3.60478	3.35216
6	5.24214	5.07569	4.91732	4.62288	4.48592	4.35526	4.23054	4.11141	3.78448
7	6.00205	5.78637	5.58238	5.20637	5.03295	4.86842	4.71220	4.56376	4.16042
8	6.73274	6.46321	6.20979	5.74664	5.53482	5.33493	5.14612	4.96764	4.48732
9	7.43533	7.10782	6.80169	6.24689	5.99525	5.75902	5.53705	5.32825	4.77158
10	8.11090	7.72173	7.36009	6.71008	6.41766	6.14457	5.88923	5.65022	5.01877

From Table 15A-2 you can see that the present value factor of an annuity of 1 for three periods at 10% is 2.48685.[1] This present value factor is the total of the three individual present value factors as shown in Illustration 15A-6. Applying this amount to the annual cash flow of $1,000 produces a present value of $2,486.85.

Let's now go back to our lottery example. We determined that you would get more money if you wait and take the $10,000,000 in three years rather than take $7,000,000 immediately. But there is still another option—to receive $3,500,000 at the end of **each year** for three years (an annuity). The computation to evaluate this option (again assuming a 9% discount rate) is as follows.

$3,500,000 × PV of 1 due yearly for 3 years at 9% =	
$3,500,000 × 2.53130 (Table 15A-2)	$8,859,550
Present value of $10,000,000 to be received in 3 years	7,721,800
Difference	$1,137,750

Illustration 15A-7
Present value of lottery payments to be received over three years

If you take the annuity of $3,500,000 for each of 3 years, you will be $1,137,750 richer as a result.

Time Periods and Discounting

We have used an **annual** interest rate to determine present value. Present value computations may also be done over shorter periods of time, such as monthly, quarterly, or semiannually. When the time frame is less than one year, it is necessary to convert the annual interest rate to the shorter time frame.

Assume, for example, that the investor in Illustration 15A-6 received $500 **semiannually** for three years instead of $1,000 annually. In this case, the number of periods becomes 6 (3 × 2), the interest rate is 5% (10% ÷ 2), the present value factor from Table 15A-2 is 5.07569, and the present value of the future cash flows is $2,537.85 (5.07569 × $500). This amount is slightly higher than the $2,486.86 computed in Illustration 15A-6 because interest is computed twice during the same year. That is, interest is earned on the first half year's interest.

Computing the Present Value of a Bond

The present value (or market price) of a bond is a function of three variables: (1) the payment amounts, (2) the length of time until the amounts are paid, and (3) the interest (discount) rate.

The first variable (dollars to be paid) is made up of two elements: (1) a series of interest payments (an annuity), and (2) the principal amount (a single sum). To compute the present value of the bond, we must discount both the interest payments and the principal amount.

When the investor's interest (discount) rate is equal to the bond's contractual interest rate, the present value of the bonds will equal the face value of the bonds. To illustrate, assume a bond issue of 10%, five-year bonds with a face value of $100,000 with interest payable **semiannually** on January 1 and July 1. If the discount rate is the same as the contractual rate, the bonds will sell **at face value**. In this case, the investor will receive: (1) $100,000 at maturity and (2) a series of ten $5,000 interest payments [$100,000 × (10% ÷ 2)] over the term of the bonds. The length of time is expressed in terms of interest periods (in this case, 10) and the discount rate per interest period (5%). The time diagram in Illustration 15A-8 (page 656) depicts the variables involved in this discounting situation.

---

[1] The difference of .00001 between 2.48686 and 2.48685 is due to rounding.

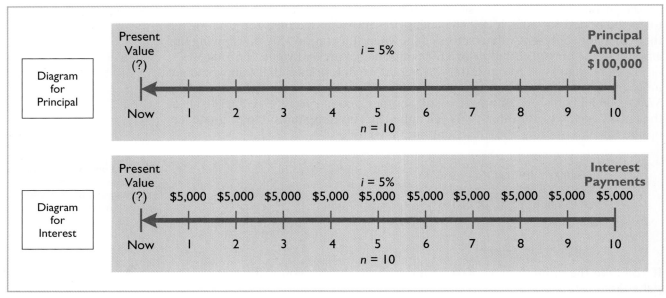

Illustration 15A-8
Time diagram for the present value of a 10%, five-year bond paying interest semiannually

Illustration 15A-9
Present value of principal and interest (face value)

The computation of the present value of Candlestick's bonds, assuming they were issued at face value (page 637), is shown below.

10% Contractual Rate—10% Discount Rate	
Present value of principal to be received at maturity	
$100,000 × PV of 1 due in 10 periods at 5%	
$100,000 × .61391 (Table 15A-1)	$ 61,391
Present value of interest to be received periodically	
over the term of the bonds	
$5,000 × PV of 1 due periodically for 10 periods at 5%	
$5,000 × 7.72173 (Table 15A-2)	38,609*
Present value of bonds	**$100,000**

*(Rounded).

Now assume that the investor's required rate of return is 12%, not 10%. The future amounts are again $100,000 and $5,000, respectively. But now we must use a discount rate of 6% (12% ÷ 2). The present value of Candlestick's bonds issued at a discount (page 638) is $92,639 as computed below.

Illustration 15A-10
Present value of principal and interest (discount)

10% Contractual Rate—12% Discount Rate	
Present value of principal to be received at maturity	
$100,000 × .55839 (Table 15A-1)	$55,839
Present value of interest to be received periodically	
over the term of the bonds	
$5,000 × 7.36009 (Table 15A-2)	36,800
Present value of bonds	**$92,639**

If the discount rate is 8% and the contractual rate is 10%, the present value of Candlestick's bonds issued at a premium (page 639) is $108,111, computed as follows.

10% Contractual Rate—8% Discount Rate	
Present value of principal to be received at maturity	
$100,000 × .67556 (Table 15A-1)	$67,556
Present value of interest to be received periodically over the term of the bonds	
$5,000 × 8.11090 (Table 15A-2)	40,555
Present value of bonds	**$108,111**

Illustration 15A-11
Present value of principal and interest (premium)

SUMMARY OF STUDY OBJECTIVE FOR APPENDIX 15A

7 Compute the market price of a bond. Time value of money concepts are useful for pricing bonds. The present value (or market price) of a bond is a function of three vari-ables: (1) the payment amounts, (2) the length of time until the amounts are paid, and (3) the interest rate.

APPENDIX 15B Effective-Interest Method of Bond Amortization

Under the **effective-interest method**, the amortization of bond discount or bond premium results in periodic interest expense equal to a **constant per-centage** of the carrying value of the bonds. The effective-interest method results in varying amounts of amortization and interest expense per period but **a constant percentage rate**.

The following steps are required under the effective-interest method.

STUDY OBJECTIVE 8
Apply the effective-interest method of amortizing bond discount and bond premium.

1. Compute the **bond interest expense**. To do so, multiply the carrying value of the bonds at the beginning of the interest period by the effective-interest rate.
2. Compute the **bond interest paid** (or accrued). To do so, multiply the face value of the bonds by the contractual interest rate.
3. Compute the **amortization amount**. To do so, determine the difference between the amounts computed in steps (1) and (2).

Illustration 15B-1 depicts these steps.

(1) Bond Interest Expense		(2) Bond Interest Paid		(3)
(Carrying Value of Bonds at Beginning of Period × Effective Interest Rate)	−	(Face Amount of Bonds × Contractual Interest Rate)	=	Amortization Amount

Illustration 15B-1
Computation of amortization—effective-interest method

When the difference between the straight-line method of amortization (Appendix 15C) and the effective-interest method is material, GAAP requires the use of the effective-interest method.

Amortizing Bond Discount

To illustrate the effective-interest method of bond discount amortization, assume that Candlestick, Inc. issues $100,000 of 10%, five-year bonds on January 1, 2008, with interest payable each July 1 and January 1 (pages 638–639). The bonds sell for $92,639 (92.639% of face value). This sales price results in bond discount of $7,361 ($100,000 − $92,639) and an effective-interest rate of 12%. A bond discount amortization schedule, as shown in Illustration 15B-2 (page 658), facilitates the recording of interest expense and the discount amortization. Note that interest expense as a percentage of carrying value remains constant at 6%.

⊠ Candlestick Inc.xls

▤ File   Edit   View   Insert   Format   Tools   Data   Window   Help

CANDLESTICK, INC.
Bond Discount Amortization
Effective-Interest Method—Semiannual Interest Payments
10% Bonds Issued at 12%

Semiannual Interest Periods	(A) Interest to Be Paid (5% × $100,000)	(B) Interest Expense to Be Recorded (6% × Preceding Bond Carrying Value)		(C) Discount Amortization (B) − (A)	(D) Unamortized Discount (D) − (C)	(E) Bond Carrying Value ($100,000 − D)
Issue date					$7,361	$92,639
1	$ 5,000	$ 5,558	(6% × $92,639)	$ 558	6,803	93,197
2	5,000	5,592	(6% × $93,197)	592	6,211	93,789
3	5,000	5,627	(6% × $93,789)	627	5,584	94,416
4	5,000	5,665	(6% × $94,416)	665	4,919	95,081
5	5,000	5,705	(6% × $95,081)	705	4,214	95,786
6	5,000	5,747	(6% × $95,786)	747	3,467	96,533
7	5,000	5,792	(6% × $96,533)	792	2,675	97,325
8	5,000	5,840	(6% × $97,325)	840	1,835	98,165
9	5,000	5,890	(6% × $98,165)	890	945	99,055
10	5,000	5,945*	(6% × $99,055)	945	–0–	100,000
	$50,000	$57,361		$7,361		

Column (A) remains constant because the face value of the bonds ($100,000) is multiplied by the semiannual contractual interest rate (5%) each period.

Column (B) is computed as the preceding bond carrying value times the semiannual effective-interest rate (6%).

Column (C) indicates the discount amortization each period.

Column (D) decreases each period until it reaches zero at maturity.

Column (E) increases each period until it equals face value at maturity.

*$2 difference due to rounding.

Illustration 15B-2
Bond discount amortization schedule

We have highlighted columns (A), (B), and (C) in the amortization schedule to emphasize their importance. These three columns provide the numbers for each period's journal entries. They are the primary reason for preparing the schedule.

For the first interest period, the computations of bond interest expense and the bond discount amortization are:

Illustration 15B-3
Computation of bond discount amortization

Bond interest expense ($92,639 × 6%)	$5,558
Contractual interest ($100,000 × 5%)	5,000
Bond discount amortization	**$ 558**

Candlestick records the payment of interest and amortization of bond discount on July 1, 2008, as follows.

```
A  =  L  +  SE
            −5,558 Exp
      +558
−5,000
```

Cash Flows
−5,000

July 1	Bond Interest Expense	5,558	
	Discount on Bonds Payable		558
	Cash		5,000
	(To record payment of bond interest and amortization of bond discount)		

For the second interest period, bond interest expense will be $5,592 ($93,197 × 6%), and the discount amortization will be $592. At December 31, Candlestick makes the following adjusting entry.

Dec. 31	Bond Interest Expense	5,592	
	Discount on Bonds Payable		592
	Bond Interest Payable		5,000
	(To record accrued interest and amortization of bond discount)		

A	=	L	+	SE
				−5,592 Exp
		+592		
		+5,000		

Cash Flows
no effect

Total bond interest expense for 2008 is $11,150 ($5,558 + $5,592). On January 1, Candlestick records payment of the interest by a debit to Bond Interest Payable and a credit to Cash.

Amortizing Bond Premium

The amortization of bond premium by the effective-interest method is similar to the procedures described for bond discount. For example, assume that Candlestick, Inc. issues $100,000, 10%, five-year bonds on January 1, 2008, with interest payable on July 1 and January 1 (pages 639–640). In this case, the bonds sell for $108,111. This sales price results in bond premium of $8,111 and an effective-interest rate of 8%. Illustration 15-4 shows the bond premium amortization schedule.

HELPFUL HINT

When a bond sells for $108,111, it is quoted as 108.111% of face value. Note that $108,111 can be proven as shown in Appendix 15A.

Illustration 15B-4
Bond premium amortization schedule

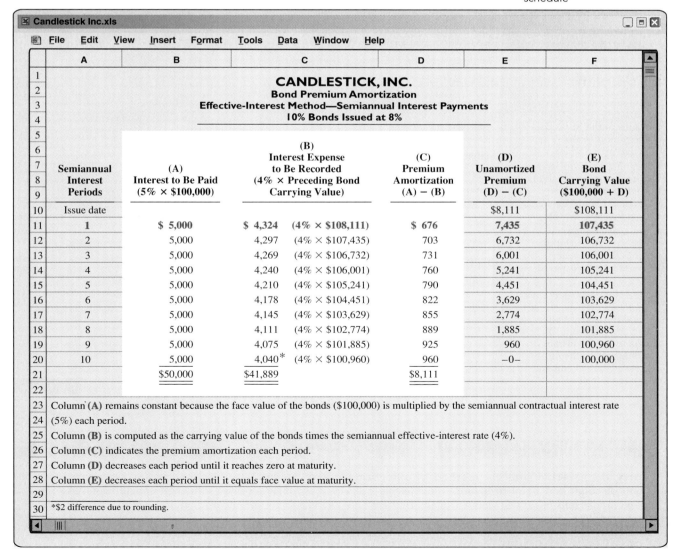

CANDLESTICK, INC.
Bond Premium Amortization
Effective-Interest Method—Semiannual Interest Payments
10% Bonds Issued at 8%

Semiannual Interest Periods	(A) Interest to Be Paid (5% × $100,000)	(B) Interest Expense to Be Recorded (4% × Preceding Bond Carrying Value)		(C) Premium Amortization (A) − (B)	(D) Unamortized Premium (D) − (C)	(E) Bond Carrying Value ($100,000 + D)
Issue date					$8,111	$108,111
1	$ 5,000	$ 4,324	(4% × $108,111)	$ 676	7,435	107,435
2	5,000	4,297	(4% × $107,435)	703	6,732	106,732
3	5,000	4,269	(4% × $106,732)	731	6,001	106,001
4	5,000	4,240	(4% × $106,001)	760	5,241	105,241
5	5,000	4,210	(4% × $105,241)	790	4,451	104,451
6	5,000	4,178	(4% × $104,451)	822	3,629	103,629
7	5,000	4,145	(4% × $103,629)	855	2,774	102,774
8	5,000	4,111	(4% × $102,774)	889	1,885	101,885
9	5,000	4,075	(4% × $101,885)	925	960	100,960
10	5,000	4,040*	(4% × $100,960)	960	−0−	100,000
	$50,000	$41,889		$8,111		

Column (A) remains constant because the face value of the bonds ($100,000) is multiplied by the semiannual contractual interest rate (5%) each period.

Column (B) is computed as the carrying value of the bonds times the semiannual effective-interest rate (4%).

Column (C) indicates the premium amortization each period.

Column (D) decreases each period until it reaches zero at maturity.

Column (E) decreases each period until it equals face value at maturity.

*$2 difference due to rounding.

For the first interest period, the computations of bond interest expense and the bond premium amortization are:

Illustration 15B-5
Computation of bond premium amortization

Bond interest expense ($108,111 × 4%)	$4,324
Contractual interest ($100,000 × 5%)	5,000
Bond premium amortization	$ 676

Candlestick records payments on the first interest date as follows.

A	=	L	+	SE
				−4,324 Exp
		−676		
−5,000				

Cash Flows
−5,000

July 1	Bond Interest Expense		4,324	
	Premium on Bonds Payable		676	
	Cash			5,000
	(To record payment of bond interest and			
	amortization of bond premium)			

For the second interest period, interest expense will be $4,297, and the premium amortization will be $703. Total bond interest expense for 2008 is $8,621 ($4,324 + $4,297).

Demonstration Problem for Appendix15B

Gardner Corporation issues $1,750,000, 10-year, 12% bonds on January 1, 2008, at $1,820,000, to yield 10%. The bonds pay semiannual interest July 1 and January 1. Gardner uses the effective-interest method of amortization.

Instructions

(a) Prepare the journal entry to record the issuance of the bonds.
(b) Prepare the journal entry to record the payment of interest on July 1, 2008.

action plan

✔ Compute interest expense by multiplying bond carrying value at the beginning of the period by the effective-interest rate.

✔ Compute credit to cash (or bond interest payable) by multiplying the face value of the bonds by the contractual interest rate.

✔ Compute bond premium or discount amortization, which is the difference between interest expense and cash paid.

✔ Interest expense decreases when the effective-interest method is used for bonds issued at a premium. The reason is that a constant percentage is applied to a decreasing book value to compute interest expense.

Solution to Demonstration Problem

(a) 2008

Jan. 1	Cash		1,820,000	
	Bonds Payable			1,750,000
	Premium on Bonds Payable			70,000
	(To record issuance of bonds at a premium)			

(b) 2008

July 1	Bond Interest Expense		91,000*	
	Premium on Bonds Payable		14,000**	
	Cash			105,000
	(To record payment of semiannual interest			
	and amortization of bond premium)			
	*($1,820,000 × 5%)			
	**($105,000 − $91,000)			

✔ *The Navigator*

SUMMARY OF STUDY OBJECTIVE FOR APPENDIX 15B

8 **Apply the effective-interest method of amortizing bond discount and bond premium.** The effective-interest method results in varying amounts of amortization and interest expense per period but a *constant percentage rate* of interest. When the difference between the straight-line and effective-interest method is material, GAAP requires the use of the effective-interest method.

Effective-interest method of amortization   A method of amortizing bond discount or bond premium that results in periodic interest expense equal to a constant percentage of the carrying value of the bonds. (p. 657).

APPENDIX 15C **Straight-Line Amortization**

Amortizing Bond Discount

To follow the matching principle, companies should allocate bond discount systematically to each period in which the bonds are outstanding. The straight-line method of amortization allocates the **same amount to interest expense** in each interest period. The amount is determined using the formula in Illustration 15C-1.

> **STUDY OBJECTIVE 9**
> Apply the straight-line method of amortizing bond discount and bond premium.

Bond Discount	÷	Number of Interest Periods	=	Bond Discount Amortization

Illustration 15C-1
Formula for straight-line method of bond discount amortization

In the Candlestick, Inc. example (page 638), the company sold $100,000, five-year, 10% bonds on January 1, 2008, for $92,639. This price resulted in a $7,361 bond discount ($100,000 − $92,639). Interest is payable on July 1 and January 1. The bond discount amortization for each interest period is $736 ($7,361 ÷ 10). Candlestick records the payment of bond interest and the amortization of bond discount on the first interest date (July 1, 2008) as follows.

July 1	Bond Interest Expense	5,736	
	Discount on Bonds Payable		736
	Cash		5,000
	(To record payment of bond interest and amortization of bond discount)		

A	=	L	+	SE
				−5,736 Exp
		+736		
−5,000				

Cash Flows
−5,000

At December 31, Candlestick makes the following adjusting entry.

Dec. 31	Bond Interest Expense	5,736	
	Discount on Bonds Payable		736
	Bond Interest Payable		5,000
	(To record accrued bond interest and amortization of bond discount)		

A	=	L	+	SE
				−5,736 Exp
		+736		
		+5,000		

Cash Flows
no effect

Over the term of the bonds, the balance in Discount on Bonds Payable will decrease annually by the **same amount** until it has a zero balance at the maturity date of the bonds. Thus, the carrying value of the bonds at maturity will be equal to the face value.

It is useful to prepare a bond discount amortization schedule as shown in Illustration 15C-2 (page 662). The schedule shows interest expense, discount amortization, and the carrying value of the bond for each interest period. As indicated, the interest expense recorded **each period** for the Candlestick bond is $5,736. Also note that the carrying value of the bond increases $736 each period until it reaches its face value $100,000 at the end of period 10.

Illustration 15C-2
Bond discount amortization schedule

Candlestick Inc.xls					
File Edit View Insert Format Tools Data Window Help					
	A	B	C	D	E	F

CANDLESTICK, INC.
Bond Discount Amortization
Straight-Line Method—Semiannual Interest Payments

Semiannual Interest Periods	(A) Interest to Be Paid (5% × $100,000)	(B) Interest Expense to Be Recorded (A) + (C)	(C) Discount Amortization ($7,361 ÷ 10)	(D) Unamortized Discount (D) − (C)	(E) Bond Carrying Value ($100,000 − D)
Issue date				$7,361	$92,639
1	$ 5,000	$ 5,736	$ 736	6,625	93,375
2	5,000	5,736	736	5,889	94,111
3	5,000	5,736	736	5,153	94,847
4	5,000	5,736	736	4,417	95,583
5	5,000	5,736	736	3,681	96,319
6	5,000	5,736	736	2,945	97,055
7	5,000	5,736	736	2,209	97,791
8	5,000	5,736	736	1,473	98,527
9	5,000	5,736	736	737	99,263
10	5,000	5,737*	737*	–0–	100,000
	$50,000	$57,361	$7,361		

Column **(A)** remains constant because the face value of the bonds ($100,000) is multiplied by the semiannual contractual interest rate (5%) each period.
Column **(B)** is computed as the interest paid (Column A) plus the discount amortization (Column C).
Column **(C)** indicates the discount amortization each period.
Column **(D)** decreases each period by the same amount until it reaches zero at maturity.
Column **(E)** increases each period by the same amount of discount amortization until it equals the face value at maturity.
*One dollar difference due to rounding.

We have highlighted columns (A), (B), and (C) in the amortization schedule to emphasize their importance. These three columns provide the numbers for each period's journal entries. They are the primary reason for preparing the schedule.

Amortizing Bond Premium

The amortization of bond premium parallels that of bond discount. Illustration 15C-3 presents the formula for determining bond premium amortization under the straight-line method.

Illustration 15C-3
Formula for straight-line method of bond premium amortization

Bond Premium	÷	Number of Interest Periods	=	Bond Premium Amortization

Continuing our example, assume that Candlestick sells the bonds for $108,111, rather than $92,639 (page 639). This sale price results in a bond premium of $8,111 ($108,111 − $100,000). The bond premium amortization for each interest period is $811 ($8,111 ÷ 10). Candlestick records the first payment of interest on July 1 as follows.

A	=	L	+	SE
				−4,189 Exp
		−811		
−5,000				

Cash Flows
−5,000

July 1	Bond Interest Expense	4,189	
	Premium on Bonds Payable	811	
	Cash		5,000
	(To record payment of bond interest and amortization of bond premium)		

At December 31, the company makes the following adjusting entry.

Dec. 31	Bond Interest Expense		4,189	
	Premium on Bonds Payable		811	
	Bond Interest Payable			5,000
	(To record accrued bond interest and			
	amortization of bond premium)			

A	=	L	+	SE
				−4,189 Exp
		−811		
		+5,000		

Cash Flows
no effect

Over the term of the bonds, the balance in Premium on Bonds Payable will decrease annually **by the same amount** until it has a zero balance at maturity.

It is useful to prepare a bond premium amortization schedule as shown in Illustration 15C-4. It shows interest expense, premium amortization, and the carrying value of the bond. The interest expense recorded each period for the Candlestick bond is $4,189. Also note that the carrying value of the bond decreases $811 each period until it reaches its face value $100,000 at the end of period 10.

Illustration 15C-4
Bond premium amortization schedule

Candlestick Inc.xls

File   Edit   View   Insert   Format   Tools   Data   Window   Help

CANDLESTICK, INC.
Bond Premium Amortization
Straight-Line Method—Semiannual Interest Payments

Semiannual Interest Periods	(A) Interest to Be Paid (5% × $100,000)	(B) Interest Expense to Be Recorded (A) − (C)	(C) Premium Amortization ($8,111 ÷ 10)	(D) Unamortized Premium (D) − (C)	(E) Bond Carrying Value ($100,000 + D)
Issue date				$8,111	$108,111
1	$ 5,000	$ 4,189	$ 811	7,300	107,300
2	5,000	4,189	811	6,489	106,489
3	5,000	4,189	811	5,678	105,678
4	5,000	4,189	811	4,867	104,867
5	5,000	4,189	811	4,056	104,056
6	5,000	4,189	811	3,245	103,245
7	5,000	4,189	811	2,434	102,434
8	5,000	4,189	811	1,623	101,623
9	5,000	4,189	811	812	100,812
10	5,000	4,188*	812*	−0−	100,000
	$50,000	$41,889	$8,111		

Column **(A)** remains constant because the face value of the bonds ($100,000) is multiplied by the semiannual contractual interest rate (5%) each period.
Column **(B)** is computed as the interest paid (Column A) less the premium amortization (Column C).
Column **(C)** indicates the premium amortization each period.
Column **(D)** decreases each period by the same amount until it reaches zero at maturity.
Column **(E)** decreases each period by the amount of premium amortization until it equals the face value at maturity.
*One dollar difference due to rounding.

Demonstration Problem for Appendix 15C

Glenda Corporation issues $1,750,000, 10-year, 12% bonds on January 1, 2008, for $1,820,000 to yield 10%. The bonds pay semiannual interest July 1 and January 1. Glenda uses the straight-line method of amortization.

Instructions

(a) Prepare the journal entry to record the issuance of the bonds.
(b) Prepare the journal entry to record the payment of interest on July 1, 2008.

action plan

✔ Compute credit to cash (or bond interest payable) by multiplying the face value of the bonds by the contractual interest rate.

✔ Compute bond premium or discount amortization by dividing bond premium or discount by the total number of periods.

✔ Understand that interest expense decreases when bonds are issued at a premium. The reason is that the amortization of premium reduces the total cost of borrowing.

Solution to Demonstration Problem

(a) 2008

Jan. 1	Cash	1,820,000	
	Bonds Payable		1,750,000
	Premium on Bonds Payable		70,000

(b) 2008

July 1	Bond Interest Expense	101,500**	
	Premium on Bonds Payable	3,500*	
	Cash		105,000
	*$70,000 ÷ 20		
	**$105,000 − $3,500		

 The Navigator

SUMMARY OF STUDY OBJECTIVE FOR APPENDIX 15C

9 Apply the straight-line method of amortizing bond discount and bond premium. The straight-line method of amortization results in a *constant amount* of amortization and interest expense per period.

GLOSSARY FOR APPENDIX 15C

Straight-line method of amortization. A method of amortizing bond discount or bond premium that results in allocating the same amount to interest expense in each interest period. (p. 661)

---

*Note: All asterisked Questions, Exercises, and Problems relate to material in the appendices to the chapter.

SELF-STUDY QUESTIONS

Answers are at the end of the chapter.

(SO 1) **1.** The term used for bonds that are unsecured is:
   a. callable bonds.
   b. indenture bonds.
   c. debenture bonds.
   d. bearer bonds.

(SO 2) **2.** Karson Inc. issues 10-year bonds with a maturity value of $200,000. If the bonds are issued at a premium, this indicates that:
   a. the contractual interest rate exceeds the market interest rate.
   b. the market interest rate exceeds the contractual interest rate.
   c. the contractual interest rate and the market interest rate are the same.
   d. no relationship exists between the two rates.

(SO 3) **3.** Gester Corporation retires its $100,000 face value bonds at 105 on January 1, following the payment of semiannual interest. The carrying value of the bonds at the redemption date is $103,745. The entry to record the redemption will include a:
   a. credit of $3,745 to Loss on Bond Redemption.
   b. debit of $3,745 to Premium on Bonds Payable.

   c. credit of $1,255 to Gain on Bond Redemption.
   d. debit of $5,000 to Premium on Bonds Payable.

4. Colson Inc. converts $600,000 of bonds sold at face value (SO into 10,000 shares of common stock, par value $1. Both the bonds and the stock have a market value of $760,000. What amount should be credited to Paid-in Capital in Excess of Par as a result of the conversion?
   a. $10,000.
   b. $160,000.
   c. $600,000.
   d. $590,000.

5. Andrews Inc. issues a $497,000, 10% 3-year mortgage note (SO on January 1. The note will be paid in three annual installments of $200,000, each payable at the end of the year. What is the amount of interest expense that should be recognized by Andrews Inc. in the second year?
   a. $16,567.
   b. $49,700.
   c. $34,670.
   d. $346,700.

6. Lease A does not contain a bargain purchase option, but (SO the lease term is equal to 90 percent of the estimated economic life of the leased property. Lease B does not transfer ownership of the property to the lessee by the end of the lease term, but the lease term is equal to 75 percent of the estimated economic life of the leased property. How should the lessee classify these leases?

	Lease A	Lease B
a.	Operating lease	Capital lease
b.	Operating lease	Operating lease
c.	Capital lease	Operating lease
d.	Capital lease	Capital lease

(SO 8) *7. On January 1, Besalius Inc. issued $1,000,000, 9% bonds for $939,000. The market rate of interest for these bonds is 10%. Interest is payable annually on December 31. Besalius uses the effective-interest method of amortizing bond discount. At the end of the first year, Besalius should report unamortized bond discount of:
a. $54,900.   c. $51,610.
b. $57,100.   d. $51,000.

(SO 8) *8. On January 1, Dias Corporation issued $1,000,000, 14%, 5-year bonds with interest payable on July 1 and January 1. The bonds sold for $1,098,540. The market rate of interest for these bonds was 12%. On the first interest date, using

the effective-interest method, the debit entry to Bond Interest Expense is for:
a. $60,000.   c. $65,912.
b. $76,898.   d. $131,825.

*9. On January 1, Hurley Corporation issues $500,000, 5-year, (SO 9) 12% bonds at 96 with interest payable on July 1 and January 1. The entry on July 1 to record payment of bond interest and the amortization of bond discount using the straight-line method will include a:
a. debit to Interest Expense $30,000.
b. debit to Interest Expense $60,000.
c. credit to Discount on Bonds Payable $4,000.
d. credit to Discount on Bonds Payable $2,000.

*10. For the bonds issued in question 9, above, what is the carry- (SO 9) ing value of the bonds at the end of the third interest period?
a. $486,000.   c. $472,000.
b. $488,000.   d. $464,000.

Go to the book's website,
www.wiley.com/college/weygandt,
for Additional Self-Study questions.

QUESTIONS

1. (a) What are long-term liabilities? Give three examples. (b) What is a bond?

2. (a) As a source of long-term financing, what are the major advantages of bonds over common stock? (b) What are the major disadvantages in using bonds for long-term financing?

3. Contrast the following types of bonds: (a) secured and unsecured, (b) term and serial, (c) registered and bearer, and (d) convertible and callable.

4. The following terms are important in issuing bonds: (a) face value, (b) contractual interest rate, (c) bond indenture, and (d) bond certificate. Explain each of these terms.

5. Describe the two major obligations incurred by a company when bonds are issued.

6. Assume that Koslowski Inc. sold bonds with a par value of $100,000 for $104,000. Was the market interest rate equal to, less than, or greater than the bonds' contractual interest rate? Explain.

7. If a 7%, 10-year, $800,000 bond is issued at par and interest is paid semiannually, what is the amount of the interest payment at the end of the first semiannual period?

8. If the Bonds Payable account has a balance of $900,000 and the Discount on Bonds Payable account has a balance of $40,000, what is the carrying value of the bonds?

9. Which accounts are debited and which are credited if a bond issue originally sold at a premium is redeemed before maturity at 97 immediately following the payment of interest?

10. Henricks Corporation is considering issuing a convertible bond. What is a convertible bond? Discuss the advantages of a convertible bond from the standpoint of (a) the bondholders and (b) the issuing corporation.

11. Tim Brown, a friend of yours, has recently purchased a home for $125,000, paying $25,000 down and the remainder financed by a 10.5%, 20-year mortgage, payable at $998.38 per month. At the end of the first month, Tim receives a statement from the bank indicating that only $123.38 of principal was paid during the month. At this rate, he calculates that it will take over 67 years to pay off the mortgage. Is he right? Discuss.

12. (a) What is a lease agreement? (b) What are the two most common types of leases? (c) Distinguish between the two types of leases.

13. Clooney Company rents a warehouse on a month-to-month basis for the storage of its excess inventory. The company periodically must rent space when its production greatly exceeds actual sales. What is the nature of this type of lease agreement, and what accounting treatment should be used?

14. Rondelli Company entered into an agreement to lease 12 computers from Estes Electronics Inc. The present value of the lease payments is $186,300. Assuming that this is a capital lease, what entry would Rondelli Company make on the date of the lease agreement?

15. In general, what are the requirements for the financial statement presentation of long-term liabilities?

16. Laura Hiatt is discussing the advantages of the effective-interest method of bond amortization with her accounting staff. What do you think Laura is saying?

17. Markham Corporation issues $500,000 of 9%, 5-year bonds on January 1, 2008, at 104. If Markham uses the effective-interest method in amortizing the premium, will the annual interest expense increase or decrease over the life of the bonds? Explain.

*18. Tina Cruz and Dale Commons are discussing how the market price of a bond is determined. Tina believes that the market price of a bond is solely a function of the amount of the principal payment at the end of the term of a bond. Is she right? Discuss.

*19. Explain the straight-line method of amortizing discount and premium on bonds payable.

*20. DeWeese Corporation issues $400,000 of 8%, 5-year bonds on January 1, 2008, at 105. Assuming that the straight-line method is used to amortize the premium, what is the total amount of interest expense for 2008?

BRIEF EXERCISES

Compare bond versus stock financing.

(SO 1)

BE15-1   Mareska Inc. is considering two alternatives to finance its construction of a new $2 million plant.

(a) Issuance of 200,000 shares of common stock at the market price of $10 per share.
(b) Issuance of $2 million, 8% bonds at par.

Complete the following table, and indicate which alternative is preferable.

	Issue Stock	Issue Bond
Income before interest and taxes	$700,000	$700,000
Interest expense from bonds		
Income before income taxes	$	$
Income tax expense (30%)		
Net income	$	$
Outstanding shares		500,000
Earnings per share		

Prepare entries for bonds issued at face value.

(SO 2)

BE15-2   Pruitt Corporation issued 3,000, 8%, 5-year, $1,000 bonds dated January 1, 2008, at 100.

(a) Prepare the journal entry to record the sale of these bonds on January 1, 2008.
(b) Prepare the journal entry to record the first interest payment on July 1, 2008 (interest payable semiannually), assuming no previous accrual of interest.
(c) Prepare the adjusting journal entry on December 31, 2008, to record interest expense.

Prepare entries for bonds sold at a discount and a premium.

(SO 2)

BE15-3   Ratzlaff Company issues $2 million, 10-year, 8% bonds at 97, with interest payable on July 1 and January 1.

(a) Prepare the journal entry to record the sale of these bonds on January 1, 2008.
(b) Assuming instead that the above bonds sold for 104, prepare the journal entry to record the sale of these bonds on January 1, 2008.

Prepare entries for bonds issued.

(SO 2)

BE15-4   Halloway Company has issued three different bonds during 2008. Interest is payable semiannually on each of these bonds.

1. On January 1, 2008, 1,000, 8%, 5-year, $1,000 bonds dated January 1, 2008, were issued at face value.
2. On July 1, $800,000, 9%, 5-year bonds dated July 1, 2008, were issued at 102.
3. On September 1, $200,000, 7%, 5-year bonds dated September 1, 2008, were issued at 98.

Prepare the journal entry to record each bond transaction at the date of issuance.

Prepare entry for redemption of bonds.

(SO 3)

BE15-5   The balance sheet for Lemay Company reports the following information on July 1, 2008.

Long-term liabilities
Bonds payable $1,000,000
Less: Discount on bonds payable   60,000 $940,000

Lemay decides to redeem these bonds at 101 after paying semiannual interest. Prepare the journal entry to record the redemption on July 1, 2008.

Prepare entries for long-term notes payable.

(SO 4)

BE15-6   Pickeril Inc. issues a $600,000, 10%, 10-year mortgage note on December 31, 2008, to obtain financing for a new building. The terms provide for semiannual installment payments of $48,145. Prepare the entry to record the mortgage loan on December 31, 2008, and the first installment payment.

BE15-7 Prepare the journal entries that the lessee should make to record the following transactions.

Contrast accounting for operating and capital lease.

(SO 5)

1. The lessee makes a lease payment of $80,000 to the lessor in an operating lease transaction.
2. Veatch Company leases a new building from Joel Construction, Inc. The present value of the lease payments is $700,000. The lease qualifies as a capital lease.

BE15-8 Presented below are long-term liability items for Molini Company at December 31, 2008. Prepare the long-term liabilities section of the balance sheet for Molini Company.

Prepare statement presentation of long-term liabilities.

(SO 6)

Bonds payable, due 2010	$500,000
Lease liability	70,000
Notes payable, due 2013	80,000
Discount on bonds payable	45,000

*BE15-9 (a) What is the present value of $10,000 due 8 periods from now, discounted at 10%?
(b) What is the present value of $20,000 to be received at the end of each of 6 periods, discounted at 8%?

Determine present value.

(SO 7)

*BE15-10 Presented below is the partial bond discount amortization schedule for Morales Corp. Morales uses the effective-interest method of amortization.

Use effective-interest method of bond amortization.

(SO 8)

Semiannual Interest Periods	Interest to Be Paid	Interest Expense to Be Recorded	Discount Amortization	Unamortized Discount	Bond Carrying Value
Issue date				$62,311	$937,689
1	$45,000	$46,884	$1,884	60,427	939,573
2	45,000	46,979	1,979	58,448	941,552

Instructions
(a) Prepare the journal entry to record the payment of interest and the discount amortization at the end of period 1.
(b) Explain why interest expense is greater than interest paid.
(c) Explain why interest expense will increase each period.

*BE15-11 Deane Company issues $5 million, 10-year, 9% bonds at 96, with interest payable on July 1 and January 1. The straight-line method is used to amortize bond discount.

Prepare entries for bonds issued at a discount.

(SO 9)

(a) Prepare the journal entry to record the sale of these bonds on January 1, 2008.
(b) Prepare the journal entry to record interest expense and bond discount amortization on July 1, 2008, assuming no previous accrual of interest.

*BE15-12 Coates Inc. issues $3 million, 5-year, 10% bonds at 102, with interest payable on July 1 and January 1. The straight-line method is used to amortize bond premium.

Prepare entries for bonds issued at a premium.

(SO 9)

(a) Prepare the journal entry to record the sale of these bonds on January 1, 2008.
(b) Prepare the journal entry to record interest expense and bond premium amortization on July 1, 2008, assuming no previous accrual of interest.

EXERCISES

E15-1 Jim Thome has prepared the following list of statements about bonds.

Evaluate statements about bonds.

(SO 1)

1. Bonds are a form of interest-bearing notes payable. T
2. When seeking long-term financing, an advantage of issuing bonds over issuing common stock is that stockholder control is not affected. T
3. When seeking long-term financing, an advantage of issuing common stock over issuing bonds is that tax savings result.
4. Secured bonds have specific assets of the issuer pledged as collateral for the bonds. T
5. Secured bonds are also known as debenture bonds. F
6. Bonds that mature in installments are called term bonds. F
7. A conversion feature may be added to bonds to make them more attractive to bond buyers. T
8. The rate used to determine the amount of cash interest the borrower pays is called the stated rate.
9. Bond prices are usually quoted as a percentage of the face value of the bond.
10. The present value of a bond is the value at which it should sell in the marketplace. F

Instructions

Identify each statement on page 667 as true or false. If false, indicate how to correct the statement.

Compare two alternatives of financing—issuance of common stock vs. issuance of bonds.

(SO 1)

E15-2   Northeast Airlines is considering two alternatives for the financing of a purchase of a fleet of airplanes. These two alternatives are:

1. Issue 60,000 shares of common stock at $45 per share. (Cash dividends have not been paid nor is the payment of any contemplated).
2. Issue 10%, 10-year bonds at par for $2,700,000.

It is estimated that the company will earn $800,000 before interest and taxes as a result of this purchase. The company has an estimated tax rate of 30% and has 90,000 shares of common stock outstanding prior to the new financing.   *EPS stock: $3 73   , Bond $4.13*

Instructions

Determine the effect on net income and earnings per share for these two methods of financing.

Prepare entries for issuance of bonds, and payment and accrual of bond interest.

(SO 2)

E15-3   On January 1, Neuer Company issued $500,000, 10%, 10-year bonds at par. Interest is payable semiannually on July 1 and January 1.

Instructions

Present journal entries to record the following.

Interest Pd $25,000
Interest accrued $25,000

(a) The issuance of the bonds.
(b) The payment of interest on July 1, assuming that interest was not accrued on June 30.
(c) The accrual of interest on December 31.

Prepare entries for bonds issued at face value.

(SO 2)

E15-4   On January 1, Flory Company issued $300,000, 8%, 5-year bonds at face value. Interest is payable semiannually on July 1 and January 1.

Instructions

Prepare journal entries to record the following events.

(a) The issuance of the bonds.
(b) The payment of interest on July 1, assuming no previous accrual of interest.   *Interest expense $12,000*
(c) The accrual of interest on December 31.

Prepare entries for bonds issued at face value.

(SO 2, 3)

E15-5   Jaurez Company issued $400,000 of 9%, 10-year bonds on January 1, 2008, at face value. Interest is payable semiannually on July 1 and January 1.

Instructions

Prepare the journal entries to record the following events.

(a) The issuance of the bonds.
(b) The payment of interest on July 1, assuming no previous accrual of interest.   *Interest expense $18,000*
(c) The accrual of interest on December 31.
(d) The redemption of bonds at maturity, assuming interest for the last interest period has been paid and recorded.

Prepare entries for issuance, retirement, and conversion of bonds.

(SO 2, 3)

E15-6   Nocioni Company issued $1,000,000 of bonds on January 1, 2008.

Instructions

(a) Prepare the journal entry to record the issuance of the bonds if they are issued at (1) 100, (2), 98, and (3) 103.
(b) Prepare the journal entry to record the retirement of the bonds at maturity, assuming the bonds were issued at 100.
(c) Prepare the journal entry to record the retirement of the bonds before maturity at 98. Assume the balance in Premium on Bonds Payable is $9,000.   *Gain on redemption $29,000*
(d) Prepare the journal entry to record the conversion of the bonds into 30,000 shares of $10 par value common stock. Assume the bonds were issued at par.

Prepare entries to record issuance of bonds at discount and premium.

(SO 2)

E15-7   Deng Company issued $500,000 of 5-year, 8% bonds at 97 on January 1, 2008. The bonds pay interest twice a year.

Instructions

(a) (1) Prepare the journal entry to record the issuance of the bonds.
     (2) Compute the total cost of borrowing for these bonds.
(b) Repeat the requirements from part (a), assuming the bonds were issued at 105.

E15-8 The following section is taken from Budke Corp.'s balance sheet at December 31, 2007.

Prepare entries for bond inter-est and redemption.

(SO 2, 3)

Current liabilities	
Bond interest payable	$ 72,000
Long-term liabilities	
Bonds payable, 9%, due January 1, 2012	1,600,000

Interest is payable semiannually on January 1 and July 1. The bonds are callable on any interest date.

Instructions
(a) Journalize the payment of the bond interest on January 1, 2008.
(b) Assume that on January 1, 2008, after paying interest, Budke calls bonds having a face value of $600,000. The call price is 104. Record the redemption of the bonds.
(c) Prepare the entry to record the payment of interest on July 1, 2008, assuming no previous ac-crual of interest on the remaining bonds.

E15-9 Presented below are three independent situations.

Prepare entries for redemption of bonds and conversion of bonds into common stock.

(SO 3)

1. Sigel Corporation retired $130,000 face value, 12% bonds on June 30, 2008, at 102. The carry-ing value of the bonds at the redemption date was $117,500. The bonds pay semiannual inter-est, and the interest payment due on June 30, 2008, has been made and recorded.
2. Diaz Inc. retired $150,000 face value, 12.5% bonds on June 30, 2008, at 98. The carrying value of the bonds at the redemption date was $151,000. The bonds pay semiannual interest, and the interest payment due on June 30, 2008, has been made and recorded.
3. Haas Company has $80,000, 8%, 12-year convertible bonds outstanding. These bonds were sold at face value and pay semiannual interest on June 30 and December 31 of each year. The bonds are convertible into 30 shares of Haas $5 par value common stock for each $1,000 worth of bonds. On December 31, 2008, after the bond interest has been paid, $20,000 face value bonds were converted. The market value of Haas common stock was $44 per share on December 31, 2008.

Instructions
For each independent situation above, prepare the appropriate journal entry for the redemption or conversion of the bonds.

E15-10 Leoni Co. receives $240,000 when it issues a $240,000, 10%, mortgage note payable to finance the construction of a building at December 31, 2008. The terms provide for semiannual installment payments of $20,000 on June 30 and December 31.

Prepare entries to record mortgage note and installment payments.

(SO 4)

Instructions
Prepare the journal entries to record the mortgage loan and the first two installment payments.

E15-11 TPo1 Company borrowed $300,000 on January 1, 2008, by issuing a $300,000, 8% mortgage note payable. The terms call for semiannual installment payments of $20,000 on June 30 and December 31.

Prepare entries to record mort-gage note and installment pay-ments.

(SO 4)

Instructions
(a) Prepare the journal entries to record the mortgage loan and the first two installment payments.
(b) Indicate the amount of mortgage note payable to be reported as a current liability and as a long-term liability at December 31, 2008.

E15-12 Presented below are two independent situations.

Prepare entries for operating lease and capital lease.

(SO 5)

1. Speedy Car Rental leased a car to Mayfield Company for one year. Terms of the operating lease agreement call for monthly payments of $500.
2. On January 1, 2008, Olsen Inc. entered into an agreement to lease 20 computers from Gage Electronics. The terms of the lease agreement require three annual rental payments of $30,000 (including 10% interest) beginning December 31, 2008. The present value of the three rental payments is $74,606. Olsen considers this a capital lease.

Instructions
(a) Prepare the appropriate journal entry to be made by Mayfield Company for the first lease payment.
(b) Prepare the journal entry to record the lease agreement on the books of Olsen Inc. on January 1, 2008.

Prepare long-term liabilities section.

(SO 6)

E15-13 The adjusted trial balance for Gilligan Corporation at the end of the current year contained the following accounts.

Bond Interest Payable	$ 9,000
Lease Liability	89,500
Bonds Payable, due 2013	180,000
Premium on Bonds Payable	32,000

Instructions

Prepare the long-term liabilities section of the balance sheet.

Compute debt to total assets and times interest earned ratios.

(SO 6)

E15-14 Seven Corporation reports the following amounts in their 2008 financial statements:

	At December 31, 2008	For the Year 2008
Total assets	$1,000,000	
Total liabilities	620,000	
Total stockholders' equity	?	
Interest expense		$ 7,000
Income tax expense		100,000
Net income		150,000

Instructions

(a) Compute the December 31, 2008, balance in stockholders' equity.

(b) Compute the debt to total assets ratio at December 31, 2008.

(c) Compute times interest earned for 2008.

Compute market price of bonds.

(SO 7)

*E15-15 Banzai Corporation is issuing $200,000 of 8%, 5-year bonds when potential bond investors want a return of 10%. Interest is payable semiannually.

Instructions

Compute the market price (present value) of the bonds.

Prepare entries for issuance of bonds, payment of interest, and amortization of discount using effective-interest method

(SO 8)

*E15-16 Hrabik Corporation issued $600,000, 9%, 10-year bonds on January 1, 2008, for $562,613. This price resulted in an effective-interest rate of 10% on the bonds. Interest is payable semiannually on July 1 and January 1. Hrabik uses the effective-interest method to amortize bond premium or discount.

Instructions

Prepare the journal entries to record the following. (Round to the nearest dollar.)

(a) The issuance of the bonds.

(b) The payment of interest and the discount amortization on July 1, 2008, assuming that interest was not accrued on June 30.

(c) The accrual of interest and the discount amortization on December 31, 2008.

Prepare entries for issuance of bonds, payment of interest, and amortization of premium using effective-interest method.

(SO 8)

*E15-17 Siburo Company issued $300,000, 11%, 10-year bonds on January 1, 2008, for $318,694. This price resulted in an effective-interest rate of 10% on the bonds. Interest is payable semiannually on July 1 and January 1. Siburo uses the effective-interest method to amortize bond premium or discount.

Instructions

Prepare the journal entries to record the following. (Round to the nearest dollar).

(a) The issuance of the bonds.

(b) The payment of interest and the premium amortization on July 1, 2008, assuming that interest was not accrued on June 30.

(c) The accrual of interest and the premium amortization on December 31, 2008.

Prepare entries to record issuance of bonds, payment of interest, amortization of premium, and redemption at maturity.

(SO 3, 9)

*E15-18 Patino Company issued $400,000, 9%, 20-year bonds on January 1, 2008, at 103. Interest is payable semiannually on July 1 and January 1. Patino uses straight-line amortization for bond premium or discount.

Instructions

Prepare the journal entries to record the following.

(a) The issuance of the bonds.

(b) The payment of interest and the premium amortization on July 1, 2008, assuming that interest was not accrued on June 30.

(c) The accrual of interest and the premium amortization on December 31, 2008.

(d) The redemption of the bonds at maturity, assuming interest for the last interest period has been paid and recorded.

*E15-19   Joseph Company issued $800,000, 11%, 10-year bonds on December 31, 2007, for $730,000. Interest is payable semiannually on June 30 and December 31. Joseph Company uses the straight-line method to amortize bond premium or discount.

Prepare entries to record issuance of bonds, payment of interest, amortization of discount, and redemption at maturity.

(SO 3, 9)

Instructions
Prepare the journal entries to record the following.

(a) The issuance of the bonds.

(b) The payment of interest and the discount amortization on June 30, 2008.

(c) The payment of interest and the discount amortization on December 31, 2008.

(d) The redemption of the bonds at maturity, assuming interest for the last interest period has been paid and recorded.

EXERCISES: SET B

Visit the book's website at **www.wiley.com/college/weygandt**, and choose the Student Companion site, to access Exercise Set B.

PROBLEMS: SET A

P15-1A   On May 1, 2008, Newby Corp. issued $600,000, 9%, 5-year bonds at face value. The bonds were dated May 1, 2008, and pay interest semiannually on May 1 and November 1. Financial statements are prepared annually on December 31.

Prepare entries to record issuance of bonds, interest accrual, and bond redemption.

(SO 2, 3, 6)

Instructions

(a) Prepare the journal entry to record the issuance of the bonds.

(b) Prepare the adjusting entry to record the accrual of interest on December 31, 2008.

(c) Show the balance sheet presentation on December 31, 2008.

(d) Prepare the journal entry to record payment of interest on May 1, 2009, assuming no accrual of interest from January 1, 2009, to May 1, 2009.

(d) Int. exp. $18,000

(e) Prepare the journal entry to record payment of interest on November 1, 2009.

(f) Assume that on November 1, 2009, Newby calls the bonds at 102. Record the redemption of the bonds.

(f) Loss $12,000

P15-2A   Kusmaul Electric sold $500,000, 10%, 10-year bonds on January 1, 2008. The bonds were dated January 1 and paid interest on January 1 and July 1. The bonds were sold at 104.

Prepare entries to record issuance of bonds, interest accrual, and bond redemption.

(SO 2, 3, 6)

Instructions

(a) Prepare the journal entry to record the issuance of the bonds on January 1, 2008.

(b) At December 31, 2008, the balance in the Premium on Bonds Payable account is $18,000. Show the balance sheet presentation of accrued interest and the bond liability at December 31, 2008.

(c) On January 1, 2010, when the carrying value of the bonds was $516,000, the company redeemed the bonds at 105. Record the redemption of the bonds assuming that interest for the period has already been paid.

(c) Loss $9,000

P15-3A   Fordyce Electronics issues a $400,000, 8%, 10-year mortgage note on December 31, 2007. The proceeds from the note are to be used in financing a new research laboratory. The terms of the note provide for semiannual installment payments, exclusive of real estate taxes and insurance, of $29,433. Payments are due June 30 and December 31.

Prepare installment payments schedule and journal entries for a mortgage note payable.

(SO 4)

Instructions

(a) Prepare an installment payments schedule for the first 2 years.

(b) Prepare the entries for (1) the loan and (2) the first two installment payments.

(b) June 30 Mortgage Notes Payable $13,433

(c) Show how the total mortgage liability should be reported on the balance sheet at December 31, 2008.

(c) Current liability—2008: $29,639

Analyze three different lease situations and prepare journal entries.

(SO 5)

P15-4A Presented below are three different lease transactions that occurred for Kear Inc. in 2008. Assume that all lease contracts start on January 1, 2008. In no case does Kear receive title to the properties leased during or at the end of the lease term.

	Lessor		
	Jansen Delivery	**Flood Co.**	**Louis Auto**
Type of property	Computer	Delivery equipment	Automobile
Yearly rental	$ 6,000	$ 4,200	$ 3,700
Lease term	6 years	4 years	2 years
Estimated economic life	7 years	7 years	5 years
Fair market value of lease asset	$33,000	$19,000	$11,000
Present value of the lease rental payments	$31,000	$13,000	$ 6,400
Bargain purchase option	None	None	None

Instructions
(a) Which of the leases above are operating leases and which are capital leases? Explain.
(b) How should the lease transaction for Flood Co. be recorded in 2008?
(c) How should the lease transaction for Jansen Delivery be recorded on January 1, 2008?

Prepare entries to record issuance of bonds, payment of interest, and amortization of bond premium using effective-interest method.

(SO 2, 8)

*P15-5A On July 1, 2008, Atwater Corporation issued $2,000,000 face value, 10%, 10-year bonds at $2,271,813. This price resulted in an effective-interest rate of 8% on the bonds. Atwater uses the effective-interest method to amortize bond premium or discount. The bonds pay semi-annual interest July 1 and January 1.

Instructions
(Round all computations to the nearest dollar.)
(a) Prepare the journal entry to record the issuance of the bonds on July 1, 2008.
(b) Prepare an amortization table through December 31, 2009 (3 interest periods) for this bond issue.

(c) Amortization $9,127

(c) Prepare the journal entry to record the accrual of interest and the amortization of the premium on December 31, 2008.

(d) Amortization $9,493

(d) Prepare the journal entry to record the payment of interest and the amortization of the premium on July 1, 2009, assuming no accrual of interest on June 30.

(e) Amortization $9,872

(e) Prepare the journal entry to record the accrual of interest and the amortization of the premium on December 31, 2009.

Prepare entries to record issuance of bonds, payment of interest, and amortization of discount using effective-interest method. In addition, answer questions.

(SO 2, 8)

*P15-6A On July 1, 2008, Rossillon Company issued $4,000,000 face value, 8%, 10-year bonds at $3,501,514. This price resulted in an effective-interest rate of 10% on the bonds. Rossillon uses the effective-interest method to amortize bond premium or discount. The bonds pay semiannual interest July 1 and January 1.

Instructions
(Round all computations to the nearest dollar.)
(a) Prepare the journal entries to record the following transactions.
  (1) The issuance of the bonds on July 1, 2008.
  (2) The accrual of interest and the amortization of the discount on December 31, 2008.

(a) (3) Amortization $15,830

  (3) The payment of interest and the amortization of the discount on July 1, 2009, assuming no accrual of interest on June 30.

(a) (4) Amortization $16,621

  (4) The accrual of interest and the amortization of the discount on December 31, 2009.

(b) Bond carrying value $3,549,041

(b) Show the proper balance sheet presentation for the liability for bonds payable on the December 31, 2009, balance sheet.
(c) ━━━ Provide the answers to the following questions in letter form.
  (1) What amount of interest expense is reported for 2009?
  (2) Would the bond interest expense reported in 2009 be the same as, greater than, or less than the amount that would be reported if the straight-line method of amortization were used?
  (3) Determine the total cost of borrowing over the life of the bond.
  (4) Would the total bond interest expense be greater than, the same as, or less than the total interest expense that would be reported if the straight-line method of amortization were used?

*P15-7A   Soprano Electric sold $3,000,000, 10%, 10-year bonds on January 1, 2008. The bonds were dated January 1 and pay interest July 1 and January 1. Soprano Electric uses the straight-line method to amortize bond premium or discount. The bonds were sold at 104. Assume no interest is accrued on June 30.

Prepare entries to record issuance of bonds, interest accrual, and straight-line amortization for 2 years.

(SO 6, 9)

Instructions
(a) Prepare the journal entry to record the issuance of the bonds on January 1, 2008.
(b) Prepare a bond premium amortization schedule for the first 4 interest periods.
(c) Prepare the journal entries for interest and the amortization of the premium in 2008 and 2009.
(d) Show the balance sheet presentation of the bond liability at December 31, 2009.

(b) Amortization $6,000

(d) Premium on bonds
  payable $96,000

*P15-8A   Elkins Company sold $2,500,000, 8%, 10-year bonds on July 1, 2008. The bonds were dated July 1, 2008, and pay interest July 1 and January 1. Elkins Company uses the straight-line method to amortize bond premium or discount. Assume no interest is accrued on June 30.

Prepare entries to record issuance of bonds, interest, and straight-line amortization of bond premium and discount.

(SO 6, 9)

Instructions
(a) Prepare all the necessary journal entries to record the issuance of the bonds and bond interest expense for 2008, assuming that the bonds sold at 104.
(b) Prepare journal entries as in part (a) assuming that the bonds sold at 98.
(c) Show balance sheet presentation for each bond issue at December 31, 2008.

(a) Amortization $5,000
(b) Amortization $2,500
(c) Premium on bonds
  payable $95,000
  Discount on bonds
  payable $47,500

*P15-9A   The following is taken from the Pinkston Company balance sheet.

Prepare entries to record interest payments, straight-line premium amortization, and redemption of bonds.

(SO 2, 3, 9)

PINKSTON COMPANY
Balance Sheet (partial)
December 31, 2008

Current liabilities		
Bond interest payable (for 6 months		
from July 1 to December 31)		$ 105,000
Long-term liabilities		
Bonds payable, 7% due January 1, 2019	$3,000,000	
Add: Premium on bonds payable	200,000	$3,200,000

Interest is payable semiannually on January 1 and July 1. The bonds are callable on any semiannual interest date. Pinkston uses straight-line amortization for any bond premium or discount. From December 31, 2008, the bonds will be outstanding for an additional 10 years (120 months).

Instructions
(a) Journalize the payment of bond interest on January 1, 2009.
(b) Prepare the entry to amortize bond premium and to pay the interest due on July 1, 2009, assuming no accrual of interest on June 30.
(c) Assume that on July 1, 2009, after paying interest, Pinkston Company calls bonds having a face value of $1,200,000. The call price is 101. Record the redemption of the bonds.
(d) Prepare the adjusting entry at December 31, 2009, to amortize bond premium and to accrue interest on the remaining bonds.

(b) Amortization $10,000

(c) Gain $64,000

(d) Amortization $6,000

PROBLEMS: SET B

P15-1B   On June 1, 2008, Logsdon Corp. issued $1,500,000, 8%, 5-year bonds at face value. The bonds were dated June 1, 2008, and pay interest semiannually on June 1 and December 1. Financial statements are prepared annually on December 31.

Prepare entries to record issuance of bonds, interest accrual, and bond redemption.

(SO 2, 3, 6)

Instructions
(a) Prepare the journal entry to record the issuance of the bonds.
(b) Prepare the adjusting entry to record the accrual of interest on December 31, 2008.
(c) Show the balance sheet presentation on December 31, 2008.
(d) Prepare the journal entry to record payment of interest on June 1, 2009, assuming no accrual of interest from January 1, 2009, to June 1, 2009.
(e) Prepare the journal entry to record payment of interest on December 1, 2009.
(f) Assume that on December 1, 2009, Logsdon calls the bonds at 102. Record the redemption of the bonds.

(d) Int. exp. $50,000

(f) Loss $30,000

Prepare entries to record issuance of bonds, interest accrual, and bond redemption.

(SO 2, 3, 6)

P15-2B Merendo Co. sold $600,000, 9%, 10-year bonds on January 1, 2008. The bonds were dated January 1, and interest is paid on January 1 and July 1. The bonds were sold at 105.

Instructions
(a) Prepare the journal entry to record the issuance of the bonds on January 1, 2008.
(b) At December 31, 2008, the balance in the Premium on Bonds Payable account is $27,000. Show the balance sheet presentation of accrued interest and the bond liability at December 31, 2008.

(c) Loss $6,000

(c) On January 1, 2010, when the carrying value of the bonds was $624,000, the company redeemed the bonds at 105. Record the redemption of the bonds assuming that interest for the period has already been paid.

Prepare installment payments schedule and journal entries for a mortgage note payable.

(SO 4)

P15-3B Egan Electronics issues an $500,000, 8%, 10-year mortgage note on December 31, 2008, to help finance a plant expansion program. The terms provide for semiannual installment payments, not including real estate taxes and insurance, of $36,791. Payments are due June 30 and December 31.

Instructions
(a) Prepare an installment payments schedule for the first 2 years.

(b) June 30 Mortgage Notes Payable $16,791

(b) Prepare the entries for (1) the mortgage loan and (2) the first two installment payments.

(c) Current liability—2009: $37,049

(c) Show how the total mortgage liability should be reported on the balance sheet at December 31, 2009.

Analyze three different lease situations and prepare journal entries.

(SO 5)

P15-4B Presented below are three different lease transactions in which Gomez Enterprises engaged in 2008. Assume that all lease transactions start on January 1, 2008. In no case does Gomez receive title to the properties leased during or at the end of the lease term.

	Lessor		
	Schoen Co.	**Didde Co.**	**Krumme Inc.**
Type of property	Bulldozer	Truck	Furniture
Bargain purchase option	None	None	None
Lease term	4 years	6 years	3 years
Estimated economic life	8 years	7 years	5 years
Yearly rental	$13,000	$18,000	$ 4,000
Fair market value of leased asset	$80,000	$86,000	$27,500
Present value of the lease rental payments	$48,000	$74,000	$12,000

Instructions
(a) Identify the leases above as operating or capital leases. Explain.
(b) How should the lease transaction for Didde Co. be recorded on January 1, 2008?
(c) How should the lease transaction for Krumme Inc. be recorded in 2008?

Prepare entries to record issuance of bonds, payment of interest, and amortization of bond discount using effective-interest method.

(SO 2, 8)

*P15-5B On July 1, 2008, Matlock Satellites issued $2,700,000 face value, 9%, 10-year bonds at $2,531,760. This price resulted in an effective-interest rate of 10% on the bonds. Matlock uses the effective-interest method to amortize bond premium or discount. The bonds pay semiannual interest July 1 and January 1.

Instructions
(Round all computations to the nearest dollar.)
(a) Prepare the journal entry to record the issuance of the bonds on July 1, 2008.
(b) Prepare an amortization table through December 31, 2009 (3 interest periods) for this bond issue.

(c) Amortization $5,088

(c) Prepare the journal entry to record the accrual of interest and the amortization of the discount on December 31, 2008.

(d) Amortization $5,342

(d) Prepare the journal entry to record the payment of interest and the amortization of the discount on July 1, 2009, assuming that interest was not accrued on June 30.

(e) Amortization $5,610

(e) Prepare the journal entry to record the accrual of interest and the amortization of the discount on December 31, 2009.

*P15-6B   On July 1, 2008, S. Posadas Chemical Company issued $3,000,000 face value, 10%, 10-year bonds at $3,407,720. This price resulted in an 8% effective-interest rate on the bonds. Posadas uses the effective-interest method to amortize bond premium or discount. The bonds pay semi-annual interest on each July 1 and January 1.

Prepare entries to record issuance of bonds, payment of interest, and amortization of premium using effective-interest method. In addition, answer questions.

(SO 2, 8)

Instructions

(Round all computations to the nearest dollar.)

(a) Prepare the journal entries to record the following transactions.
  (1) The issuance of the bonds on July 1, 2008.
  (2) The accrual of interest and the amortization of the premium on December 31, 2008.
  (3) The payment of interest and the amortization of the premium on July 1, 2009, assuming no accrual of interest on June 30.
  (4) The accrual of interest and the amortization of the premium on December 31, 2009.
(b) Show the proper balance sheet presentation for the liability for bonds payable on the December 31, 2009, balance sheet.
(c) ◄━━━━━ Provide the answers to the following questions in letter form.
  (1) What amount of interest expense is reported for 2009?
  (2) Would the bond interest expense reported in 2009 be the same as, greater than, or less than the amount that would be reported if the straight-line method of amortization were used?
  (3) Determine the total cost of borrowing over the life of the bond.
  (4) Would the total bond interest expense be greater than, the same as, or less than the total interest expense if the straight-line method of amortization were used?

(a) (2) Amortization $13,691
(a) (3) Amortization $14,239

(a) (4) Amortization $14,808
(b) Bond carrying value
$3,364,982

*P15-7B   Roeder Company sold $4,000,000, 9%, 20-year bonds on January 1, 2008. The bonds were dated January 1, 2008, and pay interest on January 1 and July 1. Roeder Company uses the straight-line method to amortize bond premium or discount. The bonds were sold at 96. Assume no interest is accrued on June 30.

Prepare entries to record issuance of bonds, interest accrual, and straight-line amortization for 2 years.

(SO 6, 9)

Instructions

(a) Prepare the journal entry to record the issuance of the bonds on January 1, 2008.
(b) Prepare a bond discount amortization schedule for the first 4 interest periods.
(c) Prepare the journal entries for interest and the amortization of the discount in 2008 and 2009.
(d) Show the balance sheet presentation of the bond liability at December 31, 2009.

(b) Amortization $4,000

(d) Discount on bonds payable $144,000

*P15-8B   Karjala Corporation sold $5,000,000, 8%, 10-year bonds on January 1, 2008. The bonds were dated January 1, 2008, and pay interest on July 1 and January 1. Karjala Corporation uses the straight-line method to amortize bond premium or discount. Assume no interest is accrued on June 30.

Prepare entries to record issuance of bonds, interest, and straight-line amortization of bond premium and discount.

(SO 6, 9)

Instructions

(a) Prepare all the necessary journal entries to record the issuance of the bonds and bond interest expense for 2008, assuming that the bonds sold at 103.
(b) Prepare journal entries as in part (a) assuming that the bonds sold at 96.
(c) Show balance sheet presentation for each bond issue at December 31, 2008.

(a) Amortization $7,500
(b) Amortization $10,000
(c) Premium on bonds payable $135,000
Discount on bonds payable $180,000

*P15-9B   The following is taken from the Magana Corp. balance sheet.

Prepare entries to record interest payments, straight-line discount amortization, and redemption of bonds.

(SO 2, 3, 9)

MAGANA CORPORATION
Balance Sheet (partial)
December 31, 2008

Current liabilities		
Bond interest payable (for 6 months from July 1 to December 31)		$ 84,000
Long-term liabilities		
Bonds payable, 7%, due January 1, 2019	$2,400,000	
Less: Discount on bonds payable	90,000	$2,310,000

Interest is payable semiannually on January 1 and July 1. The bonds are callable on any semi-annual interest date. Magana uses straight-line amortization for any bond premium or discount. From December 31, 2008, the bonds will be outstanding for an additional 10 years (120 months).

Instructions

(Round all computations to the nearest dollar).

(b) Amortization $4,500

(c) Loss $36,500

(d) Amortization $3,000

(a) Journalize the payment of bond interest on January 1, 2009.

(b) Prepare the entry to amortize bond discount and to pay the interest due on July 1, 2009, assuming that interest was not accrued on June 30.

(c) Assume that on July 1, 2009, after paying interest, Magana Corp. calls bonds having a face value of $800,000. The call price is 101. Record the redemption of the bonds.

(d) Prepare the adjusting entry at December 31, 2009, to amortize bond discount and to accrue interest on the remaining bonds.

PROBLEMS: SET C

Visit the book's website at **www.wiley.com/college/weygandt**, and choose the Student Companion site, to access Problem Set C.

COMPREHENSIVE PROBLEM: CHAPTERS 13–15

Nordham Corporation's trial balance at December 31, 2008, is presented below. All 2008 transactions have been recorded except for the items described below and on the next page.

	Debit	Credit
Cash	$ 23,000	
Accounts Receivable	51,000	
Merchandise Inventory	22,700	
Land	65,000	
Building	95,000	
Equipment	40,000	
Allowance for Doubtful Accounts		$ 450
Accumulated Depreciation—Building		30,000
Accumulated Depreciation—Equipment		14,400
Accounts Payable		19,300
Bond Interest Payable		–0–
Dividends Payable		–0–
Unearned Rent Revenue		8,000
Bonds Payable (10%)		50,000
Common Stock ($10 par)		30,000
Paid-in Capital in Excess of Par—Common Stock		6,000
Preferred Stock ($20 par)		–0–
Paid-in Capital in Excess of Par—Preferred Stock		–0–
Retained Earnings		75,050
Treasury Stock	–0–	
Dividends	–0–	
Sales		570,000
Rent Revenue		–0–
Bad Debts Expense	–0–	
Bond Interest Expense	2,500	
Cost of Goods Sold	400,000	
Depreciation Expense—Buildings	–0–	
Depreciation Expense—Equipment	–0–	
Other Operating Expenses	39,000	
Salaries Expense	65,000	
Total	$803,200	$803,200

Unrecorded transactions

1. On January 1, 2008, Nordham issued 1,000 shares of $20 par, 6% preferred stock for $22,000.
2. On January 1, 2008, Nordham also issued 1,000 shares of common stock for $23,000.
3. Nordham reacquired 300 shares of its common stock on July 1, 2008, for $49 per share.

4. On December 31, 2008, Nordham declared the annual preferred stock dividend and a $1.50 per share dividend on the outstanding common stock, all payable on January 15, 2009.
5. Nordham estimates that uncollectible accounts receivable at year-end is $5,100.
6. The building is being depreciated using the straight-line method over 30 years. The salvage value is $5,000.
7. The equipment is being depreciated using the straight-line method over 10 years. The salvage value is $4,000.
8. The unearned rent was collected on October 1, 2008. It was receipt of 4 months' rent in advance (October 1, 2008 through January 31, 2009).
9. The 10% bonds payable pay interest every January 1 and July 1. The interest for the 6 months ended December 31, 2008, has not been paid or recorded.

Instructions
(Ignore income taxes.)

(a) Prepare journal entries for the transactions listed above.
(b) Prepare an updated December 31, 2008, trial balance, reflecting the unrecorded transactions.
(c) Prepare a multiple-step income statement for the year ending December 31, 2008.
(d) Prepare a statement of retained earnings for the year ending December 31, 2008.
(e) Prepare a classified balance sheet as of December 31, 2008.

CONTINUING COOKIE CHRONICLE

(Note: This is a continuation of the Cookie Chronicle from Chapters 1 through 14.)

CCC15 Natalie and Curtis have been experiencing great demand for their cookies and muffins. As a result, they are now thinking about buying a commercial oven. They know which oven they want and how much it will cost. They have some cash set aside for the purchase and will need to borrow the rest. They met with a bank manager to discuss their options.

Go to the book's website,
www.wiley.com/college/weygandt,
to see the completion of this problem.

BROADENING YOUR PERSPECTIVE

FINANCIAL REPORTING AND ANALYSIS

Financial Reporting Problem:
PepsiCo, Inc.

BYP15-1 Refer to the financial statements of PepsiCo and the Notes to Consolidated Financial Statements in Appendix A.

Instructions
(a) What was PepsiCo's total long-term debt at December 31, 2005? What was the increase/decrease in total long-term debt from the prior year? What does Note 9 to the financial statements indicate about the composition of PepsiCo's long-term debt obligation?
(b) What type of leases, operating or capital, does PepsiCo report? (See Note 9.) Are these leases reported on PepsiCo's financial statements?
(c) What are the total long-term contractual commitments that PepsiCo reports as of December 31, 2005? (See Note 9.)

Comparative Analysis Problem:
PepsiCo, Inc. vs. The Coca-Cola Company

BYP15-2 PepsiCo's financial statements are presented in Appendix A. Coca-Cola's financial statements are presented in Appendix B.

Instructions
(a) Based on the information contained in these financial statements, compute the following 2005 ratios for each company.
   (1) Debt to total assets.
   (2) Times interest earned.
(b) What conclusions concerning the companies' long-run solvency can be drawn from these ratios?
(c) Which company has reported the greater amount of future long-term commitments for the 5 succeeding years?

Exploring the Web

BYP15-3 Bond or debt securities pay a stated rate of interest. This rate of interest is dependent on the risk associated with the investment. Moody's Investment Service provides ratings for companies that issue debt securities.

Address: www.moodys.com, or go to **www.wiley.com/college/weygandt**

Steps: From Moody's homepage, choose **About Moody's**.

Instructions
(a) What year did Moody's introduce the first bond rating? (See Moody's History.)
(b) What is the total amount of debt securities that Moody's analysts "track"? (See **An Introduction**.)
(c) What characteristics must debt ratings have in order to be useful to the capital markets? (See **Understand Risk: The Truth About Credit Ratings**.)

CRITICAL THINKING

Decision Making Across the Organization

*BYP15-4 On January 1, 2006, Carlin Corporation issued $2,400,000 of 5-year, 8% bonds at 95; the bonds pay interest semiannually on July 1 and January 1. By January 1, 2008, the market rate of interest for bonds of risk similar to those of Carlin Corporation had risen. As a result the market value of these bonds was $2,000,000 on January 1, 2008—below their carrying value. Andrea Carlin, president of the company, suggests repurchasing all of these bonds in the open market at the $2,000,000 price. To do so the company will have to issue $2,000,000 (face value) of new 10-year, 11% bonds at par. The president asks you, as controller, "What is the feasibility of my proposed repurchase plan?"

Instructions
With the class divided into groups, answer the following.

(a) What is the carrying value of the outstanding Carlin Corporation 5-year bonds on January 1, 2008? (Assume straight-line amortization.)
(b) Prepare the journal entry to retire the 5-year bonds on January 1, 2008. Prepare the journal entry to issue the new 10-year bonds.
(c) Prepare a short memo to the president in response to her request for advice. List the economic factors that you believe should be considered for her repurchase proposal.

Communication Activity

BYP15-5 Joe Penner, president of the Penner Corporation, is considering the issuance of bonds to finance an expansion of his business. He has asked you to (1) discuss the advantages of bonds over common stock financing, (2) indicate the types of bonds he might issue, and (3) explain the issuing procedures used in bond transactions.

Instructions
Write a memo to the president, answering his request.

Ethics Case

BYP15-6   Sam Farr is the president, founder, and majority owner of Galena Medical Corporation, an emerging medical technology products company. Galena is in dire need of additional capital to keep operating and to bring several promising products to final development, testing, and production. Sam, as owner of 51% of the outstanding stock, manages the company's operations. He places heavy emphasis on research and development and on long-term growth. The other principal stockholder is Jill Hutton who, as a nonemployee investor, owns 40% of the stock. Jill would like to deemphasize the R&D functions and emphasize the marketing function, to maximize short-run sales and profits from existing products. She believes this strategy would raise the market price of Galena's stock.

All of Sam's personal capital and borrowing power is tied up in his 51% stock ownership. He knows that any offering of additional shares of stock will dilute his controlling interest because he won't be able to participate in such an issuance. But, Jill has money and would likely buy enough shares to gain control of Galena. She then would dictate the company's future direction, even if it meant replacing Sam as president and CEO.

The company already has considerable debt. Raising additional debt will be costly, will adversely affect Galena's credit rating, and will increase the company's reported losses due to the growth in interest expense. Jill and the other minority stockholders express opposition to the assumption of additional debt, fearing the company will be pushed to the brink of bankruptcy. Wanting to maintain his control and to preserve the direction of "his" company, Sam is doing everything to avoid a stock issuance. He is contemplating a large issuance of bonds, even if it means the bonds are issued with a high effective-interest rate.

Instructions
(a) Who are the stakeholders in this situation?
(b) What are the ethical issues in this case?
(c) What would you do if you were Sam?

"All About You" Activity

BYP15-7   Numerous articles have been written that identify early warning signs that you might be getting into trouble with your personal debt load. You can find many good articles on this topic on the Web.

Instructions
Find an article that identifies early warning signs of personal debt trouble. Write up a summary of the article and bring your summary and the article to class to share.

Answers to Insight and Accounting Across the Organization Questions

p. 636 When to Go Long-Term
Q: Based on this story, what is a good general rule to use in choosing between short-term and long-term financing?
A: *In general, it is best to finance short-term assets with short-term liabilities and long-term assets with long-term liabilities, in order to reduce the likelihood of a liquidity crunch such as this.*

p. 644 Search for Your Best Rate
Q: What should you do if the dealer "trash-talks" your lender, or refuses to sell you the car for the agreed-upon price unless you get your car loan through the dealer?
A: *Experts suggest that if the dealer "trash-talks" your lender or refuses to sell you the car at the agreed-upon price unless you get your financing through the dealer, get up and leave, and buy your car somewhere else.*

p. 647 They Thought It Was Easy Money

Q: What do you think happens when a company violates its debt covenants?

A: *If a company violates its debt covenants the lender can "call the loan." This means that the company is required to repay the loan immediately, even though the maturity date of the loan has not been reached. In practice, many lenders will renegotiate the terms of the loan rather than force the company to repay immediately.*

Authors' Comments on *All About You*: The Risks of Adjustable Rates (p. 648)

A big part of the American dream is home ownership. In the past, homes have enjoyed a relatively steady and safe increase in value; thus many people are eager to quit renting and become homeowners.

But home ownership is not without risks. In recent years home prices increased so much that economists expect that in some parts of the country home prices could fall by as much as 30%. In the example above, if the house lost 30% of its value it would be worth only $140,000—much less than the amount owed. Another risk is that, as interest rates increase, people with adjustable-rate mortgages can experience huge increases in their mortgage payments. In the example given here, if the loan rate hit the cap of 10.5%, the monthly payment would jump to $1,647. That represents a 61% increase. We don't want to discourage you from home ownership, but we do want to encourage you to get educated about mortgage terms.

Answer to PepsiCo Review It Question 2, p. 642

An examination of PepsiCo's statement of cash flows indicates the following reductions of debt: payments of long-term debt, $177 million, and payments of short-term borrowings of more than 3 months, $85 million.

Answers to Self-Study Questions

1. c   **2.** a   **3.** b   **4.** d   **5.** c   **6.** d   ***7.** b   ***8.** c   ***9.** d   ***10.** a

Chapter 16

Investments

Feature Story

"IS THERE ANYTHING ELSE WE CAN BUY?"

In a rapidly changing world you must change rapidly or suffer the consequences. In business, change requires investment.

A case in point is found in the entertainment industry. Technology is bringing about innovations so quickly that it is nearly impossible to guess which technologies will last and which will soon fade away. For example, will both satellite TV and cable TV survive, or will just one succeed, or will both be replaced by something else? Or consider the publishing industry. Will paper newspapers and magazines be replaced by online news via the World Wide Web? If you are a publisher, you have to make your best guess about what the future holds and invest accordingly.

Time Warner, Inc. (*www.timewarner.com*) lives at the center of this arena. It is not an environment for the timid, and Time Warner's philosophy is anything but timid. It might be characterized as, "If we can't beat you, we will buy you." Its mantra is "invest, invest, invest." A list of Time Warner's holdings gives an idea of its reach. Magazines: *People, Time, Life, Sports Illustrated, Fortune.* Book publishers: Time-Life Books, Book-of-the-Month Club, Little, Brown & Co, Sunset Books. Television and movies: Warner Bros. ("ER," "Without a Trace," the WB Network), HBO, and movies like *Harry Potter and the Goblet of Fire, and Batman Begins.* Broadcasting: TNT, CNN news, and Turner's library of thousands of classic movies. Internet: America Online, and AOL Anywhere. Time Warner owns more information and entertainment copyrights and brands than any other company in the world.

So what has Time Warner's aggressive acquisition spree meant for the bottom line? It has left the company with an accumulated deficit of approximately $93 billion. Some of the acquisitions have not come cheap, resulting in large amounts of reported goodwill and related intangible assets. The merger of America Online (AOL) with Time Warner was billed as a merger of equals. But, it was AOL's phenomenal growth and astronomical stock price that made this merger possible. Unfortunately, investors involved in this merger have faired poorly. From a high of $95.80, Time Warner's stock price recently sold at $17.08 per share.

✓ The Navigator

Inside Chapter 16...

Time Warner's management believes in aggressive growth through investing in the stock of existing companies. Besides purchasing stock, companies also purchase other securities such as bonds issued by corporations or by governments. Companies can make investments for a short or long period of time, as a passive investment, or with the intent to control another company. As you will see in this chapter, the way in which a company accounts for its investments is determined by a number of factors.

The content and organization of Chapter 16 are as follows.

Investments

Why Corporations Invest	**Accounting for Debt Investments**	**Accounting for Stock Investments**	**Valuing and Reporting Investments**
• Cash management • Investment income • Strategic reasons	• Recording acquisition of bonds • Recording bond interest • Recording sale of bonds	• Holdings of less than 20% • Holdings between 20% and 50% • Holdings of more than 50%	• Categories of securities • Balance sheet presentation • Realized and unrealized gain or loss • Classified balance sheet

✓ *The Navigator*

WHY CORPORATIONS INVEST

Corporations purchase investments in debt or stock securities generally for one of three reasons. First, a corporation may **have excess cash** that it does not need for the immediate purchase of operating assets. For example, many companies experience seasonal fluctuations in sales. A Cape Cod marina has more sales in the spring and summer than in the fall and winter. At the end of an operating cycle, the marina may have cash on hand that is temporarily idle until the start of another operating cycle. It may invest the excess funds to earn a greater return than it would get by just holding the funds in the bank. Illustration 16-1 depicts the role that such temporary investments play in the operating cycle.

Illustration 16-1
Temporary investments and the operating cycle

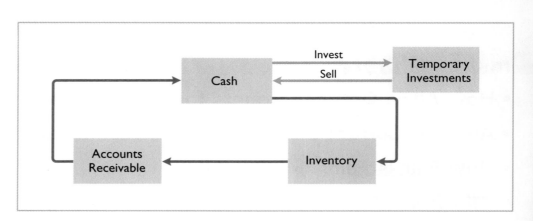

Excess cash may also result from economic cycles. For example, when the economy is booming, General Electric generates considerable excess cash. It uses some of this cash to purchase new plant and equipment and pays out some of the cash in dividends. But it may also invest excess cash in liquid assets in anticipation of a future downturn in the economy. It can then liquidate these investments during a recession, when sales slow and cash is scarce.

When investing excess cash for short periods of time, corporations invest in low-risk, highly liquid securities—most often short-term government securities. It is generally not wise to invest short-term excess cash in shares of common stock because stock investments can experience rapid price changes. If you did invest your short-term excess cash in stock and the price of the stock declined significantly just before you needed cash again, you would be forced to sell your stock investment at a loss.

A second reason some companies purchase investments is to generate **earnings from investment income**. For example, banks make most of their earnings by lending money, but they also generate earnings by investing in debt. Conversely, mutual stock funds invest primarily in equity securities in order to benefit from stock-price appreciation and dividend revenue.

Third, companies also invest for **strategic reasons**. A company can exercise some influence over a customer or supplier by purchasing a significant, but not controlling, interest in that company. Or, a company may purchase a noncontrolling interest in another company in a related industry in which it wishes to establish a presence. For example, Time Warner initially purchased an interest of less than 20% in Turner Broadcasting to have a stake in Turner's expanding business opportunities. At a later date Time Warner acquired the remaining 80%. Subsequently, Time Warner merged with AOL and became AOL Time Warner, Inc. Now, it is again just Time Warner, Inc., having dropped the "AOL" from its name in late 2003.

A corporation may also choose to purchase a controlling interest in another company. For example, in the *Accounting Across the Organization* box on page 691, Philip Morris purchased Kraft Foods. Such purchases might be done to enter a new industry without incurring the tremendous costs and risks associated with starting from scratch. Or a company might purchase another company in its same industry.

In summary, businesses invest in other companies for the reasons shown in Illustration 16-2.

Illustration 16-2
Why corporations invest

Reason	Typical Investment
To house excess cash until needed	Low-risk, high-liquidity, short-term securities such as government-issued securities
To generate earnings	Debt securities (banks and other financial institutions); and stock securities (mutual funds and pension funds)
To meet strategic goals	Stocks of companies in a related industry or in an unrelated industry that the company wishes to enter

ACCOUNTING FOR DEBT INVESTMENTS

Debt investments are investments in government and corporation bonds. In accounting for debt investments, companies make entries to record (1) the acquisition, (2) the interest revenue, and (3) the sale.

Recording Acquisition of Bonds

At acquisition, the cost principle applies. Cost includes all expenditures necessary to acquire these investments, such as the price paid plus brokerage fees (commissions), if any.

Assume, for example, that Kuhl Corporation acquires 50 Doan Inc. 8%, 10-year, $1,000 bonds on January 1, 2008, for $54,000, including brokerage fees of $1,000. The entry to record the investment is:

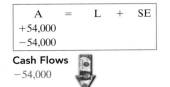

Jan. 1	Debt Investments	54,000	
	Cash		54,000
	(To record purchase of 50 Doan Inc. bonds)		

Recording Bond Interest

The Doan, Inc. bonds pay interest of $2,000 semiannually on July 1 and January 1 ($50,000 × 8% × ½). The entry for the receipt of interest on July 1 is:

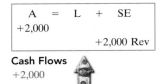

July 1	Cash	2,000	
	Interest Revenue		2,000
	(To record receipt of interest on Doan Inc. bonds		

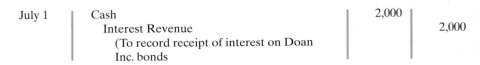

If Kuhl Corporation's fiscal year ends on December 31, it accrues the interest of $2,000 earned since July 1. The adjusting entry is:

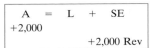

Dec. 31	Interest Receivable	2,000	
	Interest Revenue		2,000
	(To accrue interest on Doan Inc. bonds)		

Kuhl reports Interest Receivable as a current asset in the balance sheet. It reports Interest Revenue under "Other revenues and gains" in the income statement.

Kuhl reports receipt of the interest on January 1 as follows.

Jan. 1	Cash	2,000	
	Interest Receivable		2,000
	(To record receipt of accrued interest)		

A credit to Interest Revenue at this time is incorrect because the company earned and accrued interest revenue in the *preceding* accounting period.

Recording Sale of Bonds

When Kuhl sells the bonds, it credits the investment account for the cost of the bonds. Kuhl records as a gain or loss any difference between the net proceeds from the sale (sales price less brokerage fees) and the cost of the bonds.

Assume, for example, that Kuhl Corporation receives net proceeds of $58,000 on the sale of the Doan Inc. bonds on January 1, 2009, after receiving the interest due. Since the securities cost $54,000, the company realizes a gain of $4,000. It records the sale as:

Jan. 1	Cash	58,000	
	Debt Investments		54,000
	Gain on Sale of Debt Investments		4,000
	(To record sale of Doan Inc. bonds)		

A	=	L	+	SE
+58,000				
−54,000				
				+4,000 Rev

Cash Flows
+58,000

Kuhl reports the gain on sale of debt investments under "Other revenues and gains" in the income statement and reports losses under "Other expenses and losses."

Before You Go On...

REVIEW IT
1. Why might a company make investments in debt or stock securities?
2. What entries are required in accounting for debt investments?
3. How do companies report gains and losses from the sale of bonds in the income statement?

DO IT
Waldo Corporation had the following transactions pertaining to debt investments.

Jan. 1   Purchased 30, $1,000 Hillary Co. 10% bonds for $30,000, plus brokerage fees of $900. Interest is payable semiannually on July 1 and January 1.
July 1   Received semiannual interest on Hillary Co. bonds.
July 1   Sold 15 Hillary Co. bonds for $15,000, less $400 brokerage fees.

(a) Journalize the transactions, and **(b)** prepare the adjusting entry for the accrual of interest on December 31.

Action Plan
■ Record bond investments at cost.
■ Record interest when received and/or accrued.
■ When bonds are sold, credit the investment account for the cost of the bonds.
■ Record any difference between the cost and the net proceeds as a gain or loss.

Solution

(a) Jan. 1	Debt Investments	30,900	
	Cash		30,900
	(To record purchase of 30 Hillary Co. bonds)		
July 1	Cash	1,500	
	Interest Revenue ($30,000 × .10 × 6/12)		1,500
	(To record receipt of interest on Hillary Co. bonds)		
July 1	Cash	14,600	
	Loss on Sale of Debt Investments	850	
	Debt Investments ($30,900 × 15/30)		15,450
	(To record sale of 15 Hillary Co. bonds)		
(b) Dec. 31	Interest Receivable	750	
	Interest Revenue ($15,000 × .10 × 6/12)		750
	(To accrue interest on Hillary Co. bonds)		

Related exercise material: *BE16-1, E16-2, and E16-3.*

The Navigator

ACCOUNTING FOR STOCK INVESTMENTS

STUDY OBJECTIVE 3
Explain the accounting for stock investments.

Stock investments are investments in the capital stock of other corporations. When a company holds stock (and/or debt) of several different corporations, the group of securities is identified as an **investment portfolio**.

The accounting for investments in common stock depends on the extent of the investor's influence over the operating and financial affairs of the issuing corporation (the **investee**). Illustration 16-3 shows the general guidelines.

Illustration 16-3
Accounting guidelines for stock investments

Investor's Ownership Interest in Investee's Common Stock	Presumed Influence on Investee	Accounting Guidelines
Less than 20%	Insignificant	Cost method
Between 20% and 50%	Significant	Equity method
More than 50%	Controlling	Consolidated financial statements

Companies are required to use judgment instead of blindly following the guidelines.[1] On the following pages we will explain the application of each guideline.

Holdings of Less than 20%

HELPFUL HINT
The entries for investments in common stock also apply to investments in preferred stock.

In accounting for stock investments of less than 20%, companies use the cost method. Under the **cost method**, companies record the investment at cost, and recognize revenue only when cash dividends are received.

RECORDING ACQUISITION OF STOCK INVESTMENTS

At acquisition, the cost principle applies. Cost includes all expenditures necessary to acquire these investments, such as the price paid plus any brokerage fees (commissions).

Assume, for example, that on July 1, 2008, Sanchez Corporation acquires 1,000 shares (10% ownership) of Beal Corporation common stock. Sanchez pays $40 per share plus brokerage fees of $500. The entry for the purchase is:

A	=	L	+	SE
+40,500				
−40,500				

Cash Flows
−40,500

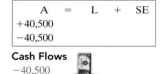

July 1	Stock Investments	40,500	
	Cash		40,500
	(To record purchase of 1,000 shares of Beal Corporation common stock)		

---

[1]Among the questions that are considered in determining an investor's influence are these: (1) Does the investor have representation on the investee's board? (2) Does the investor participate in the investee's policy-making process? (3) Are there material transactions between the investor and investee? (4) Is the common stock held by other stockholders concentrated or dispersed?

RECORDING DIVIDENDS

During the time Sanchez owns the stock, it makes entries for any cash dividends received. If Sanchez receives a $2 per share dividend on December 31, the entry is:

Dec. 31	Cash (1,000 × $2)	2,000	
	Dividend Revenue		2,000
	(To record receipt of a cash dividend)		

A	=	L	+	SE
+2,000				
				+2,000 Rev

Cash Flows
+2,000

Sanchez reports Dividend Revenue under "Other revenues and gains" in the income statement. Unlike interest on notes and bonds, dividends do not accrue. Therefore, companies do not make adjusting entries to accrue dividends.

RECORDING SALE OF STOCK

When a company sells a stock investment, it recognizes as a gain or a loss the difference between the net proceeds from the sale (sales price less brokerage fees) and the cost of the stock.

Assume that Sanchez Corporation receives net proceeds of $39,500 on the sale of its Beal stock on February 10, 2009. Because the stock cost $40,500, Sanchez incurred a loss of $1,000. The entry to record the sale is:

Feb. 10	Cash	39,500	
	Loss on Sale of Stock Investments	1,000	
	Stock Investments		40,500
	(To record sale of Beal common stock)		

A	=	L	+	SE
+39,500				
				−1,000 Exp
−40,500				

Cash Flows
+39,500

Sanchez reports the loss under "Other expenses and losses" in the income statement. It would show a gain on sale under "Other revenues and gains."

Holdings Between 20% and 50%

When an investor company owns only a small portion of the shares of stock of another company, the investor cannot exercise control over the investee. But, when an investor owns between 20% and 50% of the common stock of a corporation, it is presumed that the investor has significant influence over the financial and operating activities of the investee. The investor probably has a representative on the investee's board of directors, and through that representative, may exercise some control over the investee. The investee company in some sense becomes part of the investor company.

For example, even prior to purchasing all of Turner Broadcasting, Time Warner owned 20% of Turner. Because it exercised significant control over major decisions made by Turner, Time Warner used an approach called the equity method. Under the **equity method**, **the investor records its share of the net income of the investee in the year when it is earned**. An alternative might be to delay recognizing the investor's share of net income until the investee declares a cash dividend. But that approach would ignore the fact that the investor and investee are, in some sense, one company, making the investor better off by the investee's earned income.

Under the equity method, the investor company initially records the investment in common stock at cost. After that, it **annually adjusts** the investment account to show the investor's equity in the investee. Each year, the investor does the following: (1) It increases (debits) the investment account and increases (credits) revenue for its share of the investee's net income.[2] (2) The investor also decreases

HELPFUL HINT

Under the equity method, the investor recognizes revenue on the accrual basis—i.e., when it is earned by the investee.

---

[2]Or, the investor increases (debits) a loss account and decreases (credits) the investment account for its share of the investee's net loss.

(credits) the investment account for the amount of dividends received. The investment account is reduced for dividends received, because payment of a dividend decreases the net assets of the investee.

RECORDING ACQUISITION OF STOCK INVESTMENTS

Assume that Milar Corporation acquires 30% of the common stock of Beck Company for $120,000 on January 1, 2008. Milar records this transaction as:

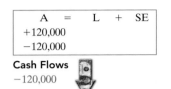

A	=	L	+	SE
+120,000				
−120,000				

Cash Flows
−120,000

Jan. 1	Stock Investments	120,000	
	Cash		120,000
	(To record purchase of Beck common stock)		

RECORDING REVENUE AND DIVIDENDS

For 2008, Beck reports net income of $100,000. It declares and pays a $40,000 cash dividend. Milar records (1) its share of Beck's income, $30,000 (30% × $100,000) and (2) the reduction in the investment account for the dividends received, $12,000 ($40,000 × 30%). The entries are:

A	=	L	+	SE
+30,000				
				+30,000 Rev

Cash Flows
no effect

A	=	L	+	SE
+12,000				
−12,000				

Cash Flows
+12,000

(1)

Dec. 31	Stock Investments	30,000	
	Revenue from Investment in Beck Company		30,000
	(To record 30% equity in Beck's 2008 net income)		

(2)

Dec. 31	Cash	12,000	
	Stock Investments		12,000
	(To record dividends received)		

After Milar posts the transactions for the year, its investment and revenue accounts will show the following.

Illustration 16-4
Investment and revenue accounts after posting

	Stock Investments				Revenue from Investment in Beck Company	
Jan. 1	120,000	Dec. 31	**12,000**		Dec. 31	**30,000**
Dec. 31	**30,000**					
Dec. 31 Bal.	138,000					

During the year, the net increase in the investment account was $18,000. As indicated above, the investment account increased by $30,000 due to Milar's share of Beck's income, and it decreased by $12,000 due to dividends received from Beck. In addition, Milar reports $30,000 of revenue from its investment, which is 30% of Beck's net income of $100,000.

Note that the difference between reported revenue under the cost method and reported revenue under the equity method can be significant. For example, Milar would report only $12,000 of dividend revenue (30% × $40,000) if it used the cost method.

Holdings of More than 50%

STUDY OBJECTIVE 4
Describe the use of consolidated financial statements.

A company that owns more than 50% of the common stock of another entity is known as the **parent company**. The entity whose stock the parent company owns is called the **subsidiary (affiliated) company**. Because of its stock ownership, the parent company has a <u>controlling interest</u> in the subsidiary.

When a company owns more than 50% of the common stock of another company, it usually prepares **consolidated financial statements**. These statements present the total assets and liabilities controlled by the parent company. They also present the total revenues and expenses of the subsidiary companies. Companies prepare consolidated statements **in addition to** the financial statements for the parent and individual subsidiary companies.

As noted earlier, when Time Warner had a 20% investment in Turner, it reported this investment in a single line item—Other Investments. After the merger, Time Warner instead consolidated Turner's results with its own. Under this approach, Time Warner included Turner's individual assets and liabilities with its own: its plant and equipment were added to Time Warner's plant and equipment, its receivables were added to Time Warner's receivables, and so on.

> **HELPFUL HINT**
>
> If parent (A) has three wholly owned subsidiaries (B, C, & D), there are four separate legal entities. From the viewpoint of the shareholders of the parent company, there is only one economic entity.

CCOUNTING ACROSS THE ORGANIZATION

How Altria Group Accounts for Kraft Foods

Altria Group Inc. (formerly Philip Morris) owns 98.3% of the common stock of Kraft Foods, Inc. The common stockholders of Altria elect the board of directors of the company, who, in turn, select the officers and managers of the company. Altria's board of directors controls the property owned by the corporation, which includes the common stock of Kraft. Thus, they are in a position to elect the board of directors of Kraft and, in effect, control its operations. These relationships are graphically illustrated here.

 Where on Altria Group's balance sheet will you find its investment in Kraft Foods, Inc.?

Consolidated statements are useful to the stockholders, board of directors, and managers of the parent company. These statements indicate the magnitude and scope of operations of the companies under common control. For example, regulators and the courts undoubtedly used the consolidated statements of AT&T to determine whether a breakup of AT&T was in the public interest. Listed at the top of page 692 are three companies that prepare consolidated statements and some of the companies they have owned. One, Disney, is Time Warner's arch rival.

Illustration 16-5
Examples of consolidated companies and their subsidiaries

Toys "R" Us, Inc.	Cendant	The Disney Company
Kids "R" Us	Howard Johnson	Capital Cities/ABC, Inc.
Babies "R" Us	Ramada Inn	Disneyland, Disney World
Imaginarium	Century 21	Mighty Ducks
Toysrus.com	Coldwell Banker	Anaheim Angels
	Avis	ESPN

Before You Go On...

REVIEW IT

1. What are the accounting entries for stock investments of less than 20%?
2. What entries are made under the equity method when (a) the investor receives a cash dividend from the investee and (b) the investee reports net income for the year?
3. What is the purpose of consolidated financial statements?
4. What does PepsiCo state regarding its accounting policy involving consolidated financial statements? The answer to this question appears on page 717.

DO IT

Presented below are two independent situations.

1. Rho Jean Inc. acquired 5% of the 400,000 shares of common stock of Stillwater Corp. at a total cost of $6 per share on May 18, 2008. On August 30, Stillwater declared and paid a $75,000 dividend. On December 31, Stillwater reported net income of $244,000 for the year.
2. Debbie, Inc. obtained significant influence over North Sails by buying 40% of North Sails' 60,000 outstanding shares of common stock at a cost of $12 per share on January 1, 2008. On April 15, North Sails declared and paid a cash dividend of $45,000. On December 31, North Sails reported net income of $120,000 for the year.

Prepare all necessary journal entries for 2008 for (1) Rho Jean Inc. and (2) Debbie, Inc.

Action Plan

■ Presume that the investor has relatively little influence over the investee when an investor owns less than 20% of the common stock of another corporation. In this case, net income earned by the investee is not considered a proper basis for recognizing income from the investment by the investor.
■ Presume significant influence for investments of 20%–50%. Therefore, record the investor's share of the net income of the investee.

Solution

(1) May 18	Stock Investments (20,000 × $6)		120,000	
	Cash			120,000
	(To record purchase of 20,000 shares of Stillwater Co. stock)			
Aug. 30	Cash		3,750	
	Dividend Revenue ($75,000 × 5%)			3,750
	(To record receipt of cash dividend)			

(2) Jan. 1	Stock Investments (60,000 × 40% × $12)	288,000	
	Cash		288,000
	(To record purchase of 24,000 shares of North Sails' stock)		
Apr. 15	Cash	18,000	
	Stock Investments ($45,000 × 40%)		18,000
	(To record receipt of cash dividend)		
Dec. 31	Stock Investments ($120,000 × 40%)	48,000	
	Revenue from Investment in North Sails		48,000
	(To record 40% equity in North Sails' net income)		

Related exercise material: *BE16-2, BE16-3, E16-4, E16-5, E16-6, E16-7, and E16-8.*

The Navigator

VALUING AND REPORTING INVESTMENTS

STUDY OBJECTIVE 5

Indicate how debt and stock investments are reported in financial statements.

The value of debt and stock investments may fluctuate greatly during the time they are held. For example, in one 12-month period, the stock price of Dell Computer Corp. hit a high of $41.99 and a low of $23.60. In light of such price fluctuations, how should companies value investments at the balance sheet date? Valuation could be at cost, at fair value (market value), or at the lower-of-cost-or-market value.

Many people argue that fair value offers the best approach because it represents the expected cash realizable value of securities. **Fair value** is the amount for which a security could be sold in a normal market. Others counter that, unless a security is going to be sold soon, the fair value is not relevant because the price of the security will likely change again.

Categories of Securities

For purposes of valuation and reporting at a financial statement date, companies classify debt and stock investments into three categories:

1. **Trading securities** are bought and held primarily for sale in the near term to generate income on short-term price differences.
2. **Available-for-sale securities** are held with the intent of selling them sometime in the future.
3. **Held-to-maturity securities** are debt securities that the investor has the intent and ability to hold to maturity.[3]

Illustration 16-6 (on page 694) shows the valuation guidelines for these securities. **These guidelines apply to all debt securities and all stock investments in which the holdings are less than 20%.**

TRADING SECURITIES

Companies hold trading securities with the intention of selling them in a short period (generally less than a month). *Trading* means frequent buying and selling. Companies report trading securities at fair value, and report changes from cost as part of net income. The changes are reported as **unrealized gains or losses** because

---

[3]This category is provided for completeness. The accounting and valuation issues related to held-to-maturity securities are discussed in more advanced accounting courses.

Trading	Available-for-sale	Held-to-maturity
"We'll sell within ten days."	"We'll hold the stock for a while to see how it performs."	"We intend to hold until maturity."
At fair value with changes reported in net income	At fair value with changes reported in the stockholders' equity section	At amortized cost

Illustration 16-6
Valuation guidelines

the securities have not been sold. The unrealized gain or loss is the difference between the **total cost** of trading securities and their **total fair value**. Companies classify trading securities as current assets.

Illustration 16-7 shows the cost and fair values for investments Pace classified as trading securities on December 31, 2008. Pace has an unrealized gain of $7,000 because total fair value of $147,000 is $7,000 greater than total cost of $140,000.

Illustration 16-7
Valuation of trading securities

Trading Securities, December 31, 2008			
Investments	**Cost**	**Fair Value**	**Unrealized Gain (Loss)**
Yorkville Company bonds	$ 50,000	$ 48,000	$ (2,000)
Kodak Company stock	90,000	99,000	9,000
Total	$140,000	$147,000	$ 7,000

HELPFUL HINT

The fact that trading securities are short-term investments increases the likelihood that they will be sold at fair value (the company may not be able to time their sale) and the likelihood that there will be realized gains or losses.

A	=	L	+	SE
+7,000				
				+7,000 Rev

Cash Flows
no effect

Pace records fair value and unrealized gain or loss through an adjusting entry at the time it prepares financial statements. In this entry, the company uses a valuation allowance account, Market Adjustment—Trading, to record the difference between the total cost and the total fair value of the securities. The adjusting entry for Pace Corporation is:

Dec. 31	Market Adjustment—Trading	7,000	
	Unrealized Gain—Income		7,000
	(To record unrealized gain on trading securities)		

Use of a Market Adjustment—Trading account enables Pace to maintain a record of the investment cost. It needs actual cost to determine the gain or loss realized when it sells the securities. Pace adds the Market Adjustment—Trading balance to the cost of the investments to arrive at a fair value for the trading securities.

The fair value of the securities is the amount Pace reports on its balance sheet. It reports the unrealized gain in the income statement in the "Other revenues and gains" section. The term "Income" in the account title indicates that the gain affects net income.

If the total cost of the trading securities is greater than total fair value, an unrealized loss has occurred. In such a case, the adjusting entry is a debit to Unrealized Loss—Income and a credit to Market Adjustment—Trading. Companies report the unrealized loss under "Other expenses and losses" in the income statement.

The market adjustment account is carried forward into future accounting periods. The company does not make any entry to the account until the end of each reporting period. At that time, the company adjusts the balance in the account to the difference between cost and fair value. For trading securities, it closes the Unrealized Gain (Loss)—Income account at the end of the reporting period.

CCOUNTING ACROSS THE ORGANIZATION

And the Correct Way to Report Investments Is...?

The accompanying graph presents an estimate of the percentage of companies on the major exchanges that have investments in the equity of other entities.

As the graph indicates, many companies have equity investments of some type. These investments can be substantial. For example, the total amount of equity-method investments appearing on company balance sheets is approximately $403 billion, and the amount shown in the income statements in any one year for all companies is approximately $38 billion.

Source: "Report and Recommendations Pursuant to Section 401(c) of the Sarbanes-Oxley Act of 2002 on Arrangements with Off-Balance Sheet Implications, Special Purpose Entities, and Transparency of Filings by Issuers," United States Securities and Exchange Commission—Office of Chief Accountant, Office of Economic Analyses, Division of Corporation Finance (June 2005), pp. 36–39.

? Why might the use of the equity method not lead to full disclosure in the financial statements?

AVAILABLE-FOR-SALE SECURITIES

As indicated earlier, companies hold available-for-sale securities with the intent of selling these investments sometime in the future. If the intent is to sell the securities within the next year or operating cycle, the investor classifies the securities as current assets in the balance sheet. Otherwise, it classifies them as long-term assets in the investments section of the balance sheet.

Companies report available-for-sale securities at fair value. The procedure for determining fair value and the unrealized gain or loss for these securities is the same as for trading securities. To illustrate, assume that Ingrao Corporation has two securities that it classifies as available-for-sale. Illustration 16-8 provides information on their valuation. There is an unrealized loss of $9,537 because total cost of $293,537 is $9,537 more than total fair value of $284,000.

> **ETHICS NOTE**
> Some managers seem to hold their available-for-sale securities that have experienced losses, while selling those that have gains, thus increasing income. Do you think this is ethical?

Available-for-Sale Securities, December 31, 2008			
Investments	**Cost**	**Fair Value**	**Unrealized Gain (Loss)**
Campbell Soup Corporation 8% bonds	$ 93,537	$103,600	$10,063
Hershey Corporation stock	200,000	180,400	(19,600)
Total	$293,537	$284,000	$(9,537)

Illustration 16-8
Valuation of available-for-sale securities

Both the adjusting entry and the reporting of the unrealized gain or loss for Ingrao's available-for-sale securities differ from those illustrated for trading securities. The differences result because Ingrao does not expect to sell these securities in the near term. Thus, prior to actual sale it is more likely that changes in fair value may change either unrealized gains or losses. Therefore, Ingrao does not report an unrealized gain or loss in the income statement. Instead, it reports it as a **separate component of stockholders' equity**.

In the adjusting entry, Ingrao identifies the market adjustment account with available-for-sale securities, and it identifies the unrealized gain or loss account with stockholders' equity. Ingrao records the unrealized loss of $9,537 as follows:

A = L + SE
                 −9,537 Exp
−9,537

Cash Flows
no effect

Dec. 31	Unrealized Gain or Loss—Equity	9,537	
	Market Adjustment—Available-for-Sale		9,537
	(To record unrealized loss on available-for-sale securities)		

If total fair value exceeds total cost, Ingrao debits Market Adjustment—Available for Sale and credits Unrealized Gain or Loss—Equity.

For available-for-sale securities, the company carries forward the Unrealized Gain or Loss—Equity account to future periods. At each future balance sheet date, Ingrao adjusts the market adjustment account to show the difference between cost and fair value at that time.

ACCOUNTING ACROSS THE ORGANIZATION

How Fair Is Fair?

In the fall of 2000, Wall Street brokerage firm Morgan Stanley told investors that rumors of big losses in its bond portfolio were "greatly exaggerated." As it turns out, Morgan Stanley also was exaggerating.

Recently, the SEC accused Morgan Stanley of violating securities laws by overstating the value of certain bonds by $75 million. The overvaluations stemmed more from wishful thinking than reality, the SEC said. "In effect, Morgan Stanley valued its positions at the price at which it thought a willing buyer and seller should enter into an exchange, rather than at a price at which a willing buyer and a willing seller would enter into a current exchange," the SEC wrote.

The SEC also noted that Morgan Stanley in some instances used its own more optimistic assumptions as a substitute for external pricing sources. "What that is saying is: 'Fair value is what you want the value to be. Pick a number...' That's especially troublesome."

 What do you believe is a major concern in valuing securities at fair value in the financial statements?

Balance Sheet Presentation

In the balance sheet, companies classify investments as either short-term or long-term.

SHORT-TERM INVESTMENTS

Short-term investments (also called **marketable securities**) are securities held by a company that are (1) **readily marketable** and (2) **intended to be converted into cash** within the next year or operating cycle, whichever is longer. Investments that do not meet **both criteria** are classified as **long-term investments**.

Valuing and Reporting Investments **697**

Readily Marketable. **An investment is readily marketable when it can be sold easily whenever the need for cash arises.** Short-term paper[4] meets this criterion. It can be readily sold to other investors. Stocks and bonds traded on organized securities exchanges, such as the New York Stock Exchange, are readily marketable. They can be bought and sold daily. In contrast, there may be only a limited market for the securities issued by small corporations, and no market for the securities of a privately held company.

Intent to Convert. **Intent to convert means that management intends to sell the investment within the next year or operating cycle, whichever is longer.** Generally, this criterion is satisfied when the investment is considered a resource that the investor will use whenever the need for cash arises. For example, a ski resort may invest idle cash during the summer months with the intent to sell the securities to buy supplies and equipment shortly before the winter season. This investment is considered short-term even if lack of snow cancels the next ski season and eliminates the need to convert the securities into cash as intended.

Because of their high liquidity, short-term investments appear immediately below Cash in the "Current assets" section of the balance sheet. They are reported at fair value. For example, Pace Corporation would report its trading securities as shown in Illustration 16-9.

> **HELPFUL HINT**
> Trading securities are always classified as short-term. Available-for-sale securities can be either short-term or long-term.

PACE CORPORATION	
Balance Sheet (partial)	
Current assets	
Cash	$ 21,000
Short-term investments, at fair value	147,000

Illustration 16-9
Presentation of short-term investments

> **HELPFUL HINT**
> In a recent survey of 600 large U.S. companies, 242 reported short-term investments.

LONG-TERM INVESTMENTS

Companies generally report long-term investments in a separate section of the balance sheet immediately below "Current assets," as shown later in Illustration 16-12 (page 699). Long-term investments in available-for-sale securities are reported at fair value. Investments in common stock accounted for under the equity method are reported at their equity value.

Presentation of Realized and Unrealized Gain or Loss

Companies must present in the financial statements gains and losses on investments, whether realized or unrealized. In the income statement, companies report gains and losses in the nonoperating activities section under the categories listed in Illustration 16-10. Interest and dividend revenue are also reported in that section.

Other Revenue and Gains	Other Expenses and Losses
Interest Revenue	Loss on Sale of Investments
Dividend Revenue	Unrealized Loss—Income
Gain on Sale of Investments	
Unrealized Gain—Income	

Illustration 16-10
Nonoperating items related to investments

---

[4]**Short-term paper** includes (1) certificates of deposit (CDs) issued by banks, (2) money market certificates issued by banks and savings and loan associations, (3) Treasury bills issued by the U.S. government, and (4) commercial paper (notes) issued by corporations with good credit ratings.

As indicated earlier, companies report an unrealized gain or loss on available-for-sale securities as a separate component of stockholders' equity. To illustrate, assume that Dawson Inc. has common stock of $3,000,000, retained earnings of $1,500,000, and an unrealized loss on available-for-sale securities of $100,000. Illustration 16-11 shows the balance sheet presentation of the unrealized loss.

Illustration 16-11
Unrealized loss in stockholders' equity section

DAWSON INC. Balance Sheet (partial)	
Stockholders' equity	
Common stock	$3,000,000
Retained earnings	1,500,000
Total paid-in capital and retained earnings	4,500,000
Less: Unrealized loss on available-for-sale securities	(100,000)
Total stockholders' equity	$4,400,000

Note that the loss decreases stockholders' equity. An unrealized gain is added to stockholders' equity. Reporting the unrealized gain or loss in the stockholders' equity section serves two purposes: (1) It reduces the volatility of net income due to fluctuations in fair value. (2) It informs the financial statement user of the gain or loss that would occur if the securities were sold at fair value.

Companies must report items such as this, which affect stockholders' equity but are not included in the calculation of net income, as part of a more inclusive measure called *comprehensive income*. We discuss comprehensive income briefly in Chapter 18.

Classified Balance Sheet

We have presented many sections of classified balance sheets in this and preceding chapters. The classified balance sheet in Illustration 16-12 includes, in one place, key topics from previous chapters: the issuance of par value common stock, restrictions of retained earnings, and issuance of long-term bonds. From this chapter, the statement includes (highlighted in red) short-term and long-term investments. The investments in short-term securities are considered trading securities. The long-term investments in stock of less than 20% owned companies are considered available-for-sale securities. Illustration 16-12 also includes a long-term investment reported at equity and descriptive notations within the statement, such as the basis for valuing merchandise and one note to the statement.

Before You Go On...

REVIEW IT

1. What is the proper valuation and reporting of trading and available-for-sale securities on a balance sheet?
2. Explain how companies report the unrealized gain or loss for both trading and available-for-sale securities.
3. Explain where to report short- and long-term investments on a balance sheet.

 The Navigator

 Be sure to read **ALL ABOUT YOU: A Good Day to Start Saving** on page 700 for information on how topics in this chapter apply to you.

Illustration 16-12
Classified balance sheet

PACE CORPORATION
Balance Sheet
December 31, 2008

Assets

Current assets			
Cash			$ 21,000
Short-term investments, at fair value			147,000
Accounts receivable		$ 84,000	
Less: Allowance for doubtful accounts		4,000	80,000
Merchandise inventory, at FIFO cost			43,000
Prepaid insurance			23,000
Total current assets			314,000
Investments			
Investments in stock of less than 20% owned companies, at fair value		50,000	
Investment in stock of 20–50% owned company, at equity		150,000	
Total investments			200,000
Property, plant, and equipment			
Land		200,000	
Buildings	$800,000		
Less: Accumulated depreciation	200,000	600,000	
Equipment	180,000		
Less: Accumulated depreciation	54,000	126,000	
Total property, plant, and equipment			926,000
Intangible assets			
Goodwill			270,000
Total assets			$1,710,000

Liabilities and Stockholders' Equity

Current liabilities			
Accounts payable			$185,000
Federal income taxes payable			60,000
Bond interest payable			10,000
Total current liabilities			255,000
Long-term liabilities			
Bonds payable, 10%, due 2019		$ 300,000	
Less: Discount on bonds		10,000	
Total long-term liabilities			290,000
Total liabilities			545,000
Stockholders' equity			
Paid-in capital			
Common stock, $10 par value, 200,000 shares authorized, 80,000 shares issued and outstanding		800,000	
Paid-in capital in excess of par value		100,000	
Total paid-in capital		900,000	
Retained earnings (Note 1)		255,000	
Total paid-in capital and retained earnings		1,155,000	
Add: Unrealized gain on available-for-sale securities		10,000	
Total stockholders' equity			1,165,000
Total liabilities and stockholders' equity			$1,710,000

Note 1. Retained earnings of $100,000 is restricted for plant expansion.

A Good Day to Start Saving

Compared to citizens in many other nations, Americans are very poor savers. It isn't that we don't know that we should save. It is just that we would rather spend. When *is* a good time to get serious about saving? Maybe you should start saving when you've graduated and have a good job, but then there will be those student loans to pay off, and your car loans as well. Maybe you should start after you've purchased your first home—and furnished it. Oh, and you might have kids, so you might wait until after they've gone off to college. You get the picture: there's always a reason not to start saving. Given that, *today* is as good a day as any to start saving.

✹ Some Facts

* Only about 48% of people in their twenties whose employers have a 401(k) plan participate in that plan. [401(k) plans allow you to put part of your pre-tax salary into investments. The investment and its earnings are not taxed until you withdraw them in retirement.] Many employers automatically enroll employees in 401(k) plans when they hire them.

* Only 40% of working couples currently are covered by pension plans, but 61% of workers expect to get income from a company pension plan.

* More than half of workers age 55 and older have less than $50,000 in retirement savings.

* 80% of individuals between the ages of 18 to 26 said that, if given $10,000, they would deposit the money into a traditional bank savings account rather than invest in the stock market. Many stated that they are intimidated by the stock market, and choose to give up the added returns the stock market offers over the long run, rather than face the market.

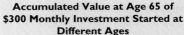

✹ About the Numbers

The message to start saving early has been presented in many different ways. Th[e] chart below presents the facts in very blunt terms. When you are 25 years old, if [you] start putting $300 per month into an investment earning 8%, by the age of 65 y[ou] will have accumulated more than $1 million. But if you wait until age 55, you wi[ll] accumulate only about $55,000. Notice the sharp drop-off between ages 25 and [35.]

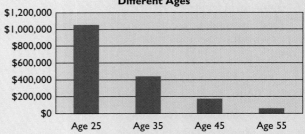

Accumulated Value at Age 65 of $300 Monthly Investment Started at Different Ages

✹ What Do You Think?

You've got $3,000 in credit card bills at an 18% interest rate. Your employe[r] has a 401(k) plan in which it will match your contributions, up to 10% of y[our] annual salary. Should you pay off your credit card bills before you start putting money into the 401(k)?

YES: Paying off an 18% debt, and thus avoiding 18% interest payments, [is] essentially equivalent to earning 18% on investments. Reducing your debts reduces your financial vulnerability.

NO: You need to get in the savings habit as soon as possible. You should take part of the money you would have used to pay off your debt each mon[th] and instead put it into the 401(k).

Sources: Kelly Greene, "Workers' Views On Retirement May Be Too Rosy," *Wall Street Journal*, Ap[ril] 4, 2006, p. D2; Ron Lieber, "Getting Younger Folk to Save," *Wall Street Journal*, June 17, 2006, p. B1; Eric A. Henon, "Why and How Generation Y Saves and Spends," *Benefits & Compensation Digest*, February 2006, pp. 30–32.

Demonstration Problem

In its first year of operations, DeMarco Company had the following selected transactions in stock investments that are considered trading securities.

June 1   Purchased for cash 600 shares of Sanburg common stock at $24 per share, plus $300 brokerage fees.

July 1   Purchased for cash 800 shares of Cey common stock at $33 per share, plus $600 brokerage fees.

Sept. 1   Received a $1 per share cash dividend from Cey Corporation.

Nov. 1   Sold 200 shares of Sanburg common stock for cash at $27 per share, less $150 brokerage fees.

Dec. 15   Received a $0.50 per share cash dividend on Sanburg common stock.

At December 31, the fair values per share were: Sanburg $25 and Cey $30.

Instructions

(a) Journalize the transactions.

(b) Prepare the adjusting entry at December 31 to report the securities at fair value.

Solution to Demonstration Problem

(a) June 1	Stock Investments	14,700	
	Cash (600 × $24) + $300		14,700
	(To record purchase of 600 shares of		
	Sanburg common stock)		
July 1	Stock Investments	27,000	
	Cash (800 × $33) + $600		27,000
	(To record purchase of 800 shares of Cey		
	common stock)		
Sept. 1	Cash (800 × $1.00)	800	
	Dividend Revenue		800
	(To record receipt of $1 per share cash		
	dividend from Cey Corporation)		
Nov. 1	Cash (200 × $27) − $150	5,250	
	Stock Investments ($14,700 × 200/600)		4,900
	Gain on Sale of Stock Investments		350
	(To record sale of 200 shares of Sanburg		
	common stock)		
Dec. 15	Cash (600 − 200) × $0.50	200	
	Dividend Revenue		200
	(To record receipt of $0.50 per share		
	dividend from Sanburg Corporation)		
(b) Dec. 31	Unrealized Loss—Income	2,800	
	Market Adjustment—Trading		2,800
	(To record unrealized loss on trading		
	securities)		

action plan

✔ Include the price paid plus brokerage fees in the cost of the investment.

✔ Compute the gain or loss on sales as the difference between net selling price and the cost of the securities.

✔ Base the adjustment to fair value on the total difference between the cost and the fair value of the securities.

Investment	Cost	Fair Value	Unrealized Gain (Loss)
Sanburg common stock	$ 9,800	$10,000	$ 200
Cey common stock	27,000	24,000	(3,000)
Totals	$36,800	$34,000	$(2,800)

✓ The Navigator

SUMMARY OF STUDY OBJECTIVES

1 **Discuss why corporations invest in debt and stock securities.** Corporations invest for three primary reasons: (a) They have excess cash. (b) They view investments as a significant revenue source. (c) They have strategic goals such as gaining control of a competitor or moving into a new line of business.

2 **Explain the accounting for debt investments.** Companies record investments in debt securities when they purchase bonds, receive or accrue interest, and sell the bonds. They report gains or losses on the sale of bonds in the "Other revenues and gains" or "Other expenses and losses" sections of the income statement.

3 **Explain the accounting for stock investments.** Companies record investments in common stock when they purchase the stock, receive dividends, and sell the stock. When ownership is less than 20%, the cost method is used. When ownership is between 20% and 50%, the equity method should be used. When ownership is more than 50%, companies prepare consolidated financial statements.

4 **Describe the use of consolidated financial statements.** When a company owns more than 50% of the common stock of another company, it usually prepares consolidated financial statements. These statements indicate the magnitude and scope of operations of the companies under common control.

5 **Indicate how debt and stock investments are reported in financial statements.** Investments in debt and stock securities are classified as trading, available-for-sale, or held-to-maturity securities for valuation and reporting purposes. Trading securities are reported as current assets at fair value, with changes from cost reported in net income. Available-for-sale securities are also reported at fair value, with the changes from cost reported in stockholders' equity. Available-for-sale securities are classified as short-term or long-term depending on their expected future sale date.

6 **Distinguish between short-term and long-term investments.** Short-term investments are securities that are (a) readily marketable and (b) intended to be converted to cash within the next year or operating cycle, whichever is longer. Investments that do not meet both criteria are classified as long-term investments.

GLOSSARY

Available-for-sale securities Securities that are held with the intent of selling them sometime in the future. (p. 693).

Consolidated financial statements Financial statements that present the assets and liabilities controlled by the parent company and the total revenues and expenses of the subsidiary companies. (p. 691).

Controlling interest Ownership of more than 50% of the common stock of another entity. (p. 691).

Cost method An accounting method in which the investment in common stock is recorded at cost, and revenue is recognized only when cash dividends are received. (p. 688).

Debt investments Investments in government and corporation bonds. (p. 686).

Equity method An accounting method in which the investment in common stock is initially recorded at cost, and the investment account is then adjusted annually to show the investor's equity in the investee. (p. 689).

Fair value Amount for which a security could be sold in a normal market. (p. 693).

Held-to-maturity securities Debt securities that the investor has the intent and ability to hold to their maturity date. (p. 693).

Investment portfolio A group of stocks and/or debt securities in different corporations held for investment purposes. (p. 688).

Long-term investments Investments that are not readily marketable or that management does not intend to convert into cash within the next year or operating cycle, whichever is longer. (p. 696).

Parent company A company that owns more than 50% of the common stock of another entity. (p. 690).

Short-term investments Investments that are readily marketable and intended to be converted into cash within the next year or operating cycle, whichever is longer. (p. 696).

Stock investments Investments in the capital stock of other corporations. (p. 688).

Subsidiary (affiliated) company A company in which more than 50% of its stock is owned by another company. (p. 690).

Trading securities Securities bought and held primarily for sale in the near term to generate income on short-term price differences. (p. 693).

SELF-STUDY QUESTIONS

Answers are at the end of the chapter.

(SO 2) **1.** Debt investments are initially recorded at:
  a. cost.
  b. cost plus accrued interest.
  c. fair value.
  d. None of the above.

(SO 2) **2.** Hanes Company sells debt investments costing $26,000 for $28,000, plus accrued interest that has been recorded. In journalizing the sale, credits are to:
  a. Debt Investments and Loss on Sale of Debt Investments.
  b. Debt Investments, Gain on Sale of Debt Investments, and Bond Interest Receivable.
  c. Stock Investments and Bond Interest Receivable.
  d. No correct answer given.

(SO 3) **3.** Pryor Company receives net proceeds of $42,000 on the sale of stock investments that cost $39,500. This transaction will result in reporting in the income statement a:
  a. loss of $2,500 under "Other expenses and losses."
  b. loss of $2,500 under "Operating expenses."
  c. gain of $2,500 under "Other revenues and gains."
  d. gain of $2,500 under "Operating revenues."

(SO 3) **4.** The equity method of accounting for long-term investments in stock should be used when the investor has significant influence over an investee and owns:
  a. between 20% and 50% of the investee's common stock.
  b. 20% or more of the investee's common stock.
  c. more than 50% of the investee's common stock.
  d. less than 20% of the investee's common stock.

(SO 4) **5.** Which of the following statements is *not true*? Consolidated financial statements are useful to:
  a. determine the profitability of specific subsidiaries.
  b. determine the total profitability of enterprises under common control.
  c. determine the breadth of a parent company's operations.
  d. determine the full extent of total obligations of enterprises under common control.

(SO 5) **6.** At the end of the first year of operations, the total cost of the trading securities portfolio is $120,000. Total fair value is $115,000. The financial statements should show:
  a. a reduction of an asset of $5,000 and a realized loss of $5,000.
  b. a reduction of an asset of $5,000 and an unrealized loss of $5,000 in the stockholders' equity section.
  c. a reduction of an asset of $5,000 in the current assets section and an unrealized loss of $5,000 in "Other expenses and losses."
  d. a reduction of an asset of $5,000 in the current assets section and a realized loss of $5,000 in "Other expenses and losses."

(SO 5) **7.** In the balance sheet, a debit balance in Unrealized Gain or Loss—Equity is reported as a:
  a. contra asset account.
  b. contra stockholders' equity account.
  c. loss in the income statement.
  d. loss in the retained earnings statement.

(SO 6) **8.** Short-term debt investments must be readily marketable and be expected to be sold within:
  a. 3 months from the date of purchase.
  b. the next year or operating cycle, whichever is shorter.
  c. the next year or operating cycle, whichever is longer.
  d. the operating cycle.

Go to the book's website,
www.wiley.com/college/ weygandt,
for Additional Self-Study questions.

The Navigator

QUESTIONS

1. What are the reasons that corporations invest in securities?

2. (a) What is the cost of an investment in bonds?
(b) When is interest on bonds recorded?

3. Tino Martinez is confused about losses and gains on the sale of debt investments. Explain to Tino (a) how the gain or loss is computed, and (b) the statement presentation of the gains and losses.

4. Olindo Company sells Gish's bonds costing $40,000 for $45,000, including $500 of accrued interest. In recording the sale, Olindo books a $5,000 gain. Is this correct? Explain.

5. What is the cost of an investment in stock?

6. To acquire Kinston Corporation stock, R. Neal pays $62,000 in cash, plus $1,200 broker's fees. What entry should be made for this investment, assuming the stock is readily marketable?

7. (a) When should a long-term investment in common stock be accounted for by the equity method? (b) When is revenue recognized under this method?

8. Rijo Corporation uses the equity method to account for its ownership of 30% of the common stock of Pippen Packing. During 2008 Pippen reported a net income of $80,000 and declares and pays cash dividends of $10,000. What recognition should Rijo Corporation give to these events?

9. What constitutes "significant influence" when an investor's financial interest is below the 50% level?

10. Distinguish between the cost and equity methods of accounting for investments in stocks.

11. What are consolidated financial statements?

12. What are the valuation guidelines for investments at a balance sheet date?

13. Tina Eddings is the controller of Mendez Inc. At December 31, the company's investments in trading securities cost $74,000. They have a fair value of $70,000. Indicate how Tina would report these data in the financial statements prepared on December 31.

14. Using the data in question 13, how would Tina report the data if the investment were long-term and the securities were classified as available-for-sale?

15. Hashmi Company's investments in available-for-sale securities at December 31 show total cost of $195,000 and total fair value of $205,000. Prepare the adjusting entry.

16. Using the data in question 15, prepare the adjusting entry assuming the securities are classified as trading securities.

17. What is the proper statement presentation of the account Unrealized Loss—Equity?

18. What purposes are served by reporting Unrealized Gains (Losses)—Equity in the stockholders' equity section?

19. Altoona Wholesale Supply owns stock in Key Corporation. Altoona intends to hold the stock indefinitely because of some negative tax consequences if sold. Should the investment in Key be classified as a short-term investment? Why or why not?

BRIEF EXERCISES

Journalize entries for debt investments.

(SO 2)

BE16-1 Coffey Corporation purchased debt investments for $52,000 on January 1, 2008. On July 1, 2008, Coffey received cash interest of $2,340. Journalize the purchase and the receipt of interest. Assume that no interest has been accrued.

Journalize entries for stock investments.

(SO 3)

BE16-2 On August 1, Wade Company buys 1,000 shares of Morgan common stock for $35,000 cash, plus brokerage fees of $700. On December 1, Wade sells the stock investments for $40,000 in cash. Journalize the purchase and sale of the common stock.

Record transactions under the equity method of accounting.

(SO 3)

BE16-3 Kayser Company owns 25% of Fort Company. For the current year Fort reports net income of $180,000 and declares and pays a $50,000 cash dividend. Record Kayser's equity in Fort's net income and the receipt of dividends from Fort.

Prepare adjusting entry using fair value.

(SO 5)

BE16-4 The cost of the trading securities of Cepeda Company at December 31, 2008, is $62,000. At December 31, 2008, the fair value of the securities is $59,000. Prepare the adjusting entry to record the securities at fair value.

Indicate statement presentation using fair value.

(SO 5, 6)

BE16-5 For the data presented in BE16-4, show the financial statement presentation of the trading securities and related accounts.

Prepare adjusting entry using fair value.

(SO 5)

BE16-6 Garrett Corporation holds as a long-term investment available-for-sale stock securities costing $72,000. At December 31, 2008, the fair value of the securities is $66,000. Prepare the adjusting entry to record the securities at fair value.

Indicate statements presentation using fair value.

(SO 5, 6)

BE16-7 For the data presented in BE16-6, show the financial statement presentation of the available-for-sale securities and related accounts. Assume the available-for-sale securities are noncurrent.

Prepare investments section of balance sheet.

(SO 5, 6)

BE16-8 Gowdy Corporation has the following long-term investments: (1) Common stock of Dixen Co. (10% ownership) held as available-for-sale securities, cost $108,000, fair value $115,000. (2) Common stock of Ely Inc. (30% ownership), cost $210,000, equity $270,000. Prepare the investments section of the balance sheet.

EXERCISES

Understand debt and stock investments.

(SO 1)

E16-1 Max Weinberg is studying for an accounting test and has developed the following questions about investments.

1. What are three reasons why companies purchase investments in debt or stock securities?
2. Why would a corporation have excess cash that it does not need for operations?
3. What is the typical investment when investing cash for short periods of time?
4. What is the typical investment when investing cash to generate earnings?

5. Why would a company invest in securities that provide no current cash flows?
6. What is the typical investment when investing cash for strategic reasons?

Instructions
Provide answers for Max.

E16-2   Foren Corporation had the following transactions pertaining to debt investments.

Jan. 1 Purchased 50 8%, $1,000 Choate Co. bonds for $50,000 cash plus brokerage fees of $900. Interest is payable semiannually on July 1 and January 1.
July 1 Received semiannual interest on Choate Co. bonds.
July 1 Sold 30 Choate Co. bonds for $34,000 less $500 brokerage fees.

Journalize debt investment transactions and accrue interest.
(SO 2)

Instructions
(a) Journalize the transactions. *GAIN ON SALE $2,960*
(b) Prepare the adjusting entry for the accrual of interest at December 31. *Accrued interest $800*

E16-3   EmmyLou Company purchased 70 Harris Company 12%, 10-year, $1,000 bonds on January 1, 2008, for $73,000. EmmyLou Company also had to pay $500 of broker's fees. The bonds pay interest semiannually. On January 1, 2009, after receipt of interest, EmmyLou Company sold 40 of the bonds for $40,100. *Loss on sale $1,900*

Journalize debt investment transactions, accrue interest, and record sale.
(SO 2)

Instructions
Prepare the journal entries to record the transactions described above.

E16-4   Dossett Company had the following transactions pertaining to stock investments.

Feb. 1 Purchased 600 shares of Goetz common stock (2%) for $6,000 cash, plus brokerage fees of $200.
July 1 Received cash dividends of $1 per share on Goetz common stock.
Sept. 1 Sold 300 shares of Goetz common stock for $4,400, less brokerage fees of $100.
Dec. 1 Received cash dividends of $1 per share on Goetz common stock.

Journalize stock investment transactions.
(SO 3)

Instructions
(a) Journalize the transactions. *total DIVIDEND Revenue $900*
(b) Explain how dividend revenue and the gain (loss) on sale should be reported in the income statement. *Loss on sale*

E16-5   Wyrick Inc. had the following transactions pertaining to investments in common stock.

Jan. 1 Purchased 2,500 shares of Murphy Corporation common stock (5%) for $140,000 cash plus $2,100 broker's commission.
July 1 Received a cash dividend of $3 per share.
Dec. 1 Sold 500 shares of Murphy Corporation common stock for $32,000 cash, less $800 broker's commission.
Dec. 31 Received a cash dividend of $3 per share.

Journalize transactions for investments in stocks.
(SO 3)

Instructions
Journalize the transactions. *GAIN ON SALE $2,780*

E16-6   On February 1, Neil Company purchased 500 shares (2% ownership) of Young Company common stock for $30 per share plus brokerage fees of $400. On March 20, Neil Company sold 100 shares of Young stock for $2,900, less a $50 brokerage fee. Neil received a dividend of $1.00 per share on April 25. On June 15, Neil sold 200 shares of Young stock for $7,400, less a $90 brokerage fee. On July 28, Neil received a dividend of $1.25 per share.

Journalize transactions for investments in stocks.
(SO 3)

Instructions
Prepare the journal entries to record the transactions described above. *Loss on sale $230*

E16-7   On January 1 Kwun Corporation purchased a 25% equity in Connors Corporation for $180,000. At December 31 Connors declared and paid a $60,000 cash dividend and reported net income of $200,000.

Journalize and post transactions, and contrast cost and equity method results.
(SO 3)

Instructions
(a) Journalize the transactions.
(b) Determine the amount to be reported as an investment in Connors stock at December 31.

Journalize entries under cost and equity methods.

(SO 3)

E16-8 Presented below are two independent situations.

1. Heath Cosmetics acquired 15% of the 200,000 shares of common stock of Van Fashion at a total cost of $13 per share on March 18, 2008. On June 30, Van declared and paid a $60,000 dividend. On December 31, Van reported net income of $122,000 for the year. At December 31, the market price of Van Fashion was $15 per share. The stock is classified as available-for-sale.

2. Yoder, Inc., obtained significant influence over Parks Corporation by buying 30% of Parks 30,000 outstanding shares of common stock at a total cost of $9 per share on January 1, 2008. On June 15, Parks declared and paid a cash dividend of $30,000. On December 31, Parks reported a net income of $80,000 for the year.

Instructions

Prepare all the necessary journal entries for 2008 for (a) Heath Cosmetics and (b) Yoder, Inc.

Understand the usefulness of consolidated statements.

(SO 4)

E16-9 Ryan Company purchased 70% of the outstanding common stock of Wayne Corporation.

Instructions

(a) Explain the relationship between Ryan Company and Wayne Corporation.

(b) How should Ryan account for its investment in Wayne?

(c) Why is the accounting treatment described in (b) useful?

Prepare adjusting entry to record fair value, and indicate statement presentation.

(SO 5, 6)

E16-10 At December 31, 2008, the trading securities for Natoli, Inc. are as follows.

Security	Cost	Fair Value
A	$17,500	$16,000
B	12,500	14,000
C	23,000	19,000
	$53,000	$49,000

Instructions

(a) Prepare the adjusting entry at December 31, 2008, to report the securities at fair value.

(b) Show the balance sheet and income statement presentation at December 31, 2008, after adjustment to fair value.

Prepare adjusting entry to record fair value, and indicate statement presentation.

(SO 5, 6)

E16-11 Data for investments in stock classified as trading securities are presented in E16-10. Assume instead that the investments are classified as available-for-sale securities. They have the same cost and fair value. The securities are considered to be a long-term investment.

Instructions

(a) Prepare the adjusting entry at December 31, 2008, to report the securities at fair value.

(b) Show the statement presentation at December 31, 2008, after adjustment to fair value.

(c) ━━━ M. Linquist, a member of the board of directors, does not understand the reporting of the unrealized gains or losses. Write a letter to Mr. Linquist explaining the reporting and the purposes that it serves.

Prepare adjusting entries for fair value, and indicate statement presentation for two classes of securities.

(SO 5, 6)

E16-12 McGee Company has the following data at December 31, 2008.

Securities	Cost	Fair Value
Trading	$120,000	$124,000
Available-for-sale	100,000	94,000

The available-for-sale securities are held as a long-term investment.

Instructions

(a) Prepare the adjusting entries to report each class of securities at fair value.

(b) Indicate the statement presentation of each class of securities and the related unrealized gain (loss) accounts.

EXERCISES: SET B

Visit the book's website at **www.wiley.com/college/weygandt**, and choose the Student Companion site, to access Exercise Set B.

PROBLEMS: SET A

P16-1A   Davison Carecenters Inc. provides financing and capital to the health-care industry, with a particular focus on nursing homes for the elderly. The following selected transactions re-late to bonds acquired as an investment by Davison, whose fiscal year ends on December 31.

Journalize debt investment transactions and show financial statement presentation.

(SO 2, 5, 6)

2008

Jan.   1   Purchased at par $2,000,000 of Hannon Nursing Centers, Inc., 10-year, 8% bonds dated January 1, 2008, directly from Hannon.
July   1   Received the semiannual interest on the Hannon bonds.
Dec. 31   Accrual of interest at year-end on the Hannon bonds.

(Assume that all intervening transactions and adjustments have been properly recorded and that the number of bonds owned has not changed from December 31, 2008, to December 31, 2010.)

2011

Jan.   1   Received the semiannual interest on the Hannon bonds.
Jan.   1   Sold $1,000,000 Hannon bonds at 106. The broker deducted $6,000 for commissions and fees on the sale.
July   1   Received the semiannual interest on the Hannon bonds.
Dec. 31   Accrual of interest at year-end on the Hannon bonds.

Instructions

(a) Journalize the listed transactions for the years 2008 and 2011.
(b) Assume that the fair value of the bonds at December 31, 2008, was $2,200,000. These bonds are classified as available-for-sale securities. Prepare the adjusting entry to record these bonds at fair value.
(c) Based on your analysis in part (b), show the balance sheet presentation of the bonds and interest receivable at December 31, 2008. Assume the investments are considered long-term. Indicate where any unrealized gain or loss is reported in the financial statements.

(a) Gain on sale of debt investment $54,000

P16-2A   In January 2008, the management of Noble Company concludes that it has sufficient cash to permit some short-term investments in debt and stock securities. During the year, the following transactions occurred.

Journalize investment transactions, prepare adjusting entry, and show statement presentation.

(SO 2, 3, 5, 6)

Feb.   1   Purchased 600 shares of Hiens common stock for $31,800, plus brokerage fees of $600.
Mar.   1   Purchased 800 shares of Pryce common stock for $20,000, plus brokerage fees of $400.
Apr.   1   Purchased 50 $1,000, 7% Roy bonds for $50,000, plus $1,000 brokerage fees. Interest is payable semiannually on April 1 and October 1.
July   1   Received a cash dividend of $0.60 per share on the Hiens common stock.
Aug.   1   Sold 200 shares of Hiens common stock at $58 per share less brokerage fees of $200.
Sept. 1   Received a $1 per share cash dividend on the Pryce common stock.
Oct.   1   Received the semiannual interest on the Roy bonds.
Oct.   1   Sold the Roy bonds for $50,000 less $1,000 brokerage fees.

At December 31, the fair value of the Hiens common stock was $55 per share. The fair value of the Pryce common stock was $24 per share.

Instructions

(a) Journalize the transactions and post to the accounts Debt Investments and Stock Investments. (Use the T-account form.)
(b) Prepare the adjusting entry at December 31, 2008, to report the investment securities at fair value. All securities are considered to be trading securities.
(c) Show the balance sheet presentation of investment securities at December 31, 2008.
(d) Identify the income statement accounts and give the statement classification of each account.

(a) Gain on stock sale $600

P16-3A   On December 31, 2008, Ramey Associates owned the following securities, held as a long-term investment. The securities are not held for influence or control of the investee.

Journalize transactions and adjusting entry for stock investments.

(SO 3, 5, 6)

Common Stock	Shares	Cost
Hurst Co.	2,000	$60,000
Pine Co.	5,000	45,000
Scott Co.	1,500	30,000

On December 31, 2008, the total fair value of the securities was equal to its cost. In 2009, the following transactions occurred.

July   1   Received $1 per share semiannual cash dividend on Pine Co. common stock.
Aug. 1   Received $0.50 per share cash dividend on Hurst Co. common stock.
Sept. 1   Sold 1,500 shares of Pine Co. common stock for cash at $8 per share, less brokerage fees of $300.
Oct.   1   Sold 800 shares of Hurst Co. common stock for cash at $33 per share, less brokerage fees of $500.
Nov. 1   Received $1 per share cash dividend on Scott Co. common stock.
Dec. 15 Received $0.50 per share cash dividend on Hurst Co. common stock.
       31 Received $1 per share semiannual cash dividend on Pine Co. common stock.

At December 31, the fair values per share of the common stocks were: Hurst Co. $32, Pine Co. $8, and Scott Co. $18.

Instructions
(a) Journalize the 2009 transactions and post to the account Stock Investments. (Use the T-account form.)

(b) Unrealized loss $4,100

(b) Prepare the adjusting entry at December 31, 2009, to show the securities at fair value. The stock should be classified as available-for-sale securities.
(c) Show the balance sheet presentation of the investments at December 31, 2009. At this date, Ramey Associates has common stock $1,500,000 and retained earnings $1,000,000.

Prepare entries under the cost and equity methods, and tabulate differences.

(SO 3)

P16-4A   Glaser Services acquired 30% of the outstanding common stock of Nickels Company on January 1, 2008, by paying $800,000 for the 45,000 shares. Nickels declared and paid $0.30 per share cash dividends on March 15, June 15, September 15, and December 15, 2008. Nickels reported net income of $320,000 for the year. At December 31, 2008, the market price of Nickels common stock was $24 per share.

Instructions

(a) Total dividend revenue $54,000

(a) Prepare the journal entries for Glaser Services for 2008 assuming Glaser cannot exercise significant influence over Nickels. (Use the cost method and assume that Nickels common stock should be classified as a trading security.)

(b) Revenue from investments $96,000

(b) Prepare the journal entries for Glaser Services for 2008, assuming Glaser can exercise significant influence over Nickels. Use the equity method.
(c) In tabular form, indicate the investment and income statement account balances at December 31, 2008, under each method of accounting.

Journalize stock investment transactions and show statement presentation.

(SO 3, 5, 6)

P16-5A   The following securities are in Pascual Company's portfolio of long-term available-for-sale securities at December 31, 2008.

	Cost
1,000 shares of Abel Corporation common stock	$52,000
1,400 shares of Frey Corporation common stock	84,000
1,200 shares of Weiss Corporation preferred stock	33,600

On December 31, 2008, the total cost of the portfolio equaled total fair value. Pascual had the following transactions related to the securities during 2009.

Jan. 20 Sold 1,000 shares of Abel Corporation common stock at $55 per share less brokerage fees of $600.
     28 Purchased 400 shares of $70 par value common stock of Rosen Corporation at $78 per share, plus brokerage fees of $480.
     30 Received a cash dividend of $1.15 per share on Frey Corp. common stock.
Feb. 8 Received cash dividends of $0.40 per share on Weiss Corp. preferred stock.
     18 Sold all 1,200 shares of Weiss Corp. preferred stock at $27 per share less brokerage fees of $360.
July 30 Received a cash dividend of $1.00 per share on Frey Corp. common stock.
Sept. 6 Purchased an additional 900 shares of $10 par value common stock of Rosen Corporation at $82 per share, plus brokerage fees of $1,200.
Dec. 1 Received a cash dividend of $1.50 per share on Rosen Corporation common stock.

At December 31, 2009, the fair values of the securities were:

Frey Corporation common stock	$64 per share
Rosen Corporation common stock	$72 per share

Pascual Company uses separate account titles for each investment, such as "Investment in Frey Corporation Common Stock."

Instructions
(a) Prepare journal entries to record the transactions.
(b) Post to the investment accounts. (Use T accounts.)
(c) Prepare the adjusting entry at December 31, 2009 to report the portfolio at fair value.
(d) Show the balance sheet presentation at December 31, 2009.

(a) Loss on sale of preferred
stock $1,560

(c) Unrealized loss $7,480

P16-6A   The following data, presented in alphabetical order, are taken from the records of Urbina Corporation.

Prepare a balance sheet.
(SO, 5, 6)

Accounts payable	$ 240,000
Accounts receivable	140,000
Accumulated depreciation—building	180,000
Accumulated depreciation—equipment	52,000
Allowance for doubtful accounts	6,000
Bonds payable (10%, due 2016)	500,000
Buildings	950,000
Cash	42,000
Common stock ($10 par value; 500,000 shares authorized, 150,000 shares issued)	1,500,000
Dividends payable	80,000
Equipment	275,000
Goodwill	200,000
Income taxes payable	120,000
Investment in Flott common stock (10% ownership), at cost	278,000
Investment in Portico common stock (30% ownership), at equity	380,000
Land	390,000
Market adjustment—available-for-sale securities (Dr)	8,000
Merchandise inventory	170,000
Notes payable (due 2009)	70,000
Paid-in capital in excess of par value	130,000
Premium on bonds payable	40,000
Prepaid insurance	16,000
Retained earnings	103,000
Short-term stock investment, at fair value (and cost)	180,000
Unrealized gain—available-for-sale securities	8,000

The investment in Flott common stock is considered to be a long-term available-for-sale security.

Instructions
Prepare a balance sheet at December 31, 2008.

Total assets $2,791,000

PROBLEMS: SET B

P16-1B   Marshall Farms is a grower of hybrid seed corn for DeKalb Genetics Corporation. It has had two exceptionally good years and has elected to invest its excess funds in bonds. The following selected transactions relate to bonds acquired as an investment by Marshall Farms, whose fiscal year ends on December 31.

Journalize debt investment transactions and show financial statement presentation.
(SO 2, 5, 6)

2008

Jan. 1   Purchased at par $600,000 of Kenner Corporation 10-year, 9% bonds dated January 1, 2008, directly from the issuing corporation.
July 1   Received the semiannual interest on the Kenner bonds.
Dec. 31   Accrual of interest at year-end on the Kenner bonds.

(Assume that all intervening transactions and adjustments have been properly recorded and the number of bonds owned has not changed from December 31, 2008, to December 31, 2010.)

2011

Jan. 1 Received the semiannual interest on the Kenner bonds.
Jan. 1 Sold $300,000 Kenner bonds at 114. The broker deducted $7,000 for commissions and fees on the sale.
July 1 Received the semiannual interest on the Kenner bonds.
Dec. 31 Accrual of interest at year-end on the Kenner bonds.

Instructions

(a) Gain on sale of debt investments $35,000

(a) Journalize the listed transactions for the years 2008 and 2011.
(b) Assume that the fair value of the bonds at December 31, 2008, was $580,000. These bonds are classified as available-for-sale securities. Prepare the adjusting entry to record these bonds at fair value.
(c) Based on your analysis in part (b) show the balance sheet presentation of the bonds and interest receivable at December 31, 2008. Assume the investments are considered long-term. Indicate where any unrealized gain or loss is reported in the financial statements.

Journalize investment transactions, prepare adjusting entry, and show statement presentation.

(SO 2, 3, 5, 6)

GLS

P16-2B In January 2008, the management of Pandya Company concludes that it has sufficient cash to purchase some short-term investments in debt and stock securities. During the year, the following transactions occurred.

Feb. 1 Purchased 600 shares of EMP common stock for $40,000, plus brokerage fees of $800.
Mar. 1 Purchased 500 shares of SEK common stock for $15,000, plus brokerage fees of $300.
Apr. 1 Purchased 60 $1,000, 9% CRE bonds for $60,000, plus $1,200 brokerage fees. Interest is payable semiannually on April 1 and October 1.
July 1 Received a cash dividend of $0.60 per share on the EMP common stock.
Aug. 1 Sold 300 shares of EMP common stock at $72 per share, less brokerage fees of $350.
Sept. 1 Received a $1 per share cash dividend on the SEK common stock.
Oct. 1 Received the semiannual interest on the CRE bonds.
Oct. 1 Sold the CRE bonds for $64,000, less $1,000 brokerage fees.

At December 31, the fair value of the EMP common stock was $66 per share. The fair value of the SEK common stock was $29 per share.

Instructions

(b) Unrealized loss $1,400

(a) Journalize the transactions and post to the accounts Debt Investments and Stock Investments. (Use the T-account form.)
(b) Prepare the adjusting entry at December 31, 2008, to report the investments at fair value. All securities are considered to be trading securities.
(c) Show the balance sheet presentation of investment securities at December 31, 2008.
(d) Identify the income statement accounts and give the statement classification of each account.

Journalize transactions and adjusting entry for stock investments.

(SO 3, 5, 6)

GLS

P16-3B On December 31, 2008, Hastco Associates owned the following securities, held as long-term investments.

Common Stock	Shares	Cost
Agee Co.	3,000	$60,000
Burns Co.	6,000	36,000
Corea Co.	1,200	24,000

On this date, the total fair value of the securities was equal to its cost. The securities are not held for influence or control over the investees. In 2009, the following transactions occurred.

July 1 Received $1 per share semiannual cash dividend on Burns Co. common stock.
Aug. 1 Received $0.50 per share cash dividend on Agee Co. common stock.
Sept. 1 Sold 2,000 shares of Burns Co. common stock for cash at $8 per share, less brokerage fees of $300.
Oct. 1 Sold 600 shares of Agee Co. common stock for cash at $28 per share, less brokerage fees of $600.
Nov. 1 Received $1 per share cash dividend on Corea Co. common stock.
Dec. 15 Received $0.50 per share cash dividend on Agee Co. common stock.
     31 Received $1 per share semiannual cash dividend on Burns Co. common stock.

At December 31, the fair values per share of the common stocks were: Agee Co. $18, Burns Co. $6, and Corea Co. $19.

Instructions

(a) Journalize the 2009 transactions and post to the account Stock Investments. (Use the T-account form.)

(b) Prepare the adjusting entry at December 31, 2009, to show the securities at fair value. The stock should be classified as available-for-sale securities.

(c) Show the balance sheet presentation of the investments at December 31, 2009. At this date, Hastco Associates has common stock $2,000,000 and retained earnings $1,200,000.

(a) Gain on sale, $3,700 and $4,200

P16-4B   Keady's Concrete acquired 30% of the outstanding common stock of Washburn, Inc. on January 1, 2008, by paying $1,600,000 for 60,000 shares. Washburn declared and paid a $0.50 per share cash dividend on June 30 and again on December 31, 2008. Washburn reported net income of $600,000 for the year. At December 31, 2008, the market price of Washburn's common stock was $30 per share.

Prepare entries under the cost and equity methods, and tabulate differences.

(SO 3)

Instructions

(a) Prepare the journal entries for Keady's Concrete for 2008 assuming Keady's cannot exercise significant influence over Washburn. (Use the cost method and assume Washburn common stock should be classified as available-for-sale.)

(b) Prepare the journal entries for Keady's Concrete for 2008, assuming Keady's can exercise significant influence over Washburn. (Use the equity method.)

(c) In tabular form, indicate the investment and income account balances at December 31, 2008, under each method of accounting.

(a) Total dividend revenue $60,000

(b) Revenue from investments $180,000

P16-5B   The following are in Madisen Company's portfolio of long-term available-for-sale securities at December 31, 2008.

Journalize stock investment transactions and show statement presentation.

(SO 3, 5, 6)

	Cost
500 shares of Bonds Corporation common stock	$26,000
700 shares of Mays Corporation common stock	42,000
600 shares of Dukakis Corporation preferred stock	16,800

On December 31, the total cost of the portfolio equaled total fair value. Madisen Company had the following transactions related to the securities during 2009.

Jan.	7	Sold 500 shares of Bonds Corporation common stock at $56 per share, less brokerage fees of $700.
	10	Purchased 200 shares, $70 par value common stock of Petengill Corporation at $78 per share, plus brokerage fees of $240.
	26	Received a cash dividend of $1.15 per share on Mays Corporation common stock.
Feb.	2	Received cash dividends of $0.40 per share on Dukakis Corporation preferred stock.
	10	Sold all 600 shares of Dukakis Corporation preferred stock at $26 per share less brokerage fees of $180.
July	1	Received a cash dividend of $1.00 per share on Mays Corporation common stock.
Sept.	1	Purchased an additional 600 shares of the $70 par value common stock of Petengill Corporation at $75 per share, plus brokerage fees of $900.
Dec.	15	Received a cash dividend of $1.50 per share on Petengill Corporation common stock.

At December 31, 2009, the fair values of the securities were:

Mays Corporation common stock	$63 per share
Petengill Corporation common stock	$72 per share

Madisen uses separate account titles for each investment, such as Investment in Mays Corporation Common Stock.

Instructions

(a) Prepare journal entries to record the transactions.

(b) Post to the investment accounts. (Use T accounts.)

(c) Prepare the adjusting entry at December 31, 2009, to report the portfolio at fair value.

(d) Show the balance sheet presentation at December 31, 2009.

(a) Loss on sale $1,380

(c) Unrealized loss $2,040

P16-6B   The following data, presented in alphabetical order, are taken from the records of Manning Corporation.

Prepare a balance sheet.

(SO 5, 6)

Accounts payable	$ 250,000
Accounts receivable	90,000
Accumulated depreciation—building	180,000
Accumulated depreciation—equipment	52,000
Allowance for doubtful accounts	6,000
Bonds payable (10%, due 2018)	400,000
Buildings	900,000
Cash	142,000
Common stock ($5 par value; 500,000 shares authorized, 300,000 shares issued)	1,500,000
Discount on bonds payable	20,000
Dividends payable	50,000
Equipment	275,000
Goodwill	200,000
Income taxes payable	120,000
Investment in Tabares Inc. stock (30% ownership), at equity	600,000
Land	520,000
Merchandise inventory	170,000
Notes payable (due 2009)	70,000
Paid-in capital in excess of par value	200,000
Prepaid insurance	16,000
Retained earnings	290,000
Short-term stock investment, at fair value (and cost)	185,000

Instructions

Total assets $2,860,000

Prepare a balance sheet at December 31, 2008.

PROBLEMS: SET C

Visit the book's website at **www.wiley.com/college/weygandt**, and choose the Student Companion site, to access Problem Set C.

COMPREHENSIVE PROBLEM: CHAPTERS 12 TO 16

Part I

Mindy Feldkamp and her two colleagues, Oscar Lopez and Lori Melton, are personal trainers at an upscale health spa/resort in Tampa, Florida. They want to start a health club that specializes in health plans for people in the 50+ age range. The growing population in this age range and strong consumer interest in the health benefits of physical activity have convinced them they can profitably operate their own club. In addition to many other decisions, they need to determine what type of business organization they want. Oscar believes there are more advantages to the corporate form than a partnership, but he hasn't yet convinced Mindy and Lori. They have come to you, a small business consulting specialist, seeking information and advice regarding the choice of starting a partnership versus a corporation.

Instructions

(a) ✏️ Prepare a memo (dated May 26, 2007) that describes the advantages and disadvantages of both partnerships and corporations. Advise Mindy, Oscar, and Lori regarding which organizational form you believe would better serve their purposes. Make sure to include reasons supporting your advice.

Part II

After deciding to incorporate, each of the three investors receives 20,000 shares of $2 par common stock on June 12, 2007, in exchange for their co-owned building ($200,000 market value) and $100,000 total cash they contributed to the business. The next decision that Mindy, Oscar, and Lori need to make is how to obtain financing for renovation and equipment. They understand the difference between equity securities and debt securities, but do not understand the tax, net income, and earnings per share consequences of equity versus debt financing on the future of their business.

Instructions

(b) Prepare notes for a discussion with the three entrepreneurs in which you will compare the consequences of using equity versus debt financing. As part of your notes, show the differences in interest and tax expense assuming $1,400,000 is financed with common stock, and then alternatively with debt. Assume that when common stock is used, 140,000 shares will be issued. When debt is used, assume the interest rate on debt is 9%, the tax rate is 32%, and income before interest and taxes is $300,000. (You may want to use an electronic spreadsheet.)

Part III

During the discussion about financing, Lori mentions that one of her clients, Roberto Marino, has approached her about buying a significant interest in the new club. Having an interested investor sways the three to issue equity securities to provide the financing they need. On July 21, 2007, Mr. Marino buys 90,000 shares at a price of $10 per share.

The club, LifePath Fitness, opens on January 12, 2008, and after a slow start, begins to produce the revenue desired by the owners. The owners decide to pay themselves a stock dividend, since cash has been less than abundant since they opened their doors. The 10% stock dividend is declared by the owners on July 27, 2008. The market value of the stock is $3 on the declaration date. The date of record is July 31, 2008 (there have been no changes in stock ownership since the initial issuance), and the issue date is August 15, 2008. By the middle of the fourth quarter of 2008, the cash flow of LifePath Fitness has improved to the point that the owners feel ready to pay themselves a cash dividend. They declare a $0.05 cash dividend on December 4, 2008. The record date is December 14, 2008, and the payment date is December 24, 2008.

Instructions

(c) (1) Record all of the transactions related to the common stock of LifePath Fitness during the years 2007 and 2008. **(2)** Indicate how many shares are issued and outstanding after the stock dividend is issued.

Part IV

Since the club opened, a major concern has been the pool facilities. Although the existing pool is adequate, Mindy, Oscar, and Lori all desire to make LifePath a cutting-edge facility. Until the end of 2008, financing concerns prevented this improvement. However, because there has been steady growth in clientele, revenue, and income since the fourth quarter of 2008, the owners have explored possible financing options. They are hesitant to issue stock and change the ownership mix because they have been able to work together as a team with great effectiveness. They have formulated a plan to issue secured term bonds to raise the needed $600,000 for the pool facilities. By the end of April 2009 everything was in place for the bond issue to go ahead. On June 1, 2009, the bonds were issued for $548,000. The bonds pay semiannual interest of 3% (6% annual) on December 1 and June 1 of each year. The bonds mature in 10 years, and amortization is computed using the straight-line method.

Instructions

(d) Record **(1)** the issuance of the secured bonds, **(2)** the interest payment made on December 1, 2009, **(3)** the adjusting entry required at December 31, 2009, and **(4)** the interest payment made on June 1, 2010.

Part V

Mr. Marino's purchase of LifePath Fitness was done through his business. The investment has always been accounted for using the cost method on his firm's books. However, early in 2010 he decided to take his company public. He is preparing an IPO (initial public offering), and he needs to have the firm's financial statements audited. One of the issues to be resolved is to restate the investment in LifePath Fitness using the equity method, since Mr. Marino's ownership percentage is greater than 20%.

Instructions

(e) (1) Give the entries that would have been made on Marino's books if the equity method of accounting for investments had been used since the initial investment. Assume the following data for LifePath.

	2007	**2008**	**2009**
Net income	$30,000	$70,000	$105,000
Total cash dividends	$ 2,100	$20,000	$ 50,000

(2) Compute the balance in the LifePath Investment account at the end of 2009.

CONTINUING COOKIE CHRONICLE

(Note: This is a continuation of the Cookie Chronicle from Chapters 1 through 15.)

CCC 16 Natalie has been approached by Ken Thornton, a shareholder of The Beanery Coffee Inc. Ken wants to retire and would like to sell his 1,000 shares in The Beanery Coffee, which represents 20% of all shares issued. The Beanery is currently operated by Ken's twin daughters, who each own 40% of the common shares. The Beanery not only operates a coffee shop but also roasts and sells beans to retailers, under the name "Rocky Mountain Beanery."

Ken has met with Curtis and Natalie to discuss the business operation. All have concluded that there would be many advantages for Cookie & Coffee Creations Inc. to acquire an interest in The Beanery Coffee. Despite the apparent advantages, Natalie and Curtis are still not convinced that they should participate in this business venture.

Go to the book's website,
www.wiley.com/college/weygandt,
to see the completion of this problem.

BROADENING YOUR PERSPECTIVE

FINANCIAL REPORTING AND ANALYSIS

Financial Reporting Problem:

Pepsico, Inc.

BYP16-1 The annual report of PepsiCo. is presented in Appendix A.

Instructions
(a) See Note 1 to the financial statements and indicate what the consolidated financial statements include.
(b) Using PepsiCo's consolidated statement of cash flows, determine how much was spent for capital acquisitions during the current year.

Comparative Analysis Problem:

PepsiCo, Inc. vs. The Coca-Cola Company

BYP16-2 PepsiCo's financial statements are presented in Appendix A. Coca-Cola's financial statements are presented in Appendix B.

Instructions
(a) Based on the information contained in these financial statements, determine each of the following for each company.
  (1) Net cash used for investing (investment) activities for the current year (from the statement of cash flows).
  (2) Cash used for capital expenditures during the current year.
(b) Each of PepsiCo's financial statements is labeled "consolidated." What has been consolidated? That is, from the contents of PepsiCo's annual report, identify by name the corporations that have been consolidated (parent and subsidiaries).

Exploring the Web

BYP16-3 Most publicly traded companies are analyzed by numerous analysts. These analysts often don't agree about a company's future prospects. In this exercise you will find analysts' rat-

ings about companies and make comparisons over time and across companies in the same industry. You will also see to what extent the analysts experienced "earnings surprises." Earnings surprises can cause changes in stock prices.

Address: biz.yahoo.com/i, or go to **www.wiley.com/college/weygandt**

Steps
1. Choose a company.
2. Use the index to find the company's name.
3. Choose **Research**.

Instructions
(a) How many analysts rated the company?
(b) What percentage rated it a strong buy?
(c) What was the average rating for the week?
(d) Did the average rating improve or decline relative to the previous week?
(e) How do the analysts rank this company among all the companies in its industry?
(f) What was the amount of the earnings surprise percentage during the last quarter?

CRITICAL THINKING

Decision Making Across the Organization

BYP16-4   At the beginning of the question and answer portion of the annual stockholders' meeting of Kemper Corporation, stockholder Mike Kerwin asks, "Why did management sell the holdings in UMW Company at a loss when this company has been very profitable during the period its stock was held by Kemper?"

Since president Tony Chavez has just concluded his speech on the recent success and bright future of Kemper, he is taken aback by this question and responds, "I remember we paid $1,300,000 for that stock some years ago, and I am sure we sold that stock at a much higher price. You must be mistaken."

Kerwin retorts, "Well, right here in footnote number 7 to the annual report it shows that 240,000 shares, a 30% interest in UMW, were sold on the last day of the year. Also, it states that UMW earned $520,000 this year and paid out $160,000 in cash dividends. Further, a summary statement indicates that in past years, while Kemper held UMW stock, UMW earned $1,240,000 and paid out $440,000 in dividends. Finally, the income statement for this year shows a loss on the sale of UMW stock of $180,000. So, I doubt that I am mistaken."

Red-faced, president Chavez turns to you.

Instructions
With the class divided into groups, answer the following.

(a) What dollar amount did Kemper receive upon the sale of the UMW stock?
(b) Explain why both stockholder Kerwin and president Chavez are correct.

Communication Activity

BYP16-5   Bunge Corporation has purchased two securities for its portfolio. The first is a stock investment in Longley Corporation, one of its suppliers. Bunge purchased 10% of Longley with the intention of holding it for a number of years, but has no intention of purchasing more shares. The second investment was a purchase of debt securities. Bunge purchased the debt securities because its analysts believe that changes in market interest rates will cause these securities to increase in value in a short period of time. Bunge intends to sell the securities as soon as they have increased in value.

Instructions
Write a memo to Max Scholes, the chief financial officer, explaining how to account for each of these investments. Explain what the implications for reported income are from this accounting treatment.

Ethics Case

BYP16-6   Bartlet Financial Services Company holds a large portfolio of debt and stock securities as an investment. The total fair value of the portfolio at December 31, 2008, is greater than total cost. Some securities have increased in value and others have decreased. Deb Faust, the financial vice president, and Jan McCabe, the controller, are in the process of classifying for the first time the securities in the portfolio.

Faust suggests classifying the securities that have increased in value as trading securities in order to increase net income for the year. She wants to classify the securities that have decreased in value as long-term available-for-sale securities, so that the decreases in value will not affect 2008 net income.

McCabe disagrees. She recommends classifying the securities that have decreased in value as trading securities and those that have increased in value as long-term available-for-sale securities. McCabe argues that the company is having a good earnings year and that recognizing the losses now will help to smooth income for this year. Moreover, for future years, when the company may not be as profitable, the company will have built-in gains.

Instructions
(a) Will classifying the securities as Faust and McCabe suggest actually affect earnings as each says it will?
(b) Is there anything unethical in what Faust and McCabe propose? Who are the stakeholders affected by their proposals?
(c) Assume that Faust and McCabe properly classify the portfolio. Assume, at year-end, that Faust proposes to sell the securities that will increase 2008 net income, and that McCabe proposes to sell the securities that will decrease 2008 net income. Is this unethical?

✳ "All About You" Activity

BYP16-7   The Securities and Exchange Commission (SEC) is the primary regulatory agency of U.S. financial markets. Its job is to ensure that the markets remain fair for all investors. The following SEC sites provide useful information for investors.

Address: **www.sec.gov/answers.shtml** and **http://www.sec.gov/investor/tools/quiz.htm**, or go to **www.wiley.com/college/weygandt**.

Instructions
(a) Go to the first SEC site and find the definition of the following terms.
   (i)   Ask price.
   (ii) Margin account.
   (iii) Prospectus.
   (iv) Index fund.
(b) Go to the second SEC site and take the short quiz.

? Answers to Insight and Accounting Across the Organization Questions

p. 691 How Altria Group Accounts for Kraft Foods
Q: Where on Altria Group's balance sheet will you find its investment in Kraft Foods, Inc.?
A: *Because Altria owns 98.3% of Kraft, Altria Group does not report Kraft in the investment section of its balance sheet. Instead, Kraft's assets and liabilities are included and commingled with the assets and liabilities of Altria Group.*

p. 695 And the Correct Way to Report Investments Is ... ?
Q: Why might the use of the equity method not lead to full disclosure in the financial statements?
A: *Under the equity method, the investment in common stock of another company is initially recorded at cost. After that, the investment account is adjusted at each reporting date to show the investor's equity in the investee. However, on the investor's balance sheet, only the investment account is shown. The pro-rata share of the investee's assets and liabilities are not reported. Because the pro-rata share of the investee's assets and liabilities are not shown, some argue that the full disclosure principle is violated.*

p. 696 How Fair Is Fair?

Q: What do you believe is a major concern in valuing securities at fair value in the financial statements?

A: *Some question the relevance of fair value measures for investments in securities, arguing in favor of reporting based on cost. They believe that cost provides relevant information: it focuses on the decision to acquire the asset, the earning effects of that decision that will be realized over time, and the ultimate recoverable value of the asset. They argue that fair value ignores those concepts. Instead, fair value focuses on the effects of transactions and events that do not involve the company, reflecting opportunity gains and losses whose recognition in the financial statements is, in their view, not appropriate until realized.*

Authors' Comments on *All About You:* A Good Day to Start Saving (p. 700)

We believe that the correct answer to this situation is both *yes* and *no.* Here is what we propose: You need to cut up your credit cards, and then pay down your credit card debt. You should prepare a budget and figure out an affordable monthly payment that will pay off your debt as fast as possible. After you have paid off the credit card, you should continue to make this same payment into some form of savings account. If your employer has a 401(k) plan, then you should put the payment into that, since it has significant tax advantages. Otherwise set up an Individual Retirement Account (IRA). Most local banks or brokerage houses would be happy to help you set up an account.

A final note: All of us want to have financial security when we retire. We don't want to be a burden to anyone. That means that we should, whenever possible, participate in any tax-advantaged savings programs available to us, such as the 401(k) and IRAs. This is especially true given the concerns that many people have about the long-term viability of Social Security.

Answer to PepsiCo Review It Question 4, page 692

In Note 1, the following statement is made regarding PepsiCo's consolidation policy:

> Our financial statements include the consolidated accounts of PepsiCo, Inc. and the affiliates that we control. In addition, we include our share of the results of certain other affiliates based on our economic ownership interest. We do not control these other affiliates, as our ownership in these other affiliates is generally less than fifty percent. Our share of the net income of noncontrolled bottling affiliates is reported in our income statement as bottling equity income. Bottling equity income also includes any changes in our ownership interests of these affiliates. In 2005, bottling equity income includes $126 million of pre-tax gains on our sales of PBG stock. See Note 8 for additional information on our noncontrolled bottling affiliates. Our share of other noncontrolled affiliates is included in division operating profit. Intercompany balances and transactions are eliminated.

Answers to Self-Study Questions

1. a   **2.** b   **3.** c   **4.** a   **5.** a   **6.** c   **7.** b   **8.** c

Statement of Cash Flows

Feature Story

GOT CASH?

In today's environment, companies must be ready to respond to changes quickly in order to survive and thrive. They need to produce new products and expand into new markets continually. To do this takes cash—lots and lots of cash. Keeping lots of cash available is a real challenge for a young company. It requires careful cash management and attention to cash flow.

One company that managed cash successfully in its early years was Microsoft (*www.microsoft.com*). During those years the company paid much of its payroll with stock options (rights to purchase company stock in the future at a given price) instead of cash. This strategy conserved cash, and turned more than a thousand of its employees into millionaires during the company's first 20 years of business.

In recent years Microsoft has had a different kind of cash problem. Now that it has reached a more "mature" stage in life, it generates so much cash—roughly $1 billion per month—that it cannot always figure out what to do with it. By 2004 Microsoft had accumulated $60 billion.

The company said it was accumulating cash to invest in new opportunities, buy other companies, and pay off pending lawsuits. But for years, the federal government has blocked attempts by Microsoft to buy anything other than small firms because it feared that purchase of a large firm would only increase Microsoft's monopolistic position. In addition, even the largest estimates of Microsoft's legal obligations related to pending lawsuits would use up only about $6 billion in cash.

Microsoft's stockholders have complained for years that holding all this cash was putting a drag on the company's profitability. Why? Because Microsoft had the cash invested in very low-yielding government securities. Stockholders felt that the company either should find new investment projects that would bring higher returns, or return some of the cash to stockholders.

Finally, in July 2004 Microsoft announced a plan to return cash to stockholders, by paying a special one-time $32 billion dividend in December 2004. This special dividend was so large that, according to the U.S. Commerce Department, it caused total personal income in the United States to rise by 3.7% in one month—the largest monthly increase ever recorded by the agency. (It also made the holiday season brighter, especially for retailers in the Seattle area.) Microsoft also doubled its regular annual dividend to $3.50 per share. Further, it announced that it would spend another $30 billion over the next four years buying treasury stock. These actions will help to deplete some of its massive cash horde, but as you will see in this chapter, for a cash-generating machine like Microsoft, the company will be anything but cash-starved.

Source: "Business: An End to Growth? Microsoft's Cash Bonanza," *The Economist,* July 23, 2005, p. 61.

✓ The Navigator

Inside Chapter 17...

The balance sheet, income statement, and retained earnings statement do not always show the whole picture of the financial condition of a company or institution. In fact, looking at the financial statements of some well-known companies, a thoughtful investor might ask questions like these: How did Eastman Kodak finance cash dividends of $649 million in a year in which it earned only $17 million? How could United Airlines purchase new planes that cost $1.9 billion in a year in which it reported a net loss of over $2 billion? How did the companies that spent a combined fantastic $3.4 trillion on mergers and acquisitions in a recent year finance those deals? Answers to these and similar questions can be found in this chapter, which presents the statement of cash flows.

The content and organization of this chapter are as follows.

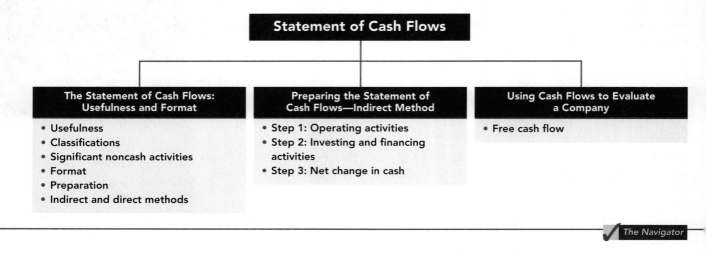

The Navigator

THE STATEMENT OF CASH FLOWS: USEFULNESS AND FORMAT

The balance sheet, income statement, and retained earnings statement provide only limited information about a company's cash flows (cash receipts and cash payments). For example, comparative balance sheets show the increase in property, plant, and equipment during the year. But they do not show how the additions were financed or paid for. The income statement shows net income. But it does not indicate the amount of cash generated by operating activities. The retained earnings statement shows cash dividends declared but not the cash dividends paid during the year. None of these statements presents a detailed summary of where cash came from and how it was used.

Usefulness of the Statement of Cash Flows

STUDY OBJECTIVE 1

Indicate the usefulness of the statement of cash flows.

The <u>statement of cash flows</u> reports the cash receipts, cash payments, and net change in cash resulting from operating, investing, and financing activities during a period. The information in a statement of cash flows should help investors, creditors, and others assess:

1. **The entity's ability to generate future cash flows.** By examining relationships between items in the statement of cash flows, investors can make predictions of the amounts, timing, and uncertainty of future cash flows better than they can from accrual basis data.

2. **The entity's ability to pay dividends and meet obligations.** If a company does not have adequate cash, it cannot pay employees, settle debts, or pay dividends. Employees, creditors, and stockholders should be particularly interested in this statement, because it alone shows the flows of cash in a business.

3. **The reasons for the difference between net income and net cash provided (used) by operating activities.** Net income provides information on the success or failure of a business enterprise. However, some financial statement users are critical of accrual-basis net income because it requires many estimates. As a result, users often challenge the reliability of the number. Such is not the case with cash. Many readers of the statement of cash flows want to know the reasons for the difference between net income and net cash provided by operating activities. Then they can assess for themselves the reliability of the income number.

4. **The cash investing and financing transactions during the period.** By examining a company's investing and financing transactions, a financial statement reader can better understand why assets and liabilities changed during the period.

> **ETHICS NOTE**
>
> Though we would discourage reliance on cash flows to the exclusion of accrual accounting, comparing cash from operations to net income can reveal important information about the "quality" of reported net income. Such a comparison can reveal the extent to which net income provides a good measure of actual performance.

Classification of Cash Flows

The statement of cash flows classifies cash receipts and cash payments as operating, investing, and financing activities. Transactions and other events characteristic of each kind of activity are as follows.

> **STUDY OBJECTIVE 2**
>
> Distinguish among operating, investing, and financing activities.

1. **Operating activities** include the cash effects of transactions that create revenues and expenses. They thus enter into the determination of net income.

2. **Investing activities** include (a) acquiring and disposing of investments and property, plant, and equipment, and (b) lending money and collecting the loans.

3. **Financing activities** include (a) obtaining cash from issuing debt and repaying the amounts borrowed, and (b) obtaining cash from stockholders, repurchasing shares, and paying dividends.

The operating activities category is the most important. It shows the cash provided by company operations. This source of cash is generally considered to be the best measure of a company's ability to generate sufficient cash to continue as a going concern.

Illustration 17-1 (page 722) lists typical cash receipts and cash payments within each of the three classifications. **Study the list carefully.** It will prove very useful in solving homework exercises and problems.

Note the following general guidelines:

1. Operating activities involve income statement items.

2. Investing activities involve cash flows resulting from changes in investments and long-term asset items.

3. Financing activities involve cash flows resulting from changes in long-term liability and stockholders' equity items.

Companies classify as operating activities some cash flows related to investing or financing activities. For example, receipts of investment revenue (interest and dividends) are classified as operating activities. So are payments of interest to lenders. Why are these considered operating activities? **Because companies report these items in the income statement, where results of operations are shown.**

Illustration 17-1
Typical receipt and payment classifications

Operating activities

Investing activities

Financing activities

TYPES OF CASH INFLOWS AND OUTFLOWS

Operating activities—Income statement items
Cash inflows:
    From sale of goods or services.
    From interest received and dividends received.
Cash outflows:
    To suppliers for inventory.
    To employees for services.
    To government for taxes.
    To lenders for interest.
    To others for expenses.

Investing activities—Changes in investments and long-term assets
Cash inflows:
    From sale of property, plant, and equipment.
    From sale of investments in debt or equity securities of other entities.
    From collection of principal on loans to other entities.
Cash outflows:
    To purchase property, plant, and equipment.
    To purchase investments in debt or equity securities of other entities.
    To make loans to other entities.

Financing activities—Changes in long-term liabilities and stockholders' equity
Cash inflows:
    From sale of common stock.
    From issuance of long-term debt (bonds and notes).
Cash outflows:
    To stockholders as dividends.
    To redeem long-term debt or reacquire capital stock (treasury stock).

Significant Noncash Activities

Not all of a company's significant activities involve cash. Examples of significant noncash activities are:

1. Direct issuance of common stock to purchase assets.
2. Conversion of bonds into common stock.
3. Direct issuance of debt to purchase assets.
4. Exchanges of plant assets.

    Companies do not report in the body of the statement of cash flows significant financing and investing activities that do not affect cash. Instead, they report these activities in either a **separate schedule** at the bottom of the statement of cash flows or in a **separate note or supplementary schedule** to the financial statements. The reporting of these noncash activities in a separate schedule satisfies the **full disclosure principle**.

    In solving homework assignments you should present significant noncash investing and financing activities in a separate schedule at the bottom of the statement of cash flows. (See the last entry in Illustration 17-2, at the bottom of page 723, for an example.)

HELPFUL HINT

Do not include **noncash** investing and financing activities in the body of the statement of cash flows. Report this information in a separate schedule.

ACCOUNTING ACROSS THE ORGANIZATION

Net What?

Net income is not the same as net cash provided by operating activities. Below are some results from recent annual reports (dollars in millions). Note the wide disparity among these companies, all of which engaged in retail merchandising.

Company	Net Income	Net Cash Provided by Operating Activities
Kohl's Corporation	$ 730	$ 948
Wal-Mart Stores, Inc.	10,267	15,044
J. C. Penney Company, Inc.	524	61
Costco Wholesale Corp.	882	2,099
Target Corporation	3,198	3,195

? In general, why do differences exist between net income and net cash provided by operating activities?

Format of the Statement of Cash Flows

The general format of the statement of cash flows presents the results of the three activities discussed previously—operating, investing, and financing—plus the significant noncash investing and financing activities. Illustration 17–2 shows a widely used form of the statement of cash flows.

Illustration 17-2
Format of statement of cash flows

COMPANY NAME
Statement of Cash Flows
Period Covered

Cash flows from operating activities		
(List of individual items)	XX	
Net cash provided (used) by operating activities		XXX
Cash flows from investing activities		
(List of individual inflows and outflows)	XX	
Net cash provided (used) by investing activities		XXX
Cash flows from financing activities		
(List of individual inflows and outflows)	XX	
Net cash provided (used) by financing activities		XXX
Net increase (decrease) in cash		XXX
Cash at beginning of period		XXX
Cash at end of period		XXX
Noncash investing and financing activities		
(List of individual noncash transactions)		XXX

The cash flows from operating activities section always appears first, followed by the investing activities section and then the financing activities section.

Before You Go On...

REVIEW IT

1. Why is the statement of cash flows useful?
2. What are the major classifications of cash flows on the statement of cash flows?
3. What are some examples of significant noncash activities?
4. What is the general format of the statement of cash flows? In what sequence are the three types of business activities presented?
5. In its 2005 statement of cash flows, what amounts did PepsiCo report for net cash (a) provided by operating activities, (b) used for investing activities, and (c) used for financing activities? The answer to this question appears on page 777.

DO IT

During its first week, Duffy & Stevenson Company had these transactions.

1. Issued 100,000 shares of $5 par value common stock for $800,000 cash.
2. Borrowed $200,000 from Castle Bank, signing a 5-year note bearing 8% interest.
3. Purchased two semi-trailer trucks for $170,000 cash.
4. Paid employees $12,000 for salaries and wages.
5. Collected $20,000 cash for services provided.

Classify each of these transactions by type of cash flow activity.

Action Plan

- Identify the three types of activities used to report all cash inflows and outflows.
- Report as operating activities the cash effects of transactions that create revenues and expenses and enter into the determination of net income.
- Report as investing activities transactions that (a) acquire and dispose of investments and productive long-lived assets and (b) lend money and collect loans.
- Report as financing activities transactions that (a) obtain cash from issuing debt and repay the amounts borrowed and (b) obtain cash from stockholders and pay them dividends.

Solution

1. Financing activity
2. Financing activity
3. Investing activity
4. Operating activity
5. Operating activity

The Navigator

Preparing the Statement of Cash Flows

Companies prepare the statement of cash flows differently from the three other basic financial statements. First, it is not prepared from an adjusted trial balance. It requires detailed information concerning the changes in account balances that occurred between two points in time. An adjusted trial balance will not provide the necessary data. Second, the statement of cash flows deals with cash receipts and payments. As a result, the company **must adjust** the effects of the use of accrual accounting **to determine cash flows**.

The information to prepare this statement usually comes from three sources:

- **Comparative balance sheets.** Information in the comparative balance sheets indicates the amount of the changes in assets, liabilities, and stockholders' equities from the beginning to the end of the period.

- **Current income statement.** Information in this statement helps determine the amount of cash provided or used by operations during the period.

- **Additional information.** Such information includes transaction data that are needed to determine how cash was provided or used during the period.

Preparing the statement of cash flows from these data sources involves three major steps, explained in Illustration 17-3 below.

Step 1: Determine net cash provided/used by operating activities by converting net income from an accrual basis to a cash basis.

This step involves analyzing not only the current year's income statement but also comparative balance sheets and selected additional data.

Step 2: Analyze changes in noncurrent asset and liability accounts and record as investing and financing activities, or disclose as noncash transactions.

This step involves analyzing comparative balance sheet data and selected additional information for their effects on cash.

Step 3: Compare the net change in cash on the statement of cash flows with the change in the cash account reported on the balance sheet to make sure the amounts agree.

The difference between the beginning and ending cash balances can be easily computed from comparative balance sheets.

Illustration 17-3
Three major steps in preparing the statement of cash flows

Indirect and Direct Methods

In order to perform step 1, a company **must convert net income from an accrual basis to a cash basis**. This conversion may be done by either of two methods: (1) the indirect method or (2) the direct method. **Both methods arrive at the same total amount** for "Net cash provided by operating activities." They differ in **how** they arrive at the amount.

The indirect method adjusts net income for items that do not affect cash. A great majority of companies (98.8%) use this method, as shown in the nearby chart.[1] Companies favor the indirect method for two reasons: (1) It is easier and

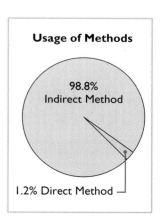

Usage of Methods

98.8% Indirect Method

1.2% Direct Method

[1] *Accounting Trends and Techniques—2005* (New York: American Institute of Certified Public Accountants, 2005).

less costly to prepare, and (2) it focuses on the differences between net income and net cash flow from operating activities.

The **direct method** shows operating cash receipts and payments, making it more consistent with the objective of a statement of cash flows. The FASB has expressed a preference for the direct method, but allows the use of either method.

The next section illustrates the more popular indirect method. Appendix 17B illustrates the direct method.

INVESTOR INSIGHT

Cash Flow Isn't Always What It Seems

Some managers have taken actions that artificially increase cash flow from operating activities. They do this by moving negative amounts out of the operating section and into the investing or financing section.

For example, WorldCom, Inc. disclosed that it had improperly capitalized expenses: It had moved $3.8 billion of cash outflows from the "Cash from operating activities" section of the cash flow statement to the "Investing activities" section, thereby greatly enhancing cash provided by operating activities. Similarly, Dynegy, Inc. restated its cash flow statement because it had improperly included in operating activities, instead of in financing activities, $300 million from natural gas trading. The restatement resulted in a drop of 37% in cash flow from operating activities.

Source: Henny Sender, "Sadly, These Days Even Cash Flow Isn't Always What It Seems To Be," *Wall Street Journal*, May 8, 2002.

? For what reasons might managers at WorldCom and at Dynegy take the actions noted above?

Before You Go On...

REVIEW IT
1. What are the three major steps in preparing a statement of cash flows?
2. What is the primary difference between the indirect and direct approaches to the statement of cash flows?
3. Which method of preparing the statement of cash flows is more commonly used in practice?

The Navigator

PREPARING THE STATEMENT OF CASH FLOWS—INDIRECT METHOD

STUDY OBJECTIVE 3

Prepare a statement of cash flows using the indirect method.

To explain how to prepare a statement of cash flows using the indirect method, we use financial information from Computer Services Company. Illustration 17-4 presents Computer Services' current and previous-year balance sheets, its current-year income statement, and related financial information for the current year.

			Change in Account Balance
COMPUTER SERVICES COMPANY Comparative Balance Sheets December 31			

Illustration 17-4
Comparative balance sheets, income statement, and additional information for Computer Services Company

Assets	2008	2007	Increase/Decrease
Current assets			
Cash	$ 55,000	$ 33,000	$ 22,000 Increase
Accounts receivable	20,000	30,000	10,000 Decrease
Merchandise inventory	15,000	10,000	5,000 Increase
Prepaid expenses	5,000	1,000	4,000 Increase
Property, plant, and equipment			
Land	130,000	20,000	110,000 Increase
Building	160,000	40,000	120,000 Increase
Accumulated depreciation—building	(11,000)	(5,000)	6,000 Increase
Equipment	27,000	10,000	17,000 Increase
Accumulated depreciation—equipment	(3,000)	(1,000)	2,000 Increase
Total assets	$398,000	$138,000	
Liabilities and Stockholders' Equity			
Current liabilities			
Accounts payable	$ 28,000	$ 12,000	$ 16,000 Increase
Income tax payable	6,000	8,000	2,000 Decrease
Long-term liabilities			
Bonds payable	130,000	20,000	110,000 Increase
Stockholders' equity			
Common stock	70,000	50,000	20,000 Increase
Retained earnings	164,000	48,000	116,000 Increase
Total liabilities and stockholders' equity	$398,000	$138,000	

COMPUTER SERVICES COMPANY
Income Statement
For the Year Ended December 31, 2008

Revenues		$507,000
Cost of goods sold	$150,000	
Operating expenses (excluding depreciation)	111,000	
Depreciation expense	9,000	
Loss on sale of equipment	3,000	
Interest expense	42,000	315,000
Income before income tax		192,000
Income tax expense		47,000
Net income		$145,000

Additional information for 2008:
1. The company declared and paid a $29,000 cash dividend.
2. Issued $110,000 of long-term bonds in direct exchange for land.
3. A building costing $120,000 was purchased for cash. Equipment costing $25,000 was also purchased for cash.
4. The company sold equipment with a book value of $7,000 (cost $8,000, less accumulated depreciation $1,000) for $4,000 cash.
5. Issued common stock for $20,000 cash.
6. Depreciation expense was comprised of $6,000 for building and $3,000 for equipment.

We will now apply the three steps to the information provided for Computer Services Company.

Step 1: Operating Activities

DETERMINE NET CASH PROVIDED/USED BY OPERATING ACTIVITIES BY CONVERTING NET INCOME FROM AN ACCRUAL BASIS TO A CASH BASIS

To determine net cash provided by operating activities under the indirect method, companies **adjust net income in numerous ways**. A useful starting point is to understand **why** net income must be converted to net cash provided by operating activities.

Under generally accepted accounting principles, most companies use the accrual basis of accounting. As you have learned, this basis requires that companies record revenue when earned and record expenses when incurred. Earned revenues may include credit sales for which the company has not yet collected cash. Expenses incurred may include some items that it has not yet paid in cash. Thus, under the accrual basis of accounting, net income is not the same as net cash provided by operating activities.

Therefore, under the indirect method, companies must adjust net income to convert certain items to the cash basis. The indirect method (or reconciliation method) starts with net income and converts it to net cash provided by operating activities. Illustration 17-5 lists the three types of adjustments.

Illustration 17-5
Three types of adjustments to convert net income to net cash provided by operating activities

Net Income	+/−	Adjustments	=	Net Cash Provided/ Used by Operating Activities
		• **Add back noncash expenses**, such as depreciation expense, amortization, or depletion.		
		• **Deduct gains and add losses** that resulted from investing and financing activities.		
		• **Analyze changes** to noncash current asset and current liability accounts.		

We explain the three types of adjustments in the next three sections.

DEPRECIATION EXPENSE

Computer Services' income statement reports depreciation expense of $9,000. Although depreciation expense reduces net income, it does not reduce cash. In other words, depreciation expense is a noncash charge. The company must add it back to net income to arrive at net cash provided by operating activities. Computer Services reports depreciation expense as follows in the statement of cash flows.

HELPFUL HINT

Depreciation is similar to any other expense in that it reduces net income. It differs in that it does not involve a current cash outflow; that is why it must be *added back* to net income to arrive at cash provided by operating activities.

Illustration 17-6
Adjustment for depreciation

Cash flows from operating activities	
Net income	$145,000
Adjustments to reconcile net income to net cash provided by operating activities:	
Depreciation expense	**9,000**
Net cash provided by operating activities	$154,000

As the first adjustment to net income in the statement of cash flows, companies frequently list depreciation and similar noncash charges such as amortization of intangible assets, depletion expense, and bad debt expense.

LOSS ON SALE OF EQUIPMENT

Illustration 17-1 states that the investing activities section should report cash received from the sale of plant assets. Because of this, **companies must eliminate from net income all gains and losses related to the disposal of plant assets, to arrive at cash provided by operating activities**.

In our example, Computer Services' income statement reports a $3,000 loss on the sale of equipment (book value $7,000, less $4,000 cash received from sale of equipment). The company's loss of $3,000 should not be included in the operating activities section of the statement of cash flows. Illustration 17-7 shows that the $3,000 loss is eliminated by adding $3,000 back to net income to arrive at net cash provided by operating activities.

Cash flows from operating activities		
Net income		$145,000
Adjustments to reconcile net income to net cash provided by operating activities:		
Depreciation expense	$9,000	
Loss on sale of equipment	**3,000**	12,000
Net cash provided by operating activities		$157,000

Illustration 17-7
Adjustment for loss on sale of equipment

If a gain on sale occurs, the company deducts the gain from its net income in order to determine net cash provided by operating activities. **In the case of either a gain or a loss, companies report as a source of cash in the investing activities section of the statement of cash flows the actual amount of cash received from the sale.**

CHANGES TO NONCASH CURRENT ASSET AND CURRENT LIABILITY ACCOUNTS

A final adjustment in reconciling net income to net cash provided by operating activities involves examining all changes in current asset and current liability accounts. The accrual accounting process records revenues in the period earned and expenses in the period incurred. For example, companies use Accounts Receivable to record amounts owed to the company for sales that have been made but for which cash collections have not yet been received. They use the Prepaid Insurance account to reflect insurance that has been paid for, but which has not yet expired, and therefore has not been expensed. Similarly, the Salaries Payable account reflects salaries expense that has been incurred by the company but has not been paid.

As a result, we need to adjust net income for these accruals and prepayments to determine net cash provided by operating activities. Thus we must analyze the change in each current asset and current liability account to determine its impact on net income and cash.

CHANGES IN NONCASH CURRENT ASSETS. The adjustments required for changes in noncash current asset accounts are as follows: **Deduct from net income increases in current asset accounts, and add to net income decreases in current asset accounts, to arrive at net cash provided by operating activities.** We can observe these relationships by analyzing the accounts of Computer Services Company.

Decrease in Accounts Receivable. Computer Services Company's accounts receivable decreased by $10,000 (from $30,000 to $20,000) during the period. For Computer Services this means that cash receipts were $10,000 higher than revenues. The Accounts Receivable account in Illustration 17-8 shows that Computer Services Company had $507,000 in revenues (as reported on the income statement), but it collected $517,000 in cash. As shown in Illustration 17-9 (below), to adjust net income to net cash provided by operating activities, the company adds to net income the decrease of $10,000 in accounts receivable.

Illustration 17-8
Analysis of accounts receivable

Accounts Receivable				
1/1/08	Balance	30,000	**Receipts from customers**	**517,000**
	Revenues	**507,000**		
12/31/08	Balance	20,000		

When the Accounts Receivable balance increases, cash receipts are lower than revenue earned under the accrual basis. Therefore, the company deducts from net income the amount of the increase in accounts receivable, to arrive at net cash provided by operating activities.

Increase in Merchandise Inventory. Computer Services Company's Merchandise Inventory balance increased $5,000 (from $10,000 to $15,000) during the period. The change in the Merchandise Inventory account reflects the difference between the amount of inventory purchased and the amount sold. For Computer Services this means that the cost of merchandise purchased exceeded the cost of goods sold by $5,000. As a result, cost of goods sold does not reflect $5,000 of cash payments made for merchandise. The company deducts from net income this inventory increase of $5,000 during the period, to arrive at net cash provided by operating activities (see Illustration 17-9). If inventory decreases, the company adds to net income the amount of the change, to arrive at net cash provided by operating activities.

Increase in Prepaid Expenses. Computer Services' prepaid expenses increased during the period by $4,000. This means that cash paid for expenses is higher than expenses reported on an accrual basis. In other words, the company has made cash payments in the current period, but will not charge expenses to income until future periods (as charges to the income statement). To adjust net income to net cash provided by operating activities, the company deducts from net income the $4,000 increase in prepaid expenses (see Illustration 17-9).

Illustration 17-9
Adjustments for changes in current asset accounts

Cash flows from operating activities		
Net income		$145,000
Adjustments to reconcile net income to net cash		
provided by operating activities:		
Depreciation expense	$ 9,000	
Loss on sale of equipment	3,000	
Decrease in accounts receivable	10,000	
Increase in merchandise inventory	(5,000)	
Increase in prepaid expenses	(4,000)	13,000
Net cash provided by operating activities		$158,000

If prepaid expenses decrease, reported expenses are higher than the expenses paid. Therefore, the company adds to net income the decrease in prepaid expenses, to arrive at net cash provided by operating activities.

CHANGES IN CURRENT LIABILITIES.   The adjustments required for changes in current liability accounts are as follows: **Add to net income increases in current liability accounts, and deduct from net income decreases in current liability accounts, to arrive at net cash provided by operating activities.**

Increase in Accounts Payable.   For Computer Services Company, Accounts Payable increased by $16,000 (from $12,000 to $28,000) during the period. That means the company received $16,000 more in goods than it actually paid for. As shown in Illustration 17-10 (below), to adjust net income to determine net cash provided by operating activities, the company adds to net income the $16,000 increase in Accounts Payable.

Decrease in Income Taxes Payable.   When a company incurs income tax expense but has not yet paid its taxes, it records income tax payable. A change in the Income Tax Payable account reflects the difference between income tax expense incurred and income tax actually paid. Computer Services' Income Tax Payable account decreased by $2,000. That means the $47,000 of income tax expense reported on the income statement was $2,000 less than the amount of taxes paid during the period of $49,000. As shown in Illustration 17-10, to adjust net income to a cash basis, the company must reduce net income by $2,000.

Cash flows from operating activities		
Net income		$145,000
Adjustments to reconcile net income to net cash provided by operating activities:		
Depreciation expense	$ 9,000	
Loss on sale of equipment	3,000	
Decrease in accounts receivable	10,000	
Increase in merchandise inventory	(5,000)	
Increase in prepaid expenses	(4,000)	
Increase in accounts payable	**16,000**	
Decrease in income tax payable	**(2,000)**	27,000
Net cash provided by operating activities		$172,000

Illustration 17-10
Adjustments for changes in current liability accounts

Illustration 17-10 shows that, after starting with net income of $145,000, the sum of all of the adjustments to net income was $27,000. This resulted in net cash provided by operating activities of $172,000.

Summary of Conversion to Net Cash Provided by Operating Activities—Indirect Method

As shown in the previous illustrations, the statement of cash flows prepared by the indirect method starts with net income. It then adds or deducts items to arrive at net cash provided by operating activities. The required adjustments are of three types:

1. Noncash charges such as depreciation, amortization, and depletion.
2. Gains and losses on the sale of plant assets.
3. Changes in noncash current asset and current liability accounts.

Illustration 17-11 (page 732) provides a summary of these changes.

Illustration 17-11
Adjustments required to convert net income to net cash provided by operating activities

		Adjustment Required to Convert Net Income to Net Cash Provided by Operating Activities
Noncash Charges	Depreciation expense	Add
	Patent amortization expense	Add
	Depletion expense	Add
Gains and Losses	Loss on sale of plant asset	Add
	Gain on sale of plant asset	Deduct
Changes in Current Assets and Current Liabilities	Increase in current asset account	Deduct
	Decrease in current asset account	Add
	Increase in current liability account	Add
	Decrease in current liability account	Deduct

ACCOUNTING ACROSS THE ORGANIZATIO

GM Must Sell More Cars

Market share matters—and it shows up in the accounting numbers. Just ask General Motors. In recent years GM has seen its market share erode until, at 25.6% of the market, the company reached the point where it actually consumed more cash than it generated. It isn't time to panic yet—GM has about $20 billion in cash on hand—but it is time to come up with a plan.

To address immediate cash needs, GM management may have to quit paying its $1.1 billion annual dividend, and it may have to sell off some assets and businesses. But in the long term, GM must either increase its market share, or shrink its operations to fit its sales figures. The following table shows net income and cash provided by operating activities at various market-share levels.

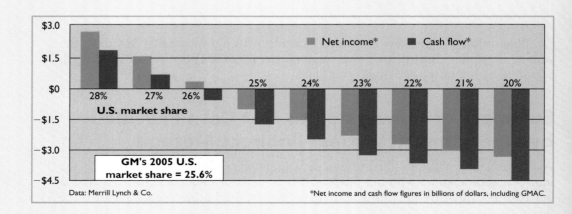

Data: Merrill Lynch & Co.   *Net income and cash flow figures in billions of dollars, including GMAC.

Source: David Welch and Dan Beucke, "Why GM's Plan Won't Work," *Business Week*, May 9, 2005, pp. 85–93.

? Why does GM's cash provided by operating activities drop so precipitously when the company's sales figures decline?

Step 2: Investing and Financing Activities

ANALYZE CHANGES IN NONCURRENT ASSET AND LIABILITY ACCOUNTS AND RECORD AS INVESTING AND FINANCING ACTIVITIES, OR AS NONCASH INVESTING AND FINANCING ACTIVITIES

Increase in Land.   As indicated from the change in the Land account and the additional information, the company purchased land of $110,000 through the issuance of long-term bonds. The issuance of bonds payable for land has no effect on cash. But it is a significant noncash investing and financing activity that merits disclosure in a separate schedule. (See Illustration 17-13 on page 734.)

Increase in Building.   As the additional data indicate, Computer Services Company acquired an office building for $120,000 cash. This is a cash outflow reported in the investing section. (See Illustration 17-13 on page 734.)

Increase in Equipment.   The Equipment account increased $17,000. The additional information explains that this was a net increase that resulted from two transactions: (1) a purchase of equipment of $25,000, and (2) the sale for $4,000 of equipment costing $8,000. These transactions are investing activities. The company should report each transaction separately. Thus it reports the purchase of equipment as an outflow of cash for $25,000. It reports the sale as an inflow of cash for $4,000. The T account below shows the reasons for the change in this account during the year.

Equipment			
1/1/08 Balance	10,000	Cost of equipment sold	8,000
Purchase of equipment	25,000		
12/31/08 Balance	27,000		

Illustration 17-12
Analysis of equipment

The following entry shows the details of the equipment sale transaction.

Cash	4,000	
Accumulated Depreciation	1,000	
Loss on Sale of Equipment	3,000	
Equipment		8,000

A	=	L	+	SE
+4,000				
+1,000				
				−3,000 Exp
−8,000				

Cash Flows
+4,000

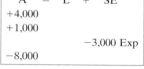

Increase in Bonds Payable.   The Bonds Payable account increased $110,000. As indicated in the additional information, the company acquired land from the issuance of these bonds. It reports this noncash transaction in a separate schedule at the bottom of the statement.

Increase in Common Stock.   The balance sheet reports an increase in Common Stock of $20,000. The additional information section notes that this increase resulted from the issuance of new shares of stock. This is a cash inflow reported in the financing section.

Increase in Retained Earnings.   Retained earnings increased $116,000 during the year. This increase can be explained by two factors: (1) Net income of $145,000 increased retained earnings. (2) Dividends of $29,000 decreased retained earnings. The company adjusts net income to net cash provided by operating activities in the operating activities section. Payment of the dividends (not the declaration) is a **cash outflow that the company reports as a financing activity**.

Illustration 17-13
Statement of cash flows,
2008—indirect method

STATEMENT OF CASH FLOWS—2008

Using the previous information, we can now prepare a statement of cash flows for 2008 for Computer Services Company as shown in Illustration 17-13.

COMPUTER SERVICES COMPANY Statement of Cash Flows—Indirect Method For the Year Ended December 31, 2008		
Cash flows from operating activities		
Net income		$145,000
Adjustments to reconcile net income to net cash		
provided by operating activities:		
Depreciation expense	$ 9,000	
Loss on sale of equipment	3,000	
Decrease in accounts receivable	10,000	
Increase in merchandise inventory	(5,000)	
Increase in prepaid expenses	(4,000)	
Increase in accounts payable	16,000	
Decrease in income tax payable	(2,000)	27,000
Net cash provided by operating activities		172,000
Cash flows from investing activities		
Purchase of building	(120,000)	
Purchase of equipment	(25,000)	
Sale of equipment	4,000	
Net cash used by investing activities		(141,000)
Cash flows from financing activities		
Issuance of common stock	20,000	
Payment of cash dividends	(29,000)	
Net cash used by financing activities		(9,000)
Net increase in cash		22,000
Cash at beginning of period		33,000
Cash at end of period		$ 55,000
Noncash investing and financing activities		
Issuance of bonds payable to purchase land		$110,000

> **HELPFUL HINT**
> Note that in the investing and financing activities sections, positive numbers indicate cash inflows (receipts), and negative numbers indicate cash outflows (payments).

Step 3: Net Change in Cash

COMPARE THE NET CHANGE IN CASH ON THE STATEMENT OF CASH FLOWS WITH THE CHANGE IN THE CASH ACCOUNT REPORTED ON THE BALANCE SHEET TO MAKE SURE THE AMOUNTS AGREE

Illustration 17-13 indicates that the net change in cash during the period was an increase of $22,000. This agrees with the change in Cash account reported on the balance sheet in Illustration 17-4 (page 727).

Before You Go On...

REVIEW IT
1. What is the format of the operating activities section?
2. Where is depreciation expense shown on a statement of cash flows?
3. Where are significant noncash investing and financing activities shown?

DO IT
Use the information on page 735 to prepare a statement of cash flows using the indirect method.

REYNOLDS COMPANY
Comparative Balance Sheets
December 31

Assets	2008	2007	Change Increase/Decrease
Cash	$ 54,000	$ 37,000	$ 17,000 Increase
Accounts receivable	68,000	26,000	42,000 Increase
Inventories	54,000	–0–	54,000 Increase
Prepaid expenses	4,000	6,000	2,000 Decrease
Land	45,000	70,000	25,000 Decrease
Buildings	200,000	200,000	–0–
Accumulated depreciation—buildings	(21,000)	(11,000)	10,000 Increase
Equipment	193,000	68,000	125,000 Increase
Accumulated depreciation—equipment	(28,000)	(10,000)	18,000 Increase
Totals	$569,000	$386,000	

Liabilities and Stockholders' Equity			
Accounts payable	$ 23,000	$ 40,000	$ 17,000 Decrease
Accrued expenses payable	10,000	–0–	10,000 Increase
Bonds payable	110,000	150,000	40,000 Decrease
Common stock ($1 par)	220,000	60,000	160,000 Increase
Retained earnings	206,000	136,000	70,000 Increase
Totals	$569,000	$386,000	

REYNOLDS COMPANY
Income Statement
For the Year Ended December 31, 2008

Revenues		$890,000
Cost of goods sold	$465,000	
Operating expenses	221,000	
Interest expense	12,000	
Loss on sale of equipment	2,000	700,000
Income before income taxes		190,000
Income tax expense		65,000
Net income		$125,000

Additional information:
1. Operating expenses include depreciation expense of $33,000 and charges from prepaid expenses of $2,000.
2. Land was sold at its book value for cash.
3. Cash dividends of $55,000 were declared and paid in 2008.
4. Interest expense of $12,000 was paid in cash.
5. Equipment with a cost of $166,000 was purchased for cash. Equipment with a cost of $41,000 and a book value of $36,000 was sold for $34,000 cash.
6. Bonds of $10,000 were redeemed at their book value for cash. Bonds of $30,000 were converted into common stock.
7. Common stock ($1 par) of $130,000 was issued for cash.
8. Accounts payable pertain to merchandise suppliers.

Action Plan
■ Determine net cash provided/used by operating activities by adjusting net income for items that did not affect cash.

- Determine net cash provided/used by investing activities and financing activities.
- Determine the net increase/decrease in cash.

Solution

REYNOLDS COMPANY
Statement of Cash Flows—Indirect Method
For the Year Ended December 31, 2008

Cash flows from operating activities		
Net income		$125,000
Adjustments to reconcile net income to net cash provided by operating activities:		
Depreciation expense	$ 33,000	
Loss on sale of equipment	2,000	
Increase in accounts receivable	(42,000)	
Increase in inventories	(54,000)	
Decrease in prepaid expenses	2,000	
Decrease in accounts payable	(17,000)	
Increase in accrued expenses payable	10,000	(66,000)
Net cash provided by operating activities		59,000
Cash flows from investing activities		
Sale of land	25,000	
Sale of equipment	34,000	
Purchase of equipment	(166,000)	
Net cash used by investing activities		(107,000)
Cash flows from financing activities		
Redemption of bonds	(10,000)	
Sale of common stock	130,000	
Payment of dividends	(55,000)	
Net cash provided by financing activities		65,000
Net increase in cash		17,000
Cash at beginning of period		37,000
Cash at end of period		$ 54,000
Noncash investing and financing activities		
Conversion of bonds into common stock		$ 30,000

Related exercise material: BE17-4, BE17-5, BE17-6, BE17-7, E17-4, E17-5, and E17-6.

✓ *The Navigator*

USING CASH FLOWS TO EVALUATE A COMPANY

Traditionally, investors and creditors have most commonly used ratios based on accrual accounting. These days, cash-based ratios are gaining increased acceptance among analysts.

Free Cash Flow

In the statement of cash flows, cash provided by operating activities is intended to indicate the cash-generating capability of the company. Analysts have noted, however, that **cash provided by operating activities fails to take into account that a company must invest in new fixed assets** just to maintain its current level of operations. Companies also must at least **maintain dividends at current levels** to satisfy investors. The measurement of free cash flow provides additional insight regarding a company's cash-generating ability. **Free cash flow** describes the cash remaining from operations after adjustment for capital expenditures and dividends.

Consider the following example: Suppose that MPC produced and sold 10,000 personal computers this year. It reported $100,000 cash provided by operating activities. In order to maintain production at 10,000 computers, MPC invested $15,000 in equipment. It chose to pay $5,000 in dividends. Its free cash flow was $80,000 ($100,000 − $15,000 − $5,000). The company could use this $80,000 either to purchase new assets to expand the business or to pay an $80,000 dividend and continue to produce 10,000 computers. In practice, free cash flow is often calculated with the formula in Illustration 17-14. Alternative definitions also exist.

Free Cash Flow	=	Cash Provided by Operating Activities	−	Capital Expenditures	−	Cash Dividends

Illustration 17-14
Free cash flow

Illustration 17-15 provides basic information excerpted from the 2004 statement of cash flows of Microsoft Corporation.

MICROSOFT CORPORATION
Statement of Cash Flows (partial)
2004

Cash provided by operating activities		$14,626
Cash flows from investing activities		
Additions to property and equipment	$ (1,109)	
Purchases of investments	(92,495)	
Sales of investments	85,302	
Acquisitions of companies	(4)	
Maturities of investments	5,561	
Cash used by investing activities		(2,745)
Cash paid for dividends		(1,729)

Illustration 17-15
Microsoft cash flow information ($ in millions)

Microsoft's free cash flow is calculated as shown in Illustration 17-16.

Cash provided by operating activities	$14,626
Less: Expenditures on property, plant, and equipment	1,109
Dividends paid	1,729
Free cash flow	$11,788

Illustration 17-16
Calculation of Microsoft's free cash flow ($ in millions)

This is a tremendous amount of cash generated in a single year. It is available for the acquisition of new assets, the retirement of stock or debt, or the payment of dividends. Also note that this amount far exceeds Microsoft's 2004 net income of $8,168 million. This lends additional credibility to Microsoft's income number as an indicator of potential future performance. If anything, Microsoft's net income might understate its actual performance.

Oracle Corporation is one of the world's largest sellers of database software and information management services. Like Microsoft, its success depends on continuing to improve its existing products while developing new products to keep pace with rapid changes in technology. Oracle's free cash flow for 2004 was $2,988 million. This is impressive, but significantly less than Microsoft's amazing ability to generate cash.

Be sure to read **ALL ABOUT YOU: *Where Does the Money Go?*** on page 738 for information on how topics in this chapter apply to you.

Where Does the Money Go?

When a company's cash flow from operating activities does not cover its cash needs, it must borrow money. In the short term this is OK, but in the long-term it can spell disaster. Sooner or later the company needs to increase its cash from operations or cut back on its expenditures, or it will go broke. Guess what? The same is true for you and me.

Where do you spend your cash? Most of us know how much we spend each month on rent and car payments. But how much do you spend each month on soda, coffee, pizza, video rentals, music downloads, and your cell phone service? Don't think it matters? Suppose you spend an average of only $4 per day on unneeded "incidentals." That's $120 a month, or almost $1,500 per year.

✷ About the Numbers

College students spend an average of $287 per month on discretionary items (defined as anything other than tuition, room/board, rent, books, and school fee A large chunk of that—more than $11 billion—is spent on beverages and snac foods. Maybe this would be a good place to start cutting your expenditures.

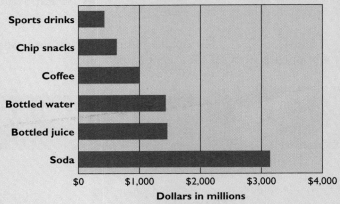

Annual Spending by College Students on Beverages and Snacks

Dollars in millions

Source: "College Students Spend $200 Billion per Year," HarrisInteractive, *www.harrisinteractive.com/news/allnewsbydate.asp?NewsID=480* (accessed May 2006).

✷ Some Facts

* College students spend about $200 billion per year on consumer products. Of that amount, $41 billion is "discretionary" in nature.

* More than 70% of college students own a cell phone, and 71% own a car.

* College students spend more than $8 billion per year purchasing DVDs, CDs, music downloads, and video games.

* Annual spending on travel by college students is about $4.6 billion.

* 78% of college students work, earning an average of $821 per month.

✷ What Do You Think?

Let's say that you live on campus and own a car. You use the car for pleasur and to drive to a job that is three miles away. Suppose your annual cash fl statement includes the following items.

Cash inflows:	
Wages	$ 9,000
Student loans	5,000
Credit card debt	4,000
Cash outflows:	
Tuition, books, room, and board	13,000
Vehicle costs	2,000
Vacation	2,000
Cell phone service	500
Snacks and beverages	500

Should you get rid of your car and cell phone, quit eating snacks, and give the idea of a vacation?

YES: At this rate you will accumulate nearly $40,000 in debts by the tim you graduate. It is not fun to spend most of the paycheck of your post-graduation job paying off the debts you accumulated while in school.

NO: Give me a break. A person has to have some fun. Life wouldn't be worth living if I couldn't be drinking a Starbucks while cruising down the road talking on my cell phone.

Sources: Becky Ebenkamp, "College Communications 101," *Brandweek*, August 22-29, 2005, p.

Before You Go On...

REVIEW IT
1. What is the difference between cash from operations and free cash flow?
2. What does it mean if a company has negative free cash flow?

 The Navigator

Demonstration Problem 1

 WILEY PLUS

The income statement for the year ended December 31, 2008, for John Kosinski Manufacturing Company contains the following condensed information.

JOHN KOSINSKI MANUFACTURING COMPANY
Income Statement

Revenues		$6,583,000
Operating expenses (excluding depreciation)	$4,920,000	
Depreciation expense	880,000	5,800,000
Income before income taxes		783,000
Income tax expense		353,000
Net income		$ 430,000

Included in operating expenses is a $24,000 loss resulting from the sale of machinery for $270,000 cash. Machinery was purchased at a cost of $750,000.

The following balances are reported on Kosinski's comparative balance sheets at December 31.

JOHN KOSINSKI MANUFACTURING COMPANY
Comparative, Balance Sheets (partial)

	2008	**2007**
Cash	$672,000	$130,000
Accounts receivable	775,000	610,000
Inventories	834,000	867,000
Accounts payable	521,000	501,000

Income tax expense of $353,000 represents the amount paid in 2008. Dividends declared and paid in 2008 totaled $200,000.

Instructions

Prepare the statement of cash flows using the indirect method.

Solution to Demonstration Problem 1

JOHN KOSINSKI MANUFACTURING COMPANY
Statement of Cash Flows—Indirect Method
For the Year Ended December 31, 2008

Cash flows from operating activities		
Net income		$ 430,000
Adjustments to reconcile net income to net cash provided by operating activities:		
Depreciation expense	$ 880,000	
Loss on sale of machinery	24,000	
Increase in accounts receivable	(165,000)	
Decrease in inventories	33,000	
Increase in accounts payable	20,000	792,000
Net cash provided by operating activities		1,222,000

action plan

✔ Determine net cash from operating activities. Operating activities generally relate to changes in current assets and current liabilities.

✔ Determine net cash from investing activities. Investing activities generally relate to changes in noncurrent assets.

✔ Determine net cash from financing activities. Financing activities generally relate to changes in long-term liabilities and stockholders' equity accounts.

Cash flows from investing activities			
Sale of machinery		270,000	
Purchase of machinery		(750,000)	
Net cash used by investing activities			(480,000)
Cash flows from financing activities			
Payment of cash dividends			(200,000)
Net increase in cash			542,000
Cash at beginning of period			130,000
Cash at end of period			$ 672,000

The Navigator

SUMMARY OF STUDY OBJECTIVES

1 Indicate the usefulness of the statement of cash flows. The statement of cash flows provides information about the cash receipts, cash payments, and net change in cash resulting from the operating, investing, and financing activities of a company during the period.

2 Distinguish among operating, investing, and financing activities. Operating activities include the cash effects of transactions that enter into the determination of net income. Investing activities involve cash flows resulting from changes in investments and long-term asset items. Financing activities involve cash flows resulting from changes in long-term liability and stockholders' equity items.

3 Prepare a statement of cash flows using the indirect method. The preparation of a statement of cash flows involves three major steps: (1) Determine net cash provided/used by operating activities by converting net income from an accrual basis to a cash basis. (2) Analyze changes in noncurrent asset and liability accounts and record as investing and financing activities, or disclose as noncash transactions. (3) Compare the net change in cash on the statement of cash flows with the change in the cash account reported on the balance sheet to make sure the amounts agree.

4 Analyze the statement of cash flows. Free cash flow indicates the amount of cash a company generated during the current year that is available for the payment of additional dividends or for expansion.

The Navigator

GLOSSARY

Direct method A method of determining net cash provided by operating activities by adjusting each item in the income statement from the accrual basis to the cash basis. (p. 726)

Financing activities Cash flow activities that include (a) obtaining cash from issuing debt and repaying the amounts borrowed and (b) obtaining cash from stockholders, repurchasing shares, and paying dividends. (p. 721).

Free cash flow Cash provided by operating activities adjusted for capital expenditures and dividends paid. (p. 737).

Indirect method A method of preparing a statement of cash flows in which net income is adjusted for items that do not affect cash, to determine net cash provided by operating activities. (pp. 725, 728).

Investing activities Cash flow activities that include (a) purchasing and disposing of investments and property, plant, and equipment using cash and (b) lending money and collecting the loans. (p. 721).

Operating activities Cash flow activities that include the cash effects of transactions that create revenues and expenses and thus enter into the determination of net income. (p. 721).

Statement of cash flows A basic financial statement that provides information about the cash receipts, cash payments, and net change in cash during a period, resulting from operating, investing, and financing activities. (p. 720).

APPENDIX 17A Using a Worksheet to Prepare the Statement of Cash Flows—Indirect Method

When preparing a statement of cash flows, companies may need to make numerous adjustments of net income. In such cases, they often use **a worksheet to assemble and classify the data that will appear on the statement**. The worksheet is merely an aid in preparing the statement. Its use is optional. Illustration 17A-1 shows the skeleton format of the worksheet for preparation of the statement of cash flows.

STUDY OBJECTIVE 5

Explain how to use a worksheet to prepare the statement of cash flows using the indirect method.

XYZ Company.xls

File   Edit   View   Insert   Format   Tools   Data   Window   Help

	A	B	C	D	E
1		**XYZ COMPANY**			
2					
3		Worksheet			
4		Statement of Cash Flows For the Year Ended . . .			
5					
6		**End of Last Year Balances**	**Reconciling Items**		**End of Current Year Balances**
7					
8	**Balance Sheet Accounts**		**Debit**	**Credit**	
9	Debit balance accounts	XX	XX	XX	XX
10		XX	XX	XX	XX
11	Totals	XXX			XXX
12	Credit balance accounts	XX	XX	XX	XX
13		XX	XX	XX	XX
14	Totals	XXX			XXX
15	**Statement of Cash**				
16	**Flows Effects**				
17	Operating activities				
18	Net income		XX		
19	Adjustments to net income		XX	XX	
20	Investing activities				
21	Receipts and payments		XX	XX	
22	Financing activities				
23	Receipts and payments		XX	XX	
24	Totals		XXX	XXX	
25	Increase (decrease) in cash		(XX)	XX	
26	Totals		XXX	XXX	
27					

Illustration 17A-1
Format of worksheet

The following guidelines are important in preparing a worksheet.

1. In the balance sheet accounts section, **list accounts with debit balances separately from those with credit balances**. This means, for example, that Accumulated Depreciation appears under credit balances and not as a contra account under debit balances. Enter the beginning and ending balances of each account in the appropriate columns. Enter as reconciling items in the two middle columns the transactions that caused the change in the account balance during the year.

    After all reconciling items have been entered, each line pertaining to a balance sheet account should "foot across." That is, the beginning balance plus or minus the reconciling item(s) must equal the ending balance. When this agreement exists for all balance sheet accounts, all changes in account balances have been reconciled.

2. The bottom portion of the worksheet consists of the operating, investing, and financing activities sections. It provides the information necessary to prepare the formal statement of cash flows. **Enter inflows of cash as debits in the reconciling columns. Enter outflows of cash as credits in the reconciling columns.** Thus, in this section, the sale of equipment for cash at book value appears as a debit under investing activities. Similarly, the purchase of land for cash appears as a credit under investing activities.

3. **The reconciling items shown in the worksheet are not entered in any journal or posted to any account.** They do not represent either adjustments or corrections of the balance sheet accounts. They are used only to facilitate the preparation of the statement of cash flows.

Preparing the Worksheet

As in the case of worksheets illustrated in earlier chapters, preparing a worksheet involves a series of prescribed steps. The steps in this case are:

1. Enter in the balance sheet accounts section the balance sheet accounts and their beginning and ending balances.

2. Enter in the reconciling columns of the worksheet the data that explain the changes in the balance sheet accounts other than cash and their effects on the statement of cash flows.

3. Enter on the cash line and at the bottom of the worksheet the increase or decrease in cash. This entry should enable the totals of the reconciling columns to be in agreement.

To illustrate the preparation of a worksheet, we will use the 2008 data for Computer Services Company. Your familiarity with these data (from the chapter) should help you understand the use of a worksheet. For ease of reference, the comparative balance sheets, income statement, and selected data for 2008 are presented in Illustration 17A-2 (on page 743).

DETERMINING THE RECONCILING ITEMS

Companies can use one of several approaches to determine the reconciling items. For example, they can first complete the changes affecting net cash provided by operating activities, and then can determine the effects of financing and investing transactions. Or, they can analyze the balance sheet accounts in the order in which they are listed on the worksheet. We will follow this latter approach for Computer Services, except for cash. As indicated in step 3, **cash is handled last**.

Accounts Receivable   The decrease of $10,000 in accounts receivable means that cash collections from revenues are higher than the revenues reported in the income statement. To convert net income to net cash provided by operating activities, we add the decrease of $10,000 to net income. The entry in the reconciling columns of the worksheet is:

(a)	Operating—Decrease in Accounts Receivable	10,000	
	Accounts Receivable		10,000

Merchandise Inventory   Computer Services Company's Merchandise Inventory balance increases $5,000 during the period. The Merchandise Inventory account reflects the difference between the amount of inventory that the company purchased and the amount that it sold. For Computer Services this means that the cost of merchandise purchased exceeds the cost of goods sold by $5,000. As a

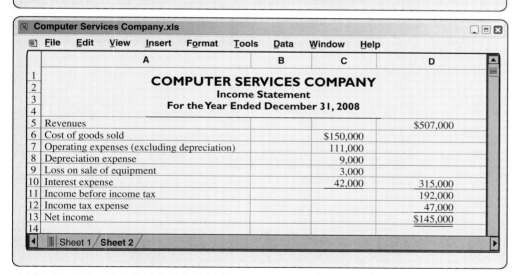

Illustration 17A-2
Comparative balance sheets, income statement, and additional information for Computer Services Company

Computer Services Company.xls

File Edit View Insert Format Tools Data Window Help

	A	B	C	D
1	COMPUTER SERVICES COMPANY			
2	Comparative Balance Sheets			
3	December 31			
4				**Change in Account Balance Increase/Decrease**
5				
6	**Assets**	**2008**	**2007**	
7	Current assets			
8	Cash	$ 55,000	$ 33,000	$ 22,000 Increase
9	Accounts receivable	20,000	30,000	10,000 Decrease
10	Merchandise inventory	15,000	10,000	5,000 Increase
11	Prepaid expenses	5,000	1,000	4,000 Increase
12	Property, plant, and equipment			
13	Land	130,000	20,000	110,000 Increase
14	Building	160,000	40,000	120,000 Increase
15	Accumulated depreciation—building	(11,000)	(5,000)	6,000 Increase
16	Equipment	27,000	10,000	17,000 Increase
17	Accumulated depreciation—equipment	(3,000)	(1,000)	2,000 Increase
18	Total	$398,000	$138,000	
19				
20	**Liabilities and Stockholders' Equity**			
21	Current liabilities			
22	Accounts payable	$ 28,000	$ 12,000	$ 16,000 Increase
23	Income tax payable	6,000	8,000	2,000 Decrease
24	Long-term liabilities			
25	Bonds payable	130,000	20,000	110,000 Increase
26	Stockholders' equity			
27	Common stock	70,000	50,000	20,000 Increase
28	Retained earnings	164,000	48,000	116,000 Increase
29	Total liabilities and stockholders' equity	$398,000	$138,000	

Sheet 1 Sheet 2

Computer Services Company.xls

File Edit View Insert Format Tools Data Window Help

	A	B	C	D
1	COMPUTER SERVICES COMPANY			
2	Income Statement			
3	For the Year Ended December 31, 2008			
4				
5	Revenues			$507,000
6	Cost of goods sold		$150,000	
7	Operating expenses (excluding depreciation)		111,000	
8	Depreciation expense		9,000	
9	Loss on sale of equipment		3,000	
10	Interest expense		42,000	315,000
11	Income before income tax			192,000
12	Income tax expense			47,000
13	Net income			$145,000
14				

Sheet 1 Sheet 2

Additional information for 2008:
1. The company declared and paid a $29,000 cash dividend.
2. Issued $110,000 of long-term bonds in direct exchange for land.
3. A building costing $120,000 was purchased for cash. Equipment costing $25,000 was also purchased for cash.
4. The company sold equipment with a book value of $7,000 (cost $8,000, less accumulated depreciation $1,000) for $4,000 cash.
5. Issued common stock for $20,000 cash.
6. Depreciation expense was comprised of $6,000 for building and $3,000 for equipment.

result, cost of goods sold does not reflect $5,000 of cash payments made for merchandise. We deduct this inventory increase of $5,000 during the period from net income to arrive at net cash provided by operating activities. The worksheet entry is:

(b)	Merchandise Inventory	5,000	
	Operating—Increase in Merchandise Inventory		5,000

Prepaid Expenses An increase of $4,000 in prepaid expenses means that expenses deducted in determining net income are less than expenses that were paid in cash. We deduct the increase of $4,000 from net income in determining net cash provided by operating activities. The worksheet entry is:

(c)	Prepaid Expenses	4,000	
	Operating—Increase in Prepaid Expenses		4,000

HELPFUL HINT
These amounts are asterisked in the worksheet to indicate that they result from a significant noncash transaction.

Land The increase in land of $110,000 resulted from a purchase through the issuance of long-term bonds. The company should report this transaction as a significant noncash investing and financing activity. The worksheet entry is:

(d)	Land	110,000	
	Bonds Payable		110,000

Building The cash purchase of a building for $120,000 is an investing activity cash outflow. The entry in the reconciling columns of the worksheet is:

(e)	Building	120,000	
	Investing—Purchase of Building		120,000

Equipment The increase in equipment of $17,000 resulted from a cash purchase of $25,000 and the sale of equipment costing $8,000. The book value of the equipment was $7,000, the cash proceeds were $4,000, and a loss of $3,000 was recorded. The worksheet entries are:

(f)	Equipment	25,000	
	Investing—Purchase of Equipment		25,000

(g)	Investing—Sale of Equipment	4,000	
	Operating—Loss on Sale of Equipment	3,000	
	Accumulated Depreciation—Equipment	1,000	
	Equipment		8,000

Accounts Payable We must add the increase of $16,000 in accounts payable to net income to determine net cash provided by operating activities. The worksheet entry is:

(h)	Operating—Increase in Accounts Payable	16,000	
	Accounts Payable		16,000

Income Taxes Payable When a company incurs income tax expense but has not yet paid its taxes, it records income tax payable. A change in the Income Tax Payable account reflects the difference between income tax expense incurred and income tax actually paid. Computer Services' Income Tax Payable account decreases by $2,000. That means the $47,000 of income tax expense reported on the income statement was $2,000 less than the amount of taxes paid during the period of $49,000. To adjust net income to a cash basis, we must reduce net income by $2,000. The worksheet entry is:

(i)	Income Taxes Payable	2,000	
	Operating—Decrease in Income Taxes		
	Payable		2,000

Bonds Payable   The increase of $110,000 in this account resulted from the issuance of bonds for land. This is a significant noncash investing and financing activity. Worksheet entry (d) above is the only entry necessary.

Common Stock   The balance sheet reports an increase in Common Stock of $20,000. The additional information section notes that this increase resulted from the issuance of new shares of stock. This is a cash inflow reported in the financing section. The worksheet entry is:

| (j) | Financing—Issuance of Common Stock | 20,000 | |
| | Common Stock | | 20,000 |

Accumulated Depreciation—Building, and Accumulated Depreciation—Equipment   Increases in these accounts of $6,000 and $3,000, respectively, resulted from depreciation expense. Depreciation expense is a **noncash charge that we must add to net income** to determine net cash provided by operating activities. The worksheet entries are:

| (k) | Operating—Depreciation Expense—Building | 6,000 | |
| | Accumulated Depreciation—Building | | 6,000 |

| (l) | Operating—Depreciation Expense—Equipment | 3,000 | |
| | Accumulated Depreciation—Equipment | | 3,000 |

Retained Earnings   The $116,000 increase in retained earnings resulted from net income of $145,000 and the declaration and payment of a $29,000 cash dividend. Net income is included in net cash provided by operating activities, and the dividends are a financing activity cash outflow. The entries in the reconciling columns of the worksheet are:

| (m) | Operating—Net Income | 145,000 | |
| | Retained Earnings | | 145,000 |

| (n) | Retained Earnings | 29,000 | |
| | Financing—Payment of Dividends | | 29,000 |

Disposition of Change in Cash   The firm's cash increased $22,000 in 2008. The final entry on the worksheet, therefore, is:

| (o) | Cash | 22,000 | |
| | Increase in Cash | | 22,000 |

As shown in the worksheet, we enter the increase in cash in the reconciling credit column as a **balancing** amount. This entry should complete the reconciliation of the changes in the balance sheet accounts. Also, it should permit the totals of the reconciling columns to be in agreement. When all changes have been explained and the reconciling columns are in agreement, the reconciling columns are ruled to complete the worksheet. The completed worksheet for Computer Services Company is shown in Illustration 17A-3 (page 746).

Illustration 17A-3
Completed worksheet—
indirect method

☒ Computer Services Company.xls ▢◨☒

🗐 File   Edit   View   Insert   Format   Tools   Data   Window   Help

	A	B	C		D	E
1	COMPUTER SERVICES COMPANY					
2	Worksheet					
3	Statement of Cash Flows For the Year Ended December 31, 2008					
4						
5		Balance	Reconciling Items			Balance
6	Balance Sheet Accounts	12/31/07	Debit		Credit	12/31/08
7	Debits					
8	Cash	33,000	(o) 22,000			55,000
9	Accounts Receivable	30,000		(a)	10,000	20,000
10	Merchandise Inventory	10,000	(b) 5,000			15,000
11	Prepaid Expenses	1,000	(c) 4,000			5,000
12	Land	20,000	(d) 110,000*			130,000
13	Building	40,000	(e) 120,000			160,000
14	Equipment	10,000	(f) 25,000	(g)	8,000	27,000
15	Total	144,000				412,000
16	Credits					
17	Accounts Payable	12,000		(h)	16,000	28,000
18	Income Taxes Payable	8,000	(i) 2,000			6,000
19	Bonds Payable	20,000		(d)	110,000*	130,000
20	Accumulated Depreciation—Building	5,000		(k)	6,000	11,000
21	Accumulated Depreciation—Equipment	1,000	(g) 1,000	(l)	3,000	3,000
22	Common Stock	50,000		(j)	20,000	70,000
23	Retained Earnings	48,000	(n) 29,000	(m)	145,000	164,000
24	Total	144,000				412,000
25	**Statement of Cash Flows Effects**					
26	Operating activities					
27	Net income		(m) 145,000			
28	Decrease in accounts receivable		(a) 10,000			
29	Increase in merchandise inventory			(b)	5,000	
30	Increase in prepaid expenses			(c)	4,000	
31	Increase in accounts payable		(h) 16,000			
32	Decrease in income taxes payable			(i)	2,000	
33	Depreciation expense—building		(k) 6,000			
34	Depreciation expense—equipment		(l) 3,000			
35	Loss on sale of equipment		(g) 3,000			
36	Investing activities					
37	Purchase of building			(e)	120,000	
38	Purchase of equipment			(f)	25,000	
39	Sale of equipment		(g) 4,000			
40	Financing activities					
41	Issuance of common stock		(j) 20,000			
42	Payment of dividends			(n)	29,000	
43	Totals		525,000		503,000	
44	Increase in cash			(o)	22,000	
45	Totals		525,000		525,000	
46						

* Significant noncash investing and financing activity.

◀ ||| ▶

SUMMARY OF STUDY OBJECTIVE FOR APPENDIX 17A

5 Explain how to use a worksheet to prepare the statement of cash flows using the indirect method. When there are numerous adjustments, a worksheet can be a helpful tool in preparing the statement of cash flows. Key guidelines for using a worksheet are: (1) List accounts with debit balances separately from those with credit balances. (2) In the reconciling columns in the bottom portion of the worksheet, show cash inflows as debits and cash outflows as credits. (3) Do not enter reconciling items in any journal or account, but use them only to help prepare the statement of cash flows.

The steps in preparing the worksheet are: (1) Enter beginning and ending balances of balance sheet accounts. (2) Enter debits and credits in reconciling columns. (3) Enter the increase or decrease in cash in two places as a balancing amount.

APPENDIX 17B **Statement of Cash Flows— Direct Method**

To explain and illustrate the direct method, we will use the transactions of Juarez Company for 2008, to prepare a statement of cash flows. Illustration 17B-1 presents information related to 2008 for Juarez Company.

STUDY OBJECTIVE 6

Prepare a statement of cash flows using the direct method.

Illustration 17B-1
Comparative balance sheets, income statement, and additional information for Juarez Company

JUAREZ COMPANY
Comparative Balance Sheets
December 31

Assets	2008	2007	Change Increase/Decrease
Cash	$191,000	$159,000	$ 32,000 Increase
Accounts receivable	12,000	15,000	3,000 Decrease
Inventory	170,000	160,000	10,000 Increase
Prepaid expenses	6,000	8,000	2,000 Decrease
Land	140,000	80,000	60,000 Increase
Equipment	160,000	–0–	160,000 Increase
Accumulated depreciation—equipment	(16,000)	–0–	16,000 Increase
Total	$663,000	$422,000	

Liabilities and Stockholders' Equity			
Accounts payable	$ 52,000	$ 60,000	$ 8,000 Decrease
Accrued expenses payable	15,000	20,000	5,000 Decrease
Income taxes payable	12,000	–0–	12,000 Increase
Bonds payable	130,000	–0–	130,000 Increase
Common stock	360,000	300,000	60,000 Increase
Retained earnings	94,000	42,000	52,000 Increase
Total	$663,000	$422,000	

JUAREZ COMPANY
Income Statement
For the Year Ended December 31, 2008

Revenues		$975,000
Cost of goods sold	$660,000	
Operating expenses (excluding depreciation)	176,000	
Depreciation expense	18,000	
Loss on sale of store equipment	1,000	855,000
Income before income taxes		120,000
Income tax expense		36,000
Net income		$ 84,000

Additional information:
1. In 2008, the company declared and paid a $32,000 cash dividend.
2. Bonds were issued at face value for $130,000 in cash.
3. Equipment costing $180,000 was purchased for cash.
4. Equipment costing $20,000 was sold for $17,000 cash when the book value of the equipment was $18,000.
5. Common stock of $60,000 was issued to acquire land.

Preparing the Statement of Cash Flows—Direct Method

To prepare a statement of cash flows under the direct approach, we will apply the three steps outlined in Illustration 17-3 (page 725).

STEP 1: OPERATING ACTIVITIES

DETERMINE NET CASH PROVIDED/USED BY OPERATING ACTIVITIES BY CONVERTING NET INCOME FROM AN ACCRUAL BASIS TO A CASH BASIS

Under the **direct method**, companies compute net cash provided by operating activities by **adjusting each item in the income statement** from the accrual basis to the cash basis. To simplify and condense the operating activities section, companies **report only major classes of operating cash receipts and cash payments**. For these major classes, the difference between cash receipts and cash payments is the net cash provided by operating activities. These relationships are as shown in Illustration 17B-2.

Illustration 17B-2
Major classes of cash receipts and payments

Cash Receipts — Cash Payments = Net Cash Provided by Operating Activities

From sales of goods and services to customers

From receipts of interest and dividends on loans and investments

To suppliers

To employees

For operating expenses

For interest

For taxes

Net cash provided by operating activities

An efficient way to apply the direct method is to analyze the items reported in the income statement in the order in which they are listed. We then determine cash receipts and cash payments related to these revenues and expenses. The following pages present the adjustments required to prepare a statement of cash flows for Juarez Company using the direct approach.

Cash Receipts From Customers. The income statement for Juarez Company reported revenues from customers of $975,000. How much of that was cash receipts? To answer that, companies need to consider the change in accounts receivable during the year. When accounts receivable increase during the year, revenues on an accrual basis are higher than cash receipts from customers. Operations led to revenues, but not all of these revenues resulted in cash receipts.

To determine the amount of cash receipts, the company deducts from sales revenues the increase in accounts receivable. On the other hand, there may be a decrease in accounts receivable. That would occur if cash receipts from customers exceeded sales revenues. In that case, the company adds to sales revenues the decrease in accounts receivable.

For Juarez Company, accounts receivable decreased $3,000. Thus, cash receipts from customers were $978,000, computed as shown in Illustration 17B-3.

Revenues from sales	$ 975,000
Add: Decrease in accounts receivable	3,000
Cash receipts from customers	**$ 978,000**

Illustration 17B-3
Computation of cash receipts from customers

Juarez can also determine cash receipts from customers from an analysis of the Accounts Receivable account, as shown in Illustration 17B-4.

Accounts Receivable

1/1/08	Balance	15,000	**Receipts from customers**	**978,000**
	Revenues from sales	975,000		
12/31/08	Balance	12,000		

Illustration 17B-4
Analysis of accounts receivable

HELPFUL HINT
The T account shows that revenue plus decrease in receivables equals cash receipts.

Illustration 17B-5 shows the relationships among cash receipts from customers, revenues from sales, and changes in accounts receivable.

Cash Receipts from Customers	=	Revenues from Sales	+ Decrease in Accounts Receivable or − Increase in Accounts Receivable

Illustration 17B-5
Formula to compute cash receipts from customers—direct method

Cash Payments to Suppliers.   Juarez Company reported cost of goods sold of $660,000 on its income statement. How much of that was cash payments to suppliers? To answer that, it is first necessary to find purchases for the year. To find purchases, companies adjust cost of goods sold for the change in inventory. When inventory increases during the year, purchases for the year have exceeded cost of goods sold. As a result, to determine the amount of purchases, the company adds to cost of goods sold the increase in inventory.

In 2008, Juarez Company's inventory increased $10,000. It computes purchases as follows.

Cost of goods sold	$660,000
Add: Increase in inventory	10,000
Purchases	**$670,000**

Illustration 17B-6
Computation of purchases

After computing purchases, a company can determine cash payments to suppliers. This is done by adjusting purchases for the change in accounts payable.

When accounts payable increase during the year, purchases on an accrual basis are higher than they are on a cash basis. As a result, to determine cash payments to suppliers, a company deducts from purchases the increase in accounts payable. On the other hand, if cash payments to suppliers exceed purchases, there will be a decrease in accounts payable. In that case, a company adds to purchases the decrease in accounts payable.

For Juarez Company, cash payments to suppliers were $678,000, computed as follows.

Illustration 17B-7
Computation of cash payments to suppliers

Purchases	$670,000
Add: Decrease in accounts payable	8,000
Cash payments to suppliers	**$678,000**

Juarez also can determine cash payments to suppliers from an analysis of the Accounts Payable account, as shown in Illustration 17B-8.

Illustration 17B-8
Analysis of accounts payable

Accounts Payable

Payments to suppliers	**678,000**	1/1/08	Balance	60,000
			Purchases	670,000
		12/31/08	Balance	52,000

HELPFUL HINT
The T account shows that purchases plus decrease in accounts payable equals payments to suppliers.

Illustration 17B-9 shows the relationships among cash payments to suppliers, cost of goods sold, changes in inventory, and changes in accounts payable.

Illustration 17B-9
Formula to compute cash payments to suppliers—direct method

Cash Payments for Operating Expenses. Juarez reported on its income statement operating expenses of $176,000. How much of that amount was cash paid for operating expenses? To answer that, we need to adjust this amount for any changes in prepaid expenses and accrued expenses payable. For example, if prepaid expenses increased during the year, cash paid for operating expenses is higher than operating expenses reported on the income statement. To convert operating expenses to cash payments for operating expenses, a company adds the increase to operating expenses. On the other hand, if prepaid expenses decrease during the year, it deducts the decrease from operating expenses.

Companies must also adjust operating expenses for changes in accrued expenses payable. When accrued expenses payable increase during the year, operating expenses on an accrual basis are higher than they are in a cash basis. As a result, to determine cash payments for operating expenses, a company deducts from operating expenses an increase in accrued expenses payable. On the other hand, a company adds to operating expenses a decrease in accrued expenses payable because cash payments exceed operating expenses.

Juarez Company's cash payments for operating expenses were $179,000, computed as follows.

Operating expenses	$176,000
Deduct: Decrease in prepaid expenses	(2,000)
Add: Decrease in accrued expenses payable	5,000
Cash payments for operating expenses	**$179,000**

Illustration 17B-10
Computation of cash payments for operating expenses

Illustration 17B-11 shows the relationships among cash payments for operating expenses, changes in prepaid expenses, and changes in accrued expenses payable.

| Cash Payments for Operating Expenses | = | Operating Expenses | { | + Increase in Prepaid Expense or − Decrease in Prepaid Expense | } | { | + Decrease in Accrued Expenses Payable or − Increase in Accrued Expenses Payable | } |

Illustration 17B-11
Formula to compute cash payments for operating expenses—direct method

Depreciation Expense and Loss on Sale of Equipment. Companies show operating expenses exclusive of depreciation. Juarez's depreciation expense in 2008 was $18,000. Depreciation expense is not shown on a statement of cash flows because it is a noncash charge. If the amount for operating expenses includes depreciation expense, the company must reduce operating expenses by the amount of depreciation to determine cash payments for operating expenses.

The loss on sale of equipment of $1,000 is also a noncash charge. The loss on sale of equipment reduces net income, but it does not reduce cash. Thus, companies do not report on a statement of cash flows the loss on sale of equipment.

Other charges to expense that do not require the use of cash, such as the amortization of intangible assets, depletion expense, and bad debt expense, are treated in the same manner as depreciation.

Cash Payments For Income Taxes. Juarez reported income tax expense of $36,000 on the income statement. Income taxes payable, however, increased $12,000. This increase means that the company has not yet paid $12,000 of the income taxes. As a result, income taxes paid were less than income taxes reported in the income statement. Cash payments for income taxes were, therefore, $24,000 as shown below.

Income tax expense	$36,000
Deduct: Increase in income taxes payable	12,000
Cash payments for income taxes	**$24,000**

Illustration 17B-12
Computation of cash payments for income taxes

Illustration 17B-13 shows the relationships among cash payments for income taxes, income tax expense, and changes in income taxes payable.

| Cash Payments for Income Taxes | = | Income Tax Expense | { | + Decrease in Income Taxes Payable or − Increase in Income Taxes Payable | } |

Illustration 17B-13
Formula to compute cash payments for income taxes—direct method

The operating activities section of the statement of cash flows of Juarez Company is shown in Illustration 17B-14.

Illustration 17B-14
Operating activities section of the statement of cash flows

Cash flows from operating activities		
Cash receipts from customers		$978,000
Less: Cash payments:		
To suppliers	$678,000	
For operating expenses	179,000	
For income taxes	24,000	881,000
Net cash provided by operating activities		$ 97,000

When a company uses the direct method, it must also provide in a **separate schedule** (not shown here) the net cash flows from operating activities as computed under the indirect method.

STEP 2: INVESTING AND FINANCING ACTIVITIES

ANALYZE CHANGES IN NONCURRENT ASSET AND LIABILITY ACCOUNTS AND RECORD AS INVESTING AND FINANCING ACTIVITIES, OR AS SIGNIFICANT NONCASH TRANSACTIONS

Increase in Land. Juarez's land increased $60,000. The additional information section indicates that the company issued common stock to purchase the land. The issuance of common stock for land has no effect on cash. But it is a **significant noncash investing and financing transaction**. This transaction requires disclosure in a separate schedule at the bottom of the statement of cash flows.

Increase in Equipment. The comparative balance sheets show that equipment increased $160,000 in 2008. The additional information in Illustration 17B-1 indicated that the increase resulted from two investing transactions: (1) Juarez purchased for cash equipment costing $180,000. And (2) it sold for $17,000 cash equipment costing $20,000, whose book value was $18,000. The relevant data for the statement of cash flows is the cash paid for the purchase and the cash proceeds from the sale. For Juarez Company, the investing activities section will show the following: The $180,000 purchase of equipment as an outflow of cash, and the $17,000 sale of equipment as an inflow of cash. The company **should not net** the two amounts. **Both individual outflows and inflows of cash should be shown.**

The analysis of the changes in equipment should include the related Accumulated Depreciation account. These two accounts for Juarez Company are shown in Illustration 17B-15.

Illustration 17B-15
Analysis of equipment and related accumulated depreciation

Equipment				
1/1/08	Balance	–0–	Cost of equipment sold	20,000
	Cash purchase	**180,000**		
12/31/08	Balance	160,000		

Accumulated Depreciation—Equipment				
Sale of equipment	2,000	1/1/08	Balance	–0–
			Depreciation expense	18,000
		12/31/08	Balance	16,000

Increase in Bonds Payable. Bonds Payable increased $130,000. The additional information in Illustration 17B-1 indicated that Juarez issued, for $130,000 cash, bonds with a face value of $130,000. The issuance of bonds is a financing activity. For Juarez Company, there is an inflow of cash of $130,000 from the issuance of bonds.

Increase in Common Stock. The Common Stock account increased $60,000. The additional information indicated that Juarez acquired land from the issuance of common stock. This transaction is a **significant noncash investing and financing transaction** which the company should report separately at the bottom of the statement.

Increase in Retained Earnings. The $52,000 net increase in Retained Earnings resulted from net income of $84,000 and the declaration and payment of a cash dividend of $32,000. Companies **do not report net income in the statement of cash flows under the direct method**. Cash dividends paid of $32,000 are reported in the financing activities section as an outflow of cash.

Statement of Cash Flows—2008   Illustration 17B-16 shows the statement of cash flows for Juarez.

<table>
<tr><td colspan="3">JUAREZ COMPANY
Statement of Cash Flows—Direct Method
For the Year Ended December 31, 2008</td></tr>
<tr><td>Cash flows from operating activities</td><td></td><td></td></tr>
<tr><td>Cash receipts from customers</td><td></td><td>$ 978,000</td></tr>
<tr><td>Less: Cash payments:</td><td></td><td></td></tr>
<tr><td>To suppliers</td><td>$ 678,000</td><td></td></tr>
<tr><td>For operating expenses</td><td>179,000</td><td></td></tr>
<tr><td>For income taxes</td><td>24,000</td><td>881,000</td></tr>
<tr><td>Net cash provided by operating activities</td><td></td><td>97,000</td></tr>
<tr><td>Cash flows from investing activities</td><td></td><td></td></tr>
<tr><td>Purchase of equipment</td><td>(180,000)</td><td></td></tr>
<tr><td>Sale of equipment</td><td>17,000</td><td></td></tr>
<tr><td>Net cash used by investing activities</td><td></td><td>(163,000)</td></tr>
<tr><td>Cash flows from financing activities</td><td></td><td></td></tr>
<tr><td>Issuance of bonds payable</td><td>130,000</td><td></td></tr>
<tr><td>Payment of cash dividends</td><td>(32,000)</td><td></td></tr>
<tr><td>Net cash provided by financing activities</td><td></td><td>98,000</td></tr>
<tr><td>Net increase in cash</td><td></td><td>32,000</td></tr>
<tr><td>Cash at beginning of period</td><td></td><td>159,000</td></tr>
<tr><td>Cash at end of period</td><td></td><td>$ 191,000</td></tr>
<tr><td>Noncash investing and financing activities</td><td></td><td></td></tr>
<tr><td>Issuance of common stock to purchase land</td><td></td><td>$ 60,000</td></tr>
</table>

Illustration 17B-16
Statement of cash flows, 2008—direct method

STEP 3: NET CHANGE IN CASH

COMPARE THE NET CHANGE IN CASH ON THE STATEMENT OF CASH FLOWS WITH THE CHANGE IN THE CASH ACCOUNT REPORTED ON THE BALANCE SHEET TO MAKE SURE THE AMOUNTS AGREE

Illustration 17B-16 indicates that the net change in cash during the period was an increase of $32,000. This agrees with the change in balances in the cash account reported on the balance sheets in Illustration 17B-1 (page 747).

6 Prepare a statement of cash flows using the direct method. The preparation of the statement of cash flows involves three major steps: (1) Determine net cash provided/ used by operating activities by converting net income from an accrual basis to a cash basis. (2) Analyze changes in noncurrent asset and liability accounts and record as investing and financing activities, or disclose as noncash transactions. (3) Compare the net change in cash on the statement of cash flows with the change in the cash account reported on the balance sheet to make sure the amounts agree. The direct method reports cash receipts less cash payments to arrive at net cash provided by operating activities.

GLOSSARY FOR APPENDIX 17B

Direct method A method of determining net cash provided by operating activities by adjusting each item in the income statement from the accrual basis to the cash basis. (pp. 748)

Demonstration Problem 2

The income statement for Kosinski Manufacturing Company contains the following condensed information.

KOSINSKI MANUFACTURING COMPANY
Income Statement
For the Year Ended December 31, 2008

Revenues		$6,583,000
Operating expenses, excluding depreciation	$4,920,000	
Depreciation expense	880,000	5,800,000
Income before income taxes		783,000
Income tax expense		353,000
Net income		$ 430,000

Included in operating expenses is a $24,000 loss resulting from the sale of machinery for $270,000 cash. Machinery was purchased at a cost of $750,000. The following balances are reported on Kosinski's comparative balance sheet at December 31.

	2008	2007
Cash	$672,000	$130,000
Accounts receivable	775,000	610,000
Inventories	834,000	867,000
Accounts payable	521,000	501,000

Income tax expense of $353,000 represents the amount paid in 2008. Dividends declared and paid in 2008 totaled $200,000.

Instructions

Prepare the statement of cash flows using the direct method.

KOSINSKI MANUFACTURING COMPANY
Statement of Cash Flows—Direct Method
For the Year Ended December 31, 2008

Cash flows from operating activities		
Cash collections from customers		$6,418,000*
Cash payments:		
For operating expenses	$4,843,000**	
For income taxes	353,000	5,196,000
Net cash provided by operating activities		1,222,000
Cash flows from investing activities		
Sale of machinery	270,000	
Purchase of machinery	(750,000)	
Net cash used by investing activities		(480,000)
Cash flows from financing activities		
Payment of cash dividends	(200,000)	
Net cash used by financing activities		(200,000)
Net increase in cash		542,000
Cash at beginning of period		130,000
Cash at end of period		$ 672,000

Direct-Method Computations:

*Computation of cash collections from customers:		
Revenues per the income statement		$6,583,000
Deduct: Increase in accounts receivable		(165,000)
Cash collections from customers		$6,418,000
**Computation of cash payments for operating expenses:		
Operating expenses per the income statement		$4,920,000
Deduct: Loss from sale of machinery		(24,000)
Deduct: Decrease in inventories		(33,000)
Deduct: Increase in accounts payable		(20,000)
Cash payments for operating expenses		$4,843,000

action plan

✔ Determine net cash from operating activities. Each item in the income statement must be adjusted to the cash basis.

✔ Determine net cash from investing activities. Investing activities generally relate to changes in noncurrent assets.

✔ Determine net cash from financing activities. Financing activities generally relate to changes in long-term liabilities and stockholders' equity accounts.

Note: All Questions, Exercises, and Problems marked with an asterisk relate to material in the appendices to the chapter.

SELF-STUDY QUESTIONS

Answers are at the end of the chapter.

1) **1.** Which of the following is *incorrect* about the statement of cash flows?
   a. It is a fourth basic financial statement.
   b. It provides information about cash receipts and cash payments of an entity during a period.
   c. It reconciles the ending cash account balance to the balance per the bank statement.
   d. It provides information about the operating, investing, and financing activities of the business.

2) **2.** The statement of cash flows classifies cash receipts and cash payments by these activities:
   a. operating and nonoperating.
   b. investing, financing, and operating.
   c. financing, operating, and nonoperating.
   d. investing, financing, and nonoperating.

3. Which is an example of a cash flow from an operating (SO 2) activity?
   a. Payment of cash to lenders for interest.
   b. Receipt of cash from the sale of capital stock.
   c. Payment of cash dividends to the company's stock-holders.
   d. None of the above.

4. Which is an example of a cash flow from an investing (SO 2) activity?
   a. Receipt of cash from the issuance of bonds payable.
   b. Payment of cash to repurchase outstanding capital stock.

c. Receipt of cash from the sale of equipment.
d. Payment of cash to suppliers for inventory.

(SO 2) 5. Cash dividends paid to stockholders are classified on the statement of cash flows as:
a. operating activities.
b. investing activities.
c. a combination of (a) and (b).
d. financing activities.

(SO 2) 6. Which is an example of a cash flow from a financing activity?
a. Receipt of cash from sale of land.
b. Issuance of debt for cash.
c. Purchase of equipment for cash.
d. None of the above

(SO 2) 7. Which of the following is *incorrect* about the statement of cash flows?
a. The direct method may be used to report cash provided by operations.
b. The statement shows the cash provided (used) for three categories of activity.
c. The operating section is the last section of the statement.
d. The indirect method may be used to report cash provided by operations.

Questions 8 and 9 apply only to the indirect method.

(SO 3) 8. Net income is $132,000, accounts payable increased $10,000 during the year, inventory decreased $6,000 during the year, and accounts receivable increased $12,000 during the year. Under the indirect method, what is net cash provided by operating activities?
a. $102,000.   c. $124,000.
b. $112,000.   d. $136,000.

(SO 3) 9. Items that are added back to net income in determining cash provided by operating activities under the indirect method do *not* include:
a. depreciation expense.
b. an increase in inventory.
c. amortization expense.
d. loss on sale of equipment.

10. The statement of cash flows should *not* be used to evalu- (S ate an entity's ability to:
a. earn net income.
b. generate future cash flows.
c. pay dividends.
d. meet obligations.

11. Free cash flow provides an indication of a company's abil- (S ity to:
a. generate net income.
b. generate cash to pay dividends.
c. generate cash to invest in new capital expenditures.
d. both (b) and (c).

*12. In a worksheet for the statement of cash flows, a decrease in (S accounts receivable is entered in the reconciling columns as a credit to Accounts Receivable and a debit in the:
a. investing activities section.
b. operating activities section.
c. financing activities section.
d. None of the above.

Questions 13 and 14 apply only to the direct method.

*13. The beginning balance in accounts receivable is $44,000, (S the ending balance is $42,000, and sales during the period are $129,000. What are cash receipts from customers?
a. $127,000.   c. $131,000.
b. $129,000.   d. $141,000.

*14. Which of the following items is reported on a cash flow (S statement prepared by the direct method?
a. Loss on sale of building.
b. Increase in accounts receivable.
c. Depreciation expense.
d. Cash payments to suppliers.

Go to the book's website,
www.wiley.com/college/weygandt,
for Additional Self-Study questions.

 The Navigator

QUESTIONS

1. (a) What is a statement of cash flows?
(b) John Norris maintains that the statement of cash flows is an optional financial statement. Do you agree? Explain.

2. What questions about cash are answered by the statement of cash flows?

3. Distinguish among the three types of activities reported in the statement of cash flows.

4. (a) What are the major sources (inflows) of cash in a statement of cash flows?
(b) What are the major uses (outflows) of cash?

5. Why is it important to disclose certain noncash transactions? How should they be disclosed?

6. Wilma Flintstone and Barny Rublestone were discussing the format of the statement of cash flows of Hart Candy Co. At the bottom of Hart Candy's statement of cash flows

was a separate section entitled "Noncash investing and financing activities." Give three examples of significant noncash transactions that would be reported in this section.

7. Why is it necessary to use comparative balance sheets, a current income statement, and certain transaction data in preparing a statement of cash flows?

8. Contrast the advantages and disadvantages of the direct and indirect methods of preparing the statement of cash flows. Are both methods acceptable? Which method is preferred by the FASB? Which method is more popular?

9. When the total cash inflows exceed the total cash outflows in the statement of cash flows, how and where is this excess identified?

10. Describe the indirect method for determining net cash provided (used) by operating activities.

11. Why is it necessary to convert accrual-based net income to cash-basis income when preparing a statement of cash flows?

12. The president of Ferneti Company is puzzled. During the last year, the company experienced a net loss of $800,000, yet its cash increased $300,000 during the same period of time. Explain to the president how this could occur.

13. Identify five items that are adjustments to convert net income to net cash provided by operating activities under the indirect method.

14. Why and how is depreciation expense reported in a statement prepared using the indirect method?

15. Why is the statement of cash flows useful?

16. During 2008 Doubleday Company converted $1,700,000 of its total $2,000,000 of bonds payable into common stock. Indicate how the transaction would be reported on a statement of cash flows, if at all.

***17.** Why is it advantageous to use a worksheet when preparing a statement of cash flows? Is a worksheet required to prepare a statement of cash flows?

***18.** Describe the direct method for determining net cash provided by operating activities.

***19.** Give the formulas under the direct method for computing (a) cash receipts from customers and (b) cash payments to suppliers.

***20.** Garcia Inc. reported sales of $2 million for 2008. Accounts receivable decreased $200,000 and accounts payable increased $300,000. Compute cash receipts from customers, assuming that the receivable and payable transactions related to operations.

***21.** In the direct method, why is depreciation expense not reported in the cash flows from operating activities section?

BRIEF EXERCISES

BE17-1 Each of these items must be considered in preparing a statement of cash flows for Kiner Co. for the year ended December 31, 2008. For each item, state how it should be shown in the statement of cash flows for 2008.

Indicate statement presentation of selected transactions.
(SO 2)

(a) Issued bonds for $200,000 cash.
(b) Purchased equipment for $150,000 cash.
(c) Sold land costing $20,000 for $20,000 cash.
(d) Declared and paid a $50,000 cash dividend.

BE17-2 Classify each item as an operating, investing, or financing activity. Assume all items involve cash unless there is information to the contrary.

Classify items by activities.
(SO 2)

(a) Purchase of equipment.   **(d)** Depreciation.
(b) Sale of building.   **(e)** Payment of dividends.
(c) Redemption of bonds.   **(f)** Issuance of capital stock.

BE17-3 The following T account is a summary of the cash account of Edmonds Company.

Identify financing activity transactions.
(SO 2)

Cash (Summary Form)

Balance, Jan. 1	8,000		
Receipts from customers	364,000	Payments for goods	200,000
Dividends on stock investments	6,000	Payments for operating expenses	140,000
Proceeds from sale of equipment	36,000	Interest paid	10,000
Proceeds from issuance of		Taxes paid	8,000
bonds payable	300,000	Dividends paid	50,000
Balance, Dec. 31	306,000		

What amount of net cash provided (used) by financing activities should be reported in the statement of cash flows?

BE17-4 Martinez, Inc. reported net income of $2.5 million in 2008. Depreciation for the year was $160,000, accounts receivable decreased $350,000, and accounts payable decreased $280,000. Compute net cash provided by operating activities using the indirect method.

Compute cash provided by operating activities—indirect method.
(SO 3)

BE17-5 The net income for Adcock Co. for 2008 was $280,000. For 2008 depreciation on plant assets was $70,000, and the company incurred a loss on sale of plant assets of $12,000. Compute net cash provided by operating activities under the indirect method.

Compute cash provided by operating activities—indirect method.
(SO 3)

BE17-6 The comparative balance sheets for Goltra Company show these changes in noncash current asset accounts: accounts receivable decrease $80,000, prepaid expenses increase $28,000, and inventories increase $30,000. Compute net cash provided by operating activities using the indirect method assuming that net income is $200,000.

Compute net cash provided by operating activities—indirect method.
(SO 3)

Determine cash received from sale of equipment.
(SO 3)

BE17-7 The T accounts for Equipment and the related Accumulated Depreciation for Pettengill Company at the end of 2008 are shown here.

Equipment					Accumulated Depreciation			
Beg. bal.	80,000	Disposals	22,000		Disposals	5,500	Beg. bal.	44,500
Acquisitions	41,600						Depr. exp.	12,000
End. bal.	99,600						End. bal.	51,000

In addition, Pettengill Company's income statement reported a loss on the sale of equipment of $5,500. What amount was reported on the statement of cash flows as "cash flow from sale of equipment"?

Calculate free cash flow.
(SO 4)

BE17-8 In a recent year, Cypress Semiconductor Corporation reported cash provided by operating activities of $155,793,000, cash used in investing of $207,826,000, and cash used in financing of $33,372,000. In addition, cash spent for fixed assets during the period was $132,280,000. No dividends were paid. Calculate free cash flow.

Calculate free cash flow.
(SO 4)

BE17-9 Lott Corporation reported cash provided by operating activities of $360,000, cash used by investing activities of $250,000, and cash provided by financing activities of $70,000. In addition, cash spent for capital assets during the period was $200,000. No dividends were paid. Calculate free cash flow.

Calculate free cash flow.
(SO 4)

BE17-10 Alliance Atlantis Communications Inc. reported a $35.8 million increase in operating cash flow for its first quarter of 2005. Alliance reported cash provided by operating activities of $45,600,000 and revenues of $264,800,000. Cash spent on plant asset additions during the quarter was $1,600,000. Calculate free cash flow.

Calculate and analyze free cash flow.
(SO 4)

BE17-11 The management of Radar Inc. is trying to decide whether it can increase its dividend. During the current year it reported net income of $875,000. It had cash provided by operating activities of $734,000, paid cash dividends of $70,000, and had capital expenditures of $280,000. Compute the company's free cash flow, and discuss whether an increase in the dividend appears warranted. What other factors should be considered?

Indicate entries in worksheet.
(SO 5)

*BE17-12 During the year, prepaid expenses decreased $6,600, and accrued expenses increased $2,400. Indicate how the changes in prepaid expenses and accrued expenses payable should be entered in the reconciling columns of a worksheet. Assume that beginning balances were: Prepaid expenses $18,600 and Accrued expenses payable $8,200.

Compute receipts from customers—direct method.
(SO 6)

*BE17-13 Columbia Sportswear Company had accounts receivable of $206,024,000 at the beginning of a recent year, and $267,653,000 at year-end. Sales revenues were $1,095,307,000 for the year. What is the amount of cash receipts from customers?

Compute cash payments for income taxes—direct method.
(SO 6)

*BE17-14 Young Corporation reported income taxes of $340,000,000 on its 2008 income statement and income taxes payable of $277,000,000 at December 31, 2007, and $522,000,000 at December 31, 2008. What amount of cash payments were made for income taxes during 2008?

Compute cash payments for operating expenses—direct method.
(SO 6)

*BE17-15 Flynn Corporation reports operating expenses of $80,000 excluding depreciation expense of $15,000 for 2008. During the year prepaid expenses decreased $6,600 and accrued expenses payable increased $4,400. Compute the cash payments for operating expenses in 2008.

EXERCISES

Classify transactions by type of activity.
(SO 2)

E17-1 Pioneer Corporation had these transactions during 2008.

(a) Issued $50,000 par value common stock for cash.
(b) Purchased a machine for $30,000, giving a long-term note in exchange.
(c) Issued $200,000 par value common stock upon conversion of bonds having a face value of $200,000.
(d) Declared and paid a cash dividend of $18,000.
(e) Sold a long-term investment with a cost of $15,000 for $15,000 cash.
(f) Collected $16,000 of accounts receivable.
(g) Paid $18,000 on accounts payable.

Instructions

Analyze the transactions and indicate whether each transaction resulted in a cash flow from operating activities, investing activities, financing activities, or noncash investing and financing activities.

E17-2   An analysis of comparative balance sheets, the current year's income statement, and the general ledger accounts of Gagliano Corp. uncovered the following items. Assume all items involve cash unless there is information to the contrary.

Classify transactions by type of activity.

(SO 2)

(a) Payment of interest on notes payable. *operating activity*
(b) Exchange of land for patent. *noncash financing & investing*
(c) Sale of building at book value. *non cash investing*
(d) Payment of dividends. *financing activities*
(e) Depreciation. *operating activities*
(f) Receipt of dividends on investment in stock. *operating activities*
(g) Receipt of interest on notes receivable. *operating activities*
(h) Issuance of capital stock. *financing activity*
(i) Amortization of patent. *operating activity*
(j) Issuance of bonds for land. *Non cash financing + investing*
(k) Purchase of land. *investing*
(l) Conversion of bonds into common stock. *Non-cash. investing + financing*
(m) Loss on sale of land. *operating*
(n) Retirement of bonds. *financing*

Instructions

Indicate how each item should be classified in the statement of cash flows using these four major classifications: operating activity (indirect method), investing activity, financing activity, and significant noncash investing and financing activity.

E17-3   Rachael Ray Corporation had the following transactions.

Prepare journal entry and determine effect on cash flows.

(SO 2)

1. Sold land (cost $12,000) for $15,000.
2. Issued common stock for $20,000.
3. Recorded depreciation of $17,000.
4. Paid salaries of $9,000.
5. Issued 1,000 shares of $1 par value common stock for equipment worth $8,000.
6. Sold equipment (cost $10,000, accumulated depreciation $7,000) for $1,200.

Instructions

For each transaction above, **(a)** prepare the journal entry, and **(b)** indicate how it would affect the statement of cash flows.

E17-4   Villa Company reported net income of $195,000 for 2008. Villa also reported depreciation expense of $45,000 and a loss of $5,000 on the sale of equipment. The comparative balance sheet shows a decrease in accounts receivable of $15,000 for the year, a $17,000 increase in accounts payable, and a $4,000 decrease in prepaid expenses.

Prepare the operating activities section—indirect method.

(SO 3)

Instructions

Prepare the operating activities section of the statement of cash flows for 2008. Use the indirect method.

E17-5   The current sections of Bellinham Inc.'s balance sheets at December 31, 2007 and 2008, are presented here.

Prepare the operating activities section—indirect method.

(SO 3)

Bellinham's net income for 2008 was $153,000. Depreciation expense was $24,000.

	2008	2007
Current assets		
Cash	$105,000	$ 99,000
Accounts receivable	110,000	89,000
Inventory	158,000	172,000
Prepaid expenses	27,000	22,000
Total current assets	$400,000	$382,000
Current liabilities		
Accrued expenses payable	$ 15,000	$ 5,000
Accounts payable	85,000	92,000
Total current liabilities	$100,000	$ 97,000

Instructions
Prepare the net cash provided by operating activities section of the company's statement of cash flows for the year ended December 31, 2008, using the indirect method.

Prepare partial statement of cash flows—indirect method.

(SO 3)

E17-6 The three accounts shown below appear in the general ledger of Cesar Corp. during 2008.

Equipment

Date			Debit	Credit	Balance
Jan.	1	Balance			160,000
July	31	Purchase of equipment	70,000		230,000
Sept.	2	Cost of equipment constructed	53,000		283,000
Nov.	10	Cost of equipment sold		49,000	234,000

Accumulated Depreciation—Equipment

Date			Debit	Credit	Balance
Jan.	1	Balance			71,000
Nov.	10	Accumulated depreciation on equipment sold	30,000		41,000
Dec.	31	Depreciation for year		28,000	69,000

Retained Earnings

Date			Debit	Credit	Balance
Jan.	1	Balance			105,000
Aug.	23	Dividends (cash)	14,000		91,000
Dec.	31	Net income		67,000	158,000

Instructions
From the postings in the accounts, indicate how the information is reported on a statement of cash flows using the indirect method. The loss on sale of equipment was $5,000. (*Hint:* Cost of equipment constructed is reported in the investing activities section as a decrease in cash of $53,000.)

Prepare statement of cash flows and compute free cash flow.

(SO 3, 4)

E17-7 Scully Corporation's comparative balance sheets are presented below.

SCULLY CORPORATION
Comparative Balance Sheets
December 31

	2008	2007
Cash	$ 14,300	$ 10,700
Accounts receivable	21,200	23,400
Land	20,000	26,000
Building	70,000	70,000
Accumulated depreciation	(15,000)	(10,000)
Total	$110,500	$120,100
Accounts payable	$12,370	$31,100
Common stock	75,000	69,000
Retained earnings	23,130	20,000
Total	$110,500	$120,100

Additional information:

1. Net income was $22,630. Dividends declared and paid were $19,500.
2. All other changes in noncurrent account balances had a direct effect on cash flows, except the change in accumulated depreciation. The land was sold for $4,900.

Instructions

(a) Prepare a statement of cash flows for 2008 using the indirect method.

(b) Compute free cash flow.

E17-8 Here are comparative balance sheets for Taguchi Company.

Prepare a statement of cash flows—indirect method.

(SO 3)

TAGUCHI COMPANY
Comparative Balance Sheets
December 31

Assets	2008	2007	
Cash	$ 73,000	$ 22,000	
Accounts receivable	85,000	76,000	(9,000)
Inventories	170,000	189,000	19,000
Land	75,000	100,000	25,000
Equipment	260,000	200,000	
Accumulated depreciation	(66,000)	(32,000)	34,000
Total	$597,000	$555,000	

Liabilities and Stockholders' Equity	2008	2007	
Accounts payable	$ 39,000	$ 47,000	(8000)
Bonds payable	150,000	200,000	42,000
Common stock ($1 par)	216,000	174,000	
Retained earnings	192,000	134,000	
Total	$597,000	$555,000	

Additional information:

1. Net income for 2008 was $103,000.
2. Cash dividends of $45,000 were declared and paid.
3. Bonds payable amounting to $50,000 were redeemed for cash $50,000.
4. Common stock was issued for $42,000 cash.
5. No equipment was sold during 2008.

Instructions

Prepare a statement of cash flows for 2008 using the indirect method.

E17-9 Muldur Corporation's comparative balance sheets are presented below.

Prepare statement of cash flows and compute free cash flow.

(SO 3, 4)

MULDUR CORPORATION
Comparative Balance Sheets
December 31

	2008	2007
Cash	$ 15,200	$ 17,700
Accounts receivable	25,200	22,300
Investments	20,000	16,000
Equipment	60,000	70,000
Accumulated depreciation	(14,000)	(10,000)
Total	$106,400	$116,000
Accounts payable	$ 14,600	$ 11,100
Bonds payable	10,000	30,000
Common stock	50,000	45,000
Retained earnings	31,800	29,900
Total	$106,400	$116,000

Additional information:

1. Net income was $18,300. Dividends declared and paid were $16,400.
2. Equipment which cost $10,000 and had accumulated depreciation of $1,200 was sold for $3,300.
3. All other changes in noncurrent account balances had a direct effect on cash flows, except the change in accumulated depreciation.

Instructions
(a) Prepare a statement of cash flows for 2008 using the indirect method.
(b) Compute free cash flow.

Prepare a worksheet.

(SO 5)

*E17-10 Comparative balance sheets for Eddie Murphy Company are presented below.

EDDIE MURPHY COMPANY
Comparative Balance Sheets
December 31

Assets	2008	2007
Cash	$ 63,000	$ 22,000
Accounts receivable	85,000	76,000
Inventories	180,000	189,000
Land	75,000	100,000
Equipment	260,000	200,000
Accumulated depreciation	(66,000)	(42,000)
Total	$597,000	$545,000

Liabilities and Stockholders' Equity	2008	2007
Accounts payable	$ 34,000	$ 47,000
Bonds payable	150,000	200,000
Common stock ($1 par)	214,000	164,000
Retained earnings	199,000	134,000
Total	$597,000	$545,000

Additional information:

1. Net income for 2008 was $125,000.
2. Cash dividends of $60,000 were declared and paid.
3. Bonds payable amounting to $50,000 were redeemed for cash $50,000.
4. Common stock was issued for $50,000 cash.
5. Depreciation expense was $24,000.
6. Sales for the year were $978,000.

Instructions
Prepare a worksheet for a statement of cash flows for 2008 using the indirect method. Enter the reconciling items directly on the worksheet, using letters to cross-reference each entry.

Compute cash provided by operating activities—direct method.

(SO 6)

*E17-11 Hairston Company completed its first year of operations on December 31, 2008. Its initial income statement showed that Hairston had revenues of $192,000 and operating expenses of $78,000. Accounts receivable and accounts payable at year-end were $60,000 and $23,000, respectively. Assume that accounts payable related to operating expenses. Ignore income taxes.

Instructions
Compute net cash provided by operating activities using the direct method.

Compute cash payments— direct method.

(SO 6)

*E17-12 The 2004 income statement for McDonald's Corporation shows cost of goods sold $4,852.7 million and operating expenses (including depreciation expense of $1,201 million) $10,671.5 million. The comparative balance sheet for the year shows that inventory increased $18.1 million, prepaid expenses increased $56.3 million, accounts payable (merchandise suppliers) increased $136.9 million, and accrued expenses payable increased $160.9 million.

Instructions
Using the direct method, compute (a) cash payments to suppliers and (b) cash payments for operating expenses.

*E17-13 The 2008 accounting records of Verlander Transport reveal these transactions and events.

Compute cash flow from operating activities—direct method.
(SO 6)

Payment of interest	$ 10,000	Collection of accounts receivable	$182,000
Cash sales	48,000	Payment of salaries and wages	53,000
Receipt of dividend revenue	18,000	Depreciation expense	16,000
Payment of income taxes	12,000	Proceeds from sale of vehicles	12,000
Net income	38,000	Purchase of equipment for cash	22,000
Payment of accounts payable		Loss on sale of vehicles	3,000
for merchandise	115,000	Payment of dividends	14,000
Payment for land	74,000	Payment of operating expenses	28,000

Instructions
Prepare the cash flows from operating activities section using the direct method. (Not all of the items will be used.)

*E17-14 The following information is taken from the 2008 general ledger of Pierzynski Company.

Calculate cash flows—direct method.
(SO 6)

Rent	Rent expense	$ 40,000
	Prepaid rent, January 1	5,900
	Prepaid rent, December 31	9,000
Salaries	Salaries expense	$ 54,000
	Salaries payable, January 1	10,000
	Salaries payable, December 31	8,000
Sales	Revenue from sales	$170,000
	Accounts receivable, January 1	16,000
	Accounts receivable, December 31	7,000

Instructions
In each case, compute the amount that should be reported in the operating activities section of the statement of cash flows under the direct method.

EXERCISES: SET B

Visit the book's website at **www.wiley.com/college/weygandt**, and choose the Student Companion site, to access Exercise Set B.

PROBLEMS: SET A

P17-1A You are provided with the following transactions that took place during a recent fiscal year.

Distinguish among operating, investing, and financing activities.
(SO 2)

Transaction	Where Reported on Statement	Cash Inflow, Outflow, or No Effect?
(a) Recorded depreciation expense on the plant assets.		
(b) Recorded and paid interest expense.		
(c) Recorded cash proceeds from a sale of plant assets.		
(d) Acquired land by issuing common stock.		
(e) Paid a cash dividend to preferred stockholders.		
(f) Distributed a stock dividend to common stockholders.		
(g) Recorded cash sales.		
(h) Recorded sales on account.		
(i) Purchased inventory for cash.		
(j) Purchased inventory on account.		

Instructions

Complete the table indicating whether each item (1) should be reported as an operating (O) activity, investing (I) activity, financing (F) activity, or as a noncash (NC) transaction reported in a separate schedule, and (2) represents a cash inflow or cash outflow or has no cash flow effect. Assume use of the indirect approach.

Determine cash flow effects of changes in equity accounts.

(SO 3)

P17-2A The following account balances relate to the stockholders' equity accounts of Gore Corp. at year-end.

	2008	2007
Common stock, 10,500 and 10,000 shares, respectively, for 2008 and 2007	$160,000	$140,000
Preferred stock, 5,000 shares	125,000	125,000
Retained earnings	300,000	260,000

A small stock dividend was declared and issued in 2008. The market value of the shares was $10,500. Cash dividends were $15,000 in both 2008 and 2007. The common stock has no par or stated value.

Instructions

(a) Net income $65,500

(a) What was the amount of net income reported by Gore Corp. in 2008?

(b) Determine the amounts of any cash inflows or outflows related to the common stock and dividend accounts in 2008.

(c) Indicate where each of the cash inflows or outflows identified in (b) would be classified on the statement of cash flows.

Prepare the operating activities section—indirect method.

(SO 3)

P17-3A The income statement of Elbert Company is presented here.

ELBERT COMPANY
Income Statement
For the Year Ended November 30, 2008

Sales		$7,700,000
Cost of goods sold		
Beginning inventory	$1,900,000	
Purchases	4,400,000	
Goods available for sale	6,300,000	
Ending inventory	1,400,000	
Total cost of goods sold		4,900,000
Gross profit		2,800,000
Operating expenses		
Selling expenses	450,000	
Administrative expenses	700,000	1,150,000
Net income		$1,650,000

Additional information:

1. Accounts receivable increased $250,000 during the year, and inventory decreased $500,000.
2. Prepaid expenses increased $150,000 during the year.
3. Accounts payable to suppliers of merchandise decreased $340,000 during the year.
4. Accrued expenses payable decreased $100,000 during the year.
5. Administrative expenses include depreciation expense of $90,000.

Cash from operations $1,400,000

Instructions

Prepare the operating activities section of the statement of cash flows for the year ended November 30, 2008, for Elbert Company, using the indirect method.

Prepare the operating activities section—direct method.

(SO 6)

*P17-4A Data for Elbert Company are presented in P17-3A.

Instructions
Prepare the operating activities section of the statement of cash flows using the direct method.

P17-5A Grania Company's income statement contained the condensed information below.

Cash from operations
$1,400,000

Prepare the operating activities section—indirect method.

(SO 3)

GRANIA COMPANY
Income Statement
For the Year Ended December 31, 2008

Revenues		$970,000
Operating expenses, excluding depreciation	$624,000	
Depreciation expense	60,000	
Loss on sale of equipment	16,000	700,000
Income before income taxes		270,000
Income tax expense		40,000
Net income		$230,000

Grania's balance sheet contained the comparative data at December 31, shown below.

	2008	2007
Accounts receivable	$75,000	$60,000
Accounts payable	41,000	28,000
Income taxes payable	11,000	7,000

Accounts payable pertain to operating expenses.

Instructions
Prepare the operating activities section of the statement of cash flows using the indirect method.

*P17-6A Data for Grania Company are presented in P17-5A.

Instructions
Prepare the operating activities section of the statement of cash flows using the direct method.

P17-7A Presented below are the financial statements of Weller Company.

Cash from operations
$308,000

Prepare the operating activities section—direct method.

(SO 6)   Cash from operations $308,000

Prepare a statement of cash flows—indirect method, and compute free cash flow.

(SO 3, 4)

WELLER COMPANY
Comparative Balance Sheets
December 31

Assets	**2008**	**2007**
Cash	$ 35,000	$ 20,000
Accounts receivable	33,000	14,000
Merchandise inventory	27,000	20,000
Property, plant, and equipment	60,000	78,000
Accumulated depreciation	(29,000)	(24,000)
Total	$126,000	$108,000
Liabilities and Stockholders' Equity		
Accounts payable	$ 29,000	$ 15,000
Income taxes payable	7,000	8,000
Bonds payable	27,000	33,000
Common stock	18,000	14,000
Retained earnings	45,000	38,000
Total	$126,000	$108,000

WELLER COMPANY
Income Statement
For the Year Ended December 31, 2008

Sales		$242,000
Cost of goods sold		175,000
Gross profit		67,000
Selling expenses	$18,000	
Administrative expenses	6,000	24,000
Income from operations		43,000
Interest expense		3,000
Income before income taxes		40,000
Income tax expense		8,000
Net income		$ 32,000

Additional data:

1. Dividends declared and paid were $25,000.
2. During the year equipment was sold for $8,500 cash. This equipment cost $18,000 originally and had a book value of $8,500 at the time of sale.
3. All depreciation expense, $14,500, is in the selling expense category.
4. All sales and purchases are on account.

Instructions

(a) Prepare a statement of cash flows using the indirect method.
(b) Compute free cash flow.

(a) Cash from operations
$33,500

Prepare a statement of cash flows—direct method, and compute free cash flow.

(SO 4, 6)

(a) Cash from operations
$33,500

Prepare a statement of cash flows—indirect method.

(SO 3)

*P17-8A Data for Weller Company are presented in P17-7A. Further analysis reveals the following.

1. Accounts payable pertain to merchandise suppliers.
2. All operating expenses except for depreciation were paid in cash.

Instructions

(a) Prepare a statement of cash flows for Weller Company using the direct method.
(b) Compute free cash flow.

P17-9A Condensed financial data of Arma Inc. follow.

ARMA INC.
Comparative Balance Sheets
December 31

Assets	2008	2007
Cash	$ 90,800	$ 48,400
Accounts receivable	92,800	33,000
Inventories	112,500	102,850
Prepaid expenses	28,400	26,000
Investments	138,000	114,000
Plant assets	270,000	242,500
Accumulated depreciation	(50,000)	(52,000)
Total	$682,500	$514,750

Liabilities and Stockholders' Equity	2008	2007
Accounts payable	$112,000	$ 67,300
Accrued expenses payable	16,500	17,000
Bonds payable	110,000	150,000
Common stock	220,000	175,000
Retained earnings	224,000	105,450
Total	$682,500	$514,750

ARMA INC.
Income Statement
For the Year Ended December 31, 2008

Sales		$392,780
Less:		
Cost of goods sold	$135,460	
Operating expenses, excluding depreciation	12,410	
Depreciation expense	46,500	
Income taxes	27,280	
Interest expense	4,730	
Loss on sale of plant assets	7,500	233,880
Net income		$158,900

Additional information:

1. New plant assets costing $85,000 were purchased for cash during the year.
2. Old plant assets having an original cost of $57,500 were sold for $1,500 cash.
3. Bonds matured and were paid off at face value for cash.
4. A cash dividend of $40,350 was declared and paid during the year.

Instructions

Prepare a statement of cash flows using the indirect method.

Cash from operations
$185,250

*P17-10A   Data for Arma Inc. are presented in P17-9A. Further analysis reveals that accounts payable pertain to merchandise creditors.

Prepare a statement of cash flows—direct method.
(SO 6)

Instructions

Prepare a statement of cash flows for Arma Inc. using the direct method.

Cash from operations
$185,250

P17-11A   The comparative balance sheets for Ramirez Company as of December 31 are presented below.

Prepare a statement of cash flows—indirect method.
(SO 3)

RAMIREZ COMPANY
Comparative Balance Sheets
December 31

Assets	2008	2007
Cash	$ 71,000	$ 45,000
Accounts receivable	44,000	62,000
Inventory	151,450	142,000
Prepaid expenses	15,280	21,000
Land	105,000	130,000
Equipment	228,000	155,000
Accumulated depreciation—equipment	(45,000)	(35,000)
Building	200,000	200,000
Accumulated depreciation—building	(60,000)	(40,000)
Total	$709,730	$680,000

Liabilities and Stockholders' Equity	2008	2007
Accounts payable	$ 47,730	$ 40,000
Bonds payable	260,000	300,000
Common stock, $1 par	200,000	160,000
Retained earnings	202,000	180,000
Total	$709,730	$680,000

Additional information:

1. Operating expenses include depreciation expense of $42,000 and charges from prepaid expenses of $5,720.
2. Land was sold for cash at book value.

3. Cash dividends of $15,000 were paid.
4. Net income for 2008 was $37,000.
5. Equipment was purchased for $95,000 cash. In addition, equipment costing $22,000 with a book value of $10,000 was sold for $6,000 cash.
6. Bonds were converted at face value by issuing 40,000 shares of $1 par value common stock.

Cash from operations
$105,000

Instructions

Prepare a statement of cash flows for the year ended December 31, 2008, using the indirect method.

Prepare a worksheet—indirect method.

(SO 5)

*P17-12A   Condensed financial data of Oprah Company appear below.

OPRAH COMPANY
Comparative Balance Sheets
December 31

Assets	2008	2007
Cash	$ 92,700	$ 47,250
Accounts receivable	90,800	57,000
Inventories	121,900	102,650
Investments	84,500	87,000
Plant assets	250,000	205,000
Accumulated depreciation	(49,500)	(40,000)
	$590,400	$458,900

Liabilities and Stockholders' Equity	2008	2007
Accounts payable	$ 57,700	$ 48,280
Accrued expenses payable	12,100	18,830
Bonds payable	100,000	70,000
Common stock	250,000	200,000
Retained earnings	170,600	121,790
	$590,400	$458,900

OPRAH COMPANY
Income Statement
For the Year Ended December 31, 2008

Sales		$297,500
Gain on sale of plant assets		8,750
		306,250
Less:		
Cost of goods sold	$99,460	
Operating expenses (excluding depreciation expense)	14,670	
Depreciation expense	49,700	
Income taxes	7,270	
Interest expense	2,940	174,040
Net income		$132,210

Additional information:

1. New plant assets costing $92,000 were purchased for cash during the year.
2. Investments were sold at cost.
3. Plant assets costing $47,000 were sold for $15,550, resulting in gain of $8,750.
4. A cash dividend of $83,400 was declared and paid during the year.

Instructions

Reconciling items
total $610,210

Prepare a worksheet for the statement of cash flows using the indirect method. Enter the reconciling items directly in the worksheet columns, using letters to cross-reference each entry.

PROBLEMS: SET B

P17-1B   You are provided with the following transactions that took place during a recent fiscal year.

Distinguish among operating, investing, and financing activities.

(SO 2)

Transaction	Where Reported on Statement	Cash Inflow, Outflow, or No Effect?
(a) Recorded depreciation expense on the plant assets.		
(b) Incurred a loss on disposal of plant assets.		
(c) Acquired a building by paying cash.		
(d) Made principal repayments on a mortgage.		
(e) Issued common stock.		
(f) Purchased shares of another company to be held as a long-term equity investment.		
(g) Paid dividends to common stockholders.		
(h) Sold inventory on credit. The company uses a perpetual inventory system.		
(i) Purchased inventory on credit.		
(j) Paid wages to employees.		

Instructions
Complete the table indicating whether each item (1) should be reported as an operating (O) activity, investing (I) activity, financing (F) activity, or as a noncash (NC) transaction reported in a separate schedule, and (2) represents a cash inflow or cash outflow or has no cash flow effect. Assume use of the indirect approach.

P17-2B   The following selected account balances relate to the plant asset accounts of Zambia Inc. at year-end.

Determine cash flow effects of changes in plant asset accounts.

(SO 3)

	2008	2007
Accumulated depreciation—buildings	$337,500	$300,000
Accumulated depreciation—equipment	144,000	96,000
Buildings	750,000	750,000
Depreciation expense	101,500	85,500
Equipment	300,000	240,000
Land	100,000	70,000
Loss on sale of equipment	3,000	0

Additional information:

1. Zambia purchased $85,000 of equipment and $30,000 of land for cash in 2008.
2. Zambia also sold equipment in 2008.
3. Depreciation expense in 2008 was $37,500 on building and $64,000 on equipment.

Instructions
(a) Determine the amounts of any cash inflows or outflows related to the plant asset accounts in 2008.
(b) Indicate where each of the cash inflows or outflows identified in (a) would be classified on the statement of cash flows.

(a) Cash proceeds $6,000

P17-3B   The income statement of Marquette Company is presented on page 770.

Additional information:

1. Accounts receivable decreased $520,000 during the year, and inventory increased $140,000.
2. Prepaid expenses increased $175,000 during the year.
3. Accounts payable to merchandise suppliers increased $50,000 during the year.
4. Accrued expenses payable increased $165,000 during the year.

Prepare the operating activities section—indirect method.

(SO 3)

MARQUETTE COMPANY
Income Statement
For the Year Ended December 31, 2008

Sales		$5,400,000
Cost of goods sold		
Beginning inventory	$1,780,000	
Purchases	3,430,000	
Goods available for sale	5,210,000	
Ending inventory	1,920,000	
Total cost of goods sold		3,290,000
Gross profit		2,110,000
Operating expenses		
Selling expenses	420,000	
Administrative expense	525,000	
Depreciation expense	105,000	
Amortization expense	20,000	1,070,000
Net income		$1,040,000

Instructions

Cash from operations $1,585,000

Prepare the operating activities section of the statement of cash flows for the year ended December 31, 2008, for Marquette Company, using the indirect method.

Prepare the operating activities section—direct method.

(SO 6)

Cash from operations $1,585,000

Prepare the operating activities section—indirect method.

(SO 3)

*P17-4B   Data for Marquette Company are presented in P17-3B.

Instructions

Prepare the operating activities section of the statement of cash flows using the direct method.

P17-5B   The income statement of Shapiro Inc. reported the following condensed information.

SHAPIRO INC.
Income Statement
For the Year Ended December 31, 2008

Revenues	$545,000
Operating expenses	400,000
Income from operations	145,000
Income tax expense	47,000
Net income	$ 98,000

Shapiro's balance sheet contained these comparative data at December 31.

	2008	2007
Accounts receivable	$50,000	$75,000
Accounts payable	30,000	51,000
Income taxes payable	10,000	4,000

Shapiro has no depreciable assets. Accounts payable pertain to operating expenses.

Cash from operations $108,000

Instructions

Prepare the operating activities section of the statement of cash flows using the indirect method.

Prepare the operating activities section—direct method.

(SO 6)

Cash from operations $108,000

*P17-6B   Data for Shapiro Inc. are presented in P17-5B.

Instructions

Prepare the operating activities section of the statement of cash flows using the direct method.

P17-7B   Presented below are the financial statements of Molina Company.

Prepare a statement of cash flows—indirect method, and compute free cash flow.

(SO 3, 4)

MOLINA COMPANY
Comparative Balance Sheets
December 31

Assets		2008		2007
Cash		$ 28,000		$ 33,000
Accounts receivable		23,000		14,000
Merchandise inventory		41,000		25,000
Property, plant, and equipment	$ 70,000		$ 78,000	
Less: Accumulated depreciation	(27,000)	43,000	(24,000)	54,000
Total		$135,000		$126,000

Liabilities and Stockholders' Equity	2008	2007
Accounts payable	$ 31,000	$ 43,000
Income taxes payable	26,000	20,000
Bonds payable	20,000	10,000
Common stock	25,000	25,000
Retained earnings	33,000	28,000
Total	$135,000	$126,000

MOLINA COMPANY
Income Statement
For the Year Ended December 31, 2008

Sales		$286,000
Cost of goods sold		194,000
Gross profit		92,000
Selling expenses	$28,000	
Administrative expenses	9,000	37,000
Income from operations		55,000
Interest expense		7,000
Income before income taxes		48,000
Income tax expense		10,000
Net income		$ 38,000

Additional data:

1. Dividends of $33,000 were declared and paid.
2. During the year equipment was sold for $10,000 cash. This equipment cost $13,000 originally and had a book value of $10,000 at the time of sale.
3. All depreciation expense, $6,000, is in the selling expense category.
4. All sales and purchases are on account.
5. Additional equipment was purchased for $5,000 cash.

Instructions
(a) Prepare a statement of cash flows using the indirect method.
(b) Compute free cash flow.

(a) Cash from operations $13,000

*P17-8B   Data for Molina Company are presented in P17-7B. Further analysis reveals the following.

Prepare a statement of cash flows—direct method, and compute free cash flow.

(SO 4, 6)

1. Accounts payable pertains to merchandise creditors.
2. All operating expenses except for depreciation are paid in cash.

Instructions
(a) Prepare a statement of cash flows using the direct method.
(b) Compute free cash flow.

(a) Cash from operations $13,000

P17-9B   Condensed financial data of Yaeger Company are shown below.

YAEGER COMPANY
Comparative Balance Sheets
December 31

Assets	2008	2007
Cash	$ 97,700	$ 33,400
Accounts receivable	70,800	37,000
Inventories	121,900	102,650
Investments	89,500	107,000
Plant assets	310,000	205,000
Accumulated depreciation	(49,500)	(40,000)
Total	$640,400	$445,050

Liabilities and Stockholders' Equity	2008	2007
Accounts payable	$ 62,700	$ 48,280
Accrued expenses payable	15,100	18,830
Bonds payable	140,000	70,000
Common stock	250,000	200,000
Retained earnings	172,600	107,940
Total	$640,400	$445,050

YAEGER COMPANY
Income Statement
For the Year Ended December 31, 2008

Sales		$297,500
Gain on sale of plant assets		5,000
		302,500
Less:		
Cost of goods sold	$99,460	
Operating expenses, excluding depreciation expense	14,670	
Depreciation expense	35,500	
Income taxes	27,270	
Interest expense	2,940	179,840
Net income		$122,660

Additional information:

1. New plant assets costing $141,000 were purchased for cash during the year.
2. Investments were sold at cost.
3. Plant assets costing $36,000 were sold for $15,000, resulting in a gain of $5,000.
4. A cash dividend of $58,000 was declared and paid during the year.

Instructions
Prepare a statement of cash flows using the indirect method.

*P17-10B   Data for Yaeger Company are presented in P17-9B. Further analysis reveals that accounts payable pertain to merchandise creditors.

Instructions
Prepare a statement of cash flows for Yaeger Company using the direct method.

P17-11B Presented below are the comparative balance sheets for Lewis Company at December 31.

Prepare a statement of cash flows—indirect method.
(SO 3)

LEWIS COMPANY
Comparative Balance Sheets
December 31

Assets	2008	2007
Cash	$ 31,000	$ 57,000
Accounts receivable	77,000	64,000
Inventory	192,000	140,000
Prepaid expenses	12,140	16,540
Land	100,000	150,000
Equipment	215,000	175,000
Accumulated depreciation—equipment	(70,000)	(42,000)
Building	250,000	250,000
Accumulated depreciation—building	(70,000)	(50,000)
Total	$737,140	$760,540

Liabilities and Stockholders' Equity	2008	2007
Accounts payable	$ 58,000	$ 45,000
Bonds payable	235,000	265,000
Common stock, $1 par	280,000	250,000
Retained earnings	164,140	200,540
Total	$737,140	$760,540

Additional information:

1. Operating expenses include depreciation expense $65,000 and charges from prepaid expenses of $4,400.
2. Land was sold for cash at cost.
3. Cash dividends of $69,290 were paid.
4. Net income for 2007 was $32,890.
5. Equipment was purchased for $80,000 cash. In addition, equipment costing $40,000 with a book value of $23,000 was sold for $25,000 cash.
6. Bonds were converted at face value by issuing 30,000 shares of $1 par value common stock.

Instructions
Prepare a statement of cash flows for 2008 using the indirect method.

Cash from operations $48,290

PROBLEMS: SET C

Visit the book's website at **www.wiley.com/college/weygandt** and choose the Student Companion site to access Problem Set C.

CONTINUING COOKIE CHRONICLE

(*Note:* This is a continuation of the Cookie Chronicle from Chapters 1 through 16.)

CCC17 Natalie has prepared the balance sheet and income statement of Cookie & Coffee Creations Inc. and would like you to prepare the cash flow statement.

Go to the book's website,
www.wiley.com/college/weygandt,
to see the completion of this problem.

BROADENING YOUR PERSPECTIVE

FINANCIAL REPORTING AND ANALYSIS

Financial Reporting Problem:
PepsiCo, Inc.

BYP17-1 Refer to the financial statements of PepsiCo, presented in Appendix A, and answer the following questions.

(a) What was the amount of net cash provided by operating activities for the year ended December 31, 2005? For the year ended December 25, 2004?

(b) What was the amount of increase or decrease in cash and cash equivalents for the year ended December 31, 2005? For the year ended December 25, 2004?

(c) Which method of computing net cash provided by operating activities does PepsiCo use?

(d) From your analysis of the 2005 statement of cash flows, did the change in accounts and notes receivable require or provide cash? Did the change in inventories require or provide cash? Did the change in accounts payable and other current liabilities require or provide cash?

(e) What was the net outflow or inflow of cash from investing activities for the year ended December 31, 2005?

(f) What was the amount of interest paid in the year ended December 31, 2005? What was the amount of income taxes paid in the year ended December 31, 2005? (See Note 14.)

Comparative Analysis Problem:
PepsiCo, Inc. vs. The Coca-Cola Company

BYP17-2 PepsiCo's financial statements are presented in Appendix A. Coca-Cola's financial statements are presented in Appendix B.

Instructions
(a) Based on the information contained in these financial statements, compute free cash flow for each company.
(b) What conclusions concerning the management of cash can be drawn from these data?

Exploring the Web

BYP17-3 Purpose: Learn about the SEC.

Address:www.sec.gov/index.html, or go to **www.wiley.com/college/weygandt**

From the SEC homepage, choose **About the SEC**.

Instructions
Answer the following questions.

(a) How many enforcement actions does the SEC take each year against securities law violators? What are typical infractions?

(b) After the Depression, Congress passed the Securities Acts of 1933 and 1934 to improve investor confidence in the markets. What two "common sense" notions are these laws based on?

(c) Who was the President of the United States at the time of the creation of the SEC? Who was the first SEC Chairperson?

BYP17-4 Purpose: Use the Internet to view SEC filings.

Address: biz.yahoo.com/i, or go to **www.wiley.com/college/weygandt**

Steps
1. Type in a company name.
2. Choose **Profile**.
3. Choose **SEC**. (This will take you to Yahoo-Edgar Online.)

Instructions

Answer the following questions.

(a) What company did you select?

(b) Which filing is the most recent? What is the date?

(c) What other recent SEC filings are available for your viewing?

CRITICAL THINKING

Decision Making Across the Organization

BYP17-5 Ron Nord and Lisa Smith are examining the following statement of cash flows for Carpino Company for the year ended January 31, 2008.

CARPINO COMPANY
Statement of Cash Flows
For the Year Ended January 31, 2008

Sources of cash	
From sales of merchandise	$380,000
From sale of capital stock	420,000
From sale of investment (purchased below)	80,000
From depreciation	55,000
From issuance of note for truck	20,000
From interest on investments	6,000
Total sources of cash	961,000
Uses of cash	
For purchase of fixtures and equipment	330,000
For merchandise purchased for resale	258,000
For operating expenses (including depreciation)	160,000
For purchase of investment	75,000
For purchase of truck by issuance of note	20,000
For purchase of treasury stock	10,000
For interest on note payable	3,000
Total uses of cash	856,000
Net increase in cash	$ 105,000

Ron claims that Carpino's statement of cash flows is an excellent portrayal of a superb first year with cash increasing $105,000. Lisa replies that it was not a superb first year. Rather, she says, the year was an operating failure, that the statement is presented incorrectly, and that $105,000 is not the actual increase in cash. The cash balance at the beginning of the year was $140,000.

Instructions

With the class divided into groups, answer the following.

(a) Using the data provided, prepare a statement of cash flows in proper form using the indirect method. The only noncash items in the income statement are depreciation and the gain from the sale of the investment.

(b) With whom do you agree, Ron or Lisa? Explain your position.

Communication Activity

BYP17-6 Kyle Benson, the owner-president of Computer Services Company, is unfamiliar with the statement of cash flows that you, as his accountant, prepared. He asks for further explanation.

Instructions

Write him a brief memo explaining the form and content of the statement of cash flows as shown in Illustration 17-13 (page 734).

Ethics Case

BYP17-7   Tappit Corp. is a medium-sized wholesaler of automotive parts. It has 10 stock-holders who have been paid a total of $1 million in cash dividends for 8 consecutive years. The board's policy requires that, for this dividend to be declared, net cash provided by operating activities as reported in Tappit's current year's statement of cash flows must exceed $1 million. President and CEO Willie Morton's job is secure so long as he produces annual operating cash flows to support the usual dividend.

At the end of the current year, controller Robert Jennings presents president Willie Morton with some disappointing news: The net cash provided by operating activities is calculated by the indirect method to be only $970,000. The president says to Robert, "We must get that amount above $1 million. Isn't there some way to increase operating cash flow by another $30,000?" Robert answers, "These figures were prepared by my assistant. I'll go back to my office and see what I can do." The president replies, "I know you won't let me down, Robert."

Upon close scrutiny of the statement of cash flows, Robert concludes that he can get the operating cash flows above $1 million by reclassifying a $60,000, 2-year note payable listed in the financing activities section as "Proceeds from bank loan—$60,000." He will report the note instead as "Increase in payables—$60,000" and treat it as an adjustment of net income in the operating activities section. He returns to the president, saying, "You can tell the board to declare their usual dividend. Our net cash flow provided by operating activities is $1,030,000." "Good man, Robert! I knew I could count on you," exults the president.

Instructions
(a) Who are the stakeholders in this situation?
(b) Was there anything unethical about the president's actions? Was there anything unethical about the controller's actions?
(c) Are the board members or anyone else likely to discover the misclassification?

"All About You" Activity

BYP17-8   In this chapter you learned that companies prepare a statement of cash flows in order to keep track of their sources and uses of cash and to help them plan for their future cash needs. Planning for your own short- and long-term cash needs is every bit as important as it is for a company.

Instructions
Read the article provided at **www.fool.com/savings/shortterm/02.htm**, and answer the following questions.
(a) Describe the three factors that determine how much money you should set aside for short-term needs.
(b) How many months of living expenses does the article suggest to set aside?
(c) Estimate how much you should set aside based upon your current situation. Are you closer to Cliff's scenario or to Prudence's?

Answers to Insight and Accounting Across the Organization Questions

p. 723 Net *What?*
Q: In general, why do differences exist between net income and net cash provided by operating activities?
A: *The differences are explained by differences in the timing of the reporting of revenues and expenses under accrual accounting versus cash. Under accrual accounting, companies report revenues when earned, even if cash hasn't been received, and they report expenses when incurred, even if cash hasn't been paid.*

p. 726 Cash Flow Isn't Always What It Seems
Q: For what reasons might managers at WorldCom and at Dynegy take the actions noted above?
A: *Analysts increasingly use cash-flow-based measures of income, such as cash flow provided by operations, in addition to net income. More investors now focus on cash flow from operations, and some compensation contracts now have bonuses tied to cash-flow numbers. Thus, some managers have taken actions that artificially increase cash flow from operations.*

p. 732 GM Must Sell More Cars

Q: Why does GM's cash provided by operating activities drop so precipitously when the company's sales figures decline?

A: *GM's cash inflow is directly related to how many cars it sells. But many of its cash outflows are not tied to sales—they are "fixed." For example, many of its employee payroll costs are very rigid due to labor contracts. Therefore, even though sales (and therefore cash inflows) fall, these cash outflows don't decline.*

Authors' Comments on *All About You:* Where Does the Money Go? (p. 738)

There are really two issues to consider here. The first centers on the problems associated with accumulating debt to support discretionary expenditures. If you think that you will simply pay off your debts when you graduate, consider the fact that it is not unusual for people to spend 10 years to pay off the debts they accumulated during college.

A second issue relates to the impact that working so many hours can have on your academic performance. Research shows that college students today spend more hours working at jobs and fewer hours studying than at any time in the past. This same research shows that academic performance declines when students work too many hours at their jobs. If you could cut back on your discretionary expenditures, you could quit working so many hours, which would mean that you would do better in school, which would mean that you would have a better shot at a good job after college.

The bottom line: While we think that borrowing to invest in yourself through your education makes good sense, we think that borrowing to support a Starbucks habit is a bad idea. For more ideas on how to get your cash flow under control, see *http://financialplan.about.com/cs/college/a/MoneyCollege.htm*.

Answer to PepsiCo Review It Question 4, p. 724

In its 2005 statement of cash flows, PepsiCo reported:

(1) net cash provided by operating activities of $5.852 billion;
(2) net cash used for investing activities of $3.517 million; and
(3) net cash used for financing activities of $1.878 billion.

Answers to Self-Study Questions

1. c   2. b   3. a   4. c   5. d   6. b   7. c   8. d   9. b   10. a   11. d   *12. b   *13. c
*14. d

✓ *Remember to go back to the Navigator box on the chapter-opening page and check off your completed work.*

Chapter 18

Financial Statement Analysis

STUDY OBJECTIVES

After studying this chapter, you should be able to:

1 Discuss the need for comparative analysis.
2 Identify the tools of financial statement analysis.
3 Explain and apply horizontal analysis.
4 Describe and apply vertical analysis.
5 Identify and compute ratios used in analyzing a firm's liquidity, profitability, and solvency.
6 Understand the concept of earning power, and how irregular items are presented.
7 Understand the concept of quality of earnings.

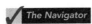

✓ The Navigator

Scan **Study Objectives**	▪
Read **Feature Story**	▪
Read **Preview**	▪
Read text and answer **Before You Go On** p. 787 ▪ p. 798 ▪ p. 803 ▪ p. 806 ▪	
Work **Demonstration Problems**	▪
Review **Summary of Study Objectives**	▪
Answer **Self-Study Questions**	▪
Complete **Assignments**	▪

Feature Story

"FOLLOW THAT STOCK!"

If you thought cab drivers with cell phones were scary, how about a cab driver with a trading desk in the front seat?

When a stoplight turns red or traffic backs up, New York City cabby Carlos Rubino morphs into a day trader, scanning real-time quotes of his favorite stocks as they spew across a PalmPilot mounted next to the steering wheel. "It's kind of stressful," he says, "but I like it."

Itching to know how a particular stock is doing? Mr. Rubino is happy to look up quotes for passengers. Yahoo! and Amazon.com are two of the most requested ones. He even lets customers use his laptop computer to send urgent e-mails from the back seat. Aware of a local law prohibiting cabbies from using cell phones while they're driving, Mr. Rubino extends that rule to his trading. "I stop the cab at the side of the road if I have to make a trade," he says. "Safety first."

Originally from São Paulo, Brazil, Mr. Rubino has been driving his cab since 1987, and started trading stocks a few years ago. His curiosity grew as he began to educate himself by reading business publications. The Wall Street brokers he picks up are usually impressed with his knowledge, he says. But the feeling generally isn't mutual. Some of them "don't know much," he says. "They buy what people tell them to buy—they're like a toll collector."

Mr. Rubino is an enigma to his fellow cab drivers. A lot of his colleagues say they want to trade too. "But cab drivers are a little cheap," he says. "The [real-time] quotes cost $100 a month. The wireless Internet access is $54 a month."

Will he give up his brokerage firm on wheels for a stationary job? Not likely. Though he claims a 70% return on his investments in some months, he says he makes $1,300 and up a week driving his cab—more than he does trading. Besides, he adds, "Why go somewhere and have a boss?"

Source: Excerpted from Barbara Boydston, "With This Cab, People Jump in and Shout, 'Follow that Stock!'," *Wall Street Journal*, August 18, 1999, p. C1. Reprinted by permission of the Wall Street Journal © 1999 Dow Jones & Company, Inc. All Rights Reserved Worldwide.

Inside Chapter 18...

We can learn an important lesson from the Feature Story: Experience is the best teacher. By now you have learned a significant amount about financial reporting by U.S. companies. Using some of the basic decision tools presented in this book, you can perform a rudimentary analysis on any U.S. company and draw basic conclusions about its financial health. Although it would not be wise for you to bet your life savings on a company's stock relying solely on your current level of knowledge, we strongly encourage you to practice your new skills wherever possible. Only with practice will you improve your ability to interpret financial numbers.

Before unleashing you on the world of high finance, we will present a few more important concepts and techniques, as well as provide you with one more comprehensive review of corporate financial statements. We use all of the decision tools presented in this text to analyze a single company—J.C. Penney Company, one of the country's oldest and largest retail store chains.

The content and organization of Chapter 18 are as follows.

The Navigator

BASICS OF FINANCIAL STATEMENT ANALYSIS

Analyzing financial statements involves evaluating three characteristics: a company's liquidity, profitability, and solvency. A **short-term creditor**, such as a bank, is primarily interested in liquidity—the ability of the borrower to pay obligations when they come due. The liquidity of the borrower is extremely important in evaluating the safety of a loan. A **long-term creditor**, such as a bondholder, looks to profitability and solvency measures that indicate the company's ability to survive over a long period of time. Long-term creditors consider such measures as the amount of debt in the company's capital structure and its ability to meet interest payments. Similarly, **stockholders** look at the profitability and solvency of the company. They want to assess the likelihood of dividends and the growth potential of the stock.

Need for Comparative Analysis

STUDY OBJECTIVE 1

Discuss the need for comparative analysis.

Every item reported in a financial statement has significance. When J.C. Penney Company, Inc. reports cash of $3,016 million on its balance sheet, we know the company had that amount of cash on the balance sheet date. But, we do not know whether the amount represents an increase over prior years, or whether it is adequate in relation to the company's need for cash. To obtain such information, we need to compare the amount of cash with other financial statement data.

Comparisons can be made on a number of different bases. Three are illustrated in this chapter:

1. **Intracompany basis.** This basis compares an item or financial relationship **within a company** in the current year with the same item or relationship in one or more prior years. For example, J.C. Penney can compare its cash balance at the end of the current year with last year's balance to find the amount of the increase or decrease. Likewise, J.C. Penney can compare the percentage of cash to current assets at the end of the current year with the percentage in one or more prior years. Intracompany comparisons are useful in detecting changes in financial relationships and significant trends.

2. **Industry averages.** This basis compares an item or financial relationship of a company with **industry averages** (or **norms**) published by financial ratings organizations such as Dun & Bradstreet, Moody's, and Standard & Poor's. For example, J.C. Penney's net income can be compared with the average net income of all companies in the retail chain-store industry. Comparisons with industry averages provide information as to a company's relative performance within the industry.

3. **Intercompany basis.** This basis compares an item or financial relationship of one company with the same item or relationship in **one or more competing companies**. Analysts make these comparisons on the basis of the published financial statements of the individual companies. For example, we can compare J.C. Penney's total sales for the year with the total sales of a major competitor such as Kmart. Intercompany comparisons are useful in determining a company's competitive position.

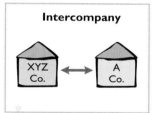

Tools of Analysis

We use various tools to evaluate the significance of financial statement data. Three commonly used tools are these:

STUDY OBJECTIVE 2
Identify the tools of financial statement analysis.

- **Horizontal analysis** evaluates a series of financial statement data over a period of time.

- **Vertical analysis** evaluates financial statement data by expressing each item in a financial statement as a percent of a base amount.

- **Ratio analysis** expresses the relationship among selected items of financial statement data.

Horizontal analysis is used primarily in intracompany comparisons. Two features in published financial statements facilitate this type of comparison: First, each of the basic financial statements presents comparative financial data for a minimum of two years. Second, a summary of selected financial data is presented for a series of five to ten years or more. *Vertical analysis* is used in both intra- and intercompany comparisons. *Ratio analysis* is used in all three types of comparisons. In the following sections, we explain and illustrate each of the three types of analysis.

HORIZONTAL ANALYSIS

Horizontal analysis, also called **trend analysis**, is a technique for evaluating a series of financial statement data over a period of time. Its purpose is to determine the increase or decrease that has taken place. This change

STUDY OBJECTIVE 3
Explain and apply horizontal analysis.

may be expressed as either an amount or a percentage. For example, the recent net sales figures of J.C. Penney Company are as follows.

Illustration 18-1
J.C. Penney Company's
net sales

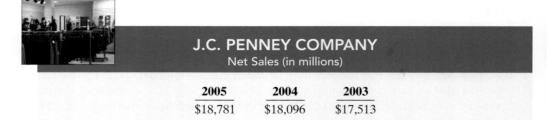

J.C. PENNEY COMPANY
Net Sales (in millions)

2005	2004	2003
$18,781	$18,096	$17,513

If we assume that 2003 is the base year, we can measure all percentage increases or decreases from this base period amount as follows.

Illustration 18-2
Formula for horizontal
analysis of changes since
base period

$$\text{Change Since Base Period} = \frac{\text{Current Year Amount} - \text{Base Year Amount}}{\text{Base Year Amount}}$$

For example, we can determine that net sales for J.C. Penney increased from 2003 to 2004 approximately 3.3% [($18,096 − $17,513) ÷ $17,513]. Similarly, we can determine that net sales increased from 2003 to 2005 approximately 7.2% [($18,781 − $17,513) ÷ $17,513].

Alternatively, we can express current year sales as a percentage of the base period. We do this by dividing the current year amount by the base year amount, as shown below.

Illustration 18-3
Formula for horizontal
analysis of current year in
relation to base year

$$\text{Current Results in Relation to Base Period} = \frac{\text{Current Year Amount}}{\text{Base Year Amount}}$$

Illustration 18-4 presents this analysis for J.C. Penney for a three-year period using 2003 as the base period.

Illustration 18-4
Horizontal analysis of J.C.
Penney Company's net sales
in relation to base period

J.C. PENNEY COMPANY
Net Sales (in millions)
in relation to base period 2003

2005	2004	2003
$18,781	$18,096	$17,513
107.2%	103.3%	100.0%

Balance Sheet

To further illustrate horizontal analysis, we will use the financial statements of Quality Department Store Inc., a fictional retailer. Illustration 18-5 presents a horizontal analysis of its two-year condensed balance sheets, showing dollar and percentage changes.

Illustration 18-5
Horizontal analysis of
balance sheets

QUALITY DEPARTMENT STORE INC.
Condensed Balance Sheets
December 31

	2005	2004	Increase or (Decrease) during 2005 Amount	Percent
Assets				
Current assets	$1,020,000	$ 945,000	$ 75,000	7.9%
Plant assets (net)	800,000	632,500	167,500	26.5%
Intangible assets	15,000	17,500	(2,500)	(14.3%)
Total assets	$1,835,000	$1,595,000	$240,000	15.0%
Liabilities				
Current liabilities	$ 344,500	$ 303,000	$ 41,500	13.7%
Long-term liabilities	487,500	497,000	(9,500)	(1.9%)
Total liabilities	832,000	800,000	32,000	4.0%
Stockholders' Equity				
Common stock, $1 par	275,400	270,000	5,400	2.0%
Retained earnings	727,600	525,000	202,600	38.6%
Total stockholders' equity	1,003,000	795,000	208,000	26.2%
Total liabilities and stockholders' equity	$1,835,000	$1,595,000	$240,000	15.0%

The comparative balance sheets in Illustration 18-5 show that a number of significant changes have occurred in Quality Department Store's financial structure from 2004 to 2005:

- In the assets section, plant assets (net) increased $167,500, or 26.5%.
- In the liabilities section, current liabilities increased $41,500, or 13.7%.
- In the stockholders' equity section, retained earnings increased $202,600, or 38.6%.

These changes suggest that the company expanded its asset base during 2005 and **financed this expansion primarily by retaining income** rather than assuming additional long-term debt.

Income Statement

Illustration 18-6 (page 784) presents a horizontal analysis of the two-year condensed income statements of Quality Department Store Inc. for the years 2005 and 2004. Horizontal analysis of the income statements shows the following changes:

- Net sales increased $260,000, or 14.2% ($260,000 ÷ $1,837,000).
- Cost of goods sold increased $141,000, or 12.4% ($141,000 ÷ $1,140,000).
- Total operating expenses increased $37,000, or 11.6% ($37,000 ÷ $320,000).

Overall, gross profit and net income were up substantially. Gross profit increased 17.1%, and net income, 26.5%. Quality's profit trend appears favorable.

Illustration 18-6
Horizontal analysis of
income statements

QUALITY DEPARTMENT STORE INC.
Condensed Income Statements
For the Years Ended December 31

	2005	2004	Increase or (Decrease) during 2005 Amount	Percent
Sales	$2,195,000	$1,960,000	$235,000	12.0%
Sales returns and allowances	98,000	123,000	(25,000)	(20.3%)
Net sales	2,097,000	1,837,000	260,000	14.2%
Cost of goods sold	1,281,000	1,140,000	141,000	12.4%
Gross profit	816,000	697,000	119,000	17.1%
Selling expenses	253,000	211,500	41,500	19.6%
Administrative expenses	104,000	108,500	(4,500)	(4.1%)
Total operating expenses	357,000	320,000	37,000	11.6%
Income from operations	459,000	377,000	82,000	21.8%
Other revenues and gains Interest and dividends	9,000	11,000	(2,000)	(18.2%)
Other expenses and losses Interest expense	36,000	40,500	(4,500)	(11.1%)
Income before income taxes	432,000	347,500	84,500	24.3%
Income tax expense	168,200	139,000	29,200	21.0%
Net income	$ 263,800	$ 208,500	$ 55,300	26.5%

HELPFUL HINT

Note that though the amount column is additive (the total is $55,300), the percentage column is not additive (26.5% is not the total). A separate percentage has been calculated for each item.

Retained Earnings Statement

Illustration 18-7 presents a horizontal analysis of Quality Department Store's comparative retained earnings statements. Analyzed horizontally, net income increased $55,300, or 26.5%, whereas dividends on the common stock increased only $1,200, or 2%. We saw in the horizontal analysis of the balance sheet that ending retained earnings increased 38.6%. As indicated earlier, the company retained a significant portion of net income to finance additional plant facilities.

Illustration 18-7
Horizontal analysis of
retained earnings statements

QUALITY DEPARTMENT STORE INC.
Retained Earnings Statements
For the Years Ended December 31

	2005	2004	Increase or (Decrease) during 2005 Amount	Percent
Retained earnings, Jan. 1	$525,000	$376,500	$148,500	39.4%
Add: Net income	263,800	208,500	55,300	26.5%
	788,800	585,000	203,800	
Deduct: Dividends	61,200	60,000	1,200	2.0%
Retained earnings, Dec. 31	$727,600	$525,000	$202,600	38.6%

Horizontal analysis of changes from period to period is relatively straightforward and is quite useful. But complications can occur in making the computations. If an item has no value in a base year or preceding year but does have a value in the next year, we cannot compute a percentage change. Similarly, if a negative amount appears in the base or preceding period and a positive amount exists the following year (or vice versa), no percentage change can be computed.

VERTICAL ANALYSIS

Vertical analysis, also called **common-size analysis**, is a technique that expresses each financial statement item as a percent of a base amount. On a balance sheet we might say that current assets are 22% of total assets—*total assets* being the base amount. Or on an income statement, we might say that selling expenses are 16% of net sales—*net sales* being the base amount.

STUDY OBJECTIVE 4
Describe and apply vertical analysis.

Balance Sheet

Illustration 18-8 presents the vertical analysis of Quality Department Store Inc.'s comparative balance sheets. The base for the asset items is **total assets**. The base for the liability and stockholders' equity items is **total liabilities and stockholders' equity**.

Illustration 18-8
Vertical analysis of balance sheets

QUALITY DEPARTMENT STORE INC.
Condensed Balance Sheets
December 31

	2005 Amount	2005 Percent	2004 Amount	2004 Percent
Assets				
Current assets	$1,020,000	55.6%	$ 945,000	59.2%
Plant assets (net)	800,000	43.6%	632,500	39.7%
Intangible assets	15,000	0.8%	17,500	1.1%
Total assets	$1,835,000	100.0%	$1,595,000	100.0%
Liabilities				
Current liabilities	$ 344,500	18.8%	$ 303,000	19.0%
Long-term liabilities	487,500	26.5%	497,000	31.2%
Total liabilities	832,000	45.3%	800,000	50.2%
Stockholders' Equity				
Common stock, $1 par	275,400	15.0%	270,000	16.9%
Retained earnings	727,600	39.7%	525,000	32.9%
Total stockholders' equity	1,003,000	54.7%	795,000	49.8%
Total liabilities and stockholders' equity	$1,835,000	100.0%	$1,595,000	100.0%

HELPFUL HINT
The formula for calculating these balance sheet percentages is:
$$\frac{\text{Each item on B/S}}{\text{Total assets}} = \%$$

Vertical analysis shows the relative size of each category in the balance sheet. It also can show the **percentage change** in the individual asset, liability, and stockholders' equity items. For example, we can see that current assets decreased from 59.2% of total assets in 2004 to 55.6% in 2005 (even though the absolute dollar amount increased $75,000 in that time). Plant assets (net) have increased from 39.7% to 43.6% of total assets. Retained earnings have increased from 32.9% to 39.7% of total liabilities and stockholders' equity. These results reinforce the earlier observations that **Quality is choosing to finance its growth through retention of earnings rather than through issuing additional debt.**

Income Statement

Illustration 18-9 (page 786) shows vertical analysis of Quality's income statements. Cost of goods sold as a percentage of net sales declined 1% (62.1% vs. 61.1%), and total operating expenses declined 0.4% (17.4% vs. 17.0%). As a result, it is not surprising to see net income as a percent of net sales increase from 11.4% to 12.6%. Quality appears to be a profitable enterprise that is becoming even more successful.

Illustration 18-9
Vertical analysis of income statements

QUALITY DEPARTMENT STORE INC.
Condensed Income Statements
For the Years Ended December 31

	2005		2004	
	Amount	**Percent**	**Amount**	**Percent**
Sales	$2,195,000	104.7%	$1,960,000	106.7%
Sales returns and allowances	98,000	4.7%	123,000	6.7%
Net sales	2,097,000	100.0%	1,837,000	100.0%
Cost of goods sold	1,281,000	61.1%	1,140,000	62.1%
Gross profit	816,000	38.9%	697,000	37.9%
Selling expenses	253,000	12.0%	211,500	11.5%
Administrative expenses	104,000	5.0%	108,500	5.9%
Total operating expenses	357,000	17.0%	320,000	17.4%
Income from operations	459,000	21.9%	377,000	20.5%
Other revenues and gains				
Interest and dividends	9,000	0.4%	11,000	0.6%
Other expenses and losses				
Interest expense	36,000	1.7%	40,500	2.2%
Income before income taxes	432,000	20.6%	347,500	18.9%
Income tax expense	168,200	8.0%	139,000	7.5%
Net income	$ 263,800	12.6%	$ 208,500	11.4%

HELPFUL HINT

The formula for calculating these income statement percentages is:

$$\frac{\text{Each item on I/S}}{\text{Net sales}} = \%$$

An associated benefit of vertical analysis is that it enables you to compare companies of different sizes. For example, Quality's main competitor is a JC Penney store in a nearby town. Using vertical analysis, we can compare the condensed income statements of Quality Department Store Inc. (a small retail company) with J.C. Penney Company, Inc. (a giant international retailer), as shown in Illustration 18-10.

Illustration 18-10
Intercompany income statement comparison

CONDENSED INCOME STATEMENTS
(in thousands)

	Quality Department Store Inc.		J. C. Penney Company[1]	
	Dollars	**Percent**	**Dollars**	**Percent**
Net sales	$2,097	100.0%	$18,781,000	100.0%
Cost of goods sold	1,281	61.1%	11,405,000	60.7%
Gross profit	816	38.9%	7,376,000	39.3%
Selling and administrative expenses	357	17.0%	5,799,000	30.9%
Income from operations	459	21.9%	1,577,000	8.4%
Other expenses and revenues (including income taxes)	195	9.3%	489,000	2.6%
Net income	$ 264	12.6%	$ 1,088,000	5.8%

[1] *2005 Annual Report* J.C. Penney Company, Inc. (Dallas, Texas).

J.C. Penney's net sales are 8,956 times greater than the net sales of relatively tiny Quality Department Store. But vertical analysis eliminates this difference in size. The percentages show that Quality's and J.C. Penney's gross profit rates were comparable at 38.9% and 39.3%. However, the percentages related to income from operations were significantly different at 21.9% and 8.4%. This disparity can be attributed to Quality's selling and administrative expense percentage (17%) which is much lower than J.C. Penney's (30.9%). Although J.C. Penney earned net income more than 4,121 times larger than Quality's, J.C. Penney's net income as a **percent of each sales dollar** (5.8%) is only 46% of Quality's (12.6%).

Before You Go On...

REVIEW IT

1. What are the different tools that might be used to compare financial information?
2. What is horizontal analysis?
3. What is vertical analysis?
4. Identify the specific sections in PepsiCo's 2005 Annual Report where horizontal and vertical analysis of financial data is presented. The answer to this question is provided on page 829.

DO IT

Summary financial information for Rosepatch Company is as follows.

	December 31, 2008	December 31, 2007
Current assets	$234,000	$180,000
Plant assets (net)	756,000	420,000
Total assets	$990,000	$600,000

Compute the amount and percentage changes in 2008 using horizontal analysis, assuming 2007 is the base year.

Action Plan

■ Find the percentage change by dividing the amount of the increase by the 2007 amount (base year).

Solution

	Increase in 2008	
	Amount	**Percent**
Current assets	$ 54,000	30% [($234,000 − $180,000) ÷ $180,000]
Plant assets (net)	336,000	80% [($756,000 − $420,000) ÷ $420,000]
Total assets	$390,000	65% [($990,000 − $600,000) ÷ $600,000]

Related exercise material: *BE18-2, BE18-3, BE18-5, BE18-6, BE18-7, E18-1, E18-3, and E18-4.*

The Navigator

RATIO ANALYSIS

Ratio analysis expresses the relationship among selected items of financial statement data. A **ratio** expresses the mathematical relationship between one quantity and another. The relationship is expressed in terms of either a percentage, a rate, or a simple proportion. To illustrate, in 2005 Nike, Inc., had current assets of $6,351.1

STUDY OBJECTIVE 5
Identify and compute ratios used
in analyzing a firm's liquidity,
profitability, and solvency.

million and current liabilities of $1,999.2 million. We can find the relation-ship between these two measures by dividing current assets by current li-abilities. The alternative means of expression are:

Percentage:	Current assets are 318% of current liabilities.
Rate:	Current assets are 3.18 times current liabilities.
Proportion:	The relationship of current assets to liabilities is 3.18:1.

To analyze the primary financial statements, we can use ratios to evaluate liq-uidity, profitability, and solvency. Illustration 18-11 describes these classifications.

Illustration 18-11
Financial ratio classifications

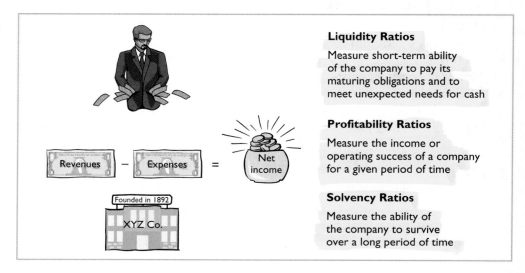

Liquidity Ratios

Measure short-term ability
of the company to pay its
maturing obligations and to
meet unexpected needs for cash

Profitability Ratios

Measure the income or
operating success of a company
for a given period of time

Solvency Ratios

Measure the ability of
the company to survive
over a long period of time

Ratios can provide clues to underlying conditions that may not be apparent from individual financial statement components. However, a single ratio by itself is not very meaningful. Thus, in the discussion of ratios we will use the following types of comparisons.

1. **Intracompany comparisons** for two years for Quality Department Store.
2. **Industry average comparisons** based on median ratios for department stores.
3. **Intercompany comparisons** based on J.C. Penney Company as Quality De-partment Store's principal competitor.

Liquidity Ratios

Liquidity ratios measure the short-term ability of the company to pay its matur-ing obligations and to meet unexpected needs for cash. Short-term creditors such as bankers and suppliers are particularly interested in assessing liquidity. The ratios we can use to determine the enterprise's short-term debt-paying abil-ity are the current ratio, the acid-test ratio, receivables turnover, and inventory turnover.

1. CURRENT RATIO

The **current ratio** is a widely used measure for evaluating a company's liquidity and short-term debt-paying ability. The ratio is computed by dividing current assets by current liabilities. Illustration 18-12 shows the 2005 and 2004 current ratios for Quality Department Store and comparative data.

Illustration 18-12
Current ratio

$$\text{Current Ratio} = \frac{\text{Current Assets}}{\text{Current Liabilities}}$$

Quality Department Store

2005	2004
$\dfrac{\$1,020,000}{\$344,500} = 2.96:1$	$\dfrac{\$945,000}{\$303,000} = 3.12:1$
Industry average	J.C. Penney Company
1.28:1	5.72:1

HELPFUL HINT

Can any company operate successfully without working capital? Yes, if it has very predictable cash flows and solid earnings. A number of companies (e.g., Whirlpool, American Standard, and Campbell's Soup) are pursuing this goal. The rationale: Less money tied up in working capital means more money to invest in the business.

What does the ratio actually mean? The 2005 ratio of 2.96:1 means that for every dollar of current liabilities, Quality has $2.96 of current assets. Quality's current ratio has decreased in the current year. But, compared to the industry average of 1.28:1, Quality appears to be reasonably liquid. J.C. Penney has a very high current ratio of 5.72 which indicates it has considerable current assets relative to its current liabilities.

The current ratio is sometimes referred to as the **working capital ratio**; **working capital** is current assets minus current liabilities. The current ratio is a more dependable indicator of liquidity than working capital. Two companies with the same amount of working capital may have significantly different current ratios.

The current ratio is only one measure of liquidity. It does not take into account the **composition** of the current assets. For example, a satisfactory current ratio does not disclose the fact that a portion of the current assets may be tied up in slow-moving inventory. A dollar of cash would be more readily available to pay the bills than a dollar of slow-moving inventory.

CCOUNTING ACROSS THE ORGANIZATION

How to Manage the Current Ratio

The apparent simplicity of the current ratio can have real-world limitations. An addition of equal amounts to both the numerator and the denominator causes the ratio to change.

Assume, for example, that a company has $2,000,000 of current assets and $1,000,000 of current liabilities. Its current ratio is 2:1. If it purchases $1,000,000 of inventory on account, it will have $3,000,000 of current assets and $2,000,000 of current liabilities. Its current ratio will decrease to 1.5:1. If, instead, the company pays off $500,000 of its current liabilities, it will have $1,500,000 of current assets and $500,000 of current liabilities, and its current ratio will increase to 3:1. Thus, any trend analysis should be done with care, because the ratio is susceptible to quick changes and is easily influenced by management.

 How might management influence the company's current ratio?

2. ACID-TEST RATIO

The **acid-test (quick) ratio** is a measure of a company's immediate short-term liquidity. We compute this ratio by dividing the sum of cash, short-term investments, and net receivables by current liabilities. Thus, it is an important complement to the current ratio. For example, assume that the current assets of Quality Department Store for 2005 and 2004 consist of the items shown in Illustration 18-13 (page 790).

ALTERNATIVE TERMINOLOGY

The acid-test ratio is also called the *quick ratio*.

Illustration 18-13
Current assets of Quality
Department Store

QUALITY DEPARTMENT STORE INC.
Balance Sheet (partial)

	2005	2004
Current assets		
Cash	$ 100,000	$155,000
Short-term investments	20,000	70,000
Receivables (net*)	230,000	180,000
Inventory	620,000	500,000
Prepaid expenses	50,000	40,000
Total current assets	$1,020,000	$945,000

*Allowance for doubtful accounts is $10,000 at the end of each year.

Cash, short-term investments, and receivables (net) are highly liquid compared to inventory and prepaid expenses. The inventory may not be readily saleable, and the prepaid expenses may not be transferable to others. Thus, the acid-test ratio measures **immediate** liquidity. The 2005 and 2004 acid-test ratios for Quality Department Store and comparative data are as follows.

Illustration 18-14
Acid-test ratio

$$\text{Acid-Test Ratio} = \frac{\text{Cash + Short-Term Investments + Receivables (Net)}}{\text{Current Liabilities}}$$

Quality Department Store

2005	2004
$\dfrac{\$100,000 + \$20,000 + \$230,000}{\$344,500} = 1.02:1$	$\dfrac{\$155,000 + \$70,000 + \$180,000}{\$303,000} = 1.34:1$
Industry average 0.33:1	J.C. Penney Company 1.19:1

The ratio has declined in 2005. Is an acid-test ratio of 1.02:1 adequate? This depends on the industry and the economy. When compared with the industry average of 0.33:1 and Penney's of 1.19:1, Quality's acid-test ratio seems adequate.

3. RECEIVABLES TURNOVER

We can measure liquidity by how quickly a company can convert certain assets to cash. How liquid, for example, are the receivables? The ratio used to assess the liquidity of the receivables is **receivables turnover**. It measures the number of times, on average, the company collects receivables during the period. We compute receivables turnover by dividing net credit sales (net sales less cash sales) by the average net receivables. Unless seasonal factors are significant, average net receivables can be computed from the beginning and ending balances of the net receivables.[2]

Assume that all sales are credit sales. The balance of net receivables at the beginning of 2004 is $200,000. Illustration 18-15 shows the receivables turnover for Quality Department Store and comparative data. Quality's receivables turnover improved in 2005. The turnover of 10.2 times is substantially lower than J.C. Penney's 69 times, but is similar to the department store industry's average of 10.8 times.

---

[2]If seasonal factors are significant, the average receivables balance might be determined by using monthly amounts.

Illustration 18-15
Receivables turnover

Average Collection Period.   A popular variant of the receivables turnover ratio is to convert it to an **average collection period** in terms of days. To do so, we divide the receivables turnover ratio into 365 days. For example, the receivables turnover of 10.2 times divided into 365 days gives an average collection period of approximately 36 days. This means that receivables are collected on average every 36 days, or about every 5 weeks. Analysts frequently use the average collection period to assess the effectiveness of a company's credit and collection policies. The general rule is that the collection period should not greatly exceed the credit term period (the time allowed for payment).

4. INVENTORY TURNOVER

Inventory turnover measures the number of times, on average, the inventory is sold during the period. Its purpose is to measure the liquidity of the inventory. We compute the inventory turnover by dividing cost of goods sold by the average inventory. Unless seasonal factors are significant, we can use the beginning and ending inventory balances to compute average inventory.

Assuming that the inventory balance for Quality Department Store at the beginning of 2004 was $450,000, its inventory turnover and comparative data are as shown in Illustration 18-16. Quality's inventory turnover declined slightly in 2005. The turnover of 2.3 times is relatively low compared with the industry average of 6.7 and J.C. Penney's 3.6. Generally, the faster the inventory turnover, the less cash a company has tied up in inventory and the less the chance of inventory obsolescence.

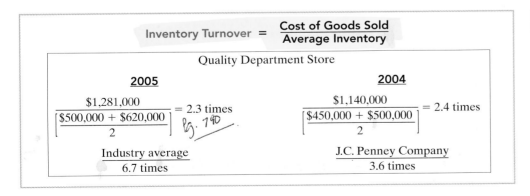

Illustration 18-16
Inventory turnover

Days in Inventory.   A variant of inventory turnover is the **days in inventory**. We calculate it by dividing the inventory turnover into 365. For example, Quality's 2005 inventory turnover of 2.3 times divided into 365 is approximately 159 days. An average selling time of 159 days is also relatively high compared with the industry average of 54.5 days (365 ÷ 6.7) and J.C. Penney's 101.4 days (365 ÷ 3.6).

Inventory turnover ratios vary considerably among industries. For example, grocery store chains have a turnover of 10 times and an average selling period of 37 days. In contrast, jewelry stores have an average turnover of 1.3 times and an average selling period of 281 days.

Profitability Ratios

Profitability ratios measure the income or operating success of a company for a given period of time. Income, or the lack of it, affects the company's ability to obtain debt and equity financing. It also affects the company's liquidity position and the company's ability to grow. As a consequence, both creditors and investors are interested in evaluating earning power—profitability. Analysts frequently use profitability as the ultimate test of management's operating effectiveness.

ALTERNATIVE TERMINOLOGY

Profit margin is also called the *rate of return on sales*.

5. PROFIT MARGIN

Profit margin is a measure of the percentage of each dollar of sales that results in net income. We can compute it by dividing net income by net sales. Illustration 18-17 shows Quality Department Store's profit margin and comparative data.

Illustration 18-17
Profit margin

$$\text{Profit Margin} = \frac{\text{Net Income}}{\text{Net Sales}}$$

Quality Department Store

2005	2004
$\dfrac{\$263,800}{\$2,097,000} = 12.6\%$	$\dfrac{\$208,500}{\$1,837,000} = 11.4\%$
Industry average 3.6%	J.C. Penney Company 3.7%

Quality experienced an increase in its profit margin from 2004 to 2005. Its profit margin is unusually high in comparison with the industry average of 3.6% and J.C. Penney's 3.7%.

High-volume (high inventory turnover) enterprises such as grocery stores (Safeway or Kroger) and discount stores (Kmart or Wal-Mart) generally experience low profit margins. In contrast, low-volume enterprises such as jewelry stores (Tiffany & Co.) or airplane manufacturers (Boeing Co.) have high profit margins.

6. ASSET TURNOVER

Asset turnover measures how efficiently a company uses its assets to generate sales. It is determined by dividing net sales by average assets. The resulting number shows the dollars of sales produced by each dollar invested in assets. Unless seasonal factors are significant, we can use the beginning and ending balance of total assets to determine average total assets. Assuming that total assets at the beginning of 2004 were $1,446,000, the 2005 and 2004 asset turnover for Quality Department Store and comparative data are Shown in Illustration 18-18.

Illustration 18-18
Asset turnover

$$\text{Asset Turnover} = \frac{\text{Net Sales}}{\text{Average Assets}}$$

Quality Department Store

2005	**2004**
$\dfrac{\$2,097,000}{\left[\dfrac{\$1,595,000 + \$1,835,000}{2}\right]} = 1.22$ times	$\dfrac{\$1,837,000}{\left[\dfrac{\$1,446,000 + \$1,595,000}{2}\right]} = 1.21$ times
Industry average 2.37 times	J.C. Penney Company 1.41 times

Asset turnover shows that in 2005 Quality generated sales of $1.22 for each dollar it had invested in assets. The ratio changed little from 2004 to 2005. Quality's asset turnover is below the industry average of 2.37 times and J.C. Penney's ratio of 1.41 times.

Asset turnover ratios vary considerably among industries. For example, a large utility company like Consolidated Edison (New York) has a ratio of 0.49 times, and the large grocery chain Kroger Stores has a ratio of 4.34 times.

7. RETURN ON ASSETS

An overall measure of profitability is **return on assets**. We compute this ratio by dividing net income by average assets. The 2005 and 2004 return on assets for Quality Department Store and comparative data are shown below.

Illustration 18-19
Return on assets

$$\text{Return on Assets} = \frac{\text{Net Income}}{\text{Average Assets}}$$

Quality Department Store

2005	**2004**
$\dfrac{\$263,800}{\left[\dfrac{\$1,595,000 + \$1,835,000}{2}\right]} = 15.4\%$	$\dfrac{\$208,500}{\left[\dfrac{\$1,446,000 + \$1,595,000}{2}\right]} = 13.7\%$
Industry average 8.3%	J.C. Penney Company 8.2%

Quality's return on assets improved from 2004 to 2005. Its return of 15.4% is very high compared with the department store industry average of 8.3% and J.C. Penney's 8.2%.

8. RETURN ON COMMON STOCKHOLDERS' EQUITY

Another widely used profitability ratio is **return on common stockholders' equity**. It measures profitability from the common stockholders' viewpoint. This ratio shows how many dollars of net income the company earned for each dollar invested by the owners. We compute it by dividing net income by average common stockholders' equity. Assuming that common stockholders' equity at the beginning of 2004 was $667,000, Illustration 18-20 shows the 2005 and 2004 ratios for Quality Department Store and comparative data.

Illustration 18-20
Return on common stockholders' equity

$$\text{Return on Common Stockholders' Equity} = \frac{\text{Net Income}}{\text{Average Common Stockholders' Equity}}$$

Quality Department Store

2005	2004
$\dfrac{\$263,800}{\left[\dfrac{\$795,000 + \$1,003,000}{2}\right]} = 29.3\%$	$\dfrac{\$208,500}{\left[\dfrac{\$667,000 + \$795,000}{2}\right]} = 28.5\%$
Industry average 20.5%	J. C. Penney Company 24.6%

Quality's rate of return on common stockholders' equity is high at 29.3%, considering an industry average of 20.5% and a rate of 24.6% for J.C. Penney.

With Preferred Stock. When a company has preferred stock, we must deduct **preferred dividend** requirements from net income to compute income available to common stockholders. Similarly, we deduct the par value of preferred stock (or call price, if applicable) from total stockholders' equity to determine the amount of common stockholders' equity used in this ratio. The ratio then appears as follows.

Illustration 18-21
Return on common stockholders' equity with preferred stock

$$\text{Return on Common Stockholders' Equity} = \frac{\text{Net Income} - \text{Preferred Dividends}}{\text{Average Common Stockholders' Equity}}$$

Note that Quality's rate of return on stockholders' equity (29.3%) is substantially higher than its rate of return on assets (15.4%). The reason is that Quality has made effective use of **leverage**. **Leveraging** or **trading on the equity** at a gain means that the company has borrowed money at a lower rate of interest than it is able to earn by using the borrowed money. Leverage enables Quality Department Store to use money supplied by nonowners to increase the return to the owners. A comparison of the rate of return on total assets with the rate of interest paid for borrowed money indicates the profitability of trading on the equity. Quality Department Store earns more on its borrowed funds than it has to pay in the form of interest. Thus the return to stockholders exceeds the return on the assets, due to benefits from the positive leveraging.

9. EARNINGS PER SHARE (EPS)

Earnings per share (EPS) is a measure of the net income earned on each share of common stock. It is computed by dividing net income by the number of weighted average common shares outstanding during the year. A measure of net income earned on a per share basis provides a useful perspective for determining profitability. Assuming that there is no change in the number of outstanding shares during 2004 and that the 2005 increase occurred midyear, Illustration 18-22 shows the net income per share for Quality Department Store for 2005 and 2004.

Illustration 18-22
Earnings per share

$$\text{Earnings per Share} = \frac{\text{Net Income}}{\text{Weighted Average Common Shares Outstanding}}$$

Quality Department Store

2005	2004
$\dfrac{\$263,800}{\left[\dfrac{270,000 + 275,400}{2}\right]} = \$0.97$	$\dfrac{\$208,500}{270,000} = \$0.77$

Note that no industry or J.C. Penney data are presented. Such comparisons are not meaningful because of the wide variations in the number of shares of outstanding stock among companies. The only meaningful EPS comparison is an intracompany trend comparison: Quality's earnings per share increased 20 cents per share in 2005. This represents a 26% increase over the 2004 earnings per share of 77 cents.

The terms "earnings per share" and "net income per share" refer to the amount of net income applicable to each share of **common stock**. Therefore, in computing EPS, if there are preferred dividends declared for the period, we must deduct them from net income to determine income available to the common stockholders.

10. PRICE-EARNINGS RATIO

The **price-earnings (P-E) ratio** is an oft-quoted measure of the ratio of the market price of each share of common stock to the earnings per share. The price-earnings (P-E) ratio reflects investors' assessments of a company's future earnings. We compute it by dividing the market price per share of the stock by earnings per share. Assuming that the market price of Quality Department Store Inc. stock is $8 in 2004 and $12 in 2005, the price-earnings ratio computation is as follows.

Illustration 18-23
Price-earnings ratio

$$\text{Price-Earnings Ratio} = \frac{\text{Market Price per Share of Stock}}{\text{Earnings per Share}}$$

Quality Department Store

2005	2004
$\dfrac{\$12.00}{\$0.97} = 12.4$ times	$\dfrac{\$8.00}{\$0.77} = 10.4$ times
Industry average	J.C. Penney Company
26 times	13 times

In 2005 each share of Quality's stock sold for 12.4 times the amount that the company earned on each share. Quality's price-earnings ratio is lower than the industry average of 26 times, but almost the same as the ratio of 13 times for J.C. Penney. The average price-earnings ratio for the stocks that constitute the Standard and Poor's 500 Index (500 largest U.S. firms) in early 2006 was a little less than 20 times.

11. PAYOUT RATIO

The **payout ratio** measures the percentage of earnings distributed in the form of cash dividends. We compute it by dividing cash dividends by net income. Companies that have high growth rates generally have low payout ratios because they reinvest most of their net income into the business. The 2005 and 2004 payout ratios for Quality Department Store are computed as shown in Illustration 18-24 (page 796).

Illustration 18-24
Payout ratio

Quality's payout ratio is higher than J.C. Penney's payout ratio of 12.0%. As indicated earlier (page 785), Quality funded its purchase of plant assets through retention of earnings but still is able to pay dividends.

Solvency Ratios

Solvency ratios measure the ability of a company to survive over a long period of time. Long-term creditors and stockholders are particularly interested in a company's ability to pay interest as it comes due and to repay the face value of debt at maturity. Debt to total assets and times interest earned are two ratios that provide information about debt-paying ability.

12. DEBT TO TOTAL ASSETS RATIO

The **debt to total assets ratio** measures the percentage of the total assets that creditors provide. We compute it by dividing total debt (both current and long-term liabilities) by total assets. This ratio indicates the company's degree of leverage. It also provides some indication of the company's ability to withstand losses without impairing the interests of creditors. The higher the percentage of debt to total assets, the greater the risk that the company may be unable to meet its maturing obligations. The 2005 and 2004 ratios for Quality Department Store and comparative data are as follows.

Illustration 18-25
Debt to total assets ratio

A ratio of 45.3% means that creditors have provided 45.3% of Quality Department Store's total assets. Quality's 45.3% is above the industry average of 40.1%. It is considerably below the high 67.8% ratio of J.C. Penney. The lower the ratio, the more equity "buffer" there is available to the creditors. Thus, from the creditors' point of view, a low ratio of debt to total assets is usually desirable.

The adequacy of this ratio is often judged in the light of the company's earnings. Generally, companies with relatively stable earnings (such as public utilities) have higher debt to total assets ratios than cyclical companies with widely fluctuating earnings (such as many high-tech companies).

13. TIMES INTEREST EARNED

Times interest earned provides an indication of the company's ability to meet interest payments as they come due. We compute it by dividing income before interest expense and income taxes by interest expense. Illustration 18-26 shows the 2005 and 2004 ratios for Quality Department Store and comparative data. Note that times interest earned uses income before income taxes and interest expense. This represents the amount available to cover interest. For Quality Department Store the 2005 amount of $468,000 is computed by taking the income before income taxes of $432,000 and adding back the $36,000 of interest expense.

ALTERNATIVE TERMINOLOGY

Times interest earned is also called *interest coverage.*

Illustration 18-26
Times interest earned

$$\text{Times Interest Earned} = \frac{\text{Income before Income Taxes and Interest Expense}}{\text{Interest Expense}}$$

Quality Department Store

2005	2004
$\dfrac{\$468,000}{\$36,000} = 13 \text{ times}$	$\dfrac{\$388,000}{\$40,500} = 9.6 \text{ times}$
Industry average	J.C. Penney Company
12 times	10.2 times

Quality's interest expense is well covered at 13 times, compared with the industry average of 12 times and J.C. Penney's 10.2 times.

INVESTOR INSIGHT

Keeping Up to Date as an Investor

Today, investors have access to information provided by corporate managers that used to be available only to professional analysts. Corporate managers have always made themselves available to security analysts for questions at the end of every quarter. Now, because of a combination of new corporate disclosure requirements by the Securities and Exchange Commission and technologies that make communication to large numbers of people possible at a very low price, the average investor can listen in on these discussions. For example, one individual investor, Matthew Johnson, a Nortel Networks local area network engineer in Belfast, Northern Ireland, "stayed up past midnight to listen to Apple Computer's recent Internet conference call. Hearing the company's news 'from the dog's mouth,' he says 'gave me better information' than hunting through chat-rooms."

Source: Jeff D. Opdyke, "Individuals Pick Up on Conference Calls," *Wall Street Journal*, November 20, 2000.

? If you want to keep current with the financial and operating developments of a company in which you own shares, what are some ways you can do so?

Summary of Ratios

Illustration 18-27
Summary of liquidity, profitability, and solvency ratios

Illustration 18-27 summarizes the ratios discussed in this chapter. The summary includes the formula and purpose or use of each ratio.

Ratio	Formula	Purpose or Use
Liquidity Ratios		
1. Current ratio	$\dfrac{\text{Current assets}}{\text{Current liabilities}}$:1	Measures short-term debt-paying ability.
2. Acid-test (quick) ratio	$\dfrac{\text{Cash + Short-term investments + Receivables (net)}}{\text{Current liabilities}}$	Measures immediate short-term liquidity.
3. Receivables turnover	$\dfrac{\text{Net credit sales}}{\text{Average net receivables}}$ Times	Measures liquidity of receivables.
4. Inventory turnover	$\dfrac{\text{Cost of goods sold}}{\text{Average inventory}}$ Times	Measures liquidity of inventory.
Profitability Ratios		
5. Profit margin	$\dfrac{\text{Net income}}{\text{Net sales}}$ %	Measures net income generated by each dollar of sales.
6. Asset turnover	$\dfrac{\text{Net sales}}{\text{Average assets}}$ times	Measures how efficiently assets are used to generate sales.
7. Return on assets	$\dfrac{\text{Net income}}{\text{Average assets}}$ %	Measures overall profitability of assets.
8. Return on common stockholders' equity	$\dfrac{\text{Net income}}{\text{Average common stockholders' equity}}$ %	Measures profitability of owners' investment.
9. Earnings per share (EPS)	$\dfrac{\text{Net income}}{\text{Weighted average common shares outstanding}}$	Measures net income earned on each share of common stock.
10. Price-earnings (P-E) ratio	$\dfrac{\text{Market price per share of stock}}{\text{Earnings per share}}$ times	Measures the ratio of the market price per share to earnings per share.
11. Payout ratio	$\dfrac{\text{Cash dividends}}{\text{Net income}}$ %	Measures percentage of earnings distributed in the form of cash dividends.
Solvency Ratios		
12. Debt to total assets ratio	$\dfrac{\text{Total debt}}{\text{Total assets}}$ %	Measures the percentage of total assets provided by creditors.
13. Times interest earned	$\dfrac{\text{Income before income taxes and interest expense}}{\text{Interest expense}}$ times	Measures ability to meet interest payments as they come due.

Before You Go On...

REVIEW IT

1. What are liquidity ratios? Explain the current ratio, acid-test ratio, receivables turnover, and inventory turnover.
2. What are profitability ratios? Explain the profit margin, asset turnover ratio, return on assets, return on common stockholders' equity, earnings per share, price-earnings ratio, and payout ratio.
3. What are solvency ratios? Explain the debt to total assets ratio and times interest earned.

EARNING POWER AND IRREGULAR ITEMS

Users of financial statements are interested in the concept of earning power. **Earning power** means the normal level of income to be obtained in the future. Earning power differs from actual net income by the amount of irregular revenues, expenses, gains, and losses. Users are interested in earning power because it helps them derive an estimate of future earnings without the "noise" of irregular items.

For users of financial statements to determine earning power or regular income, the "irregular" items are separately identified on the income statement. Companies report two types of "irregular" items.

1. Discontinued operations.
2. Extraordinary items.

These "irregular" items are reported net of income taxes. That is, the income statement first reports income tax on the income before "irregular" items. Then the amount of tax for each of the listed "irregular" items is computed. The general concept is "let the tax follow income or loss."

Discontinued Operations

Discontinued operations refers to the disposal of a **significant component** of a business. Examples involve stopping an entire activity or eliminating a major class of customers. For example, Kmart reported as discontinued operations its decision to terminate its interest in four business activities, including PACE Membership Warehouse and PayLess Drug Stores Northwest.

Following the disposal of a significant component, the company should report on its income statement both income from continuing operations and income (or loss) from discontinued operations. **The income (loss) from discontinued operations consists of two parts: the income (loss) from operations** and **the gain (loss) on disposal of the segment**.

To illustrate, assume that during 2008 Acro Energy Inc. has income before income taxes of $800,000. During 2008 Acro discontinued and sold its unprofitable chemical division. The loss in 2008 from chemical operations (net of $60,000 taxes) was $140,000. The loss on disposal of the chemical division (net of $30,000 taxes) was $70,000. Assuming a 30% tax rate on income, Illustration 18-28 shows Acro's income statement presentation.

HELPFUL HINT
Observe the dual disclosures: (1) The results of operations of the discontinued division must be eliminated from the results of continuing operations. (2) The company must also report the disposal of the operation.

ACRO ENERGY INC.		
Income Statement (partial)		
For the Year Ended December 31, 2008		
Income before income taxes		$800,000
Income tax expense		240,000
Income from continuing operations		560,000
Discontinued operations		
Loss from operations of chemical division, net of $60,000 income tax saving	$140,000	
Loss from disposal of chemical division, net of $30,000 income tax saving	70,000	210,000
Net income		$350,000

Note that the statement uses the caption "Income from continuing operations," and adds a new section "Discontinued operations". **The new section reports both the operating loss and the loss on disposal net of applicable income taxes.** This presentation clearly indicates the separate effects of continuing operations and discontinued operations on net income.

Extraordinary Items

Extraordinary items are events and transactions that meet two conditions: They are (1) **unusual in nature,** and (2) **infrequent in occurrence.** To be *unusual*, the item should be abnormal and only incidentally related to the company's customary activities. To be *infrequent*, the item should not be reasonably expected to recur in the foreseeable future.

A company must evaluate both criteria in terms of its operating environment. Thus, Weyerhaeuser Co. reported the $36 million in damages to its timberland caused by the volcanic eruption of Mount St. Helens as an extraordinary item. The eruption was both unusual and infrequent. In contrast, Florida Citrus Company does not report frost damage to its citrus crop as an extraordinary item, because frost damage is not infrequent. Illustration 18-29 shows the classification of extraordinary and ordinary items.

Companies report extraordinary items net of taxes in a separate section of the income statement, immediately below discontinued operations. To illustrate, assume that in 2008 a foreign government expropriated property held as an investment by Acro Energy Inc. If the loss is $70,000 before applicable income taxes of $21,000, the income statement will report a deduction of $49,000, as shown in Illustration 18-30 (page 801). When there is an extraordinary item to report, the company adds the caption "Income before extraordinary item" immediately before the section for the extraordinary item. This presentation clearly indicates the effect of the extraordinary item on net income.

What if a transaction or event meets one (but not both) of the criteria for an extraordinary item? In that case the company reports it under either "Other revenues and gains" or "Other expenses and losses" at its gross amount (not net of

Extraordinary items

1. Effects of major natural casualties, if rare in the area.

2. Expropriation (takeover) of property by a foreign government.

3. Effects of a newly enacted law or regulation, such as a property condemnation action.

Ordinary items

1. Effects of major natural casualties, not uncommon in the area.

2. Write-down of inventories or write-off of receivables.

3. Losses attributable to labor strikes.

4. Gains or losses from sales of property, plant, or equipment.

Illustration 18-29
Examples of extraordinary and ordinary items

tax). This is true, for example, of gains (losses) resulting from the sale of property, plant, and equipment, as explained in Chapter 10. It is quite common for companies to use the label "Nonrecurring charges" for losses that do not meet the extraordinary item criteria.

Illustration 18-30
Statement presentation of extraordinary items

ACRO ENERGY INC.
Income Statement (partial)
For the Year Ended December 31, 2008

Income before income taxes		$800,000
Income tax expense		240,000
Income from continuing operations		560,000
Discontinued operations		
Loss from operations of chemical division, net of $60,000 income tax saving	$140,000	
Loss from disposal of chemical division, net of $30,000 income tax saving	70,000	210,000
Income before extraordinary item		350,000
Extraordinary item		
Expropriation of investment, net of $21,000 income tax saving		49,000
Net income		$301,000

HELPFUL HINT

If there are no discontinued operations, the third line of the income statement would be labeled "Income before extraordinary item."

INVESTOR INSIGHT

What Is Extraordinary?

Many companies these days are incurring restructuring charges as a result of attempting to reduce costs. Are these costs ordinary or extraordinary? Some companies report "one-time" restructuring charges over and over. Case in point: Toothpaste and diapers giant Procter & Gamble Co. reported a restructuring charge in 12 consecutive quarters, and Motorola had "special" charges 14 quarters in a row. On the other hand, some companies take a restructuring charge only once in five years. The one-size-fits-all classification therefore will not work. There appears to be no substitute for a careful analysis of the numbers that comprise net income.

 If a company takes a large restructuring charge, what is the effect on the company's current income statement versus future ones?

Changes in Accounting Principle

For ease of comparison, users of financial statements expect companies to prepare such statements on a basis **consistent** with the preceding period. A change in accounting principle occurs when the principle used in the current year is different from the one used in the preceding year. Accounting rules permit a change when management can show that the new principle is preferable to the old principle. An example is a change in inventory costing methods (such as FIFO to average cost).

Companies report most changes in accounting principle retroactively. That is, they report both the current period and previous periods using the new principle. As a result the same principle applies in all periods. This treatment improves the ability to compare results across years.

Comprehensive Income

The income statement reports most revenues, expenses, gains, and losses recognized during the period. However, over time, specific exceptions to this general practice have developed. Certain items now bypass income and are reported directly in stockholders' equity.

For example, in Chapter 16 you learned that companies do not include in income any unrealized gains and losses on available-for-sale securities. Instead, they report such gains and losses in the balance sheet as adjustments to stockholders' equity. Why are these gains and losses on available-for-sale securities excluded from net income? Because disclosing them separately (1) reduces the volatility of net income due to fluctuations in fair value, yet (2) informs the financial statement user of the gain or loss that would be incurred if the securities were sold at fair value.

Many analysts have expressed concern over the significant increase in the number of items that bypass the income statement. They feel that such reporting has reduced the usefulness of the income statement. To address this concern, in addition to reporting net income, a company must also report comprehensive income. Comprehensive income includes all changes in stockholders' equity during a period except those resulting from investments by stockholders and distributions to stockholders. A number of alternative formats for reporting comprehensive income are allowed. These formats are discussed in advanced accounting courses.

Before You Go On...

REVIEW IT
1. What are the similarities and differences in reporting material items not typical of regular operations?
2. What is included in comprehensive income?

DO IT
In its proposed 2008 income statement, AIR Corporation reports income before income taxes $400,000, extraordinary loss $100,000, income taxes (30%) $120,000, and net income $210,000. Prepare a correct income statement, beginning with income before income taxes.

Action Plan
- Recall that the loss is extraordinary because it meets the criteria of being both unusual and infrequent.
- Disclose the income tax effect of each component of income, beginning with income before any irregular items.
- Report irregular items net of any income tax effect.

Solution

AIR CORPORATION
Income Statement (partial)

Income before income taxes	$400,000
Income tax expense (30%)	120,000
Income before extraordinary item	280,000
Extraordinary loss net of $30,000 income tax saving	70,000
Net income	$210,000

Related exercise material: *BE18-14, BE18-15, E18-12, and E18-13.*

 The Navigator

QUALITY OF EARNINGS

In evaluating the financial performance of a company, the quality of a company's earnings is of extreme importance to analysts. A company that has a high **quality of earnings** provides full and transparent information that will not confuse or mislead users of the financial statements.

STUDY OBJECTIVE 7
Understand the concept of quality of earnings.

The issue of quality of earnings has taken on increasing importance because recent accounting scandals suggest that some companies are spending too much time managing their income and not enough time managing their business. Here are some of the factors affecting quality of earnings.

Alternative Accounting Methods

Variations among companies in the application of generally accepted accounting principles may hamper comparability and reduce quality of earnings. For example, one company may use the FIFO method of inventory costing, while another company in the same industry may use LIFO. If inventory is a significant asset to both companies, it is unlikely that their current ratios are comparable. For example, if General Motors Corporation had used FIFO instead of LIFO for inventory valuation, its inventories in a recent year would have been 26% higher, which significantly affects the current ratio (and other ratios as well).

In addition to differences in inventory costing methods, differences also exist in reporting such items as depreciation, depletion, and amortization. Although these differences in accounting methods might be detectable from reading the notes to the financial statements, adjusting the financial data to compensate for the different methods is often difficult, if not impossible.

Pro Forma Income

Companies whose stock is publicly traded are required to present their income statement following generally accepted accounting principles (GAAP). In recent years, many companies have also reported a second measure of income, called pro forma income. **Pro forma income** usually excludes items that the company thinks are unusual or nonrecurring. For example, in a recent year, Cisco Systems (a high-tech company) reported a quarterly net loss under GAAP of $2.7 billion. Cisco reported pro forma income for the same quarter as a profit of $230 million. This large difference in profits between GAAP income numbers and pro forma income is not unusual these days. For example, during one recent 9-month period the 100 largest firms on the Nasdaq stock exchange reported a total pro forma income of $19.1 billion, but a total loss as measured by GAAP of $82.3 billion—a difference of about $100 billion!

To compute pro forma income, companies generally can exclude any items they deem inappropriate for measuring their performance. Many analysts and investors are critical of the practice of using pro forma income because these numbers often make companies look better than they really are. As the financial press noted, pro forma numbers might be called EBS, which stands for "earnings before bad stuff." Companies, on the other hand, argue that pro forma numbers more clearly indicate sustainable income because they exclude unusual and nonrecurring expenses. "Cisco's technique gives readers of financial statements a clear picture of Cisco's normal business activities," the company said in a statement issued in response to questions about its pro forma income accounting.

Recently, the SEC provided some guidance on how companies should present pro forma information. Stay tuned: Everyone seems to agree that pro forma numbers can be useful if they provide insights into determining a company's sustainable income. However, many companies have abused the flexibility that pro forma numbers allow and have used the measure as a way to put their companies in a good light.

Improper Recognition

Because some managers have felt pressure from Wall Street to continually increase earnings, they have manipulated the earnings numbers to meet these expectations. The most common abuse is the improper recognition of revenue. One practice that companies are using is *channel stuffing*: Offering deep discounts on their products to customers, companies encourage their customers to buy early (stuff the channel) rather than later. This lets the company report good earnings in the current period, but it often leads to a disaster in subsequent periods because customers have no need for additional goods. To illustrate, Bristol-Myers Squibb recently indicated that it used sales incentives to encourage wholesalers to buy more drugs than needed to meet patients' demands. As a result, the company had to issue revised financial statements showing corrected revenues and income.

Another practice is the improper capitalization of operating expenses. The classic case is WorldCom. It capitalized over $7 billion dollars of operating expenses so that it would report positive net income. In other situations, companies fail to report all their liabilities. Enron had promised to make payments on certain contracts if financial difficulty developed, but these guarantees were not reported as liabilities. In addition, disclosure was so lacking in transparency that it was impossible to understand what was happening at the company.

 Be sure to read **ALL ABOUT YOU:** *Should I Play the Market Yet?* on the next page for information on how topics in this chapter apply to you.

Should I Play the Market Yet?

this chapter you learned how to use many tools
performing a financial analysis of a company.
metimes companies fail even though they have a
od product and good sales growth. All too often
cause of failure is something that should have
used only momentary discomfort. But if a company
ks sufficient liquidity, a momentary hiccup can be
al. This is true for individuals as well.

For example, the decision to invest in common
ck can be risky. As a company's net income changes,
stock price can be volatile. You must take this into
sideration when deciding whether to buy stock.
don't want to be in a situation where you have to
a stock whose price has fallen in order to raise
h to pay your bills.

✹Some Facts

3.4 million Americans own stock investments,
ither through mutual funds or individual stocks;
9% of stock investors own stock mutual funds.

4% of the people who own stock bought their first
tock before 1990.

he typical equity investor is in his or her late 40s,
married, is employed, and has a household
come in the low $60,000s.

8% of people who own stock said that they rely on
rofessional financial advisors when making
ecisions regarding the purchase and sale of stock.

6% of people who own stock used the Internet to
heck stock prices, and 38% use it to read online
nancial publications.

✹About the Numbers

The percentage of Americans who buy stock, either through mutual funds or individual shares, has increased significantly in recent years. A big part of this increase is due to the increasing prevalence of employer-sponsored retirement plans, such as 401(k) plans.

Equity Ownership in the U.S., 1983–2002, Selected Years
(number and percent of U.S. households)

U.S. Households (millions)	15.9	30.2	34.6	40.6	49.2	52.7

Source: "Equity Ownership in America," Investment Company Institute and the Securities Industry Association, 2002, p. 1.

✹What Do You Think?

Rachael West has been working at her new job for six months. She has a good salary, with lots of opportunities for growth. She has already accumulated $8,000 in savings, which right now is sitting in a bank savings account earning very little interest. She decided to take $7,000 out of this savings account and buy common stock of her employer, a young company that has been in business for two years. Rachael's liquid assets, including her savings account, total $10,000. Her monthly expenses are approximately $3,000. Should Rachael make this investment?

YES: She has a good income, and this is a great opportunity for her to get in on the ground floor of her employer's fast-growing company.

NO: She shouldn't invest all of her money in one company, particularly the company at which she works.

Source: "Equity Ownership in America," Investment Company Institute and the Securities Industry Association, 2002.

authors' comments on this situation appear on p. 828.

Before You Go On...

REVIEW IT

1. What is meant by *quality of earnings?*
2. Give examples of alternative accounting methods that hamper comparability.
3. What is pro forma income and why are analysts often critical of this number?

 The Navigator

 WILEY PLUS

Demonstration Problem 1

The condensed financial statements ot The Estée Lauder Companies, Inc., for the years ended June 30, 2005 and 2004, are presented below.

THE ESTÉE LAUDER COMPANIES, INC.
Balance Sheets
June 30

Assets	(in millions)	
	2005	2004
Current assets		
Cash and cash equivalents	$ 553.3	$ 611.6
Accounts receivable (net)	776.6	664.9
Inventories	768.3	653.5
Prepaid expenses and other current assets	204.4	269.2
Total current assets	2,302.6	2,199.2
Property, plant, and equipment (net)	694.2	647.0
Investments	12.3	12.6
Intangibles and other assets	876.7	849.3
Total assets	$3,885.8	$3,708.1
Liabilities and Stockholders' Equity		
Current liabilities	$1,497.7	$1,322.0
Long-term liabilities	679.5	637.1
Stockholders' equity—common	1,708.6	1,749.0
Total liabilities and stockholders' equity	$3,885.8	$3,708.1

THE ESTÉE LAUDER COMPANIES, INC.
Income Statements
For the Year Ended June 30

	(in millions)	
	2005	2004
Revenues	$6,336.3	$5,790.4
Costs and expenses		
Cost of goods sold	1,617.4	1,476.3
Selling and administrative expenses	4,007.6	3,679.0
Interest expense	13.9	27.1
Total costs and expenses	5,638.9	5,182.4
Income before income taxes	697.4	608.0
Income tax expense	291.3	232.6
Net income	$ 406.1	$ 375.4

Instructions

Compute the following ratios for 2005 and 2004.

(a) Current ratio.
(b) Inventory turnover. (Inventory on 6/30/03 was $599.0.)
(c) Profit margin ratio.
(d) Return on assets. (Assets on 6/30/03 were $3,349.9.)
(e) Return on common stockholders' equity. (Equity on 6/30/03 was $1,795.9.)
(f) Debt to total assets ratio.
(g) Times interest earned.

Solution to Demonstration Problem 1

	2005	2004
(a) Current ratio:		
$2,302.6 ÷ $1,497.7 =	1.5:1	
$2,199.2 ÷ $1,322.0 =		1.7:1
(b) Inventory turnover:		
$1,617.4 ÷ [($768.3 + $653.5) ÷ 2] =	2.3 times	
$1,476.3 ÷ [($653.5 + $599.0) ÷ 2] =		2.4 times
(c) Profit margin:		
$406.1 ÷ $6,336.3	6.4%	
$375.4 ÷ $5,790.4		6.5%
(d) Return on assets:		
$406.1 ÷ [($3,885.8 + $3,708.1) ÷ 2] =	10.7%	
$375.4 ÷ [($3,708.1 + $3,349.9) ÷ 2] =		10.6%
(e) Return on common stockholders' equity:		
$406.1 ÷ [($1,708.6 + $1,749.0) ÷ 2] =	23.5%	
$375.4 ÷ [($1,749.0 + $1,795.9) ÷ 2] =		21.2%
(f) Debt to total assets ratio:		
($1,497.7 + $679.5) ÷ $3,885.8 =	56.0%	
($1,322.0 + $637.1) ÷ $3,708.1 =		52.8%
(g) Times interest earned:		
($406.1 + $291.3 + $13.9) ÷ $13.9 =	51.2 times	
($375.4 + $232.6 + $27.1) ÷ $27.1 =		23.4 times

The Navigator

action plan

✔ Remember that the current ratio includes all current assets. The acid-test ratio uses only cash, short-term investments, and net receivables.

✔ Use average balances for turnover ratios like inventory, receivables, and assets.

Demonstration Problem 2

The events and transactions of Dever Corporation for the year ending December 31, 2008, resulted in the following data.

Cost of goods sold	$2,600,000
Net sales	4,400,000
Other expenses and losses	9,600
Other revenues and gains	5,600
Selling and administrative expenses	1,100,000
Income from operations of plastics division	70,000
Gain from disposal of plastics division	500,000
Loss from tornado disaster (extraordinary loss)	600,000

Analysis reveals that:

1. All items are before the applicable income tax rate of 30%.
2. The plastics division was sold on July 1.
3. All operating data for the plastics division have been segregated.

Instructions

Prepare an income statement for the year.

action plan

✔ Report material items not typical of operations in separate sections, net of taxes.

✔ Associate income taxes with the item that affects the taxes.

✔ Apply the corporate tax rate to income before income taxes to determine tax expense.

✔ Recall that all data presented in determining income before income taxes are the same as for unincorporated companies.

Solution to Demonstration Problem 2

DEVER CORPORATION
Income Statement
For the Year Ended December 31, 2008

Net sales		$4,400,000
Cost of goods sold		2,600,000
Gross profit		1,800,000
Selling and administrative expenses		1,100,000
Income from operations		700,000
Other revenues and gains	$5,600	
Other expenses and losses	9,600	4,000
Income before income taxes		696,000
Income tax expense ($696,000 × 30%)		208,800
Income from continuing operations		487,200
Discontinued operations		
Income from operations of plastics division, net of $21,000 income taxes ($70,000 × 30%)	49,000	
Gain from disposal of plastics division, net of $150,000 income taxes ($500,000 × 30%)	350,000	399,000
Income before extraordinary item		886,200
Extraordinary item		
Tornado loss, net of $180,000 income tax saving ($600,000 × 30%)		420,000
Net income		$ 466,200

SUMMARY OF STUDY OBJECTIVES

1 Discuss the need for comparative analysis. There are three bases of comparison: (1) Intracompany, which compares an item or financial relationship with other data within a company. (2) Industry, which compares company data with industry averages. (3) Intercompany, which compares an item or financial relationship of a company with data of one or more competing companies.

2 Identify the tools of financial statement analysis. Financial statements can be analyzed horizontally, vertically, and with ratios.

3 Explain and apply horizontal analysis. Horizontal analysis is a technique for evaluating a series of data over a period of time to determine the increase or decrease that has taken place, expressed as either an amount or a percentage.

4 Describe and apply vertical analysis. Vertical analysis is a technique that expresses each item within a financial statement in terms of a percentage of a relevant total or a base amount.

5 Identify and compute ratios used in analyzing a firm's liquidity, profitability, and solvency. The formula and purpose of each ratio was presented in Illustration 18-27 (page 798).

6 Understand the concept of earning power, and how irregular items are presented. Earning power refers to a company's ability to sustain its profits from operations. "Irregular items"—discontinued operations and extraordinary items—are presented net of tax below income from continuing operations to highlight their unusual nature.

7 Understand the concept of quality of earnings. A high quality of earnings provides full and transparent information that will not confuse or mislead users of the financial statements. Issues related to quality of earnings are (1) alternative accounting methods, (2) pro forma income, and (3) improper recognition.

GLOSSARY

Acid-test (quick) ratio A measure of a company's immediate short-term liquidity; computed by dividing the sum of cash, short-term investments, and net receivables by current liabilities. (p. 789).

Asset turnover A measure of how efficiently a company uses its assets to generate sales; computed by dividing net sales by average assets. (p. 792).

Change in accounting principle The use of a principle in the current year that is different from the one used in the preceding year. (p. 802).

Comprehensive income Includes all changes in stockholders' equity during a period except those resulting from investments by stockholders and distributions to stockholders. (p. 802).

Current ratio A measure used to evaluate a company's liquidity and short-term debt-paying ability; computed by dividing current assets by current liabilities. (p. 788).

Debt to total assets ratio Measures the percentage of total assets provided by creditors; computed by dividing total debt by total assets. (p. 796).

Discontinued operations The disposal of a significant segment of a business. (p. 799).

Earnings per share (EPS) The net income earned on each share of common stock; computed by dividing net income by the number of weighted average common shares outstanding. (p. 794).

Extraordinary items Events and transactions that are unusual in nature and infrequent in occurrence. (p. 800).

Horizontal analysis A technique for evaluating a series of financial statement data over a period of time, to determine the increase (decrease) that has taken place, expressed as either an amount or a percentage. (p. 781).

Inventory turnover A measure of the liquidity of inventory; computed by dividing cost of goods sold by average inventory. (p. 791).

Leveraging See Trading on the equity.

Liquidity ratios Measures of the short-term ability of the enterprise to pay its maturing obligations and to meet unexpected needs for cash. (p. 788).

Payout ratio Measures the percentage of earnings distributed in the form of cash dividends; computed by dividing cash dividends by net income. (p. 795).

Price-earnings (P-E) ratio Measures the ratio of the market price of each share of common stock to the earnings per share; computed by dividing the market price of the stock by earnings per share. (p. 795).

Profit margin Measures the percentage of each dollar of sales that results in net income; computed by dividing net income by net sales. (p. 792).

Profitability ratios Measures of the income or operating success of an enterprise for a given period of time. (p. 792).

Pro forma income A measure of income that usually excludes items that a company thinks are unusual or nonrecurring. (p. 804).

Quality of earnings Indicates the level of full and transparent information provided to users of the financial statements (p. 803).

Ratio An expression of the mathematical relationship between one quantity and another. The relationship may be expressed either as a percentage, a rate, or a simple proportion. (p. 787).

Ratio analysis A technique for evaluating financial statements that expresses the relationship between selected financial statement data. (p. 787).

Receivables turnover A measure of the liquidity of receivables; computed by dividing net credit sales by average net receivables. (p. 790).

Return on assets An overall measure of profitability; computed by dividing net income by average assets. (p. 793).

Return on common stockholders' equity Measures the dollars of net income earned for each dollar invested by the owners; computed by dividing net income by average common stockholders' equity. (p. 793).

Solvency ratios Measures of the ability of the enterprise to survive over a long period of time. (p. 796).

Times interest earned Measures a company's ability to meet interest payments as they come due; computed by dividing income before interest expense and income taxes by interest expense. (p. 797).

Trading on the equity Borrowing money at a lower rate of interest than can be earned by using the borrowed money. (p. 794).

Vertical analysis A technique for evaluating financial statement data that expresses each item within a financial statement as a percent of a base amount. (p. 785).

Answers are at the end of the chapter.

1. Comparisons of data within a company are an example of the following comparative basis:
   a. Industry averages.
   b. Intracompany.
   c. Intercompany.
   d. Both (b) and (c).

2. In horizontal analysis, each item is expressed as a percentage of the:
   a. net income amount.
   b. stockholders' equity amount.
   c. total assets amount.
   d. base year amount.

3. In vertical analysis, the base amount for depreciation expense is generally: (SO 4)
   a. net sales.
   b. depreciation expense in a previous year.
   c. gross profit.
   d. fixed assets.

4. The following schedule is a display of what type of analysis? (SO 4)

	Amount	Percent
Current assets	$200,000	25%
Property, plant, and equipment	600,000	75%
Total assets	$800,000	

a. Horizontal analysis.
b. Differential analysis.
c. Vertical analysis.
d. Ratio analysis.

(SO 3) **5.** Sammy Corporation reported net sales of $300,000, $330,000, and $360,000 in the years, 2006, 2007, and 2008, respectively. If 2006 is the base year, what is the trend percentage for 2008?
a. 77%.
b. 108%.
c. 120%.
d. 130%.

(SO 5) **6.** Which of the following measures is an evaluation of a firm's ability to pay current liabilities?
a. Acid-test ratio.
b. Current ratio.
c. Both (a) and (b).
d. None of the above.

(SO 5) **7.** A measure useful in evaluating the efficiency in managing inventories is:
a. inventory turnover.
b. average days to sell inventory.
c. Both (a) and (b).
d. None of the above.

(SO 6) **8.** In reporting discontinued operations, the income statement should show in a special section:

a. gains and losses on the disposal of the discontinued segment.
b. gains and losses from operations of the discontinued segment.
c. Both (a) and (b).
d. Neither (a) nor (b).

9. Scout Corporation has income before taxes of $400,000 (S and an extraordinary loss of $100,000. If the income tax rate is 25% on all items, the income statement should show income before extraordinary items and extraordinary items, respectively, of:
a. $325,000 and $100,000.
b. $325,000 and $75,000.
c. $300,000 and $100,000
d. $300,000 and $75,000.

10. Which situation below might indicate a company has a (S low quality of earnings?
a. The same accounting principles are used each year.
b. Revenue is recognized when earned.
c. Maintenance costs are expensed as incurred.
d. The company is continually reporting pro forma income numbers.

Go to the book's website,
www.wiley.com/college/weygandt,
for Additional Self-Study questions.

 The Navigator

QUESTIONS

1. (a) Juan Marichal believes that the analysis of financial statements is directed at two characteristics of a company: liquidity and profitability. Is Juan correct? Explain.
(b) Are short-term creditors, long-term creditors, and stockholders interested primarily in the same characteristics of a company? Explain.

2. (a) Distinguish among the following bases of comparison: (1) intracompany, (2) industry averages, and (3) intercompany.
(b) Give the principal value of using each of the three bases of comparison.

3. Two popular methods of financial statement analysis are horizontal analysis and vertical analysis. Explain the difference between these two methods.

4. (a) If Leonard Company had net income of $360,000 in 2008 and it experienced a 24.5% increase in net income for 2009, what is its net income for 2009?
(b) If six cents of every dollar of Leonard revenue is net income in 2008, what is the dollar amount of 2008 revenue?

5. What is a ratio? What are the different ways of expressing the relationship of two amounts? What information does a ratio provide?

6. Name the major ratios useful in assessing (a) liquidity and (b) solvency.

7. Raphael Ochoa is puzzled. His company had a profit margin of 10% in 2008. He feels that this is an indication that the company is doing well. Cindy Lore, his accountant, says that more information is needed to determine the firm's financial well-being. Who is correct? Why?

8. What do the following classes of ratios measure? (a) Liquidity ratios. (b) Profitability ratios. (c) Solvency ratios.

9. What is the difference between the current ratio and the acid-test ratio?

10. Donte Company, a retail store, has a receivables turnover of 4.5 times. The industry average is 12.5 times. Does Donte have a collection problem with its receivables?

11. Which ratios should be used to help answer the following questions?
(a) How efficient is a company in using its assets to produce sales?
(b) How near to sale is the inventory on hand?
(c) How many dollars of net income were earned for each dollar invested by the owners?
(d) How able is a company to meet interest charges as they fall due?

12. The price-earnings ratio of General Motors (automobile builder) was 8, and the price-earnings ratio of Microsoft (computer software) was 38. Which company did the stock market favor? Explain.

13. What is the formula for computing the payout ratio? Would you expect this ratio to be high or low for a growth company?

14. Holding all other factors constant, indicate whether each of the following changes generally signals good or bad news about a company.
    (a) Increase in profit margin.
    (b) Decrease in inventory turnover.
    (c) Increase in the current ratio.
    (d) Decrease in earnings per share.
    (e) Increase in price-earnings ratio.
    (f) Increase in debt to total assets ratio.
    (g) Decrease in times interest earned.

15. The return on assets for Tresh Corporation is 7.6%. During the same year Tresh's return on common stockholders' equity is 12.8%. What is the explanation for the difference in the two rates?

16. Which two ratios do you think should be of greatest interest to:
    (a) A pension fund considering the purchase of 20-year bonds?
    (b) A bank contemplating a short-term loan?
    (c) A common stockholder?

17. Why must preferred stock dividends be subtracted from net income in computing earnings per share?

18. (a) What is meant by trading on the equity?
    (b) How would you determine the profitability of trading on the equity?

19. Hillman Inc. has net income of $160,000, weighted average shares of common stock outstanding of 50,000, and pre-ferred dividends for the period of $40,000. What is Hillman's earnings per share of common stock? Kate Hillman, the president of Hillman Inc., believes the computed EPS of the company is high. Comment.

20. Why is it important to report discontinued operations separately from income from continuing operations?

21. You are considering investing in Shawnee Transportation. The company reports 2008 earnings per share of $6.50 on income before extraordinary items and $4.75 on net income. Which EPS figure would you consider more relevant to your investment decision? Why?

22. STL Inc. reported 2007 earnings per share of $3.20 and had no extraordinary items. In 2008, EPS on income before extraordinary items was $2.99, and EPS on net income was $3.49. Is this a favorable trend?

23. Indicate which of the following items would be reported as an extraordinary item in Mordica Corporation's income statement.
    (a) Loss from damages caused by volcano eruption.
    (b) Loss from sale of temporary investments.
    (c) Loss attributable to a labor strike.
    (d) Loss caused when manufacture of a product was prohibited by the Food and Drug Administration.
    (e) Loss from flood damage. (The nearby Black River floods every 2 to 3 years.)
    (f) Write-down of obsolete inventory.
    (g) Expropriation of a factory by a foreign government.

24. Identify and explain factors that affect quality of earnings.

BRIEF EXERCISES

WILEY PLUS

Follow the rounding procedures used in the chapter.

BE18-1 You recently received a letter from your Uncle Frank. A portion of the letter is presented below.

Discuss need for comparative analysis.

(SO 1)

> You know that I have a significant amount of money I saved over the years. I am thinking about starting an investment program. I want to do the investing myself, based on my own research and analysis of financial statements. I know that you are studying accounting, so I have a couple of questions for you. I have heard that different users of financial statements are interested in different characteristics of companies. Is this true, and, if so, why? Also, some of my friends, who are already investing, have told me that comparisons involving a company's financial data can be made on a number of different bases. Can you explain these bases to me?

Instructions
Write a letter to your Uncle Frank which answers his questions.

BE18-2 Drew Carey Corporation reported the following amounts in 2007, 2008, and 2009.

Identify and use tools of financial statement analysis.

(SO 2, 3, 4, 5)

	2007	2008	2009
Current assets	$200,000	$230,000	$240,000
Current liabilities	$160,000	$168,000	$184,000
Total assets	$500,000	$600,000	$620,000

Instructions
(a) Identify and describe the three tools of financial statement analysis. (b) Perform each of the three types of analysis on Drew Carey's current assets.

Prepare horizontal analysis.
(SO 3)

BE18-3   Using the following data from the comparative balance sheet of Rodenbeck Company, illustrate horizontal analysis.

	December 31, 2009	December 31, 2008
Accounts receivable	$ 520,000	$ 400,000
Inventory	$ 840,000	$ 600,000
Total assets	$ 3,000,000	$2,500,000

Prepare vertical analysis.
(SO 4)

BE18-4   Using the same data presented above in BE18-3 for Rodenbeck Company, illustrate vertical analysis.

Calculate percentage of change.
(SO 3)

BE18-5   Net income was $500,000 in 2007, $450,000 in 2008, and $522,000 in 2009. What is the percentage of change from **(a)** 2007 to 2008 and **(b)** 2008 to 2009? Is the change an increase or a decrease?

Calculate net income.
(SO 3)

BE18-6   If Soule Company had net income of $585,000 in 2009 and it experienced a 30% increase in net income over 2008, what was its 2008 net income?

Calculate change in net income.
(SO 3)

BE18-7   Horizontal analysis (trend analysis) percentages for Epstein Company's sales, cost of goods sold, and expenses are shown below.

Horizontal Analysis	2009	2008	2007
Sales	96.2	106.8	100.0
Cost of goods sold	102.0	97.0	100.0
Expenses	109.6	98.4	100.0

Did Epstein's net income increase, decrease, or remain unchanged over the 3-year period?

Calculate change in net income.
(SO 4)

BE18-8   Vertical analysis (common size) percentages for Charles Company's sales, cost of goods sold, and expenses are shown below.

Vertical Analysis	2009	2008	2007
Sales	100.0	100.0	100.0
Cost of goods sold	59.2	62.4	64.5
Expenses	25.0	25.6	27.5

Did Charles's net income as a percent of sales increase, decrease, or remain unchanged over the 3-year period? Provide numerical support for your answer.

Calculate liquidity ratios.
(SO 5)

BE18-9   Selected condensed data taken from a recent balance sheet of Perkins Inc. are as follows.

PERKINS INC.
Balance Sheet (partial)

Cash	$ 8,041,000
Short-term investments	4,947,000
Accounts receivable	12,545,000
Inventories	14,814,000
Other current assets	5,571,000
Total current assets	$45,918,000
Total current liabilities	$40,644,000

What are the **(a)** working capital, **(b)** current ratio, and **(c)** acid-test ratio?

Calculate profitability ratios.
(SO 5)

BE18-10   McLaren Corporation has net income of $11.44 million and net revenue of $80 million in 2008. Its assets are $14 million at the beginning of the year and $18 million at the end of the year. What are McLaren's **(a)** asset turnover and **(b)** profit margin?

BE18-11 The following data are taken from the financial statements of Morino Company.

Evaluate collection of accounts receivable.

(SO 5)

	2009	2008
Accounts receivable (net), end of year	$ 550,000	$ 520,000
Net sales on account	3,960,000	3,100,000
Terms for all sales are 1/10, n/60.		

1,070,000 ÷ 2
= 535,000

(a) Compute for each year (1) the receivables turnover and (2) the average collection period. At the end of 2007, accounts receivable (net) was $480,000.
(b) ▬▬▬▬▶ What conclusions about the management of accounts receivable can be drawn from these data?

BE18-12 The following data are from the income statements of Huntsinger Company.

Evaluate management of inventory.

(SO 5)

	2009	2008
Sales	$6,420,000	$6,240,000
Beginning inventory	980,000	860,000
Purchases	4,340,000	4,661,000
Ending inventory	1,020,000	980,000

(a) Compute for each year (1) the inventory turnover and (2) the average days to sell the inventory.
▬▬▬▶ **(b)** What conclusions concerning the management of the inventory can be drawn from these data?

BE18-13 Gladow Company has owners' equity of $400,000 and net income of $66,000. It has a payout ratio of 20% and a rate of return on assets of 15%. How much did Gladow pay in cash dividends, and what were its average assets? B)440,000
A) 13,200

Calculate profitability ratios.

(SO 5)

BE18-14 An inexperienced accountant for Ming Corporation showed the following in the income statement: income before income taxes and extraordinary item $400,000, and extraordinary loss from flood (before taxes) $70,000. The extraordinary loss and taxable income are both subject to a 30% tax rate. Prepare a correct income statement. +PRESENT NET OF the tax.

Prepare income statement including extraordinary items.

(SO 6)

BE18-15 On June 30, Reeves Corporation discontinued its operations in Mexico. During the year, the operating loss was $300,000 before taxes. On September 1, Reeves disposed of the Mexico facility at a pretax loss of $120,000. The applicable tax rate is 30%. Show the discontinued operations section of the income statement.

Prepare discontinued operations section of income statement.

(SO 6)

EXERCISES

Follow the rounding procedures used in the chapter.

E18-1 Financial information for Blevins Inc. is presented below.

Prepare horizontal analysis.

(SO 3)

	December 31, 2009	December 31, 2008
Current assets	$125,000	$100,000
Plant assets (net)	396,000	330,000
Current liabilities	91,000	70,000
Long-term liabilities	133,000	95,000
Common stock, $1 par	161,000	115,000
Retained earnings	136,000	150,000

Instructions
Prepare a schedule showing a horizontal analysis for 2009 using 2008 as the base year.

E18-2 Operating data for Gallup Corporation are presented below.

Prepare vertical analysis.

(SO 4)

	2009	2008
Sales	$750,000	$600,000
Cost of goods sold	465,000	390,000
Selling expenses	120,000	72,000
Administrative expenses	60,000	54,000
Income tax expense	33,000	24,000
Net income	72,000	60,000

Instructions
Prepare a schedule showing a vertical analysis for 2009 and 2008.

Prepare horizontal and vertical analyses.
(SO 3, 4)

E18-3 The comparative condensed balance sheets of Conard Corporation are presented below.

CONARD CORPORATION
Comparative Condensed Balance Sheets
December 31

	2009	2008
Assets		
Current assets	$ 74,000	$ 80,000
Property, plant, and equipment (net)	99,000	90,000
Intangibles	27,000	40,000
Total assets	$200,000	$210,000
Liabilities and stockholders' equity		
Current liabilities	$ 42,000	$ 48,000
Long-term liabilities	143,000	150,000
Stockholders' equity	15,000	12,000
Total liabilities and stockholders' equity	$200,000	$210,000

Instructions

(a) Prepare a horizontal analysis of the balance sheet data for Conard Corporation using 2008 as a base.

(b) Prepare a vertical analysis of the balance sheet data for Conard Corporation in columnar form for 2009.

Prepare horizontal and vertical analyses.
(SO 3, 4)

E18-4 The comparative condensed income statements of Hendi Corporation are shown below.

HENDI CORPORATION
Comparative Condensed Income Statements
For the Years Ended December 31

	2009	2008
Net sales	$600,000	$500,000
Cost of goods sold	483,000	420,000
Gross profit	117,000	80,000
Operating expenses	57,200	44,000
Net income	$ 59,800	$ 36,000

Instructions

(a) Prepare a horizontal analysis of the income statement data for Hendi Corporation using 2008 as a base. (Show the amounts of increase or decrease.)

(b) Prepare a vertical analysis of the income statement data for Hendi Corporation in columnar form for both years.

Compute liquidity ratios and compare results.
(SO 5)

E18-5 Nordstrom, Inc. operates department stores in numerous states. Selected financial statement data for the year ending January 29, 2005, are as follows.

NORDSTROM, INC.
Balance Sheet (partial)

(in millions)	End-of-Year	Beginning-of-Year
Cash and cash equivalents	$ 361	$ 340
Receivables (less allowance of 19 and 20)	646	667
Merchandise inventory	917	902
Prepaid expenses	53	46
Other current assets	595	570
Total current assets	$2,572	$2,525
Total current liabilities	$1,341	$1,123

For the year, net sales were $7,131, and cost of goods sold was $4,559 (in millions).

Instructions

(a) Compute the four liquidity ratios at the end of the year.

(b) Using the data in the chapter, compare Nordstrom's liquidity with (1) that of J.C. Penney Company, and (2) the industry averages for department stores.

E18-6 Leach Incorporated had the following transactions occur involving current assets and current liabilities during February 2008.

Perform current and acid-test ratio analysis.

(SO 5)

Feb.	3	Accounts receivable of $15,000 are collected.
	7	Equipment is purchased for $28,000 cash.
	11	Paid $3,000 for a 3-year insurance policy.
	14	Accounts payable of $12,000 are paid.
	18	Cash dividends of $5,000 are declared.

Additional information:

1. As of February 1, 2008, current assets were $130,000, and current liabilities were $50,000.
2. As of February 1, 2008, current assets included $15,000 of inventory and $2,000 of prepaid expenses.

Instructions

(a) Compute the current ratio as of the beginning of the month and after each transaction.

(b) Compute the acid-test ratio as of the beginning of the month and after each transaction.

E18-7 Bennis Company has the following comparative balance sheet data.

Compute selected ratios.

(SO 5)

BENNIS COMPANY
Balance Sheets
December 31

	2009	2008
Cash	$ 15,000	$ 30,000
Receivables (net)	70,000	60,000
Inventories	60,000	50,000
Plant assets (net)	200,000	180,000
	$345,000	$320,000
Accounts payable	$50,000	$60,000
Mortgage payable (15%)	100,000	100,000
Common stock, $10 par	140,000	120,000
Retained earnings	55,000	40,000
	$345,000	$320,000

Additional information for 2009:

1. Net income was $25,000.
2. Sales on account were $410,000. Sales returns and allowances were $20,000.
3. Cost of goods sold was $198,000.
4. The allowance for doubtful accounts was $2,500 on December 31, 2009, and $2,000 on December 31, 2008.

Instructions

Compute the following ratios at December 31, 2009.

(a) Current.

(b) Acid-test.

(c) Receivables turnover.

(d) Inventory turnover.

E18-8 Selected comparative statement data for Willingham Products Company are presented on the next page. All balance sheet data are as of December 31.

Compute selected ratios.

(SO 5)

	2009	2008
Net sales	$760,000	$720,000
Cost of goods sold	480,000	440,000
Interest expense	7,000	5,000
Net income	50,000	42,000
Accounts receivable	120,000	100,000
Inventory	85,000	75,000
Total assets	580,000	500,000
Total common stockholders' equity	430,000	325,000

Instructions
Compute the following ratios for 2009.

(a) Profit margin.
(b) Asset turnover.
(c) Return on assets.
(d) Return on common stockholders' equity.

Compute selected ratios.
(SO 5)

E18-9   The income statement for Christensen, Inc., appears below.

CHRISTENSEN, INC.
Income Statement
For the Year Ended December 31, 2008

Sales	$400,000
Cost of goods sold	230,000
Gross profit	170,000
Expenses (including $16,000 interest and $24,000 income taxes)	105,000
Net income	$ 65,000

Additional information:

1. The weighted average common shares outstanding in 2008 were 30,000 shares.
2. The market price of Christensen, Inc. stock was $13 in 2008.
3. Cash dividends of $26,000 were paid, $5,000 of which were to preferred stockholders.

Instructions
Compute the following ratios for 2008.

(a) Earnings per share.
(b) Price-earnings.
(c) Payout.
(d) Times interest earned.

Compute amounts from ratios.
(SO 5)

E18-10   Rees Corporation experienced a fire on December 31, 2009, in which its financial records were partially destroyed. It has been able to salvage some of the records and has ascertained the following balances.

	December 31, 2009	December 31, 2008
Cash	$ 30,000	$ 10,000
Receivables (net)	72,500	126,000
Inventory	200,000	180,000
Accounts payable	50,000	90,000
Notes payable	30,000	60,000
Common stock, $100 par	400,000	400,000
Retained earnings	113,500	101,000

Additional information:

1. The inventory turnover is 3.5 times.
2. The return on common stockholders' equity is 24%. The company had no additional paid-in capital.
3. The receivables turnover is 8.8 times.
4. The return on assets is 20%.
5. Total assets at December 31, 2008, were $605,000.

Instructions
Compute the following for Rees Corporation.

(a) Cost of goods sold for 2009.
(b) Net sales (credit) for 2009.
(c) Net income for 2009.
(d) Total assets at December 31, 2009.

E18-11 Scully Corporation's comparative balance sheets are presented below.

Compute ratios.
(SO 5)

SCULLY CORPORATION
Balance Sheets
December 31

	2008	2007
Cash *C A*	$ 4,300	$ 3,700
Accounts receivable *CA*	21,200	23,400
Inventory *CA*	10,000	7,000
Land	20,000	26,000
Building	70,000	70,000
Accumulated depreciation	(15,000)	(10,000)
Total	$110,500	$120,100
Accounts payable *CL*	$ 12,370	$ 31,100
Common stock *SHE*	75,000	69,000
Retained earnings *SHE*	23,130	20,000
Total	$110,500	$120,100

Scully's 2008 income statement included net sales of $100,000, cost of goods sold of $60,000, and net income of $15,000.

Instructions
Compute the following ratios for 2008.

(a) Current ratio.
(b) Acid-test ratio.
(c) Receivables turnover.
(d) Inventory turnover.
(e) Profit margin.
(f) Asset turnover.
(g) Return on assets.
(h) Return on common stockholders' equity.
(i) Debt to total assets ratio.

E18-12 For its fiscal year ending October 31, 2008, Molini Corporation reports the following partial data.

Prepare a correct income statement.
(SO 6)

Income before income taxes	$540,000
Income tax expense (30% × $390,000)	117,000
Income before extraordinary items	423,000
Extraordinary loss from flood	150,000
Net income	$273,000

The flood loss is considered an extraordinary item. The income tax rate is 30% on all items.

Instructions
(a) Prepare a correct income statement, beginning with income before income taxes.
(b) Explain in memo form why the income statement data are misleading.

E18-13 Yadier Corporation has income from continuing operations of $290,000 for the year ended December 31, 2008. It also has the following items (before considering income taxes).

Prepare income statement.
(SO 6)

1. An extraordinary loss of $80,000.
2. A gain of $30,000 on the discontinuance of a division.

3. A correction of an error in last year's financial statements that resulted in a $20,000 understatement of 2007 net income.

Assume all items are subject to income taxes at a 30% tax rate.

Instructions
(a) Prepare an income statement, beginning with income from continuing operations.
(b) Indicate the statement presentation of any item not included in (a) above.

EXERCISES: SET B

Visit the book's website at **www.wiley.com/college/weygandt**, and choose the Student Companion site, to access Exercise Set B.

PROBLEMS

Follow the rounding procedures used in the chapter.

Prepare vertical analysis and comment on profitability.

(SO 4, 5)

P18-1 Comparative statement data for Douglas Company and Maulder Company, two competitors, appear below. All balance sheet data are as of December 31, 2009, and December 31, 2008.

	Douglas Company		Maulder Company	
	2009	**2008**	**2009**	**2008**
Net sales	$1,549,035		$339,038	
Cost of goods sold	1,080,490		241,000	
Operating expenses	302,275		79,000	
Interest expense	8,980		2,252	
Income tax expense	54,500		6,650	
Current assets	325,975	$312,410	83,336	$ 79,467
Plant assets (net)	521,310	500,000	139,728	125,812
Current liabilities	65,325	75,815	35,348	30,281
Long-term liabilities	108,500	90,000	29,620	25,000
Common stock, $10 par	500,000	500,000	120,000	120,000
Retained earnings	173,460	146,595	38,096	29,998

Instructions
(a) Prepare a vertical analysis of the 2009 income statement data for Douglas Company and Maulder Company in columnar form.
(b) Comment on the relative profitability of the companies by computing the return on assets and the return on common stockholders' equity ratios for both companies.

Compute ratios from balance sheet and income statement.

(SO 5)

P18-2 The comparative statements of Villa Tool Company are presented below.

VILLA TOOL COMPANY
Income Statement
For the Year Ended December 31

	2009	**2008**
Net sales	$1,818,500	$1,750,500
Cost of goods sold	1,011,500	996,000
Gross profit	807,000	754,500
Selling and administrative expense	516,000	479,000
Income from operations	291,000	275,500
Other expenses and losses		
Interest expense	18,000	14,000
Income before income taxes	273,000	261,500
Income tax expense	81,000	77,000
Net income	$ 192,000	$ 184,500

VILLA TOOL COMPANY
Balance Sheets
December 31

Assets	2009	2008
Current assets		
Cash	$ 60,100	$ 64,200
Short-term investments	69,000	50,000
Accounts receivable (net)	117,800	102,800
Inventory	123,000	115,500
Total current assets	369,900	332,500
Plant assets (net)	600,300	520,300
Total assets	$970,200	$852,800
Liabilities and Stockholders' Equity		
Current liabilities		
Accounts payable	$160,000	$145,400
Income taxes payable	43,500	42,000
Total current liabilities	203,500	187,400
Bonds payable	200,000	200,000
Total liabilities	403,500	387,400
Stockholders' equity		
Common stock ($5 par)	280,000	300,000
Retained earnings	286,700	165,400
Total stockholders' equity	566,700	465,400
Total liabilities and stockholders' equity	$970,200	$852,800

All sales were on account. The allowance for doubtful accounts was $3,200 on December 31, 2009, and $3,000 on December 31, 2008.

Instructions
Compute the following ratios for 2009. (Weighted average common shares in 2009 were 57,000.)

(a) Earnings per share. (f) Receivables turnover.
(b) Return on common stockholders' equity. (g) Inventory turnover.
(c) Return on assets. (h) Times interest earned.
(d) Current. (i) Asset turnover.
(e) Acid-test. (j) Debt to total assets.

P18-3 Condensed balance sheet and income statement data for Kersenbrock Corporation appear below.

Perform ratio analysis, and evaluate financial position and operating results.

(SO 5)

KERSENBROCK CORPORATION
Balance Sheets
December 31

	2009	2008	2007
Cash	$ 25,000	$ 20,000	$ 18,000
Receivables (net)	50,000	45,000	48,000
Other current assets	90,000	95,000	64,000
Investments	75,000	70,000	45,000
Plant and equipment (net)	400,000	370,000	358,000
	$640,000	$600,000	$533,000
Current liabilities	$ 75,000	$ 80,000	$ 70,000
Long-term debt	80,000	85,000	50,000
Common stock, $10 par	340,000	310,000	300,000
Retained earnings	145,000	125,000	113,000
	$640,000	$600,000	$533,000

KERSENBROCK CORPORATION
Income Statement
For the Year Ended December 31

	2009	2008
Sales	$740,000	$700,000
Less: Sales returns and allowances	40,000	50,000
Net sales	700,000	650,000
Cost of goods sold	420,000	400,000
Gross profit	280,000	250,000
Operating expenses (including income taxes)	235,000	220,000
Net income	$ 45,000	$ 30,000

Additional information:

1. The market price of Kersenbrock's common stock was $4.00, $5.00, and $8.00 for 2007, 2008, and 2009, respectively.
2. All dividends were paid in cash.

Instructions

(a) Compute the following ratios for 2008 and 2009.
   (1) Profit margin.
   (2) Asset turnover.
   (3) Earnings per share. (Weighted average common shares in 2009 were 32,000 and in 2008 were 31,000.)
   (4) Price-earnings.
   (5) Payout.
   (6) Debt to total assets.

(b) ◖▬▬▬ Based on the ratios calculated, discuss briefly the improvement or lack thereof in financial position and operating results from 2008 to 2009 of Kersenbrock Corporation.

Compute ratios, and comment on overall liquidity and profitability.
(SO 5)

P18-4 Financial information for Hanshew Company is presented below.

HANSHEW COMPANY
Balance Sheets
December 31

Assets	2009	2008
Cash	$ 70,000	$ 65,000
Short-term investments	52,000	40,000
Receivables (net)	98,000	80,000
Inventories	125,000	135,000
Prepaid expenses	29,000	23,000
Land	130,000	130,000
Building and equipment (net)	180,000	175,000
	$684,000	$648,000
Liabilities and Stockholders' Equity		
Notes payable	$100,000	$100,000
Accounts payable	48,000	42,000
Accrued liabilities	50,000	40,000
Bonds payable, due 2012	150,000	150,000
Common stock, $10 par	200,000	200,000
Retained earnings	136,000	116,000
	$684,000	$648,000

HANSHEW COMPANY
Income Statement
For the Years Ended December 31

	2009	2008
Sales	$850,000	$790,000
Cost of goods sold	620,000	575,000
Gross profit	230,000	215,000
Operating expenses	187,000	173,000
Net income	$ 43,000	$ 42,000

Additional information:

1. Inventory at the beginning of 2008 was $118,000.
2. Receivables (net) at the beginning of 2008 were $88,000. The allowance for doubtful accounts was $4,000 at the end of 2009, $3,800 at the end of 2008, and $3,700 at the beginning of 2008.
3. Total assets at the beginning of 2008 were $630,000.
4. No common stock transactions occurred during 2008 or 2009.
5. All sales were on account.

Instructions

(a) Indicate, by using ratios, the change in liquidity and profitability of Hanshew Company from 2008 to 2009. (*Note*: Not all profitability ratios can be computed.)

(b) Given below are three independent situations and a ratio that may be affected. For each situation, compute the affected ratio (1) as of December 31, 2009, and (2) as of December 31, 2010, after giving effect to the situation. Net income for 2010 was $50,000. Total assets on December 31, 2010, were $700,000.

Situation	Ratio
(1) 18,000 shares of common stock were sold at par on July 1, 2010.	Return on common stockholders' equity
(2) All of the notes payable were paid in 2010. The only change in liabilities was that the notes payable were paid.	Debt to total assets
(3) Market price of common stock was $9 on December 31, 2009, and $12.80 on December 31, 2010.	Price-earnings ratio

P18-5   Selected financial data of Target and Wal-Mart for 2005 are presented here (in millions).

Compute selected ratios, and compare liquidity, profitability, and solvency for two companies.

(SO 5)

	Target Corporation	Wal-Mart Stores, Inc.
	Income Statement Data for Year	
Net sales	$45,682	$285,222
Cost of goods sold	31,445	219,793
Selling and administrative expenses	10,480	51,354
Interest expense	570	986
Other income (expense)	1,157	2,767
Income tax expense	1,146	5,589
Net income	$ 3,198	$ 10,267
	Balance Sheet Data (End of Year)	
Current assets	$13,922	$ 38,491
Noncurrent assets	18,371	81,732
Total assets	$32,293	$120,223
Current liabilities	$ 8,220	$ 42,888
Long-term debt	11,044	27,939
Total stockholders' equity	13,029	49,396
Total liabilities and stockholders' equity	$32,293	$120,223

	Beginning-of-Year Balances	
Total assets	$31,416	$105,405
Total stockholders' equity	11,132	43,623
Current liabilities	8,314	40,364
Total liabilities	20,284	61,782
	Other Data	
Average net receivables	$4,845	$ 1,485
Average inventory	4,958	28,030
Net cash provided by operating activities	3,821	15,044

Instructions
(a) For each company, compute the following ratios.

(1) Current.	**(7)** Asset turnover.
(2) Receivables turnover.	**(8)** Return on assets.
(3) Average collection period.	**(9)** Return on common stockholders' equity.
(4) Inventory turnover.	**(10)** Debt to total assets.
(5) Days in inventory.	**(11)** Times interest earned.
(6) Profit margin.	

(b) Compare the liquidity, solvency, and profitability of the two companies.

Compute numerous ratios.
(SO 5)

P18-6 The comparative statements of Dillon Company are presented below.

DILLON COMPANY
Income Statement
For Year Ended December 31

	2009	2008
Net sales (all on account)	$600,000	$520,000
Expenses		
Cost of goods sold	415,000	354,000
Selling and administrative	120,800	114,800
Interest expense	7,800	6,000
Income tax expense	18,000	14,000
Total expenses	561,600	488,800
Net income	$ 38,400	$ 31,200

DILLON COMPANY
Balance Sheets
December 31

Assets	2009	2008
Current assets		
Cash	$ 21,000	$ 18,000
Short-term investments	18,000	15,000
Accounts receivable (net)	86,000	74,000
Inventory	90,000	70,000
Total current assets	215,000	177,000
Plant assets (net)	423,000	383,000
Total assets	$638,000	$560,000

Liabilities and Stockholders' Equity

Current liabilities		
Accounts payable	$122,000	$110,000
Income taxes payable	23,000	20,000
Total current liabilities	145,000	130,000
Long-term liabilities		
Bonds payable	120,000	80,000
Total liabilities	265,000	210,000
Stockholders' equity		
Common stock ($5 par)	150,000	150,000
Retained earnings	223,000	200,000
Total stockholders' equity	373,000	350,000
Total liabilities and stockholders' equity	$638,000	$560,000

Additional data:

The common stock recently sold at $19.50 per share.

The year-end balance in the allowance for doubtful accounts was $3,000 for 2009 and $2,400 for 2008.

Instructions

Compute the following ratios for 2009.

(a) Current.   (h) Return on common stockholders' equity.
(b) Acid-test.   (i) Earnings per share.
(c) Receivables turnover.   (j) Price-earnings.
(d) Inventory turnover.   (k) Payout.
(e) Profit margin.   (l) Debt to total assets.
(f) Asset turnover.   (m) Times interest earned.
(g) Return on assets.

P18-7   Presented below is an incomplete income statement and an incomplete comparative balance sheet of Cotte Corporation.

Compute missing information given a set of ratios.

(SO 5)

COTTE CORPORATION
Income Statement
For the Year Ended December 31, 2009

Sales	$11,000,000
Cost of goods sold	?
Gross profit	?
Operating expenses	1,665,000
Income from operations	?
Other expenses and losses	
Interest expense	?
Income before income taxes	?
Income tax expense	560,000
Net income	$?

COTTE CORPORATION
Balance Sheets
December 31

Assets	2009	2008
Current assets		
Cash	$ 450,000	$ 375,000
Accounts receivable (net)	?	950,000
Inventory	?	1,720,000
Total current assets	?	3,045,000
Plant assets (net)	4,620,000	3,955,000
Total assets	$?	$7,000,000
Liabilities and Stockholders' Equity		
Current liabilities	$?	$ 825,000
Long-term notes payable	?	2,800,000
Total liabilities	?	3,625,000
Common stock, $1 par	3,000,000	3,000,000
Retained earnings	400,000	375,000
Total stockholders' equity	3,400,000	3,375,000
Total liabilities and stockholders' equity	$?	$7,000,000

Additional information:

1. The receivables turnover for 2009 is 10 times.
2. All sales are on account.
3. The profit margin for 2009 is 14.5%.
4. Return on assets is 22% for 2009.
5. The current ratio on December 31, 2009, is 3.0.
6. The inventory turnover for 2009 is 4.8 times.

Instructions

Compute the missing information given the ratios above. Show computations. (*Note*: Start with one ratio and derive as much information as possible from it before trying another ratio. List all missing amounts under the ratio used to find the information.)

Prepare income statement with discontinued operations and extraordinary loss.

(SO 6)

P18-8   Cheaney Corporation owns a number of cruise ships and a chain of hotels. The hotels, which have not been profitable, were discontinued on September 1, 2008. The 2008 operating results for the company were as follows.

Operating revenues	$12,850,000
Operating expenses	8,700,000
Operating income	$ 4,150,000

Analysis discloses that these data include the operating results of the hotel chain, which were: operating revenues $2,000,000 and operating expenses $2,400,000. The hotels were sold at a gain of $200,000 before taxes. This gain is not included in the operating results. During the year, Cheaney suffered an extraordinary loss of $800,000 before taxes, which is not included in the operating results. In 2008, the company had other revenues and gains of $100,000, which are not included in the operating results. The corporation is in the 30% income tax bracket.

Instructions

Prepare a condensed income statement.

Prepare income statement with nontypical items.

(SO 6)

P18-9   The ledger of LaRussa Corporation at December 31, 2008, contains the following summary data.

Net sales	$1,700,000	Cost of goods sold	$1,100,000
Selling expenses	120,000	Administrative expenses	150,000
Other revenues and gains	20,000	Other expenses and losses	28,000

Your analysis reveals the following additional information that is not included in the above data.

1. The entire puzzles division was discontinued on August 31. The income from operations for this division before income taxes was $20,000. The puzzles division was sold at a loss of $90,000 before income taxes.
2. On May 15, company property was expropriated for an interstate highway. The settlement resulted in an extraordinary gain of $120,000 before income taxes.
3. The income tax rate on all items is 30%.

Instructions

Prepare an income statement for the year ended December 31, 2008. Use the format illustrated in Demonstration Problem 2 (p. 808).

PROBLEMS: SET B

Visit the book's website at **www.wiley.com/college/weygandt**, and choose the Student Companion site, to access Problem Set B.

CONTINUING COOKIE CHRONICLE

(Note: This is a continuation of the Cookie Chronicle from Chapters 1-17.)

CCC18   Natalie and Curtis have comparative balance sheets and income statements for Cookie & Coffee Creations Inc. They have been told that they can use these financial statements to prepare horizontal and vertical analyses, and to calculate financial ratios, to analyze how their business is doing and to make some decisions they have been considering.

Go to the book's website,
www.wiley.com/college/weygandt,
to see the completion of this problem.

BROADENING YOUR PERSPECTIVE

FINANCIAL REPORTING AND ANALYSIS

Financial Reporting Problem
PepsiCo, Inc.

BYP18-1   Your parents are considering investing in PepsiCo, common stock. They ask you, as an accounting expert, to make an analysis of the company for them. Fortunately, excerpts from a current annual report of PepsiCo are presented in Appendix A of this textbook. Note that all dollar amounts are in millions.

Instructions

(Follow the approach in the chapter for rounding numbers.)

(a) Make a 5-year trend analysis, using 2001 as the base year, of (1) net sales and (2) net income. Comment on the significance of the trend results.
(b) Compute for 2005 and 2004 the (1) profit margin, (2) asset turnover, (3) return on assets, and (4) return on common stockholders' equity. How would you evaluate PepsiCo's profitability? Total assets at December 27, 2003, were $25,327, and total stockholders' equity at December 27, 2003, was $11,896.
(c) Compute for 2005 and 2004 the (1) debt to total assets and (2) times interest earned ratio. How would you evaluate PepsiCo's long-term solvency?
(d) What information outside the annual report may also be useful to your parents in making a decision about PepsiCo, Inc.?

Comparative Analysis Problem
PepsiCo, Inc. vs. The Coca-Cola Company

BYP18-2   PepsiCo's financial statements are presented in Appendix A. Coca-Cola Company's financial statements are presented in Appendix B.

Instructions
(a) Based on the information contained in these financial statements, determine each of the following for each company.
  (1) The percentage increase (decrease) in (i) net sales and (ii) net income from 2004 to 2005.
  (2) The percentage increase in (i) total assets and (ii) total common stockholders' (shareholders') equity from 2004 to 2005.
  (3) The basic earnings per share and price-earnings ratio for 2005. (For Coca-Cola, use the basic earnings per share.) Coca-Cola's common stock had a market price of $43.60 at the end of fiscal-year 2005.

(b) What conclusions concerning the two companies can be drawn from these data?

Exploring the Web

BYP18-3   The Management Discussion and Analysis section of an annual report addresses corporate performance for the year, and sometimes uses financial ratios to support its claims.

Address: www.ibm.com/investor/tools/index.phtml or go to **www.wiley.com/college/weygandt**

Steps
1. From IBM's Investor Tools, choose **Investment Guides**.
2. Choose **Guide to Annual Reports**.
3. Choose **Anatomy of an Annual Report**.

Instructions
Using the information from the above site, answer the following questions.

(a) What are the optional elements that are often included in an annual report?
(b) What are the elements of an annual report that are required by the SEC?
(c) Describe the contents of the Management Discussion.
(d) Describe the contents of the Auditors' Report.
(e) Describe the contents of the Selected Financial Data.

CRITICAL THINKING

Decision Making Across the Organization

BYP18-4   As the CPA for Carismo Manufacturing Inc., you have been asked to develop some key ratios from the comparative financial statements. This information is to be used to convince creditors that the company is solvent and will continue as a going concern. The data requested and the computations developed from the financial statements follow.

	2008	2007
Current ratio	3.1 times	2.1 times
Acid-test ratio	.8 times	1.4 times
Asset turnover	2.8 times	2.2 times
Net income	Up 32%	Down 8%
Earnings per share	$3.30	$2.50
Book value per share	Up 8%	Up 11%

Instructions
With the class divided into groups, answer the following.

Carismo Manufacturing Inc. asks you to prepare a list of brief comments stating how each of these items supports the solvency and going-concern potential of the business. The company wishes to use these comments to support its presentation of data to its creditors. You are to prepare the comments as requested, giving the implications and the limitations of each item separately. Then prepare a collective inference that may be drawn from the individual items about Carismo's solvency and going-concern potential.

BYP18-5 General Dynamics develops, produces, and supports innovative, reliable, and highly sophisticated military and commercial products. In July of a recent year, the corporation announced that its Quincy Shipbuilding Division (Quincy) will be closed following the completion of the Maritime Prepositioning Ship construction program.

Prior to discontinuance, the operating results of Quincy were net sales $246.8 million, income from operations before income taxes $28.3 million, and income taxes $12.5 million. The corporation's loss on disposition of Quincy was $5.0 million, net of $4.3 million income tax benefits.

From its other operating activities, General Dynamics' financial results were net sales $8,163.8 million, cost of goods sold $6,958.8 million, and selling and administrative expenses $537.0 million. In addition, the corporation had interest expense of $17.2 million and interest revenue of $3.6 million. Income taxes were $282.9 million.

General Dynamics had an average of 42.3 million shares of common stock outstanding during the year.

Instructions

With the class divided into groups, answer the following.

(a) Prepare the income statement for the year, assuming that the year ended on December 31, 2008. Show earnings per share data on the income statement. All dollars should be stated in millions, except for per share amounts. (For example, $8 million would be shown as $8.0)

(b) In the preceding year, Quincy's earnings were $51.6 million before income taxes of $22.8 million. For comparative purposes, General Dynamics reported earnings per share of $0.61 from discontinued operations for Quincy in the preceding year.

(1) What was the average number of common shares outstanding during the preceding year?

(2) If earnings per share from continuing operations was $7.47, what was income from continuing operations during the preceding year? (Round to two decimals.)

Communication Activity

BYP18-6 Beth Harlan is the CEO of Lafferty's Electronics. Harlan is an expert engineer but a novice in accounting. She asks you to explain (1) the bases for comparison in analyzing Lafferty's financial statements, and (2) the factors affecting quality of earnings.

Instructions

Write a letter to Beth Harlan that explains the bases for comparison and factors affecting quality of earnings.

Ethics Case

BYP18-7 Jack McClintock, president of McClintock Industries, wishes to issue a press release to bolster his company's image and maybe even its stock price, which has been gradually falling. As controller, you have been asked to provide a list of twenty financial ratios along with some other operating statistics relative to McClintock Industries' first quarter financials and operations.

Two days after you provide the ratios and data requested, Jeremy Phelps, the public relations director of McClintock, asks you to prove the accuracy of the financial and operating data contained in the press release written by the president and edited by Jeremy. In the press release, the president highlights the sales increase of 25% over last year's first quarter and the positive change in the current ratio from 1.5:1 last year to 3:1 this year. He also emphasizes that production was up 50% over the prior year's first quarter.

You note that the press release contains only positive or improved ratios and none of the negative or deteriorated ratios. For instance, no mention is made that the debt to total assets ratio has increased from 35% to 55%, that inventories are up 89%, and that while the current ratio improved, the acid-test ratio fell from 1:1 to .5:1. Nor is there any mention that the reported profit for the quarter would have been a loss had not the estimated lives of McClintock's plant and machinery been increased by 30%. Jeremy emphasized, "The prez wants this release by early this afternoon."

Instructions

(a) Who are the stakeholders in this situation?

(b) Is there anything unethical in president McClintock's actions?

(c) Should you as controller remain silent? Does Jeremy have any responsibility?

 ## "All About You" Activity

BYP18-8 In this chapter you learned how to use many tools for performing a financial analysis of a company. When making personal investments, however, it is most likely that you won't be buying stocks and bonds in individual companies. Instead, when most people want to invest in stock, they buy mutual funds. By investing in a mutual fund, you reduce your risk because the fund diversifies by buying the stock of a variety of different companies, bonds, and other investments, depending on the stated goals of the fund.

Before you invest in a fund, you will need to decide what type of fund you want. For example, do you want a fund that has the potential of high growth (but also high risk), or are you looking for lower risk and a steady stream of income? Do you want a fund that invests only in U.S. companies, or do you want one that invests globally? Many resources are available to help you with these types of decisions.

Instructions

Go to **http://web.archive.org/web/20050210200843/http://www.cnb1.com/invallocmdl.htm** and complete the investment allocation questionnaire. Add up your total points to determine the type of investment fund that would be appropriate for you.

 ## Answers to Insight and Accounting Across the Organization Questions

p. 789 How to Manage the Current Ratio

Q: How might management influence the company's current ratio?

A: *Management can affect the current ratio by speeding up or withholding payments on accounts payable just before the balance sheet date. Management can alter the cash balance by increasing or decreasing long-term assets or long-term debt, or by issuing or purchasing equity shares.*

p. 797 Keeping Up to Date as an Investor

Q: If you want to keep current with the financial and operating developments of a company in which you own shares, what are some ways you can do so?

A: *You can obtain current information on your investments through a company's Web site, financial magazines and newspapers, CNBC television programs, investment letters, and a stockbroker.*

p. 802 What Is Extraordinary?

Q: If a company takes a large restructuring charge, what is the effect on the company's current income statement versus future ones?

A: *The current period's net income can be greatly diminished by a large restructuring charge, while the net income in future periods can be enhanced because they are relieved of costs (i.e., depreciation and labor expenses) that would have been charged to them.*

 ## Authors' Comments on *All About You:* Should I Play the Market Yet? (p. 805)

For a number of reasons, it is probably a bad idea for Rachael to buy her employer's stock. First, if Rachael is going to invest in the stock market, she should diversify her investments across a number of different companies. Second, you should never have more than a small portion of your total investment portfolio invested in your employer. Suppose that your employer starts to do poorly, the stock price falls, and you get laid off. You lose on two counts: You don't have income, and your net worth has been affected adversely by the drop in the stock price. (This exact situation happened to thousands of Enron employees, who not only lost their jobs, but their retirement savings as well, as Enron's stock plummeted). Third, after purchasing her employer's stock, Rachael's liquidity would be negatively affected: She would have only $3,000 of remaining liquid assets.

If Rachel invests $7,000, she actually has only enough liquid assets to cover one month's worth of expenses. It is true that she could sell her stock, but if it has fallen in value, she will be reluctant to sell. In short, if she were to buy the stock, her financial flexibility would be very limited.

The bottom line is that we think that Rachael *should* invest in something that offers a higher return than her bank savings account, but we question whether she has enough liquidity to invest in individual stocks. We would recommend that she put some money in a stock mutual fund, some in a short-term CD, and the rest in a money-market fund.

Answer to PepsiCo Review It Question 4, p. 787

PepsiCo presents horizontal analyses in its "Financial Highlights" section and its Management's Discussion and Analysis section. Vertical analysis is used in discussions presented in the Management's Discussion and Analysis section.

Answers to Self-Study Questions

1. b   **2.** d   **3.** a   **4.** c   **5.** c   **6.** c   **7.** c   **8.** c   **9.** d   **10.** d

Chapter 19

Managerial Accounting

The Navigator

Feature Story

WHAT A DIFFERENCE A DAY MAKES

In January 1998 Compaq Computer (*www.compaq.com*) had just become the largest seller of personal computers, and it was *Forbes* magazine's "company of the year." Its chief executive, Eckhard Pfeiffer, was riding high. But during the next two years Compaq lost $2 billion. The company was in chaos, and Mr. Pfeiffer was out of a job. What happened?

First, Dell happened. Dell Computer (www.dell.com) pioneered a new way of making and selling personal computers. Its customers "custom design" their computer over the Internet or phone. Dell reengineered its "supply chain": It coordinated its efforts with its suppliers and streamlined its order-taking and production process. It can ship a computer within two days of taking an order. Personal computers lose 1 percent of their value every week they sit on a shelf. Thus, having virtually no inventory is a great advantage to Dell. Compaq tried to adopt Dell's approach, but with limited success.

The second shock to Compaq came when it acquired a company even larger than itself—Digital Equipment. Digital was famous as much for its technical service as it was for its products. Mr. Pfeiffer believed that the purchase of Digital, with its huge and respected technical sales force, opened new opportunities for Compaq as a global service company. Now it could sell to and service high-end corporate customers. But combining the two companies proved to be hugely expensive and extremely complicated. Ultimately Compaq decided to merge with Hewlett-Packard (*www.hp.com*) in order to survive.

But now Hewlett-Packard is looking over its shoulder for Dell. Why? Because recently Dell moved into the computer printer business—a segment that Hewlett-Packard has long dominated. Dell currently sells only 2 million printers per year, compared to Hewlett-Packard's 42 million. But many analysts predict that by employing the same techniques that it used in its PC business, Dell will soon take a major share of the printer business—and in the process drive down prices and force some less-nimble competitors out of business.

Inside Chapter 19...

This chapter focuses on issues illustrated in the Feature Story about Compaq Computer and Dell. These include determining and controlling the costs of material, labor, and overhead and the relationship between costs and profits. In previous chapters, you learned about the form and content of **financial statements for external users** of financial information, such as stockholders and creditors. These financial statements represent the principal product of financial accounting. Managerial accounting focuses primarily on the preparation of **reports for internal users** of financial information, such as the managers and officers of a company. Managers are evaluated on the results of their decisions. In today's rapidly changing global environment, managers often make decisions that determine their company's fate—and their own. Managerial accounting provides tools for assisting management in making decisions and for evaluating the effectiveness of those decisions.

The content and organization of this chapter are as follows.

The Navigator

MANAGERIAL ACCOUNTING BASICS

Managerial accounting, also called **management accounting**, is a field of accounting that provides economic and financial information for managers and other internal users. The activities that are part of managerial accounting (and the chapters in which they are discussed in this textbook) are as follows.

1. Explaining manufacturing and nonmanufacturing costs and how they are reported in the financial statements (Chapter 19).

2. Computing the cost of providing a service or manufacturing a product (Chapters 20 and 21).

3. Determining the behavior of costs and expenses as activity levels change and analyzing cost–volume–profit relationships within a company (Chapter 22).

4. Assisting management in profit planning and formalizing these plans in the form of budgets (Chapter 23).

5. Providing a basis for controlling costs and expenses by comparing actual results with planned objectives and standard costs (Chapters 24 and 25).

6. Accumulating and presenting data for management decision making (Chapter 27).

Managerial accounting applies to all types of businesses—service, merchandising, and manufacturing. It also applies to all forms of business organizations—proprietorships, partnerships, and corporations. Managerial accounting is needed in not-for-profit entities as well as in profit-oriented enterprises.

In the past, managerial accountants were primarily engaged in cost accounting—collecting and reporting costs to management. Recently that role changed significantly. First as the business environment has become more automated, methods to determine the amount and type of cost in a product have changed. Second, managerial accountants are now held responsible for strategic cost management; that is, assisting in evaluating how well the company is employing its resources. As a result, managerial accountants now serve as team members alongside personnel from production, marketing, and engineering when critical strategic decisions are being made.

Opportunities for managerial accountants to advance within the company are considerable. Financial executives must have a background that includes an understanding of managerial accounting concepts. Whatever your position in the company—marketing, sales, or production, knowledge of managerial accounting greatly improves your opportunities for advancement. As the CEO of Microsoft noted: "If you're supposed to be making money in business and supposed to be satisfying customers and building market share, there are numbers that characterize those things. And if somebody can't sort of speak to me quantitatively about it, then I'm nervous."

Comparing Managerial and Financial Accounting

STUDY OBJECTIVE 1

Explain the distinguishing features of managerial accounting.

There are both similarities and differences between managerial and financial accounting. First, each field of accounting deals with the economic events of a business. Thus, their interests overlap. For example, determining the unit cost of manufacturing a product is part of managerial accounting. Reporting the total cost of goods manufactured and sold is part of financial accounting. In addition, both managerial and financial accounting require that a company's economic events be quantified and communicated to interested parties.

The principal differences between financial accounting and managerial accounting are summarized in Illustration 19-1. The need for various types of economic data is responsible for many of the differences.

Illustration 19-1
Differences between financial and managerial accounting

Financial Accounting		Managerial Accounting
• External users: stockholders, creditors, and regulators.	**Primary Users of Reports**	• Internal users: officers and managers.
• Financial statements. • Quarterly and annually.	**Types and Frequency of Reports**	• Internal reports. • As frequently as needed.
• General-purpose.	**Purpose of Reports**	• Special-purpose for specific decisions.
• Pertains to business as a whole. • Highly aggregated (condensed). • Limited to double-entry accounting and cost data. • Generally accepted accounting principles.	**Content of Reports**	• Pertains to subunits of the business. • Very detailed. • Extends beyond double-entry accounting to any relevant data. • Standard is relevance to decisions.
• Audit by CPA.	**Verification Process**	• No independent audits.

Management Functions

Management's activities and responsibilities can be classified into three broad functions. They are:

1. Planning.
2. Directing.
3. Controlling.

In performing these functions, managers make decisions that have a significant impact on the organization.

Planning requires management to look ahead and to establish objectives. These objectives are often diverse: maximizing short-term profits and market share, maintaining a commitment to environmental protection, and contributing to social programs. For example, Hewlett-Packard, in an attempt to gain a stronger foothold in the computer industry, has greatly reduced its prices to compete with Dell. A key objective of management is to add **value** to the business under its control. Value is usually measured by the trading price of the company's stock and by the potential selling price of the company.

Directing involves coordinating a company's diverse activities and human resources to produce a smooth-running operation. This function relates to implementing planned objectives and providing necessary incentives to motivate employees. For example, manufacturers such as Campbell Soup Company, General Motors, and Dell must coordinate purchasing, manufacturing, warehousing, and selling. Service corporations such as American Airlines, FedEx, and AT&T must coordinate scheduling, sales, service, and acquisitions of equipment and supplies. Directing also involves selecting executives, appointing managers and supervisors, and hiring and training employees.

The third management function, **controlling**, is the process of keeping the company's activities on track. In controlling operations, managers determine whether planned goals are being met. When there are deviations from targeted objectives, managers must decide what changes are needed to get back on track. Recent scandals at companies like Enron, Lucent, and Xerox attest to the fact that companies must have adequate controls to ensure that accurate information is developed.

How do managers achieve control? A smart manager in a small operation can make personal observations, ask good questions, and know how to evaluate the answers. But using this approach in a large organization would result in chaos. Imagine the president of Dell attempting to determine whether planned objectives are being met without some record of what has happened and what is expected to occur. Thus, large businesses typically use a formal system of evaluation. These systems include such features as budgets, responsibility centers, and performance evaluation reports.

MANAGEMENT INSIGHT

Automation Has Changed Management

The trend toward more automated and computerized factories has changed the way managers and employees interact. For one thing, managers have fewer direct labor employees to supervise because fewer are needed on the line. Recently, two technology giants, General Electric and Cisco Systems, joined forces to build computerized infrastructures for manufacturers. Their goal is to improve productivity by making better use of data generated by factory-automation equipment. Ultimately their systems should provide a closer link between the factory and corporate offices.

 As factories become more automated, what will managers "manage"?

Decision making is not a separate management function. Rather, it is the outcome of the exercise of good judgment in planning, directing, and controlling.

Business Ethics

As indicated in Chapter 1, all employees within an organization are expected to act ethically in their business activities. Given the importance of ethical behavior to corporations and their owners (stockholders), an increasing number of organizations provide codes of business ethics for their employees.

Despite these efforts, recent business scandals resulted in massive investment losses and numerous employee layoffs. A 2003 survey of fraud by international accounting firm KPMG reported a 13% increase in instances of corporate fraud compared to five years earlier. It noted that while employee fraud (such things as expense-account abuse, payroll fraud, and theft of assets) represented 60% of all instances of fraud, financial reporting fraud (the intentional misstatement of financial reports) was the most costly to companies. That should not be surprising given the long list of companies such as Enron, Global Crossing, WorldCom, and others that engaged in massive financial frauds which led to huge financial losses and thousands of lost jobs.

CREATING PROPER INCENTIVES

Companies like Motorola, IBM, and Nike use complex systems to control and evaluate the actions of managers. They dedicate substantial resources to monitor and effectively evaluate the actions of employees. Unfortunately, these systems and controls sometimes unwittingly create incentives for managers to take unethical actions. For example, companies prepare budgets to provide direction. Because the budget is also used as an evaluation tool, some managers try to "game" the budgeting process by underestimating their division's predicted performance so that it will be easier to meet their performance targets. On the other hand, if the budget is set at unattainable levels, managers sometimes take unethical actions to meet the targets in order to receive higher compensation or, in some cases, to keep their jobs.

For example, in recent years, airline manufacturer Boeing was plagued by a series of scandals including charges of over-billing, corporate espionage, and illegal conflicts of interest. Some long-time employees of Boeing blame the decline in ethics on a change in the corporate culture that took place after Boeing merged with McDonnell Douglas. They suggest that evaluation systems implemented after the merger to monitor results and evaluate employee performance made employees believe they needed to succeed no matter what.

As another example, manufacturing companies need to establish production goals for their processes. Again, if controls are not effective and realistic, problems develop. To illustrate, Schering-Plough, a pharmaceutical manufacturer, found that employees were so concerned with meeting production standards that they failed to monitor the quality of the product, and as a result the dosages were often wrong.

CODE OF ETHICAL STANDARDS

As noted throughout the textbook, the U.S. Congress enacted legislation to help prevent lapses in internal control. This legislation, referred to as the **Sarbanes-Oxley Act of 2002** (SOX, or Sarbox) has important implications for the financial community. One result of SOX was to clarify top management's responsibility for the company's financial statements. CEOs and CFOs must now certify that financial statements give a fair presentation of the company's operating results and its financial condition. In addition, top managers must certify that the company maintains an adequate system of internal controls to safeguard the company's assets and ensure accurate financial reports.

Another result of SOX is that companies now pay more attention to the composition of the board of directors. In particular, the audit committee of the board of directors must be comprised entirely of independent members (that is, non-employees) and must contain at least one financial expert.

Finally, to increase the likelihood of compliance with the rules that are part of the new legislation, the law substantially increases the penalties for misconduct.

To provide guidance for managerial accountants, the Institute of Management Accountants (IMA) has developed a code of ethical standards, entitled *IMA Statement of Ethical Professional Practice.* Management accountants should not commit acts in violation of these standards. Nor should they condone such acts by others within their organizations. We include the IMA code of ethical standards in Appendix E at the end of the book. Throughout the chapters on managerial accounting, we will address various ethical issues faced by managers.

Before You Go On...

REVIEW IT

1. Compare financial accounting and managerial accounting and identify the principal differences.
2. Identify and discuss the three broad functions of management.
3. What were some of the regulatory changes enacted under the Sarbanes-Oxley Act?

 The Navigator

MANAGERIAL COST CONCEPTS

For managers at companies like Dell or Hewlett-Packard to plan, direct, and control operations effectively, they need good information. One very important type of information is related to costs. Managers should ask questions such as the following.

1. What costs are involved in making a product or providing a service?
2. If we decrease production volume, will costs decrease?
3. What impact will automation have on total costs?
4. How can we best control costs?

To answer these questions, managers need reliable and relevant cost information. We now explain and illustrate the various cost categories that management uses.

Manufacturing Costs

STUDY OBJECTIVE 3

Define the three classes of manufacturing costs.

Manufacturing consists of activities and processes that convert raw materials into finished goods. Contrast this type of operation with merchandising, which sells merchandise in the form in which it is purchased. Manufacturing costs are typically classified as shown in Illustration 19-2.

Illustration 19-2
Classifications of manufacturing costs

Manufacturing Costs

Direct Materials

Direct Labor

Manufacturing Overhead

DIRECT MATERIALS

To obtain the materials that will be converted into the finished product, the manufacturer purchases raw materials. **Raw materials** are the basic materials and parts used in the manufacturing process. For example, auto manufacturers such as General Motors, Ford, and DaimlerChrysler use steel, plastics, and tires as raw materials in making cars.

Direct Materials

Raw materials that can be physically and directly associated with the finished product during the manufacturing process are called **direct materials**. Examples include flour in the baking of bread, syrup in the bottling of soft drinks, and steel in the making of automobiles. In the Feature Story, direct materials for Hewlett-Packard and Dell Computer include plastic, glass, hard drives, and processing chips.

But some raw materials cannot be easily associated with the finished product. These are called indirect materials. **Indirect materials** have one of two characteristics: Either (1) they do not physically become part of the finished product, such as lubricants and polishing compounds. Or (2) they cannot be traced because their physical association with the finished product is too small in terms of cost, such as cotter pins and lock washers. Companies account for indirect materials as part of **manufacturing overhead**.

DIRECT LABOR

The work of factory employees that can be physically and directly associated with converting raw materials into finished goods is called **direct labor**. Bottlers at Coca-Cola, bakers at Sara Lee, and typesetters at TechBooks are employees whose activities are usually classified as direct labor. **Indirect labor** refers to the work of factory employees that has no physical association with the finished product, or for which it is impractical to trace costs to the goods produced. Examples include wages of maintenance people, time-keepers, and supervisors. Like indirect materials, companies classify indirect labor as **manufacturing overhead**.

Direct Labor

MANAGEMENT INSIGHT

Productivity at Nissan

Recently a closely watched study of productivity in the automobile industry reported some encouraging improvements for U.S. auto manufacturers. For example, the U.S. unit of DaimlerChrysler improved its overall productivity 8.3%. A Nissan Motor plant in Tennessee set the standard for least amount of labor hours per vehicle: It produced Altima automobiles using only 15.74 labor hours per vehicle. Chrysler assembly plants required 28 hours per vehicle, and Ford took 26 hours.

Source: Ann Keeton, "Chrysler Leads Big Three in Productivity Gains," *Wall Street Journal*, June 18, 2003.

Why might Nissan production require significantly fewer labor hours?

MANUFACTURING OVERHEAD

Manufacturing overhead consists of costs that are indirectly associated with the manufacture of the finished product. These costs may also be manufacturing costs that cannot be classified as direct materials or direct labor. Manufacturing overhead includes indirect materials, indirect labor, depreciation on factory buildings and machines, and insurance, taxes, and maintenance on factory facilities.

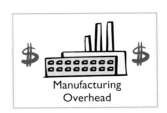
Manufacturing Overhead

One study found the following magnitudes of the three different product costs as a percentage of the total product cost: direct materials 54%, direct labor 13%, and manufacturing overhead 33%. Note that the direct labor component is the smallest. This component of product cost is dropping substantially because of automation. In some companies, direct labor has become as little as 5% of the total cost.

Allocating materials and labor costs to specific products is fairly straightforward. Good record keeping can tell a company how much plastic is used in making each type of gear, or how many hours of factory labor were used to assemble a part. But allocating overhead costs to specific products presents problems. How much of the purchasing agent's salary is attributable to the hundreds of different products made in the same plant? What about the grease that keeps the machines humming, or the computers that make sure paychecks come out on time? Boiled down to its simplest form, the question becomes: Which products cause the incurrence of which costs? In subsequent chapters we show various methods of allocating overhead to products.

Product versus Period Costs

Each of the manufacturing cost components—direct materials, direct labor, and manufacturing overhead—are product costs. As the term suggests, **product costs** are costs that are a necessary and integral part of producing the finished product. Companies record product costs, when incurred, as inventory. Under the matching principle, these costs do not become expenses until the company sells the finished goods inventory. The expense is cost of goods sold.

Period costs are costs that are matched with the revenue of a specific time period rather than included as part of the cost of a salable product. These are nonmanufacturing costs. Period costs include selling and administrative expenses. Companies deduct these costs from revenues in the period in which they are incurred in order to determine net income.

Illustration 19-3 summarizes these relationships and cost terms. Our main concern in this chapter is with product costs.

Illustration 19-3
Product versus period costs

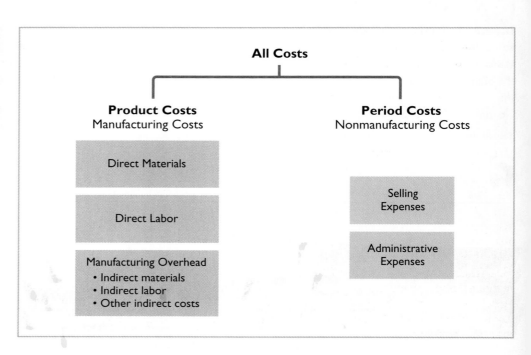

Before You Go On...

REVIEW IT

1. What are the major cost classifications involved in manufacturing a product?
2. What are product and period costs, and what is their relationship to the manufacturing process?

DO IT

A bicycle company has these costs: tires, salaries of employees who put tires on the wheels, factory building depreciation, wheel nuts, spokes, salary of factory manager, handle bars, and salaries of factory maintenance employees. Classify each cost as direct materials, direct labor, or overhead.

Action Plan

■ Classify as direct materials any raw materials that can be physically and directly associated with the finished product.

■ Classify as direct labor the work of factory employees that can be physically and directly associated with the finished product.

■ Classify as manufacturing overhead any costs that are indirectly associated with the finished product.

Solution Tires, spokes, and handle bars are direct materials. Salaries of employees who put tires on the wheels are direct labor. All of the other costs are manufacturing overhead.

Related exercise material: BE19-4, BE19-5, BE19-6, BE19-7, E19-2, E19-3, E19-4, E19-5, E19-6, and E19-7.

✓ The Navigator

MANUFACTURING COSTS IN FINANCIAL STATEMENTS

The financial statements of a manufacturer are very similar to those of a merchandiser. For example, you will find many of the same sections and same accounts in the financial statements of Procter & Gamble that you find in those of Dick's Sporting Goods. The principal differences between their financial statements pertain to the cost of goods sold section in the income statement and the current assets section in the balance sheet.

STUDY OBJECTIVE 5

Explain the difference between a merchandising and a manufacturing income statement.

Income Statement

Under a periodic inventory system, the income statements of a merchandiser and a manufacturer differ in the cost of goods sold section. Merchandisers compute cost of goods sold by adding the beginning merchandise inventory to the **cost of goods purchased** and subtracting the ending merchandise inventory. Manufacturers compute cost of goods sold by adding the beginning finished goods inventory to the **cost of goods manufactured** and subtracting the ending finished goods inventory. (See Illustration 19-4 on page 840.)

A number of accounts are involved in determining the cost of goods manufactured. To eliminate excessive detail, income statements typically show only the total cost of goods manufactured. The details are presented in a Cost of Goods Manufactured Schedule.

Illustration 19-4
Cost of goods sold components

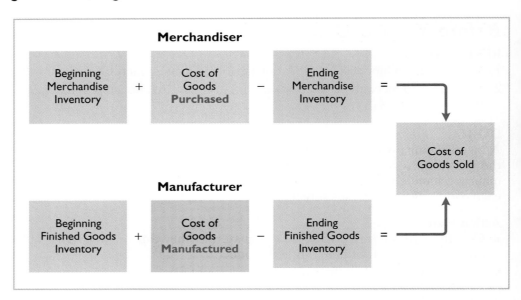

HELPFUL HINT

We assume a periodic inventory system in this illustration.

Illustration 19-5
Cost of goods sold sections of merchandising and manufacturing income statements

Illustration 19-5 shows the different presentations of the cost of goods sold sections for merchandising and manufacturing companies. The other sections of an income statement are similar for merchandisers and manufacturers.

MERCHANDISING COMPANY Income Statement (partial) For the Year Ended December 31, 2008		MANUFACTURING COMPANY Income Statement (partial) For the Year Ended December 31, 2008	
Cost of goods sold		Cost of goods sold	
Merchandise inventory, January 1	$ 70,000	Finished goods inventory, January 1	$ 90,000
Cost of goods purchased	650,000	Cost of goods manufactured (see Illustration 19-7)	370,000
Cost of goods available for sale	720,000	Cost of goods available for sale	460,000
Merchandise inventory, December 31	400,000	Finished goods inventory, December 31	80,000
Cost of goods sold	$320,000	Cost of goods sold	$380,000

DETERMINING THE COST OF GOODS MANUFACTURED

STUDY OBJECTIVE 6

Indicate how cost of goods manufactured is determined.

An example may help show how companies determine the cost of goods manufactured. Assume that Dell has a number of computers in various stages of production on January 1. In total, these partially completed units are called **beginning work in process inventory**. The costs assigned to beginning work in process inventory are based on the **manufacturing costs incurred in the prior period**.

The manufacturing costs incurred in the current year are used first to complete the work in process on January 1. They then are used to start the production of other computers. The sum of the direct materials costs, direct labor costs, and manufacturing overhead incurred in the current year is the total manufacturing costs for the current period.

We now have two cost amounts: (1) the cost of the beginning work in process and (2) the total manufacturing costs for the current period. The sum of these costs is the total cost of work in process for the year.

At the end of the year, some computers may be only partially completed. The costs of these units become the cost of the **ending work in process inventory**. To find the cost of goods manufactured, we subtract this cost from the total cost of work in process. Illustration 19-6 shows the formula for determining the cost of goods manufactured.

Illustration 19-6
Cost of goods manufactured formula

COST OF GOODS MANUFACTURED SCHEDULE

The **cost of goods manufactured schedule** is a report that shows cost elements used in calculating cost of goods manufactured. Illustration 19-7 shows the schedule for Olsen Manufacturing Company (using assumed data). The schedule presents detailed data for direct materials and for manufacturing overhead.

Review Illustration 19-6 and then examine the cost of goods manufactured schedule in Illustration 19-7. You should be able to distinguish between "Total manufacturing costs" and "Cost of goods manufactured." The difference is the effect of the change in work in process during the period.

OLSEN MANUFACTURING COMPANY
Cost of Goods Manufactured Schedule
For the Year Ended December 31, 2008

Illustration 19-7
Cost of goods manufactured schedule

Work in process, January 1			$ 18,400
Direct materials			
Raw materials inventory, January 1	$ 16,700		
Raw materials purchases	152,500		
Total raw materials available for use	169,200		
Less: Raw materials inventory, December 31	22,800		
Direct materials used		$146,400	
Direct labor		175,600	
Manufacturing overhead			
Indirect labor	14,300		
Factory repairs	12,600		
Factory utilities	10,100		
Factory depreciation	9,440		
Factory insurance	8,360		
Total manufacturing overhead		54,800	
Total manufacturing costs			376,800
Total cost of work in process			395,200
Less: Work in process, December 31			25,200
Cost of goods manufactured			$370,000

Balance Sheet

The balance sheet for a merchandising company shows just one category of inventory. In contrast, the balance sheet for a manufacturer may have three inventory accounts, as shown in Illustration 19-8.

Illustration 19-8
Inventory accounts for a manufacturer

Raw Materials Inventory	Work in Process Inventory	Finished Goods Inventory
Shows the cost of raw materials on hand.	Shows the cost applicable to units that have been started into production but are only partially completed.	Shows the cost of completed goods on hand.

Finished Goods Inventory is to a manufacturer what Merchandise Inventory is to a merchandiser. It represents the goods that are available for sale.

The current assets sections presented in Illustration 19-9 contrast the presentations of inventories for merchandising and manufacturing companies. Companies generally list manufacturing inventories in the order of their liquidity—the order in which they are expected to be realized in cash. Thus, finished goods inventory comes first. The remainder of the balance sheet is similar for the two types of companies.

Illustration 19-9
Current assets sections of merchandising and manufacturing balance sheets

MERCHANDISING COMPANY Balance Sheet December 31, 2008		MANUFACTURING COMPANY Balance Sheet December 31, 2008		
Current assets		Current assets		
Cash	$100,000	Cash		$180,000
Receivables (net)	210,000	Receivables (net)		210,000
Merchandise inventory	400,000	Inventories		
Prepaid expenses	22,000	Finished goods	$80,000	
		Work in process	25,200	
Total current assets	$732,000	Raw materials	22,800	128,000
		Prepaid expenses		18,000
		Total current assets		$536,000

For expanded coverage, go to the Student Companion site and select Chapter 19, Accounting Cycle (Worksheet) for a Manufacturing Company.

Each step in the accounting cycle for a merchandiser applies to a manufacturer. For example, prior to preparing financial statements, manufacturers make adjusting entries. The adjusting entries are essentially the same as those of a merchandiser. The closing entries are also similar for manufacturers and merchandisers.

Cost Concepts—A Review

You have learned a number of cost concepts in this chapter. Because many of these concepts are new, here we provide an extended example for review.

Assume that Northridge Company manufactures and sells pre-hung metal doors. Recently, it also has decided to start selling pre-hung wood doors. The company will use an old warehouse that it owns to manufacture the new product. Northridge identifies the following costs associated with manufacturing and selling the pre-hung wood doors.

1. The material cost (wood) for each door is $10.
2. Labor costs required to construct a wood door are $8 per door.
3. Depreciation on the factory equipment used to make the wood doors is $25,000 per year.
4. Property taxes on the factory building used to make the wood doors are $6,000 per year.
5. Advertising costs for the pre-hung wood doors total $2,500 per month or $30,000 per year.
6. Sales commissions related to pre-hung wood doors sold are $4 per door.
7. Salaries for employees who maintain the factory facilities are $28,000.
8. The salary of the plant manager in charge of pre-hung wood doors is $70,000.
9. The cost of shipping pre-hung wood doors is $12 per door sold.

Illustration 19-10 shows how these manufacturing and selling costs can be assigned to the various categories.

Cost Item	Direct Materials	Direct Labor	Manufacturing Overhead	Period Costs
1. Material cost ($10) per door	X			
2. Labor costs ($8) per door		X		
3. Depreciation on factory equipment ($25,000 per year)			X	
4. Property taxes on factory building ($6,000 per year)			X	
5. Advertising costs ($30,000 per year)				X
6. Sales commissions ($4 per door)				X
7. Maintenance salaries (factory facilities) ($28,000 per year)			X	
8. Salary of plant manager ($70,000)			X	
9. Cost of shipping pre-hung doors ($12 per door)				X

Product Costs

Illustration 19-10
Assignment of costs to cost categories

Remember that total manufacturing costs are the sum of the **product costs—** direct materials, direct labor, and manufacturing overhead. If Northridge Company produces 10,000 pre-hung wood doors the first year, the total manufacturing costs would be $309,000 as shown in Illustration 19-11 (page 844).

Illustration 19-11
Computation of total manufacturing costs

Cost Number and Item	Manufacturing Cost
1. Material cost ($10 × 10,000)	$100,000
2. Labor cost ($8 × 10,000)	80,000
3. Depreciation on factory equipment	25,000
4. Property taxes on factory building	6,000
7. Maintenance salaries (factory facilities)	28,000
8. Salary of plant manager	70,000
Total manufacturing costs	**$309,000**

Knowing the total manufacturing costs, Northridge can compute the manufacturing cost per unit. Assuming 10,000 units, the cost to produce one pre-hung wood door is $30.90 ($309,000 ÷ 10,000 units).

We will use the cost concepts discussed in this chapter extensively in subsequent chapters. Study Illustration 19-10 carefully. If you do not understand any of these classifications, go back and reread the appropriate section in this chapter.

Before You Go On...

REVIEW IT

1. How does the content of an income statement for a merchandiser differ from that for a manufacturer?
2. How do companies report the work in process inventories in the cost of goods manufactured schedule?
3. How does the content of the balance sheet for a merchandiser differ from that for a manufacturer?

 The Navigator

MANAGERIAL ACCOUNTING TODAY

STUDY OBJECTIVE 8

Identify trends in managerial accounting.

In recent years, the competitive environment for U.S. business has changed significantly. For example, the airline, financial services, and telecommunications industries have been deregulated. Global competition has intensified. The world economy now has the European Union, NAFTA, and ASEAN. Countries like China and India are becoming economic powerhouses. As indicated earlier, managerial accountants must be forward-looking, acting as advisors and information providers to different parts of the organization. Some of the issues they face are discussed below.

Service-Industry Trends

The Feature Story notes that at the peak of its success as a personal computer manufacturer, Compaq purchased Digital Equipment. Its management believed that the future of computing was in providing computer services, rather than in manufacturing computer hardware. In fact, the U.S. economy in general has shifted toward an emphasis on providing services, rather than goods. Today over 50% of U.S. workers work in service companies, and that percentage is projected to increase in coming years. Much of this chapter focused on manufacturers, but most of the techniques that you will learn in this course apply equally to service companies.

ETHICS NOTE

Do telecommunications companies have an obligation to provide service to remote or low-user areas for a fee that may be less than the cost of the service?

Managers of service companies look to managerial accounting to answer many questions. In some instances the managerial accountant may need to develop new systems for measuring the cost of serving individual customers.

In others, companies may need new operating controls to improve the quality and efficiency of specific services. Many of the examples we present in subsequent chapters will be based on service companies.

Managerial Accounting Practices

As discussed earlier, the practice of managerial accounting has changed significantly in recent years to better address the needs of managers. The following sections explain some recent managerial accounting practices.

THE VALUE CHAIN

The **value chain** refers to all activities associated with providing a product or service. For a manufacturer these include research and development, product design, acquisition of raw materials, production, sales and marketing, delivery, customer relations, and subsequent service. Illustration 19-12 depicts the value chain for a manufacturer. In recent years, companies have made huge strides in analyzing all stages of the value chain in an effort to improve productivity and eliminate waste. Japanese automobile manufacturer Toyota pioneered many of these innovations.

Illustration 19-12
A manufacturer's value chain

| Research & development and product design | Acquisition of raw materials | Production | Sales & marketing | Delivery | Customer relations and subsequent services |

In the 1980s many companies purchased giant machines to replace humans in the manufacturing process. These machines were designed to produce large batches of products. In recent years these large-batch manufacturing processes have been recognized as very wasteful. They require vast amounts of inventory storage capacity and considerable movement of materials. Consequently, many companies have reengineered their manufacturing processes. As one example, the manufacturing company Pratt and Whitney has replaced many large machines with smaller, more flexible ones and has begun reorganizing its plants for more efficient flow of goods. Pratt and Whitney was able to reduce the time that its turbine engine blades spend in the grinding section of its factory from 10 days down to 2 hours. It cut the total amount of time spent making a blade from 22 days to 7 days. Analysis of the value chain has made companies far more responsive to customer needs and has improved profitability.

JUST-IN-TIME INVENTORY METHODS

Many companies have significantly lowered inventory levels and costs using **just-in-time (JIT) inventory** methods. Under a just-in-time method, goods are manufactured or purchased just in time for use. As noted in the Feature Story, Dell is famous for having developed a system for making computers in response to individual customer requests. Even though each computer is custom-made to meet each customer's particular specifications, it takes Dell less than 48 hours to assemble the computer and put it on a truck. By integrating its information systems with those of its suppliers, Dell reduced its inventories to nearly zero. This is a huge advantage in an industry where products become obsolete nearly overnight.

ETHICS NOTE

Does just-in-time inventory justify "just-in-time" employees obtained through temporary employment services?

QUALITY

JIT inventory systems require an increased emphasis on product quality. If products are produced only as they are needed, it is very costly for the company to have to stop production because of defects or machine breakdowns. Many companies have installed **total quality management (TQM)** systems to reduce defects in finished products. The goal is to achieve zero defects. These systems require timely data on defective products, rework costs, and the cost of honoring warranty contracts. Often, companies use this information to help redesign the product in a way that makes it less prone to defect. Or they may use the information to reengineer the production process to reduce setup time and decrease the potential for error. TQM systems also provide information on nonfinancial measures such as customer satisfaction, number of service calls, and time to generate reports. Attention to these measures, which employees can control, leads to increased profitability.

ACTIVITY-BASED COSTING

As discussed earlier, overhead costs have become an increasingly large component of product and service costs. By definition, overhead costs cannot be directly traced to individual products. But to determine each product's cost, overhead must be **allocated** to the various products. In order to obtain more accurate product costs, many companies now allocate overhead using **activity-based costing (ABC)**. Under ABC, companies allocate overhead based on each product's use of activities in making the product. For example, companies can keep track of their cost of setting up machines for each batch of a production process. Then companies can allocate part of the total set-up cost to a particular product based on the number of set-ups that product required.

Activity-based costing is beneficial because it results in more accurate product costing and in more careful scrutiny of all activities in the value chain. For example, if a product's cost is high because it requires a high number of set-ups, management will be motivated to determine how to produce the product using the optimal number of machine set-ups. Both manufacturing and service companies now widely use ABC. Allied Signal and Coca-Cola have both enjoyed improved results from ABC. Fidelity Investments uses ABC to identify which customers cost the most to serve.

MANAGEMENT INSIGHT

Bananas Receive Special Treatment

When it comes to total quality management, few companies can compare with Chiquita Brands International. Grocery store customers are very picky about bananas—bad bananas are consistently the number one grocery store complaint. Because bananas often account for up to 3% of a grocery store's sales, Chiquita goes to great lengths to protect the popular fruit. While bananas are in transit from Central America, "black box" recording devices attached to shipping crates ensure that they are kept in an environment of 90% humidity and an unvarying 55-degree temperature. Upon arrival in the U.S., bananas are ripened in airtight warehouses that use carefully monitored levels of ethylene gas. Regular checks are made of each warehouse using ultrasonic detectors that can detect leaks the size of a pinhole. Says one grocery store executive, "No other item in the store has this type of attention and resources devoted to it."

Source: Devon Spurgeon, "When Grocers in U.S. Go Bananas Over Bad Fruit, They Call Laubenthal," *Wall Street Journal*, August 14, 2000, p. A1.

Why is it important to keep track of costs that are incurred to improve product quality?

BALANCED SCORECARD

As companies implement various business practice innovations, managers sometimes focus too enthusiastically on the latest innovation, to the detriment of other areas of the business. For example, in focusing on improving quality, companies sometimes have lost sight of cost/benefit considerations. Similarly, in focusing on reducing inventory levels through just-in-time, companies sometimes have lost sales due to inventory shortages. The **balanced scorecard** is a performance-measurement approach that uses both financial and nonfinancial measures to evaluate all aspects of a company's operations in an **integrated** fashion. The performance measures are linked in a cause-and-effect fashion to ensure that they all tie to the company's overall objectives.

For example, the company may desire to increase its return on assets, a common financial performance measure (calculated as net income divided by average total assets). It will then identify a series of linked goals. If the company accomplishes each goal, the ultimate result will be an increase in return on assets. For example, in order to increase return on assets, sales must increase. In order to increase sales, customer satisfaction must be increased. In order to increase customer satisfaction, product defects must be reduced. In order to reduce product defects, employee training must be increased. Note the linkage, which starts with employee training and ends with return on assets. Each objective will have associated performance measures.

The use of the balanced scorecard is widespread among well-known and respected companies. For example, Hilton Hotels Corporation uses the balanced scorecard to evaluate the performance of employees at all of its hotel chains. Wal-Mart employs the balanced scorecard, and actually extends its use to evaluation of its suppliers. For example, Wal-Mart recently awarded Welch Company the "Dry Grocery Division Supplier of the Year Award" for its balanced scorecard results. We discuss the balanced scorecard further in Chapter 25.

Before You Go On...

REVIEW IT

1. Describe, in sequence, the main components of a manufacturer's value chain.
2. Why is product quality important for companies that implement a just-in-time inventory system?
3. Explain what is meant by "balanced" in the balanced scorecard approach.

 The Navigator

 Be sure to read **ALL ABOUT YOU: *Outsourcing and Jobs*** on page 848 for information on how topics in this chapter apply to you.

all about Y✲U

Outsourcing and Jobs

As noted in this chapter, because of global competition, companies have become increasingly focused on reducing costs. To reduce costs, and remain competitive, many companies are turning to outsourcing. *Outsourcing* means hiring an outside supplier to provide elements of a product rather than producing them internally.

In many instances companies outsource jobs to foreign suppliers, which has caused considerable concern about loss of U.S. jobs. Until recently, most of the debate about outsourcing related to manufacturing. Now outsourcing is taking place in professional services like engineering and accounting. This is occurring because high-speed transmission of large amounts of data over the Internet is now cheap and easy. As a consequence, jobs that once seemed safe from foreign competition are now at risk.

✲ Some Facts

* IBM has expanded beyond information technology into providing advisory services related to outsourcing, which it believes will be a $500 billion market.

* A U.S. professional association of certified public accountants requires that its members notify clients before they share confidential client information with an outside contractor as part of an outsourcing arrangement.

* During a recent two-year period Ford Motor Co. inspected the working conditions at about 160 of the more than 2,000 foreign-owned plants in low-cost countries that supply it with outsourced parts.

* The McKinsey Global Institute predicts that white-collar overseas outsourcing will increase at a rate of 30 to 40% over the next five years. By 2015, the consultancy group Forrester predicts, roughly 3.3 million service jobs will have moved offshore, including 1.7 million "back-office" jobs such as payroll processing and accounting, and 473,000 jobs in the information technology industry.

* On the otherhand, Hewlett-Packard has begun to "insource" many of the manufacturing operations that it previously outsourced.

✲ About the Numbers

Interestingly, foreign firms doing business in the United States also hire a lot of Americans. In a recent year, U.S. subsidiaries of foreign companies employed approximately 5.3 million Americans. In comparison, in that same year 134,000 Americans lost their jobs due to outsourcing. The following graph shows which countries are the top foreign employers in the United States.

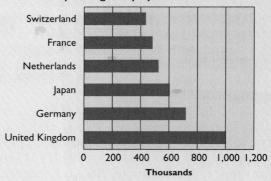

Top Foreign Employers in the U.S.

Switzerland, France, Netherlands, Japan, Germany, United Kingdom
0   200   400   600   800   1,000   1,200
Thousands

Source: Darren Dahl, "Insourcing 101," *Inc.* Magazine, April 2006, p. 50.

✲ What Do You Think?

Suppose you are the managing partner in a CPA firm with 30 full-time staf Larger firms in your community have begun to outsource basic tax-return preparation work to India. Should you outsource your basic tax return wo to India as well? You estimate that you would have to lay off six staff memb if you outsource the work.

YES: The wages paid to Indian accountants are very low relative to U.S. wages. You will not be able to compete unless you outsource.

NO: Tax-return data is highly sensitive. Many customers will be upset to learn that their data is being emailed around the world.

Sources: Jonathan Weil, "Accountants Scrutinize Outsourcing," *Wall Street Journal*, August 11, 2004, p. A2; Jeffrey McCracken, "Ford Probes Work Conditions at Part Makers in China, Mexico," *Wall Street Journal*, April 5, 2006m p. A12; Council on Foreign Affairs, "Backgrounder, Trade: Outsourcing Jobs," February 20, 2004, *cfr.org/publication* (accessed June 2006).

The authors' comments on this situation appear on pag

Demonstration Problem 1

Giant Manufacturing Co. Ltd. specializes in manufacturing many different models of bicycles. Assume that a new model, the Jaguar, has been well accepted. As a result, the company has established a separate manufacturing facility to produce these bicycles. The company produces 1,000 bicycles per month. Giant's monthly manufacturing cost and other expenses data related to these bicycles are as follows.

1. Rent on manufacturing equipment (lease cost) $2,000/month
2. Insurance on manufacturing building $750/month
3. Raw materials (frames, tires, etc.) $80/bicycle
4. Utility costs for manufacturing facility $1,000/month
5. Supplies for administrative office $800/month
6. Wages for assembly line workers in manufacturing facility $30/bicycle
7. Depreciation on office equipment $650/month

8. Miscellaneous materials (lubricants, solders, etc.) $1.20/bicycle
9. Property taxes on manufacturing building $2,400/year
10. Manufacturing supervisor's salary $3,000/month
11. Advertising for bicycles $30,000/year
12. Sales commissions $10/bicycle
13. Depreciation on manufacturing building $1,500/month

Instructions

(a) Prepare an answer sheet with the following column headings.

	Product Costs			
Cost Item	Direct Materials	Direct Labor	Manufacturing Overhead	Period Costs

Enter each cost item on your answer sheet, placing an "X" mark under the appropriate headings.

(b) Compute total manufacturing costs for the month.

Solution to Demonstration Problem 1

(a)

	Product Costs			
Cost Item	Direct Materials	Direct Labor	Manufacturing Overhead	Period Costs
1. Rent on manufacturing equipment ($2,000/month)			X	
2. Insurance on manufacturing building ($750/month)			X	
3. Raw materials ($80/bicycle)	X			
4. Manufacturing utilities ($1,000/month)			X	
5. Office supplies ($800/month)				X
6. Wages for workers ($30/bicycle)		X		

Cost Item	Product Costs			Period Costs
	Direct Materials	Direct Labor	Manufacturing Overhead	
7. Depreciation on office equipment ($650/month)				X
8. Miscellaneous materials ($1.20/bicycle)			X	
9. Property taxes on manufacturing building ($2,400/year)			X	
10. Manufacturing supervisor's salary ($3,000/month)			X	
11. Advertising cost ($30,000/year)				X
12. Sales commissions ($10/bicycle)				X
13. Depreciation on manufacturing building ($1,500/month)			X	

(b)

Cost Item	Manufacturing Cost
Rent on manufacturing equipment	$ 2,000
Insurance on manufacturing building	750
Raw materials ($80 × 1,000)	80,000
Manufacturing utilities	1,000
Labor ($30 × 1,000)	30,000
Miscellaneous materials ($1.20 × 1,000)	1,200
Property taxes on manufacturing building ($2,400 ÷ 12)	200
Manufacturing supervisor's salary	3,000
Depreciation on manufacturing building	1,500
Total manufacturing costs	$119,650

✔ *The Navigator*

Demonstration Problem 2

WILEY PLUS

Superior Manufacturing Company has the following cost and expense data for the year ending December 31, 2008.

Raw materials, 1/1/08	$ 30,000	Insurance, factory	$ 14,000
Raw materials, 12/31/08	20,000	Property taxes, factory building	6,000
Raw materials purchases	205,000	Sales (net)	1,500,000
Indirect materials	15,000	Delivery expenses	100,000
Work in process, 1/1/08	80,000	Sales commissions	150,000
Work in process, 12/31/08	50,000	Indirect labor	90,000
Finished goods, 1/1/08	110,000	Factory machinery rent	40,000
Finished goods, 12/31/08	120,000	Factory utilities	65,000
Direct labor	350,000	Depreciation, factory building	24,000
Factory manager's salary	35,000	Administrative expenses	300,000

Instructions

(a) Prepare a cost of goods manufactured schedule for Superior Company for 2008.

(b) Prepare an income statement for Superior Company for 2008.

(c) Assume that Superior Company's ledgers show the balances of the following current asset accounts: Cash $17,000, Accounts Receivable (net) $120,000, Prepaid Expenses $13,000, and Short-term Investments $26,000. Prepare the current assets section of the balance sheet for Superior Company as of December 31, 2008.

Solution to Demonstration Problem 2

(a)
SUPERIOR MANUFACTURING COMPANY
Cost of Goods Manufactured Schedule
For the Year Ended December 31, 2008

Work in process, 1/1			$ 80,000
Direct materials			
Raw materials inventory, 1/1	$ 30,000		
Raw materials purchases	205,000		
Total raw materials available for use	235,000		
Less: Raw materials inventory, 12/31	20,000		
Direct materials used		$215,000	
Direct labor		350,000	
Manufacturing overhead			
Indirect labor	90,000		
Factory utilities	65,000		
Factory machinery rent	40,000		
Factory manager's salary	35,000		
Depreciation on building	24,000		
Indirect materials	15,000		
Factory insurance	14,000		
Property taxes	6,000		
Total manufacturing overhead		289,000	
Total manufacturing costs			854,000
Total cost of work in process			934,000
Less: Work in process, 12/31			50,000
Cost of goods manufactured			$884,000

(b)
SUPERIOR MANUFACTURING COMPANY
Income Statement
For the Year Ended December 31, 2008

Sales (net)		$1,500,000
Cost of goods sold		
Finished goods inventory, January 1	$110,000	
Cost of goods manufactured	884,000	
Cost of goods available for sale	994,000	
Less: Finished goods inventory, December 31	120,000	
Cost of goods sold		874,000
Gross profit		626,000
Operating expenses		
Administrative expenses	300,000	
Sales commissions	150,000	
Delivery expenses	100,000	
Total operating expenses		550,000
Net income		$ 76,000

action plan

✔ Start with beginning work in process as the first item in the cost of goods manufactured schedule.

✔ Sum direct materials used, direct labor, and total manufacturing overhead to determine total manufacturing costs.

✔ Sum beginning work in process and total manufacturing costs to determine total cost of work in process.

✔ Cost of goods manufactured is the total cost of work in process less ending work in process.

✔ In the cost of goods sold section of the income statement, show beginning and ending finished goods inventory and cost of goods manufactured.

✔ In the balance sheet, list manufacturing inventories in the order of their expected realization in cash, with finished goods first.

(c)

SUPERIOR MANUFACTURING COMPANY
Balance Sheet (partial)
December 31, 2008

Current assets		
Cash		$ 17,000
Short-term investments		26,000
Accounts receivable (net)		120,000
Inventories		
Finished goods	$120,000	
Work in process	50,000	
Raw materials	20,000	190,000
Prepaid expenses		13,000
Total current assets		$366,000

The Navigator

SUMMARY OF STUDY OBJECTIVES

1 Explain the distinguishing features of managerial accounting. The *primary users* of managerial accounting reports are internal users, who are officers, department heads, managers, and supervisors in the company. Managerial accounting issues internal reports as frequently as the need arises. The purpose of these reports is to provide special-purpose information for a particular user for a specific decision. The content of managerial accounting reports pertains to subunits of the business and may be very detailed and may extend beyond the double-entry accounting system. The reporting standard is relevance to the decision being made. No independent audits are required in managerial accounting.

2 Identify the three broad functions of management. The three functions are planning, directing, and controlling. Planning requires management to look ahead and to establish objectives. Directing involves coordinating the diverse activities and human resources of a company to produce a smooth-running operation. Controlling is the process of keeping the activities on track.

3 Define the three classes of manufacturing costs. Manufacturing costs are typically classified as either (1) direct materials, (2) direct labor, or (3) manufacturing overhead. Raw materials that can be physically and directly associated with the finished product during the manufacturing process are called direct materials. The work of factory employees that can be physically and directly associated with converting raw materials into finished goods is considered direct labor. Manufacturing overhead consists of costs that are indirectly associated with the manufacture of the finished product.

4 Distinguish between product and period costs. Product costs are costs that are a necessary and integral part of producing the finished product. Product costs are also called inventoriable costs. Under the matching principle, these costs do not become expenses until the company sells the finished goods inventory. Period costs are costs that are identified with a specific time period rather than with a salable product. These costs relate to nonmanufacturing costs and therefore are not inventoriable costs.

5 Explain the difference between a merchandising and a manufacturing income statement. The difference between a merchandising and a manufacturing income statement is in the cost of goods sold section. A manufacturing cost of goods sold section shows beginning and ending finished goods inventories and the cost of goods manufactured.

6 Indicate how cost of goods manufactured is determined. The cost of the beginning work in process is added to the total manufacturing costs for the current year to arrive at the total cost of work in process for the year. The ending work in process is then subtracted from the total cost of work in process to arrive at the cost of goods manufactured.

7 Explain the difference between a merchandising and a manufacturing balance sheet. The difference between a merchandising and a manufacturing balance sheet is in the current assets section. The current assets section of a manufacturing company's balance sheet presents three inventory accounts: finished goods inventory, work in process inventory, and raw materials inventory.

8 Identify trends in managerial accounting. Managerial accounting has experienced many changes in recent years. Among these are a shift toward addressing the needs of service companies and improving practices to better meet the needs of managers. Improved practices include a focus on managing the value chain through techniques such as just-in-time inventory and total quality management. In addition, techniques such as activity-based costing (ABC) have been developed to improve decision making. Finally, the balanced scorecard is now used by many companies in order to attain a more comprehensive view of the company's operations. *The Navigator*

GLOSSARY

Activity-based costing (ABC)   A method of allocating overhead based on each product's use of activities in making the product. (p. 846).

Balanced scorecard   A performance-measurement approach that uses both financial and nonfinancial measures, tied to company objectives, to evaluate a company's operations in an integrated fashion. (p. 847).

Cost of goods manufactured   Total cost of work in process less the cost of the ending work in process inventory. (p. 841).

Direct labor   The work of factory employees that can be physically and directly associated with converting raw materials into finished goods. (p. 837).

Direct materials   Raw materials that can be physically and directly associated with manufacturing the finished product. (p. 837).

Indirect labor   Work of factory employees that has no physical association with the finished product, or for which it is impractical to trace the costs to the goods produced. (p. 837).

Indirect materials   Raw materials that do not physically become part of the finished product or cannot be traced because their physical association with the finished product is too small. (p. 837).

Just-in-time (JIT) inventory   Inventory system in which goods are manufactured or purchased just in time for use. (p. 845).

Managerial accounting   A field of accounting that provides economic and financial information for managers and other internal users. (p. 832).

Manufacturing overhead   Manufacturing costs that are indirectly associated with the manufacture of the finished product. (p. 837).

Period costs   Costs that are matched with the revenue of a specific time period and charged to expense as incurred. (p. 838).

Product costs   Costs that are a necessary and integral part of producing the finished product. (p. 838).

Total cost of work in process   Cost of the beginning work in process plus total manufacturing costs for the current period. (p. 840).

Total manufacturing costs   The sum of direct materials, direct labor, and manufacturing overhead incurred in the current period. (p. 840).

Total quality management (TQM)   Systems implemented to reduce defects in finished products with the goal of achieving zero defects. (p. 846).

Value chain   All activities associated with providing a product or service. (p. 845).

SELF-STUDY QUESTIONS

Answers are at the end of the chapter.

1) **1.** Managerial accounting:
   a. is governed by generally accepted accounting principles.
   b. places emphasis on special-purpose information.
   c. pertains to the entity as a whole and is highly aggregated.
   d. is limited to cost data.

2) **2.** The management of an organization performs several broad functions. They are:
   a. planning, directing, and selling.
   b. planning, directing, and controlling.
   c. planning, manufacturing, and controlling.
   d. directing, manufacturing, and controlling.

3) **3.** Direct materials are a:

	Product Cost	Manufacturing Overhead	Period Cost
a.	Yes	Yes	No
b.	Yes	No	No
c.	Yes	Yes	Yes
d.	No	No	No

4) **4.** Indirect labor is a:
   a. nonmanufacturing cost.
   b. raw material cost.
   c. product cost.
   d. period cost.

5. Which of the following costs would be included in manu- (SO 3) facturing overhead of a computer manufacturer?
   a. The cost of the disk drives.
   b. The wages earned by computer assemblers.
   c. The cost of the memory chips.
   d. Depreciation on testing equipment.

6. Which of the following is *not* an element of manufacturing (SO 3) overhead?
   a. Sales manager's salary.
   b. Plant manager's salary.
   c. Factory repairman's wages.
   d. Product inspector's salary.

7. For the year, Redder Company has cost of goods manu- (SO 5) factured of $600,000, beginning finished goods inventory of $200,000, and ending finished goods inventory of $250,000. The cost of goods sold is:
   a. $450,000.
   b. $500,000.
   c. $550,000.
   d. $600,000.

8. A cost of goods manufactured schedule shows beginning (SO 6) and ending inventories for:
   a. raw materials and work in process only.
   b. work in process only.
   c. raw materials only.
   d. raw materials, work in process, and finished goods.

(SO 7) **9.** In a manufacturer's balance sheet, three inventories may be reported: (1) raw materials, (2) work in process, and (3) finished goods. Indicate in what sequence these inventories generally appear on a balance sheet.
a. (1), (2), (3)
c. (3), (1), (2)
b. (2), (3), (1)
d. (3), (2), (1)

(SO 8) **10.** Which of the following managerial accounting techniques attempts to allocate manufacturing overhead in a more meaningful fashion?

a. Just-in-time inventory.
b. Total-quality management.
c. Balanced scorecard.
d. Activity-based costing.

Go to the book's website,
www.wiley.com/college/weygandt,
for Additional Self-Study questions.

QUESTIONS

1. (a) "Managerial accounting is a field of accounting that provides economic information for all interested parties." Do you agree? Explain.
(b) Mary Barett believes that managerial accounting serves only manufacturing firms. Is Mary correct? Explain.

2. Distinguish between managerial and financial accounting as to (a) primary users of reports, (b) types and frequency of reports, and (c) purpose of reports.

3. How does the content of reports and the verification of reports differ between managerial and financial accounting?

4. In what ways can the budgeting process create incentives for unethical behavior?

5. Karen Fritz is studying for the next accounting mid-term examination. Summarize for Karen what she should know about management functions.

6. "Decision making is management's most important function." Do you agree? Why or why not?

7. What new rules were enacted under the Sarbanes-Oxley Act to address unethical accounting practices?

8. Stan Kaiser is studying for his next accounting examination. Explain to Stan what he should know about the differences between the income statements for a manufacturing and for a merchandising company.

9. Terry Lemay is unclear as to the difference between the balance sheets of a merchandising company and a manufacturing company. Explain the difference to Terry.

10. How are manufacturing costs classified?

11. Matt Litkee claims that the distinction between direct and indirect materials is based entirely on physical association with the product. Is Matt correct? Why?

12. Megan Neill is confused about the differences between a product cost and a period cost. Explain the differences to Megan.

13. Identify the differences in the cost of goods sold section of an income statement between a merchandising company and a manufacturing company.

14. The determination of the cost of goods manufactured involves the following factors: (A) beginning work in process inventory, (B) total manufacturing costs, and (C) ending work in process inventory. Identify the meaning of x in the following formulas:
(a) $A + B = x$
(b) $A + B - C = x$

15. Ohmie Manufacturing has beginning raw materials inventory $12,000, ending raw materials inventory $15,000, and raw materials purchases $170,000. What is the cost of direct materials used?

16. Neff Manufacturing Inc. has beginning work in process $26,000, direct materials used $240,000, direct labor $200,000, total manufacturing overhead $180,000, and ending work in process $32,000. What are total manufacturing costs?

17. Using the data in Q16, what are (a) the total cost of work in process and (b) the cost of goods manufactured?

18. In what order should manufacturing inventories be listed in a balance sheet?

19. What is the value chain? Describe, in sequence, the main components of a manufacturer's value chain.

20. Why is product quality important for companies that implement a just-in-time inventory system?

21. Explain what is meant by "balanced" in the balanced scorecard approach.

22. What is activity-based costing, and what are its potential benefits?

BRIEF EXERCISES

Distinguish between managerial and financial accounting.

(SO 1)

BE19-1 Complete the following comparison table between managerial and financial accounting.

	Financial Accounting	Managerial Accounting
Primary users		
Types of reports		
Frequency of reports		
Purpose of reports		
Content of reports		
Verification		

BE19-2 The Sarbanes Oxley Act of 2002 (SOX) has important implications for the financial community. Explain two implications of SOX.

Identify important regulatory changes.

(SO 2)

BE19-3 Listed below are the three functions of the management of an organization.

1. Planning   2. Directing   3. Controlling

Identify the three management functions.

(SO 2)

Identify which of the following statements best describes each of the above functions.

(a) _____ require(s) management to look ahead and to establish objectives. A key objective of management is to add value to the business.

(b) _____ involve(s) coordinating the diverse activities and human resources of a company to produce a smooth-running operation. This function relates to the implementation of planned objectives.

(c) _____ is the process of keeping the activities on track. Management must determine whether goals are being met and what changes are necessary when there are deviations.

BE19-4 Determine whether each of the following costs should be classified as direct materials (DM), direct labor (DL), or manufacturing overhead (MO).

Classify manufacturing costs.

(SO 3)

(a) ___DM___ Frames and tires used in manufacturing bicycles.
(b) ___DL___ Wages paid to production workers.
(c) ___MO___ Insurance on factory equipment and machinery.
(d) ___MO___ Depreciation on factory equipment.

BE19-5 Indicate whether each of the following costs of an automobile manufacturer would be classified as direct materials, direct labor, or manufacturing overhead.

Classify manufacturing costs.

(SO 3)

(a) ___DM___ Windshield.
(b) ___DM___ Engine.
(c) ___DL___ Wages of assembly line worker.
(d) ___MO___ Depreciation of factory machinery.

(e) ___MO___ Factory machinery lubricants.
(f) ___DM___ Tires.
(g) ___DM___ Steering wheel.
(h) ___MO___ Salary of painting supervisor.

BE19-6 Identify whether each of the following costs should be classified as product costs or period costs.

Identify product and period costs.

(SO 4)

(a) _____ Manufacturing overhead.
(b) _____ Selling expenses.
(c) _____ Administrative expenses.

(d) _____ Advertising expenses.
(e) _____ Direct labor.
(f) _____ Direct material.

BE19-7 Presented below are Lang Company's monthly manufacturing cost data related to its personal computer products.

Classify manufacturing costs.

(SO 3)

(a) Utilities for manufacturing equipment $116,000
(b) Raw material (CPU, chips, etc.) $ 85,000
(c) Depreciation on manufacturing building $880,000
(d) Wages for production workers $191,000

Enter each cost item in the following table, placing an "X" under the appropriate headings.

	Product Costs		
	Direct Materials	**Direct Labor**	**Factory Overhead**
(a)			X
(b)	X		
(c)			X
(d)		X	

BE19-8 Francum Manufacturing Company has the following data: direct labor $229,000, direct materials used $180,000, total manufacturing overhead $208,000, and beginning work in process $25,000. Compute (a) total manufacturing costs and (b) total cost of work in process.

Compute total manufacturing costs and total cost of work in process.

(SO 6)

BE19-9 In alphabetical order below are current asset items for Dieker Company's balance sheet at December 31, 2008. Prepare the current assets section (including a complete heading).

Prepare current assets section.

(SO 7)

Accounts receivable	$200,000
Cash	62,000
Finished goods	71,000
Prepaid expenses	38,000
Raw materials	73,000
Work in process	87,000

Determine missing amounts in computing total manufacturing costs.

(SO 6)

BE19-10 Presented below are incomplete manufacturing cost data. Determine the missing amounts for three different situations.

	Direct Materials Used	Direct Labor Used	Factory Overhead	Total Manufacturing Costs
(1)	$25,000	$61,000	$ 50,000	? 136,000
(2)	81,000	$75,000	$140,000	$296,000
(3)	$55,000	144,000	$111,000	$310,000

Determine missing amounts in computing cost of goods manufactured.

(SO 6)

BE19-11 Use the same data from BE19–10 above and the data below. Determine the missing amounts.

	Total Manufacturing Costs	Work in Process (1/1)	Work in Process (12/31)	Cost of Goods Manufactured
(1)	136,000	$120,000	$82,000	174,000
(2)	$296,000	123,000	$98,000	$321,000
(3)	$310,000	$463,000	58,000	$715,000

EXERCISES

Identify distinguishing features of managerial accounting.

(SO 1)

E19-1 Chris Martin has prepared the following list of statements about managerial accounting and financial accounting.

1. Financial accounting focuses on providing information to internal users.
2. Analyzing cost-volume-profit relationships is part of managerial accounting.
3. Preparation of budgets is part of financial accounting.
4. Managerial accounting applies only to merchandising and manufacturing companies.
5. Both managerial accounting and financial accounting deal with many of the same economic events.
6. Managerial accounting reports are prepared only quarterly and annually.
7. Financial accounting reports are general-purpose reports.
8. Managerial accounting reports pertain to subunits of the business.
9. Managerial accounting reports must comply with generally accepted accounting principles.
10. Although managerial accountants are expected to behave ethically, there is no code of ethical standards for managerial accountants.

Instructions

Identify each statement as true or false. If false, indicate how to correct the statement.

Classify costs into three classes of manufacturing costs.

(SO 3)

E19-2 Presented below is a list of costs and expenses usually incurred by Burrand Corporation, a manufacturer of furniture, in its factory.

1. Salaries for assembly line inspectors.
2. Insurance on factory machines.
3. Property taxes on the factory building.
4. Factory repairs.
5. Upholstery used in manufacturing furniture.
6. Wages paid to assembly line workers.
7. Factory machinery depreciation.
8. Glue, nails, paint, and other small parts used in production.
9. Factory supervisors' salaries.
10. Wood used in manufacturing furniture.

Instructions

Classify the above items into the following categories: (a) direct materials, (b) direct labor, and (c) manufacturing overhead.

E19-3 Coldplay Corporation incurred the following costs while manufacturing its product.

Identify types of cost and explain their accounting.

(SO 3, 4)

Materials used in product	$100,000	Advertising expense	$45,000
Depreciation on plant	60,000	Property taxes on plant	14,000
Property taxes on store	7,500	Delivery expense	21,000
Labor costs of assembly-line workers	110,000	Sales commissions	35,000
Factory supplies used	13,000	Salaries paid to sales clerks	50,000

Instructions

(a) Identify each of the above costs as direct materials, direct labor, manufacturing overhead, or period costs.

(b) Explain the basic difference in accounting for product costs and period costs.

E19-4 Caroline Company reports the following costs and expenses in May.

Determine the total amount of various types of costs.

(SO 3, 4)

Factory utilities MOH	$ 11,500	Direct labor PC	$69,100
Depreciation on factory		Sales salaries Period costs	46,400
equipment MOH	12,650	Property taxes on factory MOH	
Depreciation on delivery trucks Per.Cost	3,800	building	2,500
Indirect factory labor MOH	48,900	Repairs to office equipment Period	1,300
Indirect materials MOH	80,800	Factory repairs MOH costs	2,000
Direct materials used PC	137,600	Advertising period costs	18,000
Factory manager's salary MOH	8,000	Office supplies used Period costs.	2,640

Instructions

From the information, determine the total amount of:

(a) Manufacturing overhead.

(b) Product costs.

(c) Period costs.

E19-5 Sota Company is a manufacturer of personal computers. Various costs and expenses associated with its operations are as follows.

Classify various costs into different cost categories.

(SO 3, 4)

1. Property taxes on the factory building.

2. Production superintendents' salaries.

3. Memory boards and chips used in assembling computers.

4. Depreciation on the factory equipment.

5. Salaries for assembly line quality control inspectors.

6. Sales commissions paid to sell personal computers.

7. Electrical components used in assembling computers.

8. Wages of workers assembling personal computers.

9. Soldering materials used on factory assembly lines.

10. Salaries for the night security guards for the factory building.

The company intends to classify these costs and expenses into the following categories: (a) direct materials, (b) direct labor, (c) manufacturing overhead, and (d) period costs.

Instructions

List the items (1) through (10). For each item, indicate the cost category to which it belongs.

E19-6 The administrators of San Diego County's Memorial Hospital are interested in identifying the various costs and expenses that are incurred in producing a patient's X-ray. A list of such costs and expenses in presented below.

Classify various costs into different cost categories.

(SO 3)

1. Salaries for the X-ray machine technicians.

2. Wages for the hospital janitorial personnel.

3. Film costs for the X-ray machines.

4. Property taxes on the hospital building.

5. Salary of the X-ray technicians' supervisor.

6. Electricity costs for the X-ray department.

7. Maintenance and repairs on the X-ray machines.

8. X-ray department supplies.

9. Depreciation on the X-ray department equipment.

10. Depreciation on the hospital building.

The administrators want these costs and expenses classified as: (a) direct materials, (b) direct labor, or (c) service overhead.

Instructions
List the items (1) through (10). For each item, indicate the cost category to which the item belongs.

Classify various costs into different cost categories.
(SO 4)

E19-7 Rapid Delivery Service reports the following costs and expenses in June 2008.

Indirect materials	$ 5,400	Drivers' salaries	$11,000
Depreciation on delivery equipment	11,200	Advertising	1,600
Dispatcher's salary	5,000	Delivery equipment repairs	300
Property taxes on office building	870	Office supplies	650
CEO's salary	12,000	Office utilities	990
Gas and oil for delivery trucks	2,200	Repairs on office equipment	180

Instructions
Determine the total amount of (a) delivery service (product) costs and (b) period costs.

Compute cost of goods manufactured and sold.
(SO 5, 6)

E19-8 Coldplay Corporation incurred the following costs while manufacturing its product.

Materials used in product	$100,000	Advertising expense	$45,000
Depreciation on plant	60,000	Property taxes on plant	14,000
Property taxes on store	7,500	Delivery expense	21,000
Labor costs of assembly-line workers	110,000	Sales commissions	35,000
Factory supplies used	23,000	Salaries paid to sales clerks	50,000

Work-in-process inventory was $12,000 at January 1 and $15,500 at December 31. Finished goods inventory was $60,000 at January 1 and $55,600 at December 31.

Instructions
(a) Compute cost of goods manufactured.
(b) Compute cost of goods sold.

Determine missing amounts in cost of goods manufactured schedule.
(SO 6)

E19-9 An incomplete cost of goods manufactured schedule is presented below.

CEPEDA MANUFACTURING COMPANY
Cost of Goods Manufactured Schedule
For the Year Ended December 31, 2008

Work in process (1/1)			$210,000
Direct materials			
Raw materials inventory (1/1)	$ 44,500		
Add: Raw materials purchases	158,000		
Total raw materials available for use	202,500		
Less: Raw materials inventory (12/31)	12,500		
Direct materials used		$190,000	
Direct labor		62,000	
Manufacturing overhead			
Indirect labor	$ 18,000		
Factory depreciation	36,000		
Factory utilities	68,000		
Total overhead		122,000	
Total manufacturing costs			381,000
Total cost of work in process			? 591,000
Less: Work in process (12/31)			81,000
Cost of goods manufactured			$510,000

Instructions
Complete the cost of goods manufactured schedule for Cepeda Manufacturing Company.

E19-10   Manufacturing cost data for Criqui Company are presented below.

Determine the missing amount of different cost items.

(SO 6)

	Case A	Case B	Case C
Direct materials used	(a)	$58,400	$130,000
Direct labor	$ 57,000	86,000	(g)
Manufacturing overhead	46,500	81,600	102,000
Total manufacturing costs	185,650	(d)	253,700
Work in process 1/1/08	(b)	16,500	(h)
Total cost of work in process	221,500	(e)	337,000
Work in process 12/31/08	(c)	11,000	70,000
Cost of goods manufactured	185,275	(f)	(i)

Instructions

Indicate the missing amount for each letter (a) through (i).

E19-11   Incomplete manufacturing cost data for Ikerd Company for 2008 are presented as follows for four different situations.

Determine the missing amount of different cost items, and prepare a condensed cost of goods manufactured schedule.

(SO 6)

	Direct Materials Used	Direct Labor Used	Manufacturing Overhead	Total Manufacturing Costs	Work in Process 1/1	Work in Process 12/31	Cost of Goods Manufactured
(1)	$127,000 $140,000		$ 77,000	344,000 (a)	$33,000	(b) 7,000	$360,000
(2)	118,000	200,000	132,000	$450,000 (d) 60,000		$40,000	470,000
(3)	80,000	100,000	(e) 65,000	245,000	60,000	80,000	(f) 225,000
(4)	70,000	(g) 143,000	75,000	288,000	45,000	(h) 63,000	270,000

Instructions

(a) Indicate the missing amount for each letter.

(b) Prepare a condensed cost of goods manufactured schedule for situation (1) for the year ended December 31, 2008.

E19-12   Aikman Corporation has the following cost records for June 2008.

Prepare a cost of goods manufactured schedule and a partial income statement.

(SO 5, 6)

Indirect factory labor	$ 4,500	Factory utilities	$ 400
Direct materials used	20,000	Depreciation, factory equipment	1,400
Work in process, 6/1/08	3,000	Direct labor	30,000
Work in process, 6/30/08	3,800	Maintenance, factory equipment	1,800
Finished goods, 6/1/08	5,000	Indirect materials	2,200
Finished goods, 6/30/08	7,500	Factory manager's salary	3,000

Instructions

(a) Prepare a cost of goods manufactured schedule for June 2008.

(b) Prepare an income statement through gross profit for June 2008 assuming net sales are $87,100.

E19-13   Sara Collier, the bookkeeper for Danner, Cheney, and Howe, a political consulting firm, has recently completed a managerial accounting course at her local college. One of the topics covered in the course was the cost of goods manufactured schedule. Sara wondered if such a schedule could be prepared for her firm. She realized that, as a service-oriented company, it would have no Work-in-Process inventory to consider.

Classify various costs into different categories and prepare cost of services provided schedule.

(SO 4, 5, 6)

Listed below are the costs her firm incurred for the month ended August 31, 2008.

Supplies used on consulting contracts	$ 1,200
Supplies used in the administrative offices	1,500
Depreciation on equipment used for contract work	900
Depreciation used on administrative office equipment	1,050
Salaries of professionals working on contracts	12,600
Salaries of administrative office personnel	7,700
Janitorial services for professional offices	400
Janitorial services for administrative offices	500
Insurance on contract operations	800
Insurance on administrative operations	900
Utilities for contract operations	1,400
Utilities for administrative offices	1,300

Instructions

(a) Prepare a schedule of cost of contract services provided (similar to a cost of goods manufactured schedule) for the month.

(b) For those costs not included in (a), explain how they would be classified and reported in the financial statements.

Prepare a cost of goods manufactured schedule and a partial income statement.

(SO 5, 6, 7)

E19-14 The following information is available for Sassafras Company.

	January 1, 2008	2008	December 31, 2008
Raw materials inventory	$ 21,000		$30,000
Work in process inventory	13,500		17,200
Finished goods inventory	27,000		21,000
Materials purchased		$150,000	
Direct labor		200,000	
Manufacturing overhead		180,000	
Sales		900,000	

Instructions

(a) Compute cost of goods manufactured.

(b) Prepare an income statement through gross profit.

(c) Show the presentation of the ending inventories on the December 31, 2008 balance sheet.

(d) How would the income statement and balance sheet of a merchandising company be different from Sassafras's financial statements?

Indicate in which schedule or financial statement(s) different cost items will appear.

(SO 5, 6, 7)

E19-15 Corbin Manufacturing Company produces blankets. From its accounting records it prepares the following schedule and financial statements on a yearly basis.

(a) Cost of goods manufactured schedule.

(b) Income statement.

(c) Balance sheet.

The following items are found in its ledger and accompanying data.

1. Direct labor
2. Raw materials inventory, 1/1
3. Work in process inventory, 12/31
4. Finished goods inventory, 1/1
5. Indirect labor
6. Depreciation on factory machinery
7. Work in process, 1/1
8. Finished goods inventory, 12/31

9. Factory maintenance salaries
10. Cost of goods manufactured
11. Depreciation on delivery equipment
12. Cost of goods available for sale
13. Direct materials used
14. Heat and electricity for factory
15. Repairs to roof of factory building
16. Cost of raw materials purchases

Instructions

List the items (1)–(16). For each item, indicate by using the appropriate letter or letters, the schedule and/or financial statement(s) in which the item will appear.

Prepare a cost of goods manufactured schedule, and present the ending inventories of the balance sheet.

(SO 6, 7)

E19-16 An analysis of the accounts of Chamberlin Manufacturing reveals the following manufacturing cost data for the month ended June 30, 2008.

Inventories	Beginning	Ending
Raw materials	$9,000	$13,100
Work in process	5,000	7,000
Finished goods	9,000	6,000

Costs incurred: Raw materials purchases $54,000, direct labor $57,000, manufacturing overhead $19,900. The specific overhead costs were: indirect labor $5,500, factory insurance $4,000, machinery depreciation $4,000, machinery repairs $1,800, factory utilities $3,100, miscellaneous factory costs $1,500. Assume that all raw materials used were direct materials.

Determine the amount of cost to appear in various accounts, and indicate in which financial statements these accounts would appear.

(SO 5, 6, 7)

Instructions

(a) Prepare the cost of goods manufactured schedule for the month ended June 30, 2008.

(b) Show the presentation of the ending inventories on the June 30, 2008, balance sheet.

E19-17 Todd Motor Company manufactures automobiles. During September 2008 the company purchased 5,000 head lamps at a cost of $9 per lamp. Todd withdrew 4,650 lamps from the warehouse during the month. Fifty of these lamps were used to replace the head lamps in autos used by traveling sales staff. The remaining 4,600 lamps were put in autos manufactured during the month.

Of the autos put into production during September 2008, 90% were completed and transferred to the company's storage lot. Of the cars completed during the month, 75% were sold by September 30.

Instructions
(a) Determine the cost of head lamps that would appear in each of the following accounts at September 30, 2008: Raw Materials, Work in Process, Finished Goods, Cost of Goods Sold, and Selling Expenses.
(b) Write a short memo to the chief accountant, indicating whether and where each of the accounts in (a) would appear on the income statement or on the balance sheet at September 30, 2008.

E19-18 The following is a list of terms related to managerial accounting practices.
1. Activity-based costing.
2. Just-in-time inventory.
3. Balanced scorecard.
4. Value chain.

Identify various managerial accounting practices.
(SO 8)

Instructions
Match each of the terms with the statement below that best describes the term.

(a) _____ A performance-measurement technique that attempts to consider and evaluate all aspects of performance using financial and nonfinancial measures in an integrated fashion.
(b) _____ The group of activities associated with providing a product or service.
(c) _____ An approach used to reduce the cost associated with handling and holding inventory by reducing the amount of inventory on hand.
(d) _____ A method used to allocate overhead to products based on each product's use of the activities that cause the incurrence of the overhead cost.

EXERCISES: SET B

Visit the book's website at **www.wiley.com/college/weygandt**, and choose the Student Companion site, to access Exercise Set B.

PROBLEMS: SET A

P19-1A Bjerg Company specializes in manufacturing a unique model of bicycle helmet. The model is well accepted by consumers, and the company has enough orders to keep the factory production at 10,000 helmets per month (80% of its full capacity). Bjerg's monthly manufacturing cost and other expense data are as follows.

Classify manufacturing costs into different categories and compute the unit cost.
(SO 3, 4)

Rent on factory equipment	$ 7,000
Insurance on factory building	1,500
Raw materials (plastics, polystyrene, etc.)	75,000
Utility costs for factory	900
Supplies for general office	300
Wages for assembly line workers	43,000
Depreciation on office equipment	800
Miscellaneous materials (glue, thread, etc.)	1,100
Factory manager's salary	5,700
Property taxes on factory building	400
Advertising for helmets	14,000
Sales commissions	7,000
Depreciation on factory building	1,500

Instructions

(a) Prepare an answer sheet with the following column headings.

(a) DM $75,000
DL $43,000
MO $18,100
PC $22,100

	Product Costs			
Cost Item	Direct Materials	Direct Labor	Manufacturing Overhead	Period Costs

Enter each cost item on your answer sheet, placing the dollar amount under the appropriate headings. Total the dollar amounts in each of the columns.

(b) Compute the cost to produce one helmet

Classify manufacturing costs into different categories and compute the unit cost.

(SO 3, 4)

P19-2A Copa Company, a manufacturer of stereo systems, started its production in October 2008. For the preceding 3 years Copa had been a retailer of stereo systems. After a thorough survey of stereo system markets, Copa decided to turn its retail store into a stereo equipment factory.

Raw materials cost for a stereo system will total $74 per unit. Workers on the production lines are on average paid $12 per hour. A stereo system usually takes 5 hours to complete. In addition, the rent on the equipment used to assemble stereo systems amounts to $4,900 per month. Indirect materials cost $5 per system. A supervisor was hired to oversee production; her monthly salary is $3,000.

Janitorial costs are $1,300 monthly. Advertising costs for the stereo system will be $8,500 per month. The factory building depreciation expense is $7,200 per year. Property taxes on the factory building will be $9,000 per year.

Instructions

(a) Prepare an answer sheet with the following column headings.

(a) DM $96,200
DL $78,000
MO $17,050
PC $ 8,500

	Product Costs			
Cost Item	Direct Materials	Direct Labor	Manufacturing Overhead	Period Costs

Assuming that Copa manufactures, on average, 1,300 stereo systems per month, enter each cost item on your answer sheet, placing the dollar amount per month under the appropriate headings. Total the dollar amounts in each of the columns.

(b) Compute the cost to produce one stereo system.

Indicate the missing amount of different cost items, and prepare a condensed cost of goods manufactured schedule, an income statement, and a partial balance sheet.

(SO 5, 6, 7)

P19-3A Incomplete manufacturing costs, expenses, and selling data for two different cases are as follows.

	Case 1	Case 2
Direct Materials Used	$ 7,600	$ (g)
Direct Labor	5,000	8,000
Manufacturing Overhead	8,000	4,000
Total Manufacturing Costs	(a)	18,000
Beginning Work in Process Inventory	1,000	(h)
Ending Work in Process Inventory	(b)	3,000
Sales	24,500	(i)
Sales Discounts	2,500	1,400
Cost of Goods Manufactured	17,000	22,000
Beginning Finished Goods Inventory	(c)	3,300
Goods Available for Sale	18,000	(j)
Cost of Goods Sold	(d)	(k)
Ending Finished Goods Inventory	3,400	2,500
Gross Profit	(e)	7,000
Operating Expenses	2,500	(l)
Net Income	(f)	5,000

Instructions

(a) Indicate the missing amount for each letter.

(b) Ending WIP $4,600

(b) Prepare a condensed cost of goods manufactured schedule for Case 1.

(c) Prepare an income statement and the current assets section of the balance sheet for Case 1. Assume that in Case 1 the other items in the current assets section are as follows: Cash $4,000, Receivables (net) $15,000, Raw Materials $600, and Prepaid Expenses $400.

(c) Current assets $28,000

P19-4A The following data were taken from the records of Stellar Manufacturing Company for the fiscal year ended June 30, 2008.

Prepare a cost of goods manufactured schedule, a partial income statement, and a partial balance sheet.

(SO 5, 6, 7)

Raw Materials		Factory Insurance	$ 4,600	
Inventory 7/1/07	$ 48,000	Factory Machinery		
Raw Materials		Depreciation	16,000	
Inventory 6/30/08	39,600	Factory Utilities	27,600	
Finished Goods		Office Utilities Expense	8,650	
Inventory 7/1/07	96,000	Sales	554,000	
Finished Goods		Sales Discounts	4,200	
Inventory 6/30/08	95,900	Plant Manager's Salary	29,000	
Work in Process		Factory Property Taxes	9,600	
Inventory 7/1/07	19,800	Factory Repairs	1,400	
Work in Process		Raw Materials Purchases	96,400	
Inventory 6/30/08	18,600	Cash	32,000	
Direct Labor	149,250			
Indirect Labor	24,460			
Accounts Receivable	27,000			

Instructions

(a) Prepare a cost of goods manufactured schedule. (Assume all raw materials used were direct materials.)

(b) Prepare an income statement through gross profit.

(c) Prepare the current assets section of the balance sheet at June 30, 2008.

(a) CGM $367,910

(b) Gross profit $181,790
(c) Current assets $213,100

P19-5A Tombert Company is a manufacturer of computers. Its controller resigned in October 2008. An inexperienced assistant accountant has prepared the following income statement for the month of October 2008.

Prepare a cost of goods manufactured schedule and a correct income statement.

(SO 5, 6)

TOMBERT COMPANY
Income Statement
For the Month Ended October 31, 2008

Sales (net)		$780,000
Less: Operating expenses		
Raw materials purchases	$264,000	
Direct labor cost	190,000	
Advertising expense	90,000	
Selling and administrative salaries	75,000	
Rent on factory facilities	60,000	
Depreciation on sales equipment	45,000	
Depreciation on factory equipment	31,000	
Indirect labor cost	28,000	
Utilities expense	12,000	
Insurance expense	8,000	803,000
Net loss		$(23,000)

Prior to October 2008 the company had been profitable every month. The company's president is concerned about the accuracy of the income statement. As his friend, you have been asked to review the income statement and make necessary corrections. After examining other manufacturing cost data, you have acquired additional information as follows.

1. Inventory balances at the beginning and end of October were:

	October 1	October 31
Raw materials	$18,000	$34,000
Work in process	16,000	14,000
Finished goods	30,000	48,000

2. Only 70% of the utilities expense and 60% of the insurance expense apply to factory operations. The remaining amounts should be charged to selling and administrative activities.

Instructions

(a) CGM $572,200

(b) NI $ 9,000

(a) Prepare a schedule of cost of goods manufactured for October 2008.

(b) Prepare a correct income statement for October 2008.

PROBLEMS: SET B

Classify manufacturing costs into different categories and compute the unit cost.

(SO 3, 4)

P19-1B Hite Company specializes in manufacturing motorcycle helmets. The company has enough orders to keep the factory production at 1,000 motorcycle helmets per month. Hite's monthly manufacturing cost and other expense data are as follows.

Maintenance costs on factory building	$ 600
Factory manager's salary	4,000
Advertising for helmets	8,000
Sales commissions	3,000
Depreciation on factory building	700
Rent on factory equipment	6,000
Insurance on factory building	3,000
Raw materials (plastic, polystyrene, etc.)	20,000
Utility costs for factory	800
Supplies for general office	200
Wages for assembly line workers	44,000
Depreciation on office equipment	500
Miscellaneous materials (glue, thread, etc.)	2,000

Instructions

(a) DM $20,000

DL $44,000

MO $17,100

PC $11,700

(a) Prepare an answer sheet with the following column headings.

	Product Costs			
Cost Item	Direct Materials	Direct Labor	Manufacturing Overhead	Period Costs

Enter each cost item on your answer sheet, placing the dollar amount under the appropriate headings. Total the dollar amounts in each of the columns.

(b) Compute the cost to produce one motorcycle helmet.

Classify manufacturing costs into different categories and compute the unit cost.

(SO 3, 4)

P19-2B Ladoca Company, a manufacturer of tennis rackets, started production in November 2008. For the preceding 5 years Ladoca had been a retailer of sports equipment. After a thorough survey of tennis racket markets, Ladoca decided to turn its retail store into a tennis racket factory.

Raw materials cost for a tennis racket will total $23 per racket. Workers on the production lines are paid on average $13 per hour. A racket usually takes 2 hours to complete. In addition, the rent on the equipment used to produce rackets amounts to $1,300 per month. Indirect materials cost $3 per racket. A supervisor was hired to oversee production; her monthly salary is $3,500.

Janitorial costs are $1,400 monthly. Advertising costs for the rackets will be $6,000 per month. The factory building depreciation expense is $8,400 per year. Property taxes on the factory building will be $5,400 per year.

Instructions

(a) DM $46,000

DL $52,000

MO $13,350

PC $ 6,000

(a) Prepare an answer sheet with the following column headings.

	Product Costs			
Cost Item	Direct Materials	Direct Labor	Manufacturing Overhead	Period Costs

Assuming that Ladoca manufactures, on average, 2,000 tennis rackets per month, enter each cost item on your answer sheet, placing the dollar amount per month under the appropriate headings. Total the dollar amounts in each of the columns.

(b) Compute the cost to produce one racket.

P19-3B   Incomplete manufacturing costs, expenses, and selling data for two different cases are as follows.

Indicate the missing amount of different cost items, and prepare a condensed cost of goods manufactured schedule, an income statement, and a partial balance sheet.

(SO 5, 6, 7)

	Case	
	1	**2**
Direct Materials Used	$ 8,300	$ (g)
Direct Labor	3,000	4,000
Manufacturing Overhead	6,000	5,000
Total Manufacturing Costs	(a)	18,000
Beginning Work in Process Inventory	1,000	(h)
Ending Work in Process Inventory	(b)	2,000
Sales	22,500	(i)
Sales Discounts	1,500	1,200
Cost of Goods Manufactured	15,800	20,000
Beginning Finished Goods Inventory	(c)	4,000
Goods Available for Sale	17,300	(j)
Cost of Goods Sold	(d)	(k)
Ending Finished Goods Inventory	1,200	2,500
Gross Profit	(e)	6,000
Operating Expenses	2,700	(l)
Net Income	(f)	3,200

Instructions

(a) Indicate the missing amount for each letter.

(b) Prepare a condensed cost of goods manufactured schedule for Case 1.

(c) Prepare an income statement and the current assets section of the balance sheet for Case 1. Assume that in Case 1 the other items in the current assets section are as follows: Cash $3,000, Receivables (net) $10,000, Raw Materials $700, and Prepaid Expenses $200.

(c) Current assets $17,600

P19-4B   The following data were taken from the records of Ruiz Manufacturing Company for the year ended December 31, 2008.

Prepare a cost of goods manufactured schedule, a partial income statement, and a partial balance sheet.

(SO 5, 6, 7)

Raw Materials		Factory Insurance	$ 7,400
Inventory 1/1/08	$ 47,000	Factory Machinery	
Raw Materials		Depreciation	7,700
Inventory 12/31/08	44,200	Factory Utilities	12,900
Finished Goods		Office Utilities Expense	8,600
Inventory 1/1/08	85,000	Sales	475,000
Finished Goods			
Inventory 12/31/08	77,800		
Work in Process		Sales Discounts	2,500
Inventory 1/1/08	9,500	Plant Manager's Salary	30,000
Work in Process		Factory Property Taxes	6,100
Inventory 12/31/08	8,000	Factory Repairs	800
Direct Labor	145,100	Raw Materials Purchases	67,500
Indirect Labor	18,100	Cash	28,000
Accounts Receivable	27,000		

Instructions

(a) Prepare a cost of goods manufactured schedule. (Assume all raw materials used were direct materials.)

(b) Prepare an income statement through gross profit.

(c) Prepare the current assets section of the balance sheet at December 31.

(a) CGM $299,900

(b) Gross profit $165,400
(c) Current assets $185,000

P19-5B   Agler Company is a manufacturer of toys. Its controller, Joyce Rotzen, resigned in August 2008. An inexperienced assistant accountant has prepared the following income statement for the month of August 2008.

Prepare a cost of goods manufactured schedule and a correct income statement.

(SO 5, 6)

AGLER COMPANY
Income Statement
For the Month Ended August 31, 2008

Sales (net)		$675,000
Less: Operating expenses		
Raw materials purchases	$200,000	
Direct labor cost	160,000	
Advertising expense	75,000	
Selling and administrative salaries	70,000	
Rent on factory facilities	60,000	
Depreciation on sales equipment	50,000	
Depreciation on factory equipment	35,000	
Indirect labor cost	20,000	
Utilities expense	10,000	
Insurance expense	5,000	685,000
Net loss		$(10,000)

Prior to August 2008 the company had been profitable every month. The company's president is concerned about the accuracy of the income statement. As her friend, you have been asked to review the income statement and make necessary corrections. After examining other manufacturing cost data, you have acquired additional information as follows.

1. Inventory balances at the beginning and end of August were:

	August 1	August 31
Raw materials	$19,500	$30,000
Work in process	25,000	21,000
Finished goods	40,000	64,000

2. Only 60% of the utilities expense and 70% of the insurance expense apply to factory operations; the remaining amounts should be charged to selling and administrative activities.

Instructions

(a) CGM $478,000

(b) NI $ 20,500

(a) Prepare a cost of goods manufactured schedule for August 2008.
(b) Prepare a correct income statement for August 2008.

PROBLEMS: SET C

Visit the book's website at **www.wiley.com/college/weygandt**, and choose the Student Companion site, to access Problem Set C.

BROADENING YOUR PERSPECTIVE

DECISION MAKING ACROSS THE ORGANIZATION

BYP19-1   Mismatch Manufacturing Company specializes in producing fashion outfits. On July 31, 2008, a tornado touched down at its factory and general office. The inventories in the warehouse and the factory were completely destroyed as was the general office nearby. Next morning, through a careful search of the disaster site, however, Ross Clarkson, the company's controller,

and Catherine Harper, the cost accountant, were able to recover a small part of manufacturing cost data for the current month.

"What a horrible experience," sighed Ross. "And the worst part is that we may not have enough records to use in filing an insurance claim."

"It was terrible," replied Catherine. "However, I managed to recover some of the manufacturing cost data that I was working on yesterday afternoon. The data indicate that our direct labor cost in July totaled $240,000 and that we had purchased $345,000 of raw materials. Also, I recall that the amount of raw materials used for July was $350,000. But I'm not sure this information will help. The rest of our records are blown away."

"Well, not exactly," said Ross. "I was working on the year-to-date income statement when the tornado warning was announced. My recollection is that our sales in July were $1,260,000 and our gross profit ratio has been 40% of sales. Also, I can remember that our cost of goods available for sale was $770,000 for July."

"Maybe we can work something out from this information!" exclaimed Catherine. "My experience tells me that our manufacturing overhead is usually 60% of direct labor."

"Hey, look what I just found," cried Catherine. "It's a copy of this June's balance sheet, and it shows that our inventories as of June 30 are Finished goods $38,000, Work in process $25,000, and Raw materials $19,000."

"Super," yelled Ross. "Let's go work something out."

In order to file an insurance claim, Mismatch Company must determine the amount of its inventories as of July 31, 2008, the date of the tornado touchdown.

Instructions

With the class divided into groups, determine the amount of cost in the Raw Materials, Work in Process, and Finished Goods inventory accounts as of the date of the tornado touchdown.

MANAGERIAL ANALYSIS

BYP19-2 Love All is a fairly large manufacturing company located in the southern United States. The company manufactures tennis rackets, tennis balls, tennis clothing, and tennis shoes, all bearing the company's distinctive logo, a large green question mark on a white flocked tennis ball. The company's sales have been increasing over the past 10 years.

The tennis racket division has recently implemented several advanced manufacturing techniques. Robot arms hold the tennis rackets in place while glue dries, and machine vision systems check for defects. The engineering and design team uses computerized drafting and testing of new products. The following managers work in the tennis racket division.

Andre Agassi, Sales Manager (supervises all sales representatives).
Serena Williams, technical specialist (supervises computer programmers).
Pete Sampras, cost accounting manager (supervises cost accountants).
Andy Roddick, production supervisor (supervises all manufacturing employees).
Venus Williams, engineer (supervises all new-product design teams).

Instructions
(a) What are the primary information needs of each manager?
(b) Which, if any, financial accounting report(s) is each likely to use?
(c) Name one special-purpose management accounting report that could be designed for each manager. Include the name of the report, the information it would contain, and how frequently it should be issued.

REAL-WORLD FOCUS

BYP19-3 Anchor Glass Container Corporation, the third largest manufacturer of glass containers in the U.S., supplies beverage and food producers and consumer products manufacturers nationwide. Parent company Consumers Packaging Inc. (Toronto Stock Exchange: CGC) is a leading international designer and manufacturer of glass containers.

The following management discussion appeared in a recent annual report of Anchor Glass.

ANCHOR GLASS CONTAINER CORPORATION
Management Discussion

Cost of Products Sold Cost of products sold as a percentage of net sales was 89.3% in the current year compared to 87.6% in the prior year. The increase in cost of products sold as a percentage of net sales principally reflected the impact of operational problems during the second quarter of the current year at a major furnace at one of the Company's plants, higher downtime, and costs and expenses associated with an increased number of scheduled capital improvement projects, increases in labor, and certain other manufacturing costs (with no corresponding selling price increases in the current year). Reduced fixed costs from the closing of the Streator, Illinois, plant in June of the current year and productivity and efficiency gains partially offset these cost increases.

Instructions

What factors affect the costs of products sold at Anchor Glass Container Corporation?

EXPLORING THE WEB

BYP19-4 The Institute of Management Accountants (IMA) is an organization dedicated to excellence in the practice of management accounting and financial management.

Address: www.imanet.org, or go to **www.wiley.com/college/weygandt**

Instructions

At the IMA's home page, locate the answers to the following questions.

(a) How many members does the IMA have, and what are their job titles?

(b) What are some of the benefits of joining the IMA as a student?

(c) Use the chapter locator function to locate the IMA chapter nearest you, and find the name of the chapter president.

COMMUNICATION ACTIVITY

BYP19-5 Refer to Problem 19–5A and add the following requirement.

Prepare a letter to the president of the company, Sue Tombert, describing the changes you made. Explain clearly why net income is different after the changes. Keep the following points in mind as you compose your letter.

1. This is a letter to the president of a company, who is your friend. The style should be generally formal, but you may relax some requirements. For example, you may call the president by her first name.

2. Executives are very busy. Your letter should tell the president your main results first (for example, the amount of net income).

3. You should include brief explanations so that the president can understand the changes you made in the calculations.

ETHICS CASE

BYP19-6 Wayne Terrago, controller for Robbin Industries, was reviewing production cost reports for the year. One amount in these reports continued to bother him—advertising. During the year, the company had instituted an expensive advertising campaign to sell some of its slower-moving products. It was still too early to tell whether the advertising campaign was successful.

There had been much internal debate as how to report advertising cost. The vice president of finance argued that advertising costs should be reported as a cost of production, just like direct materials and direct labor. He therefore recommended that this cost be identified as manufacturing overhead and reported as part of inventory costs until sold. Others disagreed. Terrago believed that this cost should be reported as an expense of the current period, based on the conservatism principle. Others argued that it should be reported as Prepaid Advertising and reported as a current asset.

The president finally had to decide the issue. He argued that these costs should be reported as inventory. His arguments were practical ones. He noted that the company was experiencing financial difficulty and expensing this amount in the current period might jeopardize a planned bond offering. Also, by reporting the advertising costs as inventory rather than as prepaid advertising, less attention would be directed to it by the financial community.

Instructions
(a) Who are the stakeholders in this situation?
(b) What are the ethical issues involved in this situation?
(c) What would you do if you were Wayne Terrago?

"All About You" Activity

BYP19-7   The primary purpose of managerial accounting is to provide information useful for management decisions. Many of the managerial accounting techniques that you learn in this course will be useful for decisions you make in your everyday life.

Instructions
For each of the following managerial accounting techniques, read the definition provided and then provide an example of a personal situation that would benefit from use of this technique.
(a) Break-even analysis (page 968).   **(c)** Balanced scorecard (page 847).
(b) Budgeting (page 1000).   **(d)** Capital budgeting (page 1144).

Answers to Insight and Accounting Across the Organization Questions

p. 834 Automation Has Changed Management
Q: As factories become more automated, what will managers "manage"?
A: *Managers will review production and equipment utilization data to determine if quality and quantity goals are being met. Such data should indicate which equipment and operators are most reliable and efficient.*

p. 837 Productivity at Nissan
Q: Why might Nissan production require significantly fewer labor hours?
A: *Nissan's U.S. factories are probably newer than those of Daimler-Chrysler and Ford. Newer factories tend to be more highly automated with less reliance on production-line employees.*

p. 846 Bananas Receive Special Treatment
Q: Why is it important to keep track of costs that are incurred to improve product quality?
A: *Most companies are concerned about product quality, but managers need to consider the cost/benefit tradeoff. If you spend too much on improving product quality, your customers might not be willing to pay the price needed to recover costs. Therefore it is very important that Chiquita closely track all of the costs that it incurs to protect the bananas, to ensure that these costs are factored into the price that it ultimately charges for the bananas.*

Authors' Comments on *All About You*: Outsourcing and Jobs (p. 848)

This is a difficult decision. While the direct costs of outsourced tax return preparation may in fact be lower, you must also consider other issues: Will the accuracy of the returns be as high? Will your relationships with your customers suffer due to the loss of direct contact? Will customers resent having their personal information shipped overseas? While you may not want to lay off six employees, you also don't want to put your firm at risk by not remaining competitive.

Perhaps one solution would be to outsource the most basic tasks, and then provide training to the six employees so they can perform higher-skilled services such as tax planning. Many of the techniques that you learn in the remaining chapters of this text will help you evaluate the merits of your various options.

Answers to Self-Study Questions
1. b   **2.** b   **3.** b   **4.** c   **5.** d   **6.** a   **7.** c   **8.** a   **9.** d   **10.** d

Chapter 20

Job Order Cost Accounting

Feature Story

" . . . AND WE'D LIKE IT IN RED"

Western States Fire Apparatus, Inc., of Cornelius, Oregon, is one of the few U.S. companies that makes fire trucks. The company builds about 25 trucks per year. Founded in 1941, the company is run by the children and grand-children of the original founder.

"We buy the chassis, which is the cab and the frame," says Susan Scott, the company's bookkeeper. "In our computer, we set up an account into which all of the direct material that is purchased for that particular job is charged."

SPECIMEN FINANCIAL STATEMENTS:
PepsiCo, Inc.

THE ANNUAL REPORT

Once each year a corporation communicates to its stockholders and other interested parties by issuing a complete set of audited financial statements. The **annual report**, as this communication is called, summarizes the financial results of the company's operations for the year and its plans for the future. Many annual reports are attractive, multicolored, glossy public relations pieces, containing pictures of corporate officers and directors as well as photos and descriptions of new products and new buildings. Yet the basic function of every annual report is to report financial information, almost all of which is a product of the corporation's accounting system.

The content and organization of corporate annual reports have become fairly standardized. Excluding the public relations part of the report (pictures, products, etc.), the following are the traditional financial portions of the annual report:

- Financial Highlights
- Letter to the Stockholders
- Management's Discussion and Analysis
- Financial Statements
- Notes to the Financial Statements
- Management's Report on Internal Control
- Management Certification of Financial Statements
- Auditor's Report
- Supplementary Financial Information

In this appendix we illustrate current financial reporting with a comprehensive set of corporate financial statements that are prepared in accordance with generally accepted accounting principles and audited by an international independent certified public accounting firm. We are grateful for permission to use the actual financial statements and other accompanying financial information from the annual report of a large, publicly held company, PepsiCo, Inc.

FINANCIAL HIGHLIGHTS

Companies usually present the financial highlights section inside the front cover of the annual report or on its first two pages. This section generally reports the total or per share amounts for five to ten financial items for the current year and one or more previous years. Financial items from the income statement and the balance sheet that typically are presented are sales, income from continuing operations, net income, net income per share, net cash provided by operating activities, dividends per common share, and the amount of capital expenditures. The financial highlights section from PepsiCo's Annual Report is shown on page A-2.

The financial information herein is reprinted with permission from the PepsiCo, Inc. 2005 Annual Report. The complete financial statements are available through a link at the book's companion website.

Financial Highlights

PepsiCo, Inc. and Subsidiaries
($ in millions except per share amounts; all per share amounts assume dilution)

Net Revenue
Total: $32,562

Division Operating Profit
Total: $6,710

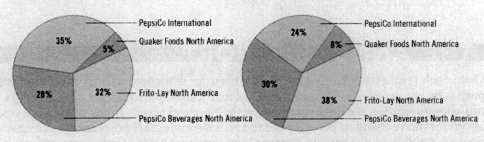

	2005	2004	% Chg[a]
Summary of Operations			
Total net revenue	$32,562	$29,261	11
Division operating profit	$6,710	$6,098	10
Total operating profit	$5,922	$5,259	13
Net income[b]	$4,536	$4,004	13
Earnings per share[b]	$2.66	$2.32	15
Other Data			
Management operating cash flow[c]	$4,204	$3,705	13
Net cash provided by operating activities	$5,852	$5,054	16
Capital spending	$1,736	$1,387	25
Common share repurchases	$3,012	$3,028	(0.5)
Dividends paid	$1,642	$1,329	24
Long-term debt	$2,313	$2,397	(3.5)

(a) Percentage changes above and in text are based on unrounded amounts.

(b) In 2005, excludes the impact of AJCA tax charge, the 53rd week and restructuring charges. In 2004, excludes certain prior year tax benefits, and restructuring and impairment charges. See page 76 for reconciliation to net income and earnings per share on a GAAP basis.

(c) Includes the impact of net capital spending. Also, see "Our Liquidity, Capital Resources and Financial Position" in Management's Discussion and Analysis.

LETTER TO THE STOCKHOLDERS

Nearly every annual report contains a letter to the stockholders from the chairman of the board or the president, or both. This letter typically discusses the company's accomplishments during the past year and highlights significant events such as mergers and acquisitions, new products, operating achievements, business philosophy, changes in officers or directors, financing commitments, expansion plans, and future prospects. The letter to the stockholders is signed by Steve Reinemund, Chairman of the Board and Chief Executive Officer, of PepsiCo.

Only a short summary of the letter is provided below. The full letter can be accessed at the book's companion website at **www.wiley.com/college/weygandt.**

Dear Shareholders:

With profitable growth across all divisions, on every continent and across both convenient food and beverage categories, PepsiCo delivered a very strong 2005. The company's continued focus on health and wellness, and innovation — coupled with its efforts to build big, muscular brands and powerful go-to-market systems — generated industry leading results.

- Volume grew 7%.
- Net revenue grew 11%.
- Division operating profit grew 10%.
- Earnings per share grew 15%.
- Total return to shareholders was 15% compared with 5% for the S&P.
- Cash flow from operations was $5.9 billion and management operating cash flow was $4.2 billion.

Steve Reinemund
Chairman and Chief Executive Officer

MANAGEMENT'S DISCUSSION AND ANALYSIS

The **management's discussion and analysis (MD&A)** section covers three financial aspects of a company: its results of operations, its ability to pay near-term obligations, and its ability to fund operations and expansion. Management must highlight favorable or unfavorable trends and identity significant events and uncertainties that affect these three factors. This discussion obviously involves a number of subjective estimates and opinions. In its MD&A section, PepsiCo breaks its discussion into three major headings: Our Business, Our Critical Accounting Policies, and Our Financial Results. PepsiCo's MD&A section is 22 pages long. You can access that section at **www.wiley.com/college/weygandt.**

FINANCIAL STATEMENTS AND ACCOMPANYING NOTES

The standard set of financial statements consists of: (1) a comparative income statement for 3 years, (2) a comparative statement of cash flows for 3 years, (3) a comparative balance sheet for 2 years, (4) a statement of stockholders' equity for 3 years, and (5) a set of accompanying notes that are considered an integral part of the financial statements. The auditor's report, unless stated otherwise, covers the financial statements and the accompanying notes. PepsiCo's financial statements and accompanying notes plus supplementary data and analyses follow.

Consolidated Statement of Income

PepsiCo, Inc. and Subsidiaries
Fiscal years ended December 31, 2005, December 25, 2004 and December 27, 2003

(in millions except per share amounts)	2005	2004	2003
Net Revenue	$32,562	$29,261	$26,971
Cost of sales	14,176	12,674	11,691
Selling, general and administrative expenses	12,314	11,031	10,148
Amortization of intangible assets	150	147	145
Restructuring and impairment charges	—	150	147
Merger-related costs	—	—	59
Operating Profit	5,922	5,259	4,781
Bottling equity income	557	380	323
Interest expense	(256)	(167)	(163)
Interest income	159	74	51
Income from Continuing Operations before Income Taxes	6,382	5,546	4,992
Provision for Income Taxes	2,304	1,372	1,424
Income from Continuing Operations	4,078	4,174	3,568
Tax Benefit from Discontinued Operations	—	38	—
Net Income	$ 4,078	$ 4,212	$ 3,568
Net Income per Common Share — Basic			
Continuing operations	$2.43	$2.45	$2.07
Discontinued operations	—	0.02	—
Total	$2.43	$2.47	$2.07
Net Income per Common Share — Diluted			
Continuing operations	$2.39	$2.41	$2.05
Discontinued operations	—	0.02	—
Total	$2.39	$2.44*	$2.05

* Based on unrounded amounts.
See accompanying notes to consolidated financial statements.

Consolidated Statement of Cash Flows

PepsiCo, Inc. and Subsidiaries
Fiscal years ended December 31, 2005, December 25, 2004 and December 27, 2003

(in millions)	2005	2004	2003
Operating Activities			
Net income	$ 4,078	$ 4,212	$ 3,568
Adjustments to reconcile net income to net cash provided by operating activities			
Depreciation and amortization	1,308	1,264	1,221
Stock-based compensation expense	311	368	407
Restructuring and impairment charges	–	150	147
Cash payments for merger-related costs and restructuring charges	(22)	(92)	(109)
Tax benefit from discontinued operations	–	(38)	–
Pension and retiree medical plan contributions	(877)	(534)	(605)
Pension and retiree medical plan expenses	464	395	277
Bottling equity income, net of dividends	(411)	(297)	(276)
Deferred income taxes and other tax charges and credits	440	(203)	(286)
Merger-related costs	–	–	59
Other non-cash charges and credits, net	145	166	101
Changes in operating working capital, excluding effects of acquisitions and divestitures			
Accounts and notes receivable	(272)	(130)	(220)
Inventories	(132)	(100)	(49)
Prepaid expenses and other current assets	(56)	(31)	23
Accounts payable and other current liabilities	188	216	(11)
Income taxes payable	609	(268)	182
Net change in operating working capital	337	(313)	(75)
Other	79	(24)	(101)
Net Cash Provided by Operating Activities	5,852	5,054	4,328
Investing Activities			
Snack Ventures Europe (SVE) minority interest acquisition	(750)	–	–
Capital spending	(1,736)	(1,387)	(1,345)
Sales of property, plant and equipment	88	38	49
Other acquisitions and investments in noncontrolled affiliates	(345)	(64)	(71)
Cash proceeds from sale of PBG stock	214	–	–
Divestitures	3	52	46
Short-term investments, by original maturity			
More than three months — purchases	(83)	(44)	(38)
More than three months — maturities	84	38	28
Three months or less, net	(992)	(963)	(940)
Net Cash Used for Investing Activities	(3,517)	(2,330)	(2,271)
Financing Activities			
Proceeds from issuances of long-term debt	25	504	52
Payments of long-term debt	(177)	(512)	(641)
Short-term borrowings, by original maturity			
More than three months — proceeds	332	153	88
More than three months — payments	(85)	(160)	(115)
Three months or less, net	1,601	1,119	40
Cash dividends paid	(1,642)	(1,329)	(1,070)
Share repurchases — common	(3,012)	(3,028)	(1,929)
Share repurchases — preferred	(19)	(27)	(16)
Proceeds from exercises of stock options	1,099	965	689
Net Cash Used for Financing Activities	(1,878)	(2,315)	(2,902)
Effect of exchange rate changes on cash and cash equivalents	(21)	51	27
Net Increase/(Decrease) in Cash and Cash Equivalents	436	460	(818)
Cash and Cash Equivalents, Beginning of Year	1,280	820	1,638
Cash and Cash Equivalents, End of Year	$ 1,716	$ 1,280	$ 820

See accompanying notes to consolidated financial statements.

Consolidated Balance Sheet

PepsiCo, Inc. and Subsidiaries
December 31, 2005 and December 25, 2004

(in millions except per share amounts)	2005	2004
ASSETS		
Current Assets		
Cash and cash equivalents	$ 1,716	$ 1,280
Short-term investments	3,166	2,165
	4,882	3,445
Accounts and notes receivable, net	3,261	2,999
Inventories	1,693	1,541
Prepaid expenses and other current assets	618	654
Total Current Assets	10,454	8,639
Property, Plant and Equipment, net	8,681	8,149
Amortizable Intangible Assets, net	530	598
Goodwill	4,088	3,909
Other nonamortizable intangible assets	1,086	933
Nonamortizable Intangible Assets	5,174	4,842
Investments in Noncontrolled Affiliates	3,485	3,284
Other Assets	3,403	2,475
Total Assets	$31,727	$27,987
LIABILITIES AND SHAREHOLDERS' EQUITY		
Current Liabilities		
Short-term obligations	$ 2,889	$ 1,054
Accounts payable and other current liabilities	5,971	5,599
Income taxes payable	546	99
Total Current Liabilities	9,406	6,752
Long-Term Debt Obligations	2,313	2,397
Other Liabilities	4,323	4,099
Deferred Income Taxes	1,434	1,216
Total Liabilities	17,476	14,464
Commitments and Contingencies		
Preferred Stock, no par value	41	41
Repurchased Preferred Stock	(110)	(90)
Common Shareholders' Equity		
Common stock, par value 1 2/3¢ per share (issued 1,782 shares)	30	30
Capital in excess of par value	614	618
Retained earnings	21,116	18,730
Accumulated other comprehensive loss	(1,053)	(886)
	20,707	18,492
Less: repurchased common stock, at cost (126 and 103 shares, respectively)	(6,387)	(4,920)
Total Common Shareholders' Equity	14,320	13,572
Total Liabilities and Shareholders' Equity	$31,727	$27,987

See accompanying notes to consolidated financial statements.

PEPSICO

Consolidated Statement of Common Shareholders' Equity

PepsiCo, Inc. and Subsidiaries
Fiscal years ended December 31, 2005, December 25, 2004 and December 27, 2003

(in millions)	2005		2004		2003	
	Shares	Amount	Shares	Amount	Shares	Amount
Common Stock	1,782	$ 30	1,782	$ 30	1,782	$ 30
Capital in Excess of Par Value						
Balance, beginning of year		618		548		207
Stock-based compensation expense		311		368		407
Stock option exercises[a]		(315)		(298)		(66)
Balance, end of year		614		618		548
Retained Earnings						
Balance, beginning of year		18,730		15,961		13,489
Net income		4,078		4,212		3,568
Cash dividends declared — common		(1,684)		(1,438)		(1,082)
Cash dividends declared — preferred		(3)		(3)		(3)
Cash dividends declared — RSUs		(5)		(2)		—
Other		—		—		(11)
Balance, end of year		21,116		18,730		15,961
Accumulated Other Comprehensive Loss						
Balance, beginning of year		(886)		(1,267)		(1,672)
Currency translation adjustment		(251)		401		410
Cash flow hedges, net of tax:						
Net derivative gains/(losses)		54		(16)		(11)
Reclassification of (gains)/losses to net income		(8)		9		(1)
Minimum pension liability adjustment, net of tax		16		(19)		7
Unrealized gain on securities, net of tax		24		6		1
Other		(2)		—		(1)
Balance, end of year		(1,053)		(886)		(1,267)
Repurchased Common Stock						
Balance, beginning of year	(103)	(4,920)	(77)	(3,376)	(60)	(2,524)
Share repurchases	(54)	(2,995)	(58)	(2,994)	(43)	(1,946)
Stock option exercises	31	1,523	32	1,434	26	1,096
Other	—	5	—	16	—	(2)
Balance, end of year	(126)	(6,387)	(103)	(4,920)	(77)	(3,376)
Total Common Shareholders' Equity		$14,320		$13,572		$11,896

	2005	2004	2003
Comprehensive Income			
Net income	$4,078	$4,212	$3,568
Currency translation adjustment	(251)	401	410
Cash flow hedges, net of tax	46	(7)	(12)
Minimum pension liability adjustment, net of tax	16	(19)	7
Unrealized gain on securities, net of tax	24	6	1
Other	(2)	—	(1)
Total Comprehensive Income	$3,911	$4,593	$3,973

(a) Includes total tax benefit of $125 million in 2005, $183 million in 2004 and $340 million in 2003.
See accompanying notes to consolidated financial statements.

Notes to Consolidated Financial Statements

Note 1 — Basis of Presentation and Our Divisions

Basis of Presentation

Our financial statements include the consolidated accounts of PepsiCo, Inc. and the affiliates that we control. In addition, we include our share of the results of certain other affiliates based on our economic ownership interest. We do not control these other affiliates, as our ownership in these other affiliates is generally less than 50%. Our share of the net income of noncontrolled bottling affiliates is reported in our income statement as bottling equity income. Bottling equity income also includes any changes in our ownership interests of these affiliates. In 2005, bottling equity income includes $126 million of pre-tax gains on our sales of PBG stock. See Note 8 for additional information on our noncontrolled bottling affiliates. Our share of other noncontrolled affiliates is included in division operating profit. Intercompany balances and transactions are eliminated. In 2005, we had an additional week of results (53rd week). Our fiscal year ends on the last Saturday of each December, resulting in an additional week of results every five or six years.

In connection with our ongoing BPT initiative, we aligned certain accounting policies across our divisions in 2005. We conformed our methodology for calculating our bad debt reserves and modified our policy for recognizing revenue for products shipped to customers by third-party carriers. Additionally, we conformed our method of accounting for certain costs, primarily warehouse and freight. These changes reduced our net revenue by $36 million and our operating profit by $60 million in 2005. We also made certain reclassifications on our Consolidated Statement of Income in the fourth quarter of 2005 from cost of sales to selling, general and administrative expenses in connection with our BPT initiative. These reclassifications resulted in reductions to cost of sales of $556 million through the third quarter of 2005, $732 million in the full year 2004 and $688 million in the full year 2003, with corresponding increases to selling, general and administrative expenses in those periods. These reclassifications had no net impact on operating profit and have been made to all periods presented for comparability.

The preparation of our consolidated financial statements in conformity with generally accepted accounting principles requires us to make estimates and assumptions that affect reported amounts of assets, liabilities, revenues, expenses and disclosure of contingent assets and liabilities. Estimates are used in determining, among other items, sales incentives accruals, future cash flows associated with impairment testing for perpetual brands and goodwill, useful lives for intangible assets, tax reserves, stock-based compensation and pension and retiree medical accruals. Actual results could differ from these estimates.

See "Our Divisions" below and for additional unaudited information on items affecting the comparability of our consolidated results, see "Items Affecting Comparability" in Management's Discussion and Analysis.

Tabular dollars are in millions, except per share amounts. All per share amounts reflect common per share amounts, assume dilution unless noted, and are based on unrounded amounts. Certain reclassifications were made to prior years' amounts to conform to the 2005 presentation.

Our Divisions

We manufacture or use contract manufacturers, market and sell a variety of salty, sweet and grain-based snacks, carbonated and non-carbonated beverages, and foods through our North American and international business divisions. Our North American divisions include the United States and Canada. The accounting policies for the divisions are the same as those described in Note 2, except for certain allocation methodologies for stock-based compensation expense and pension and retiree medical expense, as described in the unaudited information in "Our Critical Accounting Policies." Additionally, begin-

ning in the fourth quarter of 2005, we began centrally managing commodity derivatives on behalf of our divisions. Certain of the commodity derivatives, primarily those related to the purchase of energy for use by our divisions, do not qualify for hedge accounting treatment. These derivatives hedge underlying commodity price risk and were not entered into for speculative purposes. Such derivatives are marked to market with the resulting gains and losses recognized as a component of corporate unallocated expense. These gains and losses are reflected in division results when the divisions take

delivery of the underlying commodity. Therefore, division results reflect the contract purchase price of the energy or other commodities.

Division results are based on how our Chairman and Chief Executive Officer evaluates our divisions. Division results exclude certain Corporate-initiated restructuring and impairment charges, merger-related costs and divested businesses. For additional unaudited information on our divisions, see "Our Operations" in Management's Discussion and Analysis.

	2005	2004	2003	2005	2004	2003
		Net Revenue			Operating Profit	
FLNA	$10,322	$ 9,560	$ 9,091	$2,529	$2,389	$2,242
PBNA	9,146	8,313	7,733	2,037	1,911	1,690
PI	11,376	9,862	8,678	1,607	1,323	1,061
QFNA	1,718	1,526	1,467	537	475	470
Total division	32,562	29,261	26,969	6,710	6,098	5,463
Divested businesses	—	—	2	—	—	26
Corporate	—	—	—	(788)	(689)	(502)
	32,562	29,261	26,971	5,922	5,409	4,987
Restructuring and impairment charges	—	—	—	—	(150)	(147)
Merger-related costs	—	—	—	—	—	(59)
Total	$32,562	$29,261	$26,971	$5,922	$5,259	$4,781

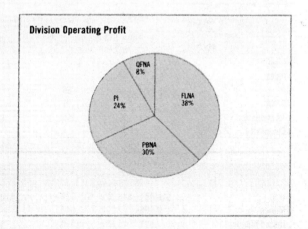

Divested Businesses
During 2003, we sold our Quaker Foods North America Mission pasta business. The results of this business are reported as divested businesses.

Corporate
Corporate includes costs of our corporate headquarters, centrally managed initiatives, such as our BPT initiative, unallocated insurance and benefit programs, foreign exchange transaction gains and losses, and certain commodity derivative gains and losses, as well as profit-in-inventory elimination adjustments for our non-controlled bottling affiliates and certain other items.

Restructuring and Impairment Charges and Merger-Related Costs — See Note 3.

Other Division Information

	2005	2004	2003	2005	2004	2003
	Total Assets			Capital Spending		
FLNA	$ 5,948	$ 5,476	$ 5,332	$ 512	$ 469	$ 426
PBNA	6,316	6,048	5,856	320	265	332
PI	9,983	8,921	8,109	667	537	521
QFNA	989	978	995	31	33	32
Total division	23,236	21,423	20,292	1,530	1,304	1,311
Corporate(a)	5,331	3,569	2,384	206	83	34
Investments in bottling affiliates	3,160	2,995	2,651	–	–	–
	$31,727	$27,987	$25,327	$1,736	$1,387	$1,345

(a) Corporate assets consist principally of cash and cash equivalents, short-term investments, and property, plant and equipment.

	2005	2004	2003	2005	2004	2003
	Amortization of Intangible Assets			Depreciation and Other Amortization		
FLNA	$ 3	$ 3	$ 3	$ 419	$ 420	$ 416
PBNA	76	75	75	264	258	245
PI	71	68	66	420	382	350
QFNA	–	1	1	34	36	36
Total division	150	147	145	1,137	1,096	1,047
Corporate	–	–	–	21	21	29
	$150	$147	$145	$1,158	$1,117	$1,076

	2005	2004	2003	2005	2004	2003
	Net Revenue(a)			Long-Lived Assets(b)		
U.S.	$19,937	$18,329	$17,377	$10,723	$10,212	$ 9,907
Mexico	3,095	2,724	2,642	902	878	869
United Kingdom	1,821	1,692	1,510	1,715	1,896	1,724
Canada	1,509	1,309	1,147	582	548	508
All other countries	6,200	5,207	4,295	3,948	3,339	3,123
	$32,562	$29,261	$26,971	$17,870	$16,873	$16,131

(a) Represents net revenue from businesses operating in these countries.

(b) Long-lived assets represent net property, plant and equipment, nonamortizable and net amortizable intangible assets and investments in noncontrolled affiliates. These assets are reported in the country where they are primarily used.

Note 2 — Our Significant Accounting Policies

Revenue Recognition

We recognize revenue upon shipment or delivery to our customers based on written sales terms that do not allow for a right of return. However, our policy for direct-store-delivery (DSD) and chilled products is to remove and replace damaged and out-of-date products from store shelves to ensure that our consumers receive the product quality and freshness that they expect. Similarly, our policy for warehouse distributed products is to replace damaged and out-of-date products. Based on our historical experience with this practice, we have reserved for anticipated damaged and out-of-date products. For additional unaudited information on our revenue recognition and related policies, including our policy on bad debts, see "Our Critical Accounting Policies" in Management's Discussion and Analysis. We are exposed to concentration of credit risk by our customers, Wal-Mart and PBG. Wal-Mart represents approximately 9% of our net revenue, including concentrate sales to our bottlers which are used in finished goods sold by them to Wal-Mart; and PBG represents approximately 10%. We have not experienced credit issues with these customers.

Sales Incentives and Other Marketplace Spending

We offer sales incentives and discounts through various programs to our customers and consumers. Sales incentives and discounts are accounted for as a reduction of revenue and totaled $8.9 billion in 2005, $7.8 billion in 2004 and $7.1 billion in 2003. While most of these incentive arrangements have terms of no more than one year, certain arrangements extend beyond one year. For example, fountain pouring rights may extend up to 15 years. Costs incurred to obtain these arrangements are recognized over the contract period and the remaining balances of $321 million at December 31, 2005 and $337 million at December 25, 2004 are included in current assets and other assets in our Consolidated Balance Sheet. For additional unaudited information on our

sales incentives, see "Our Critical Accounting Policies" in Management's Discussion and Analysis.

Other marketplace spending includes the costs of advertising and other marketing activities and is reported as selling, general and administrative expenses. Advertising expenses were $1.8 billion in 2005, $1.7 billion in 2004 and $1.6 billion in 2003. Deferred advertising costs are not expensed until the year first used and consist of:

• media and personal service prepayments,
• promotional materials in inventory, and
• production costs of future media advertising.

Deferred advertising costs of $202 million and $137 million at year-end 2005 and 2004, respectively, are classified as prepaid expenses in our Consolidated Balance Sheet.

Distribution Costs

Distribution costs, including the costs of shipping and handling activities, are reported as selling, general and administrative expenses. Shipping and handling expenses were $4.1 billion in 2005, $3.9 billion in 2004 and $3.6 billion in 2003.

Cash Equivalents

Cash equivalents are investments with original maturities of three months or less which we do not intend to rollover beyond three months.

Software Costs

We capitalize certain computer software and software development costs incurred in connection with developing or obtaining computer software for internal use. Capitalized software costs are included in property, plant and equipment on our Consolidated Balance Sheet and amortized on a straight-line basis over the estimated useful lives of the software, which generally do not exceed 5 years. Net capitalized software and development costs were $327 million at December 31, 2005 and $181 million at December 25, 2004.

Commitments and Contingencies

We are subject to various claims and contingencies related to lawsuits, taxes and environmental matters, as well as commitments under contractual and other commercial obligations. We recognize liabilities for contingencies and commitments when a loss is probable and estimable. For additional information on our commitments, see Note 9.

Other Significant Accounting Policies

Our other significant accounting policies are disclosed as follows:

• *Property, Plant and Equipment and Intangible Assets* — Note 4 and, for additional unaudited information on brands and goodwill, see "Our Critical Accounting Policies" in Management's Discussion and Analysis.
• *Income Taxes* — Note 5 and, for additional unaudited information, see "Our Critical Accounting Policies" in Management's Discussion and Analysis.
• *Stock-Based Compensation Expense* — Note 6 and, for additional unaudited information, see "Our Critical Accounting Policies" in Management's Discussion and Analysis.
• *Pension, Retiree Medical and Savings Plans* — Note 7 and, for additional unaudited information, see "Our Critical Accounting Policies" in Management's Discussion and Analysis.
• *Risk Management* — Note 10 and, for additional unaudited information, see "Our Business Risks" in Management's Discussion and Analysis.

There have been no new accounting pronouncements issued or effective during 2005 that have had, or are expected to have, a material impact on our consolidated financial statements.

Note 3 — Restructuring and Impairment Charges and Merger-Related Costs

2005 Restructuring Charges
In the fourth quarter of 2005, we incurred a charge of $83 million ($55 million after-tax or $0.03 per share) in conjunction with actions taken to reduce costs in our operations, principally through headcount reductions. Of this charge, $34 million related to FLNA, $21 million to PBNA, $16 million to PI and $12 million to Corporate (recorded in corporate unallocated expenses). Most of this charge related to the termination of approximately 700 employees. We expect the substantial portion of the cash payments related to this charge to be paid in 2006.

2004 and 2003 Restructuring and Impairment Charges
In the fourth quarter of 2004, we incurred a charge of $150 million ($96 million after-tax or $0.06 per share) in conjunction with the consolidation of FLNA's manufacturing network as part of its ongoing productivity program. Of this charge,

$93 million related to asset impairment, primarily reflecting the closure of four U.S. plants. Production from these plants was redeployed to other FLNA facilities in the U.S. The remaining $57 million included employee-related costs of $29 million, contract termination costs of $8 million and other exit costs of $20 million. Employee-related costs primarily reflect the termination costs for approximately 700 employees. Through December 31, 2005, we have paid $47 million and incurred non-cash charges of $10 million, leaving substantially no accrual.

In the fourth quarter of 2003, we incurred a charge of $147 million ($100 million after-tax or $0.06 per share) in conjunction with actions taken to streamline our North American divisions and PepsiCo International. These actions were taken to increase focus and eliminate redundancies at PBNA and PI and to improve the efficiency of the supply chain

at FLNA. Of this charge, $81 million related to asset impairment, reflecting $57 million for the closure of a snack plant in Kentucky, the retirement of snack manufacturing lines in Maryland and Arkansas and $24 million for the closure of a PBNA office building in Florida. The remaining $66 million included employee-related costs of $54 million and facility and other exit costs of $12 million. Employee-related costs primarily reflect the termination costs for approximately 850 sales, distribution, manufacturing, research and marketing employees. As of December 31, 2005, all terminations had occurred and substantially no accrual remains.

Merger-Related Costs
In connection with the Quaker merger in 2001, we recognized merger-related costs of $59 million ($42 million after-tax or $0.02 per share) in 2003.

Note 4 — Property, Plant and Equipment and Intangible Assets

	Average Useful Life	2005	2004	2003
Property, plant and equipment, net				
Land and improvements	10 – 30 yrs.	$ 685	$ 646	
Buildings and improvements	20 – 44	3,736	3,605	
Machinery and equipment, including fleet and software	5 – 15	11,658	10,950	
Construction in progress		1,066	729	
		17,145	15,930	
Accumulated depreciation		(8,464)	(7,781)	
		$ 8,681	$ 8,149	
Depreciation expense		$1,103	$1,062	$1,020
Amortizable intangible assets, net				
Brands	5 – 40	$1,054	$1,008	
Other identifiable intangibles	3 – 15	257	225	
		1,311	1,233	
Accumulated amortization		(781)	(635)	
		$ 530	$ 598	
Amortization expense		$150	$147	$145

Depreciation and amortization are recognized on a straight-line basis over an asset's estimated useful life. Land is not depreciated and construction in progress is not depreciated until ready for service. Amortization of intangible assets for each of the next five years, based on average 2005 foreign exchange rates, is expected to be $152 million in 2006, $35 million in 2007, $35 million in 2008, $34 million in 2009 and $33 million in 2010.

Depreciable and amortizable assets are only evaluated for impairment upon a significant change in the operating or macroeconomic environment. In these circumstances, if an evaluation of the undiscounted cash flows indicates impairment, the asset is written down to its estimated fair value, which is based on discounted future cash flows. Useful lives are periodically evaluated to determine whether events or circumstances have occurred which indicate the need for revision. For additional unaudited information on our amortizable brand policies, see "Our Critical Accounting Policies" in Management's Discussion and Analysis.

Nonamortizable Intangible Assets

Perpetual brands and goodwill are assessed for impairment at least annually to ensure that discounted future cash flows continue to exceed the related book value. A perpetual brand is impaired if its book value exceeds its fair value. Goodwill is evaluated for impairment if the book value of its reporting unit exceeds its fair value. A reporting unit can be a division or business within a division. If the fair value of an evaluated asset is less than its book value, the asset is written down based on its discounted future cash flows to fair value. No impairment charges resulted from the required impairment evaluations. The change in the book value of nonamortizable intangible assets is as follows:

	Balance, Beginning 2004	Acquisition	Translation and Other	Balance, End of 2004	Acquisition	Translation and Other	Balance, End of 2005
Frito-Lay North America							
Goodwill	$ 130	$ --	$ 8	$ 138	$ --	$ 7	$ 145
PepsiCo Beverages North America							
Goodwill	2,157	--	4	2,161	--	3	2,164
Brands	59	--	--	59	--	--	59
	2,216	--	4	2,220	--	3	2,223
PepsiCo International							
Goodwill	1,334	29	72	1,435	278	(109)	1,604
Brands	808	--	61	869	263	(106)	1,026
	2,142	29	133	2,304	541	(215)	2,630
Quaker Foods North America							
Goodwill	175	--	--	175	--	--	175
Corporate							
Pension intangible	2	--	3	5	--	(4)	1
Total goodwill	3,796	29	84	3,909	278	(99)	4,088
Total brands	867	--	61	928	263	(106)	1,085
Total pension intangible	2	--	3	5	--	(4)	1
	$4,665	$29	$148	$4,842	$541	$(209)	$5,174

Note 5 — Income Taxes

	2005	2004	2003
Income before income taxes — continuing operations			
U.S.	$3,175	$2,946	$3,267
Foreign	3,207	2,600	1,725
	$6,382	$5,546	$4,992
Provision for income taxes — continuing operations			
Current: U.S. Federal	$1,638	$1,030	$1,326
Foreign	426	256	341
State	118	69	80
	2,182	1,355	1,747
Deferred: U.S. Federal	137	11	(274)
Foreign	(26)	5	(47)
State	11	1	(2)
	122	17	(323)
	$2,304	$1,372	$1,424
Tax rate reconciliation — continuing operations			
U.S. Federal statutory tax rate	35.0%	35.0%	35.0%
State income tax, net of U.S. Federal tax benefit	1.4	0.8	1.0
Taxes on AJCA repatriation	7.0	—	—
Lower taxes on foreign results	(6.5)	(5.4)	(5.5)
Settlement of prior years' audit	—	(4.8)	(2.2)
Other, net	(0.8)	(0.9)	0.2
Annual tax rate	36.1%	24.7%	28.5%
Deferred tax liabilities			
Investments in noncontrolled affiliates	$ 993	$ 850	
Property, plant and equipment	772	857	
Pension benefits	863	669	
Intangible assets other than nondeductible goodwill	135	153	
Zero coupon notes	35	46	
Other	169	157	
Gross deferred tax liabilities	2,967	2,732	
Deferred tax assets			
Net carryforwards	608	666	
Stock-based compensation	426	402	
Retiree medical benefits	400	402	
Other employee-related benefits	342	379	
Other	520	460	
Gross deferred tax assets	2,296	2,309	
Valuation allowances	(532)	(564)	
Deferred tax assets, net	1,764	1,745	
Net deferred tax liabilities	$1,203	$ 987	
Deferred taxes included within:			
Prepaid expenses and other current assets	$231	$229	
Deferred income taxes	$1,434	$1,216	
Analysis of valuation allowances			
Balance, beginning of year	$564	$438	$487
(Benefit)/provision	(28)	118	(52)
Other (deductions)/additions	(4)	8	3
Balance, end of year	$532	$564	$438

For additional unaudited information on our income tax policies, including our reserves for income taxes, see "Our Critical Accounting Policies" in Management's Discussion and Analysis.

Carryforwards, Credits and Allowances

Operating loss carryforwards totaling $5.1 billion at year-end 2005 are being carried forward in a number of foreign and state jurisdictions where we are permitted to use tax operating losses from prior periods to reduce future taxable income. These operating losses will expire as follows: $0.1 billion in 2006, $4.1 billion between 2007 and 2025 and $0.9 billion may be carried forward indefinitely. In addition, certain tax credits generated in prior periods of approximately $39.4 million are available to reduce certain foreign tax liabilities through 2011. We establish valuation allowances for our deferred tax assets when the amount of expected future taxable income is not likely to support the use of the deduction or credit.

Undistributed International Earnings

The AJCA created a one-time incentive for U.S. corporations to repatriate undistributed international earnings by providing an 85% dividends received deduction. As approved by our Board of Directors in July 2005, we repatriated approximately $7.5 billion in earnings previously considered indefinitely reinvested outside the U.S. in the fourth quarter of 2005. In 2005, we recorded income tax expense of $460 million associated with this repatriation. Other than the earnings repatriated, we intend to continue to reinvest earnings outside the U.S. for the foreseeable future and, therefore, have not recognized any U.S. tax expense on these earnings. At December 31, 2005, we had approximately $7.5 billion of undistributed international earnings.

Reserves

A number of years may elapse before a particular matter, for which we have established a reserve, is audited and finally resolved. The number of years with open tax audits varies depending on the tax jurisdiction. During 2004, we recognized $266 million of tax benefits related to the favorable resolution of certain open tax issues. In addition, in 2004, we recognized a tax benefit of $38 million upon agreement with the IRS on an open issue related to our discontinued restaurant operations. At the end of 2003, we entered into agreements with the IRS for open years through 1997. These agreements resulted in a tax benefit of $109 million in the fourth quarter of 2003. As part of these agreements, we also resolved the treatment of certain other issues related to future tax years.

The IRS has initiated their audits of our tax returns for the years 1998 through 2002. Our tax returns subsequent to 2002 have not yet been examined. While it is often difficult to predict the final outcome or the timing of resolution of any particular tax matter, we believe that our reserves reflect the probable outcome of known tax contingencies. Settlement of any particular issue would usually require the use of cash. Favorable resolution would be recognized as a reduction to our annual tax rate in the year of resolution. Our tax reserves, covering all federal, state and foreign jurisdictions, are presented in the balance sheet within other liabilities (see Note 14), except for any amounts relating to items we expect to pay in the coming year which are included in current income taxes payable. For further unaudited information on the impact of the resolution of open tax issues, see "Other Consolidated Results."

Note 6 — Stock-Based Compensation

Our stock-based compensation program is a broad-based program designed to attract and retain employees while also aligning employees' interests with the interests of our shareholders. Employees at all levels participate in our stock-based compensation program. In addition, members of our Board of Directors participate in our stock-based compensation program in connection with their service on our Board. Stock options and RSUs are granted to employees under the shareholder-approved 2003 Long-Term Incentive Plan (LTIP), our only active stock-based plan. Stock-based compensation expense was $311 million in 2005, $368 million in 2004 and $407 million in 2003. Related income tax benefits recognized in earnings were $87 million in 2005, $103 million in 2004 and $114 million in 2003. At year-end 2005, 51 million shares were available for future executive and SharePower grants. For additional unaudited information on our stock-based compensation program, see "Our Critical Accounting Policies" in Management's Discussion and Analysis.

SharePower Grants

SharePower options are awarded under our LTIP to all eligible employees, based on job level or classification, and in the case of international employees, tenure as well. All stock option grants have an exercise price equal to the fair market value of our common stock on the day of grant and generally have a 10-year term with vesting after three years.

Executive Grants

All senior management and certain middle management are eligible for executive grants under our LTIP. All stock option grants have an exercise price equal to the fair market value of our common stock on the day of grant and generally have a 10-year term with vesting after three years. There have been no reductions to the exercise price of previously issued awards, and any repricing of awards would require approval of our shareholders.

Beginning in 2004, executives who are awarded long-term incentives based on their performance are offered the choice of stock options or RSUs. RSU expense is based on the fair value of PepsiCo stock on the date of grant and is amortized over the vesting period, generally three years. Each restricted stock unit can be settled in a share of our stock after the vesting period. Executives who elect RSUs receive one RSU for every four stock options that would have otherwise been granted. Senior officers do not have a choice and are granted 50% stock options and 50% RSUs. Vesting of RSU awards for senior officers is contingent upon the achievement of pre-established performance targets. We granted 3 million RSUs in both 2005 and 2004 with weighted-average intrinsic values of $53.83 and $47.28, respectively.

Method of Accounting and Our Assumptions

We account for our employee stock options under the fair value method of accounting using a Black-Scholes valuation model to measure stock-based compensation expense at the date of grant. We adopted SFAS 123R, *Share-Based Payment*, under the modified prospective method in the first quarter of 2006. We do not expect our adoption of SFAS 123R to materially impact our financial statements.

Our weighted-average Black-Scholes fair value assumptions include:

	2005	2004	2003
Expected life	6 yrs.	6 yrs.	6 yrs.
Risk free interest rate	3.8%	3.3%	3.1%
Expected volatility	23%	26%	27%
Expected dividend yield	1.8%	1.8%	1.15%

Our Stock Option Activity[a]

	2005		2004		2003	
	Options	Average Price[b]	Options	Average Price[b]	Options	Average Price[b]
Outstanding at beginning of year	174,261	$40.05	198,173	$38.12	190,432	$36.45
Granted	12,328	53.82	14,137	47.47	41,630	39.89
Exercised	(30,945)	35.40	(31,614)	30.57	(25,833)	26.74
Forfeited/expired	(5,495)	43.31	(6,435)	43.82	(8,056)	43.56
Outstanding at end of year	150,149	42.03	174,261	40.05	198,173	38.12
Exercisable at end of year	89,652	40.52	94,643	36.41	97,663	32.56

Stock options outstanding and exercisable at December 31, 2005[a]

	Options Outstanding			Options Exercisable		
Range of Exercise Price	Options	Average Price[b]	Average Life[c]	Options	Average Price[b]	Average Life[c]
$14.40 to $21.54	905	$20.01	3.56 yrs.	905	$20.01	3.56 yrs.
$23.00 to $33.75	14,559	30.46	3.07	14,398	30.50	3.05
$34.00 to $43.50	82,410	39.44	5.34	48,921	39.19	4.10
$43.75 to $56.75	52,275	49.77	7.17	25,428	49.48	6.09
	150,149	42.03	5.67	89,652	40.52	4.45

(a) Options are in thousands and include options previously granted under Quaker plans. No additional options or shares may be granted under the Quaker plans.

(b) Weighted-average exercise price.

(c) Weighted-average contractual life remaining.

Our RSU Activity[a]

	2005			2004		
	RSUs	Average Intrinsic Value[b]	Average Life[c]	RSUs	Average Intrinsic Value[b]	Average Life[c]
Outstanding at beginning of year	2,922	$47.30		–	$ –	
Granted	3,097	53.83		3,077	47.28	
Converted	(91)	48.73		(18)	47.25	
Forfeited/expired	(259)	50.51		(137)	47.25	
Outstanding at end of year	5,669	50.70	1.8 yrs.	2,922	47.30	2.2 yrs.

(a) RSUs are in thousands.

(b) Weighted-average intrinsic value.

(c) Weighted-average contractual life remaining.

Other stock-based compensation data

	Stock Options			RSUs	
	2005	2004	2003	2005	2004
Weighted-average fair value of options granted	$13.45	$12.04	$11.21		
Total intrinsic value of options/RSUs exercised/converted[a]	$632,603	$667,001	$466,719	$4,974	$914
Total intrinsic value of options/RSUs outstanding[a]	$2,553,594	$2,062,153	$1,641,505	$334,931	$151,760
Total intrinsic value of options exercisable[a]	$1,662,198	$1,464,926	$1,348,658		

(a) In thousands.

At December 31, 2005, there was $315 million of total unrecognized compensation cost related to nonvested share-based compensation grants. This unrecognized compensation is expected to be recognized over a weighted-average period of 1.6 years.

Note 7 — Pension, Retiree Medical and Savings Plans

Our pension plans cover full-time employees in the U.S. and certain international employees. Benefits are determined based on either years of service or a combination of years of service and earnings. U.S. retirees are also eligible for medical and life insurance benefits (retiree medical) if they meet age and service requirements. Generally, our share of retiree medical costs is capped at specified dollar amounts, which vary based upon years of service, with retirees contributing the remainder of the costs. We use a September 30 measurement date and all plan assets and liabilities are generally reported as of that date. The cost or benefit of plan changes that increase or decrease benefits for prior employee service (prior service cost) is included in expense on a straight-line basis over the average remaining service period of employees expected to receive benefits.

The Medicare Act was signed into law in December 2003 and we applied the provisions of the Medicare Act to our plans in 2005 and 2004. The Medicare Act provides a subsidy for sponsors of retiree medical plans who offer drug benefits equivalent to those provided under Medicare. As a result of the Medicare Act, our 2005 and 2004 retiree medical costs were $11 million and $7 million lower, respectively, and our 2005 and 2004 liabilities were reduced by $136 million and $80 million, respectively. We expect our 2006 retiree medical costs to be approximately $18 million lower than they otherwise would have been as a result of the Medicare Act.

For additional unaudited information on our pension and retiree medical plans and related accounting policies and assumptions, see "Our Critical Accounting Policies" in Management's Discussion and Analysis.

| | Pension | | | | | | Retiree Medical | | |
| | 2005 | 2004 | 2003 | 2005 | 2004 | 2003 | 2005 | 2004 | 2003 |
		U.S.			International				
Weighted-average assumptions									
Liability discount rate	5.7%	6.1%	6.1%	5.1%	6.1%	6.1%	5.7%	6.1%	6.1%
Expense discount rate	6.1%	6.1%	6.7%	6.1%	6.1%	6.4%	6.1%	6.1%	6.7%
Expected return on plan assets	7.8%	7.8%	8.3%	8.0%	8.0%	8.0%	–	–	–
Rate of compensation increases	4.4%	4.5%	4.5%	4.1%	3.9%	3.8%	–	–	–
Components of benefit expense									
Service cost	$ 213	$ 193	$ 153	$ 32	$ 27	$ 24	$ 40	$ 38	$ 33
Interest cost	296	271	245	55	47	39	78	72	73
Expected return on plan assets	(344)	(325)	(305)	(69)	(65)	(54)	–	–	–
Amortization of prior service cost/(benefit)	3	6	6	1	1	–	(11)	(8)	(3)
Amortization of experience loss	106	81	44	15	9	5	26	19	13
Benefit expense	274	226	143	34	19	14	133	121	116
Settlement/curtailment loss	–	4	–	–	1	–	–	–	–
Special termination benefits	21	19	4	–	1	–	2	4	–
Total	$ 295	$ 249	$ 147	$ 34	$ 21	$ 14	$135	$125	$116

	Pension U.S. 2005	Pension U.S. 2004	Pension International 2005	Pension International 2004	Retiree Medical 2005	Retiree Medical 2004
Change in projected benefit liability						
Liability at beginning of year	$4,968	$4,456	$ 952	$758	$1,319	$1,264
Service cost	213	193	32	27	40	38
Interest cost	296	271	55	47	78	72
Plan amendments	—	(17)	3	1	(8)	(41)
Participant contributions	—	—	10	9	—	—
Experience loss/(gain)	517	261	203	73	(45)	58
Benefit payments	(241)	(205)	(28)	(29)	(74)	(76)
Settlement/curtailment loss	—	(9)	—	(2)	—	—
Special termination benefits	21	18	—	1	2	4
Foreign currency adjustment	—	—	(68)	67	—	—
Other	(3)	—	104	—	—	—
Liability at end of year	$5,771	$4,968	$1,263	$952	$1,312	$1,319
Liability at end of year for service to date	$4,783	$4,164	$1,047	$779		
Change in fair value of plan assets						
Fair value at beginning of year	$4,152	$3,558	$ 838	$687	$ —	$ —
Actual return on plan assets	477	392	142	77	—	—
Employer contributions/funding	699	416	104	37	74	76
Participant contributions	—	—	10	9	—	—
Benefit payments	(241)	(205)	(28)	(29)	(74)	(76)
Settlement/curtailment loss	—	(9)	—	(2)	—	—
Foreign currency adjustment	—	—	(61)	59	—	—
Other	(1)	—	94	—	—	—
Fair value at end of year	$5,086	$4,152	$1,099	$838	$ —	$ —
Funded status as recognized in our Consolidated Balance Sheet						
Funded status at end of year	$ (685)	$ (817)	$(164)	$(113)	$(1,312)	$(1,319)
Unrecognized prior service cost/(benefit)	5	9	17	13	(113)	(116)
Unrecognized experience loss	2,288	2,013	474	380	402	473
Fourth quarter benefit payments	5	5	4	7	19	19
Net amounts recognized	$1,613	$1,210	$ 331	$ 287	$(1,004)	$ (943)
Net amounts as recognized in our Consolidated Balance Sheet						
Other assets	$2,068	$1,572	$367	$294	$ —	$ —
Intangible assets	—	—	1	5	—	—
Other liabilities	(479)	(387)	(41)	(37)	(1,004)	(943)
Accumulated other comprehensive loss	24	25	4	25	—	—
Net amounts recognized	$1,613	$1,210	$331	$287	$(1,004)	$(943)
Components of increase in unrecognized experience loss						
Decrease in discount rate	$ 365	$ —	$194	$ 4	$ 61	$ —
Employee-related assumption changes	57	196	2	65	—	109
Liability-related experience different from assumptions	95	65	7	4	(54)	31
Actual asset return different from expected return	(133)	(67)	(73)	(12)	—	—
Amortization of losses	(106)	(81)	(15)	(9)	(26)	(19)
Other, including foreign currency adjustments and 2003 Medicare Act	(3)	(5)	(22)	26	(52)	(82)
Total	$ 275	$108	$ 93	$ 78	$(71)	$ 39
Selected information for plans with liability for service to date in excess of plan assets						
Liability for service to date	$(374)	$(320)	$(65)	$(191)	$(1,312)	$(1,319)
Projected benefit liability	$(815)	$(685)	$(84)	$(227)	$(1,312)	$(1,319)
Fair value of plan assets	$8	$11	$33	$161	$—	$—

Of the total projected pension benefit liability at year-end 2005, $765 million relates to plans that we do not fund because the funding of such plans does not receive favorable tax treatment.

Future Benefit Payments

Our estimated future benefit payments are as follows:

	2006	2007	2008	2009	2010	2011-15
Pension	$235	$255	$275	$300	$330	$2,215
Retiree medical	$85	$90	$90	$95	$100	$545

These future benefits to beneficiaries include payments from both funded and unfunded pension plans.

Pension Assets

The expected return on pension plan assets is based on our historical experience, our pension plan investment guidelines, and our expectations for long-term rates of return. We use a market-related value method that recognizes each year's asset gain or loss over a five-year period. Therefore, it takes five years for the gain or loss from any one year to be fully included in the value of pension plan assets that is used to calculate the expected return. Our pension plan investment guidelines are established based upon an evaluation of market conditions, tolerance for risk and cash requirements for benefit payments. Our investment objective is to ensure that funds are available to meet the plans' benefit obligations when they are due. Our investment strategy is to prudently invest plan assets in high-quality and diversified equity and debt securities to achieve our long-term return expectation. Our target allocation and actual pension plan asset allocations for the plan years 2005 and 2004, are below.

Pension assets include approximately 5.5 million shares of PepsiCo common stock with a market value of $311 million in 2005, and 5.5 million shares with a market value of $267 million in 2004. Our investment policy limits the investment in PepsiCo stock at the time of investment to 10% of the fair value of plan assets.

		Actual Allocation	
Asset Category	Target Allocation	2005	2004
Equity securities	60%	60%	60%
Debt securities	40%	39%	39%
Other, primarily cash	–	1%	1%
Total	100%	100%	100%

Retiree Medical Cost Trend Rates

An average increase of 10% in the cost of covered retiree medical benefits is assumed for 2006. This average increase is then projected to decline gradually to 5% in 2010 and thereafter. These assumed health care cost trend rates have an impact on the retiree medical plan expense and liability. However, the cap on our share of retiree medical costs limits the impact. A 1 percentage point change in the assumed health care trend rate would have the following effects:

	1% Increase	1% Decrease
2005 service and interest cost components	$3	$(2)
2005 benefit liability	$38	$(33)

Savings Plans

Our U.S. employees are eligible to participate in 401(k) savings plans, which are voluntary defined contribution plans. The plans are designed to help employees accumulate additional savings for retirement. We make matching contributions on a portion of eligible pay based on years of service. In 2005 and 2004, our matching contributions were $52 million and $35 million, respectively.

Note 8 — Noncontrolled Bottling Affiliates

Our most significant noncontrolled bottling affiliates are PBG and PAS. Approximately 10% of our net revenue in 2005, 2004 and 2003 reflects sales to PBG.

The Pepsi Bottling Group

In addition to approximately 41% and 42% of PBG's outstanding common stock that we own at year-end 2005 and 2004, respectively, we own 100% of PBG's class B common stock and approximately 7% of the equity of Bottling Group, LLC, PBG's principal operating subsidiary. This gives us economic ownership of approximately 45% and 46% of PBG's combined operations at year-end 2005 and 2004, respectively. In 2005, bottling equity income includes $126 million of pre-tax gains on our sales of PBG stock.

PBG's summarized financial information is as follows:

	2005	2004	2003
Current assets	$ 2,412	$ 2,183	
Noncurrent assets	9,112	8,754	
Total assets	$11,524	$10,937	
Current liabilities	$2,598	$1,725	
Noncurrent liabilities	6,387	6,818	
Minority interest	496	445	
Total liabilities	$9,481	$8,988	
Our investment	$1,738	$1,594	
Net revenue	$11,885	$10,906	$10,265
Gross profit	$5,632	$5,250	$5,050
Operating profit	$1,023	$976	$956
Net income	$466	$457	$416

Our investment in PBG, which includes the related goodwill, was $400 million and $321 million higher than our ownership interest in their net assets at year-end 2005 and 2004, respectively. Based upon the quoted closing price of PBG shares at year-end 2005 and 2004, the calculated market value of our shares in PBG, excluding our investment in Bottling Group, LLC, exceeded our investment balance by approximately $1.5 billion and $1.7 billion, respectively.

PepsiAmericas

At year-end 2005 and 2004, we owned approximately 43% and 41% of PepsiAmericas, respectively, and their summarized financial information is as follows:

	2005	2004	2003
Current assets	$ 598	$ 530	
Noncurrent assets	3,456	3,000	
Total assets	$4,054	$3,530	
Current liabilities	$ 722	$ 521	
Noncurrent liabilities	1,763	1,386	
Total liabilities	$2,485	$1,907	
Our investment	$968	$924	
Net revenue	$3,726	$3,345	$3,237
Gross profit	$1,562	$1,423	$1,360
Operating profit	$393	$340	$316
Net income	$195	$182	$158

Our investment in PAS, which includes the related goodwill, was $292 million and $253 million higher than our ownership interest in their net assets at year-end 2005 and 2004, respectively. Based upon the quoted closing price of PAS shares at year-end 2005 and 2004, the calculated market value of our shares in PepsiAmericas exceeded our investment balance by approximately $364 million and $277 million, respectively.

In January 2005, PAS acquired a regional bottler, Central Investment Corporation. The table above includes the results of Central Investment Corporation from the transaction date forward.

Related Party Transactions

Our significant related party transactions involve our noncontrolled bottling affiliates. We sell concentrate to these affiliates, which is used in the production of carbonated soft drinks and non-carbonated beverages. We also sell certain finished goods to these affiliates and we receive royalties for the use of our trademarks for certain products. Sales of concentrate and finished goods are reported net of bottler funding. For further unaudited information on these bottlers, see "Our Customers" in Management's Discussion and Analysis. These transactions with our bottling affiliates are reflected in our consolidated financial statements as follows:

	2005	2004	2003
Net revenue	$4,633	$4,170	$3,699
Selling, general and administrative expenses	$143	$114	$128
Accounts and notes receivable	$178	$157	
Accounts payable and other current liabilities	$117	$95	

Such amounts are settled on terms consistent with other trade receivables and payables. See Note 9 regarding our guarantee of certain PBG debt.

In addition, we coordinate, on an aggregate basis, the negotiation and purchase of sweeteners and other raw materials requirements for certain of our bottlers with suppliers. Once we have negotiated the contracts, the bottlers order and take delivery directly from the supplier and pay the suppliers directly. Consequently, these transactions are not reflected in our consolidated financial statements. As the contracting party, we could be liable to these suppliers in the event of any nonpayment by our bottlers, but we consider this exposure to be remote.

Note 9 — Debt Obligations and Commitments

	2005	2004
Short-term debt obligations		
Current maturities of long-term debt	$ 143	$ 160
Commercial paper (3.3% and 1.6%)	3,140	1,287
Other borrowings (7.4% and 6.6%)	356	357
Amounts reclassified to long-term debt	(750)	(750)
	$2,889	$1,054
Long-term debt obligations		
Short-term borrowings, reclassified	$ 750	$ 750
Notes due 2006-2026 (5.4% and 4.7%)	1,161	1,274
Zero coupon notes, $475 million due 2006-2012 (13.4%)	312	321
Other, due 2006-2014 (6.3% and 6.2%)	233	212
	2,456	2,557
Less: current maturities of long-term debt obligations	(143)	(160)
	$2,313	$2,397

The interest rates in the above table reflect weighted-average rates as of year-end

Short-term borrowings are reclassified to long-term when we have the intent and ability, through the existence of the unused lines of credit, to refinance these borrowings on a long-term basis. At year-end 2005, we maintained $2.1 billion in corporate lines of credit subject to normal banking terms and conditions. These credit facilities support short-term debt issuances and remained unused as of December 31, 2005. Of the $2.1 billion, $1.35 billion expires in May 2006 with the remaining $750 million expiring in June 2009.

In addition, $181 million of our debt was outstanding on various lines of credit maintained for our international divisions.

These lines of credit are subject to normal banking terms and conditions and are committed to the extent of our borrowings.

Interest Rate Swaps

We entered into interest rate swaps in 2004 to effectively convert the interest rate of a specific debt issuance from a fixed rate of 3.2% to a variable rate. The variable weighted-average interest rate that we pay is linked to LIBOR and is subject to change. The notional amount of the interest rate swaps outstanding at December 31, 2005 and December 25, 2004 was $500 million. The terms of the interest rate swaps match the terms of the debt they modify. The swaps mature in 2007.

At December 31, 2005, approximately 78% of total debt, after the impact of the associated interest rate swaps, was exposed to variable interest rates, compared to 67% at December 25, 2004. In addition to variable rate long-term debt, all debt with maturities of less than one year is categorized as variable for purposes of this measure.

Cross Currency Interest Rate Swaps

In 2004, we entered into a cross currency interest rate swap to hedge the currency exposure on U.S. dollar denominated debt of $50 million held by a foreign affiliate. The terms of this swap match the terms of the debt it modifies. The swap matures in 2008. The unrecognized gain related to this swap was less than $1 million at December 31, 2005, resulting in a U.S. dollar liability of $50 million. At December 25, 2004, the unrecognized loss related to this swap was $3 million, resulting in a U.S. dollar liability of $53 million. We have also entered into cross currency interest rate swaps to hedge the currency exposure on U.S. dollar denominated intercompany debt of $125 million. The terms of the swaps match the terms of the debt they modify. The swaps mature over the next two years. The net unrecognized gain related to these swaps was $5 million at December 31, 2005. The net unrecognized loss related to these swaps was less than $1 million at December 25, 2004.

Long-Term Contractual Commitments

Payments Due by Period	Total	2006	2007-2008	2009-2010	2011 and beyond
Long-term debt obligations[a]	$2,313	$ —	$1,052	$ 876	$ 385
Operating leases	769	187	253	132	197
Purchasing commitments[b]	4,533	1,169	1,630	775	959
Marketing commitments	1,487	412	438	381	256
Other commitments	99	82	10	6	1
	$9,201	$1,850	$3,383	$2,170	$1,798

(a) Excludes current maturities of long-term debt of $143 million which are classified within current liabilities.

(b) Includes approximately $13 million of long-term commitments which are reflected in other liabilities in our Consolidated Balance Sheet.

The above table reflects non-cancelable commitments as of December 31, 2005 based on year-end foreign exchange rates.

Most long-term contractual commitments, except for our long-term debt obligations, are not recorded in our Consolidated Balance Sheet. Non-cancelable operating leases primarily represent building leases. Non-cancelable purchasing commitments are primarily for oranges and orange juices to be used for our Tropicana brand beverages. Non-cancelable marketing commitments primarily are for sports marketing and with our fountain customers. Bottler funding is not reflected in our long-term contractual commitments as it is negotiated on an annual basis. See Note 7 regarding our pension and retiree medical obligations and discussion below regarding our commitments to noncontrolled bottling affiliates and former restaurant operations.

Off-Balance Sheet Arrangements

It is not our business practice to enter into off-balance sheet arrangements, other than in the normal course of business, nor is it our policy to issue guarantees to our bottlers, noncontrolled affiliates or third parties. However, certain guarantees were necessary to facilitate the separation of our bottling and restaurant operations from us. In connection with these transactions, we have guaranteed $2.3 billion of Bottling Group, LLC's long-term debt through 2012 and $28 million of YUM! Brands, Inc. (YUM) outstanding obligations, primarily property leases, through 2020. The terms of our Bottling Group, LLC debt guarantee are intended to preserve the structure of PBG's separation from us and our payment obligation would be triggered if Bottling Group, LLC failed to perform under these debt obligations or the structure significantly changed. Our guarantees of certain obligations ensured YUM's continued use of certain properties. These guarantees would require our cash payment if YUM failed to perform under these lease obligations.

See "Our Liquidity, Capital Resources and Financial Position" in Management's Discussion and Analysis for further unaudited information on our borrowings.

Note 10 — Risk Management

We are exposed to the risk of loss arising from adverse changes in:
- commodity prices, affecting the cost of our raw materials and energy,
- foreign exchange risks,
- interest rates,
- stock prices, and
- discount rates affecting the measurement of our pension and retiree medical liabilities.

In the normal course of business, we manage these risks through a variety of strategies, including the use of derivatives. Certain derivatives are designated as either cash flow or fair value hedges and qualify for hedge accounting treatment, while others do not qualify and are marked to market through earnings. See "Our Business Risks" in Management's Discussion and Analysis for further unaudited information on our business risks.

For cash flow hedges, changes in fair value are deferred in accumulated other comprehensive loss within shareholders' equity until the underlying hedged item is recognized in net income. For fair value hedges, changes in fair value are recognized immediately in earnings, consistent with the underlying hedged item. Hedging transactions are limited to an underlying exposure. As a result, any change in the value of our derivative instruments would be substantially offset by an opposite change in the value of the underlying hedged items. Hedging ineffectiveness and a net earnings impact occur when the change in the value of the hedge does not offset the change in the value of the underlying hedged item. If the derivative instrument is terminated, we continue to defer the related gain or loss and include it as a component of the cost of the underlying hedged item. Upon determination that the underlying hedged item will not be part of an actual transaction, we recognize the related gain or loss in net income in that period.

We also use derivatives that do not qualify for hedge accounting treatment. We account for such derivatives at market value with the resulting gains and losses reflected in our income statement. We do not use derivative instruments for trading or speculative purposes and we limit our exposure to individual counterparties to manage credit risk.

Commodity Prices

We are subject to commodity price risk because our ability to recover increased costs through higher pricing may be limited in the competitive environment in which we operate. This risk is managed through the use of fixed-price purchase orders, pricing agreements, geographic diversity and derivatives. We use derivatives, with terms of no more than two years, to economically hedge price fluctuations related to a portion of our anticipated commodity purchases, primarily for natural gas and diesel fuel. For those derivatives that are designated as cash flow hedges, any ineffectiveness is recorded immediately. However, our commodity cash flow hedges have not had any significant ineffectiveness for all periods presented. We classify both the earnings and cash flow impact from these derivatives consistent with the underlying hedged item. During the next 12 months, we expect to reclassify gains of $24 million related to cash flow hedges from accumulated other comprehensive loss into net income.

Foreign Exchange

Our operations outside of the U.S. generate over a third of our net revenue of which Mexico, the United Kingdom and Canada comprise nearly 20%. As a result, we are exposed to foreign currency risks from unforeseen economic changes and political unrest. On occasion, we enter into hedges, primarily forward contracts with terms of no more than two years, to reduce the effect of foreign exchange rates. Ineffectiveness on these hedges has not been material.

Interest Rates

We centrally manage our debt and investment portfolios considering investment opportunities and risks, tax consequences and overall financing strategies. We may use interest rate and cross currency interest rate swaps to manage our overall interest expense and foreign exchange risk. These instruments effectively change the interest rate and currency of specific debt issuances. These swaps are entered into concurrently with the issuance of the debt that they are intended to modify. The notional amount, interest payment and maturity date of the swaps match the principal, interest payment and maturity date of the related debt. These swaps are entered into only with strong creditworthy counterparties, are settled on a net basis and are of relatively short duration.

Stock Prices

The portion of our deferred compensation liability that is based on certain market indices and on our stock price is subject to market risk. We hold mutual fund investments and prepaid forward contracts to manage this risk. Changes in the fair value of these investments and contracts are recognized immediately in earnings and are offset by changes in the related compensation liability.

Fair Value

All derivative instruments are recognized in our Consolidated Balance Sheet at fair value. The fair value of our derivative instruments is generally based on quoted market prices. Book and fair values of our derivative and financial instruments are as follows:

	2005		2004	
	Book Value	Fair Value	Book Value	Fair Value
Assets				
Cash and cash equivalents(a)	$1,716	$1,716	$1,280	$1,280
Short-term investments(b)	$3,166	$3,166	$2,165	$2,165
Forward exchange contracts(c)	$19	$19	$8	$8
Commodity contracts(d)	$41	$41	$7	$7
Prepaid forward contract(e)	$107	$107	$120	$120
Cross currency interest rate swaps(f)	$6	$6	$–	$–
Liabilities				
Forward exchange contracts(c)	$15	$15	$35	$35
Commodity contracts(d)	$3	$3	$8	$8
Debt obligations	$5,202	$5,378	$3,451	$3,676
Interest rate swaps(g)	$9	$9	$1	$1
Cross currency interest rate swaps(f)	$–	$–	$3	$3

Included in our Consolidated Balance Sheet under the captions noted above or as indicated below. In addition, derivatives are designated as accounting hedges unless otherwise noted below.

(a) Book value approximates fair value due to the short maturity.

(b) Principally short-term time deposits and includes $124 million at December 31, 2005 and $118 million at December 25, 2004 of mutual fund investments used to manage a portion of market risk arising from our deferred compensation liability.

(c) 2005 asset includes $14 million related to derivatives not designated as accounting hedges. Assets are reported within current assets and other assets and liabilities are reported within current liabilities and other liabilities.

(d) 2005 asset includes $2 million related to derivatives not designated as accounting hedges and the liability relates entirely to derivatives not designated as accounting hedges. Assets are reported within current assets and other assets and liabilities are reported within current liabilities and other liabilities.

(e) Included in current assets and other assets.

(f) Asset included within other assets and liability included in long-term debt.

(g) Reported in other liabilities.

This table excludes guarantees, including our guarantee of $2.3 billion of Bottling Group, LLC's long-term debt. The guarantee had a fair value of $47 million at December 31, 2005 and $46 million at December 25, 2004 based on an external estimate of the cost to us of transferring the liability to an independent financial institution. See Note 9 for additional information on our guarantees.

Note 11 — Net Income per Common Share from Continuing Operations

Basic net income per common share is net income available to common shareholders divided by the weighted average of common shares outstanding during the period. Diluted net income per common share is calculated using the weighted average of common shares outstanding adjusted to include the effect that would occur if

in-the-money employee stock options were exercised and RSUs and preferred shares were converted into common shares. Options to purchase 3.0 million shares in 2005, 7.0 million shares in 2004 and 49.0 million shares in 2003 were not included in the calculation of diluted earnings per common share because these

options were out-of-the-money. Out-of-the-money options had average exercise prices of $53.77 in 2005, $52.88 in 2004 and $48.27 in 2003.

The computations of basic and diluted net income per common share from continuing operations are as follows:

	2005		2004		2003	
	Income	Shares	Income	Shares	Income	Shares[a]
Net income	$4,078		$4,174		$3,568	
Preferred shares:						
Dividends	(2)		(3)		(3)	
Redemption premium	(16)		(22)		(12)	
Net income available for common shareholders	$4,060	1,669	$4,149	1,696	$3,553	1,718
Basic net income per common share	$2.43		$2.45		$2.07	
Net income available for common shareholders	$4,060	1,669	$4,149	1,696	$3,553	1,718
Dilutive securities:						
Stock options and RSUs	–	35	–	31	–	17
ESOP convertible preferred stock	18	2	24	2	15	3
Unvested stock awards	–	–	–	–	–	1
Diluted	$4,078	1,706	$4,173	1,729	$3,568	1,739
Diluted net income per common share	$2.39		$2.41		$2.05	

(a) Weighted-average common shares outstanding.

Note 12 — Preferred and Common Stock

As of December 31, 2005 and December 25, 2004, there were 3.6 billion shares of common stock and 3 million shares of convertible preferred stock authorized. The preferred stock was issued only for an employee stock ownership plan (ESOP) established by Quaker and these shares are redeemable for common stock by the ESOP participants. The preferred stock accrues dividends at an annual rate of $5.46 per share. At year-end 2005 and

2004, there were 803,953 preferred shares issued and 354,853 and 424,853 shares outstanding, respectively. Each share is convertible at the option of the holder into 4.9625 shares of common stock. The preferred shares may be called by us upon written notice at $78 per share plus accrued and unpaid dividends.

As of December 31, 2005, 0.3 million outstanding shares of preferred stock with a fair value of $104 million and 17 million

shares of common stock were held in the accounts of ESOP participants. As of December 25, 2004, 0.4 million outstanding shares of preferred stock with a fair value of $110 million and 18 million shares of common stock were held in the accounts of ESOP participants. Quaker made the final award to its ESOP plan in June 2001.

	2005		2004		2003	
	Shares	Amount	Shares	Amount	Shares	Amount
Preferred stock	0.8	$41	0.8	$41	0.8	$41
Repurchased preferred stock						
Balance, beginning of year	0.4	$ 90	0.3	$63	0.2	$48
Redemptions	0.1	19	0.1	27	0.1	15
Balance, end of year	0.5	$110*	0.4	$90	0.3	$63

*Does not sum due to rounding.

Note 13 — Accumulated Other Comprehensive Loss

Comprehensive income is a measure of income which includes both net income and other comprehensive income or loss. Other comprehensive loss results from items deferred on the balance sheet in shareholders' equity. Other comprehensive (loss)/income was $(167) million in 2005, $381 million in 2004, and $405 million in 2003. The accumulated balances for each component of other comprehensive loss were as follows:

	2005	2004	2003
Currency translation adjustment	$ (971)	$(720)	$(1,121)
Cash flow hedges, net of tax[a]	27	(19)	(12)
Minimum pension liability adjustment[b]	(138)	(154)	(135)
Unrealized gain on securities, net of tax	31	7	1
Other	(2)	–	–
Accumulated other comprehensive loss	$(1,053)	$(886)	$(1,267)

(a) Includes net commodity gains of $55 million in 2005. Also includes no impact in 2005, $6 million gain in 2004 and $8 million gain in 2003 for our share of our equity investees' accumulated derivative activity. Deferred gains/(losses) reclassified into earnings were $8 million in 2005, $(10) million in 2004 and no impact in 2003.

(b) Net of taxes of $72 million in 2005, $77 million in 2004 and $67 million in 2003. Also, includes $120 million in 2005, $121 million in 2004 and $110 million in 2003 for our share of our equity investees' minimum pension liability adjustments.

Note 14 — Supplemental Financial Information

	2005	2004	2003
Accounts receivable			
Trade receivables	$2,718	$2,505	
Other receivables	618	591	
	3,336	3,096	
Allowance, beginning of year	97	105	$116
Net amounts (credited)/charged to expense	(1)	18	32
Deductions[a]	(22)	(25)	(43)
Other[b]	1	(1)	—
Allowance, end of year	75	97	$105
Net receivables	$3,261	$2,999	
Inventory[c]			
Raw materials	$ 738	$ 665	
Work-in-process	112	156	
Finished goods	843	720	
	$1,693	$1,541	
Accounts payable and other current liabilities			
Accounts payable	$1,799	$1,731	
Accrued marketplace spending	1,383	1,285	
Accrued compensation and benefits	1,062	961	
Dividends payable	431	387	
Insurance accruals	136	131	
Other current liabilities	1,160	1,104	
	$5,971	$5,599	
Other liabilities			
Reserves for income taxes	$1,884	$1,567	
Other	2,439	2,532	
	$4,323	$4,099	
Other supplemental information			
Rent expense	$228	$245	$231
Interest paid	$213	$137	$147
Income taxes paid, net of refunds	$1,258	$1,833	$1,530
Acquisitions[d]			
Fair value of assets acquired	$ 1,089	$ 78	$178
Cash paid and debt issued	(1,096)	(64)	(71)
SVE minority interest eliminated	216	—	—
Liabilities assumed	$ 209	$ 14	$107

(a) Includes accounts written off.

(b) Includes collections of previously written-off accounts and currency translation effects.

(c) Inventories are valued at the lower of cost or market. Cost is determined using the average, first-in, first-out (FIFO) or last-in, first-out (LIFO) methods. Approximately 17% in 2005 and 15% in 2004 of the inventory cost was computed using the LIFO method. The differences between LIFO and FIFO methods of valuing these inventories were not material.

(d) In 2005, these amounts include the impact of our acquisition of General Mills, Inc.'s 40.5% ownership interest in SVE for $750 million. The excess of our purchase price over the fair value of net assets acquired is $250 million and is included in goodwill. We also reacquired rights to distribute global brands for $263 million which is included in other nonamortizable intangible assets.

ADDITIONAL INFORMATION

In addition to the financial statements and accompanying notes, companies are required to provide a report on internal control over financial reporting and to have an auditor's report on the financial statements. In addition, PepsiCo has provided a report indicating that financial reporting is management's responsibility. Finally, PepsiCo also provides selected financial data it believes is useful. The two required reports are further explained below.

Management's Report on Internal Control over Financial Reporting

The Sarbanes-Oxley Act of 2002 requires managers of publicly traded companies to establish and maintain systems of internal control over the company's financial reporting processes. In addition, management must express its responsibility for financial reporting, and it must provide certifications regarding the accuracy of the financial statements.

Auditor's Report

All publicly held corporations, as well as many other enterprises and organizations engage the services of independent certified public accountants for the purpose of obtaining an objective, expert report on their financial statements. Based on a comprehensive examination of the company's accounting system, accounting records, and the financial statements, the outside CPA issues the auditor's report.

The standard auditor's report identifies who and what was audited and indicates the responsibilities of management and the auditor relative to the financial statements. It states that the audit was conducted in accordance with generally accepted auditing standards and discusses the nature and limitations of the audit. It then expresses an informed opinion as to (1) the fairness of the financial statements and (2) their conformity with generally accepted accounting principles. It also expresses an opinion regarding the effectiveness of the company's internal controls. All of this additional information for PepsiCo is provided on the following pages.

Management's Responsibility for Financial Reporting

To Our Shareholders:

At PepsiCo, our actions — the actions of all our associates — are governed by our Worldwide Code of Conduct. This code is clearly aligned with our stated values — a commitment to sustained growth, through empowered people, operating with responsibility and building trust. Both the code and our core values enable us to operate with integrity — both within the letter and the spirit of the law. Our code of conduct is reinforced consistently at all levels and in all countries. We have maintained strong governance policies and practices for many years.

The management of PepsiCo is responsible for the objectivity and integrity of our consolidated financial statements. The Audit Committee of the Board of Directors has engaged independent registered public accounting firm, KPMG LLP, to audit our consolidated financial statements and they have expressed an unqualified opinion.

We are committed to providing timely, accurate and understandable information to investors. Our commitment encompasses the following:

Maintaining strong controls over financial reporting. Our system of internal control is based on the control criteria framework of the Committee of Sponsoring Organizations of the Treadway Commission published in their report titled, *Internal Control — Integrated Framework.* The system is designed to provide reasonable assurance that transactions are executed as authorized and accurately recorded; that assets are safeguarded; and that accounting records are sufficiently reliable to permit the preparation of financial statements that conform in all material respects with accounting principles generally accepted in the U.S. We maintain disclosure controls and procedures designed to ensure that information required to be disclosed in reports under the Securities Exchange Act of 1934 is recorded, processed, summarized and reported within the specified time periods. We monitor these internal controls through self-assessments and an ongoing program of internal audits. Our internal controls are reinforced through our Worldwide Code of Conduct, which sets forth our commitment to conduct business with integrity, and within both the letter and the spirit of the law.

Exerting rigorous oversight of the business. We continuously review our business results and strategies. This encompasses financial discipline in our strategic and daily business decisions. Our Executive Committee is actively involved — from understanding strategies and alternatives to reviewing key initiatives and financial performance. The intent is to ensure we remain objective in our assessments, constructively challenge our approach to potential business opportunities and issues, and monitor results and controls.

Engaging strong and effective Corporate Governance from our Board of Directors. We have an active, capable and diligent Board that meets the required standards for independence, and we welcome the Board's oversight as a representative of our shareholders. Our

Audit Committee comprises independent directors with the financial literacy, knowledge and experience to provide appropriate oversight. We review our critical accounting policies, financial reporting and internal control matters with them and encourage their direct communication with KPMG LLP, with our General Auditor, and with our General Counsel. In 2005, we named a senior compliance officer to lead and coordinate our compliance policies and practices.

Providing investors with financial results that are complete, transparent and understandable. The consolidated financial statements and financial information included in this report are the responsibility of management. This includes preparing the financial statements in accordance with accounting principles generally accepted in the U.S., which require estimates based on management's best judgment.

PepsiCo has a strong history of doing what's right. We realize that great companies are built on trust, strong ethical standards and principles. Our financial results are delivered from that culture of accountability, and we take responsibility for the quality and accuracy of our financial reporting.

Peter A. Bridgman
Senior Vice President and Controller

Indra K. Nooyi
President and Chief Financial Officer

Steven S Reinemund
Chairman of the Board
and Chief Executive Officer

Management's Report on Internal Control over Financial Reporting

To Our Shareholders:

Our management is responsible for establishing and maintaining adequate internal control over financial reporting, as such term is defined in Rule 13a-15(f) of the Exchange Act. Under the supervision and with the participation of our management, including our Chief Executive Officer and Chief Financial Officer, we conducted an evaluation of the effectiveness of our internal control over financial reporting based upon the framework in *Internal Control — Integrated Framework* issued by the Committee of Sponsoring Organizations of the Treadway Commission. Based on that evaluation, our management concluded that our internal control over financial reporting is effective as of December 31, 2005.

KPMG LLP, an independent registered public accounting firm, has audited the consolidated financial statements included in this Annual Report and, as part of their audit, has issued their report, included herein, (1) on our management's assessment of the effectiveness of our internal controls over financial reporting and (2) on the effectiveness of our internal control over financial reporting.

Peter A. Bridgman
Senior Vice President and Controller

Indra K. Nooyi
President and Chief Financial Officer

Steven S Reinemund
Chairman of the Board
and Chief Executive Officer

Report of Independent Registered Public Accounting Firm

Board of Directors and Shareholders PepsiCo, Inc.:

We have audited the accompanying Consolidated Balance Sheet of PepsiCo, Inc. and Subsidiaries as of December 31, 2005 and December 25, 2004 and the related Consolidated Statements of Income, Cash Flows and Common Shareholders' Equity for each of the years in the three-year period ended December 31, 2005. We have also audited management's assessment, included in Management's Report on Internal Control over Financial Reporting, that PepsiCo, Inc. and Subsidiaries maintained effective internal control over financial reporting as of December 31, 2005, based on criteria established in *Internal Control — Integrated Framework* issued by the Committee of Sponsoring Organizations of the Treadway Commission (COSO). PepsiCo, Inc.'s management is responsible for these consolidated financial statements, for maintaining effective internal control over financial reporting, and for its assessment of the effectiveness of internal control over financial reporting. Our responsibility is to express an opinion on these consolidated financial statements, an opinion on management's assessment, and an opinion on the effectiveness of PepsiCo, Inc.'s internal control over financial reporting based on our audits.

We conducted our audits in accordance with the standards of the Public Company Accounting Oversight Board (United States). Those standards require that we plan and perform the audits to obtain reasonable assurance about whether the financial statements are free of material misstatement and whether effective internal control over financial reporting was maintained in all material respects. Our audit of financial statements included examining, on a test basis, evidence supporting the amounts and disclosures in the financial statements, assessing the accounting principles used and significant estimates made by management, and evaluating the overall financial statement presentation. Our audit of internal control over financial reporting included obtaining an understanding of internal control over financial reporting, evaluating management's assessment, testing and evaluating the design and operating effectiveness of internal control, and performing such other procedures as we considered necessary in the circumstances. We believe that our audits provide a reasonable basis for our opinions.

A company's internal control over financial reporting is a process designed to provide reasonable assurance regarding the reliability of financial reporting and the preparation of financial statements for external purposes in accordance with generally accepted accounting principles. A company's internal control over financial reporting includes those policies and procedures that (1) pertain to the maintenance of records that, in reasonable detail, accurately and fairly reflect the transactions and dispositions of the assets of the company; (2) provide reasonable assurance that transactions are recorded as necessary to permit preparation of financial statements in accordance with generally accepted accounting principles, and that receipts and expenditures of the company are being made only in accordance with authorizations of management and directors of the company; and (3) provide reasonable assurance regarding prevention or timely detection of unauthorized acquisition, use, or disposition of the company's assets that could have a material effect on the financial statements.

Because of its inherent limitations, internal control over financial reporting may not prevent or detect misstatements. Also, projections of any evaluation of effectiveness to future periods are subject to the risk that controls may become inadequate because of changes in conditions, or that the degree of compliance with the policies or procedures may deteriorate.

In our opinion, the consolidated financial statements referred to above present fairly, in all material respects, the financial position of PepsiCo, Inc. and Subsidiaries as of December 31, 2005 and December 25, 2004, and the results of their operations and their cash flows for each of the years in the three-year period ended December 31, 2005, in conformity with United States generally accepted accounting principles. Also, in our opinion, management's assessment that PepsiCo, Inc. maintained effective internal control over financial reporting as of December 31, 2005, is fairly stated, in all material respects, based on criteria established in *Internal Control — Integrated Framework* issued by COSO. Furthermore, in our opinion, PepsiCo, Inc. maintained, in all material respects, effective internal control over financial reporting as of December 31, 2005, based on criteria established in *Internal Control — Integrated Framework* issued by COSO.

KPMG LLP

KPMG LLP
New York, New York
February 24, 2006

Selected Financial Data (in millions except per share amounts, unaudited)

Quarterly	First Quarter	Second Quarter	Third Quarter	Fourth Quarter
Net revenue				
2005	$6,585	$7,697	$8,184	$10,096
2004	$6,131	$7,070	$7,257	$8,803
Gross profit(a)				
2005	$3,715	$4,383	$4,669	$5,619
2004	$3,466	$4,039	$4,139	$4,943
2005 restructuring charges(b)				
2005	–	–	–	$83
2004 restructuring and impairment charges(c)				
2004	–	–	–	$150
AJCA tax charge(d)				
2005	–	–	$468	$(8)
Net income(e)				
2005	$912	$1,194	$864	$1,108
2004	$804	$1,059	$1,364	$985
Net income per common share — basic(e)				
2005	$0.54	$0.71	$0.52	$0.66
2004	$0.47	$0.62	$0.80	$0.58
Net income per common share — diluted(e)				
2005	$0.53	$0.70	$0.51	$0.65
2004	$0.46	$0.61	$0.79	$0.58
Cash dividends declared per common share				
2005	$0.23	$0.26	$0.26	$0.26
2004	$0.16	$0.23	$0.23	$0.23
2005 stock price per share(f)				
High	$55.71	$57.20	$56.73	$60.34
Low	$51.34	$51.78	$52.07	$53.55
Close	$52.62	$55.52	$54.65	$59.08
2004 stock price per share(f)				
High	$53.00	$55.48	$55.71	$53.00
Low	$45.30	$50.28	$48.41	$47.37
Close	$50.93	$54.95	$50.84	$51.94

The first, second, and third quarters consist of 12 weeks and the fourth quarter consists of 16 weeks in 2004 and 17 weeks in 2005.

(a) Reflects net reclassifications in all periods from cost of sales to selling, general and administrative expenses related to the alignment of certain accounting policies in connection with our ongoing BPT initiative. See Note 1.

(b) The 2005 restructuring charges were $83 million ($55 million or $0.03 per share after-tax). See Note 3.

(c) The 2004 restructuring and impairment charges were $150 million ($96 million or $0.06 per share after-tax). See Note 3.

(d) Represents income tax expense associated with the repatriation of earnings in connection with the AJCA. See Note 5.

(e) Fourth quarter 2004 net income reflects a tax benefit from discontinued operations of $38 million or $0.02 per share. See Note 5.

(f) Represents the composite high and low sales price and quarterly closing prices for one share of PepsiCo common stock.

Five-Year Summary	2005	2004	2003
Net revenue	$32,562	$29,261	$26,971
Income from continuing operations	$4,078	$4,174	$3,568
Net income	$4,078	$4,212	$3,568
Income per common share — basic, continuing operations	$2.43	$2.45	$2.07
Income per common share — diluted, continuing operations	$2.39	$2.41	$2.05
Cash dividends declared per common share	$1.01	$0.850	$0.630
Total assets	$31,727	$27,987	$25,327
Long-term debt	$2,313	$2,397	$1,702
Return on invested capital(a)	22.7%	27.4%	27.5%

Five-Year Summary (Cont.)	2002	2001
Net revenue	$25,112	$23,512
Net income	$3,000	$2,400
Income per common share — basic	$1.69	$1.35
Income per common share — diluted	$1.68	$1.33
Cash dividends declared per common share	$0.595	$0.575
Total assets	$23,474	$21,695
Long-term debt	$2,187	$2,651
Return on invested capital(a)	25.7%	22.1%

(a) Return on invested capital is defined as adjusted net income divided by the sum of average shareholders' equity and average total debt. Adjusted net income is defined as net income plus net interest expense after tax. Net interest expense after tax was $62 million in 2005, $60 million in 2004, $72 million in 2003, $93 million in 2002, and $99 million in 2001.

• As a result of the adoption of SFAS 142, *Goodwill and Other Intangible Assets*, and the consolidation of SVE in 2002, the data provided above is not comparable.

• Includes restructuring and impairment charges of:

	2005	2004	2003	2001
Pre-tax	$83	$150	$147	$31
After-tax	$55	$96	$100	$19
Per share	$0.03	$0.06	$0.06	$0.01

• Includes Quaker merger-related costs of:

	2002	2002	2001
Pre-tax	$59	$224	$356
After-tax	$42	$190	$322
Per share	$0.02	$0.11	$0.18

• The 2005 fiscal year consisted of fifty-three weeks compared to fifty-two weeks in our normal fiscal year. The 53rd week increased 2005 net revenue by an estimated $418 million and net income by an estimated $57 million or $0.03 per share.

• Cash dividends per common share in 2001 are those of pre-merger PepsiCo prior to the effective date of the merger.

• In the fourth quarter of 2004, we reached agreement with the IRS for an open issue related to our discontinued restaurant operations which resulted in a tax benefit of $38 million or $0.02 per share.

SPECIMEN FINANCIAL STATEMENTS:
The Coca-Cola Company

THE COCA-COLA COMPANY AND SUBSIDIARIES
CONSOLIDATED STATEMENTS OF INCOME

Year Ended December 31,	2005	2004	2003
(In millions except per share data)			
NET OPERATING REVENUES	**$ 23,104**	$ 21,742	$ 20,857
Cost of goods sold	**8,195**	7,674	7,776
GROSS PROFIT	**14,909**	14,068	13,081
Selling, general and administrative expenses	**8,739**	7,890	7,287
Other operating charges	**85**	480	573
OPERATING INCOME	**6,085**	5,698	5,221
Interest income	**235**	157	176
Interest expense	**240**	196	178
Equity income — net	**680**	621	406
Other loss — net	**(93)**	(82)	(138)
Gains on issuances of stock by equity investees	**23**	24	8
INCOME BEFORE INCOME TAXES	**6,690**	6,222	5,495
Income taxes	**1,818**	1,375	1,148
NET INCOME	**$ 4,872**	$ 4,847	$ 4,347
BASIC NET INCOME PER SHARE	**$ 2.04**	$ 2.00	$ 1.77
DILUTED NET INCOME PER SHARE	**$ 2.04**	$ 2.00	$ 1.77
AVERAGE SHARES OUTSTANDING	**2,392**	2,426	2,459
Effect of dilutive securities	**1**	3	3
AVERAGE SHARES OUTSTANDING ASSUMING DILUTION	**2,393**	2,429	2,462

Refer to Notes to Consolidated Financial Statements.

The financial information herein is reprinted with permission from The Coca-Cola Company 2005 Annual Report. The accompanying Notes are an integral part of the consolidated financial statements. The complete financial statements are available through a link at the book's companion website.

THE COCA-COLA COMPANY AND SUBSIDIARIES
CONSOLIDATED BALANCE SHEETS

December 31,	2005	2004
(In millions except par value)		
ASSETS		
CURRENT ASSETS		
Cash and cash equivalents	$ **4,701**	$ 6,707
Marketable securities	**66**	61
Trade accounts receivable, less allowances of $72 and $69, respectively	**2,281**	2,244
Inventories	**1,424**	1,420
Prepaid expenses and other assets	**1,778**	1,849
TOTAL CURRENT ASSETS	**10,250**	12,281
INVESTMENTS		
Equity method investments:		
Coca-Cola Enterprises Inc.	**1,731**	1,569
Coca-Cola Hellenic Bottling Company S.A.	**1,039**	1,067
Coca-Cola FEMSA, S.A. de C.V.	**982**	792
Coca-Cola Amatil Limited	**748**	736
Other, principally bottling companies	**2,062**	1,733
Cost method investments, principally bottling companies	**360**	355
TOTAL INVESTMENTS	**6,922**	6,252
OTHER ASSETS	**2,648**	2,981
PROPERTY, PLANT AND EQUIPMENT — net	**5,786**	6,091
TRADEMARKS WITH INDEFINITE LIVES	**1,946**	2,037
GOODWILL	**1,047**	1,097
OTHER INTANGIBLE ASSETS	**828**	702
TOTAL ASSETS	$ **29,427**	$ 31,441
LIABILITIES AND SHAREOWNERS' EQUITY		
CURRENT LIABILITIES		
Accounts payable and accrued expenses	$ **4,493**	$ 4,403
Loans and notes payable	**4,518**	4,531
Current maturities of long-term debt	**28**	1,490
Accrued income taxes	**797**	709
TOTAL CURRENT LIABILITIES	**9,836**	11,133
LONG-TERM DEBT	**1,154**	1,157
OTHER LIABILITIES	**1,730**	2,814
DEFERRED INCOME TAXES	**352**	402
SHAREOWNERS' EQUITY		
Common stock, $0.25 par value; Authorized — 5,600 shares;		
Issued — 3,507 and 3,500 shares, respectively	**877**	875
Capital surplus	**5,492**	4,928
Reinvested earnings	**31,299**	29,105
Accumulated other comprehensive income (loss)	**(1,669)**	(1,348)
Treasury stock, at cost — 1,138 and 1,091 shares, respectively	**(19,644)**	(17,625)
TOTAL SHAREOWNERS' EQUITY	**16,355**	15,935
TOTAL LIABILITIES AND SHAREOWNERS' EQUITY	$ **29,427**	$ 31,441

Refer to Notes to Consolidated Financial Statements.

THE COCA-COLA COMPANY AND SUBSIDIARIES
CONSOLIDATED STATEMENTS OF CASH FLOWS

Year Ended December 31, (In millions)	2005	2004	2003
OPERATING ACTIVITIES			
Net income	$ 4,872	$ 4,847	$ 4,347
Depreciation and amortization	932	893	850
Stock-based compensation expense	324	345	422
Deferred income taxes	(88)	162	(188)
Equity income or loss, net of dividends	(446)	(476)	(294)
Foreign currency adjustments	47	(59)	(79)
Gains on issuances of stock by equity investees	(23)	(24)	(8)
Gains on sales of assets, including bottling interests	(9)	(20)	(5)
Other operating charges	85	480	330
Other items	299	437	249
Net change in operating assets and liabilities	430	(617)	(168)
Net cash provided by operating activities	6,423	5,968	5,456
INVESTING ACTIVITIES			
Acquisitions and investments, principally trademarks and bottling companies	(637)	(267)	(359)
Purchases of investments and other assets	(53)	(46)	(177)
Proceeds from disposals of investments and other assets	33	161	147
Purchases of property, plant and equipment	(899)	(755)	(812)
Proceeds from disposals of property, plant and equipment	88	341	87
Other investing activities	(28)	63	178
Net cash used in investing activities	(1,496)	(503)	(936)
FINANCING ACTIVITIES			
Issuances of debt	178	3,030	1,026
Payments of debt	(2,460)	(1,316)	(1,119)
Issuances of stock	230	193	98
Purchases of stock for treasury	(2,055)	(1,739)	(1,440)
Dividends	(2,678)	(2,429)	(2,166)
Net cash used in financing activities	(6,785)	(2,261)	(3,601)
EFFECT OF EXCHANGE RATE CHANGES ON CASH AND CASH EQUIVALENTS	(148)	141	183
CASH AND CASH EQUIVALENTS			
Net increase (decrease) during the year	(2,006)	3,345	1,102
Balance at beginning of year	6,707	3,362	2,260
Balance at end of year	$ 4,701	$ 6,707	$ 3,362

Refer to Notes to Consolidated Financial Statements.

THE COCA-COLA COMPANY AND SUBSIDIARIES
CONSOLIDATED STATEMENTS OF SHAREOWNERS' EQUITY

Year Ended December 31, (In millions except per share data)	2005	2004	2003
NUMBER OF COMMON SHARES OUTSTANDING			
Balance at beginning of year	**2,409**	2,442	2,471
Stock issued to employees exercising stock options	**7**	5	4
Purchases of stock for treasury[1]	**(47)**	(38)	(33)
Balance at end of year	**2,369**	2,409	2,442
COMMON STOCK			
Balance at beginning of year	**$ 875**	$ 874	$ 873
Stock issued to employees exercising stock options	**2**	1	1
Balance at end of year	**877**	875	874
CAPITAL SURPLUS			
Balance at beginning of year	**4,928**	4,395	3,857
Stock issued to employees exercising stock options	**229**	175	105
Tax benefit from employees' stock option and restricted stock plans	**11**	13	11
Stock-based compensation	**324**	345	422
Balance at end of year	**5,492**	4,928	4,395
REINVESTED EARNINGS			
Balance at beginning of year	**29,105**	26,687	24,506
Net income	**4,872**	4,847	4,347
Dividends (per share — $1.12, $1.00 and $0.88 in 2005, 2004 and 2003, respectively)	**(2,678)**	(2,429)	(2,166)
Balance at end of year	**31,299**	29,105	26,687
ACCUMULATED OTHER COMPREHENSIVE INCOME (LOSS)			
Balance at beginning of year	**(1,348)**	(1,995)	(3,047)
Net foreign currency translation adjustment	**(396)**	665	921
Net gain (loss) on derivatives	**57**	(3)	(33)
Net change in unrealized gain on available-for-sale securities	**13**	39	40
Net change in minimum pension liability	**5**	(54)	124
Net other comprehensive income adjustments	**(321)**	647	1,052
Balance at end of year	**(1,669)**	(1,348)	(1,995)
TREASURY STOCK			
Balance at beginning of year	**(17,625)**	(15,871)	(14,389)
Purchases of treasury stock	**(2,019)**	(1,754)	(1,482)
Balance at end of year	**(19,644)**	(17,625)	(15,871)
TOTAL SHAREOWNERS' EQUITY	**$ 16,355**	$ 15,935	$ 14,090
COMPREHENSIVE INCOME			
Net income	**$ 4,872**	$ 4,847	$ 4,347
Net other comprehensive income adjustments	**(321)**	647	1,052
TOTAL COMPREHENSIVE INCOME	**$ 4,551**	$ 5,494	$ 5,399

[1] Common stock purchased from employees exercising stock options numbered 0.5 shares, 0.4 shares and 0.4 shares for the years ended December 31, 2005, 2004 and 2003, respectively.

Refer to Notes to Consolidated Financial Statements.

Time Value of Money

After studying this appendix, you should be able to:

1 Distinguish between simple and compound interest.
2 Identify the variables fundamental to solving present value problems.
3 Solve for present value of a single amount.
4 Solve for present value of an annuity.
5 Compute the present value of notes and bonds.

Would you rather receive $1,000 today or a year from now? You should prefer to receive the $1,000 today because you can invest the $1,000 and earn interest on it. As a result, you will have more than $1,000 a year from now. What this example illustrates is the concept of the **time value of money**. Everyone prefers to receive money today rather than in the future because of the interest factor.

NATURE OF INTEREST

Interest is payment for the use of another person's money. It is the difference between the amount borrowed or invested (called the principal) and the amount repaid or collected. The amount of interest to be paid or collected is usually stated as a **rate** over a specific period of time. The rate of interest is generally stated as an **annual rate**.

The amount of interest involved in any financing transaction is based on three elements:

1. **Principal (p):** The original amount borrowed or invested.
2. **Interest Rate (i):** An annual percentage of the principal.
3. **Time (n):** The number of years that the principal is borrowed or invested.

Simple Interest

Simple interest is computed on the principal amount only. It is the return on the principal for one period. Simple interest is usually expressed as shown in Illustration C-1 on the next page.

Illustration C-1
Interest computation

| Interest | = | Principal p | × | Rate i | × | Time n |

For example, if you borrowed $5,000 for 2 years at a simple interest rate of 12% annually, you would pay $1,200 in total interest computed as follows:

$$\text{Interest} = p \times i \times n$$
$$= \$5,000 \times .12 \times 2$$
$$= \$1,200$$

Compound Interest

Compound interest is computed on principal **and** on any interest earned that has not been paid or withdrawn. It is the return on the principal for two or more time periods. Compounding computes interest not only on the principal but also on the interest earned to date on that principal, assuming the interest is left on deposit.

To illustrate the difference between simple and compound interest, assume that you deposit $1,000 in Bank Two, where it will earn *simple interest* of 9% per year, and you deposit another $1,000 in Citizens Bank, where it will earn compound interest of 9% per year *compounded annually*. Also assume that in both cases you will not withdraw any interest until three years from the date of deposit. Illustration C-2 shows the computation of interest you will receive and the accumulated year-end balances.

Illustration C-2
Simple versus compound interest

	Bank Two				Citizens Bank		
	Simple Interest Calculation	Simple Interest	Accumulated Year-end Balance		Compound Interest Calculation	Compound Interest	Accumulated Year-end Balance
Year 1	$1,000.00 × 9%	$ 90.00	$1,090.00		Year 1 $1,000.00 × 9%	$ 90.00	$1,090.00
Year 2	$1,000.00 × 9%	90.00	$1,180.00		Year 2 $1,090.00 × 9%	98.10	$1,188.10
Year 3	$1,000.00 × 9%	90.00	$1,270.00		Year 3 $1,188.10 × 9%	106.93	$1,295.03
		$ 270.00		$25.03 Difference		$ 295.03	

Note in Illustration C-2 that simple interest uses the initial principal of $1,000 to compute the interest in all three years. Compound interest uses the accumulated balance (principal plus interest to date) at each year-end to compute interest in the succeeding year—which explains why your compound interest account is larger.

Obviously, if you had a choice between investing your money at simple interest or at compound interest, you would choose compound interest, all other things—especially risk—being equal. In the example, compounding provides $25.03 of additional interest income. For practical purposes, compounding assumes that unpaid interest earned becomes a part of the principal, and the accumulated balance at the end of each year becomes the new principal on which interest is earned during the next year.

Illustration C-2 indicates that you should invest your money at the bank that compounds interest annually. Most business situations use compound interest. Simple interest is generally applicable only to short-term situations of one year or less.

PRESENT VALUE VARIABLES

The present value is the value now of a given amount to be paid or received in the future, assuming compound interest. The present value is based on three variables: (1) the dollar amount to be received (future amount), (2) the length of time until the amount is received (number of periods), and (3) the interest rate (the discount rate). The process of determining the present value is referred to as discounting the future amount.

> **STUDY OBJECTIVE 2**
> Identify the variables fundamental to solving present value problems.

In this textbook, we use present value computations in measuring several items. For example, Chapter 15 computed the present value of the principal and interest payments to determine the market price of a bond. In addition, determining the amount to be reported for notes payable and lease liabilities involves present value computations.

PRESENT VALUE OF A SINGLE AMOUNT

To illustrate present value, assume that you want to invest a sum of money that will yield $1,000 at the end of one year. What amount would you need to invest today to have $1,000 one year from now? Illustration C-3 shows the formula for calculating present value.

> **STUDY OBJECTIVE 3**
> Solve for present value of a single amount.

Present Value = Future Value ÷ $(1 + i)^n$

Illustration C-3
Formula for present value

Thus, if you want a 10% rate of return, you would compute the present value of $1,000 for one year as follows:

$$PV = FV \div (1 + i)^n$$
$$= \$1,000 \div (1 + .10)^1$$
$$= \$1,000 \div 1.10$$
$$= \$909.09$$

We know the future amount ($1,000), the discount rate (10%), and the number of periods (1). These variables are depicted in the time diagram in Illustration C-4.

Illustration C-4
Finding present value if discounted for one period

If you receive the single amount of $1,000 **in two years**, discounted at 10% [$PV = \$1,000 \div (1 + .10)^2$], the present value of your $1,000 is $826.45 ($1,000 ÷ 1.21), depicted as shown in Illustration C-5 on the next page.

Illustration C-5
Finding present value if
discounted for two periods

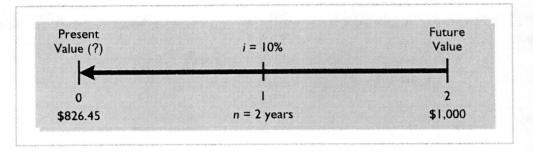

You also could find the present value of your amount through tables that show the present value of 1 for *n* periods. In Table 1, below, *n* (represented in the table's rows) is the number of discounting periods involved. The percentages (represented in the table's columns) are the periodic interest rates or discount rates. The 5-digit decimal numbers in the intersections of the rows and columns are called the **present value of 1 factors**.

When using Table 1 to determine present value, you multiply the future value by the present value factor specified at the intersection of the number of periods and the discount rate.

TABLE 1
Present Value of 1

(*n*) Periods	4%	5%	6%	8%	9%	10%	11%	12%	15%
1	.96154	.95238	.94340	.92593	.91743	.90909	.90090	.89286	.86957
2	.92456	.90703	.89000	.85734	.84168	.82645	.81162	.79719	.75614
3	.88900	.86384	.83962	.79383	.77218	.75132	.73119	.71178	.65752
4	.85480	.82270	.79209	.73503	.70843	.68301	.65873	.63552	.57175
5	.82193	.78353	.74726	.68058	.64993	.62092	.59345	.56743	.49718
6	.79031	.74622	.70496	.63017	.59627	.56447	.53464	.50663	.43233
7	.75992	.71068	.66506	.58349	.54703	.51316	.48166	.45235	.37594
8	.73069	.67684	.62741	.54027	.50187	.46651	.43393	.40388	.32690
9	.70259	.64461	.59190	.50025	.46043	.42410	.39092	.36061	.28426
10	.67556	.61391	.55839	.46319	.42241	.38554	.35218	.32197	.24719
11	.64958	.58468	.52679	.42888	.38753	.35049	.31728	.28748	.21494
12	.62460	.55684	.49697	.39711	.35554	.31863	.28584	.25668	.18691
13	.60057	.53032	.46884	.36770	.32618	.28966	.25751	.22917	.16253
14	.57748	.50507	.44230	.34046	.29925	.26333	.23199	.20462	.14133
15	.55526	.48102	.41727	.31524	.27454	.23939	.20900	.18270	.12289
16	.53391	.45811	.39365	.29189	.25187	.21763	.18829	.16312	.10687
17	.51337	.43630	.37136	.27027	.23107	.19785	.16963	.14564	.09293
18	.49363	.41552	.35034	.25025	.21199	.17986	.15282	.13004	.08081
19	.47464	.39573	.33051	.23171	.19449	.16351	.13768	.11611	.07027
20	.45639	.37689	.31180	.21455	.17843	.14864	.12403	.10367	.06110

For example, the present value factor for one period at a discount rate of 10% is .90909, which equals the $909.09 ($1,000 × .90909) computed in Illustration C-4. For two periods at a discount rate of 10%, the present value factor is .82645, which equals the $826.45 ($1,000 × .82645) computed previously.

Note that a higher discount rate produces a smaller present value. For example, using a 15% discount rate, the present value of $1,000 due one year from now is $869.57, versus $909.09 at 10%. Also note that the further removed from the present the future value is, the smaller the present value. For example, using the same discount rate of 10%, the present value of $1,000 due in **five years** is $620.92, versus the present value of $1,000 due in **one year**, which is $909.09.

The following two demonstration problems (Illustrations C-6, C-7) illustrate how to use Table 1.

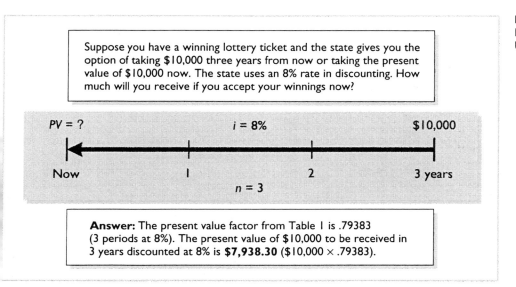

Suppose you have a winning lottery ticket and the state gives you the option of taking $10,000 three years from now or taking the present value of $10,000 now. The state uses an 8% rate in discounting. How much will you receive if you accept your winnings now?

PV = ?   i = 8% $10,000

Now   1   2   3 years

n = 3

Answer: The present value factor from Table 1 is .79383 (3 periods at 8%). The present value of $10,000 to be received in 3 years discounted at 8% is **$7,938.30** ($10,000 × .79383).

Illustration C-6
Demonstration problem—
Using Table 1 for PV of 1

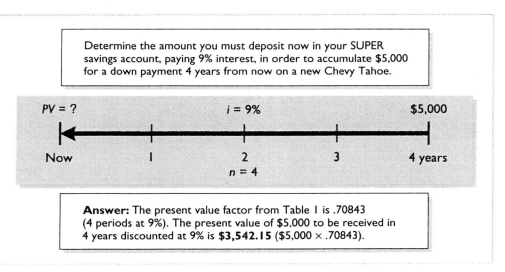

Determine the amount you must deposit now in your SUPER savings account, paying 9% interest, in order to accumulate $5,000 for a down payment 4 years from now on a new Chevy Tahoe.

PV = ?   i = 9% $5,000

Now   1   2   3   4 years

n = 4

Answer: The present value factor from Table 1 is .70843 (4 periods at 9%). The present value of $5,000 to be received in 4 years discounted at 9% is **$3,542.15** ($5,000 × .70843).

Illustration C-7
Demonstration problem—
Using Table 1 for PV of 1

PRESENT VALUE OF AN ANNUITY

The preceding discussion involved the discounting of only a single future amount. Businesses and individuals frequently engage in transactions in which a *series* of equal dollar amounts are to be received or paid periodically. Examples of a series of periodic receipts or payments are loan agreements, installment sales, mortgage notes, lease (rental) contracts, and pension obligations. As discussed in Chapter 15, these periodic receipts or payments are annuities.

The present value of an annuity is the value now of a series of future receipts or payments, discounted assuming compound interest. In computing the present value of an annuity, you need to know: (1) the discount rate, (2) the number of discount periods, and (3) the amount of the periodic receipts or payments.

STUDY OBJECTIVE 4

Solve for present value of an annuity.

To illustrate how to compute the present value of an annuity, assume that you will receive $1,000 cash annually for three years at a time when the discount rate is 10%. Illustration C-8 depicts this situation, and Illustration C-9 shows the computation of its present value.

Illustration C-8
Time diagram for a three-year annuity

Illustration C-9
Present value of a series of future amounts computation

Future Amount	×	Present Value of 1 Factor at 10%	=	Present Value
$1,000 (one year away)		.90909		$ 909.09
1,000 (two years away)		.82645		826.45
1,000 (three years away)		.75132		751.32
		2.48686		**$2,486.86**

This method of calculation is required when the periodic cash flows are not uniform in each period. However, when the future receipts are the same in each period, there are two other ways to compute present value. First, you can multiply the annual cash flow by the sum of the three present value factors. In the previous example, $1,000 × 2.48686 equals $2,486.86. The second method is to use annuity tables. As illustrated in Table 2 below, these tables show the present value of 1 to be received periodically for a given number of periods.

TABLE 2
Present Value of an Annuity of 1

(n) Periods	4%	5%	6%	8%	9%	10%	11%	12%	15%
1	.96154	.95238	.94340	.92593	.91743	.90909	.90090	.89286	.86957
2	1.88609	1.85941	1.83339	1.78326	1.75911	1.73554	1.71252	1.69005	1.62571
3	2.77509	2.72325	2.67301	2.57710	2.53130	2.48685	2.44371	2.40183	2.28323
4	3.62990	3.54595	3.46511	3.31213	3.23972	3.16986	3.10245	3.03735	2.85498
5	4.45182	4.32948	4.21236	3.99271	3.88965	3.79079	3.69590	3.60478	3.35216
6	5.24214	5.07569	4.91732	4.62288	4.48592	4.35526	4.23054	4.11141	3.78448
7	6.00205	5.78637	5.58238	5.20637	5.03295	4.86842	4.71220	4.56376	4.16042
8	6.73274	6.46321	6.20979	5.74664	5.53482	5.33493	5.14612	4.96764	4.48732
9	7.43533	7.10782	6.80169	6.24689	5.99525	5.75902	5.53705	5.32825	4.77158
10	8.11090	7.72173	7.36009	6.71008	6.41766	6.14457	5.88923	5.65022	5.01877
11	8.76048	8.30641	7.88687	7.13896	6.80519	6.49506	6.20652	5.93770	5.23371
12	9.38507	8.86325	8.38384	7.53608	7.16073	6.81369	6.49236	6.19437	5.42062
13	9.98565	9.39357	8.85268	7.90378	7.48690	7.10336	6.74987	6.42355	5.58315
14	10.56312	9.89864	9.29498	8.24424	7.78615	7.36669	6.98187	6.62817	5.72448
15	11.11839	10.37966	9.71225	8.55948	8.06069	7.60608	7.19087	6.81086	5.84737
16	11.65230	10.83777	10.10590	8.85137	8.31256	7.82371	7.37916	6.97399	5.95424
17	12.16567	11.27407	10.47726	9.12164	8.54363	8.02155	7.54879	7.11963	6.04716
18	12.65930	11.68959	10.82760	9.37189	8.75563	8.20141	7.70162	7.24967	6.12797
19	13.13394	12.08532	11.15812	9.60360	8.95012	8.36492	7.83929	7.36578	6.19823
20	13.59033	12.46221	11.46992	9.81815	9.12855	8.51356	7.96333	7.46944	6.25933

Table 2 shows that the present value of an annuity of 1 factor for three periods at 10% is 2.48685.[1] (This present value factor is the total of the three individual present value factors, as shown in Illustration C-9.) Applying this amount to the annual cash flow of $1,000 produces a present value of $2,486.85.

The following demonstration problem (Illustration C-10) illustrates how to use Table 2.

Illustration C-10
Demonstration problem—
Using Table 2 for *PV* of an
annuity of 1

Kildare Company has just signed a capitalizable lease contract for equipment that requires rental payments of $6,000 each, to be paid at the end of each of the next 5 years. The appropriate discount rate is 12%. What is the present value of the rental payments—that is, the amount used to capitalize the leased equipment?

PV = ? $6,000 $6,000 $6,000 $6,000 $6,000
i = 12%
n = 5
Now   1   2   3   4   5 years

Answer: The present value factor from Table 2 is 3.60478 (5 periods at 12%). The present value of 5 payments of $6,000 each discounted at 12% is **$21,628.68** ($6,000 × 3.60478).

TIME PERIODS AND DISCOUNTING

In the preceding calculations, the discounting was done on an *annual* basis using an *annual* interest rate. Discounting may also be done over shorter periods of time such as monthly, quarterly, or semiannually.

When the time frame is less than one year, you need to convert the annual interest rate to the applicable time frame. Assume, for example, that the investor in Illustration C-8 received $500 **semiannually** for three years instead of $1,000 annually. In this case, the number of periods becomes six (3 × 2), the discount rate is 5% (10% ÷ 2), the present value factor from Table 2 is 5.07569, and the present value of the future cash flows is $2,537.85 (5.07569 × $500). This amount is slightly higher than the $2,486.86 computed in Illustration C-9 because interest is paid twice during the same year; therefore interest is earned on the first half year's interest.

COMPUTING THE PRESENT VALUE OF A LONG-TERM NOTE OR BOND

The present value (or market price) of a long-term note or bond is a function of three variables: (1) the payment amounts, (2) the length of time until the amounts are paid, and (3) the discount rate. Our illustration uses a five-year bond issue.

The difference of .00001 between 2.48686 and 2.48685 is due to rounding.

The first variable—dollars to be paid—is made up of two elements: (1) a series of interest payments (an annuity), and (2) the principal amount (a single sum). To compute the present value of the bond, we must discount both the interest payments and the principal amount—two different computations. The time diagrams for a bond due in five years are shown in Illustration C-11.

Illustration C-11
Present value of a bond time diagram

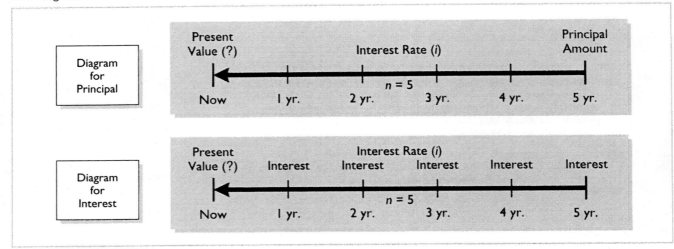

When the investor's market interest rate is equal to the bond's contractual interest rate, the present value of the bonds will *equal* the face value of the bonds. To illustrate, assume a bond issue of 10%, five-year bonds with a face value of $100,000 with interest payable **semiannually** on January 1 and July 1. If the discount rate is the same as the contractual rate, the bonds will sell at face value. In this case, the investor will receive the following: (1) $100,000 at maturity, and (2) a series of ten $5,000 interest payments [($100,000 × 10%) ÷ 2] over the term of the bonds. The length of time is expressed in terms of interest periods—in this case—10, and the discount rate per interest period, 5%. The following time diagram (Illustration C-12) depicts the variables involved in this discounting situation.

Illustration C-12
Time diagram for present value of a 10%, five-year bond paying interest semiannually

Illustration C-13 shows the computation of the present value of these bonds.

Illustration C-13
Present value of principal and interest—face value

10% Contractual Rate—10% Discount Rate	
Present value of principal to be received at maturity	
$100,000 × *PV* of 1 due in 10 periods at 5%	
$100,000 × .61391 (Table 1)	$ 61,391
Present value of interest to be received periodically	
over the term of the bonds	
$5,000 × *PV* of 1 due periodically for 10 periods at 5%	
$5,000 × 7.72173 (Table 2)	38,609*
Present value of bonds	**$100,000**

*Rounded

Now assume that the investor's required rate of return is 12%, not 10%. The future amounts are again $100,000 and $5,000, respectively, but now a discount rate of 6% (12% ÷ 2) must be used. The present value of the bonds is $92,639, as computed in Illustration C-14.

Illustration C-14
Present value of principal and interest—discount

10% Contractual Rate—12% Discount Rate	
Present value of principal to be received at maturity	
$100,000 × .55839 (Table 1)	$55,839
Present value of interest to be received periodically	
over the term of the bonds	
$5,000 × 7.36009 (Table 2)	36,800
Present value of bonds	**$92,639**

Conversely, if the discount rate is 8% and the contractual rate is 10%, the present value of the bonds is $108,111, computed as shown in Illustration C-15.

Illustration C-15
Present value of principal and interest—premium

10% Contractual Rate—8% Discount Rate	
Present value of principal to be received at maturity	
$100,000 × .67556 (Table 1)	$ 67,556
Present value of interest to be received periodically	
over the term of the bonds	
$5,000 × 8.11090 (Table 2)	40,555
Present value of bonds	**$108,111**

The above discussion relies on present value tables in solving present value problems. Many people use spreadsheets such as Excel or Financial calculators (some even on websites) to compute present values, without the use of tables. Many calculators, especially "financial calculators," have present value (*PV*) functions that allow you to calculate present values by merely inputting the proper amount, discount rate, and periods, and pressing the PV key. Appendix D illustrates how to use a financial calculator in various business situations.

SUMMARY OF STUDY OBJECTIVES

1 Distinguish between simple and compound interest. Simple interest is computed on the principal only, while compound interest is computed on the principal and any interest earned that has not been withdrawn.

2 Identify the variables fundamental to solving present value problems. The following three variables are fundamental to solving present value problems: (1) the future amount, (2) the number of periods, and (3) the interest rate (the discount rate).

3 Solve for present value of a single amount. Prepare a time diagram of the problem. Identify the future amount, the number of discounting periods, and the discount (interest) rate. Using the present value of a single amount table, multiply the future amount by the present value factor specified at the intersection of the number of periods and the discount rate.

4 Solve for present value of an annuity. Prepare a time diagram of the problem. Identify the future annuity payments, the number of discounting periods, and the discount (interest) rate. Using the present value of an annuity of 1 table, multiply the amount of the annuity payments by the present value factor specified at the intersection of the number of periods and the interest rate.

5 Compute the present value of notes and bonds. To determine the present value of the principal amount: Multiply the principal amount (a single future amount) by the present value factor (from the present value of 1 table) intersecting at the number of periods (number of interest payments) and the discount rate.

To determine the present value of the series of interest payments: Multiply the amount of the interest payment by the present value factor (from the present value of an annuity of 1 table) intersecting at the number of periods (number of interest payments) and the discount rate. Add the present value of the principal amount to the present value of the interest payments to arrive at the present value of the note or bond.

GLOSSARY

Annuity A series of equal dollar amounts to be paid or received periodically. (p. C5).

Compound interest The interest computed on the principal and any interest earned that has not been paid or withdrawn. (p. C2)

Discounting the future amount(s) The process of determining present value. (p. C3).

Interest Payment for the use of another's money. (p. C1).

Present value The value now of a given amount to be paid or received in the future assuming compound interest. (p. C3).

Present value of an annuity The value now of a series of future receipts or payments, discounted assuming compound interest. (p. C5).

Principal The amount borrowed or invested. (p. C1).

Simple interest The interest computed on the principal only. (p. C1).

BRIEF EXERCISES

Use present value tables.

Use tables to solve exercises.

BEC-1 For each of the following cases, indicate (a) to what interest rate columns, and (b) to what number of periods you would refer in looking up the discount rate.

1. In Table 1 (present value of 1):

	Annual Rate	Number of Years Involved	Discounts Per Year
(a)	12%	6	Annually
(b)	10%	15	Annually
(c)	8%	12	Semiannually

2. In Table 2 (present value of an annuity of 1):

	Annual Rate	Number of Years Involved	Number of Payments Involved	Frequency of Payments
(a)	8%	20	20	Annually
(b)	10%	5	5	Annually
(c)	12%	4	8	Semiannually

Determine present values.

BEC-2 **(a)** What is the present value of $30,000 due 8 periods from now, discounted at 8%? **(b)** What is the present value of $30,000 to be received at the end of each of 6 periods, discounted at 9%?

BEC-3   Ramirez Company is considering an investment that will return a lump sum of $600,000 5 years from now. What amount should Ramirez Company pay for this investment in order to earn a 10% return?

Compute the present value of a single-sum investment.

BEC-4   LaRussa Company earns 9% on an investment that will return $700,000 8 years from now. What is the amount LaRussa should invest now in order to earn this rate of return?

Compute the present value of a single-sum investment.

BEC-5   Polley Company sold a 5-year, zero-interest-bearing $36,000 note receivable to Valley Inc. Valley wishes to earn 10% over the remaining 4 years of the note. How much cash will Polley receive upon sale of the note?

Compute the present value of a single-sum zero-interest-bearing note.

BEC-6   Marichal Company issues a 3-year, zero-interest-bearing $60,000 note. The interest rate used to discount the zero-interest-bearing note is 8%. What are the cash proceeds that Marichal Company should receive?

Compute the present value of a single-sum zero-interest-bearing note.

BEC-7   Colaw Company is considering investing in an annuity contract that will return $40,000 annually at the end of each year for 15 years. What amount should Colaw Company pay for this investment if it earns a 6% return?

Compute the present value of an annuity investment.

BEC-8   Sauder Enterprises earns 11% on an investment that pays back $100,000 at the end of each of the next 4 years. What is the amount Sauder Enterprises invested to earn the 11% rate of return?

Compute the present value of an annuity investment.

BEC-9   Chicago Railroad Co. is about to issue $200,000 of 10-year bonds paying a 10% interest rate, with interest payable semiannually. The discount rate for such securities is 8%. How much can Chicago expect to receive for the sale of these bonds?

Compute the present value of bonds.

BEC-10   Assume the same information as in BEC-9 except that the discount rate is 10% instead of 8%. In this case, how much can Chicago expect to receive from the sale of these bonds?

Compute the present value of bonds.

BEC-11   Berghaus Company receives a $75,000, 6-year note bearing interest of 8% (paid annually) from a customer at a time when the discount rate is 9%. What is the present value of the note received by Berghaus Company?

Compute the present value of a note.

BEC-12   Troutman Enterprises issued 8%, 8-year, $1,000,000 par value bonds that pay interest semiannually on October 1 and April 1. The bonds are dated April 1, 2008, and are issued on that date. The discount rate of interest for such bonds on April 1, 2008 is 10%. What cash proceeds did Troutman receive from issuance of the bonds?

Compute the present value of bonds.

BEC-13   Ricky Cleland owns a garage and is contemplating purchasing a tire retreading machine for $16,280. After estimating costs and revenues, Ricky projects a net cash flow from the retreading machine of $2,800 annually for 8 years. Ricky hopes to earn a return of 11% on such investments. What is the present value of the retreading operation? Should Ricky Cleland purchase the retreading machine?

Compute the value of a machine for purposes of making a purchase decision.

BEC-14   Martinez Company issues a 10%, 6-year mortgage note on January 1, 2008, to obtain financing for new equipment. Land is used as collateral for the note. The terms provide for semi-annual installment payments of $78,978. What were the cash proceeds received from the issuance of the note?

Compute the present value of a note.

BEC-15   Durler Company is considering purchasing equipment. The equipment will produce the following cash flows: Year 1, $30,000; Year 2, $40,000; Year 3, $60,000. Durler requires a minimum rate of return of 12%. What is the maximum price Durler should pay for this equipment?

Compute the maximum price to pay for a machine.

BEC-16   If Carla Garcia invests $2,745 now, she will receive $10,000 at the end of 15 years. What annual rate of interest will Carla earn on her investment? (*Hint:* Use Table 1.)

Compute the interest rate on a single sum.

BEC-17   Sara Altom has been offered the opportunity of investing $51,316 now. The investment will earn 10% per year and at the end of that time will return Sara $100,000. How many years must Sara wait to receive $100,000? (*Hint:* Use Table 1.)

Compute the number of periods of a single sum.

BEC-18   Stacy Dains purchased an investment for $11,469.92. From this investment, she will receive $1,000 annually for the next 20 years, starting one year from now. What rate of interest will Stacy's investment be earning for her? (*Hint:* Use Table 2.)

Compute the interest rate on an annuity.

BEC-19   Diana Rossi invests $8,559.48 now for a series of $1,000 annual returns, beginning one year from now. Diana will earn a return of 8% on the initial investment. How many annual payments of $1,000 will Diana receive? (*Hint:* Use Table 2.)

Compute the number of periods of an annuity.

Compute the amount to be invested.

BEC-20   Minitori Company needs $10,000 on January 1, 2011. It is starting a fund on January 1, 2008.

Instructions

Compute the amount that must be invested in the fund on January 1, 2008, to produce a $10,000 balance on January 1, 2011 if.

(a) The fund earns 8% per year compounded annually.
(b) The fund earns 8% per year compounded semiannually.
(c) The fund earns 12% per year compounded annually.
(d) The fund earns 12% per year compounded semiannually.

Compute the amount to be invested.

BEC-21   Venuchi Company needs $10,000 on January 1, 2013. It is starting a fund to produce that amount.

Instructions

Compute the amount that must be invested in the fund to produce a $10,000 balance on January 1, 2013, if:

(a) The initial investment is made January 1, 2008, and the fund earns 6% per year.
(b) The initial investment is made January 1, 2010, and the fund earns 6% per year.
(c) The initial investment is made January 1, 2008, and the fund earns 10% per year.
(d) The initial investment is made January 1, 2010, and the fund earns 10% per year.

Select the better payment option.

BEC-22   Letterman Corporation is buying new equipment. It can pay $39,500 today (option 1), or $10,000 today and 5 yearly payments of $8,000 each, starting in one year (option 2).

Instructions

Which option should Letterman select? (Assume a discount rate of 10%.)

Compute the cost of an investment, amount received, and rate of return.

BEC-23   Carmen Corporation is considering several investments.

Instructions

(a) One investment returns $10,000 per year for 5 years and provides a return of 10%. What is the cost of this investment?
(b) Another investment costs $50,000 and returns a certain amount per year for 10 years, providing an 8% return. What amount is received each year?
(c) A third investment costs $70,000 and returns $11,971 each year for 15 years. What is the rate of return on this investment?

Select the best payment option.

BEC-24   You are the beneficiary of a trust fund. The fund gives you the option of receiving $5,000 per year for 10 years, $9,000 per year for 5 years, or $30,000 today.

Instructions

If the desired rate of return is 8%, which option should you select?

Compute the semiannual car payment.

BEC-25   You are purchasing a car for $24,000, and you obtain financing as follows: $2,400 down payment, 12% interest, semiannual payments over 5 years.

Instructions

Compute the payment you will make every 6 months

Compute the present value of bonds.

BEC-26   Contreras Corporation is considering purchasing bonds of Jose Company as an investment. The bonds have a face value of $40,000 with a 10% interest rate. The bonds mature in 4 years and pay interest semiannually.

Instructions

(a) What is the most Contreras should pay for the bonds if it desires a 12% return?
(b) What is the most Contreras should pay for the bonds if it desires an 8% return?

Compute the present value of bonds.

BEC-27   Garcia Corporation is considering purchasing bonds of Fred Company as an investment. The bonds have a face value of $90,000 with a 9% interest rate. The bonds mature in 6 years and pay interest semiannually.

Instructions

(a) What is the most Garcia should pay for the bonds if it desires a 10% return?
(b) What is the most Garcia should pay for the bonds if it desires an 8% return?

Using Financial Calculators

After studying this appendix, you should be able to:

1 Use a financial calculator to solve time value of money problems.

Business professionals, once they have mastered the underlying concepts in Appendix C, often use a financial (business) calculator to solve time value of money problems. In many cases, they must use calculators if interest rates or time periods do not correspond with the information provided in the compound interest tables.

STUDY OBJECTIVE 1

Use a financial calculator to solve time value of money problems.

To use financial calculators, you enter the time value of money variables into the calculator. Illustration D-1 shows the five most common keys used to solve time value of money problems.[1]

Illustration D-1
Financial calculator keys

where

N = number of periods

I = interest rate per period (some calculators use I/YR or i)

PV = present value (occurs at the beginning of the first period)

PMT = payment (all payments are equal, and none are skipped)

FV = future value (occurs at the end of the last period)

In solving time value of money problems in this appendix, you will generally be given three of four variables and will have to solve for the remaining variable. The fifth key (the key not used) is given a value of zero to ensure that this variable is not used in the computation.

PRESENT VALUE OF A SINGLE SUM

To illustrate how to solve a present value problem using a financial calculator, assume that you want to know the present value of $84,253 to be received in five years, discounted at 11% compounded annually. Illustration D-2 pictures this problem.

---

[1]On many calculators, these keys are actual buttons on the face of the calculator; on others they appear on the display after the user accesses a present value menu.

Illustration D-2
Calculator solution for present value of a single sum

The diagram shows you the information (inputs) to enter into the calculator: N = 5, I = 11, PMT = 0, and FV = 84,253. You then press PV for the answer: −$50,000. As indicated, the PMT key was given a value of zero because a series of payments did not occur in this problem.

Plus and Minus

The use of plus and minus signs in time value of money problems with a financial calculator can be confusing. Most financial calculators are programmed so that the positive and negative cash flows in any problem offset each other. In the present value problem above, we identified the $84,253 future value initial investment as a positive (inflow); the answer −$50,000 was shown as a negative amount, reflecting a cash outflow. If the 84,253 were entered as a negative, then the final answer would have been reported as a positive 50,000.

Hopefully, the sign convention will not cause confusion. If you understand what is required in a problem, you should be able to interpret a positive or negative amount in determining the solution to a problem.

Compounding Periods

In the problem above, we assumed that compounding occurs once a year. Some financial calculators have a default setting, which assumes that compounding occurs 12 times a year. You must determine what default period has been programmed into your calculator and change it as necessary to arrive at the proper compounding period.

Rounding

Most financial calculators store and calculate using 12 decimal places. As a result, because compound interest tables generally have factors only up to 5 decimal places, a slight difference in the final answer can result. In most time value of money problems, the final answer will not include more than two decimal points.

PRESENT VALUE OF AN ANNUITY

To illustrate how to solve a present value of an annuity problem using a financial calculator, assume that you are asked to determine the present value of rental receipts of $6,000 each to be received at the end of each of the next five years, when discounted at 12%, as pictured in Illustration D-3.

Illustration D-3
Calculator solution for present value of an annuity

In this case, you enter N = 5, I = 12, PMT = 6,000, FV = 0, and then press PV to arrive at the answer of $21,628.66.

USEFUL APPLICATIONS OF THE FINANCIAL CALCULATOR

With a financial calculator you can solve for any interest rate or for any number of periods in a time value of money problem. Here are some examples of these applications.

Auto Loan

Assume you are financing a car with a three-year loan. The loan has a 9.5% nominal annual interest rate, compounded monthly. The price of the car is $6,000, and you want to determine the monthly payments, assuming that the payments start one month after the purchase. This problem is pictured in Illustration D-4.

Illustration D-4
Calculator solution for auto loan payments

To solve this problem, you enter N = 36 (12 × 3), I = 9.5, PV = 6,000, FV = 0, and then press PMT. You will find that the monthly payments will be $192.20. Note that the payment key is usually programmed for 12 payments per year. Thus, you must change the default (compounding period) if the payments are other than monthly.

Mortgage Loan Amount

Let's say you are evaluating financing options for a loan on a house. You decide that the maximum mortgage payment you can afford is $700 per month. The annual interest rate is 8.4%. If you get a mortgage that requires you to make monthly payments over a 15-year period, what is the maximum purchase price you can afford? Illustration D-5 depicts this problem.

Illustration D-5
Calculator solution for mortgage amount

You enter N = 180 (12 × 15 years), I = 8.4, PMT = −700, FV = 0, and press PV. You find a present value of $71,509.81—the maximum house price you can afford, given that you want to keep your mortgage payments at $700. Note that by changing any of the variables, you can quickly conduct "what-if" analyses for different situations.

SUMMARY OF LEARNING OBJECTIVE FOR APPENDIX

1 Use a financial calculator to solve time value of money problems. Financial calculators can be used to solve the same and additional problems as those solved with time value of money tables. One enters into the financial calculator the amounts for all but one of the unknown elements of a time value of money problem (periods, interest rate, payments, future or present value). Particularly useful situations involve interest rates and compounding periods not presented in the tables.

BRIEF EXERCISES

Determine interest rate.

BED-1 Reba McEntire wishes to invest $19,000 on July 1, 2008, and have it accumulate to $49,000 by July 1, 2018.

Instructions

Use a financial calculator to determine at what exact annual rate of interest Reba must invest the $19,000.

Determine interest rate.

BED-2 On July 17, 2008, Tim McGraw borrowed $42,000 from his grandfather to open a clothing store. Starting July 17, 2009, Tim has to make 10 equal annual payments of $6,500 each to repay the loan.

Instructions

Use a financial calculator to determine what interest rate Tim is paying.

Determine interest rate.

BED-3 As the purchaser of a new house, Patty Loveless has signed a mortgage note to pay the Memphis National Bank and Trust Co. $14,000 every 6 months for 20 years, at the end of which time she will own the house. At the date the mortgage is signed the purchase price was $198,000, and Loveless made a down payment of $20,000. The first payment will be made 6 months after the date the mortgage is signed.

Instructions

Using a financial calculator, compute the exact rate of interest earned on the mortgage by the bank.

Various time value of money situations.

BED-4 Using a financial calculator, solve for the unknowns in each of the following situations.

(a) On June 1, 2008, Shelley Long purchases lakefront property from her neighbor, Joey Brenner, and agrees to pay the purchase price in seven payments of $16,000 each, the first payment to be payable June 1, 2009. (Assume that interest compounded at an annual rate of 7.35% is implicit in the payments.) What is the purchase price of the property?

(b) On January 1, 2008, Cooke Corporation purchased 200 of the $1,000 face value, 8% coupon, 10-year bonds of Howe Inc. The bonds mature on January 1, 2018, and pay interest annually beginning January 1, 2009. Cooke purchased the bonds to yield 10.65%. How much did Cooke pay for the bonds?

Various time value of money situations.

BED-5 Using a financial calculator, provide a solution to each of the following situations.

(a) Bill Schroeder owes a debt of $35,000 from the purchase of his new sport utility vehicle. The debt bears annual interest of 9.1% compounded monthly. Bill wishes to pay the debt and interest in equal monthly payments over 8 years, beginning one month hence. What equal monthly payments will pay off the debt and interest?

(b) On January 1, 2008, Sammy Sosa offers to buy Mark Grace's used snowmobile for $8,000, payable in five equal annual installments, which are to include 8.25% interest on the unpaid balance and a portion of the principal. If the first payment is to be made on December 31, 2008, how much will each payment be?

Standards of Ethical Conduct for Management Accountants

Management accountants have an obligation to the organizations they serve, their profession, the public, and themselves to maintain the highest standards of ethical conduct. In recognition of this obligation, the **Institute of Management Accountants** has published and promoted the following standards of ethical conduct for management accountants.

IMA STATEMENT OF ETHICAL PROFESSIONAL PRACTICE

Members of IMA shall behave ethically. A commitment to ethical professional practice includes: overarching principles that express our values, and standards that guide our conduct.

Principles

IMA's overarching ethical principles include: Honesty, Fairness, Objectivity, and Responsibility. Members shall act in accordance with these principles and shall encourage others within their organizations to adhere to them.

Standards

A member's failure to comply with the following standards may result in disciplinary action.

I. COMPETENCE

Each member has a responsibility to:

1. Maintain an appropriate level of professional expertise by continually developing knowledge and skills.
2. Perform professional duties in accordance with relevant laws, regulations, and technical standards.
3. Provide decision support information and recommendations that are accurate, clear, concise, and timely.
4. Recognize and communicate professional limitations or other constraints that would preclude responsible judgment or successful performance of an activity.

II. CONFIDENTIALITY

Each member has a responsibility to:

1.   Keep information confidential except when disclosure is authorized or legally required.
2.   Inform all relevant parties regarding appropriate use of confidential information. Monitor subordinates' activities to ensure compliance.
3.   Refrain from using confidential information for unethical or illegal advantage.

III. INTEGRITY

Each member has a responsibility to:

1.   Mitigate actual conflicts of interest. Regularly communicate with business associates to avoid apparent conflicts of interest. Advise all parties of any potential conflicts.
2.   Refrain from engaging in any conduct that would prejudice carrying out duties ethically.
3.   Abstain from engaging in or supporting any activity that might discredit the profession.

IV. CREDIBILITY

Each member has a responsibility to:

1.   Communicate information fairly and objectively.
2.   Disclose all relevant information that could reasonably be expected to influence an intended user's understanding of the reports, analyses, or recommendations.
3.   Disclose delays or deficiencies in information, timeliness, processing, or internal controls in conformance with organization policy and/or applicable law.

Resolution of Ethical Conflict

In applying the Standards of Ethical Professional Practice, you may encounter problems identifying unethical behavior or resolving an ethical conflict. When faced with ethical issues, you should follow your organization's established policies on the resolution of such conflict. If these policies do not resolve the ethical conflict, you should consider the following courses of action:

1.   Discuss the issue with your immediate supervisor except when it appears that the supervisor is involved. In that case, present the issue to the next level. If you cannot achieve a satisfactory resolution, submit the issue to the next management level. If your immediate superior is the chief executive officer or equivalent, the acceptable reviewing authority may be a group such as the audit committee, executive committee, board of directors, board of trustees, or owners. Contact with levels above the immediate superior should be initiated only with your superior's knowledge, assuming he or she is not involved. Communication of such problems to authorities or individuals not employed or engaged by the organization is not considered appropriate, unless you believe there is a clear violation of the law.
2.   Clarify relevant ethical issues by initiating a confidential discussion with an IMA Ethics Counselor or other impartial advisor to obtain a better understanding of possible courses of action.
3.   Consult your own attorney as to legal obligations and rights concerning the ethical conflict.

Source: Institute of Management Accountants, *www.imanct.org/pdf/981.pdf*. Reprinted by permission.

PHOTO CREDITS

SUBJECT INDEX